THE STUDY OF MEDIEVAL MANUSCRIPTS OF ENGLAND: FESTSCHRIFT IN HONOR OF RICHARD W. PFAFF

MEDIEVAL AND RENAISSANCE
TEXTS AND STUDIES

VOLUME 384

ARIZONA STUDIES IN THE
MIDDLE AGES AND THE RENAISSANCE

VOLUME 35

THE STUDY OF MEDIEVAL MANUSCRIPTS OF ENGLAND: FESTSCHRIFT IN HONOR OF RICHARD W. PFAFF

Edited by

George Hardin Brown

and

Linda Ehrsam Voigts

ACMRS
(Arizona Center for Medieval and Renaissance Studies)
Tempe, Arizona
in collaboration with
BREPOLS
2010

Published by ACMRS (Arizona Center for Medieval and Renaissance Studies)
Tempe, Arizona
and Brepols Publishers, n.v., Turnhout, Belgium.

ASMAR Volume 35: ISBN 978-2-503-53383-4   D/2010/0095/184

Library of Congress Cataloging-in-Publication Data

The study of medieval manuscripts of England : festschrift in honor of Richard W. Pfaff /
edited by George Hardin Brown and Linda Ehrsam Voigts.
   p. cm. -- (Medieval and Renaissance texts and studies ; volume 384) (Arizona
studies in the Middle Ages and the Renaissance ; volume 35)
 Includes bibliographical references and indexes.
 ISBN 978-0-86698-432-4 (acid-free paper)
 1. England--Church history--449-1066. 2. England--Church history--1066-1485.
3. Church history--Middle Ages, 600-1500. 4. Manuscripts, Medieval--England.
I. Brown, George Hardin, 1931- II. Voigts, Linda E.
 BR749.S78 2010
 274.2'03--dc22
                                                                    2010041267

Cover Art:
Salisbury Cathedral, based on etching by Wenceslaus Hollar (1607–1677), with text from
Cambridge Pembroke College MS. 302, fols. 51v, 27r.

TABLE OF CONTENTS

HISTORICAL STUDIES

INTRODUCTION

With this Festschrift we honor Richard W. Pfaff, renowned liturgist, medieval historian, academic leader, and active priest aptly named, a truly learned and gracious man. Having begun his distinguished career as an undergraduate at Harvard, he was then a Rhodes Scholar at Oxford, where he received his doctorate. Renowned as a humane, principled, and articulate scholar, Dick has now become Professor Emeritus in the History Department at the University of North Carolina, where he taught such courses as "Cathedral and Castle in Medieval England," "The Medieval Church," and "Medieval England" to both undergraduates and graduates and where he supervised graduate students now noted for their own achievements in medieval studies.

Dick's research has concentrated on the ecclesiastical, cultural, and political history of medieval England, from as early as Bede and far into the Middle Ages and its aftermath. Although his scholarship has centered on the liturgy, he has also written a highly detailed and nuanced biography of the great scholar Montague Rhodes James. Besides his half-dozen books and two-dozen scholarly articles, along with many contributions to reference works, he has every year since 1971 produced book reviews of medieval scholarship, in some years as many as a half-dozen of them. For the numerous titles, see the list of his publications at the end of this volume. Dick's writing career has been crowned with his magisterial history of the liturgy in medieval England.

Many honors have come to Dick Pfaff in his admirable life. With this Festschrift we wish to add another honor to those he has accrued as President of the Fellows of the Medieval Academy of America, Fellow of the Society of Antiquaries of London, and of the Royal Historical Society, as a research scholar with fellowships to the National Humanities Center, Magdalen College, Oxford, and Magdalene College, Cambridge, and as Honorary Vice-President of the Henry Bradshaw Society, and Doctor of Divinity of the University of Oxford.

The essays written to honor Dick in this volume reflect his own interests in the liturgy and in history. The first group of essays deals with liturgy and related topics, the second with English medieval history.

Janet Sorrentino's "Rebellion and Perseverance: The Profession of Lay Brothers in the Order of Sempringham and the Votive Mass for *Conversi*" provides the important connection between the revolt of the Gilbertine lay brothers within their order and the liturgy developed in that order to help counteract and allay their rebellion. In an extensive and closely argued essay Christopher Jones presents an overlooked redaction of a treatise by Amalarius in Salisbury Cathedral Library MS. 154, from the last quarter of the eleventh century. Elizabeth Teviotdale takes up the thorny question whether Pembroke College MS. 302 was intended as an abbreviated gospel book or as a gospel lectionary. She appends a detailed inventory of the contents of the manuscript with related manuscripts at Oxford and Florence. In a challenging analysis, titled "Page Design for the Becket Vigil: Making Something Out of Nothing," Andrew Hughes discusses principally the *prosa* and its rubric in the complex manuscript layout of the text, music, and rubrics for the Vigil of the Feast of St. Thomas Becket. William Mahrt in "The Role of Old Sarum in the Processions at Salisbury Cathedral" shows how processions on Sundays and various feasts at Salisbury imitated the original routes taken at Old Sarum, despite the notable differences in the size and layout of the new church.

In "The Sanctorals of Early Sarum Missals and Breviaries, c. 1250–c.1350" Nigel Morgan discusses how the dioceses of the province of Canterbury adopted the calendar and sanctoral of Salisbury cathedral between 1250 and 1400, processes of textual transmission so complex that surviving texts are of great diversity. In a valuable appendix Morgan lists feasts of saints not in the Sarum calendar before 1350 but which are included in the sanctorals of Sarum missals and breviaries, c. 1250-1350. In a related essay, Sherry Reames presents us with "Unexpected Texts for Saints in Some Sarum Breviary Manuscripts." She shows how the versions of the Sarum breviary are full of surprising variations from the printed versions of the late fifteenth and the sixteenth centuries. In her appendix she lists the additions she has noted in some ninety Sarum office manuscripts.

The second section of manuscript studies in this volume, broadly subsumed under the rubric "History," begins with Alan Thacker's careful recapitulation and analysis of the surviving evidence for priests and their responsibilities in Anglo-Saxon England. This study is followed by a discussion of the additions to Bede's *Historia ecclesiastica* relating to St. Wilfrid (ca. 634–709/10), in which Joshua Westgard discusses the textual tradition of these additions and edits and analyzes them using two important early manuscripts perhaps related to Mercian annals that do not survive. Joseph Wittig then examines the Latin glosses to the Boethian hymn "O qui perpetua" to try to determine whether those glosses and Bede are sources for the Old English translation of the poem, and concludes that even though there are points of similarity, the Old English text is not directly derived from the Latin but is rather made up of vignettes of current interpretations.

Jaroslav Folda's detailed analysis of one of the most spectacular of illuminated codices of William of Tyre's *History of Outremer*, BL Yates Thomson MS. 12, discusses its unique program of illustration and posits an English origin for the illumination. Focusing on a medieval English donor of manuscripts on a grand scale, Rodney Thomson brings to light much new information in "William Reed, bishop of Chichester (d. 1385)—Bibliophile?" On the basis of a detailed analysis of sources used by Gilbertus Anglicus in both his *De urinis* commentary and his own widely influential *Compendium medicine*, Michael McVaugh argues in "Who Was Gilbert the Englishman?" both for a significant re-dating of the medieval author's activity to a later period than has been assumed and for the likelihood that he was a master of medicine at Montpellier.

In "The Monks of Westminster and the *Peculium*" Barbara Harvey analyzes the extensive records of Westminster Abbey to explain how monks were allowed incomes; what they received, spent, and saved; and how these moneys largely remained within the monastery. In "Curiosities from a Sermon Book," Siegfried Wenzel edits and translates four late medieval Latin texts added to existing blank spaces in Cambridge University Library MS. Gg.6.26: a parish priest's testimony that a couple is in good standing; an episcopal *bona fides* for four pilgrims undertaking a pilgrimage to Rome; a papal letter allowing priestly privileges to a monk; and mass prayers for a pregnant woman. The final study in this collection, by Charles Briggs, "Moral Philosophy in England after Grosseteste: An 'Underground' History," is an extensive analysis and listing of moral philosophical treatises composed, written, commented on, or owned in medieval England from the mid-thirteenth century.

These studies are followed first by a list of Dick Pfaff's publications through 2009, then by brief notes on the contributors, and finally by three indices. The first two indices classify references to liturgical feasts and to manuscripts and are followed by a general index—all ably compiled by Julia McVaugh. It is important that readers be cognizant of the different uses of the three, as there is no duplication among them. A reader interested in the cult of Saint Etheldreda, for example, will not find references to her in the General Index, but will find nine citations in the Index of Feasts.

The editors wish to thank the many who made invaluable contributions to this volume: Julia McVaugh, indexer; Roy Rukkila and Todd Halvorsen, editors at the Arizona Center for Medieval and Renaissance Studies, as well as the anonymous readers and copy editor; and, of course, the learned scholars whose studies make up this volume. It is a pleasure to join them in honoring Dick Pfaff with *The Study of Medieval Manuscripts of England*.

Liturgical Studies

Rebellion and Perseverance: The Profession of Lay Brothers in the Order of Sempringham and the Votive Mass for *Conversi*

Janet Sorrentino[*]

While inheriting and self-consciously copying the liturgical traditions of established cathedral and monastic uses, the new orders of twelfth-century Europe adapted them to their individual circumstances, as an analysis of the Gilbertine Mass *De perseverentia* reveals.[1] The Order of Sempringham in England, also known as the Gilbertines after its founder Gilbert (ca.1083–1189), illustrates such adaptation particularly well. Examination of the Gilbertine customs, rule, and liturgy shows that the new order (founded in 1131) indeed borrowed heavily from other contemporary monastic groups. Their most important model was the Cistercian interpretation of Benedictine life, but the Gilbertines may also have borrowed significantly from the orders of Grandmont, Fontevrault, Arrouaise, and Prémontré as well as English Benedictine establishments. The variety of new religious organizations illustrates the dynamic character of the period.[2]

Vibrant, dynamic growth is usually, however, accompanied by its natural counterparts: instability and conflict. Thus it was that in most of these new

---

[*] I am grateful to the Pontifical Institute of Mediaeval Studies in Toronto for support during 2004–2005 in order to pursue research on this and other topics. Dr. Ann Hutchison and Dr. Jonathan Black generously read and commented on an earlier draft; I am very thankful for their help and suggestions. Any remaining errors are my own.

[1] Paul Tirot, "Un '*Ordo missae*' monastique: Cluny, Cîteaux, La Chartreuse," *Ephemerides Liturgicae* 95 (1981): 44–120, 220–51; repr. in *Bibliotheca Ephemerides Liturgicae Subsidia* 21 (Rome: Centro Liturgico Vincenziano Editioni Liturgiche, 1981).

[2] See Giles Constable, "The Diversity of Religious Life and Acceptance of Social Pluralism in the Twelfth Century," in *History, Society and the Churches: Essays in Honour of Owen Chadwick*, ed. D. Beales and G. Best (Cambridge: Cambridge University Press, 1985), 29–47; and idem and B. Smith, *Libellus de diversis ordinibus et professionibus qui sunt in aecclesia* (Oxford: Clarendon Press, 1972).

foundations, the class of men known as *conversi* or *fratres laici*, who played such a significant role in the economy of monastic houses, agitated as their status was changed and redefined. Nowhere is the link between the social milieu of twelfth-century monasticism and the liturgy more apparent than with the rebellion of the Gilbertine lay brothers in the 1160s and the subsequent response from the Order in the thirteenth century. While the revolt of the Gilbertine lay brothers has found a place in the literature, little notice has been paid to its impact on their liturgy. Scholars have rightly pointed out the impact the rebellion had on the narrative of Gilbertine origins, the evolution of the Order's Rule, and the record of these events in Gilbert's canonization dossier.[3] This paper will draw on that scholarship and argue further that the addition of a Mass for the lay brothers in the thirteenth century and the assignment of its rubric *De perseverentia* can likewise be considered a response to the lay brothers' rebellion.

There are a number of threads to this argument that need to be set out before the final argument can be woven. The paper will first present the Mass *formulae* from the Gilbertine Missal and their general distribution in Mass books from other churches. Since the rebellion of the Gilbertine lay brothers belongs to the Gilbertine narrative of its origins, the paper will continue with a short account of the foundation of the Order, the events surrounding the rebellion, and its effect on the surviving sources. Since an ambiguity about the status of men known as lay brothers and *conversi* played a part in their uprising, the paper will consider their status in its historical context and how it may have contributed to their failure to persevere. Moreover, a key issue in the investigation of the revolt was the nature of the profession taken by the lay brothers. The paper will examine the text of the profession in the *Institutes* in comparison with texts of such oaths taken by *conversi* in other contemporary orders, and demonstrate that the Gilbertine text emphasized the concept of perseverance relative to most others. The paper will argue that the rubric attached to that Mass, *De perseverentia*, represents a genuine concern on the part of the clerics to ensure that the lay brothers conform in continued obedience to the rationalized order of society as they perceived it.

---

[3] The two foundational studies of the events are David Knowles, "The Revolt of the Laybrothers of Sempringham," *English Historical Review* 50 (1935): 465–87; and Raymonde Foreville, "La crise de l'ordre de Sempringham au XIIe siècle: nouvelle approche du dossier des frères lais," *Anglo-Norman Studies* 6 (1983): 39–57. These articles as well as the following studies underscore the link between the harsh discipline and changes in status on the one hand, and the rebellion on the other. See Giles Constable, "Lay Brothers and Lay Sisters of the Order of Sempringham," in *Medieval Studies in Honour of Avrom Saltman* ed. Bat-Sheva Albert, Yvonne Friedman, and Simon Schwarzfuchs (Ramat-Gan: Bar-Ilan University Press, 1995), 83–96; Raymonde Foreville and Gillian Keir, *The Book of St. Gilbert* (Oxford: Clarendon Press, 1987), lv–lxii, 76–85, 134–67; Brian Golding, *Gilbert of Sempringham and the Gilbertine Order, c. 1130–c.1300* (Oxford: Clarendon Press, 1995), 40–51, 458–62.

Votive Mass: *De Perseverentia*

The Mass with the rubric in question occurs in one of only two Mass books that survive from the Order of Sempringham: MS. Lincoln Cathedral Chapter Library 115 [hereafter *L*] written in the twelfth and thirteenth centuries, and MS. Cambridge, St John's College 239 written in the thirteenth century. The latter contains a Bible and only an abbreviated Missal, and does not contain the votive Mass with which this paper is concerned. *L* may have belonged to the Gilbertine Priory at St. Katherine's, Lincoln.[4] It included a special Mass for St Katherine. Also, the book was prepared initially for a house of men only, then adapted for women as well by adding *sorores* (not *sanctimoniales*) in the margins. The Priory at St. Katherine's, Lincoln, was founded for canons only around 1148, but lay brothers and lay sisters worked in the nearby Hospital of the Holy Sepulchre taking care of orphans and the sick.[5]

L consists of two volumes, bound together since the thirteenth century, comprising a total of 144 folios.[6] The first volume contains a missal supplement in one main thirteenth-century hand.[7] It includes the choir chants and lections missing in the second volume, that is, the sacramentary. This first section of *L* also contains a selection of votive masses, among them *De perseverentia*, and a Common of Saints. An entry for St. Edmund of Canterbury appears in a later hand than the rest of the supplement, which places the *terminus ante quem* for this portion of the manuscript slightly before 1247, the year of his canonization.[8] The second volume of the manuscript contains a sacramentary written in the middle of the twelfth century. Parallels to Cistercian liturgy appear throughout the sacramentary.[9] Indeed, most of the sacramentary appears to have been copied from

---

[4] R.M. Woolley, *The Gilbertine Rite*, 2 vols., Henry Bradshaw Society 59–60 (London: Harrison, 1921–1922), 1: xii–xiv; R.M. Thomson, *Catalogue of the Manuscripts of Lincoln Cathedral Chapter Library*, published on behalf of the Dean and Chapter of Lincoln Cathedral (Woodbridge: D. S. Brewer, 1989), 90 (hereafter cited as Thomson, *Catalogue — Lincoln Cathedral*).

[5] Woolley, *Gilbertine Rite*, 1: xii–xiii. For the foundation of St. Katherine's, Lincoln, see also Golding, *Gilbert of Sempringham*, 230–33; and R.E.G. Cole, "The Priory of St. Katherine's without Lincoln of the Order of St. Gilbert of Sempringham," *Lincolnshire Archaeological and Architectural Society Reports and Papers* 27 (1904): 264–336.

[6] For descriptions of the manuscript, see W.H. Frere, *Bibliotheca Musico-liturgica* (London: Quaritch, 1902–1932; repr. Hildesheim: Olms, 1967), no. 597; Thomson, *Catalogue — Lincoln Cathedral*, 89–91; R.M. Woolley, *Catalogue of the Manuscripts of Lincoln Cathedral Chapter Library* (London: H. Milford, 1924). Woolley also fully discusses the Gilbertine liturgical manuscripts in his edition, *Gilbertine Rite*, 1: xi–lv.

[7] Thomson, *Catalogue — Lincoln Cathedral*, 90.

[8] *L*, fol. 62ᵛ.

[9] J. Sorrentino, "Choice Words: The Liturgy of the Order of Sempringham" (Ph.D. diss., University of North Carolina-Chapel Hill, 1999), 59–71.

a Cistercian exemplar from earlier than 1173, since the feast for St. Thomas, Martyr, instituted in that year, was added in the margin.[10] The appearance of the feasts of St. Hugh of Lincoln and St. William of York on fol. 142 indicates that new material was still being added to the sacramentary after their canonizations, 1220 and 1227 respectively. As a composite manuscript, then, *L* represents an evolution of the Mass liturgy in the Gilbertine Order. The Common of Saints especially illustrates this, since some saints provided for in the Common in the sacramentary appear in the Proper of Saints in the supplement; the reverse is also true, that saints appearing in the Proper in the twelfth-century Sacramentary drop in rank to the Common in the thirteenth-century Missal portion of the manuscript.[11]

The table below gives the priestly prayers that form the Mass set for *De perseverentia* in the Gilbertine missal *L*. These three Mass prayers are not unique to the Gilbertine Missal. They appear in a significant number of other sacramentaries and missals among the votive Masses; the table lists the relevant Mass books in the columns with the Mass prayers.

[10] *L*, fol. 77ᵛ.
[11] Sorrentino, "Choice Words," 65–71.

TABLE I. Mass forms for the Gilbertine votive Mass *De perseverentia* in *L*, and a list of other liturgical manuscripts in which those same prayers appear.[12]

Collect	Secret	Postcommunion
Deus qui nos a seculi vanitate conuersos ad superne uocacionis amorem accendis pectoribus nostris purificandis illabere; et per intercessionem gloriose dei genitricis semper uirginis marie et omnium sanctorum tuorum gratiam qua in te perseueremus infunde ut protectionis tue muniti presidiis quod te donante promisimus impleamus; et nostre professionis exsecutores effecti ad ea que perseuerantibus in te promittere dignatus es pertingamus per eundem. *L*, fols. 61ᵛ-62ᵛ	Tibi domine deus deuotionis nostre hostias immolamus hoc orantes et pariter deprecantes ut sancte dei genitricis semperque uirginis marie et omnium sanctorum tuorum supplicationibus nos sacrificium mortificatione uite carnalis effectos in odorem suauitatis accipias. ac moribus quibus nostre professioni congruamus instituas; ut quos sancte compunctionis ardore ab hominum ceterorum proposito segregasti etiam a conuersatione carnali et ab immunditia actuum terrenorum infusa nobis celitus sanctitate discernas. per eundem.	Deus qui renunciantibus seculo mansiones paras in celo, dilata fratrum nostrorum et sororum corda celestibus donis, ut teneantur fraterne compagine caritatis unanimes, precepta custodiant sobrii. simplices, et quieti gratis datam sibi professionis sue gratiam cognoscant; concordet uita eorum cum nomine professio senciatur in opere. per.
		Casinensis [Monte Cassino] Manual: 11ᵗʰ c. MS. Rome, Vat. Ottobon. lat. 145
Engolismensis [Angoulême] Sacramentary: ca.8–9ᵗʰ c. MS. Paris, Bibl. nat. lat. 816	Angoulême	Angoulême
Fulda, Sacramentary: ca.975 MS. Göttingen, Universitätsbibl., Cod. Theol. 231	Fulda	Fulda

---

12 The list of service books and manuscripts in which the three prayers appear was compiled from the tables provided in *Corpus Orationum*, ed. E. Moeller, J.-M Clément, and B. Coppieters't Wallent, 14 vols., Corpus Christianorum, Series Latina 160–160M (Turnhout: Brepols, 1980–1981), 160B, no. 1835, 58; no. 2051, 156; 160H, no. 5885b, 176.

Gellonensis [Gellone] Sacramentary: 8th c. *ex.* MS. Paris, Bibl. nat. lat. 12,048	Gellone	Gellone
Gemmeticensis [Jumièges] Missal: ca.1013–1017 MS. Rouen, Bibl. mun. Y 6		Jumièges
Gregorianum Sacramentary: *ca.*811–812 MS. Cambrai, Bibl. mun. 164	Gregorianum	Gregorianum
		Pamelius Sacramentary: 9–10th c. MS. Cologne, Bibl. met. 87, 88
Phillipps Sacramentary: *ca.*8–9th c. MS. Berlin, Öffentliche Wissenschaftliche Bibl. Phillipps, lat. 105	Phillipps	Phillipps
Praemonstratensis [Prémontré] Missal: ca.12th c. MS. Paris, Bibl. nat. lat. 833	Prémontré	
Ratisbonensis [Ratisbon] Sacramentary: ca.993–994 MS. Verona, Bibl. Capitolare 82	Ratisbon	Ratisbon
Ripoll Sacramentary: ca.11–12th c. MS. Vich, Museo episcopal 67	Ripoll	Supplementum Sacramentary: 845
		MS. Autun, Bibl. mun. 19
		Trento Sacramentary: 9th c. MS. Trento, Museo Prov. d'arte del Castello del Buon. 1590

Triplex Sacramentary: ca.1010–1030 MS. Zürich, Zentralbibl. C. 43	Triplex	
		St Dunstan[13] Pontifical: 10th c. MS. Paris, Bibl. nat. lat. 943
Carthusian Missal Printed 1560 Washington, DC, Library of Congress, Rosenwald 968	LOC, Rosenwald 968	
Carthusian Missal MS. Grenoble, Bibl. mun. 386 (olim 71)	Carthusian	

De perseverentia, the rubric under which these prayers are gathered in the Gilbertine missal, is unusual. A similar rubric appeared in two fifteenth-century Carthusian missals. Otherwise, the rubrics normally attached to these prayer forms, while clearly associated with monastic life, do not specify perseverance. The following is a list of the rubrics attached to the Mass prayers of *De Perseverentia* in the sacramentaries and missals cited above.[14]

> *Conversorum missa*
> *Litaniae per hebdomadam, fer. V*
> *Missa in monasterio*
> *Missa monachorum*
> *Missa pro his qui se Deo deuouerint*
> *Oratio in monasterio*
> *Probatio novitiorum*
> *Rituale monasticum*

We know that monastic communities stressed the importance of not only the moment of conversion to monastic life, but perseverance in it. Nevertheless, in most of the sacramentaries and missals in which these prayers appear, the rubrics indicated the population for whom prayers were offered—monks, novices, and *conversi*. In three exceptions identified by this author, the rubric emphasized instead the virtue sought through prayer: perseverance. The Gilbertine missal *L* is

---

[13] *Corpus Benedictionum Pontificalium*, ed. E. Moeller, 4 vols., Corpus Christianorum, Series Latina 162–162C (Turnhout: Brepols, 1971–1979), 1: 458.

[14] Moeller, *Corpus Orationum*, 160B, no. 1835, 58; no. 2051, 156; 160H, no. 5885b, 176.

the earliest example. Two later Carthusian missals, one in manuscript and the other in print, gather their prayers under *Pro perseverantia in ordine* and *Pro perseverantia*, respectively.[15] No doubt there are others in individual manuscripts, but in those manuscript-types representing the major monastic orders, the rubric seems to be unusual.

In the Gilbertine Order the difference may well lie in the experience of the lay brothers in the Order of Sempringham who in the 1160s did not persevere in their vocation. Their rebellion profoundly affected the order's story of origin, the development of the mature version of the Gilbertine constitution, as well as the text of the oath the lay brothers took after the rebellion. Since the Supplement portion of *L* was compiled in the early thirteenth century during the same time when the Order revised these other key documents, it appears that even the assignment of the rubric indicated an endemic nervousness about the lay brothers' rebellion. That rebellion belongs to the Order's foundation story.

Foundation Narrative of the Order of Sempringham (Gilbertine Order)

The Order of Sempringham began in 1131 when Gilbert of Sempringham in Lincolnshire dedicated his possessions for the support and enclosure of seven women who wanted to live a contemplative life. It grew to become the only exclusively English medieval foundation.[16] Gilbert, the son of a Norman knight

---

[15] *Missel cartusien*, MS. Grenoble, Bibl. mun. 386 (olim 71) of the fifteenth century. I was not able to examine this manuscript. I am very grateful for the assistance of Marie-Françoise Bois-Delatte, Chief Conservator of the Fonds Patrimoniaux at the Bibliothèque municipale of Grenoble, for examining the manuscript for me and communicating her findings. See the notice also in Victor Leroquais, *Sacramentaires et missels manuscrits des bibliothèques publiques de France*, 3 vols. (Paris: no pub., 1924), 3: 95–96. The printed missal is *Missale secundum ordinem Carthusiensium*, Washington, DC, Library of Congress, Rosenwald 968. On the development of Carthusian Mass books, see Augustin Devaux, *Les origines du missel des chartreux* (Salzburg: Institut für Anglistik, 1995). The Mass *De perseverantia* does not appear in the *Missale secundum Carthusiensium noviter impressum*, ed. L. Guinta (Vannes, 1509). I am grateful to Dr. Denis Obermeyer, Rare Books and Special Collections of The Catholic University of America, for his assistance in checking this edition.

[16] Pope Innocent III attempted to establish the Gilbertines in the basilica of San Sisto in Rome between 1202 and 1207 as part of his renovation of the basilica there and his desire to revive cloistered female monastic life in the city. The Gilbertines did not send canons to Rome to look into the matter. After Innocent III's death, Honorius III renewed the attempt, insisting that the Gilbertines send four canons to care for the foundation or lose the offer. Finally, in December of 1219 the Gilbertine Order formally requested to be released from the obligation to serve in San Sisto claiming they would

and an Anglo-Saxon mother, was born sometime before 1089. He could not follow his father in a life of military service since he apparently had some sort of physical deformity. Eventually he studied in one of the schools in France; there he earned the title "Master Gilbert" by which he was known the rest of his life. When he returned to England, his father, who as a local landowner had various parishes in his gift, appointed Gilbert as rector to the parishes of Sempringham and West Torrington.[17] Master Gilbert ran the local school for both boys and girls and lived a quasi-monastic life with the chaplain of Sempringham with whom he held regular vigils and other services.[18] The next phase of Gilbert's formation as a spiritual leader took place in Lincoln Cathedral. He became a canon in the episcopal household of Robert Bloet, bishop of Lincoln until 1123, and he remained for a time in the household of Robert's successor, Alexander (1123–1148), during whose episcopate Gilbert entered the priesthood. According to his *Vita*, even within the episcopal household his behavior was more consistent with the life of a regular canon than that of a secular clerk.[19] He wanted to draw together a group of men as a community of religious. None came forward, and so began the most remarkable aspect of his ministry: its provision of a religious life for women.[20]

Seven women among his former students approached Gilbert about wishing to live a strict religious life. He agreed to construct the necessary buildings next to the church of St Andrew in Sempringham for their enclosure. Soon afterward, upon the advice of William, abbot of the Cistercian house of Rievaulx, Master Gilbert replaced the serving girls with lay sisters so that contact with the outside world

---

be unable to do so properly, and the house was turned over instead to Dominican nuns. Golding, *Gilbert of Sempringham*, 259–61; see also Brenda Bolton, "Daughters of Rome: All One in Christ Jesus," in *Women in the Church*, ed. W.J. Sheils and D. Wood, Studies in Church History 27 (Oxford: Blackwell, 1990), 101–15.

[17] In 1086 Jocelyn, Gilbert's father, held around twelve carucates of land in Lincolnshire as a local tenant of Alfred of Lincoln, including the two demesne churches he gave to his son. Technically, Jocelyn held only one quarter of the church in Sempringham, and the church and village in West Torrington were also divided. Brian Golding has pointed out that such divided holdings not only were common in post-Conquest England, but that such division placed Gilbert in a position of dependency on the other nobles (among them Gilbert de Gant) for support for his new foundations. See Golding, *Gilbert of Sempringham*, 10, 13, 199. The records of those holdings appear in *The Lincolnshire Domesday and the Lindsey Survey*, ed. C.W. Foster and T. Longley, intro. F. M. Stenton, Lincoln Record Society 19 (Horncastle: Lincoln Record Society, 1924; repr. 1976); 126, 130.

[18] Golding, *Gilbert of Sempringham*, 12–13.

[19] Foreville, *Book of St. Gilbert*, 24–25.

[20] Foreville, *Book of St. Gilbert*, 30–31.

would not corrupt the dedication of the nuns.[21] Gilbert also included lay brothers in the nascent order to handle the heavy labor associated with the endowment.[22]

The order grew modestly between 1131 and 1139 to two houses: Sempringham and Haverholme. It is difficult to define the character of these early communities. Although Gilbert had given them instructions for living a religious life, there was no written rule as yet.[23] The women gave their profession to Bishop Alexander of Lincoln, but it cannot be said with certainty whether they were considered anchoresses or nuns.[24] Gilbert was in charge of both communities and he, together possibly with Geoffrey, the chaplain of Sempringham, and another man named Albinus, provided the necessary pastoral care.[25]

By the mid-1140s Gilbert's community had attracted attention and respect from potential benefactors. Indeed, a number of bequests for foundations from lay patrons came in between 1148 and 1154.[26] He may have known these gifts were pending, and became concerned that he would not be able to rule a large order. Perhaps his concern derived from his age, for he was nearly sixty years old by then. His *Vita* described Gilbert visiting the Continent where he attended a Cistercian General Chapter in 1147 presided over by Pope Eugenius III, himself a Cistercian monk and former disciple of Bernard of Clairvaux.[27] Gilbert asked

---

[21] Foreville, *Book of St. Gilbert*, 34–35.

[22] Foreville, *Book of St. Gilbert*, 36–39.

[23] See Golding, *Gilbert of Sempringham*, 454–55; cf. Sharon Elkins, "All Ages, Every Condition, and Both Sexes: The Emergence of a Gilbertine Identity," in *Distant Echoes: Medieval Religious Women I*, ed. John A. Nichols and Lillian Thomas Shank, Cistercian Studies Series 71 (Kalamazoo: Cistercian Publications, 1984), 169–82, here 170–75.

[24] Golding, *Gilbert of Sempringham*, 85–86. Sally Thompson, using the example of Christina of Markyate, has argued that these early communities of women in England should not be forced into the more precise terminology that emerged in the second half of the twelfth century. See S. Thompson, *Women Religious: The Founding of English Nunneries after the Norman Conquest* (Oxford: Clarendon Press, 1991), 22–23. See also Patricia Rosof, "The Anchoritic Base of the Gilbertine Rule," *American Benedictine Review* 33 (1982): 182–94.

[25] Golding, *Gilbert of Sempringham*, 86.

[26] Golding, *Gilbert of Sempringham*, 448–49.

[27] The Cistercian General Chapter of 1147 has become part of the question surrounding the chronology of Cistercian origins raised by Constance Berman in *The Cistercian Evolution: The Invention of a Religious Order in Twelfth-Century Europe* (Philadelphia: University of Pennsylvania Press, 2000). This present paper cannot address the issues raised in that important argument. Lengthy responses to Berman's challenge to the traditional Cistercian narrative can be read in Brian Patrick McGuire, "Charity and Unanimity: The Invention of the Cistercian, a Review Article," *Cîteaux* 51 (2000): 285–97, and Chrysogonus Waddell, "The Myth of Cistercian Origins: C.H. Berman and the Manuscript Sources," *Cîteaux* 51 (2000): 299–386. For a review in a non-Cistercian publication, see Constance Bouchard, *Journal of Religion* 81 (2001): 119–20.

the Cistercians to take charge of the nuns, lay sisters, and lay brothers then under his care. The Cistercians did not accept Gilbert's proposal; the *Vita* explained that "it was not proper for them to have authority over the religious life of others, least of all that of nuns."[28] Instead the pope appointed Gilbert to remain as head and pastor of the group he had gathered. During this time, Gilbert may have met and conferred with Abbot Bernard; his *Vita* claims he remained at Clairvaux, although for how long and with how much contact with Bernard is not certain.[29] Nevertheless, multiple signs of Cistercian influence appear in the Gilbertine customs and liturgy. Some time after his return to England, probably within four years, he added the fourth population to the community's structure: regular canons to oversee the spiritual welfare of the nuns and to act as administrative leaders as well.[30] The nuns were to follow the Rule of St. Benedict and the canons the Rule of St Augustine.[31]

The first generation of Gilbertines, then, participated in an experiment of joining four populations into one monastic order. The biblical image chosen by Gilbert's biographer was the chariot of Aminadab:

Hec est quadriga Aminadab, id est spontanei populi, uoluntariorum scilicet pauperum Christi, que duo habet latera, unum uidelicet uirorum, alterum mulierum; rotas iiii°r, duas masculorum, clericorum et laicorum, et duas feminarum, litteratarum et litteras nescientium; iumenta duo quadrigam trahentia, clericalem et monachicam disciplinam. Clericatui beatus presidet Augustinus, monachatum precurrit sanctus Benedictus. Quadrigam ducit per aspera et plana, alta et profunda, pater Gilebertus.

[This is the chariot of Aminadab, in other words of a willing people who of their own accord have become poor for Christ. It has two sides, one of men, the other of women; and four wheels, two of men, clerks and laymen, and two of women, educated and unlettered; the two beasts drawing the chariot are the clerical and monastic disciplines. St Augustine directs the clerks and St Benedict guides the monks while Father Gilbert drives the chariot high and low over places rough and smooth.][32]

---

[28] Foreville, *Book of St. Gilbert*, 42–43.

[29] Foreville, *Book of St. Gilbert*, 40–45; Golding, *Gilbert of Sempringham*, 28–31; idem, "St Bernard and St Gilbert," in *The Influence of St Bernard: Anglican Essays*, ed. Benedicta Ward (Oxford: S.L.G. Press, 1976), 42–54.

[30] Golding showed that several of the Order's charters issued in 1151 established houses such as Watton for nuns without mentioning the presence of canons: Golding, *Gilbert of Sempringham*, 32.

[31] For a study of the liturgical implications of having the two Rules in one institution, see J. Sorrentino, "In Houses of Nuns, In Houses of Canons: A Liturgical Dimension to Double Monasteries," *Journal of Medieval History* 28 (2002): 361–72.

[32] Foreville, *Book of St. Gilbert*, 50–53. The edition prepared by Raymonde Foreville and Gillian Keir provides the Latin text on the left pages and an English translation on

The order grew rapidly during the twelfth century, with new foundations for both men and women. At its height ca.1300, the Order comprised ten double houses, all founded before 1200, and fourteen houses for canons alone. The latest foundation was established in 1360 at Fordham in Cambridgeshire.[33] The Order's priories were disbanded during the Dissolution and did not return during the eighteenth-century revival of monasticism.[34]

Rebellion of the Gilbertine Lay Brothers

Within a period of about ten years (ca.1147–1157) the administrative structure and center of authority in the Gilbertine Order had shifted away from the lay brothers into the hands of the choir canons. By 1165, the *conversi* had become dissatisfied with their situation and rebelled against Gilbert and the Order of Sempringham. They stole property from the Order, slandered the founder and the canons, abandoned their houses and responsibilities, and lived in disruptive, undisciplined license.[35] Led by men named Ogger and Gerard, the lay brothers took their case to Pope Alexander III. They complained that they were subject to extremely strict discipline. They also reported internal scandal in the double monasteries, probably referring to the episode at Watton; with this complaint they possibly intended to undermine Master Gilbert's reputation as a leader and his ability to administer and rule the order.[36] Furthermore, they charged that

---

the right. Unless otherwise indicated, the English translations from *The Book of St. Gilbert* are those given in the edition and the pagination given in the citation will include the texts of both. It is interesting here that the literary image refers to St Benedict guiding the monks rather than nuns. The allusion is to Song of Songs 6:11; cf. Ambrose in PL 14. 527 for exegesis; also Bernard of Clairvaux, Letter 306, PL 182. 510 n.

[33] Golding, *Gilbert of Sempringham*, 448.

[34] The disposition of the twenty-four Gilbertine priories is presented by Rose Graham, *S. Gilbert of Sempringham and the Gilbertines* (London: Stock, 1901; repr. 1904), 162–208.

[35] Golding, *Gilbert of Sempringham*, 42; Foreville, *Book of St. Gilbert*, 78–81.

[36] The reference to impropriety between men and women of the order as a charge made by the lay brothers during their rebellion appears in a letter from the bishop of Norwich to the pope dated 1166. See Foreville, *Book of St. Gilbert*, 36–39. For a more detailed contemporary account of the nun of Watton, see Aelred of Rievaulx, "De sanctimoniali de Wattun," in PL 195. 789c, printed from the only copy, MS. Cambridge, Corpus Christi College 139, fols. 149ʳ–151ᵛ. The manuscript and event are analyzed in Giles Constable, "Aelred of Rievaulx and the Nun of Watton," in *Medieval Women*, ed. D. Baker, Studies in Church History, Subsidia 1 (Oxford: Blackwell, 1978), 205–26. An English translation is available in Jo Ann McNamara, "The Nun of Watton," *Magistra* (1995): 123–37. See also M.L. Dutton, "Aelred of Rievaulx on Friendship, Chastity and Sex: The Sources," *Cistercian Studies Quarterly* 29 (1994): 121–96, here 140, 160; Elkins,

they had been forced under threat of excommunication to make a new profession and to swear oaths "*secundum formam ordinis Cistercie*" [following the example of the Cistercian order].[37]

In describing the leaders of the rebellion, the *Vita* quotes passages from an account that Gilbert wrote about the founding of his religious houses.[38] One leader, Gerard, had been a poor weaver who could barely make a satisfactory living. Another, Ogger, Gilbert had taken in as a boy with three of his brothers, a sickly father, elderly mother, and two sisters, all described as ill and weak. He gave permission for Ogger and one of his brothers to be trained as blacksmiths and the other two as carpenters.[39] In general, the *Vita* refers to them as peasants.

Nevertheless, during the early stages of the rebellion they were remarkably successful in winning papal support, a fact which shows they must have had considerable skill in secular affairs, no matter what their precise social status was. Pope Alexander III, staying in Sens ca.1165, directed Archbishop Thomas Becket (then in exile) to look into the matter and to oversee correction of the problem. That investigation and subsequent inquiries led to complex negotiations in both ecclesiastical and royal courts while it threatened the integrity of the Order and its *Institutes*. Becket wrote letters instructing Gilbert to correct the problems in his Order and established a date (2 February 1166) on which Gilbert would have to answer for his compliance with Becket's directives.[40] Ogger himself delivered the disciplinary letters from Becket and the pope—the latter Gilbert claimed never to have seen. This situation must have stung the holy man sharply, since Gilbert had been already called before royal courts in 1165 to defend himself for having helped Becket escape England and go into exile.[41] The correspondence implies that Gilbert not only received Ogger and his delegation with some harshness, but he also questioned the authenticity of the papal letters.[42] At this juncture, one of Gilbert's strongest supporters, William Turbe, bishop of Norwich, wrote to Gilbert, affirming his affection and support, but urging him to

---

Holy Women, 100, 108–10, Elizabeth Freeman, "Nuns in the Public Sphere: Aelred of Rievaulx's *De sanctimoniali de Wattun* and the Gendering of Authority," *Comitatus* 27 (1996): 55–80; Golding, *Gilbert of Sempringham*, 33–38.

[37] Foreville, *Book of St. Gilbert*, 134–35.

[38] An excerpt from this original account was included in Gilbert's *Vita*. See Foreville, *Book of St. Gilbert*, 78–81. A small portion also appears in the beginning of the *Institutes*. See W. Dugdale, *Monasticon Anglicanum*, ed. J. Caley, H. Ellis, and B. Bandinel, 6 vols. in 8 (London: Longman, Hurst, 1817–1830, repr. London: Bohn, 1846), 6. 2: xxix–xxx.

[39] Foreville, *Book of St. Gilbert*, 78–79.

[40] Foreville, *Book of St. Gilbert*, 346–48.

[41] Foreville, *Book of St. Gilbert*, 72–75; Golding, *Gilbert of Sempringham*, 38–40.

[42] Foreville, *Book of St. Gilbert*, 136–37.

exercise restraint and patience in his handling of the affair and most of all to accept any future papal letters.[43]

When Gilbert did not respond to the first round of letters nor appear as required, Becket wrote him as papal legate, in this second letter mentioning the lay brothers' complaint that Gilbert had forced them to take some unusual form of oath or profession:

> ut fratres uestros, qui occasione iuramenti seruande professionis (quod nulla sicut audiuimus religionis alicuius institutio exigere consueuit) dispersi sunt, reuocaretis, remisso tanti scandali iuramento, et eos ea moderatione de cetero tractaretis, que culpas cohibere et purgare sufficiat, et patrem et pastorem deceat animarum.

> [(lay brothers) who were dispersed on the occasion of keeping the oath of profession which, as far as we understand, no other religious institution was accustomed to exact, you should be recalling, after the oath of such a great scandal has been remitted; and concerning the rest, you should be treating them with moderation; let it suffice to restrain and purge those faults as is fitting for both a father and pastor of souls.][44]

Gilbert had strong supporters among English prelates and from King Henry II. William, bishop of Norwich (mentioned above), Roger, archbishop of York, Henry of Blois, bishop of Winchester, Gregory, prior of Bridlington, and King Henry II sent letters to Pope Alexander III praising the founder of the Order of Sempringham. The letters were transmitted by royal emissaries to add strength to their contents. The letters pointed to Gilbert's wisdom, holiness, age, and nobility as reasons to support him and his work. The archbishop of York in his letter threatened that he and his barons would withdraw "possessions and estates" previously granted to the Order if a judgment was rendered against Gilbert or if the Order's organization should be altered as a result of the rebellion. In like manner, Henry II demanded that the Order remain organized as it had been with Gilbert and the canons in charge, and he further demanded that impenitent rebels be punished by diocesan bishops. He too threatened to reclaim benefactions previously granted to the Order by himself and his magnates if the Order was changed in any way.[45]

---

[43] Foreville, *Book of St. Gilbert*, 146–49.

[44] Foreville, *Book of St. Gilbert*, 347. Although most of the *Book* was translated in this edition, several letters were not, including this correspondence of Thomas Becket. The translation here is my own.

[45] Golding has suggested that the dossier of letters may represent a coordinated effort. He pointed to certain similarities in language and argument among them. Indeed, since Archbishop Becket was so involved in the matter, the papal inquiry may have been perceived as another attack by church reformers on Henry's sovereignty in church affairs

Following this outpouring of support, Pope Alexander III set up official in-vestigations in the two dioceses where the Order had a significant presence, that is, in Lincolnshire and Yorkshire. He appointed William, bishop of Norwich, and Henry of Blois, bishop of Winchester, as the judge-delegates for the province of Canterbury, and Roger, archbishop of York, and Hugh de Puiset, bishop of Durham, as judge-delegates for York.[46] He charged the judges to investigate the allegations against Gilbert, and to investigate as well how the complainants had been treated when they presented the charges. Gilbert, a group of the canons, and the lay brothers were ordered to attend so that the judges could examine the principals about the lay brothers' living and working conditions, the character of their religious profession, and the sexual innuendos along with the other charges. Furthermore, they had to determine whether Gilbert had ignored papal letters and/or treated legitimate papal communications as forgeries.

Ultimately, Pope Alexander III exonerated Gilbert and issued privileges that secured the constitution and royal support. He reconfirmed Gilbert's authority in the Order as well as the status of the Augustinian canons as administrative and spiritual leaders superior to both the *conversi* and the nuns. He issued two privi-leges in 1169 that granted to Gilbert and to his successors exclusive authority to make any necessary changes to the Rule and granted Gilbert the right to excom-municate rebels.[47] The pope also wrote to the bishops and the king, exhorting them to support the Order of Sempringham to the full extent of their jurisdiction and power.[48] The lay brothers themselves followed several paths. Some returned to the Order after receiving absolution; some left permanently, determined never to return; some tried to join other religious orders. Ogger continued to agitate for a solution that would return the lay brothers to their former position of promi-nence before the regular canons had entered the Order, demanding that the Rule be rewritten according to his directions.[49] With regard to the rumors of scandal-ous contact between nuns and men, the crises resulted in tighter enforcement of separation and subjection of the nuns to the canons' rule. The conclusions were confirmed again by papal privilege in 1178.

That these events made a lasting impression on the history of the Order is clearly shown by the surviving sources for the Gilbertines. Ralph de Insula, a can-on of Sempringham, wrote Gilbert's *Vita* in response to a request by Hubert Wal-ter, archbishop of Canterbury, as part of a plan to submit a request for canonization

---

within England. The muster of support for Gilbert, then, may also illustrate the con-tinuing tension between the king and his archbishop. Golding, *Gilbert of Sempringham*, 44–45, 458–62; Foreville, *Book of St. Gilbert*, 142–45, 160–63.

[46] Of this group of four judges, only Hugh de Puiset had not already given written support to Gilbert.

[47] Foreville, *Book of St. Gilbert*, 84–85; 156–59.

[48] Foreville, *Book of St. Gilbert*, 158–61.

[49] Golding, *Gilbert of Sempringham*, 47–48.

to the papal authorities. The *Vita*, combined with records of Gilbert's miracles and letters of support, were submitted to Pope Innocent III, who promptly began an investigation into Gibert's sanctity. The author faced a challenge to promote the cult of Gilbert and advertise his already widely-recognized sanctity while trying to deflect the criticism which naturally arose as a result of the two crises. The *Book* was completed in 1202, thirteen years after the death of the founder. It defends Gilbert and the integrity of the Order in a self-conscious way. It describes the outbreak of the rebellion, the reaction and solutions. It also contains letters that were part of the negotiations among the Order, English prelates, the king, and the papal court during the crisis. The biographer, writing nearly forty years after the rebellion and in the context of Gilbert's canonization process, justified Gilbert's treatment of the lay brothers and presented his actions in the best possible light. The *Book of St. Gilbert*, therefore, stands as both a historical source and an apology for the troublesome events of the 1160s. The record of the rebellion of lay brothers in the Order affirmed what had by then become the dominant paradigm for the social orders in medieval society between cleric and laity.

The concern to prevent a repeat of the crises of the 1160s also influenced the writing of the Gilbertine *Institutes*, an important source for tracing the development of the Order. The *Institutes* survives in a single manuscript, MS. Oxford, Bodleian Library, Douce 136. It contains a number of layers: very early provisions set out by Gilbert, the mature *Rule*, revisions made in 1238, and the records of important Gilbertine General Chapters.[50] Both Brian Golding and Sharon Elkins, in their respective studies of the Gilbertines, have argued that the earlier portions of the *Rule* derive from material written after 1167, that is, after the two crises had threatened the stability of the Order.[51]

Who were the Gilbertine *Conversi*?

Over the last several decades, medieval historians have shown renewed interest in lay brothers.[52] The literature reveals an ambiguity that surrounded the precise origins, status, and role of the lay-brother vocation within medieval mo-

---

[50] Golding, *Gilbert of Sempringham*, 455.

[51] Elkins, "Gilbertine Identity," 169–82; Golding, *Gilbert of Sempringham*, 454–55.

[52] Early studies of *conversi* focused on their old role among traditional Benedictine monasteries, such as Giles Constable, "*Famuli* and *Conversi* at Cluny: A Note on Statute 24 of Peter the Venerable," *Revue Bénédictine* 83 (1973): 326–50. Much literature about lay brothers has come from the study of Cistercian spiritual life and economy. See especially James Donnelly, *The Decline of the Mediaeval Cistercian Laybrotherhood* (New York: Fordham University Press, 1949); K. Hallinger, "Woher kommen die Laienbrüder?" *Analecta Sacri Ordinis Cisterciensis* 12 (1956): 1–104; J. Leclercq, "Comment vivaient les frères conversi," *Analecta Sacri Ordinis Cisterciensis* 21 (1965): 239–58; E. Mikkers, "L'idéal religieux

nastic life. That ambiguity led some lay brothers from several religious orders, at one time or another, to interpret their role and status differently than did choir monks and regular canons, and indeed the rest of literate medieval society. Lay brothers followed various vocational expectations during the late eleventh through thirteenth centuries, the very years when the personnel within the Order of Sempringham struggled with the definitions imposed on them; their experience reflected earlier perceptions. One could argue that the definition of a lay brother in the eleventh-century reform might not be relevant to events of the later twelfth and early thirteenth centuries, but Gilbert's extraordinary longevity coupled with the fact that he continued to be Master of his Order, receiving new lay brothers until the end of his life, draws his late eleventh-century perceptions and those of his early lay brothers forward.[53] The rebellion of the Gilbertine lay brothers cannot be separated from their status within the Order and within medieval society at large.

Gilbert incorporated as lay brothers men who had previously worked for him as household and agricultural servants (*famuli*), some of whom had been with him since their childhood. In addition, runaway serfs and beggars joined to escape their poverty and find a "life of heaven."[54] They were charged to handle "the external and more arduous tasks" for the nuns.[55] *Conversio fratrum laicorum* in the *Vita* tells us that the men who joined as lay brothers

> Qui et ipsi, tum ex inopia humane tum ex ardore celestis uite, idem quod conuersi laici appetierunt et petierunt: circa quos eodem modo quo circa illas operatus est, et tandem tam hiis quam illis quendam signatiuum humilitatis et renuntiationis mundi tradidit habitum. Indixitque illis grauia multa et pauca leuia que supra memorauimus, preter ea que sunt anime propria, ut est humilitas, obedientia et paciencia et huiusmodi, quorum est actus difficilis sed merces multa, que omnia libentissime concesserunt et seruare sub uoto spoponderunt.

---

des frères convers dan l'Ordre Cîteaux aux 12e et 13e siècles," *Collectanea Ordinis Cisterciensis* 24 (1962): 113–29; R.P. Othon (Ducourneau), "De l'institution et des us des convers dans l'Ordre de Cîteaux (XIIe et XIIIe siècles)," in *S. Bernard et son temps*, 2 vols. (Dijon: au siège de l'Academie, 1928–1929), 1:139–201. Studies of lay brothers in other new orders include C. Caby, "*Conversi, commissi et oblati:* les laics dans les établissements camaldules au Moyen Age," in *Les mouvances laïques des ordres religieux: Actes du troisième colloque international du CERCOR, Tournus*, ed. Nicole Bouter (Saint-Etienne: Publications de l'Université de Saint-Etienne, 1996), 51–65; M. Laporte, *Aux sources de la vie cartusienne*, 3, *L'institution des frères en Chartreuse* (Marienau: Kartause Marienau, 1960); F. Salvestrini, "Natura e ruolo dei *conversi* nei monachesimo vallombrosano (secoli XI–XV): Da alcuni esempi d'area Toscana," *Archivio storico italiano* 159 (2001): 49–105.
[53] He lived from approximately 1083 to 1189.
[54] Foreville, *Book of St. Gilbert*, 38.
[55] Foreville, *Book of St. Gilbert*, 36–38.

[Because all these men, spurred both by the poverty of their human life and by their longing for the life of heaven, wanted exactly what the lay sisters desired and requested, he took the same course of action in their case as in the women's and finally bestowed the habit upon both in token of humility and renunciation. He imposed on them many heavy tasks and a few light ones, which we have recorded above, as well as spiritual qualities like humility, obedience, and patience and the like, which are difficult to perform but are greatly rewarded; all these they accepted most willingly and promised under oath to observe.][56]

Three significant points arise from this passage about the entrance of lay brothers into the early Sempringham foundations. Firstly, the brothers were given a religious habit as a reward for their conversion and life; this habit marked a special kind of religious status. Secondly, the biographer claimed that Gilbert fully warned all prospective members of the Order about the rigors and hardships awaiting them. Lastly, the lay brothers accepted the life set before them under oath. The lay brothers' rebellion of the 1160s would raise the issue of extreme hardship as well as the nature of their oath. These three points—religious status, labor, and professing—supply a ready paradigm for examining the definition of *conversi* within the Order of Sempringham and the contemporary monastic culture.

Religious Status

The reception of a habit signaled the transition from ordinary worker to member of the religious community. Enrobement with a monastic habit [*conversationis habitus, habitus religionis, habitus regularis, habitus monasticus*] as early as St Benedict symbolized one's shedding of the former self with his/her property and life, and the clothing of the self with the new.[57] Although the type of clothing worn might resemble in some aspects simple clothing worn by servants and local poor, nevertheless St Benedict seems to have envisaged the granting of a special habit as a sign of consecration.[58] The *Life* of Abbot William of Hirsau, who modeled that abbey after Cluniac customs in the late eleventh century, said the abbot gave

---

[56] Foreville, *Book of St. Gilbert*, 38–39.

[57] Adalbert de Vogüé, "Aux origines de l'habit monastique," *Studia Monastica* 43 (2001): 7–20, here 14. An early standard work on the monastic habit is Philipp Oppenheim, *Das Mönchskleid im christlichen Altertum* (Freiburg im Breisgau: Herder, 1931). See also the review by Placide de Meester, *Ephemerides Liturgicae* 47 (1933): 446–58.

[58] Maria Boulding, "Background to a Theology of the Monastic Habit," *Downside Review* 98, no. 331 (1980): 110–23, here 121.

lay brothers a religious status and a habit.[59] Moreover, Thomas Aquinas confirmed the use of the phrase *conversationis habitum* in the sense of religious status in his polemical work *Contra doctrinam retrahentium a religioni* in the chapter about the practice of child oblation. He included as part of his discussion the prevailing view that St Benedict himself considered his assumption of a habit part of his entrance into religious life.[60] O. duRoy questioned whether a rite of vestment was fundamental to conversion, but otherwise, there is general agreement that receiving a religious habit conferred religious status.[61] Like their male counterparts, female religious also were given a religious habit. In all cases the gift of a habit came in a ceremony after a novitiate or time of testing.[62]

Nevertheless, the reception of a habit was only one aspect of a *conversus'* religious status. The situation was further complicated by the fact that monastic sources referred to certain men with a religious vocation but who did not possess the status of a full choir monk by a variety of terms, among them *fratres laici* and *conversi*.[63] For example, the *Vita* of St John Gualbert confirms that Gualbert accepted *fideles laici* into the monastery and that their lives hardly differed from the monks' except that they were given concessions in clothing and permission to speak for the conducting of external business.[64] The prior of Eberbach referred to them as *saecularibus et idiotis ad spiritalem conversationem conversus, quos nos conversos dicimus*.[65] Among these terms, one can discern several meanings. For example, at times *conversus* simply meant anyone who converted to monastic life. It could mean what scholars now call the "old" type of lay monks, men who converted to religious life as adults, too old to receive the instruction needed to be choir monks. They lived in the monastery as a special labor force, bound to it by religion rather than by ties of serfdom. This early type of *conversus* brought worldly, especially economic and administrative, experience to the monastery. These men with their lack of formal education differed from the *oblati* and the *nutriti* who were raised and educated within the monastery; hence the former

---

[59] Donnelly, *Cistercian Laybrotherhood*, 11; cf. *Vita beati Wilhelmi Hirsaugiensis abbatis*, ed. W. Wattenbach, Monumenta Germaniae Historica, Scriptores 12 (Hannover: Hahn, 1856), 209–25.

[60] Thomas Aquinas, *Contra doctrinam retrahentium a religioni*, ed. Robert Busa, in *Opera omnia*, Textum Leoninum (Rome: Ad Sanctae Sabinae, 1970), c. 3, in *Corpus Thomisticum*, ed. Enrique Alarcón (Pamplona: Universidad de Navarra, 2000–2006), http://www.corpusthomisticum.org/ocr.html#69833. Date accessed 20 December 2007.

[61] O. duRoy, "L'habit fait-il le moine?" *Le Supplement* 95 (1970): 460–76.

[62] de Vogüé, "Aux origines de l'habit monastique," 14, 18.

[63] Duane J. Osheim, "Conversion, *conversi* and the Christian Life in Late Medieval Tuscany," *Speculum* 58 (1983): 368–90, here 368–71.

[64] Donnelly, *Cistercian Laybrotherhood*, 9, n. 36; see also *Vita Sancti Johannis Gualberti*, in *Acta Sanctorum Bollandiana*, 30 (Jul. III), 332–33, online: http://acta.chadwyck.com.

[65] Donnelly, *Cistercian Laybrotherhood*, 26.

were called *monachi illiterati, idiotae.*[66] Nevertheless, this old type of *conversi* were
professed monks and expected if possible to become choir monks.[67]

A "new" type of *conversus* emerged with the new orders of the late eleventh
and early twelfth centuries. The new type shared certain common characteristics.
They lived according to monastic disciplines which included a real, although limited, liturgical life. They followed a rule within the domains of a monastery. They
made a profession of some kind. Furthermore, they performed manual labor including the handling of exterior business.[68] The new type of lay brother was not
a monk and was prohibited from becoming one.[69]

These *conversi* existed simultaneously with other laborers who did not have a
religious status. Servants (*famuli, mercenarii*) had been employed from the early
years to assist monks and nuns with daily chores and administration, but such
servants had no membership in the religious community, even though they were
often attached to the community's properties. The duties of such servants might
range from menial domestic and agricultural labor to carrying banners in liturgical processions. They served the monastic officials and accompanied them in
their travels.[70] No matter how integral a part of monastic life, however, these *famuli* did not receive a religious habit, profess a religious life, or follow a rule.

Manual labor and social status

Lay brothers provided manual labor and at times administration. It is possible
that the elaboration of the divine office and the increased importance of the
Eucharist in Christian devotion changed the labor needs of monasteries. Literate monks, increasingly also priests, occupied with liturgical celebrations, had
less time for manual labor.[71] Lay brothers performed a wide range of tasks in
the monasteries. Cistercian sources relate that they handled all tasks related to

[66] Donnelly, *Cistercian Laybrotherhood*, 5.

[67] This type of *conversus* appears also in Lanfranc's *Decreta*. See, for example, references to the position of lay monks in Rogation processions, to the profession of a lay
monk, to adult converts, and to the promotion of lay converts: *Decreta Lanfranci monachis
Cantuariensibus transmissa*, ed. David Knowles, Corpus Consuetudinum Monasticarum
3, ser. ed. Kassius Hallinger (Siegburg: Francis Schmitt, 1967), 23, 86, 90, 92.

[68] Leclercq, "Comment vivaient les frères convers," 240.

[69] That prohibition, among other regulations, received clear articulation in the Cis-
tercian regulation for profession in the *Usus conversorum: Cistercian Lay Brothers: Twelfth-
Century Usages with Related Texts*, ed. C. Waddell, Studia et Documenta 10 (Brecht:
Cîteaux Commentarii Cistercienses, 2000), 71. Cf. "*Usus conversorum*," ed. J.A. Lefèvre,
Collectanea Ordinis Cisterciensis 17 (1955): 65–97, here 94.

[70] Constable, "*Famuli* and *Conversi* at Cluny," 327–34.

[71] Donnelly, *Cistercian Laybrotherhood*, 6.

agriculture and animal care.[72] In that capacity, they frequently served as supervisors in granges and farms over other non-religious laborers. At Meaux in Yorkshire in 1230, for example, the monks demoted the lay brothers from supervisors to artisans as a punishment for arrogance.[73] They also practiced other crafts such as shoemaking, tanning, and the like. They managed sales and purchases of monastery property and produce.[74] Moreover, they built and renovated permanent structures such as the buildings and roads.[75] They would also accompany dignitaries on their journeys.[76] At least some lay brothers enjoyed a measure of authority as supervisors or practiced trades with the autonomy of expertise, if not full social freedom. Among the Cistercians, masters of masons, cobblers, and other craftsmen had authority over the labor force as did the grange masters over the shepherds and agricultural workers.[77]

Within the Order of Sempringham, the rigors of religious life for a lay brother indeed included the performing of heavy maintenance on the house grounds and agricultural tasks in the granges. They supervised other laborers: *mercenarii*, that is, day laborers hired by the Order for a variety of agricultural and craft work, and *nativi*, serfs attached to local patrons of Gilbertine houses whose services were donated to the Order through grants.[78] Such use of hired labor existed at least as early as 1164 when an agreement was made between the Gilbertine and Cistercian Orders not to hire away one another's laborers.[79]

Some of the ambiguity regarding status of lay brothers, then, may derive from the close proximity among the religious workers, servants, and illiterate choir monks who lived and worked in the same institution, occupied with similar activities. Monastic lay brothers as a class emerged from this general *familia* of a monastic house.[80] Confusion led to the need to legislate and define (and thereby restrict) the status and privileges of lay converts, an effort that in effect closed the doors of fully-professed monastic status.[81] In fact, although it is difficult to determine with certainty to what extent the lay brothers were bound or free in their original status, their religious status created a kind of equality among them since all were religious members of their Order.[82] Nevertheless, their purpose

---

[72] Donnelly, *Cistercian Laybrotherhood*, 19.
[73] Donnelly, *Cistercian Laybrotherhood*, 36.
[74] Donnelly, *Cistercian Laybrotherhood*, 19.
[75] Waddell, *Twelfth-Century Usages*, 65.
[76] Donnelly, *Cistercian Laybrotherhood*, 20.
[77] Waddell, *Twelfth-Century Usages*, 65.
[78] Golding, *Gilbert of Sempringham*, 412–19.
[79] *Cartularium abbathiae de Rievalli ordinis cisterciensis*, ed. J.C. Atkinson, Surtees Society 83 (Durham: Andrews & Co., 1889), 181–83.
[80] Donnelly, *Cistercian Laybrotherhood*, 9.
[81] Osheim, "Conversion," 390.
[82] Leclercq, "Comment vivaient les frères convers," 245.

was to labor in order to free the choir monks from the very tasks the lay brothers performed. Consequently, monastic communities with lay brothers of the "new" type exhibited an essential class structure: monk and lay brother.

In the new orders of the twelfth century, including the Order of Sempringham, *conversi* were drawn from the lower ranks of society. Gilbertine sources spoke of them as beggars, without a trade or skill, household servants, field laborers, and the like.[83] The *conversi* in the Cistercian Order also came from the inferior ranks, such as serfs, poor artisans, peasants, and the illiterate. These men could—and did at times—capably manage business affairs, yet for the most part the lay brothers worked in the fields, as *fratres bubulci*.[84] Although it was not unheard of for a noble to become a *conversus*, desiring to make a sacrifice of humility, increasingly such acts of piety were discouraged. Nobles were directed instead to become monks, as they were considered more useful to their order, a fact that exacerbated the division of the classes within monasteries.[85] Lay brothers were satirized in contemporary literature as village buffoons, so the perception, if not the reality, was that by the thirteenth century the *conversus* had become a character incompatible with full monastic vocation.[86]

The customs of the new orders distinguished monks and regular canons from the lay brethren in dress, food, duties, separate living quarters, and privileges. Scholars have noted that the class distinction intensified feudal values within the cloister.[87] Such division *de facto* created essentially two monasteries in one: nobles/clergy/literate and peasants/workers/illiterate.[88] As will be seen in the texts below, both the Gilbertine and Cistercian rites or *ordines* for profession of *conversi* used the gesture of homage. The *conversus* would place his hands within the hands of the abbot, master, or prior while kneeling in an act of commendation such as when a vassal did homage to his lord and became his 'man'. The noble class practiced such feudal commendation, but not only the noble class. Men at all levels of society 'commended' themselves, and became some lord's 'man'. That this commendation took place at all levels of society is illustrated anecdotally by an incident in the eleventh century when "Norman nuns complained to a local noble that their 'men', that is to say their peasants, were being forced to work at

---

[83] Constable, "Lay Brothers," 83–86.

[84] C. Van Dijk, "L'instruction et la culture des frères convers dans les premiers siècles de l'ordre de Cîteaux," *Collectanea Ordinis Cisterciensium* 24 (1962): 243–58, here 246.

[85] The Cistercian general chapter of 1188 stipulated that nobles might not enter the order as *conversi*: Canivez, *Statuta*, 1: 108 (1188).

[86] J. Batany, "Les convers chez quelques moralistes des XIIe et XIIIe siècles," *Cîteaux* 20 (1969): 241–59, here 251.

[87] Hallinger, "Woher kommen die Laïenbrüder," 99.

[88] Leclercq, "Comment vivaient les frères convers," 244; Martène, *Thesaurus novus anecdotorum,* 5: c. 1647.

the nobleman's castle by his 'men', meaning the knights who were his vassals."[89] The act of doing homage in the ceremony for professing lay brothers illustrates the way social class informed the lay brothers' initiation rite, a quasi-liturgical gathering with prayer. The novice lay brother's life was forever changed at the altar. The ceremony, then, conveyed certain societal realities: the relative rank of the various members according to their calling, and the humility of the role of the lay brother.

Social bifurcation was also manifest in educational matters between the literate and illiterate that in turn affected the labor division. Gilbert's *Vita* underlines the distinction by referring to the canons as *ecclesiasticis ordinibus insignitos, clericos*, and *litteratos*.[90] Jacques Dubois asked whether *conversus* was synonymous with *illiteratus*.[91] It was not necessarily the case that those who could read automatically entered a house as monks and those who could not became *conversi*. Cistercian statutes, for example, speak of instruction to be given to novices and monks; such monks were called lay monks. That the term designated illiteracy becomes clear from the *Dialogus inter Cluniacensem et Cisterciensem monachum*. The author stated, "It would be improper for us to call tonsured monks lay monks if we did not take the word lay in the sense of illiterate."[92]

Be that as it may, lay brothers in most of the new orders began to resent their situation. In the records of several revolts, the harshness of life led to anger and rebellion. Furthermore, in some cases the lay brothers chafed against not only the rigorous discipline but also changes that occurred when a new administration enforced the letter of the law where leniency previously had reigned. For example, at Schönau, early custom had provided the *conversi* with boots annually at the same time that the monks received them. When that practice ended during the regime of a new abbot, the lay brothers conspired to steal and destroy the monks' boots. Supposedly the plot failed, but in the case a rebellion ensued over perceived unfairness in boot distribution.[93] Again, among Cistercians, for example, wine and beer were not to be consumed on the granges, but by 1184 the Cistercians recognized in general chapter that it was a fairly common phenomenon. That year Cistercian monasteries issued bans in Flanders, England, Italy, and France. Additionally, they articulated restrictions against wine and beer for

---

[89] Marc Bloch, *Feudal Society*, trans. L.A. Manyon, 2 vols. (Chicago: University of Chicago Press, 1961), 1: 145; see also C.H. Haskins, *Norman Institutions,* Harvard Historical Society Publications 24 (Cambridge, MA: Harvard University Press, 1918), 63.

[90] Foreville, *Book of St. Gilbert*, 44–46.

[91] J. Dubois, "L'institution des convers au XIIe siècle: Forme de vie monastique propre aux laïcs," in idem, *Histoire monastique en France au XIIe siècle: Les institutions monastiques et leur évolution*, Collected Studies 161 (London: Variorum Reprints, 1982), no. VI, 215.

[92] Dubois, "L'institution des convers," 216.

[93] Donnelly, *Cistercian Laybrotherhood*, 34–35.

conversi on granges where there had been a history or suspicion of rebellion. So, oddly, the restriction of wine and beer from the granges became both a cause of revolt and a stick used to punish it.[94] Certainly in the Order of Sempringham, Gilbert himself recognized that the lay sisters followed "all the harshness of monastic life."[95]

The daily life of a lay brother was especially difficult, presenting a challenge to their perseverance. The position of the new type of lay brother demanded acceptance of their low status vis-à-vis the choir monks. What to a monastic theorist might be a pious virtue of humility no doubt was the practical humiliation common to any peasant serving a lord. Their lives were subject to extreme disciplines. They were given only a small measure of food, drink, clothing, and other basic amenities. Not surprisingly, then, crises were endemic to the institution. Many such *conversi* revolts took place in the second half of the twelfth century, although the rebellion of the Gilbertine lay brothers may well have been the earliest.[96]

Profession or oath key to religious status

Some kind of formal oath or profession sealed the status of the lay brothers as religious members of the Order of Sempringham and other monastic orders. More will be said below about the profession of the Gilbertine lay brothers and the confusion regarding its role in their rebellion in the 1160s. It is sufficient for now that taking an oath and making a profession constituted one of the key elements that separated a lay brother or convert from a non-religious servant connected to the house. Their professed status was recognized in significant documents addressed to members of the Order. For example, papal letters addressed the *conversi* as professed members of the order.[97] Papal bulls also addressed the lay brothers in the Order as professed to the regular life. Charters included them as regular members; grants made to the Order addressed the lay brothers as well as

---

[94] Donnelly, *Cistercian Laybrotherhood*, 28–30.

[95] Foreville, *Book of St. Gilbert*, 36.

[96] Donnelly listed 123 revolts that took place between 1168 and 1308, including the Gilbertine rebellion: see Donnelly, *Cistercian Laybrotherhood*, 71–80. See also Jean Becquet, "La première crise de l'ordre de Grandmont," *Bulletin de la Société archéologique et historique du Limousin* 83 (1960): 283–324. Laporte reported that among the Cistercians alone twenty revolts took place in the second half of the twelfth century, and thirty during the thirteenth: Laporte, *L'institution des frères en Chartreuse*, 111. Also see Leclercq, "Comment vivaient les frères convers," 250.

[97] C.R. Cheney, "Papal Privileges for Gilbertine Houses," in idem, *Medieval Texts and Studies* (Oxford: Clarendon Press, 1973), 39–65, here 63, 65; Constable, "Lay Brothers," 94. Also *Papsturkunden in England*, ed. W. Holtzmann, 3 vols., Abhandlungen der Gesellschaft der Wissenschaften zu Göttingen, Phil.-Hist. Klasse, neue Folge, 25, 1–2; Dritte Folge, 24–25; 33 (Berlin and Göttingen: Weidmann, 1930–1952), 1:455, no. 185.

the canons, or clerical and lay brothers.[98] The lay sisters of the Order took a *votum* after the period of probation, and it will be recalled that the initial stages of the lay brothers' experience was modeled after that of the lay sisters.[99]

Profession of the Gilbertine Lay Brothers as a Key to their Rebellion

At the heart of the entire controversy stood the concern over whether Gilbert had required the *conversi* of his Order to make a new vow or profession different from the one they had originally made, and whether that profession significantly altered their status in the Order. The *conversi* said in effect that early in the history of the Order, they had made a profession to the house of Sempringham according to the form of the order of Cîteaux, but that later they were forced to make a second, different profession at Savigny and take oaths that were detrimental to their status. This second profession (the text of which is lost) probably derived from revised Cistercian customs that defined the new style of *conversus* as constitutionally inferior to the monks.[100]

William of Norwich's letters give two accounts of this problem, although neither is as comprehensive as one might wish:

Letter 1:

conquesti sunt conuersi quod magister G[ilebertus] compulit eos nouam facere professionem abbatie de Sabaneia et iuramenta prestare contra primam professionem quam dudum fecerant uenerabili domui de Sempringham secundum formam ordinis Cistercie; et eos qui iurare nollent excommunicasset. Magister uero G[ilebertus] contra diffitebatur quod neque secundum formam ordinis Cistercie professionem unquam ei fecerant, nec illi professioni quam primo apud Senpingham [sic], postea apud Sabaneiam coacti fecerant professionem contrariam, sed nec aliquam. Verumptamen constanter astruebat quod neminem eorum coegit ad aliquod sacramentum prestandum. Quosdam tamen, qui de conseruando ordine suo iuramentum spontanei prestiterant, iampridem coram domino Lincolniensi episcopo a iuramento absoluerat. Conuersi uero ad hec, sepius interrogati utrum intentata probare possent, in probationibus defecerunt.

[The lay brethren complained that Master Gilbert forced them to make a new profession to the abbey of Savigny and to swear oaths which were contrary to their first profession, made earlier to the venerable house of

---

[98] For a list of such charters and grants see Constable, "Lay Brothers," 88–89, nn. 22–29.

[99] Foreville, *Book of St. Gilbert*, 34–36, 48–49.

[100] Golding, *Gilbert of Sempringham*, 46–47.

Sempringham, following the example of the Cistercian Order; moreover, he had excommunicated those who refused to take such an oath. Master Gilbert on the other hand denied either that these men had ever made him a profession following the custom of the Cistercian Order, or that under compulsion they later made at Savigny any profession contrary to their first profession at Sempringham—or any at all. Indeed he firmly asserted that he had not compelled any of them to take any oath. But some who of their own free will had sworn to preserve his Order he had long ago absolved from their oath in the presence of the bishop of Lincoln. On this point, when the lay brethren were asked repeatedly whether they could substantiate their charges, they failed to supply proof.][101]

Letter 2:
A conuersis suis tantum exigit ut uitam quam professi sunt inuiolabiliter conseruent; quod et ipsi me presente se deuotissime facturos promiserunt. Quod enim predecessorum uestrorum et uestra auctoritate firmatum est, et quod illi post longam experientiam profitentes deuouerunt, ipse inmutare non presumit, ne leuitatis et presumptionis arguatur. Lis tamen, quam aduersus eum suscitauerunt plus tepidi quam feruentes caritate, utinam dirimeretur talium iudicio et testimonio, qui haberent zelum Dei secundum scientiam, qui ex inspectione apostolicorum priuilegiorum et rerum ipsarum euidenti cognitione ueritatem agnoscerent, et regularis obseruantie nec inexperti essent nec ignari, et quos non tederet suscepte religionis et manu missa ad aratrum non respicerent retro.

[The only obligation the Master lays upon his lay brethren is to keep inviolable the life which they have professed; and this they have promised in my presence most faithfully to do. For what was established on your and your predecessors' authority, what those men vowed when they made their profession after a long trial of it, Master Gilbert does not presume to alter, in case he is charged with unconsidered rashness. If only the case mounted against him by those who are lukewarm in their love, rather than red-hot, might be settled by the judgment and evidence of such men as possessed zeal for God according to knowledge, recognized the truth by inspecting papal privileges, and, clearly understanding the matter itself, were neither unused to nor ignorant of observance of a rule, did not tire of the religious life they had undertaken, and did not look back when their hand was put to the plough.][102]

The lay brothers, unable to prove their charge that Gilbert had forced them under threat of excommunication to take new oaths detrimental to their status, nevertheless established that the matter of their *profession* (in addition to the

---

[101] Foreville, *Book of St. Gilbert*, 134–36.
[102] Foreville, *Book of St. Gilbert*, 140–43. The allusion is to Luke 9:62.

extreme harshness of the Rule) was key to their complaints and revolt. According to Giles Constable, "Both sides acknowledged that a profession was made at
Savigny but disagreed over whether or not it differed from the first profession at
Sempringham or resembled the profession made by the lay brothers of Citeaux
or Savigny."[103] Sharon Elkins has suggested one possible explanation for the lay
brothers' assertion. The Savignac houses were assumed into the Cistercian administration in 1147, the same year Gilbert attended the General Chapter. Since
we know Gilbert was hoping to give responsibility of his houses to another reformed monastic order, perhaps he attempted first to hand them over to Savigny
in an earlier year, and the attempt was not recorded perhaps because it was not
ultimately successful or because the Savignac group was acquired shortly thereafter by the Cistercians.[104]

The Thirteenth-Century Profession of Gilbertine Lay Brothers

Thus the rebellion and the profession of the lay brothers in the Order were closely
linked. Profession, like baptism, was part of an initiation to a new life. Experience in religious life began for each brother necessarily with a trial period, pro-
gressed to the ceremony in which he professed and was received into the community, but only reached fruition when the lay brother fulfilled his profession
by living it until his death. Although historians have discussed the requirements
for profession and daily life in the Gilbertine Order, the ritual itself, which for
the lay brethren marked a permanent separation from their previously secular
existence, deserves careful attention. Once the lay brother was admitted into the
Order, he was included fully in the larger communion of faith, the circle of those
for whom the Order prayed: patrons, rulers, the sick, the dead, and fellow community members.[105] The profession, therefore, constituted a crucial beginning
to the life of lay brethren. Unfortunately, no copy of the early form of profession
in the Gilbertine Order survives. The version of the profession in the Gilbertine
Institutes compiled after the lay brothers' crisis given below plainly corrects for
ambiguities that existed in earlier versions.[106]

---

[103] Constable, "Lay Brothers," 92.
[104] Elkins, *Holy Women*, 203 n. 97.
[105] Constable, "Lay Brothers," 86–87; Elkins, *Holy Women,* 142; Golding, *Gilbert of Sempringham*, 111–18; Graham, *S. Gilbert*, 64–67.
[106] The Gilbertine Ordinal also contains a late (fifteenth-century) introduction to a profession in English. "I make acknawlyge to gode almythty and to oure blyssyd lady and to oure Holy father seinyt gylbert and to all the fare falychyp off heueyn and to all the company that is here present thatt I may make my professyon after thys sorte." It occurs in a section of the manuscript containing a set of unrelated elements, such as a mnemonic

According to the *Institutes*, the Master of the novices taught the novice lay
brothers the Order's customs. A candidate could be professed only after spending
a year as a novice among the other brothers, and then he would make his profession in the presence of the highest-ranking prior. On all feast days and Sundays when the sacrist had rung the bell calling the chapter meeting together, the
brothers were to gather in the canons' chapter house, take part in the customary
lections, and listen to the sermon. The *Institutes* set out the *ordo* for accepting new
lay brothers as follows:

> dicat is qui capitulum tenet, "Loquamur de ordine nostro." Ad quod ver-
> bum discedant novicii. Quo dicto, si recipiendus est aliquis novicius, quod
> non sit, nisi in praesentia summi prioris, et post annum inter fratres nostros
> completum, dicat frater cui hoc pertinet, "Recipiendus est novicius." Tunc
> summus prior diligenter inquirat de ejus vita et de moralitate: et sic si fuerit
> recipiendus jussu summi prioris adducat eum frater aliquis. Cui petita venia,
> astanti ante eum, exponat breviter asperitatem et rigorem ordinis. Deinde
> oret pro <u>perseverancia</u> eius; et dicto ab omnibus "Amen" discedat novicius
> in capitulum monialium, professionem facturus . . . Finito denique capitu-
> lo, ad jussum magistri veniat novicius in capitulum monialium, coram illo,
> ubi faciat professionem hoc modo. Imprimis prostratus petat misericordiam
> Dei, et sanctae Mariae et magistri et tocius congregationis, faciendi profes-
> sionem, et <u>perseverandi</u> in ordine usque ad finem vitae suae, ubi doceatur ut
> in prima susceptione; deinde inprecetur ei gratiam Dei et <u>perseverantiam</u>
> in bono. Et sic responso ab omnibus "Amen," flexis genibus coram magis-
> tro, ponat manus suas junctas inter manus magistri in libro, et ore proprio
> renunciet diabolo et omnibus operibus et pompis eius, seculo et actibus eius
> propriae voluntati et omnimodae proprietati; et promittat humilitatem et
> castitatem, obedientiam, fidelitatem et <u>perseverantiam</u> et ordinem fratrum
> se servaturum, pro posse, usque ad finem vitae suae, secundum statuta beati
> Gileberti et successorum ejus. Deinde orari faciat magister pro ejus <u>perse-
> verantia</u>, dicens, "Det tibi Deus meritis et precibus beatae Mariae et beati
> Gileberti et omnium sanctorum <u>perseverantiam</u> in bono." Et responso ab
> omnibus "Amen," promittat ei obedientiam in bono. Dehinc, secundum
> morem ordinis, votum de se faciat super altare. Iste modus semper servetur
> in susceptione omnium canonicorum, monialium, fratrum et sororum.

> [When . . . everyone present had joined in the 'Amen', the one presiding
> over chapter should say, "Let us speak concerning our order." At that point
> the novices should depart. When this statement has been made, if some
> novice must be received, which can happen only in the presence of the
> chief prior, and after having completed one year among our brothers, let the

---

verse detailing when the *Credo* should be chanted, a table listing commemorations of the
saints, and a list of blessings for the Christmas office. MS. Cambridge, Pembroke College
226, fol. 60; Woolley, *Gilbertine Rite*, 1: 106.

brother in question say, "A novice must be received." Then let the chief prior diligently inquire concerning the novice's life and moral behavior. And if he should be received, then on the command of the chief prior, let one of the other brothers lead him. Having asked pardon for the one standing before him, let him briefly explain the severity and rigor of the order. Let him pray for the novice's <u>perseverance</u>, and when everyone has said "Amen", let the novice depart to make his profession in the nuns' chapter . . . Then, when chapter is finished, on the Master's order let the novice come into the nuns' chapter in front of him and there let him make his profession in this way: In the first place, prostrated, let the novice ask for the mercy of God, of Holy Mary, and of the Master and of the whole congregation in making his profession and <u>persevering</u> in the order to the end of his life, where he shall be taught as in the first undertaking. Then he let him beseech for him the grace of God and <u>perseverance</u> in the good. And so, with the response "Amen" by all, kneeling in front of the Master, let him place his hands together between the Master's hands in the book, and with his own mouth, let the novice renounce the devil and all his works and pomp, the world and its deeds, and of his own will every kind of property; then let him promise humility and chastity, obedience, fidelity, and <u>perseverance</u>; to keep himself in the order of brothers as far as he was able to the end of his life, according to the statutes of Blessed Gilbert and his successors. Then let the Master pray for his <u>perseverance</u>, saying "May God grant you <u>perseverance</u> in the good by the merits and prayers of Blessed Mary, Blessed Gilbert, and all the saints." When everyone had responded "Amen", the novice would then promise obedience in the good. After this, according to the customs of the order, he would make his vow upon the altar.][107]

This profession illustrates the impact of the lay brothers' rebellion in several ways. With regard to the text itself, one form or another of the word "perseverance" appears six times. In other aspects, the Gilbertine professional text resembles other *ordines* for contemporary monastic orders: the setting in chapter, community prayers, the doing of homage. The reiteration of "perseverance" seems to suggest the Gilbertine leaders feared what the lay brothers might lack.

Moreover, the placement of the lay brothers' profession within the broader organization of the *Institutes* also shows its critical importance to the Order. The *Institutes* are divided into separate sections that legislated life within the order for each of the four populations: canons, nuns, lay brothers, and lay sisters. The profession of the lay brothers, in *Scripta de fratribus*, received special emphasis by its detail relative to the initiation of the other members of the Order. The only complete description of the Gilbertine profession ceremony occurs in the division devoted to the lay brothers. Within the sections legislating matters for the canons, nuns, and lay sisters, the *Rule* indicates only the conditions of the novitiate or of

---

[107] Dugdale, *Monasticon Anglicanum*, 6.2: xxxvii.

the period immediately following profession.[108] For the lay brothers, however, the *Institutes* describe the *ordo* for profession and reception of new brothers in detail, then mandates that all members of the order, canons, nuns, and lay sisters and lay brothers alike, should follow the *ordo* for profession as set out for the lay brothers. "Iste modus semper servetur in susceptione omnium canonicorum, monialium, fratrum et sororum." ["Let this way be kept in the reception of all canons, nuns, brothers and sisters."][109]

Why should the profession of the lay brothers be set apart in this way? The fame of the Gilbertine Order among its contemporaries derived from its provision for a religious life for women, both choir nuns and lay sisters. Alternatively, the canons in the order achieved preeminence in the Order over the other three populations before the end of the twelfth century. These facts might lead one to assume that the profession of either the canons or the nuns of the Order would have received special emphasis in the *Institutes*, especially since the manuscript was written after the canons gained authority. This textual emphasis on the lay brothers' profession suggests an endemic nervousness caused by the twelfth-century rebellion and a desire in the thirteenth century to produce documents that would leave no ambiguity.

Profession of Cistercian, Carthusian, and Grandmontine Lay Brothers

The Gilbertine Order borrowed heavily from the customs of other orders, as Gilbert himself acknowledged.[110] How similar were the professions of lay brethren in other orders to the Gilbertines'? Below are transcribed and translated professions from the Cistercian, Carthusian, and Grandmontine Orders. The rationale for selecting the Cistercian rests with the large portions of Cistercian material copied by Gilbertines during their formative years. The Carthusian and Grandmontine lay brothers' professions are included because in each the lay brothers had enjoyed at one time a high degree of equality with the choir monks within their respective orders.

Cistercian

The parallel passage from the Cistercian customs is given as follows:

---

[108] Dugdale, *Monasticon Anglicanum*, 6.2: xxvii for *Capitula de canonicis et nouiciis*; li, chap. xxv in *Institutiones ad moniales ordinis pertinentes*.

[109] Dugdale, *Monasticon Anglicanum*, 6.2: xxxvii.

[110] Foreville, *Book of St. Gilbert*, 48–49.

Post annum veniat novicius in capitulum monachorum; ubi relicta prius omni proprietate, faciat professionem hoc modo. In primis prostratus petat misericordiam; deinde surgens ad abbatis imperium, et flexis genibus coram abbate iungat manus suas; et ponens eas inter manus abbatis, promittat ei obedientiam de bono usque ad mortem. Et respondeat abbas, "et dominus det tibi <u>perseverantiam</u> usque in finem," respondentibus omnibus "Amen." Tunc osculato abbate discedat.

[After a year, let the novice come to the monks' chapter. There, having earlier given up all property, let him make a profession this way. In the first place, prostrate, he should ask for mercy, then rising before the authority of the abbot. Then, having genuflected before the abbot, he should clasp his hands and, placing his hands between the hands of the abbot, let him promise him obedience in the good until death. And let the abbot respond, "And may the Lord give you <u>perseverance</u> to the end," with everyone responding, "Amen." Then having been kissed by the abbot let him leave.][111]

Grandmontine

Historians have also compared the Gilbertine lay brothers with those of the Order of Grandmont.[112] Although most of the new orders experienced some level of rebellion from the *conversi*, the lay brothers of Grandmont agitated more than most. Grandmont, founded in the region of Limoges by Stephen of Muret at the turn of the twelfth century, adopted a simple, austere Rule whose spirit was to follow only "the Gospel of Christ." Initially, the members practiced strict evangelical poverty, but the standards relaxed in the thirteenth and fourteenth centuries, mostly in response to internal dissension.[113] The tensions within the Grandmontine Order arose over the radical equality mandated by its Rule between choir monks and the lay brothers. The lay brothers were given full administrative charge of the houses, presence in chapter meetings, and (within the order) social equality. Nevertheless, they were not choir monks and were liturgically, if not practically, illiterate, though many would have been capable of conducting business affairs. When the choir monks tried to assert their authority over them, the

---

[111] Waddell, *Twelfth-Century Usages*, 71–72.

[112] Golding, *Gilbert of Sempringham*, 72–73, 112–15.

[113] For studies of the Grandmontine Order, see Jean Becquet, *Études Grandmontaines* (Ussel: Musée du pays d'Ussel; Paris: de Boccard, 1998), esp. "Le premier crise de l'ordre de Grandmont," first published in *Bulletin de la Société archéologique et historique du Limousin* 83 (1960): 283–324, repr. in *Études Grandmontaines*, 119–60; Rose Graham, "The Order of Grandmont and its Houses in England," in *English Ecclesiastical Studies* (London: Society for Promoting Christian Knowledge, 1929), 209–46, here 212; Carol A. Hutchison, *The Hermit Monks of Grandmont* (Kalamazoo: Cistercian Publications, 1989).

Grandmontine lay brothers rebelled. The similarity between the Grandmontine lay brothers and the Gilbertine situation arises from the ambiguity of status enjoyed by the early Gilbertine lay brothers. They too participated in administrative tasks such as witnessing charters, and played a significant leadership role in the priories.

Stephen Muret exhorted his followers to follow as their rule the gospel of Christ rather than man-made Rules, however venerable. The surviving texts from Grandmont indeed derive their substance from the Scriptures, so that the words relevant to this present study (perseverance, humility, profession, obedience) appear most often in quotations from scriptural text rather than proceeding from the formulations of the Grandmontine writers.

Regula

I. Et propter huiusmodi professionem, quam primo facturus est vobis, fratres carissimi, in unum congregatis, ut uno corde Deum diligatis primum praecipimus in oboedientia Dei et pastoris vestri, et fratrum invicem sine murmure et haesitatione constanter perseuerare

De perseuerantia in supradictis

LXV. Vos itaque, fratres carissimi, in praedictis, constanter perseuerate. Quod si pastor uester ab hac uia ueritatis uos ad aliud euertere conabitur, nec uestris consiliis ullo modo acquieuerit, haec institute deserens, ex auctoritate Dei uobis confidenter praecipimus quatenus ipsum sicut apostatam potius a uestra societate penitus eiciatis, quam propter eum ab hac uia declinetis.

LXXVI. De aedificio quintae porticus: His quattuor porticibus aedificatis, necessario sequitur quinta porticus quae dicitur *perseuerantia in supradictis* . . . Nam non inchoantibus sed perseuerantibus regnum Dei promittitur. Unde est illud evangelicum: *Qui perseuerauerit in finem, hic saluus erit.*

XLV. Recordamini, obsecro, qualem professionem fecistis, qualem hostiam Domino Deo uestro immolastis. Obtulistis siquidem Domino sacrificium laudis, dum promisistis quod omnia relinqueretis.

[I: And first of all, because of this kind of profession which you will have made, beloved brothers, we decree that in obedience to God and your pastor, you love God in one body and with one heart and your brother as yourselves, and persevere constantly without murmur or hesitation.

Concerning <u>perseverance</u> in the above

LXV. You, therefore, beloved brothers, <u>persevere</u> in the above-mentioned matters faithfully. If your pastor tries to turn you from this way of truth to another, one not in any way acquired through your advice, abandoning these institutes, we confidently order you by the authority of God to evict that man from your society, thoroughly uprooted as an apostate, rather than because of him be turned from this way.[114]

LXXVI. On the structure of five pillars. You will build these four pillars, so by necessity a fifth follows which is called "<u>perseverance</u> in the above." For not to those who begin but to those who <u>persevere</u> is the kingdom of God promised. Whence it is in the gospel, "He who <u>perseveres</u> to the end shall be saved."[115]

XLV. Remember, I beseech you, what sort of profession you made, what kind of sacrifice you offered to the Lord your God. You offered to the Lord a sacrifice of praise when you promised that you would give up everything.][116]

The Grandmontine Rule did not set out a profession with the same degree of formality as that found in the other examples. The prescriptions exhort the entering candidate rather than provide a specific text or ceremony. Nevertheless, it is clear that the Grandmontine order also stressed perseverance as a fundamental virtue.

Carthusian

Lay brothers also played an important role in the order founded by Bruno in 1084, the Carthusians.[117] The life of the monks of La Chartreuse and its daughter houses exemplified the eremitic spirit of the desert, following the example of John the Baptist. Bruno's *Vita* mentions that among his first companions, two lay brothers journeyed with Bruno to participate in the first foundation.[118] Lay brothers within the Carthusian Order lived in a separate dwelling known as the lower house. The community complex, however, encompassed their buildings as well as those of the choir monks, unlike the Cistercian grange system. The Carthusian way of life also required the houses to keep to the principle of small numbers, so that each house was limited to sixteen conversi, only two of whom

---

[114] *Regula*, LXV, ed. Jean Becquet, *Scriptores ordinis grandimontensis*, Corpus Christianorum, Continuatio Mediaevalis 8 (Turnhout: Brepols, 1968), 98–99.

[115] Becquet, *Scriptores*, 400–1. The allusion is to Matthew 10:22.

[116] Becquet, *Scriptores*, 69. The allusion is to Psalm 49: 14, 23.

[117] The foundational study of the *conversi* among the Carthusians is that of M. Laporte cited above, n.52.

[118] Daniel LeBlévec, "Les convers de Chartreuse d'après les textes législatifs de l'ordre (XIIe-XIIIe)," in *Les mouvances laïques des ordres religieux*, ed. Bouter, 67–79, here 67.

at any time could do demesne work and make contact with the outside world. The Carthusian lay brothers, then, enjoyed an unusual level of solitude, eating and praying in their individual cells, and therefore shared more in common with Carthusian choir monks than did lay brothers of "the new style" with monks in other orders.[119]

The customs were set out by Guigues I, fifth prior of La Chartreuse, between 1121 and 1128. Approximately one-quarter of the regulations found within them deal with one or another aspect of the life of the Carthusian lay brother. Among the provisions laid out is the following profession:

> Professio laici LXXIIII: "Ego frater ille promitto obedientiam et conversionem morum meorum et <u>perseverantiam</u> omnibus diebus vitae meae in hac heremo, coram deo et sanctis eius et reliquiis istius heremi, quae constructa est ad honorem dei et beatae semper virginis mariae, et sancti iohannis baptistae, pro timore domini nostri ihesu Christi, et remedio animae meae, in presentia domni illius prioris. Quod si aliquot tempore unquam hinc aufugere vel abire temptavero, liceat servis dei qui hic fuerint, me plena sui iuris auctoritate requirere, et coacte ac violenter in suum servicium revocare." Post haec, hanc ipsam cartulam offert super altare, et osculate altari, incurvatur ad pedes sacerdotis, tali obsecratione benedicendus. Salvum fac, mitte ei, esto ei, dominus vobiscum, oremus, domine ihesu christe qui es via.

> [Profession of lay brothers: "I, brother N, promise obedience and conversion of my life, and <u>perseverance</u> all the days of my life in this desert, before God and his saints and the relics of this hermitage, which is built for the honor of God and of the Blessed Mary ever Virgin, and of Saint John the Baptist, out of the fear of our Lord Jesus Christ and for the salvation of my soul, in the presence of Lord N, prior of this house. If at any time I should try to run away or be tempted to leave, it should be permitted to the servants of God who are here, with the full authority of the law, to search for me, and force me, even with violence, to recall me to its service." After these things, the *conversus* places the charter itself on the altar, and, having kissed the altar, he bows before the feet of the priest in order to receive the blessing given by the following prayers: *Salvum fac, Mitte ei, Esto ei, Dominus vobiscum, Oremus, Domine Iesu Christe qui es via.*[120]

The initiation of a lay brother in all the new orders necessarily underscored certain fundamental virtues, among them obedience, humility, poverty, conversion of one's life, and perseverance. The vocation demanded them. Indeed, Bruno said of the vocation, "The true obedience can never exist without great humility and

---

[119] Guigues I, *Coutumes de Chartreuse: Introduction, texte critique, traduction et notes,* ed. un Chartreux Sources Chrétiennes 313 (Paris: Les Éditions du Cerf, 1984), 54.

[120] Guigues I, *Coutumes de Chartreuse,* 280–81.

remarkable patience."[121] One sees how the orders reinforced their values in the texts just cited. Yet the emphases differ subtly. The Grandmontine Rule focused primarily on its gospel origins. In both the Gilbertine and Cistercian ceremonies, either the abbot or the master prayed for the novices to be given perseverance. While, as will have been evident, the Gilbertine *ordo* for the profession of the lay brethren contains one or another form of the word for perseverance six times, the virtue of obedience occurs only twice, and the virtues of humility, chastity, and fidelity only once. In the Cistercian profession, perseverance is mentioned only once. In fact, when one considers the profession of lay brethren in the Cistercian and Carthusian Orders, obedience to the abbot in humility remained the characteristic most desired in a lay brother. In the Grandmontine *Regula*, perseverance was heavily emphasized as well as obedience and equality. One cannot say, therefore, that the Gilbertine emphasis on perseverance in their profession was unique. Instead, the fortunate survival of the record of the rebellion, together with the revised *Rule* and additions to the Mass books, give the historian a window into the concerns surrounding the vocation of lay brothers, not only in the Gilbertine Order but elsewhere. In the Gilbertine Order, after the dust had settled from the crises in the 1160s, and after the ultimate articulation of the Gilbertine constitution in the mid-thirteenth century, the virtue *par excellence* of a lay brother would be his perseverance, and to that characteristic both his profession and a votive Mass were dedicated. Whereas the texts used in the *De perseverentia* votive Mass were typical of prayers used for the profession of monks and lay brothers, they were gathered together in the Gilbertine and Carthusian missals under an unusual rubric that ties their worship to their history.

Conclusion

As a result of their particular status and calling, lay brothers faced severe challenges and temptations to their commitment. A lay brother might be tempted in the areas of ambition, sex, and money. When the lay brothers conducted their monastery's business, they could be attracted by the money they handled, and certainly theft was one of the charges leveled at Gilbertine lay brothers. An ambitious lay brother might also aspire to full religious status. That some attempted the transition is clear from the prohibitions (among the Cistercians as well as the Gilbertines and others) forbidding lay brothers from leaving their home abbeys and attempting to become monks or regular canons in other orders.[122] To wish to quit their station or to incite rebellion was what Leclercq called a "temptation to equality."[123] Yet in the prevailing religious atmosphere of apostolic revival, the

---

[121] M. Laporte, "L'institution des frères convers," 242.

[122] Waddell, *Twelfth-Century Usages*, 71–72.

[123] Leclercq, "Comment vivaient les frères convers," 245.

possibility of equality stood before the peasants who became lay brothers. For the gospel not only lauded those who lived with all things in common, and who gave all they owned to the poor. It also exhorted believers not to consider distinctions of class or wealth, but to be "one in Christ Jesus."[124] Such a radical social interpretation of the gospel was, of course, not limited to the eleventh and twelfth centuries. German peasants influenced by the sixteenth-century reformers also interpreted their gospel liberties to include economic and social equality as well as spiritual.[125] This apostolic equality was incorporated into the organization of several of the new orders. In the Order of Grandmont, for example, lay brothers were given full administrative charge of the priories, and shared the same quarters with the choir monks. Gerard Ithier, the seventh prior of Grandmont, observed the following:

> Quorum conversatio talis est ut tam clerici quam conversi semper habeant in commune unum oratorium, unum claustrum, unum capitulum, unum refectorium, unum dormitorium, unum habitum, unum etiam vivendi modum, ut qualis clericus, talis et conversis, nec est aliqua distinctio inter eos nisi ut alibi diximus in tonsure capitis et barbarum nutrimento.

> [Their way of life is such that, whether clergy or lay brother, they always share in common one oratory, one cloister, one chapter, one refectory, one dormitory, one habit, as well as one way of living, so that however much the clerk, so much the lay brother also, there is no distinction between them unless as we said elsewhere in tonsure of the head and trim of the beard.][126]

Medieval society evidently could not bear the social upheaval associated with such radical beginnings. In the suppression of the *conversi* rebellions, ecclesiastical and secular authorities regularly criticized the pretensions of the lay brothers because of their peasant/laborer heritage. Ultimately, the Gilbertine rebellion prompted papal confirmation of the Order, but in a way that ignored the early status of the brothers and affirmed the clerical leadership.

---

[124] Galatians 3: 28. Consider, for example, the radical equality or leveling Jesus preached as characteristic of the kingdom of heaven where the first would be last and the last first, and where a poor woman's two-penny offering had more value than the endowments of the wealthy.

[125] See, for example, the "Twelve Articles of the Upper Swabian Peasants" prepared in 1525: Michael G. Baylor, ed. and trans., *The Radical Reformation*, Cambridge Texts in the History of Political Thought (Cambridge: Cambridge University Press, 1991), 231–45.

[126] Jean Becquet, "La Règle de Grandmont," *Bulletin de la Société archéologique et historique du Limousin* 87 (1958): 9–36, here 24; repr. in idem, *Études grandmontaines*, 91–118, here 106.

The situation, then, showed lay brothers caught between two periods: eleventh-century apostolic revival and twelfth- and thirteenth-century sacerdotalism. This essay has suggested that the lay brothers rebelled in part because their understanding of their role and status differed from that of the canons in the Order and from that of clergy and monks outside. Their exclusion from letters was an important part of the breach in understanding. As the new orders created their textual societies in the twelfth century, the lay brothers of the new type were excluded not only from the creation of the texts that defined their lives, but they were moreover excluded by law (more written text) from the instruction that could ever make it possible for them to participate in that community.[127] During the first years of their formation and through the early years when they entered the order, the rigid definitions of the lay brotherhood had not yet been articulated, so that their self-perception and identity was based on their lived experience. By the 1160s they came face to face with prescriptive texts that demanded that they conform their behavior to the text. From the point of view of the Gilbertine Rule, the texts only transcribed what the canons thought about the lay brothers' role and status. From the point of view of the lay brothers, their role had been redefined.[128]

The customs governing the lives of lay brothers in these orders provided a structure to help them remain faithful to their conversion. One form of such empowerment came with the profession, a solemn promise made before concerned witnesses. Medieval society depended upon such sworn declarations in most legal and social contexts. The articulation of the mature version of the Gilbertine Rule defined more carefully the role and status of the lay brothers within the Order. That definition described the boundaries that late twelfth-century society had imposed and within which they must function thereafter. Thus the written Rule established the hegemony of the clerical over the laity within the Gilbertine Order as elsewhere.

The effort to reinforce right order in society did not rest with the constitution. Monastic vocation was one of prayer; it stands to reason that another method for strengthening "the hands of the weak" would be the Mass, offered on behalf of lay brothers. Who better to enlist to keep the lay brothers in their proper order in society than the God who, as they heard from Job, keeps the

---

[127] For the prohibition in the Gilbertine *Institutes* see Dugdale, *Monasticon Anglicanum*, 6. 2: xxxvii. The Cistercian Usages for lay brothers forbid them to possess books or to advance to any learning beyond the memorization of set prayers by heart. See Dubois, "L'institution des convers," 217; Waddell, *Twelfth-Century Usages*, 68.

[128] For the importance of textual community and its implications for society, I am indebted to the work of Brian Stock, *The Implications of Literacy: Written Language and Models of Interpretation in the Eleventh and Twelfth Centuries* (Princeton: Princeton University Press, 1983).

lines of the cosmos straight and confines the seas within their boundaries?[129] With the votive Mass *De perseverentia* the Gilbertine liturgy also encouraged conformity through prayer. It is not problematic to see that another order such as the Carthusians also had the rubric in their missal. For the Gilbertines were not unique in their concern to support their lay brothers' commitment to perseverance through prayer. Rather, in their self-conscious revision of the Gilbertine documents traceable to their *conversi*'s rebellion, specific evidence survives for the concern felt by clerical orders in society to ensure that lay brothers conform to their proper rank in society.

---

[129] Job 38: 5–12.

A Lost Treatise by Amalarius:
New Evidence from the Twelfth Century

Christopher A. Jones

Though many know Richard Pfaff for his wondrously concise and illuminating discussions of liturgical manuscripts, his erudition extends also to medieval commentaries on the liturgy and to the history of liturgical studies. The latter interests happily coincided in his work on William of Malmesbury's abridgment of the prolix *Liber officialis*, a commentary on the whole of the liturgy as interpreted by the Frankish scholar Amalarius (c. 775–c. 850). The resulting publications on William's *Abbreviatio Amalarii* shed light both on the working habits of a major twelfth-century intellectual and on Amalarius's influence in the high Middle Ages.[1] More tacitly, Dick's introductory essay on William's *Abbreviatio* stands at the same time as an appreciative tribute to a great fellow-historian of liturgy, the prodigious Jean-Michel Hanssens, whose critical edition of Amalarius's works (published between 1948 and 1950) our honorand has described as "one of the high-water marks of liturgical scholarship in [the twentieth] century."[2] My hope is that the present offering, also concerned with the English transmission of Amalarian texts, will pay tribute in turn to one who stands in the same long, learned tradition as Fr. Hanssens.

1. A Lost Amalarian Work on the *Triduum*?
The State of Some Questions

Hanssens's deep researches preparatory to his edition established that the text of the *Liber officialis* underwent at least three major revisions by Amalarius himself and then became fodder for numerous post-authorial *retractationes*, including

---

[1] Richard W. Pfaff, "The 'Abbreviatio Amalarii' of William of Malmesbury," *Recherches de théologie ancienne et médiévale* 47 (1980): 77–113 (introduction), and 48 (1981): 128–71 (edition).

[2] *Medieval Latin Liturgy: A Select Bibliography*, Toronto Medieval Bibliographies 9 (Toronto: Pontifical Institute for Mediaeval Studies, 1982), 57.

The Study of Medieval Manuscripts of England: Festschrift in Honor of Richard W. Pfaff, eds. George Hardin Brown and Linda Ehrsam Voigts, MRTS 384 (Tempe: ACMRS, 2010).   [ISBN 978-0-86698-432-4]

that by William of Malmesbury.[3] In the broader context of medieval European reception of Amalarius, William's *Abbreviatio* is actually atypical both for its coherence and for its certain pedigree. Far more of the post-authorial recyclings of Amalarius survive as unstable texts by unknown compiler-editors who labored with widely differing aims and degrees of skill.

One of the earliest and most important reworkings of Amalarius's crowning, four-book version of the *Liber officialis* was a well-executed abridgment in two books that Hanssens labeled the *Retractatio prima*. Apparently the only version of the *Liber officialis* known in England before the Norman Conquest, this *Retractatio prima* itself served as the basis for further, anonymous redactions in the tenth to twelfth centuries.[4] Of those, the most interesting survives in a manuscript that Fr. Hanssens unfortunately overlooked in his otherwise thorough *recensio codicum*. The manuscript in question, now Salisbury, Cathedral Library 154, was copied in the last quarter of the eleventh century in the scriptorium of St. Osmund's recently established cathedral at Old Sarum. Salisbury 154 preserves a version of the *Retractatio prima* that has undergone further minor reorganization and some significant interpolation.[5] The interpolations include passages that, I have argued elsewhere, derive ultimately from a separate work composed by Amalarius himself, probably early in his career, and dealing with elements of

---

[3] The complex editorial history of the *Liber officialis* was authoritatively treated by Jean-M[ichel] Hanssens in a series of articles titled "Le texte du 'Liber officialis' d'Amalaire," *Ephemerides liturgicae* 47 (1933): 113–25, 225–48, 313–28, 413–24, and 493–505; 48 (1934): 66–79, 223–32, and 549–69; 49 (1935): 413–35. Much of this matter he subsequently condensed into the introduction to his monumental edition of Amalarius's works: *Amalarii episcopi Opera liturgica omnia*, 3 vols., Studi e Testi 138–140 (Vatican City: Biblioteca Apostolica Vaticana, 1948–1950), 1: 120–200. William of Malmesbury's *abbreviatio* is Hanssens's *Retractatio V* (see *Amalarii episcopi Opera* 1: 171–73). Hereafter I cite Hanssens's edition as *AEOLO* plus volume and page numbers.

[4] On the *Retractatio prima*, see Hanssens, "Le Texte" (1934), 70–73, and *AEOLO* 1: 162–69; he regarded this *retractatio* as the work of an anonymous compiler, not Amalarius himself, though the question cannot be considered closed. On the largely Breton and Anglo-Saxon transmission of the redaction, see David N. Dumville, "Breton and English Manuscripts of Amalarius's 'Liber officialis'," in *Mélanges François Kerlouégan*, ed. Danièle Conso, Nicole Fick, and Bruno Poulle (Paris: Les belles lettres, 1994), 205–14.

[5] The variant traits of this version were first noted by Neil R. Ker, "The Beginnings of Salisbury Cathedral Library," in *Medieval Learning and Literature: Essays Presented to Richard William Hunt*, ed. J. J. G. Alexander and M. T. Gibson (Oxford: Clarendon Press, 1976), 23–49, at 38, 43, and 46; reprinted in Ker's *Books, Collectors, and Libraries: Studies in the Medieval Heritage*, ed. Andrew G. Watson (London and Ronceverte, WV: Hambledon, 1985), 143–73, at 159, 166, and 170–71. See further Teresa Webber, *Scribes and Scholars at Salisbury Cathedral, c. 1175-c.1225* (Oxford: Clarendon Press, 1992), 70–71 and 152–53 (Appendix I, no. 45).

the Divine Office and of special liturgies for the last three days of Holy Week (the *triduum sacrum*).[6]

Various kinds of evidence support Amalarius's authorship of the now-lost source behind many of the Salisbury interpolations. One external clue survives in a brief reference at the end of a letter written c. 814 by Amalarius to his friend, Abbot Peter of Nonantola, mentioning a work then in hand "about the nocturnal Offices [. . .] and other Offices performed by day; and about Maundy Thursday, Good Friday, and Holy Saturday."[7] The most conspicuous interpolations spliced into the standard text of the *Retractatio prima* in Salisbury 154 pertain exactly to those topics. (For this reason, I hereafter refer to the posited source of those interpolations simply as the *De triduo*.) But the case for Amalarius as author of such a treatise depends less on the single reference in the letter to Peter than on many features of content, sources, and style in the Salisbury passages themselves.[8] Individually, internal arguments of this kind rarely attain the force of proof, however, and so the hypothesis of Amalarian authorship has persuaded some but by no means all readers.[9]

A festschrift is not the platform for rehearsing the entire case, but two of the greater difficulties about the argument need review since they bear directly on the new evidence to be presented here. The first point concerns the significance of certain stylistic traits. The *De triduo*, so far as it could be reconstructed from the Salisbury interpolations, frequently employed a pseudo-dialogic or "diatribe" style consisting of repeated, insistent rhetorical questions raised in a kind of extended apostrophe to various persons, sometimes to an unidentified but familiar *frater*, sometimes apparently to the "author" of the liturgical texts being commented upon. This distinctive rhetorical packaging is significant because it so closely resembles what is found in a pair of texts which Hanssens considered to be Amalarius's earliest (c. 814) expositions of the Mass.[10] Hanssens edited these from a single defective manuscript—the only one known at the

---

[6] Christopher A. Jones, *A Lost Work by Amalarius of Metz: Interpolations in Salisbury, Cathedral Library, MS. 154*, Henry Bradshaw Society Subsidia 2 (London: Boydell Press, for the Henry Bradshaw Society, 2001).

[7] *AEOLO* 1: 231: "de nocturnalibus officiis et de aliis quae in die aguntur; et de cena Domini et parasceve et sabbato sancto." See discussion at Jones, *A Lost Work*, 118–19.

[8] Jones, *A Lost Work*, 33–125.

[9] The persuaded include reviewers B.-M. Tock, *Scriptorium* 56.2 (2002): 205*-206*; John J. Contreni, *Journal of Ecclesiastical History* 54 (2003): 117–18; Milton McC. Gatch, *The Medieval Review* (online), 03.12.03. Unconvinced are G. R. Evans, *Journal of Theological Studies* 53 (2002): 369–70; Yitzhak Hen, *Early Medieval Europe* 11 (2002): 401–2.

[10] On the diatribe style, see discussion and numerous examples at Jones, *A Lost Work*, 40–45 and 58–62. Cf. Herbert Schneider's comparable remarks on what he terms the "epistolary" style of the *Geminus codex* in "Roman Liturgy and Frankish Allegory," in *Early Medieval Rome and the Christian West: Essays in Honour of Donald A. Bullough*, ed. Julia M. H. Smith (Leiden: Brill, 2000), 341–79, at 352–53.

time—and coined for them the title *Missae expositionis geminus codex* (hereafter simply *Geminus codex*).[11]

The case that I have made about the origins of the Salisbury interpolations does depend significantly on the correctness of Hanssens's attribution of the *Geminus codex* to Amalarius. By sheer unlucky timing, however, the passages from the Salisbury manuscript came to light just as many of Hanssens's findings, including his attribution of the *Geminus codex*, were beginning to face determined fire from Wolfgang Steck in a Munich dissertation submitted in 1998. Steck's argument in sum—that commonplace modern associations between Amalarius and the region of Metz have little basis in medieval sources, which more securely connect him to Soissons or Tours—is persuasive and has since inspired further revisionist work by David Diósi, who has clarified the comparatively more ancient and enduring ties between Amalarius's name and the see of Trier.[12]

Despite their larger contribution, however, Steck's arguments touching many minor details in the received picture of Amalarius's career sometimes strain against the evidence or overstate its weakness. Exemplifying both tendencies, Steck's dismissal of the *Geminus codex* from the Amalarian canon has to downplay the significant testimony of Hanssens's base manuscript: Zurich, Zentralbibliothek Car. C. 102. There the *Geminus codex* is preceded by the exchange of letters between Amalarius and Peter of Nonantola, the latter requesting that the former send an exposition of the Mass composed during their recent voyage together to Constantinople. Amalarius's letter of reply describes the requested exposition in terms that accord fairly closely with the content of the *Geminus codex* that follows thereafter in the manuscript. The whole assemblage, which in Zurich Car. C. 102 also includes Amalarius's poem on the Constantinopolitan embassy (the *Versus marini*), therefore looks very much to be descended

---

[11] *AEOLO* 1: 253–81, with introductory matter at 1: 106–8. Hanssens's sole manuscript was Zurich, Zentralbibliothek, Car. C. 102 (now 268), fols. 78r-93v (but lacunose and often out of order; see Hanssens's remarks at *AEOLO* 1: 95–97). Only recently have further, more extensive fragments of the *Missae expositionis geminus codex* been discovered and published by Herbert Schneider, "Roman Liturgy and Frankish Allegory" (see preceding note).

[12] Wolfgang Steck, *Der Liturgiker Amalarius—eine quellenkritische Untersuchung zu Leben und Werk eines Theologen der Karolingerzeit*, Münchener theologische Studien, historische Abteilung, 35 (St. Ottilien: Eos Verlag, 2000), 119–74 (a comparison between Amalarius's works and Messine liturgical usages) and 175–92 (on claims for Metz as Amalarius's burial place). On the Trier connections (many of which are late and dubious), see David Diósi, *Amalarius Fortunatus in der Trierer Tradition: Eine quellenkritische Untersuchung der trierischen Zeugnisse über einen Liturgiker der Karolingerzeit*, Liturgiewissenschaftliche Quellen und Forschungen 94 (Münster: Aschendorff Verlag, 2006). Diósi's study does not take account of the potentially crucial evidence for Amalarius's Trier phase and its aftermath as discussed in *A Lost Work*, 164–74; cf. Diósi, *Amalarius Fortunatus*, 60–66.

from one or the other correspondent's file-copy of the entire exchange.[13] Steck maintains that, while the letters and poem are genuine, some intervening scribe has intruded an inauthentic anonymous text, Hanssens's *Geminus codex*, wrongly believing that to be the exposition mentioned in Amalarius's letter.[14]

While discounting the manuscript setting, Steck places correspondingly greater emphasis on internal evidence against the authenticity of the *Geminus codex*. Purely formal objections rest on the facts that chapter-by-chapter summaries prefacing each half of the *Geminus codex* in Zurich Car. C. 102 do not match up exactly with the contents that follow, and that second-person plural forms of address in Amalarius's formal letter to Peter contrast with the singular forms which recur in the diatribe-style *Geminus codex*.[15] Steck presses these objections and likewise makes much of some discrepancies between the *Geminus codex* and Amalarius's *Liber officialis*.[16] The differences pertain both to details of the Mass-*ordo* underlying the exposition in either instance and to the content of the exegesis itself. For Steck, in view of all these differences,

> [t]he conclusion follows that the texts [*scil.*, the *Geminus codex* and the *Liber officialis*] do not issue from one and the same author. Certainly, it would also be conceivable, in Amalarius's case, that at different points in time he had before his eyes differing liturgical practices and that, moreover, those actions of the liturgy that did remain the same he interpreted in different ways and using a partly different terminology. But this seems improbable.[17]

---

[13] For Hanssens's discussion of the manuscript and other reasons for his attribution, see *AEOLO* 1: 97 and 106, as well as his earlier partial edition and study, "Le traité sur la messe du ms Zurich C. 102," *Ephemerides liturgicae* 41 (1927): 153–85, at 153–56.

[14] *Der Liturgiker Amalarius*, 76. The same section of Zurich Car. C. 102 preserves another work that Hanssens considered an authentic text by Amalarius, namely the *Canonis missae interpretatio*—not a commentary on the Canon of the Mass itself but rather a supplement written to accompany another, anonymous commentary on the Canon known by its opening words as the *Dominus vobiscum*. Hanssens edits the allegedly Amalarian commentary together with the anonymous target-text at *AEOLO* 1: 283–339 (the *Dominus vobiscum* on the versos, the *Canonis missae interpretatio* facing it on the rectos). Steck also rejects the *Canonis missae interpretatio* from Amalarius's canon (*Der Liturgiker Amalarius*, 66–69 and 195). As in the case of the *Geminus codex*, I question his bases for doing so, but because the authenticity of the *Canonis missae interpretatio* does not bear on the new textual evidence discussed below, it is omitted from the present discussion.

[15] *Der Liturgiker Amalarius*, 66–68.

[16] *Der Liturgiker Amalarius*, 68–75. Steck also asserts that the expository method of the *Geminus codex* differs fundamentally from that of the *Liber officialis*, in that the former (he claims) makes no explicit reference to particular *ordines* or liturgical books (*Der Liturgiker Amalarius*, 66 n. 283). In fact, the *Geminus codex* does quote *ordines*, though Hanssens does not always identify such quotations in the edition; see Jones, *A Lost Work*, 58 n. 26.

[17] *Der Liturgiker Amalarius*, 75 (translation mine): "Es liegt somit der Schluß nahe, daß die Texte nicht von ein und demselben Autor stammen. Freilich wäre es auch (für

On the contrary, the scenario that Steck describes here is not only probable but demonstrable from comparisons between the different recensions of the *Liber officialis*, or between that and other Amalarian works whose authenticity does not stand in doubt, such as the *Liber de ordine antiphonarii*.[18] In his career-long meditations on the deeper *ratio* beneath liturgical celebrations, Amalarius simply did not place much value on strict consistency; when he revisited a liturgical point already treated elsewhere in his writings, he did not feel bound to square any new interpretation with the old or to select precisely the same set of details for treatment. By the same token, he evidently felt free to lift entire clusters or "modules" of exegetical association from one liturgical context and apply them to another.[19] Finally, it must be borne in mind that Amalarius's fascination with liturgy was equal parts bookish and practical. It would certainly be a mistake to assume that he felt free only to describe and expound the *actual* liturgy as celebrated wherever he happened to be at the moment. His eager study of differing *ordines* known partly or only from books would explain why "at different points in time he had before his eyes differing liturgical practices"—a circumstance that Amalarius, with his connoisseur's interest in the subject, must have welcomed at every opportunity. Thus he repeatedly revised the *Liber officialis* to take account of an ever-changing stock of information, oral and written, at his disposal.

Hanssens's estimation of the *Geminus codex* as a genuine Amalarian work should probably therefore stand.[20] But even if doubts in that corner subside, my hypothesis that the stylistically similar Salisbury interpolations preserve remnants of an early work by Amalarius faces a more intractable challenge in the absence of an independent manuscript tradition for the posited *De triduo*. Why would an authentic early-ninth-century text by Amalarius sink, it seems, without a ripple on the Continent, only to resurface abruptly in eleventh-century English contexts?[21] Had the work in question been lost as an independent text, we might expect to find it at least mentioned in booklists and eagerly quoted with

---

Amalar) denkbar, daß dieser zu verschiedenen Zeitpunkten eine unterschiedliche liturgische Praxis vor Augen hatte, darüber hinaus gleichgebliebene liturgische Vollzüge unterschiedlich interpretierte und dabei teilweise andere Termini verwendete. Dies erscheint jedoch unwahrscheinlich."

[18] Edited at *AEOLO* 3: 13–109 (text) and 110–224 (commentary and tables); see 1: 200–2 for prolegomena.

[19] For detailed demonstration, see Jones, *A Lost Work*, 84–117. On Amalarius's essentially meditative rather than systematic habits of thought, see now the insightful study by Celia Chazelle, "Amalarius's *Liber Officialis*: Spirit and Vision in Carolingian Liturgical Thought," in *Seeing the Invisible in Late Antiquity and the Early Middle Ages*, ed. Giselle de Nie, Karl F. Morrison, and Marco Mostert, Utrecht Studies in Medieval Literacy 14 (Turnhout: Brepols, 2005), 327–57.

[20] Schneider's "Roman Liturgy and Frankish Allegory," presenting newly discovered fragments of the *Geminus codex*, retains the attribution to Amalarius.

[21] The problem is acknowledged and discussed at Jones, *A Lost Work*, 119–25.

attribution by later authors and compilers. At the time I published the Salisbury interpolations, however, I knew of only two other significant testimonies, neither of verifiably independent value. The major supporting witness I could offer was a lengthy addition, made at Exeter in the third quarter of the eleventh century, to the end of a tenth-century English copy of the *Retractatio prima* of Amalarius's *Liber officialis*, now Cambridge, Trinity College B. 11. 2. This supplement, which may have been added to remedy a physical defect in the main part of Trinity B. 11. 2, seems to preserve *en bloc* a section from the lost *De triduo* on the rituals of Good Friday.[22] In view of other evidence for exchanges of exemplars and scribal commissions between Exeter and Salisbury in the later eleventh century, however, the survival of text from the lost Amalarian work at the end of Trinity B. 11. 2 does not move us very far from the witness of Salisbury 154 itself.[23]

The same impression is given by the evidence of quotations from the *De triduo* in a monastic customary for Eynsham that the Anglo-Saxon homilist Ælfric drew up around 1005. It is clear from the manner of his citations that, when Ælfric encountered the work, it was probably already in the form we have in Salisbury 154—namely, as interpolations spliced into the appropriate passages on the Triduum in a manuscript that otherwise transmitted the standard text of the *Retractatio prima*. Ælfric's testimony thus corroborates but does not greatly enlarge the existing pattern of evidence; his monastic home prior to Eynsham was Cernel (Cerne Abbas) in Dorset and therefore in the diocese of Sherborne, the see that, after a merger with Ramsbury, would be relocated to Old Sarum in 1075. Once again, in other words, all major indicators for transmission of the lost work seem bound directly to the *Retractatio prima* and to the southwest of England in a period no earlier than the late tenth through eleventh centuries.[24]

---

[22] Jones, *A Lost Work*, 17, with edition at 200–10 (my "Add[itions]" 4.1.1 through 4.8.13). The recovery of this material is complicated by the fact that some corresponding portions of the Salisbury manuscript have been erased and written over with the standard *Retractatio prima* text; the affected text occurs in Add. 4.2 and 4.6–7 of my edition.

[23] See Teresa Webber, "Salisbury and the Exon Domesday: Some Observations Concerning the Origin of Exeter Cathedral MS 3500," *English Manuscript Studies, 1100–1700* 1 (1989): 1–18.

[24] On Ælfric's use of the interpolated *Retractatio prima*, see Jones, *A Lost Work*, 121–22, and further in *Ælfric's Letter to the Monks of Eynsham*, ed. and trans. Christopher A. Jones, Cambridge Studies in Anglo-Saxon England 24 (Cambridge: Cambridge University Press, 1998), 59–68.

2. Some New Evidence: London, Lambeth Palace
Library 1229, nos. 14–15

The preceding survey of evidence now requires some updating thanks to an identification of further excerpts that obviously derive from the *De triduo* but do so
in some measure independently of the witnesses hitherto known. To present this
material in a volume honoring Dick Pfaff is appropriate not only because of his
interest in English Amalariana: it was he, in fact, who first detected the fresh
evidence and graciously brought it to my attention.[25] The new witness survives
within Lambeth Palace Library 1229, the shelfmark assigned to what is actually a miscellaneous assortment of nineteen medieval manuscript fragments recovered from early book-bindings. The items relevant here are Lambeth 1229,
nos. 14 and 15, two bifolia constituting, in their modern cataloguer's description, "Four adjacent leaves of a text dealing with the significance of rites and observances of the church on Holy Thursday, Good Friday, and Holy Saturday."[26]
Paleographical and codicological evidence suggests that these bifolia were written in the twelfth century at the Augustinian priory of Llanthony "Secunda" in
Gloucestershire; indeed, they appear to have been detached from the end of another Llanthony manuscript still extant as Lambeth Palace Library 372, assorted
works by Augustine copied mainly during the twelfth century.[27]

The fact that the text preserved in Lambeth 1229, nos. 14–15, is incomplete
at its beginning and end suggests that these bifolia were the inner two of a quire
whose outer constituents no longer survive and were probably already missing in
the seventeenth century when early Lambeth cataloguers described the item as
"defective at both ends."[28] How much text has been lost from this or any additional quires cannot be known. The surviving bifolia, while not a *de luxe* product,
do show that the scribe treated this text as something worthy. The proportions of

---

[25] In a private letter dated 17 August 2001. Then just returned from research travels
that included a visit to Lambeth, Dick was so generous as to spend part of his time there
transcribing for me passages from the bifolia that I discuss here.

[26] E. G. W. Bill, *A Catalogue of Manuscripts in Lambeth Palace Library: MSS 1222–
1860* (Oxford: Clarendon Press, 1972), 57–60, at 59. Bill indicates ("Introduction," 7)
that the actual description of items in MS. 1229 is the work of N. R. Ker.

[27] The linkage of Lambeth 1229, nos. 14–15, to Lambeth 372 depends on codicological analysis as well as on the earliest (seventeenth-century) catalogue descriptions of
Lambeth 372 that identified its final item as a "Tractatus Anonimus utrinque mutilus
mystice exponens ritus quosdam ecclesiasticos"; see Bill, *A Catalogue of Manuscripts in
Lambeth Palace Library*, 59–60. There is evidence that the bifolia became detached from
the end of Lambeth 372 some time between c. 1633 and the time of Archbishop Sancroft
(1678–1690). On the contents of Lambeth 372, see Montague Rhodes James and Claude
Jenkins, *A Descriptive Catalogue of the Manuscripts in the Library of Lambeth Palace* (Cambridge: Cambridge University Press, 1930–1932), 513–14.

[28] "utrinque mutilus"; see preceding note.

the leaves (242 × 172 mm), written space (c. 190 × 100 mm), and outer margins are ample and the script itself highly legible, neither cramped nor densely abbreviated. Four paragraph divisions are marked by colored initials in alternating red and green.[29]

Despite these outward appearances of careful treatment, however, the quality of the text itself is remarkably poor, amounting to a farrago of excerpts, sometimes impenetrably corrupt, that an earlier compiler assembled from various sources. Among those sources was the same Amalarian *De triduo* known to the redactor of the variant *Retractatio prima* found in Salisbury 154. The context of the Lambeth passages is somewhat different, however, since in them extracts from the *De triduo* appear folded into another, less well-defined group of commentary materials that, though ultimately based on Amalarius's *Liber officialis*, have their own transmission history quite different from that work or its *Retractatio prima*. This messy textual environment makes description and analysis of contents in the Lambeth bifolia a complicated chore. But it is precisely this environment, I will suggest, that establishes a new, helpful context for understanding how the *De triduo* might have reached England and why, even then, its transmission tended to remain scrappy. The clearest way of proceeding will be to give first a general account of all the texts on the two bifolia (in their sequence 14¹r, 14¹v, 15¹r, 15¹v, 15²r, 15²v, 14²r, 14²v) and then consider in more detail what the whole artifact adds to our knowledge of the content and fortunes of the *De triduo*. A lightly edited transcription of the Lambeth bifolia, with source and critical apparatus, follows below as the first of two appendices (Appendix A). References to the texts hereafter employ the section numbers assigned in that edition.

The text-series begins in mid-sentence at the top of fol. 14¹r with a discussion of the service of Tenebrae (§ 1), followed by another paragraph (§ 2), set off by a two-line red initial, on the number and significance of the candles extinguished in that service. Both paragraphs come verbatim from portions of the *De triduo* as already known from the Salisbury interpolations. The next paragraph break and colored initial introduce a long section (from fol. 14¹r to the middle of 15¹r), beginning "Noscat uestra caritas quod in diebus solemnibus quantum possimus altaria ornamus." This section treats the significance of various observances on Maundy Thursday (the stripping of the altars and washing of the church, the *mandatum* or foot-washing service [§ 3.a–d]) and during the Triduum as a whole (the omission of certain versicles and responses from the Divine Office, the suspension of Masses and of the kiss of peace on Friday and Saturday [§ 3.e-m]). Only a few sentences in all this (§ 3.c–d) derive from the text of the *De triduo* as already known. Most of the remaining material in the section beginning "Noscat uestra caritas" comes from a different, widely transmitted work, indebted to the

---

[29] For this physical description, I have taken the measurements from Ker's entry in Bill's *Catalogue*. The other details are based on my own examination of digital images kindly provided by the Librarian and staff of Lambeth Palace Library.

Liber officialis but of unknown immediate backgrounds. (I will discuss this item further below.) The next paragraph break comes on fol. 15^{1}r and is introduced by a large four-line initial in red: "Feria .vi. post euangelium uenit pontifex [. . .]" (§ 4). This portion treats the symbolic significance of rituals specific to Good Friday and derives almost entirely, except for its closing sentences (§ 4.m), from exposition in the *De triduo*. The final section that the scribe of the Lambeth bifolia marked off with a colored initial begins "Nobis preceptum est a papa Zosimo" (§ 5) and runs from the top of fol. 15^{2}v to the bottom of 14^{2}v, the end of the surviving leaves. The contents in this section cover rituals of Holy Saturday and derive ultimately from Amalarius's *Liber officialis*, albeit heavily abridged and reworked. As I will show, there are reasons to associate a portion of this rewritten material from the *Liber officialis* (at least my § 5.e-f) with a text-group that in other manuscripts includes parts of the anonymous "Noscat uestra caritas" (viz., § 3.a and 3.e–m).

In sum, then, the Lambeth passages on the Triduum appear to derive from two or three identifiable sources: (1) the lost Amalarian *De triduo*; (2) a short, widely-known, anonymous text (or text-group) on the Triduum beginning "Noscat uestra caritas"; and (3) other quotations and adaptations of Amalarius's well-known *Liber officialis* (if these in fact derive from a proximate source different from that of "Noscat uestra caritas"). Two questions immediately arise. First, do the Lambeth passages restore anything new to the text of the *De triduo* as already partially known from the interpolations in Salisbury 154 and from the eleventh-century Exeter addition to Trinity B. 11. 2? The total gain turns out to be disappointingly slight. The beginning of the Lambeth passages on Good Friday (§ 4.a) does preserve a short amount of text that, while obviously lifted from the *De triduo*, does not appear in matter that the Salisbury or Trinity manuscripts transmit from that source. The exposition at this point concerns the custom of not kneeling at the petition for the Jews in the long series of communal prayers (*orationes solemnes*) on Good Friday. Here the Salisbury and Trinity witnesses incorporate only a single sentence attributable to the *De triduo* (the sentence underlined below), while the corresponding passage in Lambeth 1229, no. 15, has that sentence as well as two others before it (in bold type):

Salisbury 154, pp. 29–30:
Euangelio expleto, ueniens pontifex
ante altare incipit orationes solemnes
que sequuntur et dicit: "Oremus dilec-
tissimi in primis" et reliqua. Et post is-
tam statim dicit "Oremus," et diaconus
"Flectamus genua" [. . .] Per omnes
orationes genuflexionem facimus, ut
per hunc habitum corporis mentis hu-
militatem ostendamus, excepto quando oramus pro perfidis iudeis. Fugiamus eorum consensum qui dominum
irrident. Illi irridentes genua ponebant
in terra sicut scriptum est: "Et genu
flexo ante eum illudebant dicentes
'Aue rex iudeorum'" [Matt. 27: 29].

Lambeth 1229, fol. 15¹r:
(4.a) Feria .vi. post euangelium uenit
pontifex ante altare et dicit "Oremus"
et diaconus "Flectamus genua." **Mi
didascale, requiro cum omni oratione
genuflexionem facias cur in uno loco
hunc modum amittis pro iudeis tantummodo? Cur, frater mi, fuit?** Fugiamus eorum consensum qui dominum
irrident. Illi inridentes genua ponebant in terra sicut scriptum est: "Et
genu flexu [sic] ante eum inludebant
dicentes 'Aue rex iudeorum'" [Matt.
27: 29].

The sentences "Mi didascale, requiro [. . .]" and "Cur, frater [. . .]" ring with the unmistakable mannerisms of the "diatribe" characteristic of Amalarius's *Missae expositionis geminus codex* and of the reconstructed *De triduo*.[30] The correspond-ing passage in the Salisbury version (and in the addition to Trinity B. 11. 2) lacks the two sentences, though it does contain the next two ("Fugiamus [. . .]" and "Illi irridentes [. . .]") as interpolations into text that otherwise agrees with the standard *Retractatio prima* and continues discussion of this topic at greater length than Lambeth passage § 4.a. It seems, consequently, that at this point the Lam-beth text represents an abridgment of matter taken from the lost *De triduo*, but an abridgment made by someone whose access to that source was not limited only to the portions of it preserved by Salisbury 154 and the final leaves of Trinity B. 11. 2. Thus, although the Lambeth passages contribute only two new sentences to the reconstructed whole, they verify that more of the work was once available in some form, and that its telltale stylistic traits continued through those por-tions as well.

---

[30] See references at n. 10 above. Series of rhetorical questions (as here and at § 2.a–b) and the use of grecisms (such as *didascalus* here) are also hallmarks of the style of Amalarius.

3. The Lambeth Bifolia and Transmission
of the *De triduo*

If the yield of actual new text from these bifolia seems modest, they prove somewhat more valuable for what they imply about the reception history of the *De triduo*. Here I refer to the other sources mentioned above, namely the series beginning "Noscat uestra caritas" and the rewritten excerpts (mostly about Holy Saturday) from Amalarius's *Liber officialis*. Ker's description of the Lambeth bifolia offered some guidance for investigating further the context formed by these items: "The section beginning 'Noscat uestra caritas' occurs also in Salisbury Cathedral 135, Exeter Cathedral 3525, Cambridge, Fitzwilliam Museum, McClean 101, and B[ritish] M[useum] Cotton Nero A.i. In these manuscripts it is part of a text beginning 'Legitur in ecclesiastica historia quod nabuchodonosor.'"[31] As leads go, this looks promising, as if the text-blocks variously transmitted in those other manuscripts had potential to yield, at a stroke, several new partial witnesses to the *De triduo*. But that does not turn out to be the case. Although the section "Noscat uestra caritas" in Lambeth 1229 does include some sentences from the lost *De triduo* (at § 3.c-d), they seem to be an interpolation there. At least, they do not occur at the corresponding point in Ker's other manuscripts of "Noscat uestra caritas" that I have been able to consult.[32] Nor, so far as I can determine, do any compelling arguments link "Noscat uestra caritas" intrinsically, in whole or part, with the *De triduo*. The contents of "Noscat uestra caritas" derive largely from teachings of the *Liber officialis*. And, although the passage begins with the second-person appeal to "caritas uestra," that is the only such instance in the passage, and it does not greatly resemble the insistent second-person singular addresses that contribute to the distinctive diatribe style of the *Geminus codex* and *De triduo*.

To determine what the manuscript setting of Lambeth 1229 might mean for our understanding of how the *De triduo* circulated, we must nevertheless try to come to terms with the adjoined "Noscat caritas uestra." That task also proves easier said than done, however, for Ker seems to have underestimated how wide and complex was the transmission of this and related anonymous items of commentary on the liturgy. "Noscat uestra caritas," with or without its frequently accompanying text (or text-series) "Legitur in ecclesiastica historia quod Nabuchodonosor" etc., occurs not only in the four additional manuscripts that Ker noted, but also in many other English and continental copies from the eleventh century onwards.[33] Turning to this larger corpus of materials, we enter a chaotic and mostly uncharted domain of anonymous, undatable, and often unstable texts.

---

[31] Bill, *A Catalogue of Manuscripts in Lambeth Palace Library*, 59.

[32] I have checked Salisbury 135 and Cotton Nero A.i. The several other manuscripts known to Götz (discussed below) bear out this impression.

[33] See Appendix B, below.

Much of the material in question lies unedited and only glancingly inventoried. Where they exist, editions of texts from this milieu usually present one version out of several available while the relations among them all remain obscure. In view of the hideous difficulty of mapping such terrain, and given the seemingly low intrinsic value of many of the texts at issue—being often derivatives of already edited, better-known and better-organized whole treatises by Amalarius and others—researchers are hardly lining up to study them. Even so, these neglected materials deserve attention as they contribute to an important chapter in the history of western liturgical commentary by forming a bridge, as it were, between the most influential early examples of the genre (Amalarius's *Liber officialis* in the early ninth century and the Pseudo-Alcuin's *Liber de divinis officiis* in the tenth) and its reflorescence in the later eleventh and twelfth centuries. Manuscript evidence from the latter, more glamorous period indicates, as Roger Reynolds has noted, that the conservative copying, excerpting, and rewriting of older liturgical commentaries proceeded often side-by-side with the composition of new, more modern treatises.[34] The unexpected recovery and brief vogue of a lost Amalarian work *De triduo* can be best understood in this wider context, to which the other sources figuring in the Lambeth passages likewise clearly point.

Hanssens had no choice but to trawl these depths when sorting out which works of liturgical commentary likely issued from Amalarius's own pen. As his principal goal was to establish a critical text, Hanssens sifted but justifiably discarded as irrelevant a great deal of Amalarian-derived commentary in high- and late-medieval manuscripts and early printed books. A generation after Hanssens, the Franciscan historian Georg Polycarp Götz explored much of the same territory in the course of editing another popular treatise on the liturgy, the *Liber quare*. Probably the work of an eleventh-century continental scholar steeped in Amalarius's writings, the *Liber quare* consists mostly of matter from the original *Liber officialis* but greatly abridged and recast into question-and-answer format. For present purposes, more relevant than the *Liber quare* itself are Götz's generous appendices, wherein he prints hundreds of anonymous *additiones* that accumulated barnacle-like within and around the main text of the *Liber quare* through centuries of recopying. These additions vary greatly in scope from a single sentence to several printed pages. And, as it happens, among the *additiones* published by Götz appear several of the passages that form the surrounding matrix for excerpts from the *De triduo* in Lambeth 1229, nos. 14–15. Specifically, Götz edits "Noscat uestra caritas" from no fewer than six continental manuscripts copied between the twelfth and fourteenth centuries (and these six manuscripts include

---

[34] Roger E. Reynolds, "Liturgical Scholarship at the Time of the Investiture Controversy," *Harvard Theological Review* 71 (1978): 109–24, at 116–17.

none of the five already identified by Ker).[35] Götz subdivides his edition of the text into thirteen sections, of which the first ten figure as § 3.a and 3.e-m in the Lambeth passages edited below.[36] Moreover, what Götz prints as the eleventh and twelfth subsections of "Noscat uestra caritas" show up later in the Lambeth bifolia, among the comments on Holy Saturday (§ 5.e-f below).[37]

If the entire picture thus seems to grow only more complicated the more we see of it, one plain fact begins to emerge. Neither Götz's manuscripts nor those that I have been able to check from Ker's list interpolate into "Noscat uestra caritas" the sentences from *De triduo* as the Lambeth passages do (§ 3.c-d below). Only a collation of all known manuscripts of "Noscat uestra caritas" will determine whether or not the Lambeth version is absolutely unique in this regard. That labor unfortunately exceeds the scope of this paper, since the task will inevitably require examination of other widely copied, shifting texts that often traveled in the same company (especially the item "Legitur in ecclesiastica historia" mentioned by Ker and likewise edited, from three manuscripts, among Götz's *additiones*).[38] As the initial step of such a project, I include below, as Appendix B, a provisional handlist of the manuscripts of "Noscat uestra caritas" as well as of "Legitur in ecclesiastica historia"; the inventory includes the copies already cited by Ker and Götz but also lists fifteen others identified in catalogues and additional secondary sources.

Even if the Lambeth passages turn out to be unique by interpolating sections from the Amalarian *De triduo*, they still illuminate the reception of that text simply by demonstrating that, at some point, it was swept up in a vaster tide of anonymously excerpted and recycled expositions. This circumstance renders more plausible some of the complex scenarios that must be imagined in order to countenance the very survival of a rare, early Amalarian work, perhaps as never more than a series of extracts, sometimes copied out continuously as units (as witnessed in §§ 2 and most of 4 in the Lambeth excerpts), but perhaps sometimes copied at appropriate points into the margins of the *Retractatio prima* or other works.[39] The latter scenario may indeed have pertained in the now-lost exemplar of the *Retractatio prima* that stands behind the copy in Salisbury 154, which, for

---

[35] *Liber quare*, ed. Georgius Polycarp Götz, Corpus Christianorum, Continuatio mediaeualis 60 (Turnhout: Brepols, 1983), 138–39 (Appendix II, *Additio* 12). For a list of manuscripts, including those used by Götz, see my Appendix B, below.

[36] The intervening § 3.c-d is matter taken from the *De triduo*; the only passage thus not accounted for, § 3.b, is a sentence adapted from the standard *Retractatio prima* of the *Liber officialis*; see the edition and source apparatus, below.

[37] The remaining material in § 5 is mostly taken from the *Retractatio prima* of the *Liber officialis*, but often with significant reworking and abridgment.

[38] *Liber quare*, ed. Götz, 201–3 (Appendix II, *Additio* 63).

[39] There is small evidence for precisely this fate in London, British Library, Cotton Vespasian D. xv, at fol. 109r, where two short quotations from the *De triduo* appear

its part, would then reflect a further stage in the transmission, where the marginal additions have at various places been incorporated into the main text, replacing or augmenting the original. In any event, the Lambeth passages encourage a recontextualizing of the *De triduo* within broader patterns that scholars such as Götz and Reynolds have demonstrated for the transmission of much anonymous liturgical commentary to the high Middle Ages. Set against that background, the unexpected surfacing of remnants from an Amalarian treatise *De triduo* in a remote and (so far) peculiarly circumscribed setting—the west of England in the eleventh and twelfth centuries—emerges as a less far-fetched possibility than it first seems.

On the other hand, the fact that Götz's wide canvassing of eleventh- to fifteenth-century manuscripts evidently did not discover among additions to the *Liber quare* any passages manifestly from the *De triduo* confirms how comparatively rare that source must have been (whether one accepts its Amalarian authorship or not). Götz's trove of *additiones* reminds us, too, how much liturgical commentary of this sort remains to be explored in necessary depth. The two newly recovered sentences at § 4.a in the Lambeth texts betray their origin by a style immediately recognizable from the Salisbury interpolations on one hand and from the *Geminus codex* on the other. But other passages from the *De triduo* that happen not to be so rhetorically distinctive may also lurk either already in print, among materials edited by Götz and others, or in the large number of manuscripts with contents related to the surrounding texts in Lambeth 1229, nos. 14–15. In view of our as-yet inchoate knowledge of how anonymous liturgical expositions traveled and mingled through anonymously compiled florilegia, the possibility must remain open that more evidence of the treatise *De triduo* awaits discovery.

---

as marginal additions to an early-eleventh-century Worcester copy of extracts from the standard *Retractatio prima*; see Jones, *A Lost Work*, 122.

Appendix A:
Transcription of Lambeth Palace Library 1229, Nos. 14–15

For the following transcription of Lambeth Palace Library 1229, nos. 14–15, I have standardized capitalization and inserted section numbers and modern punctuation. Tailed *e*, which the Llanthony scribe used inconsistently for *e* and *ae*, I transcribe uniformly as *e*. Angled brackets enclose words supplied by conjecture or from other sources, and superscript letters, beginning anew for each section, identify all emendations and are keyed to a minimal textual apparatus that follows the edition. Regular footnotes identify whatever sources I have been able to trace, though I have not ordinarily reproduced the entire source apparatus for those passages lifted from the lost *De triduo*. The following abbreviations appear in the source-apparatus: *DT* = the lost treatise *De triduo* that I ascribe to Amalarius, cited by the section numbers assigned in Jones, *A Lost Work*; *LO* = Amalarius's *Liber officialis*, cited by book, section, and subsection numbers of Hanssens's edition in *Amalarii episcopi Opera liturgica omnia*, volume two; *LQ add.* = the *additiones* printed in Appendix II to Götz's edition of the *Liber quare*, cited by his numeration.

(1) /14¹r/ [. . .] quicquid dominus ostenderit dicemus. Sequitur: "Sed et ipsa ecclesia^a usque ad uigilias inluminata^b permanet; similiter .vi. feria, similiter et sabbato faciendum est." Omnis enim etas et omne tempus habet et mane suum in initio prosperitatis^c sue et uesperum suum in propinquitate tribulationis sue.[40]

(2.a) Viginti .iiii. candele inluminari oportet, id est^a in cene domini in parasceue et in sabbato sancto, ita uero ut unaqueque antiphona habeat suam candelam et unumquodque responsorium. Dic, frater <mi: quem>^b imitaris quando hunc numerum tenes? Quem frater nisi solem^c illum qui .xxiiii. horis diem complet. Vnde ait Salomon: "Oritur sol et occidit, et ad locum suum reuertitur ut iterum oriatur" [Eccl. 1: 5]. Omnibus notum est diem atque noctem uolui in .xxiiii. horis.[41] (2.b) Quid, frater, pertinet et causa^d de qua agimus ut extinguantur candele? Dicam, frater, si deus permiserit. Candele^e typum gerunt solis. Absentia solis facta utimur candelis pro sole absente. Sol namque typum gestat saluatoris. De quo scriptum est: "Timentibus nomen eius oritur sol iustitie" [Mal. 4: 2].[42]

(3.a) Noscat uestra caritas quod in diebus solemnibus quantum possimus altaria ornamus. In his autem tribus diebus a cena domini usque in sabbatum sanctum nudamus. Altaria in ecclesia significant eminentiores in plebe fidelium, sicuti apostoli erant; nudatio illorum fugam apostolorum. Nam scriptum est:

---

[40] *quicquid . . . tribulationis sue*: *DT* 3.6.15 (conclusion)-16.
[41] *Viginti . . . horis*: *DT* 3.2.3, with some rewording and omissions.
[42] *Quid, frater . . . iustitie*: *DT* 3.2.4, first half.

"Et relicto eo[a] omnes fugierunt" [Matt. 25: 56; cf. Mark 12: 12].[43] (3.b) In eo lauantur pedes fratrum et pauimenta ecclesie nudantur. Penitentes ueniunt ad absolutionem.[44] (3.c) In lauatione autem ecclesie lauationem intelligimus <quam exercuit>[b] erga discipulos /14¹v/ suos, per quam iterum intellegimus remissionem quam debet unusquisque exercere erga fratrem suum.[45] (3.d) Sic in expoliatione altarium[c] a uespere quinte ferie usque mane sabbato debemus intelligere quoniam expoliatus[d] est ille per quem acceptabilis sit deo oblatio nostra. De illo enim scriptum est: "Tunc milites presidis suscipientes Iesum in pretorio congregauerunt ad eum uniuersum cohortem et exuentes[e] eum . . ." [Matt. 27: 27–28]. Nam quod exuerunt eum uestimentis suis hoc sepius agit crudelitas hominum, scilicet extinguere conantes sanctos dei qui uestimenta eius sunt. Ideoque in nudatione[f] altaris et suam et apostolorum desolationem accipimus, de quibus scriptum est: "Oculi mei languerunt pre inopia" [Ps. 87: 10].[46] (3.e) Quod autem in isdem tribus diebus non dicitur "Domine labia mea" neque "Iube domine benedicere" neque "Tu autem" neque oratio post Benedictus solito more misticat quod pastor noster Christus recessit et apostoli qui iam predestinati erant, ut pastores forent ecclesie, dispersi sunt, a quibus benedictio et danda et petenda fuit[g].[47] (3.f) Inuitatorium non cantatur ut doceamur malum conuentum uitare qualis tunc temporis apud iudeos fuit de nece Christi.[48] (3.g) "Gloria patri" omnino intermittimus quia omnis salutatio deest in illis tribus diebus ad uitandam pestiferam salutationem qualem diabolus et Iudas exercuit.[49] (3.h) Nec etiam inpulsu campanarum datur signum sed per ligni sonum[h] quia humilior est eris sono. Conuenit enim ut per hos dies humiliatio offitii nostri subsequatur quia saluatoris nostri humiliatio per sepulturam triduanam celebratur.[50] (3.i) Nouem psalmi et nouem lectiones totidemque responsoria que cele- /15¹r/ brantur per illas tres noctes insinuant quod dominus descendit ad inferiora. Misticat quia tria genera hominum rapuit que[i] ad sotietatem .ix. ordinum angelorum transuexit. Hec tria genera creduntur fuisse in naturali lege et in tempore legis et in tempore prophetarum.[51] (3.j) Quod <extinguuntur lumina in his tribus>[j] noctibus aptatur ipsi soli iusticie qui

---

[43] *Noscat . . . fugierunt*: *LQ add.* 12a, based on sentences from *LO* 1.12.53 and 54 combined as in the *Retractatio prima*.

[44] *In eo . . . absolutionem*: cf. *LO* 1.12.1: "Lavantur pedes fratrum et pavimenta ecclesiae; nudantur altaria usque in sabbato sancto. In ea die paenitentes veniunt ad solutionem." Hanssens's apparatus indicates that the word *altaria* is dropped after *nudantur* in a number of copies of the *Retractatio prima*, which would explain the Lambeth passage's odd instruction that "the floors of the church are stripped."

[45] *In lauatione . . . fratrem suum*: *DT* 3.3.2

[46] *Sic in expoliatione . . . pre inopia*: most of *DT* 3.3.1.

[47] *Quod autem . . . petenda fuit*: *LQ add.* 12b, based on *LO* 4.21.4–5.

[48] *Inuitatorium . . . nece Christi*: *LQ add.* 12c, based on *LO* 4.21.6.

[49] *Gloria patri . . . exercuit*: *LQ add.* 12d, based on *LO* 4.21.6.

[50] *Nec etiam . . . celebratur*: cf. *LQ add.* 12e, based on *LO* 4.21.7 and 8.

[51] *Nouem psalmi . . . prophetarum*: cf. *LQ add.* 12f, based on *LO* 4.21.9.

extinctus est et sepultus tribus diebus et tribus noctibus.⁵² (3.k) Terror qui per sonum ligni fit post Benedictus terre motum designat qui in morte domini cruci-fixores eius terruit.⁵³ (3.l) Queritur etiam quare solito more non cantetur missa in .vi. feria et .vii. Respondetur quod apostoli biduo in tristitia et merore fuerunt et propter metum iudeorum se occuluerunt. Vnde traditio ecclesie ut in his duobus diebus sacramenta penitus non celebrentur sed orationes legantur.⁵⁴ (3.m) Quod oscula pacis amittimus ideo facimus ne perfido Iude communicemus qui per os-culum ad homicidium uenit.⁵⁵

(4.a) Feria .vi. post euangelium uenit pontifex ante altare et dicit "Oremus" et diaconus "Flectamus genua." Mi didascale, requiro cum omni oratione genu-flexionem facias cur in uno loco hunc modum amittis pro iudeis tantummodo? Cur, frater mi, fuit? Fugiamus eorum consensum qui dominum inrident. Illi in-ridentes genua ponebant in terra sicut scriptum est: "Et genu flexoᵃ ante eum in-ludebant dicentes 'Aue rex iudeorum'" [Matt. 27: 29].⁵⁶ (4.b) Quoniam et eadem die saluator tuus pro tota ecclesia orauit in cruce, te hodie oportet eius imitatione orare.⁵⁷ (4.c) Post orationes solemnes ad uesperum preparatur crux ante altare et sustentatur hinc et inde a duobus acolitis ut omnes eam per ordinem salutent. Queramus, dilectissime frater, qui sint /15¹v/ duo acoliti qui nobis crucifixio-nemᵇ humilis pueri iustiᶜ Iesu Christi presentant. Forsitan inter alios deus nobis monstrabit Petrum et Paulum, quorum unus deputatur in circumcisione, alter in preputio. Accolitusᵈ enim accensor luminum dicitur. Nonne isti sunt duo cande-labra lucentia ante dominum inluminatorem uniuerse terre? Quid dicunt, caris-sime? Quod est lumen eorum? Prior tibi dicit: "Christus passus est pro nobis, uo-bis relinquens exemplum ut sequamini uestigia eius." Alter dicit: "Non iudicaui scire me aliquid inter uos nisi dominum Iesum Christum et hunc crucifixum."⁵⁸ (4.d) Sequitur: "Presbiteri uero priores mox ut salutauerint intrant in sacrarium ubi positum fuerat corpus domini quod pridie remansit, ponentes illud in pa-tenam. Et subdiaconus teneat calicem ante ipsos cum uino non consecrato, et

---

⁵² *Quod noctibus . . . tribus noctibus*: *LQ add.* 12g, based on a variant (early) reading for *LO* 4.22.1, printed by Hanssens as *Lectio discrepans longior* I.21 (*AEOLO* 2: 552).
⁵³ *Terror . . . terruit*: *LQ add.* 12h (cf. *LQ quaestio* 13ea and 13eb [ed. Götz, 109]), perhaps distantly based on *LO* 4.21.7; cf. partly closer analogues in Honorius's *Gemma animae* 3.88 and 134 (PL 172: 666C and 679B) and Sicard of Cremona's *Mitrale* 6.11 (PL 213: 301B).
⁵⁴ *Queritur . . . legantur*: cf. *LQ add.* 12i, based on *LO* 1.13.14.
⁵⁵ *Quod oscula . . . uenit*: cf. *LQ add.* 12k, based on *LO* 1.13.18.
⁵⁶ *Feria .vi. . . . rex iudeorum*: partially (from *Fugiamus*) identical to *DT* 4.4.4; the preceding sentences (at least *Mi didascale . . .* and *Cur, frater . . .*) are from the same source but preserved only here; see above, p. 51.
⁵⁷ *Quoniam . . . orare*: last sentence of *DT* 4.6b.1.
⁵⁸ *Post orationes . . . hunc crucifixum*: cf. *DT* 4.7b.1–2.

alter subdiaconus patenam[e] cum corpore domini."[59] (4.e) Scimus enim in patena demonstrari corpus humanum quod assumpsit, in uino[f] uero animam siue
spiritum eius, quamuis unum sit.[60] (4.f) Hoc totum etiam dixi ut manifestum sit
ideo corpus dominicum[g] reseruari et sanguinem potari quoniam corpus iacuit in
sepulchro clausum et anima[h] descendit ad inferna animas sanctorum inde[i] extrahere.[61] (4.g) Modo, si[j] libet, queramus quos in euangelio uiros[k] designent illi duo
subdiaconi qui corpus dominicum et uinum[l] componunt in secretario ut presbi-
teris presentetur. Nonne tibi uidentur posse congruere Ioseph et Nichodemus?[62]
(4.h) Prout tunc congruebat, illi <corpus>[m] eius componebant; similiter et isti[n], uidelicet subdiaconi[o] prout isti tempori congruit. Illi aromata offerebant quia
uere mortuus erat corpore, isti uero uinum offerunt quod letificat cor ho- /15²r/
minis [Ps. 103: 15] qui iam[p] eruit animam suam de manu inferi.[63] (4.i) Modo
uideamus, si tue dilectioni libet, qui sint duo presbiteri qui sacramentum dictum populo presentant: angeli, uidelicet, de quibus scribit Lucas: "Ecce duo uiri
steterunt secus illas in ueste fulgenti; timuerunt autem et declinauerunt uultum
in terra. Dixerunt ad illas: 'Quid queritis uiuentem cum mortuis? Non est hic'"
[Luke 24: 4–6]. Quod sunt presbiteri angeli Malachias ostendit dicens: "Labia
sacerdotum custodiunt scientiam, et legem requirunt ex ore eius quia angelus
domini exercituum est" [Mal. 2: 7].[64] (4.j) Postquam adductum fuerit corpus
domini et calix cum uino non consecrato, sicut superius diximus, descendit pontifex ante altare et dicit: "Oremus: Preceptis salutaribus moniti" et "Pater noster" orationemque sequentem: "Libera nos quesumus domine" usque "Per omnia
secula seculorum." Hoc et saluator noster memorato tempore egit: liberauit nos,
liberauit et eos qui apud claustra inferni tenebantur fideles. Vnde liberauit, quin
ab omnibus[q] malis?[65] (4.k) Quod postea dicit "mittens de sancta, nichil dicens"
hoc significat, quod hanc horam quando reuersa sit anima ad corpus nulli morta-
lium licitum est scire.[66] (4.l) Sequitur: "Et communicant omnes cum silentio, et
expleta[r] sunt uniuersa. Hoc expleto uespertinum officium canit unusquisque pri-
uatim in loco suo. Post hoc oportet[s] singulos remeare ad sua."[67] (4.m) Triduo iacuit dominus in sepulchro secundum euangelium quod dicit: "Sicut fuit Ionas in
uentri ceti tribus diebus" et reliqua [Matt. 12: 40]. Quod ita Augustinus in libro
primo questionum euangeliorum: ".vi. ferie[t] diei partem qua sepultus est, cum

---

[59] *Sequitur . . . corpore domini*: rubrical matter identical to that quoted at opening of
DT 4.8.1.

[60] *Scimus . . . unum sit*: from *DT* 4.8.2.

[61] *Hoc totum . . . extrahere*: from *DT* 4.8.4.

[62] *Modo . . . Nichodemus*: from *DT* 4.8.5.

[63] *Prout tunc . . . manu inferi*: from *DT* 4.8.6.

[64] *Modo uideamus . . . exercituum est*: *DT* 4.8.7.

[65] *Postquam adductum . . . omnibus malis*: from *DT* 4.8.9.

[66] *Quod postea . . . scire*: from *DT* 4.8.10.

[67] *Sequitur . . . ad sua*: rubrical matter from *DT* 4.8.10 and 11.

preterita nocte <pro nocte>ᵘ et die accipiens, hoc est pro tota die; sabbatum nocte et die; et noctem dominicam cum eadem die illucente, ac /15²v/ hoc accipiendo pro toto habes triduum et tres noctes."[68]

(5.a) Nobis preceptum est a papa Zosimo benedicere cereum, romanis hoc ita agentibus. Cera humanitatem Christi designat. Vnanimitatem sanctificationisᵃ uult habere cereus iste cum columna ignis qui inluminabat populum in nocte. Vnde dicitur in consecratione cerei: "Hec igitur nox est queᵇ peccatorum tenebrasᶜ columne illuminatione purgauit." Et paulo post: "Sed etiam columne omnes preconia nouimus, quam in honore dei rutilans ignis accendit." Iste cereus qui prefigurat humanitatem Christi illuminatur et benedicitur quia humanitasᵈ Christi, postquam assumpta est a diuinitate, semper fuit illuminata, cuiᵉ semper benedicitur. Illa columna precedebat filios Israel antequam transirent mare rubrum. Nostra columna, scilicet cereus, precedebat et nostros caticuminos.[69] (5.b) Legunturque quasi due columne, ut nostra translatio tenet [viz., Exod. 13: 21]. Dominus autem precedebat eos ad ostendendam uiam per diem in columna nubis et per noctem in columna ignis. Et sicut a benedicto cereo illuminatur alter cereus, ita per partem cerei, queᶠ nondum exerit lumen suum sed estᵍ parata ut fecunditatem prestet lumini, spiritus sancti persona designatur.[70] (5.c) Sine lumine sunt cerei neofytorum usque ad tempus quo cerei ceteri inluminantur ecclesie. Solemus diferre officium illuminandorum cereorum usque ad misse offitium siue propter causam utʰ accipiant neofyti impositionem manus episcopi et sicⁱ eos credimus illuminari spiritu sancto, seu propter noctem in qua celebramus missam, ut sic gloria resurrectionis illuminata illustreturʲ lumine cereorum nostrorumᵏ.[71] (5.d) Post benedictionem cerei leguntur lectiones quattuor et .iiii. cantica /14²r/ cantantur. Cur eo numero? Quia postquam Christus in sepulchro quieuit et suos adhuc quieteˡ ardentius incitauit, quattuor euangelia scribuntur, siue unum euangelium per quattuor partes mundi.[72] (5.e) Quattuor lectiones que in sabbato leguntur ante baptismum cum canticis et orationibus ad instructionem catecuminorum pertinent. Quod pronuntianturᵐ in capite absque suo auctore, quoniam non dicitur "Lectio libri genesis" siue "exodi," hoc est ratio, quia, ut nobis ignorantia cordis illorum ad memoriam reducatur, ideo lectiones ille dissimiliter ab aliis lectionibus pronuntiantur. Frustra enim eis pronuntiaturⁿ auc-

---

[68] *Triduo iacuit . . . tres noctes*: the only portion of this segment not manifestly from *DT* (and also out of place in its present position); drawn largely verbatim from *LO* 1.12.32 (quoting Augustine, *Quaestiones evangeliorum* 1.7), with variants here characteristic of the *Retractatio prima*.

[69] *Nobis preceptum . . . nostros caticuminos*: based on *LO* 1.18.1 and 5, combined as in, and with variant readings distinctive of, the *Retractatio prima* version.

[70] *Legunturque . . . designatur*: based on *LO* 1.26.3.

[71] *Sine lumine . . . nostrorum*: based on *LO* 1.26.5.

[72] *Post benedictionem . . . partes mundi*: the opening question derives from *LO* 1.19.2, but the remainder (*Quia . . . mundi*) I cannot identify in the *Liber officialis* or any other source.

tor incognitus, qui nondum cognoscunt ciues celestes Ierusalem.[73] (5.f) Catecuminus audiens uel instructus dicitur.[74] (5.g) Prime itaque due lectiones, id est[o] "In principio creauit deus" [Gen. 1: 1] et "Factum est in uigilia matutina" [Exod. 14: 24] plano sermone referunt de creatione mundi et de formatione hominis et de liberatione[p] israhelitici populi, quibus sequitur uictorie canticum "Cantemus domino" [Exod. 15: 1]. Omnia enim <que>[q] legimus in sabbato sancto ad celebrationem baptisterii pertinent usque euangelium lectum, deinde ad celebrationem passionis domini. Quia in prima lectione audiuit catecuminus suam formationem, in secunda audiat suam redemptionem, quia sicut populum israelem liberauit dominus de manu pharaonis, quem deleuit in mari rubro, sic possit[r] et eum liberare de manu diaboli per aquam baptismi.[75] (5.h) In tertia lectione habemus sacramenta Christi et ecclesie: "Adprehendent septem mulieres uirum unum" [Isa. 4: 1]. Secundum hystoriam non legimus illud factum sed secundum allegoriam. Allegoria est, <cum>[s] uerbis[t] siue rebus[u] misticis presentia Christi et ec- **/14^{2}v/** clesie sacramenta signantur[v]. Hic demonstrat[w] caticuminis quicquid amare debeant, ut .vii. mulieres[x] significent septem dona spiritus sancti que adprehenderunt unum, id est Christum, et quid proficiat eis baptismus, id est ut per spiritum iudicii et spiritum combustionis minora et maxima peccata purgentur. Finitaque tercia lectione sequitur canticum "Vinea facta est" [Isa. 5: 1], in quo continetur sacramentum sinagoge. Si modo non est sinagoga coniuncta uiro Christo, erit cum plenitudo gentium intrauerit.[76] (5.i) Quarta lectio "Hec est hereditas seruorum domini" [Isa. 54: 17] tropologice[y] sonat. Tropologica[z] est moralis locutio uel instructionem et correctionem morum, siue apertis seu figuratis prelata sermonibus, respicit. Fas est ut, postquam docti fuerint catecumini de purgatione baptismi, instruantur moribus. Dicit in eadem quarta lectione: "Audite audientes me, et comedite bonum" et reliqua que secuntur [Isa. 55: 2].[77] (5.j) Huic lectioni sequitur canticum "Adtende celum" [Deut. 32: 1]. Sicut prime due lectiones propter historiam narrationem concludunt uno cantico, sic ista una dilatatur in duobus propter duas res sibi coniungentes, scilicet mores bonos et celestem patriam.[78] (5.k) Post .iii. canticum et orationem sacerdotis sequitur .iiii., "Sicut ceruus"[aa] [Ps. 41: 2]. Hoc canticum totum anagogicum sonat. Inter hec duo cantica non est lectio necessaria; qui, ut prediximus, in bonis moribus moratur restat ut celestia tantummodo sciat, quamuis per conuenientiam lectionis et duorum canticorum sine[bb] altera lectione congrue coniungantur. Anagoge est sensum ad superiora ducens locutio, que de premiis futuris et ea que in celis est uita futura [. . .].[79]

73 *Quattuor lectiones . . . Ierusalem*: *LQ add.* 12l, based on *LO* 1.21.4.
74 *Catecuminus . . . dicitur*: commonplace, but here closest to *LQ add.* 12k.
75 *Prime itaque . . . baptismi*: based, with much abridgment, on *LO* 1.19.3–4.
76 *In tertia . . . intrauerit*: based on *LO* 1.19.6–7 and 9.
77 *Quarta lectio . . . que secuntur*: based on *LO* 1.19.11.
78 *Huic lectioni . . . patriam*: based on *LO* 1.19.13.
79 *Post .iii. . . . uita futura*: based on *LO* 1.19.18 and 16.

Critical Apparatus

§ 1
a ecclesia]   *corr. from* ecclesiam.
b inluminata]   illumita.
c prosperitatis]   properitatis.

§ 2
a id est]   idem.
b mi: quem]   nisi so *(sic); correction supplied from DT 3.2.3.*
c solem]   solum.
d causa]   causam.
e Candele]   Cande.

§ 3
a relicto eo]   relictio ea.
b quam exercuit]   remissione; *correction supplied from DT 3.3.2.*
c altarium]   altariorum.
d expoliatus]   expoliatur.
e exuentes]   exeuntes.
f in nudatione]   inundatione.
g fuit]   sunt *abbrev.*
h sonum]   onum.
i rapuit que]   rapuitque.
j extinguuntur . . . tribus]   *omitted; supplied from LQ add. 12g.*

§ 4
a flexo]   flexu.
b crucifixionem]   crucifixione.
c pueri iusti]   *partially erased.*
d Accolitus]   *corr. from* Adcolitus.
e patenam]   patena.
f uino]   uno.
g dominicum]   domini cum; *the same error appears in the version of this passage in Salisbury 154.*
h anima]   *corrected from* animam.
i inde]   de.
j si]   *hereafter 1–2 letters erased; cf. DT 4.8.5 si tibi libet.*
k uiros]   uires.
l uinum]   unum.
m corpus]   *omitted; supplied from DT 4.8.6.*
n isti]   *corrected from* iusti.
o subdiaconi]   *corrected from* subdiani.
p qui iam]   *cf. DT 4.8.6* quia iam.
q omnibus]   hominibus; *correction supplied from DT 4.8.9.*

r expleta]	*corrected from* explete.
s oportet]	*1 letter erased between* e *and final* t.
t ferie]	feria; *correction supplied from LO 1.12.32;* feria *is a Retractatio prima reading.*
u pro nocte]	*omitted (as in some Retractatio prima manuscripts); supplied from LO 1.12.32.*

§ 5

a sanctificationis]	*Retractatio prima reading for LO 1.18.1* significationis.
b est que]	estque.
c tenebras]	tenebre.
d humanitas]	*corrected from* humanitatis.
e cui]	qui; *correction supplied from LO 1.18.5.*
f cerei que]	cereique.
g sed est]	sedem.
h ut]	*hereafter approx. 4 letters erased.*
i sic]	*hereafter approx. 2 letters erased.*
j illustretur]	illustret.
k nostrorum]	*hereafter approx. 5 letters erased.*
l quiete]	quietem.
m pronuntiantur]	pronuntiat.
n pronuntiatur]	pronuntiant.
o id est]	idem.
p liberatione]	libatione.
q que]	*omitted.*
r possit]	posse.
s cum]	*omitted; this and other corrections in this sentence supplied from LO 1.19.6 (quoting Bede, De tabernaculo 1.6).*
t uerbis]	uerbum.
u rebus]	regibus.
v signantur]	*letters* nan *illegible.*
w demonstrat]	demonstra.
x mulieres]	*hereafter approx. 2 letters erased.*
y tropologice]	tropoloice.
z Tropologica]	Tropolia.
aa ceruus]	ceruus, *but first* u *erased.*
bb sine]	*corrected from* si non ?

Appendix B:
"Legitur In ecclesiastica historia"
and "Noscat uestra caritas":
A Provisional Handlist of Manuscripts

These two anonymous texts, each ultimately a reworking of exegeses from Ama-larius's *Liber officialis* and perhaps other sources, circulated together and inde-pendently, often in the company of other, similar materials. At least one manu-script, now at Bordeaux, attributes the item beginning "Legitur in ecclesiastica historia" to Amalarius himself, but Hanssens, who knew the piece from that and three other manuscripts, dismissed it (along with many other texts) as spurious, and the more recent *Clavis* being produced by the I.R.H.T. has endorsed Hans-sens's ruling.[80] The handlist provided below is preliminary in every way; most of the notices have come to my attention through catalogues and their cross-refer-ences, through the *In principio* database, and through the invaluable inventories prefacing Götz's edition of the *Liber quare*. Many of these books include the pas-sages "Legitur in ecclesiastica historia" and "Noscat uestra caritas" within larger groupings of similar material, the exact constitution of which (and therefore the degree of overlap with like groups in other manuscripts) is seldom clear from the catalogue descriptions alone. The folio references given, therefore, sometimes re-fer to the items "Legitur" and "Noscat" precisely, but other times to the incipit and explicit of larger text-series commenting on the liturgical seasons, the Mass and Office, ecclesiastical vestments, and the liturgy of consecrating churches. Like the foliations, any dates and origins or provenances given here come from the catalogues and other sources cited in the notes. No doubt more copies—per-haps many more copies—of "Legitur," "Noscat," and related texts await discov-ery, and I would welcome any additional references that readers are inclined to forward. To give credit where due, the inventory divides into three segments, ac-knowledging what I have gleaned respectively from Ker, Götz, and others.

I. Manuscripts identified by Ker:

Ker grouped together six manuscripts as transmitting portions of a *Summa de di-vinis officiis* (the scribal title in the McClean copy), of which the items "Legitur" and "Noscat" comprised only two subsections. In fact, this description suits only the Cambridge, Exeter, and Salisbury manuscripts (for these, the foliations giv-en below pertain to the so-called *Summa* as a whole). The Cottonian manuscript

---

[80] For Hanssens's remarks, see *AEOLO* 1: 56. For the recent French *Clavis*, see *Clavis scriptorum latinorum medii aevi: Auctores Galliae, 735–987, I (Abbon de Saint-Ger-main—Ermold le Noir)*, ed. Marie-Hélène Jullien and Françoise Perelman (Turnhout: Brepols, 1994), 140 (item AMALPs 4).

contains only (and as a later addition) the items "Legitur" and "Noscat," while the Lambeth bifolia preserve the latter but not the former.

Cambridge, Fitzwilliam Museum, McClean 101 (s. xii, Germany; Weingarten provenance), fols. 169r-174v.[81]

Exeter, Cathedral Library 3525 (s. xii[in], England), pp. 121–51.[82]

London, British Library, Cotton Nero A. I (s. xi, England), fols. 106r-108v (addition of s. xii).[83]

London, Lambeth Palace 1229, nos. 14–15 (s. xii, Llanthony Secunda).

Salisbury, Cathedral Library 135 (s. xi[4/4], Salisbury), fols. 1r-23r.[84]

II. Manuscripts identified by Götz:

The large blocks of *additiones* that sometimes include "Legitur" and "Noscat" in the manuscripts inventoried in detail by Götz are too complex to summarize here, so the reader is referred to that edition for foliations and other details. It is worth pointing out, however, how closely some of the arrangements of *additiones* in Götz's manuscripts parallel the contents of the three longer versions of the so-called *Summa de divinis officiis* identified by Ker (McClean 101, Exeter 3525, and Salisbury 135).

Cambrai, Bibliothèque municipale 411 (387) (s. xii–xiii, France)

Oxford, Bodleian Library, Add. A. 373 (s. xii, Germany)

Rome, Biblioteca Vallicelliana, C. 64 (s. xii[1/3], Italy)

Vatican City, Biblioteca Apostolica Vaticana, Vat. lat. 6382 (s. xii[2/3], Italy)

Vatican City, Biblioteca Apostolica Vaticana, Vat. lat. 5093 (s. xiv[in])

Wolfenbüttel, Herzog-August-Bibliothek, lat. 722 (Helmst. 672) (s. xiii)

III. Other pertinent manuscripts not included by Ker or Götz:

For this group, I have attempted to give somewhat fuller information, where available, than for the items already discussed by Ker and Götz. Where good modern catalogues exist, the descriptions there occasionally indicate large blocks

---

[81] Montague Rhodes James, *A Descriptive Catalogue of the McClean Collection of Manuscripts in the Fitzwilliam Museum* (Cambridge: Cambridge University Press, 1912), 226–30.

[82] N. R. Ker, *Medieval Manuscripts in British Libraries, II: Abbotsford-Keele* (Oxford: Clarendon Press, 1977), 834–36, at 835.

[83] I date this addition to s. xii; cf. Henry R. Loyn's introduction to *A Wulfstan Manuscript: British Library, Cotton Nero A. i*, Early English Manuscripts in Facsimile 17 (Copenhagen: Rosenkilde and Bagger, 1971), 33, for a more general dating of s. xi or xii.

[84] Webber, *Scribes and Scholars at Salisbury Cathedral*, 152 (Appendix I, no. 40).

of material agreeing substantially in content and even arrangement with the longer versions of Ker's *Summa* and certain groupings of Götz's *additiones.*

Basel, Universitätsbibliothek, B. VII 28, part II (s. xii), fols. 39r–50v: "Legitur in ecclesiastica hystoria . . . et secundum ea non uiuere."[85]
Besançon, Bibliothèque municipale, 187 (s. xii[med], Saint-André, Avignon, provenance), fols. 69r–75v: "Incipit de ecclesie ordinibus: Legitur in ecclesiastica historia . . . Unde et microcosmus grece vocatur, id est minor mundus."[86]
Bordeaux, Bibliothèque municipale, 11 (s. xii[in], France, Abbaye de la Sauve-Majeure?), fols. 100v–103r: "Excerpta Amalarii monachi: Legitur in ecclesiastica historia . . . ite missa est et completus est."[87]
Cologne, Historisches Archiv der Stadt Köln, GB 4° 194 (s. xv[1] or xv[med], Cologne), fols. 99r–101v: "Mysticatio de septuagesima etc.: Legitur in ecclesiastica historia . . . indicta velut instructa legitur."[88]
Escorial, Real Biblioteca de San Lorenzo de El Escorial, cod. lat. R. III. 15 (s. xiii–xiv), fols. 110r–111r: "Legitur in ecclesiastica historia . . . et secundum ea non uiuere . . . Domus domini methonomice dicitur ecclesia . . ."[89]
Oxford, Bodleian Library, Bodley 719 (s. xii, England), fols. 113v–115r.[90]
Oxford, Bodleian Library, e Mus. 222 (s. xiii[1], England), fols. 112v–115v: "De Septuagesima. Legitur in ecclesiastica historia . . . agnus immolandus in domum introducitur."[91]

---

[85] Gustav Meyer and Max Burckhardt, *Die mittelalterlichen Handschriften der Universitätsbibliothek Basel: Beschreibendes Verzeichnis, Abteilung B: Theologische Pergamenthandschriften I: Signaturen B I 1 - B VIII 10* (Basel: Verlag der Universitätsbibliothek, 1960), 778–83, at 779–80.

[86] E. G. Ledos, "Un nouveau manuscrit du poème d'Achard d'Arrouaise sur le *Templum Domini*," *Bibliothèque de l'école des chartes* 77 (1916): 58–73, at 61. See also *Catalogue général des manuscrits des bibliothèques publiques de France, Départements* 32 (Paris: Plon, 1897), 128–30, at 129.

[87] Colette Jeudy and Yves-François Riou, *Les manuscrits classiques latins des bibliothèques publiques de France, I: Agen-Évreux* (Paris: Éditions du Centre national de la recherche scientifique, 1989), 278–86, at 282.

[88] Joachim Vennebusch, *Die theologischen Handschriften des Stadtarchivs Köln, Teil 2: Die Quart-Handschriften der Gymnasialbibliothek* (Cologne: Böhlau, 1980), 221–26, at 224.

[89] Guillermo Antolín, *Catálogo de los códices latinos de la Real Biblioteca del Escorial, III (L.I.2.–R.III.23)* (Madrid: Imprenta Helénica, 1913), 508–9, at 509.

[90] Copies of "Legitur" and "Noscat" (the latter headed "Hic de tristicia passionis ostenditur") in this manuscript are noted by Albinia de la Mare, *Catalogue of the Collection of Medieval Manuscripts Bequeathed to the Bodleian Library, Oxford, by James P. R. Lyell* (Oxford: Clarendon Press, 1971), 111. These texts are not mentioned in the entry for Bodley 719 in the *Summary Catalogue, II, Part I* (no. 2633).

[91] Jean Longère, *Les sermons latins de Maurice de Sully, évêque de Paris (†1196): Contribution a l'histoire de la tradition manuscrite*, Instrumenta Patristica 16 (Steenbrugge:

Oxford, Bodleian Library, Lyell 40 (s. xii, Italy?), fols. 52r–55r: "Legitur in ecclesiastica historia . . . reticent cantores agnus dei."[92]

Paris, Bibliothèque de l'Arsenal, 371 (565 T.L.), Part C (s. xii, Abbaye de Saint-
Mesmin), fols. 92v–98v: "De sexagesima, quadragesima, et caeteris solemni-
tatibus allegorica expositio: Legitur in ecclesiastica historia . . ."[93]

Paris, Bibliothèque nationale, lat. 12020 (s. xii, Saint-Germain-des-Prés provenance), fol. 97 (?).[94]

Vatican City, Biblioteca Apostolica Vaticana, Pal. lat. 98 (s. xi [Stevenson]; s. xii
[Wilmart]), fols. 52r–56v: "Legitur in ecclesiastica historia . . ."[95]

Vatican City, Biblioteca Apostolica Vaticana, Pal. lat. 482 (s. xi-xiv), fols. 170v–
176r (s. xii or xiii): "Sermo de LXXma: Legitur in ecclesiastica hystoria . . .
De Alleluia et gloria in excelsis: Duo ymni ab angelis . . ."[96]

Vatican City, Biblioteca Apostolica Vaticana, Reg. lat. 73 (s. xii), fols. 52v–
54r: "Legitur in ecclesiastica historia . . . cognoscunt ciues caelestis patriae
iherusalem."[97]

Zurich, Zentralbibliothek, Rh. 45 (s. x/xi, Rheinau provenance), p. 184 (add. of
s. xiv): "Noscat caritas vestra . . . cognoscunt cives celestis Jerusalem."[98]

Zurich, Zentralbibliothek, Rh. 147 (s. xiii, Rheinau provenance), fols. 14v–25r:
"Legitur in ecclesiastica historia . . . quasi in itinere est pergens ad patriam."[99]

Abbatia S. Petri, 1988), 181–200, at 189–90. "Legitur" = fols. 112v-113v, and "Noscat"
= fols. 113v-114r.

[92] de la Mare, *Catalogue of the Collection of Medieval Manuscripts Bequeathed to the
Bodleian Library, Oxford, by James P. R. Lyell*, 109–14, at 111. "Legitur" = fols. 52r-54r;
"Noscat vestra sanctitas [sic!]" = fols. 54r-55r.

[93] Henry Martin, *Catalogue des manuscrits de la Bibliothèque de l'Arsenal*, I (Paris:
Plon, 1885), 233–5, at 234–5.

[94] André Wilmart claims that the beginning (only?) of "Legitur" occurs on fol. 97r;
see his *Codices Reginenses latini I: Codices 1–250* (Vatican City: Bibliotheca Apostolica
Vaticana, 1937), 166; the same is reported by Ledos, "Un nouveau manuscrit," 61 n. 2.
The date of the whole manuscript is given as "XII s." by Léopold Victor Delisle, *Inventaire des manuscrits latins conservés à la Bibliothèque nationale sous les numéros 8823–1816*, 2
vols. (Paris: Durand, 1863–1871; repr. Hildesheim: Georg Olms Verlag, 1974), 2: 33.

[95] Enrico Stevenson, *Codices Palatini latini Bibliothecae Vaticanae, I* (Rome: Typographae-
um Vaticanum, 1886), 16; for the alternative dating, cf. Wilmart, *Codices Reginenses latini I:
Codices 1–250*, 166.

[96] Stevenson, *Codices Palatini latini*, 1: 152–55, at 154. "Legitur" = fols. 170v–172r;
"Noscat" = fols. 172r-173r.

[97] Wilmart, *Codices Reginenses latini I*, 165–67, at 166.

[98] Leo Cunibert Mohlberg, *Katalog der Handschriften der Zentralbibliothek Zürich, I:
Mittelalterliche Handschriften* (Zurich: Zentralbibliothek, 1951), 179 (no. 412).

[99] Mohlberg, *Katalog der Handschriften der Zentralbibliothek Zürich*, 1: 234 (no. 519).

Pembroke College 302: Abbreviated Gospel Book or Gospel Lectionary?

Elizabeth C. Teviotdale

The exhibition *The Cambridge Illuminations*, held at the Fitzwilliam Museum and Cambridge University Library in 2005, promised to ignite interest in illuminated manuscripts in Cambridge collections.[1] Most of the codices in the exhibition—including the subject of this study, Pembroke College MS. 302—had long been familiar to scholars through the manuscript catalogs of M. R. James.[2] Nevertheless, the exhibition in Cambridge lived up to its promise, and many new insights were published in the exhibition catalog and in the proceedings of the accompanying conference. Teresa Webber, who wrote the catalog entry on Pembroke 302, brought an astute paleographer's eye to a reconsideration of the script,[3] and two eminent art historians, Catherine E. Karkov and T. A. Heslop, devoted conference papers to the manuscript.[4] This study builds on the work of these scholars and others by looking more closely at the book's text, as originally constituted and as emended and supplemented in the manuscript's early history.

Pembroke College 302 is a small, handsome volume unquestionably made in England in the mid-eleventh century, although precisely where is unclear and

---

[1] 26 July–11 December 2005.

[2] On the manuscript catalogs, see Richard William Pfaff, *Montague Rhodes James* (London: Scolar Press, 1980), esp. 172–208 and 262–91. Pembroke 302 is described in Montague Rhodes James, *A Descriptive Catalogue of the Manuscripts in the Library of Pembroke College, Cambridge* (Cambridge: Cambridge University Press, 1905), 266–69.

[3] Paul Binski and Stella Panayotova, eds., *The Cambridge Illuminations: Ten Centuries of Book Production in the Medieval West* (London: Harvey Miller, 2005), no. 43 (124–25).

[4] Catherine E. Karkov, "Evangelist Portraits and Book Production in Late Anglo-Saxon England," in *The Cambridge Illuminations: The Conference Papers*, ed. Stella Panayotova (London: Harvey Miller, [2007]), 55–63 and color plate IV; T. A. Heslop, "Manuscript Illumination at Worcester c. 1055–1065: The Origins of the Pembroke Lectionary and the Caligula Troper," in *The Cambridge Illuminations: The Conference Papers*, ed. Panayotova, 65–75 and color plate V.

The Study of Medieval Manuscripts of England: Festschrift in Honor of Richard W. Pfaff, eds. George Hardin Brown and Linda Ehrsam Voigts, MRTS 384 (Tempe: ACMRS, 2010).   [ISBN 978-0-86698-432-4]

debated.[5] It generally has been referred to as a Gospel lectionary in recent scholarly literature and has also been termed a Gospel book or "Gospels."[6] Its original text can be described briefly and accurately as a series of excerpts from the four canonical Gospels in (with one exception) biblical order preceded by an incomplete set of canon tables. The book has been known to contain less than the whole text of the Gospels at least since Henry Bradshaw itemized its contents.[7] But before delving further into the book's contents, let us step back to consider the manuscript as a physical object. Unfortunately, we know nothing of the medieval binding.[8] Whether its covering was lavish or plain, however, the book is and always has been extraordinary for its tall, thin proportions.[9]

With leaves measuring 197 × 101 mm, the pages are approximately twice as tall as they are wide. Two other late Anglo-Saxon manuscripts are of similar size with leaves of comparable proportions. One, with leaves measuring 184 × 89 mm, is a tenth-century copy of the *Pentateuchos* of Cyprianus Gallus, a fifth-century biblical poem composed of hexameters in the "jeweled style."[10] Another, also dating from the tenth century and with leaves measuring 222 × 114 mm, is a copy of Paschasius Radbertus's treatise on the Eucharist, *De corpore et sanguine Domini.*[11] Almost as tall and thin as these, but not quite, is the Caligula Troper,

---

[5] Heslop summarized the literature, especially the art historical literature, on the manuscript's place of origin in "Manuscript Illumination at Worcester." Karkov's opinion ("Evangelist Portraits," 55), not included in Heslop's summary, is that the manuscript was probably produced at Canterbury.

[6] I have contributed to the trend of calling the manuscript a lectionary, especially in "The 'Hereford Troper' and Hereford," in *Medieval Art, Architecture and Archaeology at Hereford*, ed. David Whitehead, British Archaeological Association Conference Transactions 15 (Leeds: W.S. Maney and Son, 1995), 75–81. Patrick McGurk has instead termed the book a "liturgical Gospels" and, more recently, as "probably liturgical." See Patrick McGurk, "Text," in *The York Gospels*, ed. Nicholas Barker (London: Roxburghe Club, 1986), 43–63, at 45; and McGurk and Jane Rosenthal, "The Anglo-Saxon Gospelbooks of Judith, Countess of Flanders: Their Text, Make-up and Function," *Anglo-Saxon England* 24 (1995): 251–308, at 270.

[7] Pasted to the back endpaper of the manuscript is an inventory written in ink. The attribution to Bradshaw is in pencil.

[8] The present binding dates from 1973 and incorporates the surfaces of the eighteenth-century gold-tooled binding described by James.

[9] For eastern comparanda from late antiquity see Eric G. Turner, *The Typology of the Early Codex* (Philadelphia: University of Pennsylvania Press, 1977), 20–21, 28.

[10] Cambridge, Trinity College, MS. B.1.42. Leaf dimensions are taken from M. J. Toswell, "The Format of Bibliothèque nationale MS lat. 8824: The Paris Psalter," *Notes and Queries* n.s. 43 (1996): 130–33. For an edition, see *Cypriani Galli Poetae Heptateuchos*, ed. R. Peiper (Vienna: Tempsky, 1881 [recte 1891]).

[11] London, British Library, MS. Royal 8.B.xi. Leaf dimensions are taken from Toswell, "The Format." The most celebrated tall, thin manuscript produced in Anglo-Saxon

a manuscript of music for the liturgy of the Mass probably dating from the third quarter of the eleventh century, with leaves measuring 220 × 132 mm.[12] Early medieval Gospel books and lectionaries, including those from Anglo-Saxon England, are generally larger books, the proportions of the pages—roughly 4:3 in most cases—being much more typical of books of the period. Thus the late Anglo-Saxon viewer would expect from the size and shape of the manuscript neither a Gospel book nor a Gospel lectionary.[13]

Once opened, the codex presents itself, at least at first sight, as a Gospel book. The nature of the text, the presence of canon tables with painted architectural frames, and four author portraits spaced through the book, each followed by a decorated incipit page, all point to this.[14] And the handsome writing and lavishness of the illumination confirm the impression. Indeed, the painted decoration, which is both sumptuous in materials—with generous use of gold—and thoroughly engaging, has attracted scholarly attention much more than has the text. Starting with the description of the manuscript by J. O. Westwood published in 1868,[15] the illumination has drawn repeated scrutiny from art historians and has been a regular feature—together with an added text to be addressed subsequently—in discussions of the manuscript's place of origin. Catherine E. Karkov has convincingly argued that the figural decoration forms an erudite pictorial program focused on writing and the power of the word, both spoken and written.[16]

The canons, which extend over twelve pages with painted architectural surrounds and spill onto a thirteenth page, do not follow any of the formats

---

England is the Paris Psalter (Bibliothèque nationale de France, MS. lat. 8824), which is, however, much larger than the manuscripts mentioned here.

[12] London, British Library, MS. Cotton Caligula A.xiv, fols. 1–36. Webber (in *The Cambridge Illuminations*, 124–25) and Karkov ("Evangelist Portraits," 56) have remarked the similarity in proportions between Pembroke 302 and the troper. The British Library gives the leaf dimensions as 216 × 155 mm in *The Golden Age of Anglo-Saxon Art, 966–1066*, ed. Janet Backhouse, D. H. Turner, and Leslie Webster (London: British Museum, 1984), no. 71. It is not uncommon for the pages of early medieval music manuscripts with notation to be tall and narrow. I found Heslop's arguments for the probable Worcester connections of Pembroke 302 and the Caligula Troper largely persuasive ("Manuscript Illumination at Worcester"), but I remain unconvinced that the illumination in the two books is likely to be the work of the same artist.

[13] It cannot be ruled out that the manuscript owes its size and shape to a pre-existing ivory plaque intended for its front cover.

[14] All of the painted decoration is reproduced in Thomas H. Ohlgren, *Anglo-Saxon Textual Illustration: Photographs of Sixteen Manuscripts with Descriptions and Index* (Kalamazoo: Medieval Institute Publications, 1992). This manuscript is no. 14.

[15] J. O. Westwood, *Fac-Similes of the Miniatures & Ornaments of Anglo-Saxon & Irish Manuscripts* (London: B. Quaritch, 1868), 143.

[16] Karkov, "Evangelist Portraits," 59.

encountered in late Anglo-Saxon Gospel books,[17] and it is manifest that aesthetic concerns both shaped the decoration of the canon tables and forced textual
compromises. The architecture was painted first and then the text written. The
first three pages feature columns topped by two-arch arcades (fols. 1r-2r), the
next four pages (two openings) three-arch arcades over four columns (fols. 2v-
4r), the next opening columns surmounted by two-arch arcades (fols. 4v-5r), and
the last three pages paired pediments over columns (fols. 5v-6v).[18] The resultant
structural symmetry across the openings is reinforced by the harmonious decorative treatment of the architectural elements across facing pages.

The scribe does not seem to have had a plan for fitting the text into this
framework. Canon I fills the first three pages, but with disparate amounts of
text on each page.[19] Canons II and III neatly occupy the two openings with
three-arch arcades. The heading for Canon IV (which treats correspondences
among Matthew, Mark, and John) appears at the top of the next page (fol. 4v),
but the scribe must have realized immediately that a text demanding three columns would fit only very awkwardly on a page divided into two text columns by
the painted architecture, and Canon IV is omitted altogether. The text continues
with Canons V and VI occupying an opening, but with Canon VI ending *in me-
dias res*, apparently for lack of space before the page turn. Canons VII through X
occupy the last three decorated pages, with the last eleven lines of Canon X spill-
ing onto an otherwise blank page. The result is visually pleasing and orderly (at
least on the pages with the architectural surrounds), but at the expense of textual
completeness.[20]

The Gospel text displays some Irish readings but reflects Carolingian tradition and must, like the texts of the full Gospel books written in tenth- and eleventh-century England, ultimately rely on an exemplar imported from the Continent.[21] The beginning of each Gospel is included. So too is the passion narrative

---

[17] See McGurk, "Text," 46, 49–50.

[18] The switch to the steep pediments allowed for the introduction of human figures
atop the architecture on the final three pages.

[19] There are respectively twenty-five, thirty-five, and eleven lines of numbers on the
three pages.

[20] Despite the lacunae introduced to make the text fit into the framework defined by
the painted architecture, Pembroke 302's canons do not contain the omissions and errors
that Patrick McGurk found in the canon tables of three eleventh-century Anglo-Saxon
Gospel books (Cambridge, Trinity College, MS B.10.4; Cambridge, Pembroke College,
MS. 301; and London, British Library, MS. Harley 76). See Patrick McGurk, "The Disposition of Numbers in Latin Eusebian Canon Tables," in *Philologia Sacra: Biblische und
patristische Studien für Hermann J. Frede und Walter Thiele zu ihrem siebzigsten Geburtstag*,
ed. Roger Gryson, Aus der Geschichte der lateinischen Bibel 24, 2 vols. (Freiburg: Verlag
Herder, 1993), 1: 242–58, here 255.

[21] H. H. Glunz classed the text in the Insular conservative tradition and wrote:
"For though the text . . . was derived mainly from an Irish stock, there are a number of

of each Gospel. The principal subjects of the Gospels—Christ's infancy, ministry, miracles, parables, passion, and resurrection—are all present, albeit to varying degrees. The Sermon on the Mount is nearly complete,[22] with the Beatitudes
beginning on a new line with a colored capital.[23] Christ's last discourse to the
disciples as recorded in John is present in its entirety.[24] The text includes all the
New Testament canticles, each beginning (or intended to begin) with a colored
capital at the left margin.[25] Both versions of the Lord's Prayer are present, with
the opening word or words written in rustic capitals.[26]

The manuscript contains by my reckoning ninety-six Gospel excerpts,[27] including passages that probably served as Gospel pericopes in the contemporary
liturgy of the Mass[28] and others for which we have no evidence of liturgical use

---

scholastic readings included in it which must have come from the Continent": Glunz,
*History of the Vulgate in England from Alcuin to Roger Bacon: Being an Inquiry into the Text of
Some English Manuscripts of the Vulgate Gospels* (Cambridge: Cambridge University Press,
1933), 154–55. A comparison of the text of Pembroke 302 with Bonifatius Fischer's corpus of variants in pre-950 Gospel books, however, reveals it—at least in the passages
included in Fischer's study—to be less "Irish" than one would expect from Glunz's char-
acterization. Fischer's detailed study of variants is published as *Die lateinischen Evangelien
bis zum 10. Jahrhundert*, 4 vols., Aus der Geschichte der lateinischen Bibel 13, 15, 17, 18
(Freiburg: Herder, 1988–1991). On the full and nearly full Gospel books, see McGurk,
"Text," 52–53. On the fragment of a late Anglo-Saxon Gospel book with an "Irish" text
(probably derived from Brittany) in the J. Paul Getty Museum, see E. C. Teviotdale
and Adam S. Cohen, "The Getty Anglo-Saxon Leaves and New Testament Illustration
around the Year 1000," *Scriptorium* 53 (1999): 63–81.

[22] Matt. 5:1–7:29. Curiously, Matt. 5:13–19 and Matt. 7:13–14 are omitted.

[23] Matt. 5:3–12.

[24] John 13:33–16:33.

[25] The *Magnificat* (Luke 1:46–55), the *Benedictus* (Luke 1:68–79), and the *Nunc Dimittis* (Luke 2:29–32). The capital *N* of the *Nunc Dimittis* was never executed (fol. 69r).

[26] Matt. 6:9–13 and Luke 11:2–4.

[27] Twenty-four in Matthew, twenty-one in Mark, twenty-four in Luke, and twenty-seven in John. See the appendix for my understanding of the manuscript's contents.
The graphic presentation of the text, especially the marking out of a new beginning using a colored capital followed by a line of display script, guided most of my decisions
concerning what constituted a new excerpt, but I did allow for some beginnings not so
marked (see below). Bradshaw outlined the book's contents in twenty-seven portions.
Ursula Lenker's list, which omits Luke 1:1–4, suggests that there are eighty-seven. See
Ursula Lenker, *Die westsächsische Evangelienversion und die Perikopenordnungen im an-
gelsächsischen England*, Texte und Untersuchungen zur englischen Philologie 20 (Munich:
Wilhelm Fink, 1997), 462.

[28] The evidence suggests, and strongly, that a Roman tradition modified on Carolingian soil (Antoine Chavasse's Type 3B) was followed in Anglo-Saxon England. See Lenker, *Die westsächsische Evangelienversion*, 160 and passim. Florence, Biblioteca Medicea
Laurenziana, MS. Plut. xvii.20—the only complete Gospel lectionary surviving from

in Anglo-Saxon England. [29] Seven passages open with *in illo tempore* or other interpolated words used to set the stage for the Gospel reading at Mass, [30] and indeed these excerpts probably had places in the late Anglo-Saxon Mass liturgy. [31] More care seems to have been taken to begin excerpts at appropriate sense divisions (and appropriate places for liturgical use) than to end the excerpts where sense would demand an end (and the lection would end). Sometimes, but far from always, the end of a liturgically attested pericope is indicated by a line break, with a colored capital introducing the next line of text. [32] One passage — in Christ's last discourse to the apostles in the Gospel of John — appears out of order, but not wildly so. The sequence is John 16:5–15 (on Jesus' departure), John 15:26–16:5 (on the Holy Spirit), John 16:16–23 (on Jesus' return).

The apparent casualness concerning the endings of the excerpts and the instance of the passage from John copied out of order suggest that the exemplar was a full Gospel book with a series of markings, either in the text or in the margins, at the beginnings of the excerpts to be copied. The scribe probably originally missed the cue at John 15:26 and began to copy the next marked passage — at John 16:5. He then realized his mistake and inserted the required verses after finishing John 16:5–15. The skipped passage (John 15:26–6:5) is short enough, seven verses, that it could have been (and probably was) contained within an opening in the exemplar, making it easy for the scribe quickly to catch his error.

There are no marginal Eusebian numbers or chapter divisions, [33] but the text within each Gospel is articulated into sections graphically. Most excerpts as I have defined them are initiated by an enlarged single-color capital at the left margin and a line (or lines) of display script, either of predominantly rustic capital or

---

Anglo-Saxon England — belongs to this tradition, and I am treating it as our best single witness to liturgical practice. See the appendix for a more detailed comparison of the contents of Pembroke 302 with information gleaned from the Florence manuscript.

[29] Lenker's impressive and comprehensive study of the possibilities yields no liturgical assignments for passages beginning at Matt. 6:2, Matt. 6:34, Mark 2:14, Mark 3:28, Mark 3:31, Mark 13:3, Mark 13:11, Luke 1:1, Luke 2:41, Luke 18:35. See Lenker, *Die westsächsische Evangelienversion*, 529–35. The passage I am identifying as Mark 6:7–13 is called Mark 6:6–13 by Lenker.

[30] At Matt. 1:18, Matt. 5:1, Matt. 5:43, Matt. 26:1, Mark 16:14, John 18:1, and John 21:19.

[31] At the Vigil of Christmas, All Saints, the Friday before Lent, Palm Sunday, the Ascension, Good Friday, and the Feast of St. John the Evangelist.

[32] This is the case, for example, at Mark 16:7, the end of the usual pericope for Easter. The text continues to include Mark 16:8, which begins on a new line intended to begin with a colored capital never executed. The next excerpt, Mark 16:9–14, then begins with a colored capital followed by a line of display script (fol. 58v). By contrast, for example, Luke 10:38 follows immediately upon Luke 9:6 (fol. 71v).

[33] It is not unusual for the Eusebian numbers to be absent from luxury Gospel books made in late Anglo-Saxon England (McGurk, "Text," 54).

uncial letter forms. This is not always the case, however. There are five instances in which a manifestly new section of text—that is, a portion of the Gospel text that is not contiguous with the preceding text—is marked by a colored capital only.[34] In one case, a probably new section is marked by a colored capital and just one word in display script.[35] The passion narratives in Mark and John are each preceded by a line left blank for a rubric that was never written.

The Gospel text is divided into four nearly equal parts.[36] One senses that this was a deliberate and largely aesthetic choice so that the evangelist portraits—and their accompanying incipit pages—would appear at regular intervals. The equalizing of the length of the Gospels also contributes to the clarity of the cumulative iconography of the portraits, a sequence that extends from preparing to write (Matthew), to sharpening the quill (Mark), to leaning over to write (Luke), to writing (John). Indeed, Catherine E. Karkov, who studied the series in detail, characterizes the iconographic program as depicting the essential unity of the Gospels as the product of one harmonious process.[37] If we accept this understanding of the pictorial program, and I think we should, we can understand the nearly equal length of the Gospels, as well as the presence of the canon tables, as contributing to this message of unity and harmony.

For the Gospels of Matthew and Mark, the evangelist portrait appears on a recto, with the incipit page following on its verso. The portraits of Luke and John, by contrast, are each on a verso facing the incipit page. This clearly resulted from a change of approach, for the rectos of the pages with the portraits of Luke and John are blank and thus could have accommodated miniatures. The new scheme brought the second half of the book into conformity with the norm for early medieval Gospel books.[38] As in the canon tables, aesthetic considerations almost certainly played a role. An opening with a portrait on the left-hand page and a painted initial followed by display script on the right-hand page has a visual impact that exceeds the accumulated force of a portrait and an incipit page interrupted by a page turn, surely the reason that the former is the customary arrangement in early medieval Gospel books. If we assume, as I think we should, that the scribe wrote the main text leaving space for the painted decoration, then we see the scribe working out a solution as the text was being copied, much as we saw the scribe editing his text to fit the already-painted architecture of the canon tables.

---

[34] At Matt. 4:1, Matt. 5:20, Mark 3:28, Mark 8:34, and Luke 21:34. It is more difficult to ascertain the intention at Luke 24:1 and John 15:7, where the text is contiguous.

[35] At Matt. 6:34.

[36] Matthew occupies twenty-nine leaves, Mark twenty-two leaves, Luke twenty-eight leaves, and John thirty leaves.

[37] Karkov, "Evangelist Portraits," 56.

[38] Indeed, the evangelist portraits are on versos in all of the full (or nearly full) late Anglo-Saxon Gospel books with portraits, save Rheims, Bibliothèque municipale, MS. 9, in which each portrait incorporates the opening verses of the Gospel.

The scribe made some corrections as he wrote, and the text was also corrected systematically—probably by someone other than the main scribe—after the initial writing campaign. The corrections include changes in orthography, indications of the transposition of words, expunction to indicate syllables and words to be omitted (sometimes with an alternative added above), underscoring of mistakenly repeated words, superscript insertions of missing letters or syllables within words and missing words (usually with a mark of insertion), emendation by the addition of words at the ends or beginnings of lines, and emendation by added words in the margins with insertion marks in the text. The resulting text is not error-free but certainly respectable.

Further corrections and emendations were made early in the manuscript's history. Most conspicuously, letters were added interlinearly to indicate "roles" and the punctuation reworked in the passion narratives in Matthew and Mark.[39] Isolated corrections were also made by at least one scribe other than the manuscript's corrector. Some old Insular abbreviations were clarified,[40] and stress marks were added to help in the pronunciation of probably unfamiliar words. All in all, it seems that the manuscript was read with serious intent during its early history.

That the passion narratives of Matthew and Mark should attract the attention they did raises interesting questions. It is not uncommon to find letters assigning roles in the passion narratives in Gospel books and lectionaries of the early Middle Ages, starting as early as the ninth century.[41] Although the specific interpretation of the letters—employed according to a variety of systems—is open to debate, it is reasonably certain that they served as aids to the deacon in intoning the text within the context of the Mass during Holy Week.[42] Two

---

[39] Over the course of a few lines in the passion of John (on fol. 107v) slashes have been added to separate syntactical units, but there is no campaign of repunctuation comparable to what one sees in Matthew and Mark.

[40] For example, the letters *od* were added by someone other than the corrector above the old Insular abbreviation for *quod* formed by *q* with a curly line through the descender (fol. 50r, l. 6).

[41] Michel Huglo, *Les Livres de Chant Liturgique*, Typologie des Sources du Moyen Âge Occidental 52 (Turnhout: Brepols, 1988), 18–20. The passion letters appear in many of the surviving late Anglo-Saxon Gospel books. In the Florence lectionary, the letters have been added, according to two different systems, to the passions of Matthew, Luke, and John.

[42] Matthew on Palm Sunday, Mark on Tuesday, Luke on Wednesday, and John on Good Friday. Karlheinz Schlager, "Passion," in *Die Musik in Geschichte und Gegenwart.* 2nd ed., *Sachteil*, 10 vols. (Kassel: Bärenreiter, 1994–2008) 7: 1453–56, provides an excellent summary and is more circumspect than Huglo (*Les Livres*, 18–19) in interpreting the letters. See also Nigel F. Palmer, "Zur Vortragsweise der Wien-Münchner Evangelienübersetzung," *Zeitschrift für deutsches Altertum und deutsche Literatur* 114 (1985): 95–118.

different, but not unrelated, systems of letters were used in Pembroke 302.[43] In
Matthew, c indicates the narration of the evangelist, l the direct speech of Christ,
and s (either tall or round) the direct speech of others (Fig. 3.1). In Mark, c and s
are used as they are in Matthew (although only tall s is employed), but t is used to
mark the direct speech of Christ (Fig. 3.2).[44] The repunctuation of these passages
involved both modifying existing punctuation and adding punctuation marks
where originally there were none (Figs. 3.1 and 3.2).

The use of two different systems and distinctions in the letter forms themselves suggest that the passion letters were added in the two Gospels at different times and by different people. Each campaign of annotation, therefore, was
brought about by a perceived need in relation to that particular passion text, and
one is inclined to think that the cause was the impending solemn intonation
of the text.[45] That the syntax of the very passages receiving the passion letters
should be clarified by repunctuation only strengthens this impression. Furthermore, the passion narratives feature a conspicuous concentration of the added
stress marks to aid in pronunciation (Fig. 3.2). One would not (and does not)
need to be a deacon to understand the function of the passion letters; it becomes
apparent pretty quickly how they work. Nevertheless, they constitute a liturgical
apparatus, and I am convinced that at some point in the early life of the manuscript, the passions according to Matthew and Mark were intoned at Mass during Holy Week from this book.

The textual feature of Pembroke 302 that is most celebrated is a description in Old English of the eastern boundary of the diocese of Hereford added
on a blank leaf between the canon tables and the Gospel text proper (fol. 8r).[46]
Generally thought to have been inscribed into the manuscript in the second half

---

[43] The passion letters also appear only in Matthew and Mark in one of the sumptuous late Anglo-Saxon Gospel books made for Judith of Flanders (New York, The Pierpont Morgan Library, MS. M.708), but the same system of letters is used in both. See
McGurk and Rosenthal, "The Anglo-Saxon Gospelbooks of Judith, Countess of Flanders," 297.

[44] Both systems were employed in the western part of the Carolingian realm, the
system used in Matthew (c, l, s) being identified by Huglo with Paris-Normandy-Char-
tres and the system employed in Mark (c, t, s) identified as "standard" French (Huglo,
Les Livres, 20). These two systems and one other (c, +, s) are found in late Anglo-Saxon
books.

[45] Karkov did not see the marking of these passages as indicative of the book's use
in the liturgy (Karkov, "Evangelist Portraits," 57).

[46] P. H. Sawyer, *Anglo-Saxon Charters: An Annotated List and Bibliography*, Royal Historical Society Guides and Handbooks 8 (London: Offices of the Royal Historical Society, 1968), no. 1561. N. R. Ker, *Catalogue of Manuscripts containing Anglo-Saxon*
(Oxford: Clarendon Press, 1957), no. 78. This page has most recently been reproduced
in Simon Keynes, "Diocese and Cathedral before 1056," in *Hereford Cathedral: A History*,
ed. Gerald Aylmer and John Tiller (London: Hambledon Press, 2000), 3–10, Fig. 4. The

of the eleventh century, the text relates the boundary as established by Bishop Æthelstan of Hereford (1015–1056). The presence of this text has been taken until very recently as evidence that the manuscript was at Hereford Cathedral early in its history.[47] T. A. Heslop has emphasized, however, that the boundary being described is, for all intents and purposes, the one between the dioceses of Hereford and Worcester.[48] He saw this boundary as a particular concern of Bishop Ealdred, who held the see of Hereford in plurality with Worcester from 1056 to 1060, and he pointed to the real possibility that the text was written at Ealdred's home cathedral at Worcester rather than at Hereford.

Heslop did not adduce paleographic evidence to support his localization of the writing of the diocesan boundary to Worcester, but he certainly could have. The script of the Old English is in the Worcester house style of the eleventh century that finds its classic expression in the manuscripts of Old English homilies annotated by the 'tremulous hand' in the thirteenth century.[49] The writing is round and deliberate.[50] The head of e in ash is high and small, the long and low forms of s are used indifferently,[51] the ascender of eth is very tall, the ascender of d is short and nearly horizontal with a hook at the end, and the ascenders of b, h,

---

fullest discussion is that of H. P. R. Finberg in *The Early Charters of the West Midlands*, Studies in Early English History 2 (Leicester: Leicester University Press, 1961), 225–27.

[47] The claim that the manuscript was at Hereford in the eleventh century has been made by too many to name. My own certainty on this point is startling in retrospect (Teviotdale, "The 'Hereford Troper' and Hereford," 75).

[48] Heslop, "Manuscript Illumination at Worcester," 68. That the text in large part describes the boundary between the two dioceses is the case whether one assumes that the boundary extended down the Wye from Monmouth to the Severn and then up the Severn to Minsterworth to embrace all of the Forest of Dean into the diocese of Hereford (as Finberg did) or that the boundary crossed through the Forest of Dean to Minsterworth. For the former interpretation, see Finberg, *The Early Charters*, 225 and Steven Bassett, "The Administrative Landscape of the Diocese of Worcester in the Tenth Century," in *St Oswald of Worcester: Life and Influence*, ed. Nicolas Brooks and Catherine Cubitt (Leicester: Leicester University Press, 1996), 147–73, at 152, Figure 11. For the latter interpretation, see the map reproduced on page lii of *Medieval England: An Encyclopedia*, ed. Paul E. Szarmach, M. Teresa Tavormina, and Joel T. Rosenthal (New York: Garland, 1998) after W. E. Lunt, *History of England*, 4th ed. (1956).

[49] Oxford, Bodleian Library, MSS. Hatton 113 and 114 and Junius 121 (SC 5210, 5134, and 5232). Ker, *Manuscripts containing Anglo-Saxon*, nos. 331 and 338. Ker's most complete description of this script is to be found on page 417. Gameson's discussion of the script emphasizes some features not included in Ker's description: Richard Gameson, "St Wulfstan, the Library of Worcester and the Spirituality of the Medieval Book," in *St Wulfstan and His World*, ed. Julia S. Barrow and N. P. Brooks, Studies in Early Medieval Britain (Aldershot: Ashgate, 2005), 59–104, at 73–74.

[50] To Ker's eye, "clumsy" (Ker, *Manuscripts containing Anglo-Saxon*, 126).

[51] Low s is not, as Ker reported, always final (Ker, *Manuscripts containing Anglo-Saxon*, 126).

l, and thorn are tall and wedged. By contrast, the writing of the Old English documents added in the eleventh century—presumably at or near Hereford—to the early Insular Hereford Gospels is generally less round and more casually written, and the letter forms are sharply differentiated from those of Worcester's house style: the head of **e** in ash is larger, low **s** is used almost exclusively, the ascender of **d** (which is not so proportionately short) is not hooked, and the ascenders of **b**, **h**, **l**, and thorn are forked.[52]

Wherever Pembroke 302 was when the Old English text was added, and I now think Worcester very likely, it remains to be explored why this book was considered a suitable receptacle for the preservation of the document. In late Anglo-Saxon England, blank parchment in Gospel books attracted many documentary texts, and those texts often declare themselves to have been inscribed in a *Cristes boc*.[53] But, as David Dumville has emphasized, manuscripts of other religious texts, mostly liturgical but also devotional, served similarly as magnets for documentary texts.[54] A Gospel book was probably the preferred locus for sanctifying and preserving documents in late Anglo-Saxon England, but liturgical and devotional books often substituted. Pembroke 302, therefore, may have held the status of a Gospel book when the diocesan boundary was written, but the copying of the text into the manuscript cannot be a certain indicator of how the book was regarded at the time.

The late Anglo-Saxon manuscript that is most like Pembroke 302 is the Gospels of St. Margaret of Scotland.[55] Named for its late eleventh-century owner, it

---

[52] Hereford, Cathedral Library, MS. P. I. 2. On this manuscript, see R. A. B. Mynors and R. M. Thomson, *Catalogue of the Manuscripts of Hereford Cathedral Library* (Cambridge: D. S. Brewer, 1993), 65–66 and Richard Gameson, "The Insular Gospel Book at Hereford Cathedral," *Scriptorium* 56 (2002): 48–79 with reproductions.

[53] David N. Dumville, *Liturgy and the Ecclesiastical History of Late Anglo-Saxon England: Four Studies*, Studies in Anglo-Saxon History (Woodbridge: Boydell Press, 1992), 122. An example close in time and place to Pembroke 302 is one of the documents transcribed into the Hereford Gospels. See, most recently, Gameson, "The Insular Gospel Book at Hereford Cathedral," 70–72. On the term *Cristes boc*, see Helmut Gneuss, "Liturgical Books in Anglo-Saxon England and Their Old English Terminology," in *Learning and Literature in Anglo-Saxon England: Studies Presented to Peter Clemoes on the Occasion of His Sixty-Fifth Birthday*, ed. Michael Lapidge and Gneuss (Cambridge: Cambridge University Press, 1985), 91–141, at 107–8.

[54] Dumville, *Liturgy*, 119–26.

[55] Oxford, Bodleian Library, MS. Lat. liturg. f 5 (SC 29744). On this manuscript, see Richard Gameson, "The Gospels of Margaret of Scotland and the Literacy of an Eleventh-Century Queen," in *Women and the Book: Assessing the Visual Evidence*, ed. Lesley Smith and Jane H. M. Taylor, British Library Studies in Medieval Culture (London: The British Library, 1996), 149–71 and color plates 3 and 4; and Rebecca Rushforth, *St Margaret's Gospel-Book: The Favourite Book of an Eleventh-Century Queen of Scots*, Treasures from the Bodleian Library (Oxford: Bodleian Library, 2007).

is an illuminated compendium of Gospel excerpts presented in biblical order and dating from the mid-eleventh century. With leaves measuring 172 × 110 mm, it is about the same size as Pembroke 302 (197 × 101 mm), although the proportions are more typical of manuscripts of the period. The Margaret Gospels has, however, many fewer pages, its thirty-eight leaves less than a third of the Pembroke manuscript's 117. The Gospel text in Margaret's book is divided, as is that of Pembroke 302, into four roughly equal parts,[56] but Margaret's manuscript has no canon tables. Both codices include the beginnings and the passion narratives of all four Gospels, but—because of the brevity of the text—the passion narratives dominate Margaret's book more than they do Pembroke 302.

Most of the text present in Margaret's book is to be found in the more inclusive Pembroke 302, but there are three passages in the shorter text that are absent from Pembroke: the Baptism of Christ as described by Matthew (Matt. 3:13–17),[57] Christ's prediction of the passion from Matthew (Matt. 20:17–19),[58] and the death of John the Baptist from Mark (Mark 6:17–29).[59] Margaret's book excludes the Sermon on the Mount as well as the episodes in Luke that contain the New Testament canticles,[60] and neither version of the Lord's Prayer is present. The only portion of Christ's last discourse in John included in the Gospels of Margaret is John 14:23–31, the Gospel pericope for Pentecost.

Virtually all of the excerpts in Margaret's manuscript had a place in the Mass liturgy of late Anglo-Saxon England; only the opening verses of Luke find no liturgical association.[61] Each excerpt in Margaret's book is prefaced by a rubric identifying the Gospel from which the text comes,[62] a characteristic feature of

---

[56] Matthew occupies twenty pages, Mark fifteen pages, Luke seventeen pages, and John fourteen pages.

[57] Assigned to the Wednesday after Epiphany in the Roman tradition followed in late Anglo-Saxon England (Lenker, *Die westsächsische Evangelienversion*, 302).

[58] This passage is given as the Gospel for the weekly Mass of the Holy Cross in Le Havre, Bibliothèque municipale, MS 330 and Cambridge, Corpus Christi College, MS. 422 (Lenker, *Die westsächsische Evangelienversion*, 383). Rushforth was mistaken in thinking that this Mass was to be celebrated on Saturdays (Rushforth, *St Margaret's Gospel-Book*, 72). Gameson, who was writing before Lenker's study was published, identified this pericope with the feast of St. Cecilia (Gameson, "The Gospels," 150, 152).

[59] Assigned to the Decollation of John the Baptist in the Roman tradition followed in late Anglo-Saxon England (Lenker, *Die westsächsische Evangelienversion*, 366).

[60] Rushforth was mistaken when she wrote that the *Magnificat* is included (Rushforth, *St Margaret's Gospel-Book*, 73).

[61] Rushforth, *St Margaret's Gospel-Book*, 72–75.

[62] One of these rubrics takes the specific form of the introduction customarily employed in the liturgy of the Mass: *Sequentia sancti evangelii secundum . . .* (in this case, *Mattheum*, fol. 5r). See S. J. P. van Dijk, "The Bible in Liturgical Use," in *The Cambridge History of the Bible*, 3 vols. (Cambridge: Cambridge University Press, 1963–1970), 2: 220–52, esp. 225–26. This locution presumably survives from an ancient tradition of *lectio*

lectionaries and capitularies, where the liturgical arrangement of the text makes authorship a matter to be clarified. In Margaret's book, where the excerpts are in biblical order, the cumulative effect of these rubrics is very odd. Despite the clear liturgical associations of the text and its rubrication, the small size of the book and the abbreviated nature of the text—and perhaps also the knowledge of its eventual ownership by a laywoman—have prompted scholars to see it essentially as a personal devotional book. [63]

Might Pembroke 302 too be regarded as a devotional book? [64] A comparison of the book's contents with the only complete Gospel lectionary arranged in liturgical order surviving from Anglo-Saxon England suggests that over 80% of the excerpts had a place in the Mass liturgy of late Anglo-Saxon England. [65] The preponderance of "liturgical" texts, coupled with the occasional—if very occasional—inclusion of opening formulae for Gospel lections, might lead us (and has led me in the past) to think of the manuscript as a lectionary. The liturgical associations, however, were probably secondary to other concerns that shaped the manuscript's text. I have tried to show here that the illumination contributed to the determination of the manuscript's text, and this can be understood both in terms of conveying the iconographic program and in terms of creating a beautiful object to be treasured.

If we accept that the person responsible for choosing the Gospel extracts strove to equalize the length of the four Gospels, and I think we should, there remained still the question of the character of the specific texts to be included. There seems to have been a concerted effort to create a full, if not complete, picture of Christ's life, from his infancy through the ministry to his passion and death. Besides the inclusion of all four passion narratives, the most conspicuous feature of the Gospel text is the inclusion of nearly all of the Sermon on the Mount and all of Christ's last discourse to the apostles in John, two focal texts for understanding Christ's teachings.

---

continua. The "sequence," Matthew 2:1–12, is not the direct continuation of the previous excerpt, Matthew 1:1–21.

[63] Lenker, *Die westsächsische Evangelienversion*, 463. Rushforth, who thinks it possible that Margaret commissioned the manuscript, suggests that the text may reflect her devotional practice (Rushforth, *St Margaret's Gospel-Book*, 25, 72). Gameson does not rule out the possibility that the manuscript was made for Margaret, but he seems to think it unlikely (Gameson, "The Gospels," 152). He is clear that he thinks it "designed for private use by an individual reader" (Gameson, "The Gospels," 149).

[64] Lenker thought it might have been and Karkov thought more certainly that it was used in private devotions: Ursula Lenker, "The *West-Saxon Gospels* and the Gospel-lectionary in Anglo-Saxon England: Manuscript Evidence and Liturgical Practice," *Anglo-Saxon England* 28 (1999): 141–78, at 155 and Karkov, "Evangelist Portraits," 57.

[65] See the appendix.

The presence of the Sermon on the Mount (Matt. 5:1–7:29) is especially interesting because it is a portion of the Gospels, together with the passage on judgment that immediately follows it in Pembroke 302 (Matt. 25:31–26:1), frequently quoted in the *Rule* of St. Benedict.[66] The last three painted pages of the canon tables in the Pembroke manuscript feature a series of lively half-figures of monks, engaged in reading aloud, listening, and reading privately.[67] The presence of these figures points to a Benedictine context for the manuscript's manufacture or patronage or both. Ealdred, the bishop of Worcester and Hereford whom Heslop identified as someone who would be especially interested in the diocesan boundary description inscribed in the book, was — as were all bishops of Worcester in this period — a Benedictine monk. Indeed, Heslop posited that Pembroke 302 was illuminated for Ealdred in or shortly after 1056.[68] Whether or not one accepts the likelihood of Ealdred's ownership of the manuscript, one can easily imagine someone like him, a highly placed Benedictine, as the original intended owner of the book.

The codex could have been conceived and treasured as a book of private devotion, even though it was used in a liturgical context on at least two occasions not long after its making. Margaret's Gospels seems to have been used in the public recitation of one of its texts: neums datable to the second half of the eleventh century were added to the genealogy of Christ at the opening of Matthew's Gospel (Matt. 1:1–18).[69] Musical notation — both its writing and its reading — is the province of the specialist, not the laywoman, and the musical declamation

---

[66] Benedict draws much more on the Old Testemant, especially the Psalms, than on the New Testament in the *Rule*. The concentration among Gospel quotations on the Sermon on the Mount is all the more striking for the understated presence of the Gospels in the *Rule* in general. There are quotations from Matt. 5:1–7:29 (including one from a portion omitted from Pembroke 302) and Matt. 25:31–26:1 in the Prologue and in Chapters 2, 4, 5, 7, 13, 36, 53, and 64. My thanks to Annalisa Moretti for help in tracking down Benedict's quotations from the Gospels and also for help with the appendix.

[67] Karkov's suggestion that the monks and their interactions reflect an interest in the written and spoken word manifest in the sequence of evangelist portraits ("Evangelist Portraits," 57) is very attractive. Thomas H. Ohlgren's interpretation of these figures in relation to the *Rule* of St. Benedict and Psalm 38 is less convincing: Thomas H. Ohlgren, "The Grumbling Monk in the Hereford Gospels," *Old English Newsletter* 24:3 (Spring 1991): 23–24. It is unlikely that the ensemble of a tonsured figure reading between two cocks (fol. 6v) represents the Denial of Peter, as suggested by John Higgitt (Ohlgren, *Anglo-Saxon Textual Illustration*, 74), because the figure wears a hooded robe. I see no reason to doubt the identification of these figures as Benedictine monks.

[68] Heslop, "Manuscript Illumination at Worcester," 69–70.

[69] See K. D. Hartzell, *Catalogue of Manuscripts Written or Owned in England up to 1200 Containing Music* (Woodbridge: Boydell Press, 2006), no. 277. Neither Gameson nor Rushforth remarked on this feature of the manuscript.

of a text belongs to communal worship.[70] If Margaret's book can be seen as essentially devotional, then so too can Pembroke 302, with both manuscripts having been pressed into service early in their histories in liturgical or para-liturgical settings.

It is perhaps most useful to think of Pembroke 302 the way Richard Gameson characterized the Gospels of St. Margaret, as a volume that "combines elements of a gospel book, a liturgical reading book, and a private prayer-book."[71] In summary, Pembroke 302 was probably created as a private devotional book for a high-ranking Benedictine monk, a prayer book intended to resemble a Gospel book and to present a full account of the life of Christ, with a program of illumination that develops the theme of the harmony of the Gospels. The manuscript was certainly read by its early owner(s), as the layers of corrections indicate. It was considered a suitable repository for a documentary text written most probably by a monk of Worcester cathedral in the second half of the eleventh century.[72] An early owner, perhaps the very monk for whom it was created, almost certainly lent the manuscript on two occasions for use in the liturgy of the Mass, and each borrower marked up a portion of the text for solemn intonation. Perhaps the illumination of the codex fully anticipated the manuscript's use. The pair of monks on facing pages of the canon tables (fols. 5v-6r), one reading aloud and the other contemplating what is being read, points to liturgical (or at least communal) use, while the lone monk reading (fol. 6v) points to private devotional practice, with Pembroke 302 itself pictured as a book both from which a monk might read aloud and to which a monk might turn for private contemplation of the life and teachings of Christ.

---

[70] The genealogy—although ending at Matthew 1:16—has a place in the liturgy of the Mass and of the Divine Office. In Anglo-Saxon England, Matthew 1:1–16 is the Gospel lection at Mass for the Nativity of the Virgin (Lenker, *Die westsächsische Evangelienversion*, 367). In the monastic Office liturgy, the Matthew genealogy was sung at Matins on Christmas Day (Michel Huglo, "Evangelium," in *Die Musik in Geschichte und Gegenwart: Sachteil*, 3: 212–16).

[71] Gameson, "The Gospels," 152.

[72] The most evocative parallel in this respect to Pembroke 302, if we think of it as a sort of devotional book, is the Book of Nunnaminster (London, British Library, MS. Harley 2965), a prayer book to which has been added a vernacular text describing the boundaries of the estate on which the Nunnaminster was founded (Dumville, *Liturgy*, 125).

Appendix

This appendix consists of an inventory of the contents of Pembroke 302 with a comparison to the texts of Oxford, Bodleian Library, MS. Lat. liturg. f.5 ("Oxford") and Florence, Biblioteca Medicea Laurenziana, MS. Plut. xvii.20 ("Florence"). In transcribing the incipits of the excerpts in Pembroke 302, I have rendered display script as capital letters. This should help the reader understand why I chose to define the excerpts as I did. The orthography of the manuscript has been retained, abbreviations have been silently expanded, and e-caudata has been transcribed as e. In transcribing the rubrics in the Florence manuscript, which are written entirely in uncials, I have adopted a different approach to capitalization in the interest of legibility. I have retained the language and spelling of the manuscript, which seemed prudent given some of the idiosyncrasies in the naming of Sundays and feast days.

FIG. 3.1. (P. 85) Cambridge, Pembroke College, MS 302, fol. 27r
The passion letters added in Matthew are c for the narration (e.g., on line 2 at *Et*), l for the words of Christ (e.g., on line 7 at *Amen*), and s for the direct speech of others (tall s on line 10 at *Numquid* and round s on line 20, also at *Numquid*). The original punctuation by *positurae* has been reworked, increasing the use of the *punctus elevatus*. On this page, at least two *punctus* have been transformed into *punctus elevati* (on line 5 following *facto* and on line 9 following *ualde*). In one instance, a *punctus* has been transformed into a *punctus versus* (on line 6 following *suis*). A *punctus elevatus* has been inserted on line 7 between *uobis* and *quia*.

FIG. 3.2. (P. 86) Cambridge, Pembroke College, MS. 302, fol. 51v
In the passion according to Mark, the system of passion letters is c, t, s. The narration is marked by c (e.g., on line 7 at *Petrus*), the direct discourse of Christ by t (e.g., on line 9 at *Amen*), and the speech of others by s (e.g., on line 7 at *Et*). On line 9, a *punctus* has been transformed into a *punctus versus* (following *ihesus*). There are a number of corrections to the text, which may have been made by the scribe who supplied the passion letters, and there is also an added stress mark (over *bis* on line 11)

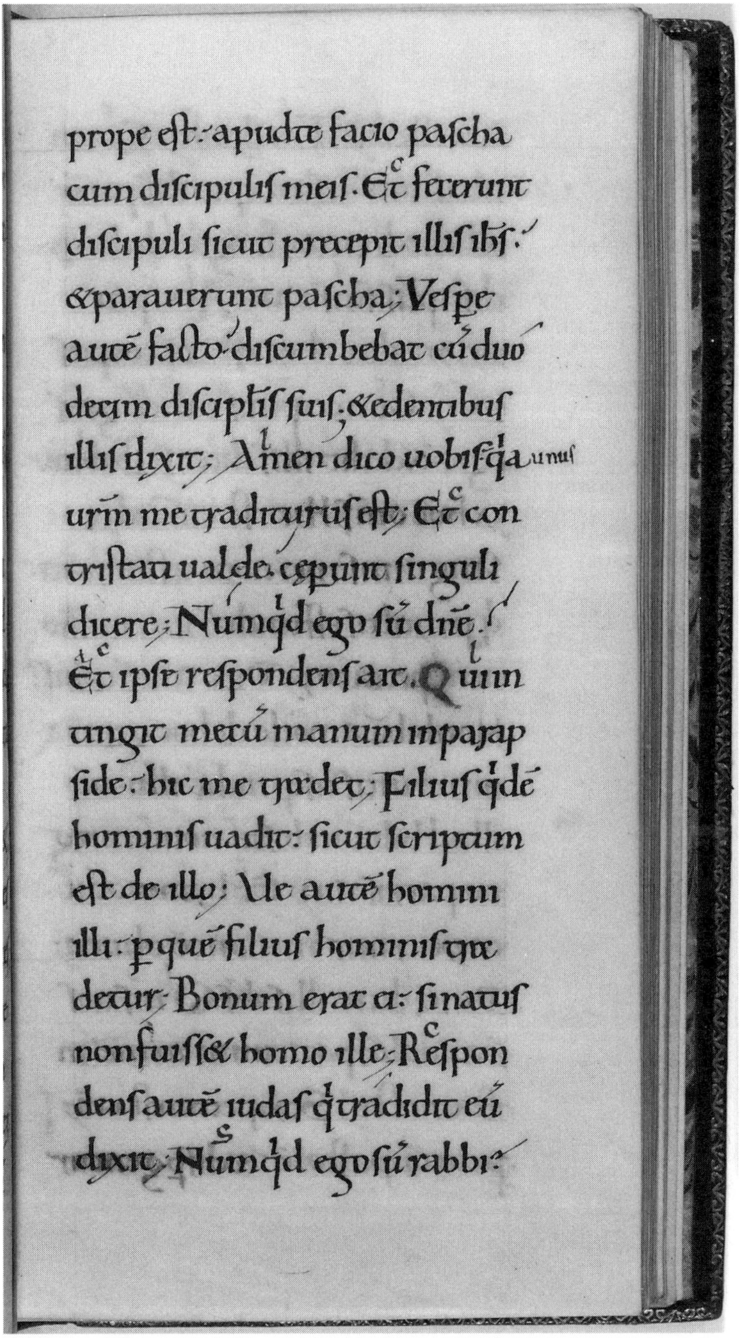

prope est· apud te facio pascha
cum discipulis meis· Et fecerunt
discipuli sicut precepit illis ihs·
&parauerunt pascha· Vespe
autem facto discumbebat cu duo
decim discipulis suis· & edentibus
illis dixit· Amen dico uobis qa unus
urm me traditurus est· Et con
tristati ualde cepunt singuli
dicere· Numqd ego su dne·
Et ipse respondens ait· Qui in
tingit mecum manum in parap
side· hic me tradet· Filius qde
hominis uadit· sicut scriptum
est de illo· Ue autem homini
illi· p que filius hominis tre
detur· Bonum erat ei· si natus
non fuisset homo ille· Respon
dens autem iudas q tradidit eu
dixit· Numqd ego su rabbi·

Fig. 3.1. Cambridge, Pembroke College, MS 302, fol. 27r

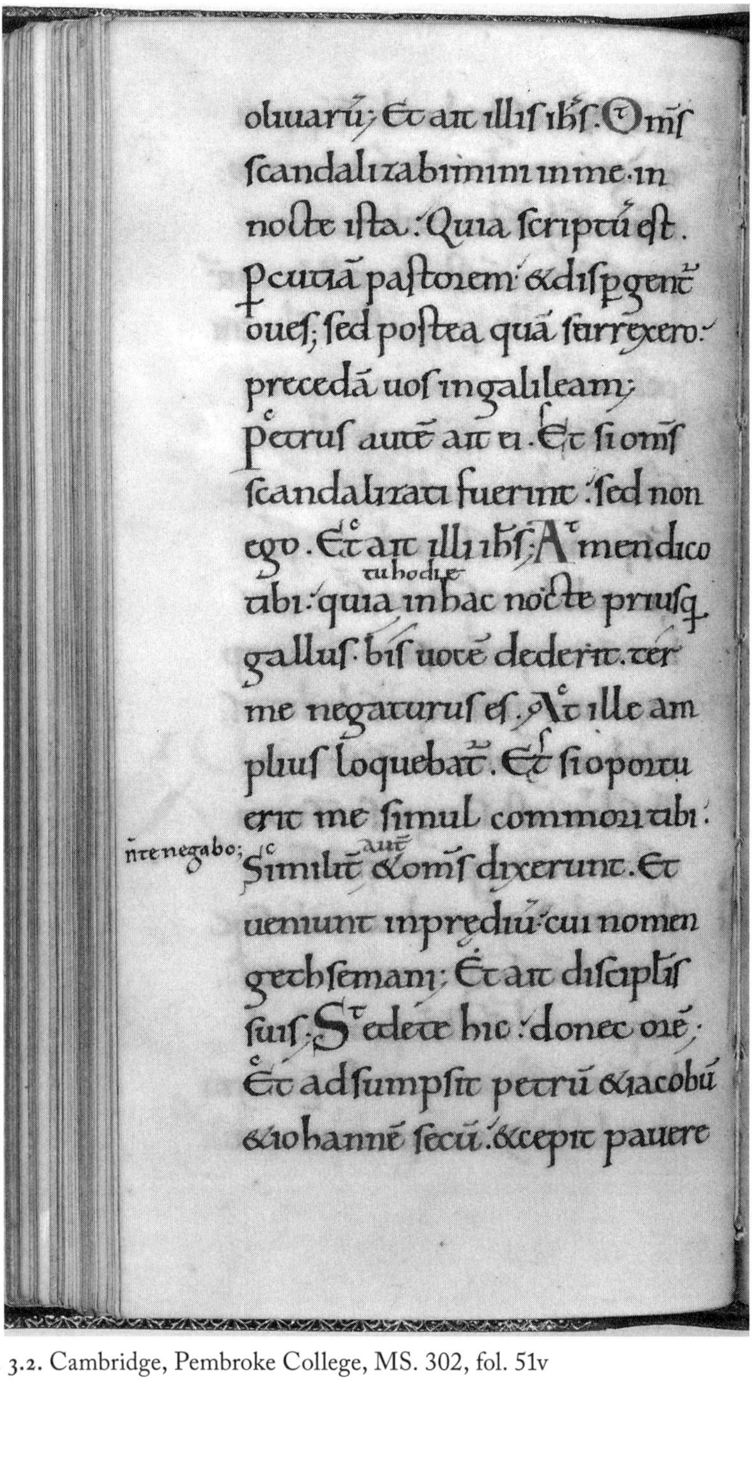

FIG. 3.2. Cambridge, Pembroke College, MS. 302, fol. 51v

fol.	passage	incipit	episode	Oxford	Florence	Florence rubric
9v	Mt 1:1–18	INITIUM SANCTI EUUANGELII DOMINI NOSTRI IHESU XPISTI SECUNDUM MATHEUM. LIBER GENERATIONIS	Genealogy of Jesus	Mt 1:1–21	Mt 1:1–16	Natiuitas sanctae Mariae
11r	Mt 1:18–21	IN ILLO TEMPORE Cum esset desponsata mater	Birth of Jesus		Mt 1:18–21	[In uigilia natalis domini]
11v	Mt 2:1–12	CUM ERGO NATUS IHESUS ESSET in bethleem iude	Visit of the Magi	Mt 2:1–12	Mt 2:1–12	In die [theophaniae]
12v	Mt 2:13–18	ECCE ANGELUS DOMINI APPAruit in sompnis ioseph	Flight into Egypt and the Massacre of the Innocents		Mt 2:13–18	In natale innocentum
13v	Mt 2:19–23	DEFUNCTO AUTEM herode ecce apparuit angelus	Return from Egypt		Mt 2:19–23	In uigilia theophaniae
14r	Mt 3:1–6	IN DIEBUS AUTEM ILLIS Uenit iohannes baptista	John the Baptist		Mt 3:1–6	Feria IIII [post Dominicam III ante natale domini]
14v	Mt 4:1–11	Tunc ihesus ductus est in desertum a spiritu	Temptations	Mt 4:1–11	Mt 4:1–11	Dominica I in quadragesima
15r	Mt 4:18–22	AMBULANS IHESUC IUXTA mare galilee uidit duos	First Disciples	Mt 4:18–22	Mt 4:18–22	In die [sancti Andreae apostoli]
15v	Mt 4:23–25	ET CIRCUIBAT IHESUC TOTAM galileam docens	Ministry in Galilee		Mt 4:23–25	Feria VI [post Dominicam III post theophaniam]

fol.	passage	incipit	episode	Oxford	Florence	Florence rubric
16r	Mt 5:1–12	IN ILLO TEMPORE UIDENS TURbas ihesuc ascendit	On the Kingdom of Heaven		Mt 5:1–2	Natale omnium sanctorum, Sanctorum Tibertii et Ualerii [incipit only], Item ut supra [i.e., In natale plurimorum sanctorum; incipit only]
16v	Mt 5:20–24	Dico enim uobis Quia nisi habundauerit iustitia	On Anger		Mt 5:20–24	Dominica VI post octabas pentecostes
17r	Mt 5:25–32	ESTO CONSENTIENS ADuersario tuo cito dum es	On the Law: Adultery, Marriage		Mt 5:25–30	Feria IIII [post Dominicam III post octabas pentecostes]
18r	Mt 5:33–42	Iterum. Audistis quia dictum est antiquis	On the Law: Oaths, Retaliation		Mt 5:33–42	Feria IIII [post Dominicam XV post octabas pentecostes]
18v	Mt 5:43–6:1	IN ILLO TEMPORE Dixit ihesus discipulis suis	On the Law: Enemies		Mt 5:43–6:4	Feria VI [post Dominicam in quinquagesima]
19r	Mt 6:2–15	CUM ERGO FACIS ELEMOsinam noli turba (*Pater noster* begins with a line of rustic capitals)	On Almsgiving, the Lord's Prayer			
20r	Mt 6:16–23	CUM AUTEM IEIUNATIS nolite fieri sicut	On Fasting and Wealth		Mt 16:16–21	Feria IIII [post dominicam quinquagesima]

fol.	passage	incipit	episode	Oxford	Florence	Florence rubric
21r	Mt 6:24–33	NEMO POTEST DUOBUS DOMInis seruire aut enim	On Discipleship and Detachment		Mt 6:24–33	Dominica XV post octabas pentecostes
22r	Mt 6:34–7:6	NOLITE ergo solliciti esse in crastinum	On Discipleship			
22v	Mt 7:7–12	PETITE ET DABITUR UOBIS Querite et inuenietis	On Discipleship			
23r	Mt 7:15–29	ADTENDITE A FALSIS prophetis qui ueniunt	On False Teachers and False Disciples		Mt 7:15–21	Dominica VIII post octabas pentecostes
24v	Mt 25:31–26:1	CUM AUTEM UENERIT FILIUS hominis in maiestate	On Judgment		Mt 25:31–46	Feria II [post Dominicam I in XL]
25v	Mt 26:2–27:66	IN ILLO TEMPORE DIXIT IHESUC DISCIPULIS SUIS Scitis quia post biduum pascha fiet et filius (first word of Mt 27:62 is in rustic capitals)	Passion and Burial of Jesus	Mt 26:2–27:66	Mt 26:2–27:66	Dominica in palmis
36r	Mt 28:1–15	UESPERE AUTEM SABbati que lucescit in prima	Empty Tomb	Mt 28:1–7	Mt 28:1–7; Mt 28:8–15	In sabbato sancto ad lateranis; Feria VI [post dominicam octabas paschae]
37r	Mt 28:16–20	UNDECIM AUTEM DISCIPULI abierunt in galileam	Final Commission of the Apostles	Mt 28:16–20	Mt 28:16–20	Feria VI [in ebdomada paschae]

fol.	passage	incipit	episode	Oxford	Florence	Florence rubric
38v	Mk 1:1–3	INCIPIT EUUANGELII SECUNDUM MARCUM. INITIUM EUUANGELII IHESU XPISTI FILII DEI SICUT SCRIPTUM	Preaching of John the Baptist	Mk 1:1–8		
38v	Mk 1:4–20	FUIT IOHANNES IN DESERTO baptizans et predicans	Baptism of Jesus, Temptations, Beginning of the Ministry, First Disciples			
40r	Mk 1:21–28	ET INGREDIUNTUR CAPHARnaum et statim sabbatis	Healing of the Man with the Unclean Spirit			
40v	Mk 1:29–39	ET PROTINUS EGREDIENTES DE sinagoga uenerunt	Healings and Preaching			
41v	Mk 1:40–45	ET UENIT AD EUM LEPROSUS DEprecans eum et	Healing of the Leper		Mk 1:40–44; Mk 1:40–45	Dominica II in XL; Feria IIII [post dominicam XIIII post octabas pentecostes]
42r	Mk 2:1–13	ET ITERUM INTRAUIT CAPHARnaum post dies et	Healing of the Paralytic			
43r	Mk 2:14–17	ET CUM PRETERIRET UIDIT LEuIN alphei sedentem	Calling of a Levite			

fol.	passage	incipit	episode	Oxford	Florence	Florence rubric
43v	Mk 3:28–30	Amen dico uobis quem omnia peccata dimittentur	On Blasphemy			
43v	Mk 3:31–35	ET UENIUNT MATER EIUS ET FRATRES et foris	Family of Jesus			
44r	Mk 6:7–13	ET CIRCUMIBAT CASTELLA IN CIRcuitu docens	Mission of the Twelve		Mk 6:7–13	In ordinatione episco-porum
44v	Mk 7:31–37	ET ITERUM EXIENS DE FINIBUS TYRI uenit per	Healing of a Deaf Man		Mk 7:31–37	Dominica XII post octabas pentecostes
45r	Mk 8:1–9	IN ILLIS DIEBUS ITERUM CUM turba esset multa	Feeding of the Crowd		Mk 8:1–9	Dominica VII post octabas pentecostes
45v	Mk 8:34–38	Et conuocata turba cum discipulis suis dixit	Prediction of the Passion			
46r	Mk 12:41–44	ET SEDENS IHESUC CONTRA GAZOphilacium et	Widow's Offering		Mk 12:41–44	Ad missa uotiua
46v	Mk 13:1–2	ET CUM EGREDERETUR DE TEMPLO ait illi unus	Prediction of the Destruction of the Temple			
46v	Mk 13:3–10	ET CUM SEDERET IN MONTE OLIUARUM cora [sic] templum	Jesus Instructs Four Disciples			

fol.	passage	incipit	episode	Oxford	Florence	Florence rubric
47r	Mk 13:11–37	ET CUM DUXERINT UOS TRADENES [sic] nolite preco-gitare	Apocalyptic Discourse to Four Disciples		Mk 13:14–23; Mk 13:33–37	Feria VI [post Dominicam XVIIII post octabas pentecostes]; Feria VI [post Dominicam V ante natale domini]
49r	Mk 14:1–16:1	ERAT AUTEM PASCHA ET AZIMA POST BIDUUM Et querebant (line left blank for a rubric)	Passion	Mk 14:1–15:46	Mk 14:1–15:46	Item [i.e., Feria III post Dominicam in palmis]
58r	Mk 16:1–8	MARIA MAGDALENE et maria iacobi et salome	Empty Tomb	Mk 16:1–7	Mk 16:1–7	Dominica in die sancto paschae
59r	Mk 16:9–14	SURGENS AUTEM IHESUS MANE prima sabbati	Post-Resurrection Appearances		Mk 16:9–13	Feria IIII [post Dominicam octabas paschae]
59r	Mk 16:14–20	RECUMBENTIBUS XI DISCIPULIS APPARUIT ILLIS IHESUC et exprobrauit incredulitatem	Final Commission of the Apostles	Mk 16:14–20	Mk 16:14–20	In die ascensionis domini
61r	Lk 1:1–4	INCIPIT EUUANGELIUM SECUNDUM LUCAM. QUONIAM QUIDEM MULTI CONATI SUNT ORDINARE NARRATIONEM	Prologue	Lk 1:1–4		

fol.	passage	incipit	episode	Oxford	Florence	Florence rubric
61v	Lk 1:5–17	FUIT IN DIEBUS HERODIS REGIS iude sacerdos	Annunciation to Zacharias		Lk 1:5–17	In uigilia sancti Iohannis baptistae
62v	Lk 1:18–26	ET DIXIT ZACHARIAS AD ANGELUM Unde hoc sciam	Annunciation to Zacharias			
63r	Lk 1:26–38	MISSUS EST GABRIHEL ANgelus a deo in ciuitatem	Annunciation to the Virgin	Lk 1:26–38	Lk 1:26–38	Feria IIII [post Dominicam II ante natale domini] mensis decimi; In conceptione [i.e., annunciatione] sanctae Mariae
64r	Lk 1:39–56	EXURGENS AUTEM MARIA in diebus illis abiit	Visitation		Lk 1:39–47	Feria VI [post Dominicam II ante natale domini]
65r	Lk 1:57–2:1	ELIZABETH AUTEM IMPLEtum est tempus pariendi	Birth and Naming of John the Baptist		Lk 1:57–68	In natale sancti Iohannis baptistae
66v	Lk 2:1–15	EXIIT EDICTUM A CESARE augusto ut describeretur	Birth of Jesus and the Annunciation to the Shepherds	Lk 2:1–14	Lk 2:1–14	Item [i.e., ad primam missam natalis domini]
67v	Lk 2:15–20	PASTORES LOQUEBANTUR AD inuicem Transeamus	Visit of the Shepherds		Lk 2:15–20	[ad secundam missam natalis domini]
68r	Lk 2:21	ET POSTQUAM CONSUMMATI sunt dies octo ut	Circumcision and Naming	Lk 2:21	Lk 2:21	In octabas domini

fol.	passage	incipit	episode	Oxford	Florence	Florence rubric
68r	Lk 2:22–32	ET POSTQUAM IMPLETI SUNT dies purgationis eius	Presentation in the Temple	Lk 2:22–32	Lk 2:22–32	Purificatio sanctae Mariae
69r	Lk 2:33–40	ET ERAT PATER EIUS ET MATER mirantes super	Prophecy of Simeon		Lk 2:33–40	Dominica I post natalem domini
70r	Lk 2:41–52	ET IBANT PARENTES EIUS PER omnes annos	Twelve-Year-Old Jesus in the Temple		Lk 2:42–52	Dominica I post theophaniam
70v	Lk 4:38–41	SURGENS AUTEM IHESUS DE SINAgoga introiuit	Healing of Simon's Mother-in-Law		Lk 4:38–43	Sabbato [in ebdomada pentecostes]
71r	Lk 9:1–6; 10:38	CONUOCATIS AUTEM DUODECIM apostolis dedit	Mission of the Twelve		Lk 9:1–6	Feria V in ebdomada pentecostes
71v	Lk 10:38–42	INTRAUIT IN QUODDAM castellum et mulier	Mary and Martha	Lk 10:38–42	Lk 10:38–42	Assumptio sanctae Mariae
72r	Lk 11:1–4	ET FACTUM EST CUM ESSET IN LOco quodam orans (the prayer begins with *Pater* in rustic capitals)	Lord's Prayer			
72v	Lk 18:9–14; 35	[D]IXIT AUTEM AD QUOS-DAM QUI IN se confidebant	Parable of the Pharisee and the Toll-Collector		Lk 18:9–14	Dominica XI post octabas pentecostes
73r	Lk 18:35–43	CUM ADPROPINQUARET HIERICHO Cecus quidam	Healing of the Blind Man at Jericho		Lk 18:31–43	Dominica in quinquagessima

fol.	passage	incipit	episode	Oxford	Florence	Florence rubric
73v	Lk 19:1-10	ET INGRESSUS PERAMBULABAT hiericho ecce uir	Zacchaeus		Lk 19:1-10	In dedicatione oratorii
74v	Lk 21:34-38	Atendite [sic] autem uobis ne forte grauentur corda	Apocalyptic Discourse		Lk 21:34-36	Feria VII [infra LX]; Feria VI [post Dominicam X post octabas pentecostes]
74v	Lk 22:1-23:56	ADPROPINQUABAT AUTEM DIES FESTUS AZIMORUM qui	Passion and the Empty Tomb	Lk 22:1-23:53	Lk 22:1-23:53	Feria IIII [post Dominicam in palmis]
84r	Lk 24:1-12	Una autem sabbati uenerunt ualde diluculo	Empty Tomb	Lk 24:1-12	Lk 24:1-12	Feria IIII [post Dominicam I post octabas paschae]
84v	Lk 24:13-36	ET ECCE DUO EX ILLIS IBANT IPSA die in castellum	Road to Emmaus		Lk 24:13-35	Feria II in ebdomada paschae
86v	Lk 24:36-53	STETIT IHESUS IN MEDIO EORUM et dixit eis pax	Final Commission of the Apostles and the Ascension		Lk 24:36-47; Lk 24:49-53	Feria III in ebdomada paschae; Feria VI [post ascensionem domini]
89r	Jn 1:1-28	INCIPIT EUUANGELII SECUNDUM IOHANNEM. IN PRINCIPIO ERAT UERBUM ET UERBUM ERAT APUD DEUM	Prologue and the Testimony of John the Baptist	Jn 1:1-14	Jn 1:1-14; Jn 1:15-18; Jn 1:19-28	In die [natalis domini]; Feria VI [post Dominicam III ante natale domini]; Dominica I ante natale domini

fol.	passage	incipit	episode	Oxford	Florence	Florence rubric
91r	Jn 1:29–34	ALTERA DIE UIDIT IOHANNES ihesum uenientem ex	Testimony of John the Baptist concerning Jesus		Jn 1:29–34	In octabas theophaniae
91v	Jn 1:35–2:1	ALTERA DIE ITERUM STABAT IOHANNES et ex	First Disciples		Jn 1:35–51	In uigilia sancti Andreae apostoli
93r	Jn 2:1–11	NUPTIE FACTE SUNT IN CHANA galilee et erat	Wedding Feast at Cana		Jn 2:1–11	Dominica II post theophaniam
93v	Jn 3:1–15	ERAT AUTEM EX PHARISEIS nichodemus nomine	Discourse with Nicodemus		Jn 3:1–15	Dominica octabas pentecostes; In pascha annotina; Inuentione sanctae crucis
95r	Jn 3:16–21	SIC ENIM DEUS DILEXIT HUNC mundum ut filium	Discourse with Nicodemus		Jn 3:16–21	Feria II in ebdomada pentecostes
95v	Jn 10:11–16	EGO SUM PASTOR BONUS Bonus pastor animam suam	Christ as the Shepherd		Jn 10:11–16	Dominica I post octabas paschae
96r	Jn 13:1–15	ANTE DIEM FESTUM PASCHE sciens ihesus	Footwashing		Jn 13:1–17:26 [8 pages and 6 lines of this pericope are written mostly on inserted leaves]	Feria V in cena domini

fol.	passage	incipit	episode	Oxford	Florence	Florence rubric
97r	Jn 13:33–38	FILIOLI ADHUC MODICUM uobiscum queritis me et	On Love		Jn 13:33–36	Feria VI [post Dominicam III post octabas paschae]
97v	Jn 14:1–13	NON TURBETUR COR UESTRUM CREditis in deum et	On Faith		Jn 14:1–13	Natale apostolorum Philippi et Iacobi
98v	Jn 14:15–23	SI DILIGITIS ME MANDATA mea seruate et ego	On the Holy Spirit		Jn 14:15–21	In sabbato uigilia pentecostes
99r	Jn 14:23–31	SI QUIS DILIGIT ME SERMONEM meum seruabit	On Rejoining the Father	Jn 14:23–31	Jn 14:23–31	In die sancto pentecostes
99v	Jn 15:1–6	EGO SUM UITIS UERA ET PATER meus agricola est	On the Vine and the Branches		Jn 15:1–7	Sancti Uitalis martyris; In uigilia omnium sanctorum [incipit only]
100r	Jn 15:7–11	Si manseritis in me et uerba mea in uobis	On the Vine and the Branches		Jn 15:7–11	Feria IIII [post Dominicam post ascensionem domini]
100v	Jn 15:12–16	HOC EST PRECEPTUM MEUM ut diligatis inuicem	On Love		Jn 15:12–16	In natale sancti Thomae apostoli; In natale plurimorum apostolorum siue unius apostoli

fol.	passage	incipit	episode	Oxford	Florence	Florence rubric
101r	Jn 15:17–25	HEC MANDO UOBIS UT DILIgatis inuicem Si mundus	On Hatred		Jn 15:17–25	In natale unde supra [i.e., apostolorum Symonis et Iudae]; Item [i.e., in natale plurimorum aposto-lorum siue unius apo-stoli; incipit only]
102r	Jn 16:5–15	UADO AD EUM QUI ME MISIT et nemo ex uobis	On Jesus' Depar-ture		Jn 16:5–14	Dominica III post octabas paschae
102v	Jn 15:26–16:5 [out of order]	CUM AUTEM UENERIT PARAclitus quem ego mittam	On the Holy Spirit		Jn 15:26–16:4	Dominica post ascensa domini
103r	Jn 16:16–23	MODICUM ET IAM NON uidebitis me et iterum	On Jesus' Return		Jn 16:16–22	Dominica II post octabas pentecosten [recte: paschae]
103v	Jn 16:23–17:1	AMEN AMEN DICO UOBIS si quid petieritis patrem	On the Coming Joy		Jn 16:23–30	Dominica IIII post octabas paschae
104v	Jn 17:1–18:1	ET SUBLEUATIS OCULIS IN CElum dixit Pater	Jesus Prays	Jn 17:1–11	Jn 17:1–11; Jn 17:11–26	In uigilia ascensio-nis domini; Feria IIII [post Dominicam III post octabas paschae]
106v	Jn 18:1–19:42	IN ILLO TEMPORE EGRES-SUS EST IHESUS trans torren-tem (line left blank for a rubric)	Passion	Jn 18:1–19:42	Jn 18:1–19:42	Feria VI in para-sceuae

fol.	passage	incipit	episode	Oxford	Florence	Florence rubric
113v	Jn 20:1–9	UNA AUTEM SABBATI MARIA magdalene uenit mane	The Empty Tomb	Jn 20:1–9	Jn 20:1–9	Sabbato in ebdomada paschae
114r	Jn 20:19–31	CUM ESSET SERO DIE ILLO UNA sabbatorum et fores	Post-Resurrection Appearances to the Disciples, Doubting of Thomas		Jn 20:19–31	Dominica octabas paschae
115r	Jn 21:1–15	POSTEA MANIFESTAUIT SE IHESUS ad mare	Post-Resurrection Appearance at the Sea of Tiberias		Jn 21:1–14	Feria IIII in ebdomada paschae
116v	Jn 21:15–19	DICIT IHESUS SIMON PETRO SIMON iohannis diligis	Risen Jesus Speaks to Peter		Jn 21:15–19	In uigilia sancti Petri apostoli
117r	Jn 21:19–25	DIXIT IHESUC PETRO SEQUERE me Conuersus petrus	On John the Disciple		Jn 21:19–24	In natale sancti Iohannis euangelistae

PAGE DESIGN FOR THE BECKET VIGIL: MAKING SOMETHING OUT OF NOTHING[1]

Andrew Hughes

Finding Waldo

Before addressing the serious matter of this study, perhaps some levity is in order. Demanding careful observation, it is not unconnected with the topic to be pursued. And it contributes a small detail to the main topic, that is, the order in which material was added to the blank leaf. There are fourteen faces on the medieval page that is the object of the first investigation (Fig. 4.1). Some are crowned with a tonsure.

The Becket vigil

Between Second Vespers of the Holy Innocents on 28 December and Matins for St Thomas Becket on 29 December in office books for use in England is a complex series of ceremonies. A lengthy rubric explains the options and rituals involved. If there is an altar to Becket, a procession to that altar takes place: otherwise a simple suffrage suffices. Following either of those ceremonies are the memorials for Stephen, John, and the Holy Innocents. The procession consisted of a responsory drawn from Matins and a *prosa* with multiple verses.[2] On its return from the altar, the choir sings Marian chants. The suffrage begins with a proper Magnificat antiphon for Thomas, *Pastor cesus*. Following either of the ceremonies and before the saints' memorials are a versicle and proper prayer for Thomas said at the altar if there was a procession, or in choir.

[1] I should like to thank Eva Branda, Pascale Duhamel, and Matthew Cheung Salisbury for editorial and bibliographical work and for many useful suggestions. All agree with the author that the reader should be reminded that to follow the details of the argument, the facsimiles must be close at hand.

[2] Terence Bailey, *The Processions of Sarum and the Western Church,* Studies and Texts 21 (Toronto: Pontifical Institute of Mediaeval Studies, 1971), 28–29.

We will be concerned principally with the *prosa* and its rubric. In a recent article, Lori Kruckenberg outlines the main features of the genre from its earliest, prose, versions.[3] She comments on controversies about what the rubrics for and the layout of such pieces in the manuscripts may tell us about the performance.[4] Clear are sources in which the chant of the texted verses is immediately repeated without text. Even clearer are those that have rubrics such as *Chorus respondeat . . .*, indicating a performance alternating solo verses with a choral melismatic response.[5] Although she does not deal with British manuscripts and practice, this type of performance is clearly indicated by layout and rubric in scores of insular sources. Kruckenberg thinks the *prosa* archaic:[6] for Stephen, John, the Holy Innocents, and Becket, however, the use of such genres continued in British sources until the Reformation ended such rituals altogether. This fact is well known for the most widespread *prosa* for Becket, *Clangat pastor*, at least to scholars of the Sarum liturgy and Becket. Kay Slocum in a recent article deals with several other *prosas* for the saint.[7] *Clangat pastor* is an eleven-stanza poem in rhymed lines of 4+6 syllables, like the rest of the office. We shall be concerned with only a few of its verses, in two manuscripts.

Here is the rubric, from the Sarum Breviary printed in 1531:[8] my editorial glosses are between brackets, and the clauses are numbered for later reference.

[1] *Tunc eat processio ad altare sancti Thome martyris habitu non mutato absque cereis in manibus cantando Responsorium cantore incipiente: Rm.* Jacet granum . . . *V.* Cadit custos . . . Celum.[9]

[2] *Deinde dicatur prosa ab omnibus qui volunt in superpelliciis coram altare.*

[3] Lori Kruckenberg, "Neumatizing the Sequence: Special Performances of Sequences in the Central Middle Ages," *Journal of the American Musicological Society* 59 (2006): 243–318. Kruckenberg notes the contributions of Michel Huglo: "Deux séquences de musique instrumentale," *Revue de musicologie* 76 (1990): 77–82; and idem, "Les séquences instrumentales," in *La sequenza medievale: Atti del convegno internazionale, Milano, 7–8 April 1984*, ed. Agostino Ziino (Lucca: Libreria musicale italiana, 1992), 3–18.

[4] Kruckenberg, "Neumatizing the Sequence," 248–49.

[5] Kruckenberg, "Neumatizing the Sequence," 245 and Figure 3.

[6] Kruckenberg, "Neumatizing the Sequence," 286.

[7] Kay Brainerd Slocum, "Prosas for Saint Thomas Becket," *Journal of the Plainsong and Medieval Music Society* 8 (1999): 39–54. In Slocum's book *Liturgies in Honour of Thomas Becket* (Toronto: University of Toronto Press, 2004) are complete editions, translations, and transcriptions of the chants of the main Thomas offices.

[8] Francis Procter and Christopher Wordsworth, eds., *Breviarium ad usum insignis ecclesiae Sarum . . .*, 3 vols. (Cambridge: Cambridge University Press, 1879, 1882, 1886), col. ccxlv.

[9] This final word is the cue pointing to the place where the choir returns after the verse. See Andrew Hughes, *Medieval Manuscripts for Mass and Office: A Guide to their Organization and Terminology*, rev. ed. (Toronto: University of Toronto Press, 1986), Fig. 2.1 and §210–11.

[3 *prosa* verse 1] Clangat pastor in tuba cornea.

[4]   *Chorus respondeat cantum prose post unumquemque versum super litteram A*

[5 verse 2] Ut libera sit christi vinea [and 9 more verses]

[6]   *Ad hanc processionem non dicatur* Gloria Patri:

[7]   *sed dum prosa canitur thurificet sacerdos altare deinde imaginem beate Thome martyris. Et postea dicat modesta voce versum:*[10] Ora pro nobis beate Thome *Oratio.* Deus pro cuius ecclesia . . .

[8]   *In redeundo dicitur responsorium vel antiphona de sancta Maria.*

[9]   *Ubi vero non fit processio de sancto Thoma tunc fiat in primis de eo memoria ante memoriam de Nativitate cum hac antiphona: A.* Pastor cesus . . . *V.* Ora pro nobis beate Thome *O.* Deus pro cuius ecclesia.

[Here memorials are recorded]

[10] *In die sancte Thoma ad matutinas Invitatorium.*

Other than alternatives of orthography and abbreviation, the rubric is reasonably consistent. A few spelling variants may be observed in later citations. Several sources have very interesting variants. I am preparing a major study of the rubric in some seventy sources, with the aim of relating the sources to each other on the basis of variants in text and chant.[11] But to pursue this aspect would require a comprehensive textual analysis of all witnesses.

Two sources have oddities of presentation that are worth pursuing. In one, a half-line of text is simply blank: in the other, no music has been added to a stave within the *prosa* otherwise fully supplied with its chant. In both cases, then, there is nothing where there should be something: no text on a line, and no pitches on a stave. In no other witnesses of the *prosa* are there lacunae of this kind. What can be deduced from these nothings?

The production of liturgical books

Can we learn anything about the way the books were produced? How did these defects arise in the process of adding rules, texts, rubrics, staves, pitches, and other elements? In both books parts of the rubric are rearranged. Were these re-arrangements the cause or the result of these defects?

To try to discern the habits of those who prepare complex liturgical books is difficult if the task is done solely from photographic resources: examination of the originals may reveal markings, prickings, and intersections that would help. But

---

[10] Strictly speaking, this word should be *versiculum.* See Hughes, *Medieval Manuscripts,* §226, 436.

[11] The research for this study has been funded by the Social Sciences and Humanities Research Council of Canada.

before work with the originals can be efficient, we must determine what should be sought. Even if a preliminary untangling of the many possibilities is unsuccessful, a good many matters about the preparation of such books that should be a part of any codicological investigation can be brought to light for later examination, and some matters may perhaps be clarified or at least made less ambiguous. In re-reading my earlier article that I knew would be of fundamental importance as background for this more specialised study, I discovered that it began with similar sentiments: "Before better answers to important questions can be found, it may be necessary to answers questions of little importance in themselves. First the latter questions must be identified and asked."[12]

It will be necessary to be precise about terminology. I will use the word "line" to mean a line of text: the drawn lines that determine where texts are placed are "rules" or "rulings." But we do not refer to a "four-rule stave": although "ruled" in a particular way, these lines are stavelines. The term "text" refers to words spoken or sung as opposed to "rubric": "chant" or "plainchant" refers to the music, the pitches on the stave. It will be necessary, too, to be clear about the various occupations in the scriptorium that are required for the production of a noted liturgical book. As will become evident when we examine the two books, a precise presentation of the options is necessary. I assume skilled, professional, knowledgeable, and competent artisans, although as we shall see that is not always true for all of the workers involved even in a superior manuscript.

We begin with three conventional and apparently common-sense premises about the order of work. One: the regulator, probably following a design laid down by the pricking or marking of the leaves, does the initial ruling of the page. Two: because of the different media required, a scribe using red worked after all the black text was completed. Three: for the same reason, artists responsible for illuminations, historiated or coloured initials, which require a number of tools and paints, worked last. We cannot doubt that premises one and three are always correct. The second is probably correct for texts with a continuous and more or less undifferentiated narrative. But for liturgical books and books with the chant, where red is required extensively for rubrics and abbreviations identifying genres, or for the staves, I have suggested that premise two may not be correct.[13]

If we set aside artwork and for the sake of simplicity minor tasks such as the addition of highlights to initials, often done in yellow, and of paraph signs, often done in blue, six distinct tasks can be identified: 1) the pricking or marking of the page; 2) the ruling of the page, done by the regulator; 3) the drawing of the staves, done by the staveliner, to coin a term; 4) the writing of the texts, done by

---

[12] Andrew Hughes, "The Scribe and the Late Medieval Liturgical Manuscript: Page Layout and Order of Work," in *The Centre and its Compass: Studies in Medieval Literature in Honor of Professor John Leyerle*, ed. Robert A. Taylor et al., Studies in Medieval Culture 33 (Kalamazoo: Western Michigan University, 1993), 151–224.

[13] Hughes, "The Scribe," 200–9.

the scribe; 5) the writing of the rubrics, done by the rubricator; 6) the addition of the chant to the stave, done by the notator. Some or perhaps all of these, of course, can be undertaken by the same person, although different skills and levels of competence are needed.

For complex books such as breviaries, a preliminary design stage setting the format of the pages in general, and specifically for individual pages, probably most of them, will always be the first task to be undertaken. Pricking or marking the leaves follows. Pricking in the margins determines the overall layout of the page, but is often not visible because of trimming. Marks or additional pricking within the writing area to determine where certain elements should appear or end, a matter dealt with in my 1993 article,[14] are perhaps characteristic of books not superior in quality or are perhaps otherwise carefully hidden under later material. Such marks are evident on one of the pages of the second manuscript discussed here: for example, on column 2, line 5 and after *Magnificat*, line 18, of Fig. 4.4. Absent such indicators, and perhaps following the specifications of the pricking, it is the regulator's job to design the layout of the page within the writing area by ruling where text is to be added. Unless an exemplar were copied in every detail, partly dependent on size, ruling each page appropriately would require considerable skill. A good manuscript, for example, leaves gaps in the ruling where staves should appear, lest the rule should be confused with a staveline or mar the spaces in the stave.[15] Fig. 4.4 has several instances of such defects, here probably indicating an incorrect layout for the page, which the staveliner or scribe was unable to follow.

Let us assume that the staveliner works next. He draws the staves, using a red medium. His task is similar to that of the regulator: the two may of course be the same person. In a simple book of music, there should be no rulings where the stave is to appear, and the staves will fill every page from top to bottom and margin to margin. Here, he has to draw lines between the pricks, or between the widely-spaced rulings for the texts, extending every stave from left to right margin or rule. In books where the stave must be interrupted, to allow for material that was not sung, his task is not a great deal more difficult: he follows the rules or gaps left by the regulator. In either case, drawing stavelines to match the rulings does not normally call for great skill.

But it is feasible, of course, that rather than the staveliner following the regulator, the scribe works next, writing the texts immediately after the rulings were laid down. In this case, the staveliner must add staves where the scribe has left gaps above the words, but must be careful not to add them where rubrics will be needed: to avoid error here he will, as before, need to observe the rulings on the page.

---

[14] Hughes, "The Scribe," 170–75.
[15] Hughes, "The Scribe," 155, 157–58.

I will now use bold to indicate elements requiring red ink or paint. The sequence of events so far established is either *ruling, stave, text*; or *ruling, text, stave.* Where shall we insert the chant and the rubrics?

It would make sense in some cases for the chant to be written before its text, so that the spacing of the latter under long melismas could be established. Nevertheless, it is a well-established feature of chant books that normally the text was written before the chants.[16] I recollect no books in which the chant is completely textless. On the contrary: a frequent feature of books with plainchant is precisely the situation in one of the books described in this study: some texts lack the music on the stave. This perhaps occurs when the manuscript was set aside for some reason and never completed, or more probably because the chant was unfamiliar or unavailable to the notator. The latter circumstance might indicate that the chant was a newly-composed proper item.

In the second of our examples, as we shall see, the chant *was* available, since the remainder of the *prosa* is noted. Indeed, even the missing piece of chant was available, since the text of that verse was written twice, on the second occasion with its chant. Thus we may start from a secure premise: text before chant. Since it is obvious that the stave must be present before the pitches are added, the addition of the chant must follow one of the alternatives set out above: *ruling, stave, text, chant*; or *ruling, text, stave, chant.*

Seeming to favour the former of these are pages on which there are only staves. But these are all in simple antiphonals, where, as already stated, the staves are regular and consistent, filling every page. I recollect no similar pages in more complex books, where the stave must be interrupted, broken, or partial to allow for rubrics and other material that was not sung. When then might the rubrics have been entered?

If the desire to minimise the alternation of red and black media were a factor, the rubrics would immediately precede or follow the addition of the staves (options A–D in the diagram below). To add them at any other point in the sequence would require exchanging ink- or paintpots (or removing the parchment to another desk) thrice rather than twice, as can be determined from the alternatives we can lay out. The exchanges are denoted by • :

DIAGRAM I

Requiring two changes of media:

A   *ruling,* • **rubric, stave,** • *text, chant*
B   *ruling,* • **stave, rubric,** • *text, chant*

---

[16] Helen Deeming's recent observations confirm this impression. Such a practice, she points out, would imply that the text scribe had knowledge of the melody, or had access to an exemplar containing it. See "Observations on the Habits of Twelfth- and Thirteenth-Century Music Scribes," *Scriptorium* 60 (2006): 38–59.

C	*ruling, text, • rubric, stave, • chant*
D	*ruling, text, • stave, rubric, • chant*

Requiring three changes of media:

E	*ruling, • stave, • text, chant, • rubric*
F	*ruling, text, • stave, • chant, • rubric*

If different personnel were used, and the preference were to minimise the rotation of bodies, keeping the linear and writing elements together, option B would be the most efficient. This option, too, is the one of those requiring lesser management of the media. Surely, however, we cannot expect a medieval scriptorium to be concerned with ergonomics of this kind. Nor can we expect there to be any consistency from scriptorium to scriptorium, or even within a single atelier. Indeed, as we shall see, it may not be possible to assign one or other of the options when looking at particular books or pages. As in the first of our sources, we will see that the process may be even more complex than any of these options or, at least, may require additional steps within some of the stages.

The production of simple antiphonals presents few problems. For our purposes there is little difference between the most complex books, Noted Breviaries, which transmit all items of the performed liturgy in its proper place for each service, including proper chants, and enhanced antiphonals, which transmit proper chants with other material.

The Wollaton Manuscript

The Wollaton manuscript is such an enhanced antiphonal, including chapters, prayers, dialogues, and extensive rubrics.[17] It is a Sarum book written in the early fifteenth century, with some adaptation for York, used in the Wollaton parish church. The Thomas office in this manuscript has been defaced in several ways (Fig. 4.1): a leaf is missing after f. 52; the opening of the rubric has been struck through line by line with extra attention to the word *Thome*.[18] The proper responsory *Jacet granum* and the prosa are lightly struck through with diagonal strokes with

---

[17] This antiphonal is now housed for restoration in the Rare Books Department of Nottingham University Library. I should like to thank Dr Dorothy Johnston, Keeper of the Manuscripts and Special Collections at Nottingham University, for her help with this book, and for permission to publish the facsimiles, acting on behalf of the parish church of St Leonard's, Wollaton.

[18] The Wollaton Antiphonal is one of the books described in Andrew Hughes, "Defacing Becket: Damaged Books for the Office," in *Hortus troporum: Florilegium in honorem Gunillae Iversen*, ed. A. André and E. Kihlman (Stockholm: Stockholm University, 2008), 162–75.

additional separate lines through the opening word *Clangat.* Several words in the prosa are worn rather than erased. The body of the rubric, however, is spared, even though it also includes the name *Thome,* and twice the short form *Th'.*

At the foot of the leaf, in a hand and ink similar to that of the strikeout lines, is a sentence that echoes the words of the various royal injunctions about Thomas:[19] *Nota quod hoc festum* [written as fâm, *factum*] *Thome Beykett abrogatum est per totum regnum Anglie in perpetuum.*[20] In the same ink are large crosses that mark the beginning and end of the Thomas office.

For some of the following paragraphs, Fig. 4.2 will be useful, although the page rules are often not visible: elsewhere the colour plate will be required.

Identical to the one already cited near the beginning of this study except where the type is **bold**, the rubric here is:

[1]   *Tunc eat processio ad altare sancti Thome martyris habitu non mutato absque cereis in manibus.* **Cantor incipiat hoc modo:** *Rm.* Jacet granum . . . *V.* Cadit custos . . . Celum.

[Added sentence:] *Iste precedens V. cantetur a tribus clericis de superiori gradu.*

[2]   *Deinde dicatur* [*prosa* omitted] *ab omnibus qui **voluerint** in superpelliciis coram altare sancti Thome martyris.* [ending halfway across the column: next sentence begins on the next line].

[7]   **Dum prosa canitur thurificet sacerdos altare sancti Thome deinde ymaginem sancti Thome. Prosa hoc modo dicatur.**

[3 *prosa* verse 1] Clangat pastor in tuba cornea.

[4]   *Chorus respondeat cantum prose post unumquemque versum super litteram* A *hoc modo.* [4 verses, the remainder cut out].

Towards the end of the normal version of the rubric, shown earlier for 1531, are the sentences [5] *Ad hanc processionem non dicatur* Gloria Patri and [7] *sed dum prosa canitur thurificet sacerdos altare deinde imaginem beate Thome martyris.* Because of the missing leaf, we cannot tell whether the former or clauses 8 and 9 were present. Clause 7 however is, as shown above, here placed before the *prosa* begins. The words *sancti Thome* are added twice. It is the space at the end of clause 2 that concerns us.

Elsewhere, this rubric is somewhat more specific about the performance than most other versions, perhaps because this is an antiphonal: the words *hoc modo* appear three times, and the words *a tribus clericis . . . gradu* qualify the per-

---

[19] Henry's injunction against Becket mandated that "[from henceforth] his ymages and pictures *through the whole realm.* . . [and] the service. . . in his name [should be] rased and put out of all books." See Hughes, "Defacing Becket."

[20] I thank George Rigg for deciphering *abrogatum est*, and correcting my reading of the last word.

formance of the verse. Terminating each verse of the *prosa*, the melisma is written out, repeating the melody of the verse, with ligatures in place of single note neumes. Under the first verses the vowel A is written three times and under other verses twice, once at the beginning of the melisma and again the end. This "double" letter is unique in the scores of sources investigated.

These variants, very important for relating the sources to each other, are mostly not noteworthy for our purposes. The feature of interest is the blank half-line at *martyris* before the sentence beginning *Dum prosa*, and above the stave with the word *Clangat*. It lacks even filler of the kind evident between the words of the responsory such as *lutea* and *Celum*. What can we infer from this "defect"?

Will a superficial investigation, using only the options already outlined, be sufficient?

Various attempts to explain the "defect" by a superficial consideration of some of the options previously identified, limited principally to the area of the defect, have all met quickly with impasses or new unanswerable questions. Let us briefly examine the two main alternatives, remembering that the black text and red stave are hand in hand, the former setting the limits for the latter, or vice versa. Henceforth, then, "black text" implies the presence of the stave or the two obviously blank lines above it.

1) *black text (and red stave), with red rubrics added later, the common assumption, options E or F of diagram 1.* But in this case, if the chant and its text—everything else of importance—were already present when the rubricator began his work, why did he begin a new line after *martyris*, leaving the remainder of the line empty? He cannot, as in the following suggestion, have miscounted the lines where the stave was to appear because the stave or its blank space and the text were already present. Nothing is omitted relative to the usual rubric at this point, and there is no obvious unique insertion that might be made.

2) *red rubrics, followed by black text, options A or B.* Two features suggest that the rubricator worked immediately after the ruling, before the addition of text and stave. Most striking is the position of *Iste*. Just before that word is *Celum*. This word points back to the beginning of the second stave of the column, the point where the choir picks up the responsory after the solo verse, sung by three clerks.[21] A comparison with the word and chant in the body of the responsory shows that the final pitch of this word, the ⁋ above *lu* (under the second stave), is omitted in its appearance before *Iste*. Here is a summary of the situation. In the body of the responsory the word is abbreviated thus *Ce- lū* with its complete melody: in the cue the word is complete, but very oddly spaced thus *Celu- m* and its melody is shortened by one pitch. Yet clearly there would have been ample room for this pitch where the rubric now sits. Had the chant been written first, with

---

[21] Hughes, *Medieval Manuscripts*, §210.

the missing pitch filling out the column, the rubric at *Iste* would have begun on the next line, pushing the following words onto the blank half-line.

From this we can infer that *Iste* and the following rubric were written before the chant, constraining the completion of *Celum* with its final pitch.

Just as convincing is the massive abbreviation, not typical elsewhere, within the line *ymaginem . . . dicatur.* Here is a possible explanation: the rubricator at *martyris* (first half-line) *thurifi-* (the second line), and *Deinde* (third line) left room for the stave and its text, not yet present. At *Deinde* he realised he had miscounted the lines, and had left space for the stave one line too high. As a consequence, to leave space in the proper position, he now had to squeeze the remaining text into a half-line. At *martyris,* he should have continued, expanding the short forms of *prosa, sacerdos, Thome* and other similar words to fill out the now blank half-line, and the three following half-lines.

But now imagine the column with only the red letters visible, that is, as the rubricator would have left it, without stave or text. How would the rubricator have known where to place the red Vs: and why would he have placed the last three of those identifying letters outside the writing area? And once again, the position of *Iste* is telling: Why would he have begun *Iste* at a very awkward position requiring the following words to be squeezed into a narrow subcolumn? How would he have known where to place it, allowing sufficient room for the long chant to be added later between *hoc modo responsorium* (near the foot of the left column) and the *Iste*? A similar question relates to the section of the rubric beginning *Chorus.* The intervening verse of the *prosa* is far shorter than the responsory, but still some expert judgment would have been required.

I have suggested elsewhere that scribes were easily able to judge areas and spaces and the amount of text that could be fitted within them much more easily than we can imagine.[22] Would such judgment of area and space be this minutely accurate?

Since neither of these two interpretations can be fully reconciled with a logical procedure, let us abandon the approach and examine the underlying design of the page. It will be necessary to proceed systematically: we will begin with the ruling and the red stave, then consider in detail the disposition of the texts, the work of the scribe, and then the placing of the rubrics and other red material. If this process, giving the scribe precedence over the rubricator, seems to endorse the conventional order, options E or F, with which we have just found problems, it is because as shown above the alternative, giving the rubricator priority, leads to far more problems. In fact, we shall find that the tasks often intersect, making some repetition inevitable and suggesting that they cannot be clearly separated, as a conventional description would prefer.

---

[22] Hughes, "The Scribe," 153, 165–66.

The design of the page

Scribes may have been able to judge areas and spaces accurately. Even so, often the positions for such "floating" elements within the page are marked with pin holes or faint lines or dots in a design stage before any text was entered. There seem to be no such design marks in this book.

The ruling, and the staves

No pricks for the ruling remain. The colour detail is important here to distinguish staves in red from the normal black or grey ruling of the page. To avoid the inelegant result in which the grey text rule shows between the red stave lines, where a stave is needed a rule is omitted.[23] In a simple antiphonal, the ruling can be consistent on every page, a format we may call "gapped ruling."[24] In antiphonals that include prayers and rubrics and other material for which the stave is not needed, the ruling cannot be consistent: each page must be ruled appropriately. The omission of the ruling can take two forms. It may extend the whole width of the column. Perhaps somewhat less common (statistics have never been collected) is partial omission within a horizontal line, not extending the whole width of the column.[25]

Because of the omission of rules, from part of the column vertically or part of the line horizontally, we can conclude that the regulator set the design of the page, knowing or estimating where staves would be needed.

The Wollaton book includes prayers and chapters and rubrics. Within the dense textual material in the left-hand column, the rules are regular, under each line. The lowest of the rules extends rightwards into the lowest line of the right-hand column. But at two places within these sections of text the pattern is broken vertically: under the ninth line from the bottom (counting the stave as two lines) where the incipit *Princeps ecclesie* occurs; and under the sixth line, where *Jacet granum* begins. In the first case, there is no need for a stave and, given the partial disappearance of some of the rules—e.g., under the third and fourth lines from the top, and in some places in the right-hand column where the rules ought to be present—we may suspect that here the rule has simply worn away: minimal signs of a rule are under the final words of the line. In the second case the stave is present, but only for the last third of the line.

The ruling of the right-hand column is much easier to describe: at first glance the ruling (not what was added afterwards) is consistently gapped, allowing for 13 potential staves, one stave at every possible position. What was actually added clearly does not follow the prescription of the rules. The rule is omitted below

---

23 Hughes, "The Scribe," 157–58.
24 Hughes, "The Scribe," 178–79.
25 Hughes, "The Scribe," 178, pertaining to Bodleian Library e Mus 2, now Salisbury Cathedral Chapter Library MS 152.

the rubrical lines *-tetur . . . Deinde dicatur* and *Dum prosa . . . thurifi-*. Where the
rubric now stands, the regulator had intended there to be staves. This circumstance suggests uncertainty about what was required. Yet beneath the line *Chorus . . . cantum* the rule extends over only the second half of the column. At this
point, the regulator mandated a stave and rubric precisely where they exist now.
The ruled half-column is appropriate and adequate for clause 4 of the rubric. This
circumstance suggests a detailed knowledge about what was required.

At *Jacet granum* in the left-hand column, the regulator omitted a whole rule
for a stave, even though only the last third was required. This circumstance again
suggests uncertainty about what was required. Interestingly, this is at the very
point where the Thomas office begins.

Even more careful perusal of the ruling discloses yet another detail: at the
end of the blank half-line is a "floating red" rule. Immediately below it is the ruling of the page. Sitting exactly above the lines of the stave at *Clangat*, it is exactly
the same length as that of the four-line stave. Barely visible in the colour reproduction, but marked (with digital enhancement) in the detail (Fig. 4.2), based
on observations by Matthew Salisbury, is another much shorter line, quite distinct in the original and beginning in the same horizontal position. According to
Salisbury, "it is roughly as far above the floating rule as the latter is above the top
staveline. Could these strokes be a sign of [stavelines] abortively drawn a short
distance . . .?" The word "roughly" is a measure of how difficult it is to obtain precise measurements even from the original: it prompts a comment with respect to
photography and digital enhancement, set aside in this footnote.[26] In addition,
the staves are done with a four-nibbed rastrum, with which these two lines of
unequal length are inconsistent.

Could these strokes, within the text space, have caused the rubricator to
halt, unsure what to do?

---

[26] It is axiomatic that the resolution of a good camera is far beyond what the human
eye can detect. Digital processes can allow such "invisible" features to appear. In an attempt to measure the distance between the stavelines, I enlarged and copied the existing
stave just below the suspect strokes. This "template" is in the margin of the detail (Fig.
4.2). I superimposed this template onto the suspect strokes. Although appearing to the
naked eye to be "clean", in fact the thickness of all of these strokes and lines, stave and
suspect, was ambiguous, especially in enlargement, where the ragged edges make it impossible to establish the true location of the line: is a light grey edge part of the line or
not? The distances could not be determined closely enough for the superimposition to be
useful. In addition, of course, the flexibility of the rastrum nibs may cause the lines to
vary in thickness and separation. Here, perhaps, the human eye is to be preferred.

The stave and notation

Using a rastrum,[27] the four stavelines were simultaneously drawn within the space taken by two lines of text or one rule. The parallel curving of the stavelines makes this evident in several places: *lutea . . . Cadit, tuba,* and *libera.*

We can be certain too that the staves were added after the text: gaps occur where there are calligraphic initials for the verses of the *prosa*. As for the notation nothing need be added beyond the observation that the pitches are sometimes extremely cramped, a "defect" caused by the actions of the scribe, which we will address. We must however comment on the *custos*. This is the mark, tick-like in this book, that ends the stave, outside the writing area: it points to the pitch of the first note on the following stave. As is evident on this page, it is present throughout the responsory, but not for the *prosa*, nor for the antiphon *Ecce vidi* for the Holy Innocents in the left column. A perusal of the whole book shows that it is present sporadically elsewhere, but on what basis it is added is not clear. I am tempted to conclude that it is used with this responsory because the tune, part of a non-standard office, was unfamiliar. But then why are they lacking in the *prosa*? Because the tune is simpler? Were they added by the notator? Or later by performers who needed the help? This aspect of medieval chant notation needs a systematic study.[28]

The scribe

Let us now track the work of the scribe. He sees a page blank except for the rules.

Perhaps recognising that an extended rubric was necessary, he declined to begin *Jacet granum* at the left-hand edge of the column, as was suggested by the ruling. This makes it impossible to give to the responsory a three-line coloured initial, as at *Clangat*.[29] But giving the *prosa* a higher rank in this way is usual, especially in sources with the chant and as in the second source studied here (Fig. 4.5). He barely leaves enough room for the beginning word of the chant, but seems to know that it will extend to the very edge of the column, requiring him to place the *t* of *Jacet* outside the column so that the *e* is under the final pitch. Elsewhere too his texting of this responsory is inaccurate, most obvious in the space allocated for the melismas. The words *palea, pravorum,* and *Celum* are spaced appropriately. For two words, however, there is inadequate space, forcing the notator to extend into the margin at *framea*, and to squeeze massively at *lutea*. In fact, as is clear from the darkened area where the staveline disappears, from

---

[27] Diane Droste, "The Musical Notation and Transmission of the Music of the Sarum Use, 1225–1500" (Ph.D. diss., University of Toronto, 1983), 104–16.

[28] Tina Marroum, one of my research assistants, has begun preliminary work, using microfilms.

[29] Hughes, *Medieval Manuscripts,* §603–610.

the lighter colour of the notation, and from the cramped note forms different in shape from those surrounding, this cadence has been erased and substantially re-written. The extra notation above this last word, in fact, obscures one of the faces with which we began this study. The face projects from the left of the calligraphic intial on *Cadit* (another face is within this initial).

Although it is of trivial importance, we can therefore establish that the graffito, the face, was added before notation, presumably by the scribe.

At *castris* and *area*, however, the scribe seems to have overestimated the space required, allowing the *s* of *castris* to extend into the margin, as at *Jacet*. This slight "defect" is not uncommon elsewhere, as at *lapides* in the left column. In addition, the second syllable of *area* is misplaced, with the last syllable under the single final pitch of this word.

At the second *Celum*, as already noted, for some reason rather than using the second syllable, he places only the *m*, not filling the end of the line. This oddity causes the staveliner to stop, and thus forces the notator to omit the last pitch.

The inaccuracies may betray an uncertainty, similar to that of the regulator, about the requirements of the office: the scribe did not know the tune, or have an exemplar with the chant. But they may not be defects. If the scribe had the chant in an exemplar before him so that he could estimate the spacing required, then either his judgement was very poor, or he saw a tune which differed from the one that was actually added. In the latter case, the chant at *framea* and *lutea* might have been shorter, and at *castris* and *area* longer. Such variants are common. But in the thirty British sources that transmit the tune (of the hundreds that must have existed),[30] and more than fifty Continental sources no variant is sufficiently shorter or longer in these places to warrant interest.[31]

We have arrived at the end of the responsory. Even though he sees space for staves immediately below, the scribe knows there should be a substantial rubric here, and declines to follow the hint given by the ruling to mandate a stave and text in the sixteenth to eighteenth lines, or to begin the stave for *Clangat* at the left-hand margin of the nineteenth to twenty-first lines.

However, he sees the partial rule now under *Chorus respondeat cantum*, and makes the correct assumption that this is for the rubric for the melisma, and precedes it with verse 1, *Clangat*. The scribe, then, knows what is required and leaves the appropriate spaces.

---

[30] Owain Tudor Edwards suggests that only one in a thousand antiphonals in England and Wales may have survived the Reformation. See "How Many Sarum Antiphonals were there in England and Wales in the Middle of the Sixteenth Century?" *Revue Bénédictine* 99 (1989): 155–80.

[31] Eva Branda, another of my research assistants, has recorded chant variants for *Jacet granum* in 72 sources, more than 50 of which are Continental sources.

Prosa

The scribe's addition of the *prosa* is largely unexceptional: the verses have no melismas, and the single vowel of the extensions requires no thought as to spacing with respect to the pitches. Nevertheless, in the last three staves he has not left space for the identifying ℣. Here, perhaps, the inelegant appearance results not so much from incompetence as a desire not to break the verses over two lines.

We are still left with our original problem: why did the rubricator leave the half-line blank?

The rubricator

I have discussed the main problems of the rubrics, and no more need be added here about the words written in red. One other feature, however, requires comment. That is the decorative filler within words whose syllables are disjoined because of melismas in the chant. It is easy to assume that the red squiggles are the work of the rubricator. Between those squiggles two tiny incises sometimes appear. They are apparently done in the same ink as the stave lines. While they are conventional throughout this antiphonal, I do not recollect seeing such incises in this position in other chant books, although unless one is primed to observe such features, they could easily escape a casual glance.

A comparison of the hairlines attached to some letters of the rubric with the incises confirms that the incises are also red: see, for instance, the incises adjacent to *clericis* and with the abbreviation sign on *sancti* two lines below. Minimal traces of red can be seen in one incise between *lutea*. Were the incises done by the staveliner? The staves are, as usual, red, although they too appear washed out and almost grey. This faded hue is probably because the nib of the rastrum is too narrow to carry the full complement of pigment. The text and its spacing were present, and the correct colour was to hand. But since the staveliner uses a four-nibbed rastrum, to do the incises—presumably with the narrow edge of a quill—he would have had to change tools quite frequently. The same condition applies to the truly red squiggles. They and the incises therefore were surely the work of the rubricator.

Scribe and rubricator

A number of features suggest that the scribe was also the rubricator, and worked by alternating rubric and text as necessary, and by changing pens and colours. In this sequential, linear approach, there is no need to judge how much space must be left for later rubrics, nor, for instance, where to place black text such as the isolated *A* within the *Chorus respondeat* clause. But rather than changing pens and colours within individual words of the chant texts, perhaps he added the red filler "hyphens" and incises later.

All of these tiny features, insignificant in themselves, point to a process of constructing the page more complex than a mere sequential alternation of colours where all the black text is completed before the red text is added. We can suggest the following order:

1. *ruling* (grey)
2. **stavelines** (red)
3. **rubric** and *text* (scribe alternating red and black, adding the filler and incises when using the red medium)
4. notation and *custodes* (black)

This layout modifies option B of diagram 1. The stavelines could just as easily be added after the rubric and text: 1 3 2 4, option C. I have separated the addition of the notation from the addition of the stavelines for this reason: it is the way I would do the job, trying to impose a time-and-motion economy on the process. After ruling the staves, the red medium is available for the rubric that is next in the process. Similarly, after finishing the red and black text, the black would be available for the notation. The assumption here is that the staveliner, scribe, rubricator, and notator are the same person. But in that case, how might we explain the discrepancies between what is prescribed and what is carried out?

The Wollaton Antiphonal: Conclusions

Unfortunately, no clear explanation of the blank half-line has yet emerged. Perhaps distracted by the absence of a rule in the lines above, and wondering why he had no stave at this point, the rubricator miscounted the lines and left the space in error. This would require option C. We have returned to an earlier suggestion. But in the process of inquiry we have isolated a number of other features of the layout and text and notation. Very few, if any, such features have been investigated, or even noticed. Yet it is only by observing such minutiae that answers about the preparation of complex books may emerge.

In this book, some of the features may suggest that the office was unfamiliar, or that its presence at this point in the antiphonal was unexpected: the discrepancies between the ruling and what was actually required; the discrepancy between the spacing of the words and what was required in the chant.

We also need to ask: was the regulator consistently correct in his design for the standard offices; was the scribe normally correct in his spacing of words under melismas elsewhere in the book? Matthew Salisbury reports that of these, which are rather few, only one, on fol. 50v, shows poor judgment as to the alignment of the pitches. Can we infer then that the Thomas office was unfamiliar? Or were other proper offices also unfamiliar, as the inconsistent use of *custodes* might suggest? Photographic reproductions are inadequate to be certain about the ruling elsewhere, and a comprehensive investigation *in situ* would be a very long undertaking.

Another question one might ask is: did the scribes and rubricators of medieval chant books work office by office? In other words, was the preceding material, texts, rubrics, and notation, for the Holy Innocents and the memorials fully complete before work on the Thomas office began? Was unfamiliar material copied in a separate stage? From a book other than the main exemplar?

By the mid-fifteenth century, the Thomas office would have been well known and its performance after the Holy Innocents would have been common knowledge. No doubt for many years after its acceptance by about 1174, the feast was performed from a separate libellus, until a liturgical book was rewritten. By the late thirteenth and early fourteenth centuries, all the known and complete British breviaries and antiphonals include it in position after Christmas and the Holy Innocents. The revision of the Sarum liturgy in the early fourteenth century would have encouraged the renewal of liturgical books.[32] Surely in the process of renewal, the Thomas office would have been incorporated in its correct position. Exemplars for a mid-fifteenth-century book would surely have been up to date. Indeed, the Thomas office is placed correctly in every relevant British liturgical book, up to and including sixteenth-century printed editions.

But we have almost no knowledge about how frequently liturgical books, the writing of which would have been a major undertaking, were renewed.[33] Perhaps among the thousands destroyed in the Reformation[34] were some "ancient" unreconstructed books. Was it possible that for the scribes of the Wollaton Antiphonal, the office was still known *only* in an independent libellus? It seems very unlikely. Yet such a libellus, called the *Officia nova*, printed in York around 1513, includes the offices of both Thomas and Edmund Rich.[35] Although Sarum in content and intent, the Wollaton book was modified for the Use of York.[36]

---

[32] See, for instance, the gradual introduction of the feast of the Transfiguration in Richard Pfaff, *New Liturgical Feasts in Later Medieval England* (Oxford: Clarendon Press, 1970), 34.

[33] In a MS of about 1450, a scribe says of the *historia* and legend of St Simpertus "quae habentur in libraria nostra in antiquissima litera" (*Analecta Hymnica Medii Aevi*, ed G.M. Dreves and C. Blume, 55 vols [Leipzig: Reisland, 1886–1922], 5: 223), but the ancient script may not have been in a liturgical book.

[34] See Edwards, "How Many Sarum Antiphonals . . .?"

[35] William K. Sessions, *Les deux Pierres: Rouen, Edinburgh, York* (York: Sessions, 1982), 24, 48–54 including black and white facsimiles; *Short Title Catalogue* 15861. The leaves survive in Emmanuel College, Cambridge, MS. 4.4.21.

[36] See Andrew Hughes, *Cataloging Discrepancies: the Printed York Breviary of 1493* (in press, University of Toronto, for fall 2010).

The Durham Noted Breviary

Our second source is a Sarum Noted Breviary of about 1480, Cosin V. I. 3 in Durham University Library.[37] A lightly erased explicit on fol. 339 points to ownership by the parish church of St John, Coltishall, near Norwich. In this book, the "defect" also leaves an unsightly visual failure: the pitches of the chant have been omitted from one stave, one verse of the *prosa*. Fig. 4.3 shows the opening of the procession and Fig. 4.4 the *prosa*. At the expense of some clarity in the scripts, the reproductions show many of the rulings of the page: the gapped ruling is clear but, as has been mentioned, on the verso page the gaps and where staves are required do not coincide, resulting in unsightly rules between the stavelines. This defect of design is not apparent once the Thomas office begins.

The stave without pitches is the *fourth* stave on Fig. 4.4.

Although the rubric, like that of Wollaton, is specific as to the purpose of the responsory verse, by *tres clerici*, it is lacking with respect to the performance of the verses of the *prosa*. The section devoted to the *prosa* as a whole is all delivered before the first verse of the *prosa*: *Deinde dicatur ab omnibus que voluerint in superpelliceis et dicatur versus [?]alterius et chorus respondeat cantum prose.* This is quite laconic with respect to most versions at this point, omitting mention of the vowel A. Indeed, the wording is unique. Otherwise there is nothing special other than the repetition in the same hand of the second verse, *Ut libera sit Christi vinea.*

The second appearance of the second verse lacks the chant, although the stave is present, empty. Why did the scribe write the words of the second verse twice? What can we deduce from these features? Whether or not the stave was already drawn, surely the textual scribe must have been aware of duplicating the second verse. Was he interrupted for a considerable time at the end of the second stave — perhaps by a service taking him away from his work? When resuming his work did he then fail to observe what he had already written — namely the second verse? But surely, after interruptions, it would have been normal to "pick up where one left off" by re-reading the text last written? It seems incomprehensible that he should not have recognised the duplication.

I believe we can reconstruct what happened by remembering the situation of other manuscripts, including the Wollaton book. It is normal, after the first verse, to include the rubrical instructions for the melismas. They should appear where the second stave and its text now occur.

Here is a possible sequence of events: in the left-hand column is the sequence if the stave has already been entered; in the other column if it has not been entered. Common elements span both columns. Failures or errors are bolded.

---

[37] The photographs are reproduced by permission of Durham University Library, Archives and Special Collections.

ONE SEQUENCE OF EVENTS	ANOTHER SEQUENCE
1. **Third stave incorrectly entered**	Staves not drawn
2. Scribe writes texts underneath it	**Scribe incorrectly writes the second verse on the ninth line and leaves space for the stave above it.**

3. Scribe realises his error and writes the second verse again correctly . . .
under the fourth stave   on the twelfth line.

4.   The scribe intends to erase the text
and the stave above
to leave space for the rubricator to add the rubric before verse 2.

5.   **The scribe forgets to erase the material**

6.   **the staveliner fails to see or recognise the duplicated verse, does not know the proper format, and draws the third stave.**

7. The notator adds the pitches to the third stave and does not know what to do with the fourth stave, which he leaves blank. **This is a failure to amend.**

8. The rubricator, expecting a space for the verse rubric, does not find it, and adapts the words to fit the space before *Clangat*. **This is a failure to amend.**

Whichever of the two options is correct, it is apparent that there are failures or errors at several points and by several of the agents, assuming that each of the stages was carried out by a different individual. In the first option, the staveliner makes a mistake; the scribe errs and fails to erase; the notator and the rubricator fail to amend. In the other option, the scribe errs, and fails to erase; the staveliner then errs; the notator and rubicator fail to amend.[38]

These two options seem not to differ or to help much; the same mistakes are made, but at different times. But here we might remember the difficulty of the tasks. We go back to the conventional view that the rubricator worked last of those in the scriptorium with which we are concerned. His job is the hardest since he has a given number of words to enter in an area already defined by the previous material. He has a good deal of leeway in the form of abbreviations, and omissions of unnecessary words.[39] The scribe of the text, too, has a similar task, but far less constrained, although in text to be sung he may avoid abbreviations. The notator has few constraints, so long as the scribe has been competent, for

[38] Yet Deeming, "Observations," notes examples where scribes seem to have been quite flexible.
[39] Hughes, "The Scribe," 181–83.

example, with respect to spacing the syllables for melismas. The staveliner has the easiest task, having only to draw lines where they should be. To determine that matter would be easiest if the scribe had already entered the chant words, leaving the appropriate blank lines: absent such textual guides or other design marks which he could follow without much thought or knowledge, the staveliner would need a reliable model and the expertise to adapt it, and expertise in knowing how the chants worked. Would it be efficient to ask a cleric with such expertise to carry out the tedious and undemanding task of drawing hundreds of lines?

Efficiency and simplicity of performance suggest that in simpler books the staveliner took his cues from the already-written text of sung items. The addition of the stave followed that of the chant texts.

We may thus favour the sequence of events in diagram 1 given by options D, E, and F. In this sequence, as we have seen, the scribe makes two errors, and the staveliner, who may not even recognise the duplicated text, can be forgiven, since he simply follows set instructions. The notator, however, is more culpable. Perhaps being a musician he, too, does not know what should be present, and does not know what to do. The rubricator is the last agent to work with the words: since he can see the whole complex of rubric, text, chant, and stave, he is perhaps the most culpable. He could have made the necessary erasures and corrections.

Or could he? Is it possible that in such situations we may have a glimpse of "task-specific" occupations? There may not have been union rules about "doing the other fellow's job," but there may have been some disdain for carrying out the less important, tedious, and mainly mechanical tasks such as erasing. The scribe and rubricator may have said: "the next person can do it." Even if such prickly sensibilities were not to be found in the scriptorium, we can confirm that erasures and corrections, at least in this case, were not carried out immediately after the error was noticed. In this case, the material is too long for immediate expunctuation, and the stave could be removed only by erasure.

Let us look briefly now at the layout and text of the rubric from its beginning on folio 24. A marginal note partly hidden in the gutter gives the location of the responsory in matins[40] (only just visible in Fig. 4.3). About the opening words of the rubric and the responsory on this page, given that *tres clerici* for the verse is common in antiphonals, nothing is particularly odd. The underlay and spacing of the chant syllables is better than that of Wollaton, although not excellent: *lutea* is poorly placed, for instance. But the chant is not cramped. There are no *custodes*. If we turn the page, however, we find that the first word of the new page, the cue for the *repetenda*, *Celum*, has no stave (Fig. 4.5). As we have seen in the other source, this cue is usually supplied with its pitches, although as here they are not strictly required. Between this cue and *Clangat* is the truncated rubric about

---

[40] I thank Ian Doyle for his assessment of this folio, and for coming to my rescue a second time with unpublished information about the book in general.

which I have already commented (Fig. 4.5). As for the remainder of the *prosa*, unlike the other source, the vowel A for the melismas is given only once, and the rubric of the verse, V, stands within the column. The calligraphic intials are small and do not require the stave to be broken, as in the Wollaton book. Moving beyond the *prosa*, we see that the proper texts after the procession are lightly crossed out and that the memorials for the preceding saints and the remainder of the rubric for Thomas are spared.[41]

In the discussion of the Durham book, which has connections with Norwich, the reader may have noticed the word *que* in the rubric where the other source (and all other sources) have *qui*. If the pronoun is correct, this book (or at least the exemplar for this rubric) was for nuns. Various reports speak of the defects in performance of language and singing that were typical of a nunnery; yet Marilyn Oliva gives considerable evidence for the reading and some writing skills of nuns in the Norwich area.[42] Does the series of errors in the recording of the *prosa* and its rubric suggest that the book was prepared in a nunnery where there might also have been a lesser competence in the scriptorium? Ian Doyle informs me that some dozen scribes and decorators were involved in the production of the book, another sign, perhaps, of a less than professional atelier. The discrepancy between rules and staves in the material preceding but not in the Thomas office, and the presence of what seem like design marks are suggestive. Perhaps evidence elsewhere in the book shows difficulties in the design. Perhaps evidence elsewhere confirms that it was intended for nuns. Investigating these matters must be deferred.

Conclusions

Intriguing are the hints that liturgical books may have been copied office by office, completing one feastday with chant and rubrics before proceeding to the next, and the likelihood that newer offices required material not always present in the current exemplar. Although in both sources studied here the signs must be confirmed by further minute investigation, the Thomas office seems to show

---

[41] See "Embedded Material" in Hughes, "Defacing Becket."

[42] Eileen Power, *Medieval Women*, ed. M. M. Postan (Cambridge: Cambridge University Press, 1976), 88–89. Carolyne Larrington, *Women and Writing in Medieval Europe: A Source Book* (London: Routledge, 1995), 187–88, 222. Marilyn Oliva, *The Convent and the Community in Late Medieval England* (Woodbridge: Boydell Press, 1998), 64–72. Perhaps the presence of Tittivulus, the demonic "verbiage collector," was keenly felt in the nunnery, as the eponymous novella by Michael Ayrton has suggested: "Where he [Tittivulus] singled out the Danglers, who lagged behind, the Gaspers, who could not keep up, and the Mumblers, who may or may not have kept up with the chant, but who were inaudible": *Tittivulus* (Frome, Somerset: Bran's Head Books, 1986), 13.

different design features: in Wollaton, its staves and rulings conflict, whereas in the Durham book, the reverse is true.

Our study of these two sources has suggested different, even conflicting, procedures. In Wollaton, many problems can be simplified by assuming that the black and red texts were added in the same stage by a single worker, the scribe: in the Durham source, the modification of the rubric suggests that the rubricator worked separately and later. In both sources, however, uncertainty, error, and possible incompetence seem to have played a part. A conclusion that the office of Becket was unfamiliar and not fully incorporated into some fifteenth-century books, although still "new" for the printer of the 1513 libellus, would be extremely surprising. Not surprising is the number of questions about the production of liturgical books that remain unanswered and unasked.

Waldo snubbed

Squeezing the pitches to complete the word *lutea* in the Wollaton Antiphonal, the notator obscured part of the scribe's playful gargoyle. Did he cut off the nose to spite the face?

Fig. 4.1. England, Nottingham University Library Special Collections, the Wollaton Antiphonal, fol. 52v.

Fig. 4.2. England, Nottingham University Library Special Collections, the Wollaton Antiphonal, fol. 52v., detail, with some editorial enhancements.

FIG. 4.3. England, Durham University Library, Cosin V. I. 3, fol. 74v. This plate has been enhanced to remove the shadow in the gutter margin.

FIG. 4.4. England, Durham University Library, Cosin V. I. 3, fols. 74v–75. At the expense of some clarity in the script, this reproduction has been exposed to reveal the rulings of the pages.

FIG. 4.5. England, Durham University Library, Cosin V.I.3, fols.74v–75.

THE ROLE OF OLD SARUM
IN THE PROCESSIONS OF SALISBURY CATHEDRAL

WILLIAM PETER MAHRT

Liturgy is a highly traditional phenomenon, and liturgical traditions persist even after their origins have been forgotten. But one might ask how liturgical traditions are transmitted, and what happens to them in a time of change. It can be that their persistence is primarily the collective memory of their participants, represented only secondarily by written documents.

This is a central question for England and its liturgical tradition in the later Middle Ages — the Sarum Rite, the usage of the diocese of Salisbury. What was nothing more than a local rite at its inception ca. 1090 gradually became a model for other dioceses; by the end of the Middle Ages, most dioceses in southern England had given up their own local usages in its favor; though still called the Sarum Rite, it became so generalized that printed "Sarum" books of the sixteenth century made special mention of usages peculiar to Salisbury cathedral itself.

Of particular interest is a crucial point in the formation, transmission, and development of the Sarum Rite: the shift of the center of the diocese from Old Fort Sarum to Salisbury and the building of the new cathedral there.[1]

The diocese of Old Sarum was established as part of William the Conqueror's reordering of the English church. A new cathedral was built within the walls of Fort Sarum upon the hill and soon a Norman, Osmund, was named bishop. Though his canonization was not achieved until 1457, Osmund was revered as the founder bishop of the cathedral chapter and of its liturgy — the rite of Sarum.[2] The principal document of this rite, the consuetudinary, acknowledges

---

[1] This move is particularly well described in Paul Binski, *Becket's Crown: Art and Imagination in Gothic England, 1170–1300* (New Haven: Yale University Press, 2004), 62–77; see also Thomas Cocke and Peter Kidson, *Salisbury Cathedral: Perspectives on the Architectural History*, Royal Commission on the Historical Monuments of England (London: HMSO, 1993).

[2] To him is ascribed, at least by legend, the invention of the four-square choir — the four principal officers of a cathedral chapter, sitting in choir at its four corners: dean,

The Study of Medieval Manuscripts of England: Festschrift in Honor of Richard W. Pfaff, eds. George Hardin Brown and Linda Ehrsam Voigts, MRTS 384 (Tempe: ACMRS, 2010). [ISBN 978-0-86698-432-4]

his role, without attributing its authorship to him: "juxta institutionem felicis
memorie Osmundi, eiusdem fundatoris episcopique" ["according to the teaching of Osmund of happy memory, its founder and bishop"]. Undoubtedly the
liturgy there underwent considerable development in the course of the century
after St. Osmund, but at the turn of the thirteenth century there was a particularly strong movement towards reinvigoration of the life of the cathedral chapter.
Under Bishop Herbert Poore and his brother Richard Poore as dean, a revision
of the liturgy seems already to have taken place at Old Sarum, and the resulting
consuetudinary, dated ca. 1210, gave the essentials of the ordering of the chapter's governance and liturgy.

An even more significant aspect of the revitalization of the life of the cathedral was its move out of the walls of the old fort on the hill to the plains below
and the building of the new cathedral—the Gothic building seen at Salisbury
today. It was rare for a cathedral to be built upon new ground; in fact, the notion
of "sacred place" is against it. Cathedrals were built upon the right place—the
place revered as the sacred location of the region.[3] Most Gothic cathedrals in
England were built upon the site, if not the structure, of a pre-existing building.
It is true that Old Sarum cathedral had itself been built anew on its site. Still,
after over a century, it, too, was received as a sacred place, and in moving to the
new site, continuity with the old one was important.[4]

Such a move could not be undertaken lightly. For the required papal permission, argument was made concerning the century-old conflict with the military,
difficulty of access for the laity, as well as harsh conditions upon the hill. The argument did not mention, however, that the space within the fort was insufficient
for a Gothic structure of the length and scope envisioned.

---

precentor, chancellor, and treasurer; see Walter Howard Frere, *The Use of Sarum, I: The
Sarum Customs as Set Forth in the Consuetudinary and Customary* (Cambridge: Cambridge
University Press, 1898), xv; for St. Osmund in general, see Daphne Stroud, *St. Osmund of
Salisbury* (Much Wenlock: R.J.L. Smith, 1994).

[3] Recall Chartres, built over a spring already dedicated to a virgin in pre-Christian
times, or Florence, where the walls of the new building were constructed around the old
cathedral, and upon its completion, the old building was taken down inside.

[4] I would distinguish "sacred place" and "sacred space." Sacred place is a specific
location, such as an altar; sacred space is the interrelation of sacred places. Anthropolo-
gists, such as Mircea Eliade (see note 6 below), emphasize the opposition between sacred
space and profane space, but in my study of the Sarum Use, I have concluded that this
opposition is not a significant feature of the Gothic conception; rather, what is important
is the hierarchical ordering of sacred places within the sacred space. Moreover, the sacred
is in part a matter of reception—it is established by convention, particularly by liturgical
repetition. I am preparing a study entitled, "Sacred Space and Sacred Time in the Processions of the Sarum Rite: An Example of Gothic Ordering."

Though papal permission was delayed by the interdict, the delay of some twenty years may also reflect a hesitation to go against the sense of sacred place.[5] The necessary link with the location of Old Sarum was even expressed by a legend, that the place of the new cathedral had been determined by shooting an arrow from Old Sarum, which hit a deer, who first ran and then died upon the new location. Such methods of discovering a sacred place are reported for ancient cultures by Mircea Eliade, and such stories are found in medieval Scandinavia. Whether this story is a fabrication or not, it shows a desire to link an ancient method of establishing a sacred place with a need to make some objective connection between the new cathedral and the old with all its history and traditions.[6]

When the removal was made, several aspects of the new building emphasized the continuity with Old Sarum. Historians of architecture speculate that certain details of the design at new Salisbury were meant to recall the old cathedral. All of the known altar dedications at Old Sarum found places in the new cathedral. Moreover, the already consolidated liturgy, represented by the consuetudinary, formed the principal basis of the liturgy at the new cathedral for more than a century, not only at Salisbury, but for the other dioceses which began to adopt it. For the new cathedral at Salisbury, beginning about 1225, the role of Old Sarum and its consuetudinary was normative. However, the topology of the new cathedral was different from the old; and certain anomalies arose, particularly in processions, the solutions of which demonstrate how normative the traditions of Old Sarum were.

I have long been interested in these processions, particularly because they reflect notions of sacred space and its ramification for sacred time.[7] My present

---

[5] A conflict between Pope Innocent III and King John concerning the appointment of Stephen Langton as archbishop of Canterbury led the pope to excommunicate the king and place the country under an interdict—a prohibition of practically all religious services—which lasted five years (1208–1213); the petition for the move went to Rome in 1217: see Binski, *Becket's Crown*, 62–65.

[6] Mircea Eliade, *The Sacred and the Profane: The Nature of Religion*, trans. Willard R. Trask (New York: Harcourt, Brace, 1959), 24–29; see also idem, *Patterns in Comparative Religion: A Study of the Element of the Sacred in the History of Religious Phenomena*, trans. Rosemary Sheed (New York: Sheed & Ward, 1958), 369–71.

[7] It is remarkable, though, that much of the major scholarship is over a century old. W.G. Henderson, Walter Howard Frere, and Christopher Wordsworth remain the principal editors of the documents: W. G. Henderson, ed., *Processionale ad usum insignis ac præclaræ ecclesiæ Sarum* (Leeds: McCorquodale, 1882; repr. Farnborough: Gregg, 1969); Walter Howard Frere, *The Use of Sarum*, 2 vols. (Cambridge: Cambridge University Press, 1898, 1901; repr. Farnborough: Gregg, 1969); *Breviarium ad usum insignis ecclesiae Sarum*, ed. Francis Procter and Christopher Wordsworth, 3 vols. (Cambridge: Cambridge University Press, 1882). William St. John Hope provided the archaeology of Old Sarum: William St. John Hope, "The Sarum Consuetudinary and its Relation to the Cathedral

purpose is to highlight the differences between the two locations and the difficulties they caused for the processions and to examine the reasons the solutions
took the shape they did; some of the reasons, I conclude, are the authority of the
tradition from Old Sarum.

The main sources for this comparison are: 1) the four manuscripts of the
consuetudinary, the first ca. 1210, and two more in the late thirteenth century,
agree substantially; the fourth, the basis of Frere's edition in *The Use of Sarum*,
shows minor alterations that pertain to the new cathedral at Salisbury; 2) the
customary, written at the new cathedral, not very specific about ceremonies but
providing some indication of the chants sung in connection with processions; 3)
the old ordinal, containing revisions at Salisbury through the late thirteenth century; 4) the new ordinal, from the latter half of the fourteenth century (before
1383), a thorough updating of the liturgy providing in a dense text the rubrics
for the processions and naming the chants;[8] and 5) the processionaries, giving
complete melodies for the processions and reproducing the rubrics of the ordinal
in varying degrees of completeness; Bailey identifies twenty-three manuscript
processionaries from the fourteenth and fifteenth centuries and some twenty-five
printed editions from the sixteenth century.[9]

Processions at Old Sarum were an important part of the liturgy, and while
their description in the consuetudinary is sometimes brief, the overall pattern
is clear. There was a procession before Mass every Sunday; on major feasts the
procession was more elaborate, during the summer season going outside and

---

Church of Old Sarum," *Archaeologia* 68 (1917): 111–26 and Plate XXI. Since then, Terence Bailey's *The Processions of the Sarum Rite and the Western Church* (Toronto: Pontifical
Institute of Mediaeval Studies, 1971) has given a synthesis from which scholars may approach the subject afresh. Leslie Anne Crawley, then a doctoral student at the University
of Toronto, presented a paper, "The Persistence of Tradition: Architecture and Processions at Old and New Sarum," at the Thirty-Third Congress on Medieval Studies, Kalamazoo, 1998; I am grateful to her for sharing her work with me. Peter Draper, *The Formation of English Gothic: Architecture and Identity* (New Haven: Yale University Press, 2006)
gives a detailed discussion in his chapter "Architecture and Liturgy," 197–215; Matthew
M. Reeve, *Thirteenth-Century Wall Painting of Salisbury Cathedral: Art, Liturgy, and Reform* (Woodbridge: Boydell Press, 2008) gives a succinct but detailed account of the reform of liturgy at Salisbury in connection with the paintings of the vault of the choir (20–
23). The function of the "singers' holes" in the west front is discussed in two important
articles: Mark Spurrell, "The Procession of Palms and West-Front Galleries," *Downside
Review* 119 (2001): 125–44, and Christopher Hohler, "The Palm Sunday Procession and
the West Front of Salisbury Cathedral," in *The Medieval Cathedral of Trondheim: Architectural and Ritual Constructions in their European Context*, ed. Margrete Syrstad Andås,
Øystein Ekroll, Andreas Haug, and Nils Holger Petersen, Ritus et Artes: Traditions and
Transformations 3 (Turnhout: Brepols, 2007), 285–90.

   [8] Bailey, *Processions*, 66–70.
   [9] Bailey, *Processions*, 3–11.

completely encircling the church. During Lent on Wednesdays and Fridays, there was a procession with litanies before Mass, and from Easter until the first Sunday of Advent there was a procession to the cross at first vespers of Sundays, that is, Saturday evening. There was a procession to the font on the vigils of Easter and Pentecost, and at vespers through the Easter week. Ash Wednesday and Holy Thursday saw the expulsion and reconciliation of penitents. Processions on the major days of Holy Week were unique and important—that on Palm Sunday was perhaps the most developed. I count roughly one hundred twenty processions in a year, on average a procession every three days.

The topological differences between the two buildings include the location of the cloister and the side doors.

At Old Sarum, ostensibly because of limitations of space imposed by the military enclosure, the cloister was in an unusual position: not only was it on the north side, it was also east of the transept. (See Fig. 5.1.) The west doors of churches were reserved for ceremonial entry on principal days; everyday entry was through a substantial porch on the south side. This porch is seen at the south end of the south transept.[10]

At Salisbury both these features are on the opposite sides—the cloister in the more normal position, west of the transept and to the south of the nave. The normal door for the entry of the laity was, on the other, hand, to the north, for the simple reason that the city was to the north. (See Fig. 5.2.) These differences were the basis for St. John Hope's demonstration that the consuetudinary pertained to Old Sarum and not Salisbury.[11]

A clear example of the differences is found on Ash Wednesday. On this day, those who had to do serious penitence during Lent were barred from entering the church, and they were symbolically (and really) ejected from the church and the doors closed behind them, to be readmitted only on Holy Thursday by a reversal of this rite. The rite began with a procession from the choir to the door that led to space outside the church. Theoretically, access to this profane space (*pro fanum,* outside the temple) is best represented by the west door, since the west portal can be seen to be the clearest boundary between less and more sacred space. The consuetudinary, however, prescribes the ejection of penitents from the south door; scholars have surmised that the west door was not used because it did not provide easy access for the laity. All sources of the consuetudinary retained this designation of the south door. By the time of the full processionaries this had been corrected, and then the rubric reads "west door," the more important portal between non-sacred and sacred space. (See Fig. 5.3.)

The normal Sunday procession reveals a similar anomaly; this procession is described in the consuetudinary for the First Sunday of Advent. It goes out the north choir door, encircles the presbytery, goes down the south aisle, past the

[10] St. John Hope, "The Sarum Consuetudinary," plate XXI.
[11] St. John Hope, "The Sarum Consuetudinary," 119–21.

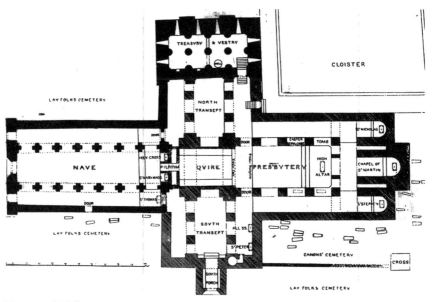

Fig. 5.1. Old Sarum

font, and up the center aisle into the choir through its west door. This is a lustral procession: the priest goes at the end of the procession and sprinkles each altar with the water blessed at the beginning of the ceremony. At Old Sarum, it seems that there were no altars in the north transept (at least this is St. John Hope's conclusion), and thus the north choir door is the most logical point to begin the lustration—starting with the three easternmost altars, then those in the south transept and then those at the choir screen.

At Salisbury, however, there were three altars in the north transept; the sprinkling of these altars would have been better accomplished if the procession had gone out the west choir door and encircled the choir.

Curiously, this is the route the later processionaries prescribed for feasts of double rank when they occur on a Sunday—leaving the shorter route for the simple Sundays. (See Fig. 5.4.) But the sprinkling was omitted on these double feasts. It seems that the lustration, having a somewhat penitential character, was thought inappropriate for festive days. Still, the route received from Old Sarum was kept literally for the simple Sundays, passing out the north choir door. Some speculate that the priest or the whole procession would have cut back to sprinkle these altars, but I suspect that they were just passed over; the terms of the processionary, "sprinkling each as they go," suggest that those they pass are sprinkled. In any case it is instructive that the rubric from Old Sarum was kept, even when it functioned differently, and this for the entire history of the processionary.

The dedications of nine altars at Old Sarum are known from documents of the twelfth century. They are: the Blessed Virgin Mary for the high altar, St.

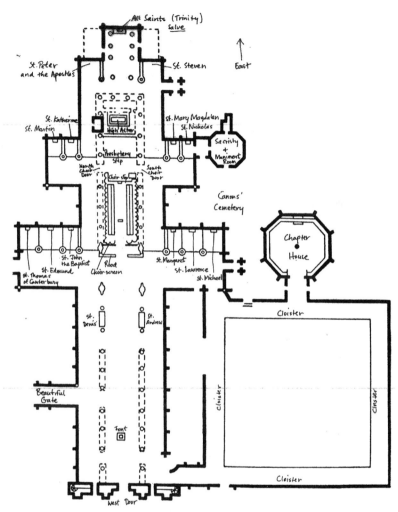

FIG. 5.2. Salisbury.

Martin for the axial chapel, St. Peter, All Saints, St. Stephen, St. Nicholas, St. Mary Magdalen, the Holy Cross (Rood), and St. Thomas of Canterbury.

There are two remarkable facts about this list. First, all of these dedications were preserved at Salisbury, including particularly the dedication of the cathedral itself, and therefore its high altar, to the Blessed Virgin Mary. Second, the ordering of these altars in the space of the cathedral was substantially revised. Usually, altars were added, one at a time, and thus there was little opportunity to coordinate their location. Indeed, the last added altar at Old Sarum, St. Thomas of Canterbury, was in a very inconvenient location.

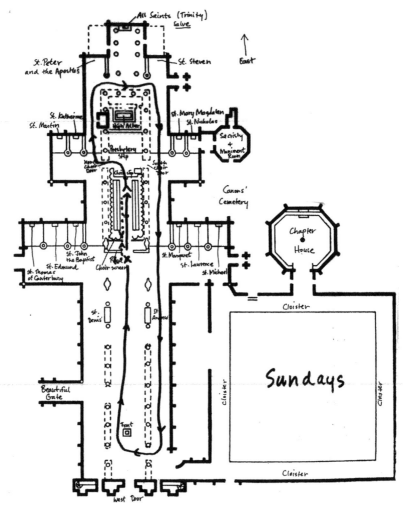

FIG. 5.3. The normal Sunday procession at Salisbury.

St. John Hope provided a conjectural plan of the location of altars at Old Sarum (see Fig. 5.1); though some of his conjecture is not entirely proven, it is enough to see that the arrangement at Salisbury must have been made on quite a different basis. Indeed, building the new Gothic cathedral at Salisbury offered the very unusual opportunity to reorder the altars (see Fig. 5.2). Just as the old Norman-style cathedral was replaced with one in the new Gothic style, so the altars as well were ordered upon a Gothic principle, that is, ordered in a decreasing hierarchy, the most important being the easternmost, with a priority given to the gospel side (the north) within that ordering.

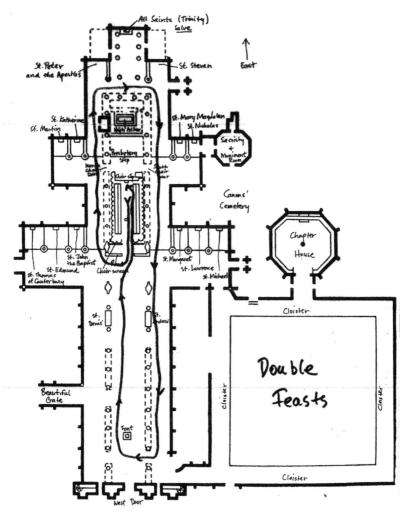

FIG. 5.4. The Sunday procession at Salisbury on double feasts.

While the easternmost, axial chapel was dedicated to St. Martin at Old Sarum, that most significant location was reserved to the Trinity itself (and later also All Saints). Of the two flanking altars, the privileged gospel side was occupied by the altar of St. Peter, the first of the apostles; that on the opposite (epistle) side, to St. Stephen, the first martyr. St. Martin, the central saint at Old Sarum, gets the far gospel side in the east transept; St. Nicholas gets the far epistle side of the east transept. At Old Sarum St. Nicholas's altar was that closest side altar to the vestry; its new location at Salisbury meant that the traditional designation of this altar as the place for blessing holy water and for the deacons' assembly to bear candles also obtained here, since the vestry at Salisbury was immediately adjacent to that altar. St. Mary Magdalen found her place on the inside altar of the gospel side of the east transept. St. Thomas of Canterbury was placed to the far gospel side in the main transept, perhaps to allow freest access of the laity to this popular saint. The altar of the cross was probably at the choir screen beneath the rood, as at Old Sarum.

This placement represents a Gothic notion of sacred space, in which the saints are placed in hierarchical order, the farthest east being the highest, and within that, the gospel side taking precedence, an order characteristic of the Gothic mentality underlying the new architecture itself.

Salisbury Cathedral had a well-developed system of processions after vespers—there was one procession per year to each of the altars in the church, generally after vespers the evening before the feast day of the saint to whom the altar was dedicated. There is a hitch in the system, though, and it has its roots at Old Sarum. Two feasts which have altars do not have processions: All Saints and Saints Peter and Paul. In these cases the vespers procession for the year had already been "used up," by the series of processions after Christmas.

The beginning of the story is at Old Sarum, where on the evening of Christmas Day all the deacons assembled at the altar of St. Nicholas, and, taking lighted candles in their hands, processed into choir, a *solemnitas diaconi*, as later sources call it, in anticipation of the feast of St. Stephen, the first deacon. The early consuetudinary sources, however, give no indication that there was a procession to the altar of St. Stephen at Old Sarum. Still, it is the root of a much larger series of vesper processions in the ritual for Salisbury Cathedral. By the latest version of the consuetudinary (Frere's Harley MS of the fourteenth century) four successive days have complete processions after vespers, each now to an altar: 25 Dec., anticipating the feast of St. Stephen to his altar; 26 Dec., anticipating the feast of St. John, to the altar of St. Peter; 27 Dec., anticipating the Holy Innocents, to Trinity and All Saints; and 28 Dec., to St. Thomas. While the procession in the position of first vespers for the feasts of St. Stephen and St. Thomas was to their altars, that of St. John was to the altar of St. Peter as representative of apostles, and that of Holy Innocents to All Saints—the altar of martyrs, St. Stephen, having been already used. Additionally, the *solemnitas diaconi*, in which the deacons sang the chant, was complemented by a *solemnitas sacerdotis*, with the priests singing the chant, and a *solemnitas pueri*, in which the boys sang the chant. Moreover, the ceremonies on Holy Innocents became the occasion for the boy-bishop celebration, on which a boy takes the role of the bishop for the day, sitting in the bishop's chair and giving the bishop's blessing. Thus, this series of days celebrating the choir actually "used up" three altars for vespers processions, and, while its realization was elaborate and "Gothic," its roots were in the tradition from Old Sarum.

That this series of processions was developed before those at first vespers throughout the year is suggested by the fact that they took priority over the normal feasts of Sts. Peter and Paul and of All Saints. Moreover, the documents from Old Sarum contain no evidence for vespers processions; thus these must have been developed first at Salisbury.

The Palm Sunday procession was one of the most elaborate of the year, and received a detailed description in the consuetudinary. Its pre-history, however, is important. As early as the Monastic Constitutions of Lanfranc, the first Norman archbishop of Canterbury, an elaborate procession with the sacrament was pre-scribed. Lanfranc had been involved in the eucharistic controversy with Beren-garius, and it stands to reason that this innovation came directly from him. As Lanfranc prescribes the procession, it has four stations (stopping places for ritual action); before the procession, the relics and the Blessed Sacrament are taken out-side the city walls, going, as the antiphon says, "out to meet the Lord." There the sacrament and relics are met and adored, and escorted into the city. At the city gate, the second station, the choir boys go atop the gate and sing the refrain of the hymn *Gloria laus et honor,* while the choir sings the verses in alternation with them. The third station is before the west door of the church, where the sacrament and the relics are placed above the door, the procession entering the church beneath them. The fourth station is at the entrance to the choir, where the cross is unveiled and adored. This constitutes a series of increasingly important portals into increas-ingly sacred spaces, making it a day of entrances.[12]

It seems that the situation inside the walls of Old Fort Sarum did not allow an easy exit and re-entrance; for the entire ceremony there was wrapped around the walls of the cathedral. (See Fig. 5.5.) The procession went from the choir out and around the cloister to the first station at the canons' cemetery; then the sec-ond station was at the south transept porch, with the boys singing atop the porch; station three was at another door on the south side, after which entrance into the west portal with relics and sacrament above led to the fourth station at the rood before the choir screen.

The transfer of this complicated procession to the new cathedral (See Fig. 5.6.) must have been provisional for quite some time, since, while the cathedral was begun ca. 1220, the cloister was not finished until ca. 1280. But by the final revision of the consuetudinary, about all that was changed was that the first sta-tion was designated at the lay folks' cemetery (on the north side of the church at Salisbury); designation of the canons' cemetery (as at Old Sarum) might have taken the procession backwards, as some have suggested, though I do not believe it. The resulting procession makes a full circle outside the church and another smaller circle inside the church, twice the distance of the Old Sarum proces-sion. These two facts, the difficulties within the old fort and the reversal of the topology at Salisbury, created a unique processional route that, because of the eventual widespread dissemination of the Sarum Rite, was observed in churches

---

[12] David Knowles, ed., *The Monastic Constitutions of Lanfranc* (New York: Oxford University Press, 1951), 22–26, 151–52.

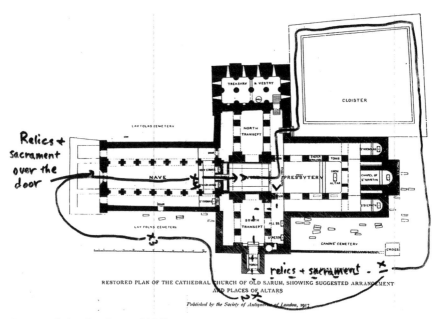

FIG. 5.5. Palm Sunday at Old Sarum.

with no memory of the reasons for the unique topology. Holding literally to the prescriptions of the Old Sarum usage created a splendid procession, one of the most extensive of the year, even though its rationale no longer existed in the new location.

It does not take long to establish a liturgical tradition; moreover, once it has been established, it can be quite durable, even after a short period of usage. Twentieth-century canon law defines a custom as something established for time out of mind, defining time out of mind in turn as about a generation, say, thirty years. My experience is that a major feast with a custom of five years' standing might as well be time out of mind; people will say, "but we've always done it that way."

That may be as it should be, since the meaning of a liturgical rite cannot be adequately spelled out in analysis; it takes on its meaning only when it is repeated as part of the annual cycle, a cycle which is experienced as an increasingly intensified repetition of the same year, rather than a succession of different years.

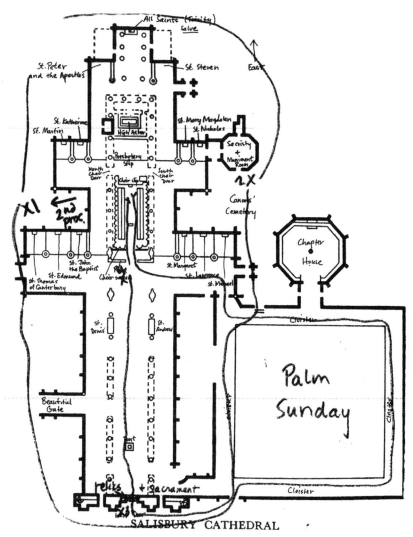

Fig. 5.6. Palm Sunday at Salisbury.

THE SANCTORALS OF EARLY SARUM MISSALS
AND BREVIARIES, C. 1250-C. 1350

NIGEL MORGAN

A significant aspect of the introduction of the Sarum Use into the dioceses of the
province of Canterbury between 1250 and 1400 was the adoption of the calendar and sanctoral of Salisbury Cathedral, and its modification for other dioceses.
This resulted in the elimination of many local saints of the various dioceses that
appear in thirteenth-century calendars of the secular church, but the retention
of some of them as supplements to the Sarum calendar.[1] Whatever other textual
differences may have existed in prayers, antiphons, verses, and responses in the
Sarum missals and breviaries of these dioceses, the taking up of the Salisbury
calendar can be seen as evidence of an intention to adopt the Sarum Use. Breviaries differ also in the number and content of proper lessons given to saints,
both those in the Sarum calendar and those that are diocesan or regional supplements to it. Some of these saints have only lessons taken from the common of the
saints. This problem of the inclusion of proper lessons and offices for the saints
in Sarum breviaries in the fourteenth and fifteenth centuries is discussed in the
paper in this volume by Sherry Reames.[2] The focus of my paper is to describe
only whether saints were mentioned in the sanctorals of missals and breviaries,

---

[1] This problem is discussed in Nigel J. Morgan, "The Introduction of the Sarum
Calendar into the Dioceses of England in the Thirteenth Century," in *Thirteenth Century
England, VIII: Proceedings of the Durham Conference 1999*, ed. Michael Prestwich, Richard Britnell, and Robin Frame (Woodbridge: Boydell Press, 2001), 179–206. Some statements in this article will need to be modified when an equivalent article on the fourteenth
century has been completed.

[2] Regrettably, two recent articles on this issue by her came to my notice too late
to be considered: Sherry L. Reames, "Lectionary Revision in Sarum Breviaries and the
Origins of the Early Printed Editions," *Journal of the Early Book Society* 9 (2006): 95–115,
and eadem, "Late Medieval Efforts at Standardization and Reform in the Sarum Lessons
for Saints' Days," in *Design and Distribution of Late Medieval Manuscripts in England*, ed.
Margaret Connolly and Linne R. Mooney (Woodbridge: York Medieval Press, 2008),
91–117. See eadem, "Unexpected Texts for Saints in some Sarum Breviary Manuscripts,"
below, 161–82.

The Study of Medieval Manuscripts of England: Festschrift in Honor of Richard W. Pfaff, eds. George Hardin Brown and
Linda Ehrsam Voigts, MRTS 384 (Tempe: ACMRS, 2010).   [ISBN 978-0-86698-432-4]

and not to detail whether there are proper prayers and offices, or directions for
these to be taken from the common of the saints. Exactly how, when, and why
a particular diocese introduced Sarum can probably never be known in view of
the extremely fragmentary surviving evidence. Also, from the evidence that *does*
survive, the Sarum texts used as models were of varying dates, some seemingly
of the Old Sarum period, before the move to the new site for the cathedral in the
second decade of the thirteenth century.[3]

Even allowing for differences between a Sarum text of c. 1200 and one of
c. 1300, some of these missals and breviaries differ from standard Sarum texts
in having alternative feasts and texts which may reveal interpolations from other
diocesan uses. In the period up to 1350 quite frequently, for example, collects,
secrets, or postcommunion prayers in missals with a Salisbury calendar are not
those texts of Sarum, and it can probably be assumed that these different prayers
have been deliberately retained from earlier diocesan uses.[4] The complete absence, to the best of my knowledge, of any non-Sarum secular diocesan missal or
breviary with a sanctoral from thirteenth-century England makes any precise assessment of this well nigh impossible.[5] From c. 1350 onwards my general impression, without having as yet undertaken any extensive text collations, is that most
missals have mainly standard Sarum texts for these prayers, but it must always
be stressed that "variation among those books nominally classed as of the Sarum
rite is enormous."[6] Breviaries, as Reames explains, seem to have more complex
text variants. This brief study will concentrate on the saints in sanctorals of surviving Sarum missals and breviaries up to c. 1350, and not attempt any analysis
of the complexities of textual variants in prayers and lessons.

From this hundred-year period only thirty-three Sarum missals and breviaries with fairly complete sanctorals have come down to us. Of Sarum-type calendars in various textual contexts many more survive, too many to survey in this
short essay. Even calendars in the missals and breviaries discussed will be rarely
commented upon, and this of course has resulted in an incomplete judgement of

---

[3] It seems likely that in most of its basic elements the Use had been formulated at
Old Sarum before the move.

[4] In order to understand better the ways in which Sarum texts were introduced into
other dioceses in the period c. 1250–1350 a study of these variant texts is an essential
task, but this time-consuming work involving so many manuscripts would perhaps best
be achieved as a collaborative rather than an individual research project.

[5] Of course, several missals and breviaries of the religious orders survive from this
century.

[6] The observation is from Richard W. Pfaff, "Prescription and Reality in the Rubrics of Sarum Rite Service Books," in *Intellectual Life in the Middle Ages: Essays Presented
to Margaret Gibson*, ed. Lesley Smith and Benedicta Ward (London: Hambledon Press,
1992), 197–205, at 204. Pfaff's study contains many judicious observations on Sarum
books, especially those of the late fourteenth and fifteenth centuries.

the text of each book as a whole. Another limitation is that five Sarum graduals, six antiphoners, two office lectionaries, one collectar, and one ordinal (the unique copy of the Old Ordinal) also survive from the pre-1350 period, and regrettably have also had to be excluded from this study, in spite of their undoubted relevance to the assessment of sanctorals.[7] Unfortunately, by far the majority of surviving manuscripts are from the first half of the fourteenth century, and those of the thirteenth century are so few that not much can be said about that period.

c. 1250–1300
Missals:

1M	Manchester, John Rylands Library, MS. lat. 24[8]	c. 1250–55
2M	Birmingham, Public Library, MS. 091/MED/2 (fragmentary)[9]	c. 1250–75
3M	Exeter, Cathedral Library, MS. 3510[10]	c. 1250–80
4M	Paris, Bibliothèque de l'Arsenal, MS. 135[11]	c. 1260–75[12]

Breviaries:

1B	Edinburgh, National Library of Scotland, MS. Adv.18.2.13B	c. 1275–1300

---

[7] Graduals include MSS. Cambridge, UL, Add. 8333; London, BL, Add. 12194; London, Lambeth Palace, 7; Oxford, Bodleian, Rawlinson liturg. d. 3; Parma, Biblioteca Palatina, 98; Antiphoners: MSS. Aberystwyth, NLW, 20541E; Cambridge, UL, Mm.2.9; Cambridge, UL, Add. 2602; Edinburgh, NLS, Adv. 18.2.13A; London, BL, Add. 28598; Paris, BnF, lat. 12036; the Office Lectionaries are Exeter, Cathedral Library, 3504–5 and London, BL, Cotton App. XXIII, the Collectar is London, BL, Royal 2 A.XIII, and the Ordinal is London, BL, Harley 1001. The text of this Ordinal is published in Walter H. Frere, *The Use of Sarum*, vol. 2 (Cambridge: Cambridge University Press, 1901), 1–193. The British Library Gradual and the Penpont Antiphoner are available in facsimiles: Walter H. Frere, *Graduale Sarisburiense* (London: Bernard Quaritch, 1894), and Owain T. Edwards, *National Library of Wales MS. 20541E: The Penpont Antiphonal* (Ottawa: Institute of Mediaeval Music, 1997).

[8] The text is printed in full in John Wickham Legg, *The Sarum Missal* (Oxford: Oxford University Press, 1916), and for problems of dating see Nigel J. Morgan, *Early Gothic Manuscripts 1250–1285*, Survey of Manuscripts Illuminated in the British Isles 4.2 (London: Harvey Miller, 1988), 57–59, no. 100.

[9] Neil R. Ker, *Medieval Manuscripts in British Libraries*, vol. 2, *Abbotsford-Keele* (Oxford: Oxford University Press, 1977), 59.

[10] Ker, *Medieval Manuscripts in British Libraries*, vol. 2, 817–18.

[11] Victor Leroquais, *Les Sacramentaires et les Missels manuscrits des bibliothèques publiques de France* (Macon: Protat Frères, 1924), 2: 132–35. The text is collated in Wickham Legg, *Sarum Missal*.

[12] Wickham Legg, *Sarum Missal*, viii, dated this manuscript to the end of the thirteenth century, but the style of its illumination suggests that it is no later than c. 1275.

c. 1300–25

Missals:

5M	Aberystwyth, National Library of Wales, MS. 15536E[13]	c. 1310–20
6M	London, British Library, Add. MS. 37519	c. 1320
7M	New York, Pierpont Morgan Library, MS. M.107[14]	c. 1320
8M	Bologna, Biblioteca Universitaria, MS. 2565[15]	c. 1320–30[16]
9M	Cardiff, Public Library, MS. 4.586[17]	c. 1320–30
10M	Cambridge, Trinity College, MS. B.10.14[18]	c. 1325

Breviaries:

2B	Cambridge, Gonville and Caius College, MS. 394/614[19]	c. 1300–25
3B	Longleat House, Collection of the Marquess of Bath, 10[20]	c. 1310–30
4B	Salisbury, Cathedral Library, MS. 224[21]	after 1320
5B	Edinburgh, University Library, MS. 26[22]	c. 1320–30
6B	Edinburgh, University Library, MS. 27[23]	c. 1320–30
7B	London, British Library, Add. MS. 52359[24]	c. 1320–30
8B	New York, Pierpont Morgan Library, MS. M.329	c. 1320–30
9B	London, British Library, MS. Stowe 12[25]	c. 1322–25

---

[13] Lucy F. Sandler, *Gothic Manuscripts 1285–1385*, Survey of Manuscripts Illuminated in the British Isles 2 (London: Harvey Miller, 1986), 73, no. 65.

[14] Sandler, *Gothic Manuscripts*, 84–86, no. 78.

[15] The text is collated in Wickham Legg, *Sarum Missal*.

[16] Wickham Legg, *Sarum Missal*, ix, dated this to the early fourteenth century, but Michael Michael in his unpublished Ph.D. thesis, "The Artists of Walter of Milemete's Treatise" (Westfield College, University of London, 1987) has related its illumination to several manuscripts for which a date in the third decade can be argued. Photographic prints are available of the manuscript in the Bodleian Library, Facs. d. 9–10.

[17] Ker, *Medieval Manuscripts in British Libraries*, vol. 2, 376–77.

[18] Montague R. James, *The Western Manuscripts in the Library of Trinity College, Cambridge: A Descriptive Catalogue* (Cambridge: Cambridge University Press, 1900), 311–12.

[19] Montague R. James, *A Descriptive Catalogue of the Manuscripts in the Library of Gonville and Caius College, Cambridge* (Cambridge: Cambridge University Press, 1907–14), 459–60.

[20] Lucy F. Sandler, "An Early Fourteenth-Century English Breviary at Longleat," *Journal of the Warburg and Courtauld Institutes* 29 (1976): 1–20.

[21] Neil R. Ker, *Medieval Manuscripts in British Libraries*, vol. 4, *Paisley-York* (Oxford: Oxford University Press, 1992), 264–66.

[22] Catherine R. Borland, *Descriptive Catalogue of Western Mediaeval Manuscripts in Edinburgh University Library* (Edinburgh: Edinburgh University Press, 1916), 36–38, plate VI.

[23] Borland, *Descriptive Catalogue*, 38–41.

[24] Derek H. Turner, "The Penwortham Breviary," *British Museum Quarterly* 23 (1964): 85–88.

[25] Sandler, *Gothic Manuscripts*, 86–87, no. 79.

c. 1325–50

Missals:

11M	Ushaw, St Cuthbert's College, MS. 18[26]	c. 1330–40
12M	London, British Library, MS. Lansdowne 432	c. 1330–50
13M	Cambridge, University Library, MS. Ff. 4. 44	c. 1340–50
14M	Munich, Bayerische Staatsbibliothek Clm 705	c. 1340–60
15M	Birkenhead, Shrewsbury Diocesan Curial Offices (Acton Burnell Missal)[27]	c. 1340–60
16M	Liverpool, Cathedral Library, MS. 29[28]	c. 1350
17M	London, British Library, Add. MS. 11414	c. 1350
18M	San Marino, CA, Huntington Library, MS. HM 19918[29]	c. 1350
19M	Oxford, Bodleian Library, MS. Don. b. 5	c. 1350–60[30]

Breviaries:

10B	Frankfurt, Stadtbibliothek, MS. lat. oct. 97[31]	c. 1325–50
11B	Liverpool, Cathedral Library, MS. 37[32]	c. 1330–50
12B	Melbourne, University of Melbourne, Baillieu Library, MS. s.n.[33]	c. 1340–50
13B	Cambridge, Clare College, MS. Kk.3.7 (G^1.3.34)[34]	c. 1350–60
14B	London, British Library, MS. Sloane 1909	c. 1350–60

Each of these manuscripts has individual characteristics, and the problems of interpretation of their sanctorals are briefly summarised in chronological order, first for the missals and then for the breviaries. Only in rare cases have additions to the sanctoral in the margins been noted, because the intention is to examine

---

[26] Ker, *Medieval Manuscripts in British Libraries*, vol. 4, 527–29.

[27] Neil R. Ker, *Medieval Manuscripts in British Libraries*, vol. 5, *Indexes and Addenda* (Oxford: Oxford University Press, 2002), 5. The manuscript is now on deposit at Liverpool University Library.

[28] Neil R. Ker, *Medieval Manuscripts in British Libraries*, vol. 3, *Lampeter-Oxford* (Oxford: Oxford University Press, 1983), 188–90.

[29] Consuelo W. Dutschke, *Guide to the Medieval and Renaissance Manuscripts in the Huntington Library*, vol. 2 (San Marino: Huntington Library, 1989), 606–8.

[30] In an earlier article, Nigel Morgan, "Some Missing Leaves from the Buckland Missal," *Bodleian Library Record* 17 (2001): 269–75, I dated this Missal c. 1360–80, but I am grateful to Michael Michael for suggesting to me that it is earlier, and unlikely to be much later than c. 1360.

[31] Karin Bredehorn and Gerhardt Powitz, *Die Handschriften der Stadt- und Universitätsbibliothek Frankfurt am Main, 3: Die mittelalterlichen Handschriften der Gruppe Manuscripta Latina* (Frankfurt am Main: Vittorio Klostermann, 1979), 101–2.

[32] Ker, *Medieval Manuscripts in British Libraries*, vol. 3, 197–98.

[33] This manuscript, which contains the sanctoral, is part of the same book as Oxford, Bodleian Library, MS. Laud Misc. 3a. On these books see Michael Michael and Nigel Morgan, "The Sarum Breviary in the Baillieu and Bodleian Libraries," *La Trobe Library Journal* 13, nos. 51–52 (1993): 30–37.

[34] Montague R. James, *A Descriptive Catalogue of the Western Manuscripts in the Library of Clare College, Cambridge* (Cambridge: Cambridge University Press, 1905), 14–15.

the original uncorrected text. If a feast is said to be in the sanctoral it means that a rubric and/or some of its propers are integral in the text.

1M   Manchester, John Rylands Library, MS. lat. 24   c. 1250–55

As this book formed the basis of Wickham Legg's edition of the Sarum Missal it is presumed to be a standard Sarum text, but if compared with a text of a century later it is not standard in many features. Possibly some of its idiosyncrasies might be explained in view of it being made for a canon of Exeter, Henry of Chichester. Since Wickham Legg's study it has now been argued with some certainty that the book was made at Salisbury itself, which makes it unique among all the other manuscripts in that we know definitely where and for whom it was made.[35] Its most unusual feature is the occurrence of Francis (4 Oct.) in the sanctoral. Although he does indeed occur in other Sarum missals and breviaries, and so probably cannot be explained as resulting from some specific requirement for the patron, Henry of Chichester, he was not part of the sanctoral of Sarum if that is looked at from the viewpoint of a mid-fourteenth-century text. Perhaps Francis was in some Sarum texts in the mid-thirteenth century, but during some sort of process of standardisation of the Use he became excluded. Why and when can probably never be determined. The feasts, normally included by the end of the century, which are lacking from this sanctoral are as follows: Octave of Thomas of Canterbury and Edward the Confessor (5 Jan.),[36] Wulfstan (9 Jan.),[37] Richard of Chichester (3 Apr.),[38] Translation of Edmund of Abingdon (9 June),[39] Translation of Richard of Chichester (16 June),[40] Translation of Thomas of Canterbury (7 July),[41] Cuthburga (31 Aug.),[42] Translation of Edward the Confessor (13

---

[35] The basic article defining this group of manuscripts is Albert Hollaender, "The Sarum Illuminator and his School," *Wiltshire Archaeological and Natural History Magazine* 50 (1943): 230–62.

[36] The memorial for Edward on that day was first decreed by the Council of Oxford in 1222. The date of the introduction of the Octave of Thomas was at some time between his canonisation in 1173 and his translation in 1220.

[37] The Commemoration of Mary from the Nativity to the Purification is in the text on that day (Wickham Legg, *Sarum Missal*, 240–41). Wulfstan had been canonised in 1203.

[38] He was canonised in 1262 after the manuscript was made.

[39] This took place in 1247/49 at about the time that the manuscript was made.

[40] This took place in 1276 after the manuscript was made.

[41] This took place in 1220 long before the manuscript was made.

[42] I have been unable to discover why her feast was entered into the Sarum sanctoral during the second half of the thirteenth century. Her relics were at Wimborne in the Salisbury diocese.

Oct.),[43] and the Conception of the Virgin Mary (8 Dec.).[44] It is significant that Hugh of Lincoln (17 Nov.) is in the sanctoral, although he is lacking from several other early Sarum texts.[45] The absence of the Conception of the Virgin, which occurs in several early Sarum texts, calls for comment. Occasionally a rubric specifically says that it should not be celebrated. However, in this missal and in some other texts, the rubric for her Nativity is "In nativitate et in concepcione sancte marie." Her feast is in the calendar, but with the annotation "Sarum nichil."

2M   Birmingham, Public Library, MS. 091/MED/2 (fragmentary)   c. 1250–75
As so much is missing from this book, were it not for its importance in view of its early date it would not be included. Nothing can be deduced about its place of production or patronage. It lacks the whole month of January, 15–30 June, 20–26 July, 8 Aug.–30 Sept., 19–31 Oct., 18 Nov.–31 Dec. The following are lacking from the sanctoral: Richard of Chichester, Translation of Edmund of Abingdon, Melor (1 Oct.),[46] Translation of Edward the Confessor, Wulfran (15 Oct.), All Souls and Eustace (2 Nov.), Edmund of Abingdon (16 Nov.), and Hugh of Lincoln. Most of these are also lacking in 1M and may generally reflect the state of the Sarum sanctoral in the middle years of the century. The fragmentary state of the text does not allow more to be said.

3M   Exeter, Cathedral Library, MS. 3510   c. 1250–80
This, like 1M, is a missal made for Exeter, perhaps even specifically for the chantry founded in 1280 by Bishop Bronescombe in the chapel of St Gabriel where he had chosen his tomb to be located.[47] The sanctoral has one non-Sarum feast, that of St Gabriel, celebrated at Exeter on the first Monday in September. Later Exeter calendars and sanctorals contain this feast, so perhaps the linking of the book with Bronescombe's chantry should be made only with caution. However, this manuscript does not contain any of the other diocesan feasts that Exeter added to Sarum.[48] The sanctoral lacks Edward the Confessor, Wulfstan,[49] Translation of Edmund of Abingdon, Translation of Richard of Chichester, Translation of Thomas of Canterbury, Cuthburga, Translation of Edward the

---

[43] This took place in 1163, and it seems that the feast was not introduced into Sarum until the second half of the thirteenth century, perhaps after the second translation of 1269.

[44] Although most English secular calendars of the first half of the thirteenth century have this feast, it was not in Sarum. It is not in the c. 1300 Ordinal, MS. BL Harley 1001.

[45] He was canonised in 1220.

[46] Melor is normally always found; his relics were in the Salisbury diocese at Amesbury.

[47] John N. Dalton, *Ordinale Exon.*, Henry Bradshaw Society 63 (London: Henry Bradshaw Society, 1925), xiii.

[48] Brannock, Kieran (Pieran), Petroc, and Sativola.

[49] It has the same Commemoration of Mary on that day as 1M.

Confessor, Edmund of Abingdon, Hugh of Lincoln, and the Conception of the
Virgin Mary. Its omissions are very similar to those of 1M and suggest a text
model for the sanctoral of c. 1250 or earlier.

4M   Paris, Bibliothèque de l'Arsenal, MS. 135   c. 1260–75

Although the sanctoral does not in any way reflect it in regard to the saints it contains, the calendar shows this missal to have been made for a patron or church
in the diocese of London.[50] There are no non-Sarum feasts in the sanctoral. The
following feasts are lacking: Octave of Thomas of Canterbury and Edward the
Confessor, Wulfstan, Richard of Chichester, Translation of Edmund of Abingdon, Translation of Richard of Chichester, Cuthburga, Melor, Translation of
Edward the Confessor, All Souls and Eustace, Edmund of Abingdon, Hugh
of Lincoln, and the Conception of the Virgin Mary.[51] These are very similar to
the omissions in the four other pre-1300 missals, and suggest a model of c. 1250
or earlier. With the exception of Melor, who should have been included, these
feasts seem to have been established in the sanctoral during the second half of
the thirteenth century.

5M   Aberystwyth, National Library of Wales, MS. 15536E   c. 1310–20

If there is a prime example of a Sarum missal with non-Sarum collects, secrets,
postcommunions, et alia, it is this manuscript. The margins and text are littered
with corrections and additions. Although it is a Sarum sanctoral, the texts for the
various feasts often came from some other source. There are no non-Sarum feasts
included, but the following Sarum sanctoral feasts are lacking: Edward the Confessor, Richard of Chichester, Translation of Richard of Chichester, Translation of Edward the Confessor, All Souls and Eustace, Hugh of Lincoln, and the
Conception of the Virgin Mary.[52] The page where Cuthburga would have been is
lacking, so it cannot be determined whether her feast was designated. Although
the manuscript is of the second decade of the fourteenth century, the text model
seems to have been of c. 1275 or earlier.

---

[50] On this London provenance see Christopher Hohler, "Reflections on Some Manuscripts Containing 13th-Century Polyphony," *Journal of the Plainsong and Mediaeval
Music Society* 1 (1978): 2–38, at 25–28, and Morgan, "Introduction of the Sarum Calendar," 174–206, at 185.

[51] The sanctoral also lacks some minor feasts which may not be significant, for they
are not always included in Graduals and Ordinals either: Gorgonius (9 Sept.), Protus and
Iacinctus (11 Sept.), Firmin (25 Sept.), Quentin (31 Oct.).

[52] In addition, some minor feasts are lacking, perhaps without significance as in the
case of those mentioned in n. 51: Agapitus (18 Aug.), Magnus (19 Aug.), Timothy and
Apollinaris (23 Aug.), Gorgonius (9 Sept.), Protus and Iacinctus (11 Sept.), Firmin (15
Sept.), Quentin (31 Oct.).

6M   London. British Library, Add. MS. 37519   c. 1320

This missal has one significant non-Sarum feast in the sanctoral, Frideswide (19 Oct.). Also a collect designated non-Sarum is inserted for St. Egidius (1 Sept.). Lacking are Richard of Chichester, Translation of Richard of Chichester, and Quentin (31 Oct.). The last is probably not significant, but the absence of Richard's feasts suggests a text model of well before 1300. In whatever way his two feast days came to be promulgated in the Sarum sanctoral, of all the additions of the second half of the thirteenth century they are the most frequently omitted in fourteenth-century texts. Whether the presence of Frideswide specifically suggests an Oxford text, or merely somewhere in the south of the diocese of Lincoln, is uncertain.

7M   New York, Pierpont Morgan Library, MS. M.107   c. 1320

The famous Tiptoft Missal has known patrons, John Clavering and his wife Hawyse Tiptoft. Their estates were in the dioceses of London, Norwich, and Lincoln, and there is no indication that it was made for any particular church associated with them. The sanctoral has no non-Sarum feasts, but the following are lacking: Richard of Chichester, Translation of Richard of Chichester, Quentin, and the Conception of the Virgin Mary. It is unusual still to find this last feast absent c. 1320, but the absence of the Richard feasts certainly suggests a text model of well before 1300.

8M   Bologna, Biblioteca Universitaria, MS. 2565   c. 1320–30

On the understanding that this was one of the earliest texts of the Sarum Missal it was collated in Wickham Legg's edition. It has one non-Sarum feast in the sanctoral, that of Frideswide (19 Oct.). Feasts lacking are as follows: Octave of Thomas of Canterbury and Edward the Confessor, Richard of Chichester, Translation of Richard of Chichester, All Souls, and the Conception of the Virgin Mary. As with 6M this may be specifically for Oxford, or merely for somewhere in the southern half of the diocese of Lincoln.

9M   Cardiff, Public Library, MS. 4.586   c. 1320–30

This book lacks large sections of its sanctoral: 25 Dec.–13 Jan. (the sanctoral of the Christmas season which is contained in the temporal), 24 Feb.–1 Apr., 29–31 July, 15 Sept.–21 Oct. There is only one non-Sarum feast in the sanctoral, that of Botulph (17 June). This saint on his own does not suggest any particular diocese. He is quite frequently found in Sarum books, doubtless because his cult was widespread throughout the country before Sarum Use was introduced, and because many wished to retain his feast.[53] The Sarum feasts lacking from the sanctoral are: Magnus (19 Aug.), All Souls, and Hugh of Lincoln. Hugh is quite

---

[53] Morgan, "Introduction of the Sarum Calendar," 204–6, lists his occurrence in thirteenth- and early fourteenth-century calendars that can be localised to the Chichester,

frequently lacking in thirteenth- and early fourteenth-century Sarum books. His
feast seems to have been introduced in the second half of the thirteenth century,
and probably this missal is based on a text model of this period.

10M   Cambridge, Trinity College, MS. B.10.14   c. 1325

This has three non-Sarum feasts in its sanctoral: Botulph (17 June), Thomas of
Hereford (2 Oct.), and the Translation of Etheldreda (17 Oct.). The only feast
lacking is Leodegarius (2 Oct.), doubtless pushed out by the insertion of Thomas
of Hereford on the same day. The only dioceses to have this combination of non-
Sarum feasts, as evident from calendars, are Ely and Norwich. However, none
of the other characteristic non-Sarum feasts of these dioceses are present, so an
attribution of the text to either of these is uncertain.[54]

11M   Ushaw, St Cuthbert's College, MS. 18   c. 1330–40

No non-Sarum feasts are in the sanctoral, but many entries are lacking: Wulfstan, Richard of Chichester, Swithun (2 July), Agapitus (18 Aug.), Magnus (19
Aug.), Timothy and Symphorian (23 Aug.), Cuthburga, Gorgonius (9 Sept.),
Protus and Iacinctus (11 Sept.), Firmin (25 Sept.), Melor, Translation of Edward
the Confessor, Quentin, All Souls and Eustace, Hugh of Lincoln, and the Conception of the Virgin. It seems that the text model must have been of c. 1275 or
even earlier. The missal belonged to Eastwell (Kent) parish church in the early
sixteenth century.

12M   London, British Library, MS. Lansdowne 432   c. 1330–50

One non-Sarum feast is in the sanctoral, Chad (2 Mar.). There are no Sarum
feasts lacking. Unfortunately the page is missing which might have contained
Winifred (3 Nov.), another diocesan supplement sometimes found for Coventry
and Lichfield. The presence of Chad, rarely found in calendars other than those
of that diocese until he was introduced into Sarum in the early fifteenth century,
suggests that this missal was intended for a church or person in the Coventry and
Lichfield diocese.

13M   Cambridge, University Library, MS. Ff. 4. 44   c. 1340–50

Two non-Sarum feasts are in the original text of the sanctoral: Translation of
Wulfstan (7 June), and Francis (4 Oct.), but both have been subsequently crossed
out. The only Sarum feasts lacking are Quentin (31 Oct.) and the Conception
of the Virgin Mary. The only diocese that celebrated the feast of the Translation
of Wulfstan as an addition to Sarum is Worcester, although the other diocesan

---

Coventry and Lichfield, Ely, Hereford, Lincoln, London, Norwich, Winchester, and
York dioceses. These in effect cover almost all of England.

[54] For Ely, the other feasts which might be expected are Ermenilda, Withburga, and
Sexburga, and for Norwich, Felix of Dunwich, Dominic, and Francis.

addition, Oswald the Bishop (28 Feb.) is not there.[55] It is probable that a Sarum-Worcester text may have been the model, but that Oswald was edited out, and the Translation of Wulfstan may have been overlooked in this editing until a later hand crossed it out.

14M Munich, Bayerische Staatsbibliothek, Clm 705 c. 1340–60

This missal belonged to the parish church of Lydd in Kent, an important town in the Romney Marsh. The calendar contains the dedication of the church in a hand contemporary to that of the main scribe. It is the earliest surviving Sarum Missal having the Feast of the Relics on the Sunday after the Translation of Thomas of Canterbury (7 July), as opposed to having it on the Octave of the Nativity of the Virgin (15 Sept.), a change which had been introduced in 1319. No surviving Sarum missal or breviary has it on the new date until the middle years of the century. The only feast additional to the Sarum sanctoral is Anne (26 July), who, although not in early fourteenth-century Sarum, seems to have been introduced at some time during the second and third quarters of the century, certainly long before the feast was officially proclaimed in England in 1383.[56] Although I have not examined its collects, secrets, and postcommunions, in respect of its sanctoral this is a completely standard Sarum text, as are by far the majority of missals from c. 1340 onwards. It may be significant that this date coincides with the period of the revision of the Sarum Ordinal.[57]

15M Birkenhead, Shrewsbury Diocesan Curial Offices (Acton Burnell Missal) c. 1340–60

This fine missal, inaccessible until fairly recently, contains only one non-Sarum entry in the sanctoral, Chad (2 Mar.). The propers for his feast are very full, and there seems little doubt that this is a Coventry and Lichfield diocese text. The calendar supports this, as does its subsequent ownership by the parish church of Frodesley (Salop.), which is in that diocese. There are no Sarum feasts lacking, and save for the inclusion of Chad it is a standard Sarum text, subject to possible variations in the collects, secrets, and postcommunions. The Feast of the Relics is on the new date of the Sunday after the Translation of Thomas of Canterbury.

---

[55] For Worcester calendars and supplements to Sarum see Nigel Morgan, "Psalter Illustration for the Diocese of Worcester in the Thirteenth Century," in *Medieval Art and Architecture in Worcester Cathedral,* British Archaeological Association Conference Transactions 1 (London: BAA, 1978), 91–104, at 99–101.

[56] It is also very frequently found in calendars long before 1383.

[57] It is frustrating that only one manuscript survives (MS. BL Harley 1001) of the Old Ordinal, and thus there is no way of knowing whether variant texts existed in copies of this which might explain the anomalies in the sanctorals of the missals and breviaries.

16M   Liverpool, Cathedral Library, MS. 29   c. 1350
Although this is of the middle years of the century it seems to derive its text
from a model of almost a century earlier. The only non-Sarum feast is Francis,
which did occur in some Sarum books (e.g. 1M) contemporary with its likely text
model. The sanctoral lacks the following Sarum feasts: Edward the Confessor
(5 Jan.), Richard of Chichester, Translation of Edmund of Abingdon, Translation of Richard of Chichester, Cuthburga, Translation of Edward the Confessor, Edmund of Abingdon, and the Conception of the Virgin Mary (the last is
there, but with the rubric "nichil Sarum"). This is the best example of how text
models for Sarum missals could often be very out-of-date! The book belonged to
the Shepton Beauchamp (Somerset) parish church and contains its dedication in
the calendar.

17M   London, British Library, Add. MS. 11414   c. 1350
This missal is one of the three or four Sarum missals that some scholars have
suggested are in part of the Use of the Lincoln diocese.[58] That may be the case,
but it cannot be decided until the complete variants of its text have been collated
with a "standard" Sarum missal. It seems that it may be essentially a Sarum text
but with the supplements for the diocese of Lincoln. The non-Sarum feasts in the
Sanctoral are as follows: Translation of Nicholas (9 May), described as non-Sarum; Botulph (17 June), described as "Sarum nihil"; Anne; Dominic (4 Aug.), described as non-Sarum; Francis (4 Oct.), described as non-Sarum; and the Translation of Hugh of Lincoln (6 Oct.). The rest of the sanctoral is completely Sarum
with nothing lacking.

18M   San Marino, CA, Huntington Library, MS. HM 19918   c. 1350
This book has the rare entry of Osburga on 23 Jan. added to the calendar. Her
relics were at Coventry and her cult was limited to that diocese, and this addition
suggests ownership within the diocese. Although Osburga is not in the sanctoral, it has non-Sarum entries some of which are also of the Coventry and Lichfield diocese: Chad (2 Mar.), Botulph (17 June), Thomas of Hereford (2 Oct.),
and the Translation of Hugh (6 Oct.). This last non-Sarum entry is characteristic
of the Lincoln diocese, and suggests that the text model was from that diocese.
The rest of the sanctoral is a Sarum text, but omitting All Souls and the Novem-
ber feast of Hugh of Lincoln. The latter is an odd omission in view of the occurrence of his Translation.

19M   Oxford, Bodleian Library, MS. Don. b. 5 c. 1350–60
As it has always been my impression that by the mid-fourteenth century some
texts of missals and breviaries are more or less standard Sarum, it is encouraging
to note that this last missal has no non-Sarum feasts in its sanctoral, and it also

---

[58] Morgan, "Introduction of the Sarum Calendar," 183.

has none of the feasts of the Sarum calendar lacking. It is possible that its collects, secrets, and postcommunions may contain non-Sarum texts, but its sanctoral is substantially a "correct" text. The book belonged first to the parish church of Adderbury (Oxon.) and then Buckland (Berks.)—their dedications are in the calendar.

Breviaries present a similar picture to missals, although their texts seem to be less often based on very old models than in the case of several of the missals. Some lack the feasts introduced into Sarum during the second half of the thirteenth century, a few have non-Sarum supplements of various dioceses, and by c. 1330 some are more or less "correct" Sarum texts.

1B   Edinburgh, National Library of Scotland, MS. Adv.18.2.13B   c. 1275–1300
Very unfortunately, this earliest surviving Sarum Breviary lacks the text of four months of the year, from 22 Feb. to 30 June. It was made for use in the diocese of Glasgow, one of the earliest dioceses for which there is evidence that the Sarum Use was taken up early in the third quarter of the thirteenth century, and it seems likely that the text model of this late thirteenth-century Breviary may be as early as c. 1225, or even before that date.[59] It has one non-Sarum feast, Kentigern (14 Jan.), with very full propers. His relics were at Glasgow Cathedral. It lacks the following Sarum feasts, and doubtless lacked more in the period from late February until late June where its text is lacking: Edward the Confessor, Wulfstan, Translation of Thomas of Canterbury, Prassede (21 July), Cuthburga, Nicomede (15 Sept.), Thecla (23 Sept.), Translation of Edward the Confessor, Eustace, Edmund of Abingdon, Hugh of Lincoln, and the Conception of the Virgin Mary.

2B   Cambridge, Gonville and Caius College, MS. 394/614 c. 1300–25
The non-Sarum feasts are: Botulph (17 June), Sexburga (6 July), Dominic (4 Aug.), Francis (4 Oct.), Translation of Etheldreda (17 Oct.). Lacking are: Richard of Chichester, Translation of Richard of Chichester, Cuthburga, and Hugh of Lincoln. The additional feasts in the sanctoral are of the diocese of Ely, although Francis and Dominic are more usually found as Norwich diocese Sarum supplements. The ownership of the breviary by a church in the diocese of Ely is further confirmed by the later addition of the propers for Ermenilda and Withburga, who should have been in the sanctoral, at the end of the book.

3B   Longleat House, Collection of the Marquess of Bath, 10   c. 1310–30
The only non-Sarum feast in the sanctoral is the Crown of Thorns (4 May). This feast is very unusual in England, save in Dominican calendars and sanctorals. Its presence as an inclusion in a Sarum breviary may imply some special patronage. Was there a church in England that possessed a relic of a thorn from the Crown which on occasion the French king gave as a gift to persons or institutions from the

---

[59] Frere, *Use of Sarum*, 1: xxviii–xxix.

relic of the Sainte-Chapelle? The text lacks a few Sarum feasts: Eustace (2 Nov.) and Hugh of Lincoln and a few other minor feasts. It belonged to the parish church of Kimbolton (Hunts.) The dedication of the church is in the calendar.

4B   Salisbury, Cathedral Library, MS. 224   after 1320

This large book includes only one non-Sarum feast in its sanctoral, Thomas of Hereford (2 Oct.). This must suggest a date after 1320 when he was canonised. He was not in the Sarum calendar, and his inclusion suggests that the book may have been made for a diocese other than Salisbury, unless an individual patron had stipulated its inclusion resulting from his recent canonisation. As there are no other non-Sarum feasts it is impossible to say which diocese this might be. The remainder of the sanctoral is standard and lacks no feasts. In the fifteenth century it belonged to the parish church of Great Bedwyn (Wilts.) in the diocese of Salisbury.

5B   Edinburgh, University Library, MS. 26   c. 1320–30

Three non-Sarum entries are in the sanctoral: Anne, Thomas of Hereford, and Francis. The feasts which are lacking are Richard of Chichester (his collect is added elsewhere) and Hugh of Lincoln (part of his office is added elsewhere). There is a short rubric recording the Translation of Richard of Chichester, but with no propers. Of the non-Sarum entries only Thomas of Hereford may be significant because Francis does occur in some earlier Sarum texts and Anne was widely introduced during the fourteenth century. Like 4B it seems to have been intended for a diocese other than Salisbury because of the inclusion of Thomas of Hereford.

6B   Edinburgh, University Library, MS. 27   c. 1320–30

This is close to a standard sanctoral text with no non-Sarum entries, and with only Hugh of Lincoln lacking. If the much-needed edition of an early Sarum Breviary is ever planned, this manuscript would be a prime candidate for a base text.

7B   London, British Library, Add. MS. 52359   c. 1320–30

There are no non-Sarum feasts, but the following are lacking: Richard of Chichester, Translation of Edmund of Abingdon, Translation of Richard of Chichester, Cuthburga, Translation of Edward the Confessor, Hugh of Lincoln, and the Conception of the Virgin Mary. This suggests a text model of at least seventy years earlier, perhaps of c. 1250.

8B   New York, Pierpont Morgan Library, MS. M.329   c. 1320–30

There are no non-Sarum feasts in the sanctoral. Two feasts are lacking: Hugh of Lincoln and the Conception of the Virgin Mary. As all the other feasts introduced in the second half of the thirteenth century (e.g. the two Richard of

Chichester feasts and Cuthburga) are present, it is odd that these two are lacking. The text model must have been of the late thirteenth century, but lacking these.

9B   London, British Library, MS. Stowe 12   c. 1322–25

This elaborately-illuminated Breviary has lost many pages and sections, but enough survives to suggest that it was intended for the diocese of Norwich and had a full set of supplements for that diocese. It was very probably made in Norwich as evidenced by its artistic relationships with other books containing evidence of connections with that region.[60] The non-Sarum feasts in the sanctoral are: Botulph, Anne, Dominic, Thomas of Hereford, and Francis. Anne, of course, later in the fourteenth century, is commonly found in Sarum texts, but this is a very early occurrence.[61] There are no Sarum sanctoral feasts lacking in the parts that survive.

10B   Frankfurt, Stadtbibliothek, MS. lat. oct. 97   c. 1325–50

The non-Sarum feasts in the sanctoral include the following: Botulph, Dominic, Thomas of Hereford, and Francis. Lacking are Richard of Chichester, Translation of Edmund of Abingdon, Translation of Richard of Chichester, Timothy and Apollinaris (23 Aug.), Cuthburga, Translation of Edward the Confessor, and Hugh of Lincoln. The non-Sarum feasts might be considered to be characteristic of the diocese of Norwich, although Felix of Dunwich (8 Mar.) is lacking, so an attribution to that diocese cannot be made with any confidence.

11B   Liverpool, Cathedral Library, MS. 37   c. 1330–50

There are no non-Sarum feasts in the sanctoral, but Hugh of Lincoln is lacking. In all other respects this is a standard Sarum sanctoral text. It still has the Feast of the Relics on the Octave of the Nativity of the Virgin.

12B   Melbourne, University of Melbourne, Baillieu Library s.n.   c. 1340–50

The sanctoral contains all the Sarum entries but has the following non-Sarum entries: Chad, Translation of Wulfstan (7 June), Botulph, and Thomas of Hereford. This suggests a Coventry and Lichfield diocese text, although the Translation of Wulfstan is a characteristic supplement for the adjacent diocese of Worcester.

---

[60] Sandler, *Gothic Manuscripts*, 86–87, no. 79, and most recently Stella Panayotova, *The Macclesfield Psalter* (London: Thames and Hudson, 2008).

[61] On the "pre-Sarum" office of St Anne in Stowe 12, see Sherry L. Reames, "Origins and Affiliations of the Pre-Sarum Office for Anne in the Stowe Breviary," in *Music and Medieval Manuscripts: Palaeography and Performance*, ed. John Hanes and Randall Rosenfeld (Aldershot: Ashgate, 2004), 349–68. The feast was officially promulgated by Archbishop William Courtenay in a mandate to the bishop of London in May 1383, following the instruction of Pope Urban VI that it should be observed throughout England: David Wilkins, *Concilia Magnae Britanniae et Hiberniae* (London, 1737), 3: 178–79.

The feast is also in the sanctoral of the missal, 13M. The office for the Feast of the Relics is set at the end of the sanctoral, and not in its correct position after the Translation of St Thomas of Canterbury. A note in the text at its former date, the Octave of the Nativity of the Virgin, says it is to be celebrated on the Sunday after the Translation of St Thomas.

13B   Cambridge, Clare College, MS. Kk.3.7 (G¹.3.34)   c. 1350–60

This has no non-Sarum entries in its original text. Four leaves containing the office for Anne were inserted in the correct position in the sanctoral shortly after the completion of the book. It lacks no feasts and is a standard sanctoral text. This contrasts with its calendar that is clearly for the diocese of Norwich. The Feast of the Relics is on the Sunday after the feast of the Translation of Thomas of Canterbury, introduced in 1319.

14B   London, British Library, MS. Sloane 1909   c. 1350–60

Several pages are lacking, so a full assessment of the content of its sanctoral is not possible. This has one non-Sarum entry, Botulph, with full propers. In other respects it is standard. As Botulph seems to have been retained as an addition to Sarum in several dioceses, such as Lincoln, London, and Norwich, it is impossible to say whether this was destined for any particular diocese. It is odd that he was never in the Sarum calendar. In thirteenth-century calendars he is very frequently found and evidently had a widespread cult. The Feast of the Relics is on the Sunday after the feast of the Translation of Thomas of Canterbury, introduced in 1319.

Many interpretations can be made from these sanctorals. It is clear that several of them derive from texts of many years earlier, and also that some have "supplements" to the Sarum calendar, which may suggest destination for specific dioceses. For some the supplementary feasts do not clearly suggest a particular diocese. The two that have the propers for Frideswide (6M, 8M) might suggest that they were made for a particular city, Oxford. Another example would be the Scottish Sarum Breviary with only Kentigern as a supplement (1B). Was this intended for the city of Glasgow? The Exeter Missal (3M), with the only supplement being Gabriel, might suggest that it was made specifically for the chapel of St Gabriel in Exeter Cathedral where Bishop Bronescombe established a chantry. Most of these books were probably destined for parish churches or chapels, belonging either to the parish or to the parish priest, although in the case of only seven (11M, 14M, 15M, 16M, 19M, 3B, 4B) is this fairly certain. It can reasonably be assumed that at the beginning of the period under investigation the missals and breviaries in the possession of parish churches and parish priests outside of the Salisbury diocese were not of Sarum Use. In the fourteenth century the situation had changed.[62] Visitation records sometimes complain that a parish church possessed a book not of Sarum Use.[63] There is the case of the parishioners of St Giles Cripplegate, who in 1376 complain that they are expected to obtain liturgical books of London Use when Sarum books are being used throughout the country.[64]

One of the matters of complaint of the parishioners of St Giles implied that London-diocese liturgical books were difficult to obtain. Presumably, with London becoming a predominant centre of book production serving other parts of the country, Sarum missals and breviaries were being produced there in large numbers in the third quarter of the fourteenth century and were easy to commission or were readily available for purchase, whereas the equivalent St Paul's-use volumes had become an expensive niche market. It can but be a matter of speculation as to how a parish in dioceses far from London, such as that of Coventry and Lichfield or Bath and Wells, obtained their missals and breviaries in the fourteenth century. It seems fairly certain that there must have been local centres of diocesan liturgical book production in great cities such as Coventry and Bristol. In the two centuries of production of Sarum liturgical books before the appearance of the first printed versions in the 1480s tens of thousands of such books must have been produced for the approximately 15,000 parish churches and chapels in the province of Canterbury.[65]

In the period surveyed in this essay, doubtless some parish churches obtained missals and breviaries that were either not of Sarum Use or very corrupt texts. Some of these contained the Sarum sanctoral but had prayers that are non-Sarum. Does this suggest an editing process of pre-existing diocesan missals that were adapted by deletion and addition to conform to the Sarum sanctoral, but retained many of the old prayers used in the diocese? Of course, it is an open question whether there were uniform diocesan Uses before Sarum was introduced, and the lack of evidence is such that that can never be known. One of the reasons for introducing the new Use could be the wish to provide a standardised

---

[62] Morgan, "Introduction of the Sarum Calendar" discusses the beginning of the process of the introduction of Sarum Use into other dioceses in regard to the calendar.

[63] Nigel Morgan, "Books for the Liturgy and Private Prayers," in *The History of the Book in Britain*, vol. 2, *1100–1400*, ed. idem and Rodney M. Thomson (Cambridge: Cambridge University Press, 2008), 291–316, at 294, 298, 299, 300, for evidence from such visitation records.

[64] John Wickham Legg, "On a Letter to the Archbishop of Canterbury from the Pope directing whether the Use of Salisbury should be followed at St. Giles Cripplegate, instead of the Use of St Paul's," *Transactions of the St Paul's Ecclesiological Society* 6 (1907): 94–96.

[65] On the incunable Sarum books see the introduction to Francis H. Dickinson, *Missale ad usum insignis et praeclarae ecclesiae Sarum* (Burntisland: Pitsligo Press, 1861–1883), lvi–lvii, and Francis Procter and Christopher Wordsworth, *Breviarium ad usum insignis ecclesiae Sarum*, vol. 3 (Cambridge: Cambridge University Press, 1886), xliii.

liturgy for a diocese in which there were no standardised texts. The introduction of Sarum into dioceses could thus be seen as part of the post-Lateran IV reform of pastoral and liturgical life in the secular church.

Another way that the early introduction of the new rite could have happened was the editing of diocesan missals from the Sarum Ordinal. This would inevitably result in old diocesan collects, secrets, and postcommunions being retained, because the Ordinal does not give full texts. Also, of course, some sectors of the diocese may have preferred to retain the old rites and not to accept Sarum without some resistance. At the Reformation the major liturgical changes resulted in much opposition in some quarters, but in that case the objection may have been primarily theological rather than liturgical. Regrettably, no documentation, other than the grumblings of the parishioners of St Giles Cripplegate, has yet come to light to assess contemporary attitudes to the introduction of Sarum Use into the dioceses of England. The situation in the diocese of London is the most extreme example of what might be called "resistance to Sarum". It was not until 1414/15 that the Bishop of London finally by official edict abandoned the Use of St Paul's for the Sarum Use.[66] The precious witness of the parishioners of St Giles Cripplegate showed that forty years earlier in London some people had indeed shown preference for Sarum.

It seems rash to speculate any more on the problems of the introduction of the Sarum sanctoral until the fifty or so missals and breviaries of the period c. 1350–1415 have been similarly investigated as in this essay. One clear lesson which can be learned from the sanctorals in the period 1250–1350 is that the absence of the feasts of Edmund of Abingdon, Richard of Chichester, Anne, and the Sarum Feast of the Relics on the Sunday after the Translation of Thomas of Canterbury are never significant for dating. Often manuscripts produced fifty years after, in the case of the canonisation of Edmund and Richard, and twenty or more years after the introduction of the new date for the Feast of the Relics, lack these feasts, and sixty years before the supposed introduction of the feast of St Anne some have her feast as an integral part of the sanctoral.[67] The next phase will be the new feasts introduced in the fifteenth century, first the 1415 introduction of David, Chad, John of Beverley, and Winifred, and then much later the introduction of the Transfiguration, Visitation, and Name of Jesus.[68]

---

[66] William Sparrow Simpson, "On a Mandate of Bishop Clifford Superseding the Ancient Use of St Paul's Cathedral by the Use of Sarum," *Proceedings of the Society of Antiquaries*, 2nd ser., 14 (1892): 118–28.

[67] The misleading list of dates of new feasts with dates by Christopher Wordsworth, *The Old Service Books of the English Church* (London: Methuen and Co., 1904), 190–93, still forms the basis of dating used by some scholars.

[68] For the period post-1415 on the introduction of the fifteenth-century Nova Festa, the analysis of the calendars and sanctorals of Sarum missals and breviaries has largely been completed in that fundamental study by the distinguished recipient of this essay:

An analogous situation occurs with that of the 1250–1350 texts, in which many years after 1415 for the early group, or after the 1470s for the second, they are not integral in the sanctoral but are added as a supplement at the end of the missal. In the case of these fifteenth-century additional feasts the situation is, however, very different from the period 1250–1350. In the earlier century the addition of new feasts to the Sarum sanctoral was complicated by the introduction of the sanctoral of the new Use *per se* into other dioceses. It seems that the processes of textual transmission were complex, and it is hardly surprising that the surviving texts are of such diversity.

Richard W. Pfaff, *New Liturgical Feasts in Late Medieval England* (Oxford: Oxford University Press, 1970). Reading that ground-breaking book was the stimulus for these preliminary investigations of the earlier period. It should be noted that for the feasts of David, Chad, and Winifred there was a preliminary instruction for their celebration at the Convocation of Canterbury in 1398: Gerald Bray, *Records of Convocation,* vol. 4, *Canterbury 1377–1414* (Woodbridge: Boydell Press, 2005), 184.

Appendix:
Saints, not in the Sarum calendar before 1350, that are included in the sanctorals of Sarum missals and breviaries c. 1250–1350

This list includes any mention of the saint in the rubrics or texts of the offices, ranging from a brief note that a memorial should be made, or an instruction that the lessons should be from the Common, or in the fullest form to the inclusion of proper lessons for the saint. I have not distinguished between these various rubrics or texts. In most cases the rubrics will define these saints as "non Sarum" or "nihil Sarum," and sometimes specify the diocese in which these feast days are observed.[69]

Anne (26 July) [ordered to be observed by Archbishop William Courtenay in 1383, and generally found in all Sarum texts from the late fourteenth century onwards]:	14M, 17M, 5B, 9B
Botulph (17 June):	9M, 10M, 17M, 18M, 2B, 9B, 10B, 12B, 14B
Chad (2 Mar.) [introduced in Sarum texts post-1398/1415]:	12M, 15M, 18M, 12B
Crown of Thorns (4 May):	3B
Dominic (4 or 5 Aug.):	17M, 2B, 9B, 10B
Ermenilda (13 Feb.):	2B (added)
Etheldreda, Trans. (17 Oct.):	10M, 2B
Francis (4 Oct.):	1M, 13M, 16M, 17M, 2B, 5B, 9B, 10B
Frideswide (19 Oct.):	6M, 8M
Gabriel (1st Monday of Sept.):	3M
Hugh of Lincoln, Trans. (6 Oct.):	17M, 18M
Kentigern (14 Jan.):	1B
Nicholas, Trans. (9 May):	17M
Sexburga (6 Jul.):	2B
Thomas of Hereford (2 Oct.):	10M, 18M, 4B, 5B, 9B, 10B, 12B
Withburga (17 Mar.):	2B (added)
Wulfstan, Trans. (7 June):	13M, 12B

---

[69] See Morgan, "Introduction of the Sarum Calendar," 204–6, for a listing of the occurrence of some of these saints in thirteenth- and early fourteenth-century English calendars, arranged according to diocese. In that list I did not include Anne and Thomas of Hereford, because their feasts were introduced later in the fourteenth century. Anne does not seem to have been specifically or consistently introduced into any particular diocese. Thomas of Hereford, canonised in 1320, was not introduced into the Sarum calendar, but is found as a supplement to Sarum in calendars of the dioceses of Coventry and Lichfield, Exeter, Hereford, and Norwich.

Unexpected Texts for Saints in Some Sarum Breviary Manuscripts

Sherry Reames

Manuscript versions of the Sarum breviary are full of surprising divergences from the versions that were chosen for printing in the late fifteenth and sixteenth centuries. Although the early printed versions — and especially the folio edition of 1531, which Procter and Wordsworth chose in the nineteenth century as the basis for their own influential edition — tend to create the illusion that the Sarum Breviary was a single, fully standardized entity with contents that hardly ever changed, the surviving manuscripts give a much more fluid and pluralistic picture.[1] Richard Pfaff knows this well, of course, and called other researchers' attention to the problem at least eighteen years ago, in his conclusions to a thought-provoking essay on rubrics in Sarum breviaries and missals:

> . . . the fact that medieval English service-books tend to be classified by Uses, and that only one such Use (that of Sarum) had any very widespread currency, encourages us to think that there is something like a normative Sarum missal or Sarum breviary as prototypical as the Book of Common Prayer or the Roman breviary or missal of 1568/70. In very broad outline this may be true, at least negatively: one can say that a book is not Sarum because it lacks such and such features, and to a degree that it is Sarum because it contains this or that. But the variation among those books nominally classed as of the Sarum rite is enormous.[2]

My own recent work has focused on one particular kind of variation in Sarum breviaries and related office manuscripts: hagiographical texts added to the normal or

---

[1] *Breviarium ad usum insignis ecclesiae Sarum*, ed. Francis Procter and Christopher Wordsworth, 3 vols. (Cambridge: Cambridge University Press, 1879–1886).

[2] R. Pfaff, "Prescription and Reality in the Rubrics of Sarum Rite Service Books," in *Intellectual Life in the Middle Ages: Essays Presented to Margaret Gibson*, ed. Lesley Smith and Benedicta Ward (London: Hambledon Press 1992), 197–205; repr. in idem, *Liturgical Calendars, Saints, and Services in Medieval England* (Aldershot: Ashgate, 1998), no. XII, quotation from 204.

The Study of Medieval Manuscripts of England: Festschrift in Honor of Richard W. Pfaff, eds. George Hardin Brown and Linda Ehrsam Voigts, MRTS 384 (Tempe: ACMRS, 2010). [ISBN 978-0-86698-432-4]

standard contents of the Sanctorale—that is, to the yearly round of texts and instructions for the celebration of saints' feasts in the daily office. For the normal contents of the Sarum Sanctorale the edition by Procter and Wordsworth is even more misleading than usual, since it includes a number of texts for strictly regional feasts (including, most obviously, the Translation of Chad, patron saint of Lichfield, and the two feasts of Erkenwald, patron of London) and some very late additions to Sarum Use that one practically never encounters in a manuscript. The norm I use instead is the Sanctorale found most regularly in Sarum breviaries and lectionaries from the late fourteenth and early fifteenth centuries, and confirmed by what their rubrics and other sources say about the perceived requirements of Sarum Use in this period. With later manuscripts, of course, it is also normal to find these basic contents supplemented by some or all of the new saints' feasts that were added to the Sarum calendar during the fifteenth century: first David, Chad, both feasts of John of Beverley, and Wenefrede; later in the century also the Visitation.[3] Texts for such new feasts will be mentioned only if their appearance in a manuscript is unexpectedly early (that is, preceding the date at which the feast was officially added to Sarum Use) or if the manuscript obviously gives a very different set of texts from the usual Sarum ones.

The Appendix to this essay gives a list of the most conspicuous and substantial additions I have found in the 90-some Sarum office manuscripts I have examined: saints' days for which some manuscripts supply a set of proper (individualized) lessons to be read at Matins, the principal service of the day, and sometimes also a full liturgical office (an extensive set of proper chant texts for Vespers, Matins, and Lauds), despite the fact that normal Sarum Use either omits these feasts entirely or limits their commemoration to a proper prayer or collect, taking the lessons and the rest of the service from the Common of Saints.[4] This choice is more significant than one might suppose, since using proper texts not only implies a heightened recognition of that saint's importance, but also tends to change the tone and focus of the Matins service by substituting lessons and sung texts based on the particular saint's legend for the more universal texts of

---

[3] Although Frideswide, the Translation of Etheldreda, and the December feast day of Osmund were also added officially to the Sarum calendar in the fifteenth century, proper lessons and offices for them occur so rarely in the surviving manuscripts that they are always unexpected, and therefore worth mentioning. By 1500, of course, the Sarum Sanctorale also included the Transfiguration and Holy Name, major new Christological feasts whose liturgical history in England—along with that of the Visitation—was documented rather definitively by Richard Pfaff in his first scholarly book, *New Liturgical Feasts in Later Medieval England* (Oxford: Clarendon Press, 1970).

[4] The texts in the Common of Saints, designed to be used multiple times each year, are organized in categories according to the type of saint, for example, Martyr, Confessor, Virgin, etc.

the Common, drawn from the sermons and biblical commentaries of writers like Gregory, Bede, and Augustine.

In some manuscripts the extra texts for saints can easily be explained as well-known regional variants of the Sarum calendar—for example, the Irish adaptations of Sarum Use, the East Anglian ones (showing the non-Sarum feast days regularly celebrated in the dioceses of Norwich and Ely), the special commemorations of Hugh's Translation in the diocese of Lincoln and of the bishops Oswald and Wulfstan in the diocese of Worcester. In other cases the extra texts can be attributed to the special veneration of a patron or local saint; obvious examples include the exceptional prominence of St. Leonard in NLW MS. 22243A (which adds a full office to the usual lessons for his major feast and also supplies lessons for his Translation), the addition of St. John of Bridlington (with a full office and six lessons) to CUL MS. Add. 4500, and the lessons for St. Erkenwald in Stonyhurst College MS. 52.

For the most part, however, the additions defy such easy categorization. In fact, certain manuscripts force themselves on our attention because they continually challenge our expectations, providing proper Matins lessons or offices, or both, for far more saints' days than Sarum Use normally allowed. The remainder of this essay will focus primarily on this subset of Sarum manuscripts, identifying and describing them first, and then attempting to show their potential value both for understanding the historical development of the Sarum breviary and for efforts to reconstruct the history of particular saints' legends and cults in England.

The manuscripts in question are these, ordered by their number of extra texts for saints.

> **Exeter Cathedral Lectionary** (hereafter cited as "Exeter"): Exeter Chapter MSS. 3504 and 3505, drawn up and personally annotated by Bishop John Grandisson in 1337–1340, and MS. 3505B, a late fourteenth-century copy of MS 3505 that makes some further additions. Thanks to J. N. Dalton, who edited these manuscripts along with the Exeter Ordinal early in the twentieth century, Grandisson's lectionary is the best known and most accessible of all Sarum office manuscripts.[5] Its distinctive lectionary of saints gives Matins lessons for thirty-four extra saints' days, plus a large number of additional lessons on saints that were designated for reading after Prime, a service later in the morning. Eight of the thirty-four sets of extra Matins lessons can easily be connected with Exeter or to Grandisson himself, but the vast majority cannot.[6]

---

[5] *Ordinale Exon[iensis]*, Appendix 3: *Legenda Exon[iensis]*, Henry Bradshaw Society 63 (London: Henry Bradshaw Society, 1926).

[6] As will be explained below, proper lessons for the Conception of the Virgin Mary (8 Dec.) appear in most of the surviving Sarum breviary manuscripts produced between about 1320 and 1370. Although they seem to have been normal during this period, I have counted them throughout as "extra" lessons because they are virtually never found in later

BL MS. Cotton Appendix 23 (hereafter "Cotton"), a Sarum office lectionary written in the first half of the fourteenth century, apparently for use in
the diocese of Worcester. This manuscript has generally been overlooked
because it is not specifically identified, much less described, in the standard
catalogues of British Library manuscripts, but it is one of the most important surviving sources for the textual history of Sarum lessons about saints.[7]
To the expected Sarum complement of its time it adds twenty-five sets of
lessons, only four of which (or possibly five, if we should count its early lessons for Chad) belong to standard Worcester feasts.

BL MS. Stowe 12 (hereafter "Stowe"), an illuminated Sarum breviary from
Norwich, produced ca. 1322–1325.[8] This beautiful manuscript is unfortunately quite incomplete, having lost the folios comprising its Sanctorale for
most of February, all of March and April, and more than half of August,
along with some smaller sections. As originally written, Stowe may well
have had even more extra proper texts for saints' days than Exeter does.
Even after its many losses it is astonishingly rich in unusual texts for such
feasts, with twenty-one surviving sets of extra proper lessons (two for standard Norwich feasts and nineteen unexpected ones), plus six extra full offices—the Conception of the Virgin, Thomas Becket's Translation, Margaret, Anne, Edmund of Canterbury, and Edmund King and Martyr.

Bodleian MS. Auct. E.1.1 (hereafter "Auct. E.1.1"), a Sarum office lectionary of ca. 1400, apparently produced for a church dedicated to St. Nicholas
in the diocese of Salisbury.[9] Besides the rare texts for Nicholas's Translation

---

Sarum breviaries (including the printed editions), which either give just a rubric or reproduce the standard lessons for the Virgin's Nativity.

[7] The 1802 *Catalogue of the Manuscripts in the Cottonian Library Deposited in the British Museum* characterizes it only as follows: "Codex membran. in folio, constans foliis
276. Lectiones in festis diebus sanctorum" (2: 615). Andrew Hughes's "Forty-Seven Medieval Office Manuscripts in the British Museum: A Provisional Inventory of Antiphonals and Breviaries" (1976 typescript), which usefully supplements much of the information in older catalogues, does not include lectionary manuscripts at all.

[8] *Catalogue of the Stowe Manuscripts in the British Museum*, vol. 1 (London: Trust-
ees of the British Museum, 1895); Paleographical Society, *Facsimiles of Manuscripts and
Inscriptions*, second series (London: Palaeographical Society, 1884–1894), vol. 2, plate
197; Andrew G. Watson, *Catalogue of Dated and Datable Manuscripts c. 700–1600 in the
Department of Manuscripts, The British Library* (London: The British Library, 1979), item
945 and plate 199.

[9] S. J. P. Van Dijk, *Handlist of the Latin Liturgical Manuscripts in the Bodleian Library, Oxford*, 7 vols. (1951, typescript on deposit in the Bodleian). Van Dijk suggests a
Salisbury provenance, presumably because of all the material on Osmund. It was presumably not closely connected with Salisbury Cathedral, however, given its many explicit departures from the Sarum ordinal and its many differences from Salisbury 224 (described
below), a manuscript for which there is specific evidence of Cathedral connections.

in its original Sanctorale and its conspicuous later additions for both Nicholas and Osmund, patron saint of Salisbury, this manuscript has eighteen unexpected sets of proper lessons, many of them accompanied by unusually interesting rubrics.

Cambridge, Gonville and Caius College, MS. 394/614 (hereafter "Gonville"), a rather eccentric Sarum breviary apparently produced in the first half of the fourteenth century for a user in the diocese of Ely.[10] The original Sanctorale of this manuscript includes extra sets of proper lessons for seventeen saints' days, including the Translation of St. Etheldreda, patron of Ely; Dominic and Francis, who also had proper lessons in other manuscripts from East Anglia; and fourteen unexpected ones, plus extra offices for the same occasions as in Stowe, except that Egidius or Giles has replaced Anne.

BL MS. Royal 2.A.XII (hereafter "Royal"), an illuminated Sarum breviary dating from the late fifteenth century and apparently produced outside England, possibly in Flanders.[11] Its Sanctorale includes extra sets of proper lessons for fifteen saints whose Sarum offices usually followed the Common instead.

BL MS. Sloane 1909 (hereafter "Sloane"), a rather plain portable breviary, apparently dating from the third quarter of the fourteenth century, with many interesting corrections and additions.[12] Its original Sanctorale includes extra sets of proper lessons for ten saints, plus extra full offices for the same five saints' days as in both Stowe and Gonville—that is, Conception of the Virgin, Thomas Becket's Translation, Margaret, and both Edmunds. In this manuscript, those offices have all been labelled as in conflict with Sarum Use, in two instances by the original scribe, and most of the office for Edmund King and Martyr (20 Nov.) has been crossed out.

---

[10] M. R. James, *Descriptive Catalogue of the Manuscripts in the Library of Gonville and Caius College* (Cambridge: Cambridge University Press, 1908), 2: 459–60. W.H. Frere, *Bibliotheca Musico-Liturgica* (London: Quaritch, 1894, repr. 1901–1932; repr. Hildesheim: Olms, 1967), vol. 2, 124 assigns this manuscript to the late 14th century, presumably on paleographical grounds, but its hagiographical contents make much better sense if one accepts the earlier date proposed by Nigel Morgan. The unusual references in this manuscript to distinctive Ely saints include a prayer for Sexburga in the original Sanctorale and (among the later additions) prayers for Ermenilda and Withburga, another prayer for Sexburga, and both the prayer and lessons needed for weekly commemorations of Etheldreda.

[11] The best available description of this manuscript is by Hughes in "Forty-Seven Medieval Office Manuscripts." Its probable Flemish origin is Pfaff's suggestion, based on the binding and the style of the illuminations (*New Liturgical Feasts*, 51).

[12] Once again, the best available description comes from Hughes, "Forty-Seven Medieval Office Manuscripts."

Salisbury Cathedral MS. 224 (hereafter "Salisbury"), a very large noted breviary, probably connected in some way with Salisbury Cathedral and dating from the third quarter of the fourteenth century.[13] Its original Sanctorale includes extra proper lessons for ten saints' days but no extra full offices except unfinished ones for the two Edmunds, which have been left with words and staves but no music, as if the scribe abandoned them when he realized that current Sarum Use required generic offices from the Common rather than the inherited proper offices for these two feasts.[14]

Edinburgh University MS. 26 (hereafter "Edinburgh 26"), a very small illuminated breviary written ca. 1350 and probably connected in some way with Hereford Cathedral, although it follows Sarum rather than Hereford Use in most respects.[15] Its Sanctorale includes proper lessons for nine extra saints' days and extra full offices for four (Conception of the Virgin, Thomas Becket's Translation, Anne, and Thomas of Hereford).

Cambridge, St. John's College MS. H.13 (hereafter "St. John's"), a large and lavishly illuminated breviary evidently produced in the later fifteenth century for Margaret of York (1446–1503), whose motto, "Bien en aviegne," frequently appears in the margins.[16] M. R. James suggests that

---

[13] This manuscript long resided at the Bodleian, where it was known as MS. E Mus. 2. N.R. Ker and A.J. Piper date it ca. 1320 (*Medieval Manuscripts in British Libraries*, 5 vols. [Oxford: Clarendon Press, 1969–2002], 4: 264–66), but it cannot be that early. Like the Exeter Breviary and Edinburgh 26, this manuscript already has incorporated some proper texts for Thomas of Hereford, who was canonized only in 1320, and it has more resemblances to manuscripts of the late 14th century than either Exeter or Edinburgh 26 does. In fact, the original state of its Sanctorale is very much like the corrected version of Sloane 1909.

[14] The unfinished state of these two offices stands out, since they are immediately preceded and followed by fully noted chants for Martin and Cecilia.

[15] C. R. Borland gives some useful information on this manuscript in *Descriptive Catalogue of the Western Medieval Manuscripts in Edinburgh University Library* (Edinburgh: Edinburgh University Press, 1916), 36–38. However, Borland's suggested date of ca. 1300 is manifestly too early, since the manuscript as originally written has already incorporated texts for Thomas of Hereford (canonized 1320), removed the Sarum Feast of Relics from its traditional September date (a change ordered in 1319), and made some other liturgical changes that were implemented rather slowly in the first half of the fourteenth century. Borland's suggestion of a connection with Chichester also needs correction, since the manuscript actually shows less interest in St. Richard than is usual for its time, not more. The most surprising and distinctive features in its Sanctorale are its full offices and proper lessons for Thomas of Hereford and for Anne; also worth noting is the provision of three extra lessons for Egidius or Giles, with a rubric identifying this departure from Sarum practice as deliberate.

[16] M. R. James, *Descriptive Catalogue of the Manuscripts in the Library of St. John's College, Cambridge* (Cambridge: Cambridge University Press, 1913), 244–45, no. 215.

the manuscript was probably written and illuminated in Flanders, and it has some oddly old-fashioned features which support the idea that it was produced abroad and based in part on a fourteenth-century model.[17] Its Sanctorale gives proper lessons for seven or eight extra saints' days.[18]

Looking back over these ten manuscripts, one notes that the majority of them were written before 1400, and the two markedly later ones (the Royal and St. John's manuscripts) were evidently produced abroad rather than in England, where the scribes would have had more up-to-date exemplars to follow. It seems reasonable, that is, to interpret the abundance of additional proper lessons and offices in these manuscripts as a manifestation of the diversity that flourished within—or cohabited with—the Sarum liturgy in the fourteenth century, and especially the earlier part of the century. Diversity does not mean, of course, that most of the surviving manuscripts from this period have an abundance of extra texts for saints. Indeed, over half do not. Although Exeter, Cotton, Gonville, and Stowe can all be dated before about 1350, so can at least five other manuscripts—NLS Advocates 18.2.13b, BL Add. 52,359, Pierpont Morgan M.329, Longleat House 10, and Edinburgh University 27—which have hardly any additions of this kind.

Besides showing how far Sarum Sanctorales were from being uniform in the fourteenth century, the manuscripts with many additions shed some light on the reasons for that lack of uniformity. Indeed, they suggest that many dioceses and individual churches adopted the Sarum liturgy piecemeal, accepting most of its calendar and ceremonial while retaining non-Sarum feasts that had local importance and continuing to use whatever legendary or lectionary of saints they already had. Retaining as many as possible of the old traditions and service books would have made good practical sense, and early versions of the ordinal (or "rules" for Sarum Use) allowed considerable latitude regarding legendaries in particular because they tended to say very little about the lessons in a saint's office, often specifying no more than the total number to be read (three or nine). Such ambiguities or loopholes in the ordinal would have invited the compilers or scribes of early Sarum breviaries to give proper lessons for the feast of any saint

---

Belatedly recognizing that the initials "C M" which sometimes accompany the motto must refer to the marriage of Margaret and Charles the Bold of Burgundy, James adds in the Corrigenda to this catalogue that the present manuscript can be dated between 1468 and 1477. For more recent discussions of this manuscript, see the bibliography provided in *The Cambridge Illuminations: Ten Centuries of Book Production in the Medieval West*, ed. Paul Binski and Stella Panayotova (London: Harvey Miller, 2005), 134–36, no. 50.

[17] Most strikingly, it still gives the office for Feast of Relics in September, although there are rubrics both there and in July that explain its changed date in the "modern" Sarum rite.

[18] The two lessons in this manuscript for Richard's Translation look like an excerpt from the saint's *vita* and may duplicate part of the text for his other feast.

in the Sarum calendar whom they deemed to be of sufficient importance and for whom such texts were locally available. In effect, then, these ambiguities created local options within Sarum Use—explaining the tendency of manuscripts like Exeter, Cotton, and Stowe to give proper lessons for many of the same "extra" saints, while other early manuscripts omit such lessons from the start.

Later revisions of the Sarum ordinal reduced the range of permissible lessons, nearly always specifying at least the general nature of the source (Common of Saints, individual saint's legend, or Gospel exposition) and the *incipit* of the first lesson. For more than twenty saints, the revised instructions prescribed—apparently for the first time—that all the lessons were to come from the Common. But the surviving manuscripts suggest that some scribes simply copied older manuscripts, oblivious to the new instructions in the ordinal, and both makers and users of breviaries apparently continued to assume, throughout the fourteenth century, that the details of Sarum Use need not always be followed, at least where lessons and offices for saints were concerned.

The feast of the Virgin Mary's Conception (8 December) provides a particularly clear illustration of both the diversity within Sarum practice in the earlier fourteenth century and the slow progress toward uniformity thereafter. Although the Conception was added to the list of obligatory Sarum feasts only in 1329, its celebration was authorized earlier as an option "for the sake of devotion," and it already has proper texts in Stowe and a few other manuscripts that predate 1329.[19] Since it was not yet an official Sarum feast, one would not expect these early manuscripts to have exactly the same texts, and indeed they do not. In fact, although they all give variants on the same full office ("Fulget dies hodierna"), the manuscripts with lessons seem to have derived them from completely different sources.[20] For a few decades after 1329, celebrating the Conception with its own office (still "Fulget dies hodierna") and nine lessons seems to have been the Sarum norm; but the lessons continue to come from a variety of different sources and to have a wide range of different *incipit*s, suggesting that no single set of

---

[19] For the statute ordering that this feast be observed in the province of Canterbury, see David Wilkins, *Concilia Magnae Britanniae et Hiberniae* (London, 1737), 2:552. The list of required Sarum feasts in Stowe says explicitly that celebration of the Conception "non imponitur necessitas nisi ex devocione velit aliquis celebrare" (fol. 154v).

[20] Besides Stowe, the Sarum office manuscripts that definitely have pre-1329 texts for the Conception are Edinburgh University 27 (which takes its lessons from Osbert of Clare's sermon on St. Anne), Longleat House 10 (with lessons apparently based on the apocryphal *De Nativitate Mariae*), and (without lessons) the four Sarum or Augustinian antiphonals listed in the Appendix. The lessons in Stowe come from the pseudo-Anselm *Sermo de Conceptione beatae Mariae* (*PL* 159. 319 et seq.) and at least one other source, which I have not yet identified. The office found in all seven manuscripts seems to be an English version of the one printed from continental sources: Guido Maria Dreves and Clemens Blume, eds., *Analecta hymnica medii aevi*, 55 vols. (Leipzig: Reisland, 1886–1922), 5: 12.

proper lessons for this feast was ever authorized and effectively disseminated.[21] A revision of the Sarum ordinal ca. 1350 or 1360 started to demand complete uniformity in this liturgy, issuing the "modern Sarum" rule that the Conception should not have its own office and lessons at all, but reuse the long-established texts for the Virgin's Nativity instead. Even manuscripts that quote the new rule, however, sometimes ignore it—as happens for example in Sloane and the late fourteenth-century copy of the Exeter Cathedral lectionary.[22] Some other manuscripts from the later fourteenth century show no awareness of the rule with which they are in conflict when they give a full office and proper lessons for the Conception.[23] Perhaps in response to the perceived chaos of the earlier period, the instructions for this feast in later Sarum breviaries become increasingly exact about the lessons, not only identifying the source from which they were to come and the place to start lesson 1, but eventually specifying all the *incipits* of lessons 2–6 and sometimes the *explicit* of lesson 6 as well.[24]

On a number of other issues, the manuscripts with many additions give us glimpses of the tensions between local traditions in the celebration of saints' feasts and a centralizing authority that was trying to establish liturgical uniformity. A few manuscripts explicitly encourage their users to tailor the services at least in part to their own customs or preferences by suggesting alternatives to the increasingly detailed instructions in the ordinal. The most conspicuous examples occur in Edinburgh 26, which provides nine hagiographical lessons each instead of the usual Sarum six for Edward, king and martyr (18 March), Augustine (28

---

[21] Altogether, the twelve Sarum manuscripts that give proper lessons for this feast are so far from unanimity that the lessons have seven different *incipits* and come from at least six different sources. Among the eleven Sarum and closely related manuscripts that give the "Fulget dies hodierna" office, on the other hand, one finds nine of them agreeing on almost every detail except the middle four antiphons at 1 Vespers which most of the manuscripts simply lack. The two manuscripts that disagree most often from the rest, primarily with regard to the selection and order of the Matins responsories, are BL Add. 28,598 and Edinburgh 26.

[22] The latter manuscript, Exeter Cathedral 3505B, inserts the following note between the modern Sarum rubric and the proper lessons from Grandisson's lectionary: "Secundum usum Exon. legantur lecc sequentes."

[23] The original scribe of Liverpool Cathedral MS. 37, for example, seems to have been oblivious to the rule; a later corrector erased the rubric that originally preceded the office and lessons and inserted the "modern Sarum" rule in its place. The late fourteenth-century scribe who wrote this part of Bodleian Rawlinson C.73 cites part of the new rule and then provides proper lessons (but no proper office).

[24] The earliest manuscript in which I have found all the *incipits* spelled out is ironically Sloane (which, as already mentioned, proceeds to give a completely different set of lessons). This detailed rubric becomes very common ca. 1400. Among the manuscripts that also prescribe the *explicit* for lec. 6 are the Chichele Breviary (Lambeth Palace 69) and half a dozen of its close relatives, all dating from the early fifteenth century.

Aug.), and Clement (23 Nov.), explaining in each case that the reader can if he prefers make six longer lessons from those nine and add the exposition of a Gospel passage as lessons 7–9. In the case of Clement, the rubric ends by acknowledging that the ordinal prescribes the latter procedure, but still suggests that one need not choose to conform.[25] Introducing the lessons for Egidius or Giles (1 Sept.), Edinburgh 26 explains that according to Sarum Use the three middle lessons should come from the Common of one martyr, but "ex devotione" it is supplying nine proper lessons for Egidius, and the reader may choose whichever he prefers: "Eligat qui voluerit unum modum vel alium" (fol. 523). For Cuthbert's Translation (4 Sept.), this manuscript finds a loophole in the ordinal's instructions and offers users both three proper lessons (to be used in years when Cuthbert's principal feast was celebrated in the spring) and a choice among several alternative sources for the lessons in years when nine are needed (fol. 525). Another rubric in this manuscript points out the difference between the "modern Sarum" directions for Vespers on 6 July, which call for the service to be devoted to Thomas Becket's Translation, and the "antiquum usum Sarum" in which this service completed the octave of Peter and Paul, and invites users of the breviary to follow the old way if devotion to the apostles prompts them to do so (fol. 472v).

The stubborn hold of older traditions is still manifested in two lectionary manuscripts produced around the end of the fourteenth century, Bodleian Auct. E.1.1 and Exeter Cathedral 3505B. In more than a dozen cases, Auct. E.1.1 quotes the revised Sarum directions, labels them "secundum ordinale," and then proceeds to give proper lessons that violate them, often adding a brief explanation. For St. Richard (2 April), for example, the rubric reads, "ix lecc fiant de communi . . . secundum ordinale, vel hic de proprietate si placuerit" (fol. 198v). For Alphege (19 April), after acknowledging that the ordinal calls for three lessons from the Common, this manuscript adds "tamen scribuntur hic de proprietate eiusdem" (fol. 200v). In the revised Exeter Cathedral lectionary, many rubrics have additions that quote the Sarum instructions and verify the Cathedral's deliberate departures from them. Some of the departures are fairly major, such as the decision to keep celebrating the non-Sarum feast of Thomas of Hereford (2 Oct.) at Exeter and to ignore the Translation of Richard of Chichester (16 June), devoting the whole service on that day to the martyrs Ciricus and Julitta. Other departures reaffirmed in this manuscript concern such details as whether to keep reading nine hagiographical lessons at Matins for Jerome (30 Sept.) and Clement (23 Nov.) or follow Sarum Use in devoting the last three lessons to an exposition of the Gospel. Even on such relatively minor details, traditions at Exeter seem to trump the revised Sarum ordinal every time. No one who has witnessed the resistance to liturgical revision in our own time will be very surprised.

---

[25] "Quod si magis placet lectori de istis ix lecc precedentibus facere vi lecc et tunc addere iii lecc de expositione ewangelii 'Homo quidam nobilis,' bene licet. Et sic forte melius concordabit ordinali" (fol. 598v).

The fourteenth-century manuscripts with a wealth of extra lessons deserve attention on many other grounds, of course, besides the light they can shed on the historical development and spread of Sarum Use. These manuscripts represent a number of different traditions. They are geographically diverse: the locations that can be identified range from Exeter northward at least to Worcester (Cotton) and east to the dioceses of Salisbury (Salisbury 224 and Auct. E.1.1), Ely (Gonville), and Norwich (Stowe). Chronologically they range only from the early 1320s (Stowe) to around 1400 (Auct. E.1.1), but the texts they give must in general be considerably older, copied or excerpted from whatever legendaries were current in their own localities before the change to Sarum Use. Even their lessons for the standard Sarum saints are often unpredictable in length, wording, and exact content, although the differences tend to be disguised at the start because they usually begin lesson 1 with the normal Sarum *incipit*.[26] Just two of these manuscripts, Cotton and Edinburgh 26, seem to belong to the same textual family as the Sarum lectionary that was printed in the folio editions of the sixteenth century and subsequently republished by Procter and Wordsworth; and these two sometimes give much fuller versions of the hagiographical texts (or, in the case of Edinburgh, excerpts from fuller versions) than do the printed editions.[27] The lessons for standard Sarum saints in Sloane and Salisbury apparently come from a second textual family, and among their cousins are the abridged lessons in the portable printed Sarum breviaries of the late fifteenth and sixteenth centuries.[28] The other four fourteenth-century manuscripts with extra lessons — Stowe, Exeter, Gonville, and Auct. E.1.1 — seem to derive from four textual traditions that rarely converge. Their lessons for the standard Sarum saints are often distinctive and far removed both from all the early printed editions and from most other Sarum manuscripts, *incipit*s and all.[29]

---

[26] My generalizations about the lessons for standard Sarum saints are based primarily on collations of all the lessons for eleven particular saints' days and octaves. For further detail, see Sherry L. Reames, "Late Medieval Efforts at Standardization and Reform in the Sarum Lessons for Saints' Days," in *Design and Distribution of Late Medieval Manuscripts in England,* ed. Margaret Connolly and Linne R. Mooney (York: University of York Medieval Press; Woodbridge, UK; Rochester, NY: in association with Boydell Press, 2008), 91–117.

[27] One striking example of the fuller lessons in Cotton is its text for Thomas Becket's Translation, which looks like the one in the printed folio breviaries throughout its first several lessons but includes two sizable and important blocks of additional material, one in the middle and one at the end. For further detail and an edition of this text, see Sherry L. Reames, "Reconstructing and Interpreting a Thirteenth-Century Office for the Translation of Thomas Becket," *Speculum* 80 (2005): 118–70.

[28] I discuss the nature and extent of this textual relationship in the closing pages of "Late Medieval Efforts at Standardization and Reform."

[29] Gonville, in fact, departs from the usual Sarum *incipit*s for most of the feast days in my sample, Exeter for half, Stowe for more than a third.

Although I have just begun to undertake detailed comparisons of the unexpected texts for saints, it is already obvious that the extra lessons in this group of manuscripts are even more diverse than their lessons for standard Sarum saints. In fact, although four of these manuscripts have proper lessons for St. Boniface on 5 June, two of them (Cotton and Gonville) actually deal with Boniface the ancient martyr and the other two (Exeter and Auct. E.1.1) with Boniface the Anglo-Saxon missionary, and all four have different *incipits*.[30] Cotton, Gonville, Exeter, and Auct. E.1.1 also have lessons for Paul's legendary female disciple Tecla on 23 September, all apparently telling the same story but starting in four different ways. Seven of the eight fourteenth-century manuscripts in the group (all except Stowe, which is missing folios at this point) have lessons for Alphege on 19 April, and a number of them are evidently based on the same ultimate source, but only two (Sloane and Salisbury) start in just the same way. Every manuscript in the group except Edinburgh 26 has lessons for Basil on 14 June, but their openings suggest that they fall into at least four subgroups: Cotton, Stowe, and Gonville beginning in much the same way; Sloane and Salisbury together as usual; Exeter and Auct. E.1.1 each different from all the rest.[31]

As I have been attempting to suggest, these manuscripts with extra texts for saints offer a number of potentially fruitful opportunities for research.[32] Some of their lessons, especially the longer ones on native saints, may be worth actually editing and publishing for the light they can shed on the textual history of other Latin accounts of these saints and the sources of vernacular ones. The manuscripts with very abbreviated lessons may be useful at least in suggesting the variety of versions and locales in which a given legend circulated, and thus indirectly illuminating the extent of that saint's cult in late medieval England and its degree of independence (or not) from the promotional efforts of a single hagiographer or cult center. The non-Sarum offices in some of these manuscripts may further illuminate the history of a given cult through their textual connections with offices in continental manuscripts or in the few surviving English monastic ones, or both. Both abridged lessons and chant texts offer additional opportunities to learn how particular saints were envisioned in this period, which aspects

---

[30] If we count the lessons in St. John's H.13 on Boniface the missionary (as perhaps we should not, since it was produced outside England), there are at least five Sarum texts for this feast day, all with different *incipits*. The lessons on Boniface in Gonville are similar at the start both to those in an earlier Sarum breviary, the thirteenth-century part of Bodleian Rawlinson C.73, and those in the Surtees Society edition of the York breviary.

[31] Lessons for Basil are also found in both fifteenth-century Sarum manuscripts with many extra lessons. Those in Royal resemble Cotton, Stowe, and Gonville at the start; those in St. John's H.13 differ from all the rest.

[32] Some examples of scholarly work already done on such texts from Sarum breviary manuscripts are cited in the notes to the Appendix; see the entries for Kentigern, Erkenwald, Anne, and Thomas Becket's Translation.

of their identity were emphasized in these inherently selective genres, and which parts of their traditional image were revised or simply ignored. Although I hope to explore a few of these possibilities before my retirement, there are far too many for any single researcher to exhaust. So I urge other scholars and students to accept the invitation implicit in the Appendix and start sampling the manuscripts and texts on those lists for themselves.

Appendix:
Hagiographical texts not found in most
Sarum manuscripts

This table is a work in progress, based on my examination of about 120 Sarum manuscripts and other English service books over a period of about twenty years. It is as accurate and complete as I could make it on the basis of my notes and the re-examination of some key manuscripts, but it undoubtedly has omissions and errors. Additions and corrections are welcome.

Unless otherwise noted, entries in this table indicate the presence of proper lessons for the feast-day in question in the manuscript's original Sanctorale. Asterisks indicate manuscripts dating from ca. 1400 or earlier. The notation "added" is used for texts inserted out of sequence, usually much later. The number of lessons is specified only when there is a Sarum version with a different number of lessons.

Short forms used in this table

BL	London, British Library
BN	Paris, Bibliothèque Nationale
Bodl	Oxford, Bodleian Library
CUL	Cambridge University Library
NLS	Edinburgh, National Library of Scotland
NLW	Aberystwyth, National Library of Wales
TCD	Dublin, Trinity College
Aberdeen	*Breviarium Aberdonense*, printed 1509–1510; republished for Bannatyne and Maitland Clubs, Edinburgh and London, 1854.
Battle Abbey	Cambridge, Trinity College MS. O.7.31
Bute	Foulis Easter breviary, published as *Breviarium Bothanum, sive portiforium secundum usum ecclesiae cujusdam in Scotia*, ed. W. D. Macray (London: Longmans, Green, 1900).
Clare	Cambridge, Clare College MS. G.3.34
Claremont	Claremont, CA, Honnold Library MS. Crispin 15
Cotton	BL MS. Cotton Appendix 23
Frankfurt	Frankfurt am Main, Stadt- und Universitätsbibliothek MS. lat. oct. 97
Gonville	Cambridge, Gonville and Caius College MS. 394/614
Helmingham	Helmingham Breviary (now in the archives adjacent to Norwich Castle Museum)
Hereford P, W, H	1505 printed edition of the Hereford breviary, Worcester manuscript, and Hereford manuscript, respectively—all published in *The Hereford Breviary*, ed. Walter Howard

	Frere and Langton E. G. Brown, Henry Bradshaw Society 26, 40, 46 (London: Harrison and Sons, 1904–1915)
Liverpool	Liverpool Cathedral MS. 37 (now in University of Liverpool Library)
Longleat	Longleat House MS. 10
Morgan	New York, Pierpont Morgan Library MS. M.329
Royal	BL MS. Royal 2.A.XII
Sloane	BL MS. Sloane 1909
Stowe	BL MS. Stowe 12
Trinity	Cambridge, Trinity College MS. O.5.3
York P	*Breviarium ad usum insignis ecclesiae Eboracensis*, printed 1493; ed. Stephen W. Lawley and republished as Surtees Society 71, 75 (Durham: Andrews, 1880–1883)

A. Unambiguously regional and local additions to the usual Sarum Sanctorale

(IRELAND)

Brigid (1 Feb.) (9 lecc + full office): NLW 21604A, Bodl Can. lit. 215 (added), TCD 80, TCD 88 [also *BN latin 12036 (office only), Aberdeen (9 lecc only)]

Canice (or Cainnech or Kenneth) (11 Oct.): TCD 88 [also Aberdeen]

Columba (9 June) (lecc + full office): NLW 21604A, Bodl Can. lit. 215 (added), TCD 88 [also Aberdeen]

Edan (or Aedh or Aidan, or Maedoc of Ferns) (31 Jan.): TCD 88

11,000 Virgins (21 Oct.) (9 lecc + full office): Bodl Can. lit. 215 (added, replacing original Sarum set of 3 lecc), TCD 88 (with further text for 6 Octave lecc) [also Aberdeen, TCD 84 (Aug./Arrouasian), with further text for Octave; Bodl Univ. College 9 (Carm.), with 8 lecc and hymns]

Finnian (12 Dec.): NLW 21604A, Bodl Can. lit. 215 (added, with full office and hymn)

Laserian (18? Apr.): TCD 88

Laurence (O'Toole), archbishop of Dublin (14 Nov.) (lecc + full office): TCD 88

Patrick (17 Mar.) (lecc + full office): NLW 21604A, Bodl Can. lit. 215 (added), TCD 80, TCD 88, TCD 79;[33] (lecc only): *Bodl Rawl. C.73 (14th-c. part) [also Aberdeen (lecc only), Bodl Univ. College 9 (Carm.), Manchester Rylands 354 (Aug.?)]

Patrick, Brigid, and Columba, Trans. (10 June) (lecc + full office): Bodl Can. lit. 215 (added), TCD 88

---

[33] This manuscript, an Irish Sarum antiphonal, gives the full office with music in calendar sequence and the lessons as a later addition (on fol.81).

(SCOTLAND) [omitting several dozen saints found only in the printed Aberdeen
   Breviary] [34]
Kentigern (14 Jan.) (lecc + full office): *NLS Advocates 18.2.13.B (added almost
   in sequence), [35] *Edinburgh Univ. 27 (added) [36] [also Aberdeen]

(EAST ANGLIA)
Dominic (4 or 5 Aug.): *Stowe, *Gonville, *Liverpool (added), *Clare (added),
   Trinity, Helmingham, BL Add. 59862, Bodl Laud Misc. 299 (added) [also
   Norwich synodal MS, [37] Bodl Univ. College 9 (Carm.)]
Edmund, King and Martyr, Transl. (29 Apr.): *Liverpool (added), *Clare
   (added), Trinity, BL Add. 59862, BL Harley 2785, Bodl Laud Misc. 299
   [also Norwich synodal MS]
Etheldreda (23 June) (full office, without lecc): *BN latin 12036
Etheldreda, Trans. (17 Oct.) [early]: *Gonville
Felix of Dunwich (8 Mar.): *Liverpool (added), *Clare, Trinity, BL Add. 59862,
   BL Harley 2785 [also Norwich synodal MS]
Francis (4 Oct.): *Stowe, *Gonville, *Liverpool (added), *Clare (added), Trinity,
   Helmingham, BL Add. 59862, Bodl Laud Misc. 299 (added) [also Norwich
   synodal MS, Exeter, Aberdeen, Bute, TCD 84 (Aug./Arrouasian), York P]
Thomas of Hereford (2 Oct.): *Liverpool (added), *Clare (added), Trinity,
   Helmingham, BL Add. 59862, Bodl Laud Misc. 299 (added) [also Norwich

---

[34] On these saints and the importance of the Aberdeen Breviary in preserving evidence of the medieval traditions surrounding them, see A. Boyle, "Some Saints' Lives in
the Breviary of Aberdeen," *Analecta Bollandiana* 94 (1976): 95–106; and Alan Macquarrie, "Medieval Scotland," in *Hagiographies: Histoire internationale de la littérature hagi-
ographique latine et vernaculaire en Occident des origines à 1550*, ed. Guy Philippart (Turnhout: Brepols, 1994), 1: 487–501, at 495–98.
   [35] The lessons from this manuscript, also known as the Sprouston Breviary, are included in A. P. Forbes' edition of the surviving sources on Kentigern, *The Lives of Saint
Ninian and Saint Kentigern*, Historians of Scotland 5 (Edinburgh: Edmonston and Douglas, 1874), and in Alan Macquarrie's historical analysis, "The Career of Saint Kentigern of
Glasgow: *Vitae, Lectiones* and Glimpses of Fact," *Innes Review* 37 (1986): 3–24.
   [36] Unfortunately, the part of Edinburgh 27 with this office (which begins at fol.
478v) is seriously damaged, with about a third of each page missing.
   [37] The manuscript in question, Cambridge St. John's College K.50, begins with the
unambiguous heading, "Hec sunt festa sinodalia Norwicensis diocesis" but also includes
proper texts for four recently added Sarum saints: David, Chad, Wenefrede, and John of
Beverley. Trinity separates out the five Norwich feasts, presenting the lessons for Felix,
Edmund's Translation, Dominic, Thomas of Hereford, and Francis in a special section
headed "Hec sunt festa sinodalia et non Sarum"; BL Add. 59862 has these five feasts integrated with the rest of its Sanctorale, with rubrics that identify each of them as belonging
to the synod rather than to wider Sarum use.

synodal MS and many printed eds. — and see "apparently non-regional" list below for MSS from other parts of England][38]

(EXETER CATHEDRAL)[39]
David (1 Mar.) [early]: *Exeter 3505, *3505B
Francis (4 Oct.): *Exeter 3505, *3505B [also E. Anglia, Aberdeen, Bute, York P, TCD 84 (Aug./ Arrouasian)]
Frideswide (19 Oct.) [early] (6 lecc): *Exeter 3505, *3505B [also Hereford *H, W, P, and Sarum printed folio eds. of 1516 and 1531]
Gabriel (first Mon. in Sept.): *Exeter 3504 (added at fols. 251v-254), *3505B (added at end of MS)
Michael, Apparicio (8 May): *Exeter 3505B (added at end of MS)
Sidwell or Sativola (2 Aug.): *Exeter 3505B (added at end of MS)
Thomas of Hereford (2 Oct.): *Exeter 3505, *3505B [also E. Anglia, many printed editions, and MSS from other parts of England (see "apparently non-regional" list below)]
Wilfrid (12 Oct.): *Exeter 3505 (added at end of MS) [also York P]

(DIOCESE OF LINCOLN)
Hugh, Trans. (6 Oct.): *Longleat (added), *Stonyhurst 44, Camb. St. John's F.24, Southwark Roman Catholic See 1 (added), Stonyhurst 40[40]

(LONDON)
Erkenwald (30 Apr.): Stonyhurst 52 (added [also Bodl Lat. lit. e.39 (Chertsey Abbey), which has lost most of the feast-day lecc but retains several sets for the ensuing Octave; Bodl Univ. College 9 (Carm.), printed folio eds. of 1516 and 1531][41]

---

[38] Stowe has just a prayer and rubric for this saint, whose 1320 canonization was still quite recent when the manuscript was produced.

[39] This lectionary also has single lessons to be read after Prime for the following saints: Audoenus (or Ouen) (24 Aug.), Bavo (1 Oct.), Christopher (25 Jul.) [also Aberdeen, on 30 Jul.], Felicitas (23 Nov.), Hermes (28 Aug.), Justus (18 Oct.), Laud (21 Sept.), Menna (11 Nov.), Nichomedis (15 Sept.), Olaf (29 Jul.), Pantaleon (28 Jul.), Potenciana (19 May), Sabina (29 Aug.), William of York (8 June).

[40] Hugh's Translation is also marked with a prayer in Sloane (added) and CUL Dd.x.66; with a prayer, gospel, and homiletic lessons in Cambridge St. John's F.9 (added). Procter and Wordsworth print the lessons for Hugh's Translation from both St. John's manuscripts at the end of vol. 3 of their edition.

[41] E. Gordon Whatley edits and translates the Stonyhurst lessons for Erkenwald's feast-day in *The Saint of London: The Life and Miracles of St. Erkenwald*, MRTS 58 (Binghamton: Medieval and Renaissance Texts and Studies, 1989), 98–99, and includes both those and the more extensive lessons from Chertsey in his magisterial analysis and interpretation of the surviving texts. For Erkenwald's Translation (14 Nov.), the only entry in

(DIOCESE OF SALISBURY)

Osmund (4 Dec.) (lecc + full office): NLW 22253A? (added)[42]

Osmund, Trans. (16 July) (lecc + full office, and usually further lessons for the Octave and weekly commemorations of Osmund): Bodl Lat. Lit. f.29 (added), Salisbury Cathedral 152 (added), Stonyhurst 52 (added) [also some printed editions]; (lecc only): *Auct. E.1.1 (added), Durham Cathedral Chapter A.IV.20

(DIOCESE OF WORCESTER)

Oswald, Bishop (28 Feb.): *Cotton, *Claremont, BL Harley 587, BL Add. 32427, Salisbury 152

Oswald, Bishop, Trans. (8 Oct.): *Cotton, *Claremont (just a one-sentence addition to the Feb. lecc)[43]

Wulfstan (19 Jan.): *Cotton, *Claremont, BL Add. 32427, Salisbury 152, BL Harley 7398B (added) [also Hereford P, Sarum printed editions that include regional feasts, and Sarum MSS from other parts of England (see below)]

Wulfstan, Trans. (7 June): *Cotton, BL Harley 587[44]

B. Apparently non-regional additions to the usual Sarum Sanctorale[45]

Alphege (19 Apr.) [proper lecc]: *Cotton, *Exeter, *Sloane, *Salisbury 224, *Edinburgh 26, *Gonville, *Auct. E.1.1, *Frankfurt, Royal, St. John's H.13 [also Battle Abbey]

---

the surviving Sarum manuscripts is a fragmentary one in Cambridge, Fitzwilliam McClean 65; too little remains to be sure it ever included proper lessons.

[42] Although Osmund's December feast-day was officially added to the Sarum calendar shortly after his canonization in 1456 and duly marked with a rubric and a prayer in many manuscripts, further proper texts for this feast were apparently never mandated, since they occur rarely, if ever, in the surviving MSS and printed editions. Even the office and lessons added near the end of NLW 22253A, which bear the heading of the December feast, "In deposicione S. Osmundi," may just be a mistitled set of the relatively common texts for Osmund's Translation (a synodal feast linked specifically to Salisbury).

[43] Oswald's Translation is marked with a prayer, but no lecc, in BL Add. 32427, Salisbury 152, and a small manuscript in the Bedford Museum called the Shillington Portiforium; with calendar entries only in BL Harley 587, BL Harley 7398B, and a few other manuscripts.

[44] Wulfstan's Translation is also marked with prayers but no lecc in *Claremont, BL Add. 32427, Salisbury 152, Harley 7398B (added), and Bodl Lat. Lit. f.29.

[45] For the many feasts listed below that normally appear in some form (usually, just a rubric and a prayer) in the Sarum Sanctorale, the table specifies the kinds of texts unexpectedly added in these particular MSS.

Anne (26 July) [early, pre-Sarum texts] (lecc + full office): *Stowe, *Edinburgh 26 [also Bodl Rawl. C.489 (monastic), Bodl Univ. College 9 (English Carm.), Hereford P and W, and some French manuscripts][46]

Arnulf (18 Jul.) [proper lecc]: *Stowe, *Cotton, *Exeter, Royal

Basil (14 June) [proper lecc]: *Stowe, *Cotton, *Exeter, *Sloane, *Salisbury 224, *Gonville, *Auct. E.1.1, Royal, St. John's H.13 [also York P, Battle Abbey]

Bathilde (30 Jan.) [proper lecc]: *Stowe, *Cotton, *Exeter, *Sloane, *Salisbury 224, *Gonville, *Auct. E.1.1, *Claremont, Royal, CUL Add. 3208 [also York P]

Bridget of Sweden (8 Oct.): BL Royal 2.A.XIV (added)

Bridget of Sweden, Trans. (28? May): BL Royal 2.A.XIV (added)

Boniface (5 June) [proper lecc]: *Cotton, *Exeter, *Gonville, *Auct. E.1.1, *Bodl Rawl. C.73 (13th c. part), St. John's H.13 [also York P]

Botulf (17 June): *Stowe, *Sloane [also York P; and an *incipit* in BL Add 28,598]

Chad (2 Mar.) [early]: *Cotton

Conception of the Virgin (8 Dec.) [early texts, predating "modern Sarum" reuse of texts from her Nativity for this feast] (lecc + full office): *Stowe, *Sloane, *Edinburgh 26, *Gonville, *Edinburgh 27, *Frankfurt, *Liverpool, *Longleat; (lecc only): *Cotton, *Exeter, *Bodl Rawl. C.73 (14th-c. part), Harley 587 [also Hereford P, some York MSS, Aberdeen, Bute, TCD 86 (Irish Carm.), Bodl Barlow 41 (monastic), and (without the lessons) *Paris BN latin 12036, *CUL Add. 2602, *BL Add. 28,598, *Cambridge St. John's D.21 (Aug.)]

Cuthbert (20 Mar.) [full office, no lecc]: *BN latin 12036

Cuthbert, Trans. (4 Sept.) [proper lecc]: *Exeter, *Edinburgh 26, *Gonville, *Auct. E.1.1, Royal [also Bute, York P][47]

Cuthburga (31 Aug.) [proper lecc]: *Exeter, Royal

David of Wales (1 Mar.)[early]: See above, under Exeter

Dominic (4 or 5 Aug.): See above, under East Anglia

Edmund of Abingdon, Archbishop of Cant. (16 Nov.) [full office besides the usual lecc]: *Stowe, *Sloane, *Gonville, *Salisbury 224, *Edinburgh 27, *BL Add. 52,359, *Stonyhurst 44 (which also gives the office in connection with his Translation, in June) [also *CUL Add. 2602 (antiphonal, no lecc), Bute]

---

[46] On this office and some of the related lessons, see Sherry L. Reames, "Origins and Affiliations of the Pre-Sarum Office for Anne in the Stowe Breviary," in *Music and Medieval Manuscripts: Paleography and Performance*, ed. John Haines and Randall Rosenfeld (Aldershot: Ashgate, 2004), 349–68.

[47] Three additional Sarum manuscripts– *Clare, *Stonyhurst 44, and Laud Misc. 299 — provide lecc for Cuthbert on the Translation date, but they seem just to be repeating the lecc for his other feast.

Edmund of Abingdon, Trans. (9 June) [proper lecc]: *Stowe, *Exeter, *Sloane, *Stonyhurst 44 (+ full office — see previous entry), BL Add. 32427, Salisbury 152 [also Hereford P]

Edmund, King and Martyr (20 Nov.) [full office besides the usual lecc]: *Stowe, *Sloane, *Salisbury 224, *Gonville [also Sarum and English Aug. antiphonals (no lessons): *Paris BN latin 12036, *Cambridge St. John's D.21, *CUL Add. 2602, *CUL Add. Mm.2.9][48]

Edward, King and Martyr, Trans. (20 June) [proper lecc]: *Stowe, *Exeter, *Morgan, Bodl Can. lit. 215 (cancelled by rubricator) [also entries for this date that just repeat the lecc from his other feast in 3 Sarum MSS: *Clare, *Stonyhurst 44, Helmingham]

Egidius or Giles (1 Sept.) [full office besides the usual lecc]: *Gonville [also Bodl. Lat. lit. c.36, Bodl. Lat. lit. b.7 (fragment, with music), some French breviaries]

Etheldreda: See above, under East Anglia

Eufemia and companions (16 Sept.) [proper lecc]: *Stowe, *Cotton, *Exeter, *Gonville, *Auct. E.1.1, Royal [also York P]

Francis (4 Oct.): See above, under East Anglia and Exeter

Gereon and companions (10 Oct.) [proper lecc]: *Cotton, *Exeter

John of Bridlington (21 Oct.): CUL Add. 4500 (lecc + full office, added at fols. 334–338)

Leonard (6 Nov.) [full office besides the usual lecc]: NLW 22423A[49]

Leonard, Trans. (19? Jun.):[50] NLW 22423A

Linus (26 Nov.) [proper lecc]: *Stowe, *Cotton, *Exeter, *Gonville, Can. lit. 215 [also York P]

Marcus and companions (7 Oct.)[proper lecc]: *Stowe, *Cotton, *Exeter (with a separate lesson for Marcellus and Apuleius and one for Sergius and Bacchus), Royal [also York P]

Margaret (20 July) [full office besides the usual lecc]: *Stowe,*Sloane, *Gonville, *Frankfurt [same office in *CUL Add. 2602, *BL Add. 28,598 (both antiphonals — no lecc), TCD 86 (Carm., Ireland)]

Melor or Mylor (1 Oct.) [proper lecc]: *Stowe, *Cotton, *Exeter, *Salisbury 224, *Auct. E.1.1 [also Bute]

---

[48] W. H. Frere published a facsimile of this manuscript in *Antiphonale Sarisburiense*, 6 vols. (London: Plainsong and Mediaeval Music Society, 1901–1925).

[49] This incomplete breviary was formerly at Hornby, where Ker described it as MS 1 (*Medieval Manuscripts in British Libraries*, 2: 986–87). Although it was evidently produced for a church dedicated to Leonard, further identification is difficult because the manuscript has only a partial Sanctorale and no calendar.

[50] Although Leonard is known to have been translated several times, the placement of his Translation feast in this manuscript does not coincide with any of the dates mentioned in standard sources.

Nicholas, Trans. (9 May): *Auct. E.1.1, Trinity, BL Add. 59862 (added, and followed by Mass texts for this feast), Bodl Laud Misc. 299 (added) [also Aberdeen, Battle Abbey]

Nicomedes (1 June) [proper lecc]: *Stowe, *Cotton,*Exeter, *BL Add. 52,359, *Auct. E.1.1, Royal, St. John's H.13, BL Add. 32427, Salisbury 152 [also York P]

Prisca (18 Jan.) [proper lecc]: *Stowe, *Exeter, *Bodl Rawl. C.73 (14th-c. part), *Auct. E.1.1, *NLS Advocates 18.2.13.B (where the lecc may be homiletic rather than hagiographic), BL Add. 32427, Salisbury 152 [also Aberdeen, Bodl Univ. College 9 (Carm.), Hereford P, York P]

Priscus (1 Sept.) [proper lecc]: *Exeter, *Auct. E.1.1 [also an *incipit* in *Longleat]

Remigius (Remi), Germanus, Vedast (Vaast) (1 Oct.) [proper lecc]: *Stowe (Remi), *Cotton (starts with Germanus), *Exeter (Remi, then separate labelled lecc for Germanus and Vedastus), *Salisbury 224 (Remi), *Gonville (starts with Germanus), *Auct. E.1.1 (Trans. Remi) [also Bute, York P (Trans. Germanus?), Battle Abbey (Trans. Remi)]

Richard of Chichester (2 Apr.) [proper lecc]: *Cotton, *Exeter, *Sloane, *Salisbury 224, *Auct. E.1.1, Royal, St. John's H.13, NLW 22253A (added), TCD 88 [also Bodl Univ. Coll 9 (Carm.)]

Richard of Chichester, Trans. (16 June) [proper lecc]: Royal (just lecc 8 & 9, and looks like an excerpt from his Life) [also Battle Abbey]

Romanus, bishop of Rouen (23 Oct.) [proper lecc]: *Cotton, *Exeter, *Gonville, *Auct. E.1.1, Royal [also Bute, which looks homiletic, and York P]

Sampson (28 Jul.) [proper lecc]: *Stowe, *Cotton, *Exeter, *Sloane, *Edinburgh 26, *Gonville, *Auct. E.1.1, Royal, St. John's H.13, Harley 7398B [also York P]

Sergius and Bacchus (7 Oct.): *Exeter (lec. 3, following Marcus and companions)

Swithun, Trans. (15 Jul.) [proper lecc]: *Stowe, *Cotton, *Exeter, *Sloane, *Salisbury 224, *Edinburgh 26, *Gonville, *Auct. E.1.1, Royal, St. John's H.13 [also Bute (added), and York P (on 2 July)][51]

Thecla (23 Sept.) [proper lecc]: *Cotton, *Exeter, *Gonville, *Auct. E.1.1 [also Bute, York P]

Thomas Becket, Trans. (7 July) [full office besides the usual lecc]: *Stowe, *Sloane, *Edinburgh 26, *Gonville [also *BL Add. 28,598 (antiphonal, no lecc)][52]

---

[51] The breviaries have a mix of lessons about Swithun's life with those that clearly pertain to his Translation, presumably because his other feast-day on 2 July was generally downgraded in liturgical status, falling as it did during the Octave of Peter and Paul and eventually on the date of the Visitation.

[52] One of these offices (preserved in Stowe and BL Add. 28,598) is edited and reconnected with Cotton's long version of the lessons in Reames, "Reconstructing and Interpreting a Thirteenth-Century Office" (text note 27). For text and discussion of the office in the other three manuscripts, see Kay Brainerd Slocum, *Liturgies in Honour of Thomas Becket* (Toronto: University of Toronto Press, 2004).

Thomas of Hereford (2 Oct.): lecc + full office in *Edinburgh 26 [also Hereford
    W and P]; lecc + noted antiphon in *Salisbury 224; lecc only in Royal,
    *Stonyhurst 44, Southwark Roman Catholic See 1, NLW 21604A (added),
    Durham Cathedral Chapter A.iv.20 [also York P, Manchester Rylands
    354 (Aug.?), and many of the printed Sarum breviaries, although some say
    explicitly that this feast is to be celebrated only in the diocese of Hereford.
    For copies from East Anglia and Exeter, see above.]
Timothy and Apollinaris (23 Aug.) [proper lecc]: *Cotton, *Exeter, Royal
Wenefrede or Winefride (3 Nov.) [full office besides the usual lecc]: Paris BN
    latin 17294, Camb. Fitzwilliam McClean 65, Helmingham
Wulfram (15 Oct.) [proper lecc]: *Stowe, *Cotton, *Exeter, *Salisbury 224, *Edin-
    burgh 26, *Gonville, *Auct. E.1.1, St. John's F.24[53] [also Bute, York P]
Wulfstan (19 Jan.) [proper lecc]: *Stowe, *Exeter, *Sloane, *Salisbury 224,
    *Edinburgh 26, *Longleat, *Morgan, *Bodl Rawl. C.73 (14th-c. part), *Auct.
    E.1.1, NLW 22253A (added), NLW 16147A, TCD 88 [also Hereford P and
    many of the printed Sarum breviaries—and see above, under diocese of
    Worcester]

---

[53] This lectionary manuscript was evidently written for a church dedicated to Wulfram, since it has 9 lecc for this feast day in place of the usual 6 and further lessons for
his Octave.

HISTORICAL STUDIES

PRIESTS AND PASTORAL CARE IN EARLY ANGLO-SAXON ENGLAND[1]

ALAN THACKER

Priests (in Latin *presbyteri*) comprise, it scarcely needs to be said, the second of the major orders of the Christian ministry, ranking immediately below bishops and above deacons. In the primitive church the two most senior grades of the hierarchy were regarded as a single order of presbyter-bishops, a view which still obtained in the early medieval Latin West, despite the increased dignity and authority of bishops in provinces with large dioceses (such as Gaul). That sharing in a single order was reflected in the fact that early medieval Latin authors could designate both priest and bishop by the single term, *sacerdos*.[2] The classic exposition is Isidore's. Priests, he says, are included with bishops among the *sacerdotes* because they offer the holy sacrifice of the mass, but they do not constitute the head of the sacerdotal order, for they cannot ordain or confirm.[3] Isidore's understanding was undoubtedly current in Bede's England. In the *Historia Ecclesiastica* itself the title *sacerdos* is awarded alike to the bishops Aidan, Tuda, and Theodore, to the priest-abbots Adomnan and Eappa, and to the martyr-priests White and Black Hewald.[4] Indeed, when Bede's diocesan Acca wrote formally to him

---

[1] I am very grateful to Catherine Cubitt for letting me consult work in advance of publication, to Andrew Wareham for assistance with recent research on the Durham *Liber Vitae*, and to John Blair and George Hardin Brown for reading and commenting on earlier drafts of this paper.

[2] For the development of the use of *sacerdos* in Gaul, see Robert Godding, *Prêtres en Gaule mérovingienne* (Brussels: Société des Bollandistes, 2001), 171–201.

[3] Isidore, *Etymologiae*, 7.12.20–21, ed. W. M. Lindsay, 2 vols. (Oxford: Oxford University Press, 1911), 1: 300–1: "Presbyteri sacerdotes vocantur, quia sacrum dant, sicut episcopi, qui licet sint sacerdotes, tamen pontificatus apicem non habent; quia nec chrismate frontem signant, nec Paracletum Spiritum dant, quod solis deberi episcopis lectio Actuum apostolorum demonstrat."

[4] Bede, *Historia Ecclesiastica Gentis Anglorum*, ed. B. Colgrave and R. A. B. Mynors, 2nd ed. (Oxford: Clarendon Press, 1991), 3. 17, 27; 4. 14; 5. 8, 10, 21.

The Study of Medieval Manuscripts of England: Festschrift in Honor of Richard W. Pfaff, eds. George Hardin Brown and Linda Ehrsam Voigts, MRTS 384 (Tempe: ACMRS, 2010).   [ISBN 978-0-86698-432-4]

to request a commentary on Luke's gospel (the letter in fact prefaces the ensuing work), he addresses him as "frater et consacerdos, Beda presbyter."[5]

The ambiguity of the word *sacerdos* in early Anglo-Saxon England and its application to men of high status is apparent from its use by Bede's contemporary Aldhelm, in a letter written when he was still abbot of Malmesbury (i.e., before 705). The letter was addressed to King Gerent and all the *sacerdotes* of Dumnonia, evidently envisaged as the local rulers of the church.[6] It is of course possible that in this case (as the most recent translators of the letter have assumed) the word simply means "bishops."[7] But it is perhaps more likely that it was intended to be more inclusive. In the opening sentence, Aldhelm refers to his attendance at a recent episcopal council (*concilium episcoporum*) attended by a great company of *sacerdotes* from all over Britain. We know from other evidence that such councils were attended by bishops and other clergy, principally priests, and so here the word may have been used deliberately to cover both grades.[8] Aldhelm goes on to say that the Dumnonian *sacerdotes* are not in harmony with catholic discipline, that certain *sacerdotes* and *clerici* obstinately refuse to adopt the petrine tonsure. He condemns this on the grounds that St Peter had chosen this distinctive hairstyle to distinguish the *sacerdotes* of the New Testament from those of the Old; here the word clearly means priests. Later he also condemns the *sacerdotes* of Dyfed (*Demetia*) for schismatically refusing to celebrate the sacraments, or even to eat, with catholics. Again, the word may not refer simply to bishops. We know that, like English church councils, those of the Britons, although doubtless convened and presided over by bishops, were afforced with other learned men. Bede, for example, relates that the councils called by Augustine were attended by British *episcopi et doctores*. He also says that these *doctores* came mostly from the monastery of Bangor, a group of whose inmates (those present at the battle of Chester) he later describes as *sacerdotes*.[9] On balance then it seems likely that in the Insular churches, both English and British, the word *sacerdos* was intended to be inclusive and that by implication therefore priests were viewed as participating with bishops in the government of the church. The high status of the priest at this

---

[5] Bede, *In Lucae Evangelium Expositio*, ed. D. Hurst, Corpus Christianorum, Series Latina 120 (Turnhout: Brepols, 1960), 5.

[6] Aldhelm, *Opera Omnia*, ed. R. Ehwald, Monumenta Germaniae Historica, Auctores Antiquissimi 15 (Berlin: Weidmann, 1919), 481–86.

[7] *Aldhelm: The Prose Works*, trans. M. Lapidge and M. Herren (Ipswich: D.S. Brewer, 1979), 155–60.

[8] E.g., the synods of Hertford (672) and Hatfield (679): Bede, *HE*, 4. 5, 17. Indeed Bede refers to the latter as a gathering of *venerabiles sacerdotes doctoresque*, also perhaps deliberately using *sacerdotes* in an inclusive sense.

[9] Bede, *HE*, 2. 2.

time is also perhaps suggested by the death notice of Bede in the *Annales Cambriae* in which his priestly rank is expressly highlighted: *Beda presbiter dormivit.*[10]

As late as the early eleventh century these attitudes remained unchanged: Ælfric follows Isidore and expressly states that bishops and priests have one and the same order, although the bishop stood higher.[11] In England, as elsewhere, that superiority was expressed in the reservation of certain functions to the bishop alone. Only he could ordain priests and deacons or confirm the recently baptized, and only he could consecrate churches. The nature of the priests' role, at once co-responsible and subordinate, is expressed in their prominence in the episcopal household, and in their performance of pastoral duties alongside the bishop when he travelled around his diocese. Outside the episcopal *familia*, they discharged their pastoral duties in locations assigned to them by bishops, and, if strange or itinerant, could exercise their office only with the local diocesan's permission.[12]

Any assessment of the priest's role in early Anglo-Saxon England has to take account of the authority of English bishops, which was far less assured than that of their Gallic counterparts.[13] English bishops were few in number—indeed they almost disappeared in the mid-seventh century—and had very large dioceses to control. As the canons of the 747 Council of Clofesho demonstrate, they lacked the power to regulate in detail the activities of local churches, evident in the conciliar canons of Merovingian Gaul and in Carolingian sources. Instead they had to be content with much vaguer requirements for correct behaviour and moral reform and unspecific penalties for non-compliance.[14] Even in such a crucial matter as retaining episcopal communities and estates under ecclesiastical control, they were dependent upon the cooperation of local priests. Two examples from the diocese of Worcester in the late eighth century illustrate this with special clarity. At Dodswell the priest-abbot Headda left his community

---

[10] "The *Annales Cambriae* and the North Welsh Genealogies from Harleian MS 3859," ed. E. Phillimore, *Y Cymmrodor* 9 (1880): 141–83, at 161.

[11] *Councils and Synods with Other Documents Relating to the English Church* I, ed. D. Whitelock, M. Brett, and C. N. L. Brooke, 2 vols. (Oxford: Oxford University Press, 1981), 1: 205, 283.

[12] Council of Clofesho, canon 9, in *Councils and Ecclesiastical Documents Relating to Great Britain and Northern Ireland*, ed. A. W. Haddan and W. Stubbs, 3 vols. (Oxford: Oxford University Press, 1871–1878), 3: 365–66; Ecgberht, *Dialogus* 9, in *Councils and Ecclesiastical Documents*, 3: 407; for their accompanying bishops see below, 196–97, 199, 200.

[13] A.T. Thacker, "Monks, Preaching and Pastoral Care in Early Anglo-Saxon England," in *Pastoral Care Before the Parish*, ed. J. Blair and R. Sharpe (Leicester: Leicester University Press, 1992), 137–70, at 149. For a much fuller discussion, the basis of the following paragraph, see now J. Blair, *The Church in Anglo-Saxon Society* (Oxford: Oxford University Press, 2005), 108–18.

[14] Godding, *Prêtres*, 240–60; Blair, *Church in Anglo-Saxon Society*, 114–15. For discussion of the regulation of priests in the 747 Council of Clofesho see below, 199–205.

and its estates to his descendants on condition that his heirs should be in priestly orders (*in ecclesiastico gradu*). At Old Sodbury Bishop Milred granted an estate to his priest Eanbald to establish a community which was similarly to remain in his family as long as it contained a member in holy orders (*godcundes hades*). Priests in such institutions may have had considerable independence of action.[15] It was not until the Council of Chelsea in 816 that the English episcopate made a really determined attempt to tackle these issues.[16]

Closely associated with the episcopate and the priesthood was the diaconate, the third of the major grades of the church. Deacons had important administrative and preaching functions, but—crucially—could not offer the sacrifice of the mass, and in seventh-century England were also forbidden to administer penance to the laity.[17] Relatively few chose to remain permanently in the diaconal grade without proceeding to the priesthood, although the select number who did included such celebrated figures as James the deacon, Paulinus's assistant at York, Sigefrith, abbot of Wearmouth, and, of course, Alcuin.[18] Like priests, they accompanied and assisted early English bishops in their pastoral journeys around their dioceses.[19]

The three grades were united in the requirement of celibacy which the church authorities sought to impose upon them. Even if married, at ordination they were supposed thereafter to remain chaste. If unmarried, they were not to take wives.[20] That undoubtedly was the position of Bede.[21] Almost certainly,

---

[15] P. H. Sawyer, *Anglo-Saxon Charters: An Annotated Bibliography* (London: Royal Historical Society, 1968); rev. version, *The Electronic Sawyer*, ed. S. Kelly and adapted for the Worldwide Web by S. M. Miller, nos. 1413, 1446. Discussed by P. Sims-Williams, *Religion and Literature in Western England, 600–800* (Cambridge: Cambridge University Press, 1990), 155–57; Blair, *Church in Anglo-Saxon Society*, 93–94, 114–15.

[16] *Councils and Ecclesiastical Documents*, 3: 579–84; Catherine Cubitt, *Anglo-Saxon Church Councils, c. 650- c. 850* (London: Leicester University Press, 1995), 191–203; Blair, *Church in Anglo-Saxon Society*, 123.

[17] Theodore, *Poenitentiale*, 12. ii, in *Die Canones Theodori Cantuariensis und ihre Überlieferungsformen*, ed. P. W. Finsterwalder (Weimar: Böhlau, 1929), 1: 313–14.

[18] Bede, *HE* 2. 16, 20; 3. 25; *Historia Abbatum*, caps. 10, 11, 12, in *Baedae Opera Historica*, ed. C. Plummer, 2 vols. (Oxford: Oxford University Press, 1896), 1: 364–87, at 374, 376; D. Bullough, *Alcuin: Achievement and Reputation* (Leiden: Brill, 2004), 306–8.

[19] E.g., Berhthun, deacon of John of Beverley, bishop of York: Bede, *HE* 5.2; and see below, 196–97. Cf. Bullough, *Alcuin*, 307–8.

[20] Theodore, *Poenitentiale*, 1. ix.4, in *Canones Theodori*, 302. For the wider picture see Godding, *Prêtres*, 111–54.

[21] Bede, *De Tabernaculo*, ed. D. Hurst, Corpus Christianorum, Series Latina 119A (Turnhout: Brepols, 1969), 121, quoted and discussed by Catherine Cubitt, "Clergy in Early Anglo-Saxon England," *Historical Research* 78 (2005): 273–87, at 284–85. For the continence expected of deacons see Bede, *In Ezram et Neemiam*, ed. D. Hurst, Corpus Christianorum, Series Latina 119A (Turnhout: Brepols, 1969), 262.

however, as Catherine Cubitt has pointed out, such ideals were not altogether enforceable. Judgements in Theodore's penitential, for example, probably reflect the difficulty of enforcing sexual abstinence on married priests.[22]

Below these senior grades lay a whole range of lesser ranks, descending from subdeacon to acolytes (assistants at mass and other liturgical ceremonies), lectors (those authorized to read texts other than the Gospel at mass), and, at the bottom, doorkeepers. Again Isidore provides the classic statement.[23] He was broadly followed in the Latin texts of the early Anglo-Saxon church which alluded to various clerical grades below bishop, priest, and deacon generically as "clerks" (*clerici*). Bede, following Gregory the Great, certainly uses *clericus* in this sense.[24] A similar application of the word to those in minor orders is also to be found in the Durham *Liber Vitae*. This book, which lists associates of a Northumbrian community (probably Wearmouth-Jarrow or Lindisfarne) for commemoration in its prayers, divided the names of those to be so remembered into various categories, distinguishing the relatively few priests and deacons from the much more plentiful *clerici* and *monachi*. Although in their present form the lists date from the earlier ninth century, they reflect a long process of collation and organization beginning perhaps in the late seventh. The arrangement into separate lists of *ordines* may go back to the earliest stratum of the text.[25]

As with *sacerdos*, however, there was ambiguity in the use of the term *clericus*. Besides defining those in minor orders, it could also be used in an inclusive sense. In the eighth-century *Dialogues* of the Northumbrian archbishop Ecgberht, for example, it was used as a generic term, covering bishops, priests, and deacons.[26] Although in the *Historia Ecclesiastica* Bede does not use the word *clericus* thus, he did use a related word, *clerus*, to apply to all the clergy of an episcopal household, including priests.[27] These ambiguities are particularly apparent in the penitential ascribed to Archbishop Ecgberht. Although the authorship of this work

---

[22] Cubitt, "Clergy in Early Anglo-Saxon England," 285.

[23] Isidore, *Etymologiae*, 7. 12.3–4 ed. Lindsay, 1:299.

[24] For Gregory see his reference to "clerici extra sacros ordines constituti" in the *Libellus Responsionum*: Bede, *HE* 1.27 (80). For Bede's own usage, "veniente in villam clerico vel presbytero," see *Vita Sancti Cuthberti prosaica*, cap. 9, in *Two Lives of Saint Cuthbert*, ed. B. Colgrave (Cambridge: Cambridge University Press, 1940); *HE* 4.27.

[25] For recent studies see Jan Gerchow, "The Origins of the Durham *Liber* Vitae," and E. Briggs, "Nothing but Names: The Original Core of the Durham *Liber Vitae*," in *The Durham Liber Vitae and its Context*, ed. D. W. Rollason, A. J. Piper, Margaret Harvey, and Linda Rollason (Woodbridge: Boydell Press, 2004), 45–61, 63–85 respectively.

[26] Ecgberht, *Dialogus*, XII, in *Councils and Ecclesiastical Documents*, 3: 408–9. Accepted as authentic by H. M. Mayr-Harting, "Ecgberht," *Oxford Dictionary of National Biography* (Oxford: Oxford University Press, 2004), 17: 635–36, and Bullough, *Alcuin*, 135, 138, 142, etc.

[27] E.g., Bede, *HE* 3. 29 where he refers to "presbyterum nomine Vighardum, de clero Deusdedit episcopi."

is controversial, and many scholars—most recently R. Haggenmüller—would place its composition in Carolingian Frankia, some of the text may be reasonably regarded as originating in eighth-century England.[28] The fact that the earliest manuscript, written at Lorsch in the late eighth century, names Ecgberht as the author is hard to account for unless there was some existing tradition linking him with the text.[29] Most plausibly, perhaps, we may postulate a text emanating from the archbishop and his circle but thereafter much adapted in Carolingian milieux.[30] If so, it is generally accepted that the prologue and the early chapters are those most likely to be of English provenance.[31] In the prologue, *clericus* appears alongside monk and layman—evidently as one of the conditions of man—rather than among the ecclesiastical grades, where bishop, priest, deacon, and subdeacon are followed by lector.[32] In chapters one and two, by contrast, *clericus* is clearly used to cover all minor grades below the office of subdeacon.[33] In chapter five, in yet another variation of usage, it refers to the whole body of ecclesiastics (including monks).[34] These uncertainties may stem from the complex origins of the text. Equally, however, they may reflect imprecision in the Latin terminology of the early English church.

Similar ambiguities in terminology are also apparent in the vernacular sources. Like *clericus*, the word *preost* could cover any member of the ecclesiastical profession. The equivalent of *sacerdos* or *presbyter* was *maesse-preost*, "mass-priest."[35] That

[28] R. Haggenmüller, *Die Überlieferung der Beda und Ecgberht zugeschriebenen Bussbücher*, Europäischen Hochschulschriften 461 (Frankfurt am Main: P. Lang, 1991).

[29] Vatican City, Bibliotheca Apostolica Vaticana, MS. Pal. Lat. 554; A. J. Frantzen, "The Penitentials Attributed to Bede," *Speculum* 58 (1983): 573–97, at 576.

[30] Mayr-Harting, "Ecgberht," 636; cf. Bullough, *Alcuin*, 234–36; R. Meens, "The Frequency and Nature of Early Medieval Penance," in *Handling Sin: Confession in the Middle Ages*, ed. P. Biller and A. J. Minnis, York Studies in Medieval Theology 2 (Woodbridge: Boydell and Brewer, 1998), 35–61, at 52, n. 77 (quoted by Bullough *Alcuin*, 236).

[31] Mayr-Harting, "Ecgberht," 636; Bullough, *Alcuin*, 174; C. Vogel, *Les "Libri Paenitentiales,"* Typologie des Sources du Moyen Âge Occidental 27 (Turnhout: Brepols, 1978), 71.

[32] *Councils and Ecclesiastical Documents*, 3: 417. In Alcuin's day at least *lector* seems to have been in England the best-known and most widely used title from among the minor grades: Bullough, *Alcuin*, 174–76.

[33] *Councils and Ecclesiastical Documents*, 3: 418–19.

[34] *Councils and Ecclesiastical Documents*, 3: 421–22.

[35] C.N.L. Brooke, "Priest, Deacon and Layman from St Peter Damian to St Francis," in *The Ministry: Clerical and Lay*, ed. W. J. Sheils and D. Wood, Studies in Church History 26 (Oxford: Blackwell, 1989), 65–85, at 72; J. Bosworth and T. Toller, *Anglo-Saxon Dictionary* (Oxford: Oxford University Press, 1898), s.v. "maesse-preost," "preost." Cf., for example, Laws of Edward and Guthrum, 3, in *Laws of the Earliest Anglo-Saxon Kings*, ed. F. L. Attenborough (Cambridge: Cambridge University Press, 1922), 102–4; *Councils and Synods*, 1: i, 204–5.

this distinction was early is apparent from a charter of 824 recording the witnesses to an oath taken at Westbury-on-Trym in Gloucestershire, which refers to
(and names) those who were mass-priests and distinguishes them from all other
preostas, that is deacons, subdeacons, and the like.[36] All this suggests that care is
required when looking for priests (i.e., mass-priests) in both the Latin and the
vernacular sources.

In ecclesiastical terms, then, priests were of high status in the early medieval
church. They alone shared with the bishop the right to celebrate mass, the central
Christian sacrament. To them too (with the bishops) was reserved in normal circumstances the right to administer baptism, the Christian rite of initiation. Their
oaths carried more weight than those of men in lesser orders; their testimony
had special authority in the oral dispositions of the dying; the penances imposed
upon them, when they lapsed into sin, were more severe.[37] Some at least of their
number were also expected to attend ecclesiastical synods and councils and share
in the governance of the church with their bishops.

Although ecclesiastical and social status need not necessarily coincide, there
is some evidence that, in the case of priests in early Anglo-Saxon England, it did.
In the *Dialogues* of Archbishop Ecgberht, for example, a blood-price or wergild is
assigned to the main ecclesiastical grades. The standing of a bishop was so great
that his was a matter of negotiation; the priest's, although measurable, was put at
800 *sicli*, almost certainly, as H. M. Chadwick long ago pointed out, the equivalent of that of a nobleman.[38] The priest's relative status within the ecclesiastical
hierarchy may be further assessed by looking at the wergilds or compensatory
payments for other ecclesiastics. In the *Dialogues* of Ecgberht, a deacon's wergild
was also comparatively high—600 *sicli*, the same perhaps as the intermediate
sixhynde men or radmen of the earlier West Saxon laws. A monk's, however, was
only 400 *sicli* (still double that of the ceorl or *twihynde* man).[39] The comparably
high legal status of the priest in the early kingdom of Kent is confirmed by the
compensation exacted for theft of his property. He was to receive ninefold, in
comparison with a bishop who received elevenfold, a deacon (sixfold), and a clerk
(threefold).[40]

---

[36] *The Electronic Sawyer*, no. 1433; *Councils and Ecclesiastical Documents*, 3: 592–4; W.
Davies and P. Fouracre, eds., *The Settlement of Disputes in Early Medieval Europe* (Cambridge: Cambridge University Press, 1986), 262.

[37] Ecgberht, *Dialogus*, 1, 2, in *Councils and Ecclesiastical Documents*, 3: 404; *Poenitentiale*, 5, in *Councils and Ecclesiastical Documents* 3: 421–23.

[38] Ecgberht, *Dialogus*, 12, in *Councils and Ecclesiastical Documents*, 3: 408–9; H. M.
Chadwick, *Studies on Anglo-Saxon Institutions* (Cambridge: Cambridge University Press,
1905), 21, 104.

[39] Ecgberht, *Dialogus*, 12; Chadwick, *Studies*, 87–90, 103–5; Laws of Ine, cap. 70,
in *Laws*, ed. Attenborough, 58.

[40] Laws of Æthelberht, para. 1, in *Laws*, ed. Attenborough, 4.

The sources leave the impression that the status of priests was perhaps highest in the essentially missionary world of the seventh century, when they were few in number and their episcopal masters had yet to consolidate their position.[41] Whereas the Council of Hertford of 672, over which Archbishop Theodore autocratically presided, was especially concerned with the role and authority of bishops, the Council of Clofesho of 747 was much more concerned with priests. By then, bishops, defined as those "promoted to be masters of others" ("praesules qui caeteris magisterii loco a Deo praelati sunt"), were at pains to prohibit priests from performing those rites which pertained to them alone.[42] Further consolidation of episcopal authority, especially over the heads of local religious communities, was enacted in the synod of Chelsea in 816.[43]

Whether the high legal status of early Anglo-Saxon priests was reflected in their social origins is less certain. Undoubtedly, they were often well-born: the narrative sources record numerous instances of priests of noble family, the companions and confidants of kings,[44] while the charters show priests frequently acting as witnesses to royal grants alongside bishops and royal *duces* and *comites*.[45] Another key to status is method of appointment. In Clovis's Gaul, it seems, the permission of king or count was required for all free men seeking to enter the clergy, unless they were of clerical descent. Royal control later slackened, but even in the 620s it was still applied to all who paid the *census publicus*.[46] In England, although kings probably had no such formal role,[47] they could still play an important part in priestly appointments, at least in the seventh century. Wilfrid, for example, was ordained priest at the command of King Alhfrith because Alhfrith wished to have a man of such learning and holy life among his companions

---

[41] Below, 196, 203.

[42] Bede, *HE* 4.5; Council, Preface, canon 12, in *Councils and Ecclesiastical Documents*, 3: 363, 366–67; Cubitt, *Anglo-Saxon Church Councils*, 62–64, 99–124, 249–50, 266–67.

[43] Above, 190.

[44] E.g., Bede, *HE* 3.15 (Utta), 3.23 (Cedd, Cælin, Cynebill, and Chad), 4.22 (Tunna); *Historia Abbatum*, cap. 8 (Eosterwine); *Vita Ceolfridi*, caps. 3–4, in *Baedae Opera Historica*, ed. Plummer, 1: 388–404, at 388–89 (Ceolfrith); Stephen, *Vita Sancti Wilfridi*, *The Life of Bishop Wilfrid by Eddius Stephanus*, ed. B. Colgrave (Cambridge: Cambridge University Press, 1927), caps. 2, 63 (Wilfrid, Tatberht).

[45] E.g., *The Electronic Sawyer*, nos. 28, 33, 35, 55, 235, 262, 1164, 1171, 1256. For the texts (in electronic versions) see *New Regesta Regum Anglorum*, devised by Sean Miller.

[46] Godding, *Prêtres*, 14–23; *Les canons des conciles mérovingiens (VIe-VIIe siècle)*, ed. J. Gaudemet and B. Basdevant-Gaudemet, Sources Chrétiennes 353–354 (Paris: Cerf, 1989), 74, 532.

[47] Wilfrid, for example, chooses and ordains Ceolfrith at Ripon, without reference it seems to the king, even though Ceolfrith was probably a royal kinsman; *Vita Ceolfridi*, cap. 3 ("a praefato episcopo . . . electus et ordinatus est").

to act as his *sacerdos et doctor.*[48] King Oethelwald of Deira may well have played a similar role in the elevation of Cælin and his brothers.[49] It may be that at York Alcuin's failure to proceed from the diaconate to which he was ordained in the 760s owes something to his non-noble origins.[50]

High status, whether determined by social origins or rank within the church, did not of course necessarily imply high standards of behaviour or even of learning. The *sacerdotes idioti*, for whom Bede had translated the Lord's Prayer and the creed, need not be regarded as men of low birth. Nor should failure to espouse the "fastidious, metropolitan, temperamentally *dirigiste*" values of the likes of Bede, Boniface, and Alcuin be similarly interpreted.[51] Bede, after all, in a moment of unusual indiscretion, famously castigated members of the household of his own bishop Wilfrid—hardly likely to be plebeian—as drunken boors.[52] Indeed, it seems inherently plausible that noblemen in particular might come from a cultural background which would predispose them to actions viewed as reprehensible by high-minded ecclesiastics—such as feasting and heavy drinking or the recitation of the liturgy in the manner of pagan bards.[53]

To set against this, there are some hints that while high social status may have been the expected norm, that norm was not always observed. The anxiety expressed in Ecgberht's *Dialogues,* for example, that *clerici* (used here in an inclusive sense) should not be of servile condition, suggests that at least a few priests may not have been socially grand.[54] Servile status of course need not imply the world of the labouring peasant. We might well suspect that noblemen had household slaves ordained to serve as compliant household priests, a phenomenon which almost certainly would have elicited clerical disapproval.[55] The most suggestive

---

[48] Bede, *HE* 5.19; Stephen, *Vita Wilfridi*, cap. 9.

[49] Bede, *HE* 3.23.

[50] Bullough, *Alcuin*, 30–33, 164–65, 306–7.

[51] Blair, *Church in Anglo-Saxon Society*, 179.

[52] Bede, *Epistola ad Pleguuinam*, in *Baedae Opera de Temporibus*, ed. C.W. Jones (Cambridge, MA: Mediaeval Academy of America, 1943), 307–15, at 307, 315.

[53] See e.g., Laws of Wihtred, cap. 6, in *Laws*, ed. Attenborough, 26/7; Council of Clofesho, canons 12, 21, in *Councils and Ecclesiastical Documents*, 3: 366–67, 369.

[54] Ecgberht, *Dialogus*, 14, in *Councils and Ecclesiastical Documents*, 3: 409–10: "Responsio: Quisquis vero secularis servitium sanctae professionis subire desiderat, si interrogatus respondeat, conditionis servilis sese non esse obnoxium. . . ." Justinian's *Novella* 123.17 disapproves of the ordination of slaves but does allow for the possibility (cf. also *Nov.* 5.2–3). See *Corpus iuris civilis*, vol. 3: *Novellae*, ed. R. Schoell and W. Kroll (Dublin/ Zürich: Weidmann, 1968), 29–32, 607–8.

[55] For the prohibition of clerical residence in lay households see Council of Clofesho, canon 29, in *Councils and Ecclesiastical Documents*, 3: 374–75. Cf. Godding, *Prêtres*, 3–5 for a different view of things in Frankia. Godding notes that the hagiographical sources generally stress the noble origins of Merovingian priests, but points out that they are mainly concerned with exceptional figures, for whom the priesthood was simply a

indicator that, nevertheless, there were rural priests of relatively modest status comes perhaps from the laws of Ine, which envisage a penalty for a priest who worked on a Sunday (the fine was to be twice that paid by a freeman).[56] Here the example of ninth-century Brittany is perhaps relevant. As Wendy Davies has shown, Breton villages might include small groups of priests, perhaps living communally in a *domus presbyteri*, who were not aristocratic but drawn from the *plebes*. Nevertheless, such figures had "very special functions" and relatively high standing. They were the serf-owning members of a local elite. In such a world the role of priest might confer status not only on the priests themselves but on their families as well.[57]

Intimately related to the question of status is the matter of numbers. How many priests were there in pre-Viking England? Although this, of course, is largely unanswerable, there are a few indications that — as might indeed be expected — they were not very numerous, especially in the first century or so after the Roman mission. One pointer is the care which the narrative sources take to note priestly rank, wherever possible.[58] Another is the fact that when priests are listed as present at church councils or as attesting royal or ecclesiastical grants, they are relatively few in number. In Kent, where they occur most frequently and most prolifically as witnesses to charters, we find that the archbishop's entourage seems never to have risen much above a handful of abbots and nine or ten priests.[59] That may well have been the maximum number of priests accompanying any bishop in early Anglo-Saxon England. Early ninth-century sources, some of which record attendance at church councils in exceptional detail, may confirm this.

In 803, for example, seventy-eight abbots, priests, and deacons attended the important council held during the week beginning 6 October at Clofesho, at which Lichfield's metropolitan status was suppressed, lay lordship of monasteries abolished, and a dispute between the bishops of Hereford and Worcester settled. The witness list records each bishop with leading members of his entourage. The archbishop of Canterbury, Æthelheard, was accompanied by his archdeacon Wulfred (who succeeded him), by the priest-abbot Feologeld (who succeeded Wulfred), by an otherwise unknown abbot named Æthelheah, and

---

stage on the way to an episcopal see or an abbacy. He argues that the ordination of former slaves, condemned but not actually outlawed by the councils, is an indication that "il n'y avait pas barrière sociale pour accéder à la cléricature." He speculates, therefore, "un grand nombre" were of modest origins, but concedes that the evidence does not permit systematic analysis.

[56] Laws of Ine, cap. 3 par. 2, in *Laws*, ed. Attenborough, 36.

[57] W. Davies, *Small Worlds* (London: Duckworth, 1988), 100–2.

[58] E.g., Felix, *Vita S. Guthlaci*, ed. B. Colgrave (Cambridge: Cambridge University Press, 1956), cap. 47; Bede's death notice in the *Annales Cambriae*; see 189 above.

[59] E.g., *The Electronic Sawyer*, no. 22; Cubitt, *Councils*, 264.

by the priests Beornmod (later bishop of Rochester), Wernoth (later abbot of SS Peter and Paul), and the unidentified Wulfheard. Aldwulf, the new incumbent of the humbled bishopric of Lichfield, was accompanied by his retired predecessor Hygeberht, designated simply "abbot," and by five priests. Similar numbers of abbots, priest-abbots, and priests, and in one or two instances the odd deacon, attended other bishops. The maximum was ten (four priest-abbots and six priests) accompanying Wernberht, bishop of Leicester. The minimum was three.[60] Such groups of signatories probably represent the norm for an episcopal entourage of this period, as far as ecclesiastics in major orders are concerned.

One exception in the early period may have been Wilfrid, whose biographer, Stephen of Ripon, dwells on the countless number of his followers and repeatedly alludes to his magnificent entourage.[61] We know, too, that Wilfrid attended the synod of Austerfield in 703 accompanied by his abbots, priests, and deacons.[62] But even Wilfrid's intimate circle may not have been so very large. When he lay dying at Ripon in 708, like the good lord that he was, he made provision for his followers from his store of treasure. Those before whom these important arrangements were made, and the gold and precious jewels displayed, numbered no more than ten: two abbots and eight faithful brethren, at least two of whom were certainly priests and one of whom was a *magister*, presumably a *clericus*.[63]

One indication of absolute numbers may be provided by the settlement in 824 of a dispute between the bishop of Worcester and the monastery (*familia*) of Berkeley (Glos.) over the monastery of Westbury-on-Trim. The settlement itself was made at a synod held at Clofesho and attended *inter alia* by the Mercian king, Beornwulf, Archbishop Wulfred of Canterbury, ten bishops of the southern province, nine ealdormen, and a papal envoy. It was agreed that the bishop was to swear the land into his own possession with an oath of the servants of God, priests, deacons, and many monks. A note in Old English included in the record of the transaction records that this later assembly, held at Westbury itself, comprised "as many as" fifty mass-priests and 180 other priests, i.e., *clerici*. A further note in Old English introduces the names of the mass-priests (forty-seven plus three abbots). Six deacons conclude the list. Clearly this last was an exceptional assembly. It is apparent that the presence of the diocesan priests conferred special validity on the oath, and the numbers — fifty as stated, if we include the three abbots (presumably priest-abbots) — may well be the entire complement for the important diocese of Worcester.[64] If we allow for a significant concentration

[60] *Councils and Ecclesiastical Documents*, 3: 541–47; Cubitt, *Councils*, 279–80.

[61] E.g., *Vita Wilfridi*, caps. 24–25; cf. the reference to abbots and priests, cap. 49.

[62] *Vita Wilfridi*, cap. 53.

[63] *Vita Wilfridi*, caps. 63–64.

[64] *Councils and Ecclesiastical Documents*, 3: 592–94; B.L. MS. Cotton Tiberius A. 13, fol. 47; Patrick Wormald, "Charters, Law and the Settlement of Disputes in Anglo-Saxon England," in *Settlement of Disputes*, ed. Davies and Fouracre, 149–68, at 152–57.

at major centres such as Worcester itself, the principal episcopal minsters, such as Fladbury, Evesham, and Berkeley, and the outstanding dynastic centres, such as Gloucester and Winchcombe, it will be seen that even as late as the early ninth century there would have been relatively few priests elsewhere. That, of course, has considerable implications for the nature and quality of pastoral care in early Anglo-Saxon England.

The Durham *Liber Vitae* also suggests that priests may not have been particularly numerous in early Anglo-Saxon England. Over the century and half of the period spanned by the earliest strand of names, that is from the late seventh century to the early ninth, abbots, including those in priestly and diaconal orders, number some 180, priests (including 68 priest-abbots) 440, and deacons (including nine deacon-abbots) 49. The lesser orders are much more plentiful—some 1175 *clerici* and 1030 *monachi*. Bishops, oddly, are not included, perhaps because the list has been lost.[65] It is worth comparing the pattern suggested by the figures for the Worcester diocese with Godding's estimates for the numbers of priests in the dioceses of Merovingian Francia. He puts the number of parishes in dioceses such as Tours and Auxerre at about 35–37 at the end of the sixth century. A large diocese such as Limoges might have 50 rural parishes. For Bourges he estimates that there may have been perhaps 130 churches altogether including parish churches, oratories, and monasteries.[66] Clearly these figures suggest (as we would expect in a country where Christianity had been well established since the fourth century) rather larger numbers than those gathering at Westbury in 824. But they are not wildly dissimilar.

Where were priests to be found? The sources suggest that they were mostly located in communities. We know that they were members of grand households, both ecclesiastical and lay, that they might travel with their lords and be sent by them on important missions. Bede, for example, relates that Utta, an "illustrious priest," honoured by secular rulers for his wisdom and probity and later abbot of Gateshead, was sent to Kent to conduct King Edwin's daughter Eanfled to Northumbria to become his successor Oswiu's queen.[67] In royal households, priests acted as chaplains, administering the sacraments in palace chapels and,

---

[65] *Liber Vitae Ecclesiae Dunelmensis*, ed. J. Stevenson, Surtees Society 13 (London: J. B. Nichols and Son, 1841); *Liber Vitae Ecclesiae Dunelmensis: A Collotype Facsimile of the Original Manuscript*, ed. A. Hamilton Thompson, Surtees Society 136 (London: Quaritch, 1923). The figures are based on the text as presented by D. Dumville and P. Stokes, "Liber Vitae Dunelmensis, BL MS Cotton Domitian A. vii" (trial version, Dept. of Anglo-Saxon, Norse and Celtic, University of Cambridge, 2001). I am grateful to Andrew Wareham for supplying me with this text.

[66] Godding, *Prêtres*, 240–43.

[67] Bede, *HE* 3.15, 21.

where appropriate (as at Bamburgh), looking after royal relics.[68] Probably, as in Frankia, certain great men may also have had priest-chaplains attached to their households. Although we have no secure knowledge of this in the seventh and eighth centuries, the fact that in 747 the Council of Clofesho found it necessary expressly to forbid clergy (*clerici*) to live among laymen in secular households ("apud laicos in domibus saecularium") suggests that this may indeed have been the case.[69] Some nobles certainly had churches on their estates.[70]

Priests were an essential element of episcopal *familiae* and seem invariably to have accompanied bishops whenever they travelled, especially on their journeys through their dioceses, when they might share in such pastoral duties as preaching.[71] Wilfrid, always grand, assigned a priest to his nephew and *clericus* Beornwine, whom he had made lord of a vast estate on the Isle of Wight, to minister word and sacraments to the newly-acquired population.[72] Above all, however, priests were concentrated in the religious communities known as *monasteria*. Canon eight of the Council of Clofesho was couched in terms which suggest that it was the norm for priests to be answerable to an abbot or abbess.[73] Moreover, canons 28 and 29 make it plain that it was also considered the norm for all ecclesiastics—whether *clerici*, monks, or nuns—to live in a community (*congregatio, monasterium*). When, in the passage already noted, the council prohibited *clerici* to live *apud laicos*, it expressly ordered that they should return to *monasteria*.[74]

Since their duties pertained particularly to the altar—to the celebration of mass—and to preaching and administering the sacraments, priests are especially mentioned in connexion with churches, *ecclesiae*.[75] Catherine Cubitt has argued

---

[68] Bede, *HE* 3.6, 23; Alcuin, *Bishops, Kings and Saints of York*, ed. P. Godman (Oxford: Clarendon Press, 1982), 30, lines 308–11.

[69] Council of Clofesho, canon 29, in *Councils and Ecclesiastical Documents*, 3: 374–75. It is not entirely clear what is meant here by *clerici*. Could the fathers of the council have been using it inclusively, rather than as elsewhere in the limited sense of minor orders?

[70] Cf. the churches which Bishop John of Hexham dedicated for the *comites* Puch and Addi. We may note, however, that in the former case the only clergy involved were the bishop, his deacon Berthun, and certain brethren of Hexham. In neither is there any mention of a local priest: Bede, *HE* 5.2, 4, 5. See now Blair, *Church in Anglo-Saxon Society*, 118–21; and S. Wood, *The Proprietary Church in the Medieval West* (Oxford: Oxford University Press, 2006) 26–27, 30 et alibi. Comparanda are found in K. Bowes, "Personal Devotions and Private Chapels," in *Late Ancient Christianity*, ed. V. Burrus (Minneapolis: Fortress Press, 2005), 188–210.

[71] E.g., Bede, *HE* 3. 30; 5: 19; idem, *Vita Cuthberti prosaica*, caps. 15, 29, 33, 35, 36; *Vita Wilfridi*, caps. 56, 63.

[72] Bede, *HE* 4.16.

[73] *Councils and Ecclesiastical Documents*, 3: 365.

[74] Canon 29, in *Councils and Ecclesiastical Documents*, 3: 374–75.

[75] E.g., Bede, *HE* 3. 22; Council of Clofesho, canons 8, 12, 14, in *Councils and Ecclesiastical Documents*, 3: 365–67.

powerfully that in some instances these are to be distinguished institutionally from *monasteria*, that they may indeed be village churches, each with its own priest and pastoral unit.[76] Now it is certainly true, as Cubitt points out, that Bede distinguishes *ecclesiae* from *monasteria*.[77] When he uses *ecclesia* in an institutional sense, he refers to an episcopal church, usually the seat of an episcopal *cathedra*, and the focus of the bishop's clerical *familia*.[78] Thus the *ecclesiae* established by Bishop Cedd in Essex at Bradwell-on-Sea and Tilbury, which Bede expressly says were staffed by priests and deacons, were clearly important episcopal communities.[79]

Elsewhere, however, in the case of village or estate churches, Bede apparently uses the term *ecclesia* to refer to a largely unendowed foundation, in other words one without permanent staff, primarily a building. Thus, in his account of the early days of the Irish mission in Northumbria, he speaks of churches as being "built" (*construebantur*) and distinguishes them from the landed communities (*monasteria*) which were "instituted."[80] No village *ecclesia* in this period is expressly mentioned as having a priest attached to it. While it is certainly true that a bishop such as Aidan maintained a church with a chamber (*cubiculum*) on a small amount of land, on at least one royal estate, there is nothing to suggest that in his day such institutions were staffed except when used as a base for a preaching expedition.[81] It is the view of the present author that the tone of both Bede and the Council of Clofesho suggests that in the seventh and earlier eighth century a permanent staff (apart perhaps from a custodian in minor orders) in such modest establishments would have been highly exceptional. There is certainly nothing to indicate that they provided a permanent station for a priest. In Bede's day when bishops went out to their dioceses to preach and administer the sacraments they seem to have been accompanied by priests from their household and not to have engaged with a locally based clergy.[82]

Another form of ecclesiastical site, the oratory (*oratorium*), offers a significant parallel. Although Bede generally uses this term to denote lesser churches or chapels in monasteries or cathedral complexes,[83] he sometimes employs it in other senses. For example, the buildings (*domus*) of Cuthbert's *mansio* on Farne include an *oratorium* and a dwelling space (*habitaculum commune*).[84] Oratories are also set beside baptisteries as places where the sacrament of baptism could be

---

[76] Cubitt, "Clergy in Early Anglo-Saxon England," 278–81.

[77] E.g., *HE* 3.23, 26; 5. 11.

[78] E.g., *HE* 2.3; 3. 22, 25; 4.2, 12; 5. 23.

[79] Bede, *HE* 3. 22.

[80] Bede, *HE* 3. 3.

[81] Bede, *HE* 3.17. The church in question later became a cult site and presumably then had permanent custodians.

[82] Above, 199.

[83] E.g., Bede, *HE* 4.3, 7, 14; *Historia Abbatum*, cap. 17.

[84] Bede, *HE* 4.28; cf. *Vita Cuthberti prosaica*, cap. 18.

administered.[85] Most interestingly, in the story of Dryhthelm's return from the dead, the protagonist is made to go at dawn to pray in a village oratory (*oratorium villulae*) in the Northumbrian district (*regio*) of *Incuneningum*. This is clearly in some sense a public building, but again there is no evidence that it was served by a resident priest or indeed that it had a local clerical custodian of any kind.[86] We may compare the situation in England with that in Frankia where *oratoria* built by the *potentes* on their domains were undoubtedly served by local priests. There they were under the direct control of bishop and archdeacon and appear frequently in the canons of Merovingian councils.[87] The silence of the English sources on such matters suggests that in the seventh and eighth centuries at least things were perhaps different there.[88]

I want now to look a little more closely at the *monasteria*, the ecclesiastical communities to which (I am arguing) most English priests belonged in the seventh and eighth centuries. The nature of these communities has been much debated. The Latin term *monasterium* undoubtedly covered a wide and varied range of institutions. While it is clear that it could embrace foundations which might in many ways resemble Benedictine monasteries, it also included the secular colleges and cathedrals known to modern historians as minsters. Scholars such as Catherine Cubitt accept that many may have been mixed communities containing both monks and clerks.[89] Numbers probably ranged from very large institutions like Wearmouth-Jarrow with several hundred inmates to quite small communities, staffed as Cubitt has suggested by a superior probably in priest's orders, a deacon, and a few clerks.[90] Debate has focused in particular upon whether—in the missionary conditions of the early English church—all such communities had pastoral responsibilities over specific *parochiae,* or whether those that were primarily monasteries in the Benedictine sense were devoted exclusively to prayer.[91]

It is clear that in England in the seventh and eighth centuries the hierarchy viewed priests as essential to all religious communities. It is equally clear, however, that there were many in which they were lacking. At the truly monastic end of the spectrum, large monasteries such as the twin communities of Wearmouth and Jarrow, reasonably regarded as closer to the traditional Benedictine ideal than most, evidently contained at their core a small group of priests, even if

---

[85] Bede, *HE* 2.14.

[86] *HE* 5.12.

[87] Godding, *Prêtres*, 255–60.

[88] A point recently made by Blair, *Church in Anglo-Saxon Society*, 118–19.

[89] Catherine Cubitt, "Pastoral Care and the Conciliar Canons: The Provisions of the 747 Council of Clofesho," in *Pastoral Care Before the Parish*, ed. Blair and Sharpe, 193–211, at 208–9.

[90] Cubitt, "Pastoral Care and the Conciliar Canons," 210.

[91] See especially the debate in *Early Medieval Europe* 4 (1995) and 5 (1996), involving Eric Cambridge, David Rollason, John Blair, and David Palliser, below, 204.

most of their inmates were probably not ordained. Although the founding abbot of Wearmouth, Benedict Biscop, was not in major orders, and one of his successors, Sigefrith, was only a deacon, priests were undoubtedly essential to the communities' proper functioning. Biscop's coadjutor, Ceolfrith, provides a particularly striking instance. Much is made of Ceolfrith's ordination and his subsequent acquisition of learning about monastic custom and *conversatio*, and he is presented as guarantor of the regular life of his monastery by virtue of these.[92] It is impossible to estimate the numbers of priests in Wearmouth and Jarrow, but Bede names at least six associated with the two communities in his hagiographical and historical works, which cover the first sixty or so years of their existence. Three—Ceolfrid, Eosterwine and Hwætbcrht—became abbots; a fourth was another very senior figure—Bede himself. In addition we know of one senior deacon—Abbot Sigefrith—and of deacons who played an important role in the ceremonies preceding Ceolfrid's departure for Italy.[93]

At the other extreme lay the so-called "pseudo-monasteries" castigated by Bede.[94] Almost certainly these aristocratic foundations, the inmates of which were often married and sexually active, contained far fewer ordained inmates. Indeed, we know from the legislation of the Council of Clofesho of 747 that by then provision had to be made for secularized communities ("monasteria . . . quae a saecularibus . . . tenentur"), which apparently had no priests at all.[95] The efforts, already alluded to, made in the diocese of Worcester in the late eighth century to ensure that minster communities remained in priestly hands suggest that such problems remained unresolved, at least until a further effort was made to deal with them in the early ninth century.[96]

In between, of course, lay a range of institutions differing greatly in size and composition. Some, such as the cathedrals and the large royal and episcopal minsters, were clearly likely to contain significant concentrations of priests. But most lesser dynastic foundations, even if more observant than those reviled by Bede, almost certainly had fewer ordained members.[97]

---

[92] *Vita Ceolfridi*, caps. 3–4, 6 ("qui et regularis obseruantium uitae pari doctrinae studio firmaret, et altaris officium sacerdotii gradu suppleret"); cf. the appointment of Hwætbert as Ceolfrid's successor, one of the justifications for which was that he was in priest's orders: *Historia Abbatum*, cap. 18.

[93] *HE* 3.15; 5.24; *Historia Abbatum*, caps. 7–8, 10, 17, 18; *Vita Cuthberti prosaica*, caps. 5, 6. In a further two instances in the *Vita Cuthberti*, priests (one from Wearmouth, the other from Jarrow) are mentioned but not named: caps. 35, 46.

[94] See especially Bede, *Epistola ad Ecgbertum Episcopum*, passim, in *Baedae Opera Historica*, ed. Plummer, 1: 405–23.

[95] Canon 5, in *Councils and Ecclesiastical Documents*, 3: 364.

[96] Above, 189–90.

[97] Cf. Blair, *Church in Anglo-Saxon Society*, 82–83.

Although indispensable, priests were, then, evidently a small and unevenly distributed minority in English *monasteria*. Even in Gaul, it has been estimated that as late as 800 as few as 20 or 30 percent of monks were ordained.[98] In England in the seventh and eighth centuries the proportion of ordained to lay in the average ecclesiastical community was undoubtedly considerably less.

The numbers and distribution of priests are key issues because of the crucial importance of priests as pastors. It is clear that they were thought of as the pastoral bedrock of the church. Bishops were very few in number and would (or should) have been largely occupied in carrying out the work specific to them, through the visitation of their vast dioceses. Such duties, as well as their inevitable involvement in secular affairs, would have left them with little time for day-to-day ministrations to the laity. Moreover, as we have seen, they do not appear to have the authority to intervene effectively in the affairs of local churches for much of this period. Bede is especially emphatic about the heavy responsibilities of priests as coadjutors of overburdened (or inadequate) bishops. For him, theirs was above all the office of dispensing the sacraments, namely baptism, penance, and the eucharist.[99] With this went the duty to preach, a wide-ranging obligation to exhort the faithful and convert the heathen, which Bede laid upon all *doctores* charged with pastoral responsibility. Although that term, as I have argued elsewhere, designated a category which overlapped with, but was not identical to, the ordained priesthood, in practice it was almost certainly the latter upon whom Bede probably envisaged such duties as falling most heavily.[100]

As a member of what appears to have been a community which genuinely followed Benedictine spiritual ideals, Bede interpreted the priestly role from an austerely monastic viewpoint.[101] Priests were at the core of his order of teachers and preachers and were expected to conform to high ascetic standards. He did not think that they should marry.[102] Any dereliction was vigorously denounced. Bede was especially severe upon ignorant priests, who knew no Latin, and avaricious,

---

[98] G. Constable, "Monasteries, Rural Churches, and the *Cura Animarum* in the Early Middle Ages," *Settimane di Studio del Centro Italiano di Studi sull'Alto Medioevo* 28 (1982 for 1980): 350–89, at 359–60.

[99] T. A. Carroll, *The Venerable Bede and His Spiritual Teachings,* Studies in Medieval History, New Series, 9 (Washington, DC: Catholic University of America Press, 1946), 82–84; Bede, *Opera Homiletica*, 1. 12, 20, ed. D. Hurst, Corpus Christianorum, Series Latina 122 (Turnhout: Brepols, 1955), 84, 146.

[100] A. T. Thacker, "Bede's Ideal of Reform," in *Ideal and Reality in Frankish and Anglo-Saxon Society*, ed. C. P. Wormald et al. (Oxford: Blackwell, 1983), 130–53; Bede, *Epistola ad Ecgbertum*, para. 5; Bede, *In Ezram* 277, 379–80; but cf. Carroll, *The Venerable Bede*, 83; Cubitt, "Pastoral Care and the Conciliar Canons," 204, n. 38.

[101] See Carroll, *The Venerable Bede*, 239–49.

[102] See for example, Bede, *De Tabernaculo*, 95–97; above, 190–91.

weak, and idle *famuli Dei* consumed with the fire of cupidity rather than with heavenly love, or lacking the diligence to administer correction to their flock.[103]

Bede's stress upon the dispensing of the sacraments as the key element in the priest's role is echoed in Theodore's penitential, where there is frequent reference to their special responsibility for baptism, the eucharist, and the administration of penance (although the reconciliation of penitents is seen as the function of the bishop alone).[104] The canons of the eighth- and early ninth-century councils, particularly the 747 Council of Clofesho, provide further evidence. There again, the priest's sacramental role is emphasized,[105] but—even more significantly—the canons also allude to units of pastoral care (*loca* or *regiones laicorum*) assigned to priests by their bishops, within which they were to discharge their apostolic commission of baptizing, teaching, and visiting.[106]

This brings us finally to the vexed question of the main focus of pastoral care in early Anglo-Saxon England. Over the last fifteen years there has been much debate over whether we can take at face value the bishop- and priest-centred model implicit in the church canons and in other sources already cited in this paper, including the penitentials and the *Dialogues* of Archbishop Ecgberht. In particular, that model has been set against the depiction of monasteries and their inmates as the focal points of pastoral activity in early narrative sources such as the history and hagiography of Bede, and the episcopal Lives written by Stephen of Ripon and the anonymous monk of Lindisfarne.[107]

This debate poses an unnecessary dichotomy. The key to the problem lies in the number of priests and the nature of early Anglo-Saxon religious communities from which they operated. Priests, as has just been argued, were of high status, crucial to pastoral care, but comparatively thin on the ground and concentrated principally in the varied communities collectively designated *monasteria*. That they had a key role in pastoral activity in any institution with which they were associated is implied by a ruling in Theodore's penitential to the effect that if anyone wished to set his monastery in another place, he was to release a priest

---

[103] *Epistola ad Ecgbertum*, paras. 3–5, 16–17 (1: 406–9, 419–23). It is not clear whether in his diatribes against the false servants of God Bede is thinking primarily of bishops or of priests and perhaps abbots as well.

[104] E.g., Theodore, *Poenitentiale*, 1. xiv.28; 2. ii.2, 7, 9, 12, 15; 2:ii. 3; *Canones Theodori*, 310, 313, 314, 315.

[105] Council of Clofesho, canons 8, 10, 11, in *Councils and Ecclesiastical Documents*, 3: 365, 366.

[106] Council of Clofesho, canon 9, in *Councils and Ecclesiastical Documents*, 3: 365–66.

[107] See especially E. Cambridge and D. W. Rollason, "The Pastoral Organization of the Anglo-Saxon Church: Review of the Minster Hypothesis," *Early Medieval Europe* 4 (1995): 87–104; J. Blair, "Ecclesiastical Organization and Pastoral Care in Anglo-Saxon England," *Early Medieval Europe* 4 (1995): 193–212; Thacker, "Monks, Preaching and Pastoral Care," 137–70; S. Foot, "Anglo-Saxon Minsters: A Review of Terminology," in *Pastoral Care Before the Parish*, ed. Blair and Sharpe, 212–25.

to minister to the church at the original site.[108] The assumption behind this ruling seems to be that it was the norm for a monastery to have such responsibilities. That would seem likely in a society like that of the English in the seventh and early eighth centuries where the church was less well established than in, say, neighbouring Gaul, and still had essentially a missionary role.[109]

It is clear that at the Council of Clofesho of 747 the legislators distinguished various ecclesiastical grades and conditions. In particular, *monasteria*, *monachi*, and *sanctimoniales* appear to be set against *ecclesiae*, *sacerdotes*, *presbyteri*, and *clerici*.[110] These distinctions, as Catherine Cubitt has pointed out, are primarily functional, "office-centered."[111] Although the distinctions in the functions are clear, the institutional operation of these modes of activity is much more opaque. *Monasteria*, as has already been shown, could clearly contain priests and *clerici* as well as *monachi* or *monasteriales*.[112] And those who served both *ecclesiae* and *monasteria* had the same duty to keep the canonical hours.[113]

At the very least, then, those who performed these various functions could live in institutions of the same name. In many instances we may suspect that they lived in the same institutions, indeed may have been the same persons. From the perspective of those drafting the canons, a single individual might be termed a *monasterialis* in relation to some of his activities and a priest or *clericus* in relation to others. Ecgberht's reference in his *Dialogues* to the *clericus sine voto monachi* surely implies that *clerici* could also be monks.[114] The way in which distinctions were drawn in the council of 747 also suggests this. We invariably read inclusively of *monasteriales* and *clerici* in *monasteria* and *ecclesiae* rather than more precisely (and exclusively) of *monasteriales* in *monasteria* and *presbyteri* or *clerici* in *ecclesiae*.[115] The point is that a *monasterium* might house both monks (*monasteriales*) given over to primarily to the contemplative life and an *ecclesia* staffed by *presbyteri* and *clerici*. Viewed from one angle it is a *monasterium* with an *abbas* to whom all its inmates were subject, whilst from another it contained an *ecclesia* with a priest serving a *regio laicorum* over whose pastoral activities the bishop had special authority.

---

[108] Theodore, *Poenitentiale*, 2: vi, 7, *Canones Theodori*, 320.

[109] For a different view of this canon see Richard Morris, *Churches in the Landscape* (London: Dent, 1989), 132. Discussed by Thacker, "Monks, Preaching and Pastoral Care," 145–46.

[110] See especially Cubitt, "Pastoral Care and the Conciliar Canons."

[111] Cubitt, "Pastoral Care and the Conciliar Canons," 207.

[112] E.g., Canons 5, 8, 29, in *Councils and Ecclesiastical Documents* 3: 364, 365, 374–75.

[113] Canon 15, in *Councils and Ecclesiastical Documents*, 3: 367.

[114] The ruling is somewhat garbled, and the heavy penalty for the unidentified ecclesiastic *sine voto monachi* should perhaps be read as (*clericus*) *cum voto monachi*: *Dialogus*, 5: 7, in *Councils and Ecclesiastical Documents*, 3: 422.

[115] But cf. Cubitt, "Clergy in Early Anglo-Saxon England," 282–83.

The ambiguities of the canons find a parallel in the title *presbyter-abbas*, by the later eighth century so widely used that it looks as if it denotes a special rank or at least a person performing a distinctive and easily recognisable role. Could they be the equivalent of Frankish archpriests? In Frankia this designation (or *prior presbyter*) was generally used for those responsible for a large rural parish staffed by a group of clergy, which might comprise at least one other priest, a deacon or deacons, and several minor clergy. The archpriest was the ordinary minister of the sacraments within his *vicus* and had supervision over the other priests, deacons, and *clerici* within his parish as a whole.[116] Many English priest-abbots may have ruled quite small establishments (still nevertheless probably termed minsters, *monasteria*) of the kind described by Catherine Cubitt, staffed by perhaps a deacon or two and some *clerici*.[117] It is surely significant that the monastic title was chosen for the archpriest's English equivalent—a further indication of the elision of the two kinds of ministry. Interestingly, in the laws of Wihtred it was expressly stated that the head of a minster (*mynstres aldor*) should clear himself of an accusation by the same formula as that to be used by a priest—an indication that in early Kent headship of a minster was regarded as a priestly office.[118]

Clearly, it was no part of an abbot's role *per se* to act as a pastor to the laity outside his monastery, and so such duties could be devolved upon one of his ordained subordinates. In some cases, however, the abbot himself may have taken responsibility for the *regio laicorum* assigned to his house. A particularly striking instance comes from Breedon in Leicestershire. One of the conditions of the gift in the late seventh century to the monks of Medeshamstede of land there for a monastery was that the brethren should provide a priest to baptise and preach to the local people. The brethren chose as abbot for the new community one of their number, the priest Haedda, who was so diligent in preaching to the people assigned to him that the founder, the *princeps* Frithuric, augmented the endowment. Haedda was thus both priest-abbot and pastor.[119]

I am arguing, then, that in England a *presbyter-abbas* may have been an ecclesiastic who was at once the superior of a community and the pastor of a *regio laicorum*. Others designated simply as *abbas* were presumably not ordained or at least without such pastoral responsibilities, either because no *regio laicorum* was attached to their community or because the pastorate was exercised by a senior priested colleague.

---

[116] Godding, *Prêtres*, 240–47. See, for example, Council of Tours II (567), canon 20, in *Canons des conciles mérovingiens*, ed. Gaudemet and Basdevant, 364–68.

[117] Cubitt, "Pastoral Care and the Conciliar Canons," 206, 210; eadem, "Clergy in Early Anglo-Saxon England," 277–78.

[118] Laws of Wihtred, caps. 17–18, in *Laws*, ed. Attenborough, 29.

[119] Thacker, "Monks, Preaching and Pastoral Care," 140, 145–46; F. M. Stenton, *Preparatory to Anglo-Saxon England,* 3rd ed. (Oxford: Oxford University Press, 1971), 181–83. For a different view again see Morris, *Churches in the Landscape*, 132.

To sum up, the *monasteria* and *ecclesiae*, about which there has been so much debate, were not necessarily distinct. They were rather two ways of looking at a single complex institution. From a pastoral perspective the important thing was the *ecclesia*, the focus of the *regio laicorum* and centre of the priest-pastor's ministry. Yet such churches were (I would argue) generally embedded in communities, *monasteria*, presided over by an *abbas*, most characteristically a *presbyter-abbas*. Abbots had duties as rulers of those communities, priest-pastors as ministers to the laity outside. Both required regulation, and the two interwoven strands are separated in the canons.

The canons, it has already been noted, speak as if priests were expected as a matter of course to exercise a pastoral ministry, to baptise, teach, and visit. In the still missionary English church, it seems likely that the great majority of priests wherever they were located were called upon to minister in some way to the local laity. Almost certainly priests did not operate alone. They would have been based in communities—sometimes, as in the great royal and episcopal churches, with several of their fellows, elsewhere in a less grand establishment as the only one of their order. Even when married, it would seem likely that they lived in such institutions; certainly Bede's letter to Ecgberht shows that the members of *monasteria* might have wives and children.[120] In all cases, however, they would have been senior figures, if not themselves abbot, then charged with heavy responsibilities.

These arrangements were probably at their most flexible in the earliest days of the English church, from the arrival of the Roman mission to the mid-eighth century. By the later eighth century, however, there may have been a growing consciousness of the need to distinguish more formally between monks and secular clergy; at the legatine synod of 786, for example, the legislators contrasted monks and nuns living according to the rule (*regulariter*) from *canonici* living canonically (*canonice*).[121] Such distinctions may reflect those emerging under the influence of Chrodegang of Metz in contemporary Carolingian Frankia, where separate *ordines* of monks and canons are referred to for the first time in 755 at the Council of Ver.[122]

---

[120] *Epistola ad Ecgbertum*, para. 12 (1. 415–16).

[121] Report of the Legates, 4, in *Councils and Ecclesiastical Documents*, 3: 450.

[122] *Concilium Vernense*, canons 5, 8, 11, in *Capitularia Regum Francorum*, ed. A. Boretius, Monumenta Germaniae Historica, Legum 2.1 (Hannover: Hahn, 1883), 14: 32–37, at 34–55; J. M. Wallace-Hadrill, *The Frankish Church* (Oxford: Oxford University Press, 1983), 170–71; R. D. McKitterick, *Frankish Kingdoms under the Carolingians 751–987* (London: Longman, 1983), 58–59.

Conclusions

This paper has presented pastoral arrangements, which, although in many ways ad hoc and dysfunctional, were intended to reach out to the ordinary people. It is based on the conviction that the pre-Viking church was not purely confined to royal courts and dynastic centres but was intended to embrace the *gentes* as well as their rulers. There is evidence that some at least of the hierarchy and some monastic founders made a serious effort to preach and to bring the sacraments to those who lived outside the monasteries and the royal courts. The priesthood was a key element in this endeavour. On the other hand, we cannot assume that there were numerous priests scattered through early English settlements, or that they were drawn from accessible local stock. It is much more likely that most priests would have seemed as remote and grand as the bishop himself (and perhaps were seen scarcely more often).

Although it is possible that in founding royal monasteries, or in authorizing the foundation of monasteries by their nobles, kings and bishops had an orderly vision of an interlocking network of pastoral centres, that is clearly not what happened in practice. In some areas there were too many, in others too few communities. In a few foundations there may have been a high concentration of priests, in others none at all. Not all the founders would have shared the royal and episcopal vision. Indeed, the difficulties which modern historians have encountered in determining the nature of pastoral activity reflect the high degree of contemporary imprecision and experiment which such foundations entailed. Nevertheless, this was the period in which in some sense England became part of Christendom. A change took place—and for this the early communities, not least their priestly inmates, were largely responsible.

The Wilfridian Annals in Winchester Cathedral Library, MS 1 and Durham Cathedral Library, MS B. ii. 35[*]

Joshua A. Westgard

On a list of the many virtues of Charles Plummer's edition of Bede's historical works, one that surely ranks high is the fact that it is possible, using the critical notes, to gain some sense of the texts' transmission-histories.[1] This feature is particularly useful for students of the *Historia ecclesiastica gentis Anglorum* (*HE*), a work with a literary *Nachleben* that is extensive to say the least. Admittedly, the picture of the text's transmission that is painted by Plummer's edition has a noticeable insular tint; nevertheless it is a valuable starting point for further study. The same cannot be said of the critical notes in the edition of Bertram Colgrave and R. A. B. Mynors, from which one would be hard-pressed to discern anything more than the faintest outlines of the differences between the circulating versions of Bede's text.[2] The paucity of the edition's critical notes stands in sharp

---

[*] It was Richard Pfaff who first suggested that I investigate the transmission of Bede's *Ecclesiastical History* in my doctoral dissertation (University of North Carolina–Chapel Hill, 2005), which he directed with equal parts wisdom and equanimity; I am pleased to offer him this study as a small token of gratitude. I would like to express my thanks to Michael Gullick and Joanna Story for many helpful comments on an earlier draft of this paper; and to Julian Harrison, who currently is engaged in a much more wide-ranging study of Bede's annalistic recapitulation than what I have undertaken here, for sharing the results of his research in advance of publication.

[1] *Venerabilis Bedae Opera Historica*, ed. C. Plummer, 2 vols. (Oxford: Clarendon Press, 1896; repr. 2 vols. in 1, 1946).

[2] See Bertram Colgrave and R. A. B. Mynors, eds., *Bede's Ecclesiastical History of the English People*, Oxford Medieval Texts (Oxford: Clarendon Press, 1969; rev. ed. 1991), esp. xxxix–xlvi. Mynors' textual notes are for the most part limited to displaying the differences between the two main recensions (*c* and *m*), which were first established by Plummer, and which have been the starting-point for all subsequent discussion of the transmission of the text. Mynors generally, though not exclusively, follows the *m*-recension in the main text, confining the readings of the *c*-recension to the notes. He does not

The Study of Medieval Manuscripts of England: Festschrift in Honor of Richard W. Pfaff, eds. George Hardin Brown and Linda Ehrsam Voigts, MRTS 384 (Tempe: ACMRS, 2010). [ISBN 978-0-86698-432-4]

contrast to the fullness of Mynors' "Textual Introduction," which is brimming with useful information concerning the relationships of the medieval copies of Bede's *magnum opus*. In this introduction, Mynors offers a nearly complete list of surviving manuscripts, and divides them into five "textual provinces."[3] Unfortunately, because most of Mynors' assertions about the relationships among the manuscripts are not backed up by textual evidence in the form of critical notes, it is impossible to evaluate the evidentiary basis for his opinions and difficult to build upon his groupings. Fortunately, for these purposes one may still fruitfully turn to Plummer.

A case in point is a set of additions relating to St. Wilfrid (ca. 634–709/10) that were inserted into the annalistic recapitulation at the end of the *HE* (v.24), right before Bede's autobiographical sketch.[4] Mynors mentions these additions in passing in his introduction, but makes no note of their presence in the edition itself, and neither discusses their origin nor investigates their contents.[5] The additions survive in at least twelve copies of the *HE*, and they must have been

---

reproduce the readings of individual MSS, though he does take care to distinguish readings he considered to be characteristic of the archetype of the *c*-recension—which can be established with reasonable certainty from MSS C (London, British Library, MS. Cotton Tiberius C. ii), K (Kassel, Gesamthochschulbibliothek, 4° MS. theol. 2), and O (Oxford, Bodleian Library, MS. Hatton 43 [*SC* 4106])—from certain other readings he attributes to *c2*. As he notes (xliii), Mynors believed that C and O shared an eighth-century ancestor, but that readings unique to this ancestor could only be discerned where C and O agreed against K. Since K is a fragmentary MS containing books IV–V, it follows that the readings Mynors attributes to *c2* could only be distinguished from those of the *c*-archetype in those two books, or where another early witness independent of C and O was available (such as I.27, where Mynors used the tenth-century Zürich MS of the *Libellus responsionum* mentioned on xliii). Thus, when Mynors gives readings from *c2* in books IV–V, they probably represent the hyparchetype of C and O, but in books I-III (with I.27 excluded), the readings given as *c2* may represent this hyparchetype or they may equally represent the archetype of the *c*-recension. Confusingly, at two points outside of I.27 and IV–V, namely III.15 (260) and III.19 (270), Mynors prints *c2*-readings alongside *c*-readings, presumably relying on some other manuscript he believed to of a 'pure' c-type (perhaps the three he lists on xlviii, or extrapolating back from the Old English version, which Dorothy Whitelock had previously demonstrated was based on a good *c*-type MS, as noted by Mynors [xliii, n. 2]). In Mynors' defense it is only fair to point out that the lack of detail in the critical notes is in keeping with the stated purpose of the OMT series, namely "for the average student, to provide the best possible text" (vii).

[3] Colgrave and Mynors, *Bede's Ecclesiastical History*, xxxix-lxxvi. See Appendix below.

[4] A wide-ranging summary of Wilfrid's career and influence is Alan Thacker, "Wilfrid," in *Oxford Dictionary of National Biography* (Oxford: Oxford University Press, 2004), 58: 944–50.

[5] Mynors mentions the presence of "annals betraying a special interest in St. Wilfrid" (xlix), but does not give any further details, nor does he mention them at the appropriate point in the textual notes (564–66).

compiled between the work's completion in 731 and ca. 1000, which is the approximate date of the earliest manuscript containing them, Winchester Cathedral Library, MS. 1 (hereafter Win).[6] Because, as will be shown, the annals are clearly not original to Win but instead are derived from one of its ancestors, there is no way to date their composition any more precisely on the basis of codicological evidence.

Transmission

Plummer was the first to recognize and collate these additions, and to locate them in nine manuscripts besides Win.[7] He considered two of the manuscripts—Oxford, Bodleian Library, Bodley 163 (*SC* 2016) (s. xi[1], Peterborough); and Oxford, Balliol College 176 (s. xii[2])—to be descendants of Win, and he therefore referred to the three manuscripts together as the Winchester group.[8] The seven other manuscripts he identified, however, seemed to him to represent an independent branch in the transmission of the Wilfridian annals: Cambridge, Pembroke College 82 (s. xii, Tynemouth); Durham Cathedral Library, B. ii. 35 (s. xi[2], Durham); London, British Library MSS. Harley 4124 (s. xii, Worksop), Additional 25014 (s. xii[2], Newminster, Northumb.), and Burney 310 (A.D. 1381, Durham or Finchale); Oxford, Corpus Christi College 279 (s. xiv) and Bodleian Library, Bodley 302 (*SC* 2086) (s. xv[1]). For both textual reasons and reasons of manuscript context, Plummer believed that the earliest of these manuscripts, Durham B. ii. 35 (hereafter Dur), was the parent from which the six later copies ultimately derived, and for this reason he referred to these manuscripts together as the Durham group.[9] Subsequently, Mynors added two manuscripts to this group: Vatican Library, Reg. lat. 694 (s. xiii, Coupar) and Edinburgh, National Library of Scotland, Adv. 18. 5. 1 (s. xiv[in], Exeter Cathedral) (hereafter Edi).[10]

---

[6] Dated s. x/xi by N. R. Ker and A. J. Piper, *Medieval Manuscripts in British Libraries*, vol. 4 (Oxford: Clarendon Press, 1992), 578–79.

[7] *Opera*, 1: civ–cxiii (the manuscripts) and 354–56 (the collations).

[8] The evidence for the derivation of MS. Balliol 176 from Win includes the former manuscript's incorporation of a twelfth-century marginal addition in Win (fol. 91r) as an alternative opening for *HE* v.9. In the case of MS. Bodley 163, the evidence for descent from Win includes some common errors in the Wilfrid additions, as well as a large number of shared readings in their respective texts of Æthelwulf's *Carmen de abbatibus*. Numerous correspondences among the three manuscripts are summarized by Plummer on pp. cxii–cxiii. See also Alistair Campbell, ed., *Æthelwulf: De abbatibus* (Oxford: Clarendon Press, 1967), esp. xix.

[9] Four of these MSS also contain Bede's *Historia abbatum*; numerous affinities in their respective texts of the *HE* are described by Plummer, *Opera*, cviii–cix.

[10] The second-folio reference given for the copy of the *HE* listed in the 1506 catalogue of the library of Exeter Cathedral matches the Edinburgh MS (Edi), and certain

Despite the availability of Plummer's collations, the nature and sources of these annals have never been investigated. In 1919 Reginald L. Poole made passing reference to them, but failed to notice that what he characterized as a "stupid repetition" is an error of transmission confined to the manuscripts of the Winchester group.[11] Indeed, because Plummer was primarily interested in demonstrating the relationships between the various manuscripts containing these additions rather than establishing the original text, his collations may give the impression that the annalist was not up to his task. But while it is true that the annals are of limited value for the historical information they contain, virtually all of which is derived directly from the main text of the *HE*, nevertheless the annals are not without interest, as I hope to demonstrate below.

As noted above, Plummer believed that Win and Dur were the manuscripts from which all the others were derived, a conclusion which seems reasonably well supported by the evidence of the collations he provides.[12] It is furthermore clear from Plummer's collations that the Durham manuscript, the younger of the two parents, cannot be derived from a manuscript of the other branch. Perhaps the clearest indicator of this is the annal for A.D. 687, which is the erroneous repetition referred to by Poole, as mentioned above. Under this year, Win recounts

---

marginalia (fol. 64v) confirm its Exeter provenance. Edi is clearly a member of the Durham (as opposed to Winchester) group, but having carried out test collations, I am reasonably confident that Edi is not a descendant of Dur, but rather its sibling, both MSS being derived independently from some common parent. The presence at Exeter Cathedral of a text of the *HE* close to Dur, though attested here only by this late (s. xiv) manuscript, is of particular interest given that the Exeter library is known to have been built up under its Norman bishop, Osbern (1072–1103), much as the Durham library was under its first Norman bishop, William of St. Calais (1081–1096). It is possible that Osbern obtained books from some of the the the same sources (whether Norman or English) as William, and that Edi is a descendant of a book first acquired under Osbern, which in turn may have been copied from the same exemplar as Dur. On the two Norman bishops' book-collecting activities, see Michael Gullick, "The Scribe of the Carilef Bible: A New Look at Some Late-Eleventh-Century Durham Cathedral Manuscripts," in *Medieval Book Production: Assessing the Evidence*, ed. Linda L. Brownrigg (Los Altos Hills, CA and Hitchin Herts.: Anderson-Lovelace/Red Gull Press, 1990), 61–83, at 61–62; idem, "Manuscrits et copistes normands en Angleterre (xie-xiie siècles)," in *Manuscrits et enluminures dans le monde normand (x[e]-xve siècles)*, ed. Pierre Bouet and Monique Dosdat (Caen: Presses Unversitaires de Caen, 1999; 2nd ed. [unseen], 2005), 83–93; and Richard Gameson, "Manuscrits normands à Exeter aux xie et xiie siècles," in *Manuscrits et enluminures*, 107–27.

[11] R. L. Poole, "Saint Wilfrid and the See of Ripon," *English Historical Review* 34 (1919): 1–24, at 3.

[12] The exception to this is Edi, as noted above (n. 10). Since Plummer gives readings from later manuscripts only when they "seemed to be of interest," the evidence for the relationships of the manuscripts of these families is, for the most part, confined to the notes for *HE* v.24 (354–56).

Wilfrid's expulsion at the hands of King Ecgfrith, in much the same language as the account of his first expulsion in the annal for 678, even though in the previous annal (685) Ecgfrith's death had just been reported. Dur's version of this annal (recorded under 686, but this after correction) is historically accurate and clearly superior, in that instead of Wilfrid's expulsion (*repulsus est*) it recounts his reception back into his see (*receptus est*) under Ecgfrith's successor Aldfrith. But this is by no means the only place where Win records erroneous information not in Dur. Win's annal for 673 reads *Ecgfrid* instead of *Ecgberct*, perhaps as a result of some confusion with the mention of Ecgfrith of Northumbria's accession in the previous annal. Similarly, in the annal for 675, Win reads *Aedilfrido* in place of *Aedilredo*. Neither of these historically inaccurate readings is found in Dur. Win's errors are, furthermore, not limited to the text of the Wilfridian additions. In the annals for A.D. 189 and 449, Win omits entire phrases (*xvii . . . qui* and *suscipiens . . . tenuit*, respectively) not omitted by Dur, and similarly in the autobiographical sketch which follows the annals, Win omits the phrases *et pauli* and *ad annum*, neither of which is omitted by Dur.[13] Further comparison of the texts of Dur and Win undoubtedly would yield additional evidence about their relationships, but it seems reasonably safe to conclude from the evidence here presented that the two branches are derived independently from a lost archetype that first contained the Wilfrid additions (hereafter Δ). Furthermore, the balance of the evidence would seem to point toward Dur as the superior witness of the text of the additions. One possible exception is the rather cryptic annal for A.D. 667, about which more will be explained below.

Text[14]

The following edition of the annals is based upon the collation of Dur and Win. In addition, I have collated Edi, but because it agrees so closely with Dur, I generally have not included its readings in the edition. I have adopted Dur as the base text, and with a few exceptions have confined the readings unique to Win to the notes.

---

[13] For the text of the two annals, see Plummer, *Opera*, 352, or Colgrave-Mynors, *History*, 562. The omissions from the autobiographical sketch are noted by Plummer, *Opera*, 357, nn. 2 and 4, but they are not mentioned by Mynors (*History*, 566).

[14] This edition records all substantive differences between the texts of the annals in Win and Dur. Differences in spelling have not been recorded, except in proper names, though Dur's frequent attaching of the *-us* ending to names has been ignored. Capitalization has been normalized to agree with modern usage. The runic character *wynn* used by the scribe of Win is represented by 'w'. No attempt has been made to reproduce manuscript punctuation. References to the editions of Plummer and Colgrave-Mynors are given in the following form: P/CM + page. It is important to remember that in the manuscripts these annals appear intermixed with the original, Bedan annals.

But while Dur often preserves superior readings, it also bears the signs of editorial intervention on the part of its scribe, William. As a result, even though in general Dur seems more correct than Win, it is not always the better witness of the original text of the annals. Where Dur presents an intelligible text without evidence of correction, I have followed it, but in problem passages (e.g., the annal for 667) or where disagreements with Win appear to be the result of scribal intervention in Dur (as in the annal for 692), I have followed the text of Win.

[658] Anno DCLVIII Uulfhere[15] subleuatus in regnum.[16]
In the year 658 Wulfhere was raised up to the throne.

[667] Anno DCLXVII nr̄ aƀƀ scr̄i.[17]
In the year 667 . . .

[670] Anno DCLXX Osuiu rex Nordanhymbrorum obiit; Ecgfrid regnum suscepit.[18]
In the year 670 Oswy, King of the Northumbrians, died; Ecgfrith took up the kingdom.

---

[15] *Uulfhere*] *Uulfere* Win
[16] The presence of a corrupt version of this annal ("Anno LXLVIIII Wulf sub*leuatus* in regem") as a later (s. ix?) addition in C (P 354, n. 8) would seem to provide a further clue as to the date of the Wilfridian additions' composition. Caution is warranted, however, as we cannot discount the possibility that this annal circulated separately from the other additions found in Δ and may have a different pedigree.
[17] Dur has *hâb* for Win's *ab˙b*. Plummer does not mention Dur's reading, and this is the one case in which Plummer has omitted a variant from either Dur or Win in the text of the additions. He confidently expands the abbreviations to read: *Noster abbas scripsit.* This problematic annal will be discussed further below. Edi has a completely different annal here: "Anno DCLXVII D*ominus* p*apa* ad consulta regum de statu eccl*esiae*," which would seem to be a reference to the letter, excerpted by Bede in iii.29, that Pope Vitalian sent to Oswy in response to Oswy's and Egbert of Kent's sending the priest Wigheard to Rome for consecration as archbishop of Canterbury. Wigheard died in a plague at Rome, and ultimately Theodore of Tarsus was made archbishop. One might hope that the annal in Edi could help resolve the textual problem in Dur/Win, but it is difficult to see how some corruption of the text in Edi (if we assume it reflects the reading of Δ) could have resulted in the text found in Dur and Win. It seems more likely that the 667 annal is a later insertion by a scribe who, perhaps, could not make sense of the text in the exemplar he was copying, and who sought out a relevant event from the main text of the *HE*.
[18] The first half of this annal is in Bede's text; *Ecgfrid . . . suscepit* is the addition of our annalist.

[687] Anno DCLXXXVII[19] Wilfrid in sedem[20] receptus est ab Aldfrido rege.[21]
In the year 687 Wilfrid was received [back] into his see by King Aldfrith.

[692] Anno DCXCII Uuilfrid ab[22] Aldfrido[23] rege iterum expulsus est, et XIII annos exulabat;[24] et primo Romam[25] adiit, et inde rediit, et in Mediterraneorum Anglorum[26] regione morabatur, multaque diu loca peruagatus; Romam adiit; Brittanniam rediit;[27] diuertens[28] ad Australium Saxonum, pagano adhuc cultura[29] dediti,[30] illis[31] illa patria per V annos docebat euangelium.[32]

---

[19] So the year is given in Win; Dur reads 786, but the passage has been corrected, and probably read 787 originally.

[20] *sedem*] *sedem* *suam*/ Dur.

[21] In Win the complete annal reads "Anno DCLXXXVII Wilfrid a sede repulsus ab ecgfrido rege," which would seem to be the result of conflation with Bede's annal for 678; Win's version of the 687 annal makes little sense, since Ecgfrith's death has just been recorded in Bede's previous annal (for 685).

[22] *ab*] *ab ab* Win

[23] *Aldfrido*] *Alfrido* Win

[24] *exulabat*] *ex*/*ulabat* Win

[25] *Romam*] *Roma* Dur

[26] The statement that Wilfrid was, particularly, among the "Midland English," a name Bede uses to distinguish the Middle Angles from the Mercians, is intriguing. Bede does not mention this fact in v.19 (P 321–30, CM 516–30), but it could perhaps be extrapolated from the reference in HE iv.21 (P 255, CM 410 [numbered iv.23 (21) in the latter edition; I follow Michael Lapidge's lead in accepting Plummer's chapter numbering (i.e., the numbers given in parentheses by Mynors) as the correct, Bedan chapter numbers; see *Beda: Storia degli Inglesi (Historia ecclesiastica gentis Anglorum)*, ed. Michael Lapidge, trans. Paolo Chiesa, vol. 1 (Milan: Fondazione Lorenzo Valla/Arnoldo Mondadori, 2008), cxxv]). Stephen of Ripon (*Vita Wilfridi*, ch. 45) says that he ruled Seaxwulf's former see, but as Bede (iv.12; P 229, CM 370) makes clear, Seaxwulf ruled over a larger see that included the Mercians, the Middle Angles, and the people of Lindsey. Here and subsequently I cite the *Vita Wilfridi* from the edition of Bertram Colgrave, *The Life of Bishop Wilfrid by Eddius Stephanus* (Cambridge: Cambridge University Press, 1927).

[27] *rediit*] *et rediit* Win

[28] *diuertens*] *diuertens* *prouinciam*/ Dur; it seems as though a later scribe has attempted to improve the wording of this annal, inserting *prouinciam* above the line to serve as the object of *ad* and the referent of the genitive *Australium Saxonum* (cf. also HE v.13 [P 230, CM 372]), and then changing the participle from *dediti* to *deditam* to agree with it. Because these are later editorial interventions in Dur, I follow the text of Win.

[29] *cultura*] *cultui* Dur (post corr.)

[30] *dediti*] *deditam* Dur (post corr.)

[31] *illis*] *ibi in* Dur

[32] The second half of this annal (everything after *peruagatus*) would seem to belong in Bede's annal for the year 678 (P 355, CM 564) which mentions Wilfrid's expulsion during the reign of Ecgfrith. According to Stephen (*Vita Wilfridi*, ch. 41), the mission to

In the year 692 Wilfrid was again expelled [this time] by King Aldfrith, and he was in exile for thirteen years. First, he went to Rome, and upon returning from there, he stayed in the land of the Middle Angles, and spent a long time wandering through many places. He went to Rome. He returned to Britain. Turning aside to the [province of the] South Saxons, who to that point were [still] devoted to pagan worship, for five years he preached the Gospel to them in their homeland.

[705] Anno DCCV Aldfrid[33] rex Nordanhymbrorum defunctus est[34] et Osred regnum suscepit. Et Uilfrid episcopus in suam receptus est sedem; et iiii[or] annos, id est usque ad diem obitus sui, uitam duxit in pace.[35] Et[36] sicque eximius uir uitae[37] uenerabilis uictor conscendit altithronum.[38]
In the year 705 Aldfrith, King of the Northumbrians, died, and Osred took up the realm; Bishop Wilfrid was received back into his see, and for four years, that is until the day of his death, he lived out his life in peace. And so this venerable man, renowned [for the conduct?] of his life, ascended victoriously to his heavenly throne.

If we set aside for a moment the mysterious annal for 667, it is clear that the source of nearly all the information in these annals is the main text of the *HE* itself. Indeed, in places the annals are direct echoes of passages from Bede's main text, as can be seen clearly from the notes. The content of the additions is somewhat out of keeping with the rest of Bede's annals in that the additions include much more detail, but with the exception of the last line, there is nothing particularly "hagiographical" about the annals. It seems that anyone in possession of a copy of the *HE* prior to ca. 1000 could have made these additions. In spite of these obstacles, it remains to investigate the evidence for the circumstances of their creation.

the South Saxons took place during this first period of exile, in the early 680s, Sussex being at that time the one place where Wilfrid could elude Ecgfrith's grasp.
   [33] *Aldfrid*] *Al\h/frid* Win
   [34] The first part of this annal is in Bede's text; from "et Osred . . ." it is an addition by our annalist.
   [35] The passage "id est . . . pace" is taken verbatim from *HE* v.19 (P 330, CM 528).
   [36] *Et*] erased in Dur
   [37] *uir uitae* is the reading of both Dur and Win; Plummer's *uirtute* (P 356, n. 1) is a plausible conjecture which would seem to improve what is otherwise an awkward passage, but it is not found in either of the main MSS.
   [38] Osred's accession is mentioned by Bede in *HE* v.18 (P 320, CM 512). The last line gives the annal a clear hagiographical tone; in terms of phrasing, its source is probably not the main text of the *HE*—although it should be mentioned that Bede does use the heavenly epithet *altithronus* twice in his hymn for St. Æthelthryth (P 248, CM 400)—but rather it is an echo of his *Vita Cuthberti metrica*, line 723: "Qui cupit altithronum victor conscendere regnum . . .," which in turn echoes Prudentius, *Peristephanon* 8.7. See Werner Jaager, ed., *Bedas metrische Vita sancti Cuthberti*, Palaestra 198 (Leipzig: Mayer and Müller, 1935), 113.

Origin

Plummer believed that the additions were probably of Northern origin. He seems to have been drawn to this conclusion by several misleading assumptions. First, he believed that C was probably a Durham or Lindisfarne manuscript. As noted above, Δ was probably derived from a manuscript close to C, and so for Plummer, it was logical to assume that the copying of Δ took place in the North. As has been shown subsequently, however, and most recently emphasized by Michael Lapidge, C is not a Northern book, but almost certainly comes from Canterbury, though it remains possible that it was for a time owned by a community connected to Lindisfarne, where the word *nostro* was added to it in reference to St. Cuthbert.[39] Second, Plummer seems to have believed that interest in St. Wilfrid naturally would have been confined to the North. This, too, is hardly persuasive given what we know of Wilfrid's activities in Mercia, Sussex, and even among the West Saxons, not to mention his spreading cult in the period after his death.[40] Third, Plummer may have been influenced by the additions' transmission in two manuscripts alongside Æthelwulf's *Carmen de abbatibus*, an 819-line hexameter poem which was almost certainly composed in a community connected to Lindisfarne.[41] But it is only the Winchester family in which this pairing is found, and therefore we have no reason to conclude that the *Carmen de abbatibus* was necessarily also found in Δ.

From the mid-tenth century, Wilfrid's bones were housed at Canterbury, having been brought there during the pontificate of Oda (941–958). The holy theft may have been carried out in connection with a military campaign of King Eadred (946–955) during which the church of Ripon, where Wilfrid had been buried, was burned down.[42] Oda subsequently commissioned the Frankish scholar Frithegod (fl. 950) to compose a versification of the *Vita Wilfridi* by Stephen of Ripon.[43] Thus we know that there was interest in Wilfrid's life and career at

---

[39] On the Canterbury affinities of C, see David H. Wright, review of Peter Hunter Blair, *The Moore Bede, Anglia* 82 (1964): 110–17, at 116–17. The evidence for C's origins is summarized by Lapidge in *Storia degli Inglesi*, 1: civ–cxi. Plummer's main evidence for Lindisfarne origins was the reference to Cuthbert as "our father," and a single reading in C that is also found in Symeon of Durham.

[40] As Thacker ("Wilfrid," 950) notes, his feast is in most early calendars, and forty-eight churches were dedicated to him.

[41] See Campbell, *De Abbatibus*, xxi–xxiii.

[42] Described in the *Anglo-Saxon Chronicle*, MS. D (London, British Library, Cotton Tib. B. iv), s.a. 948.

[43] As Oda indicates in his prefatory letter attached to Frithegod's poem: "[I]gitur uenerabillimas beati confessoris Christi Wilfridi reliquias indecenti senticosae uoraginis situ marcidas, immo, quod dictu quoque meticulosum est, praelatorum horripilatione neglectas, cum inde, favente Deo, scilicet a loco sepulchri eius, quidam transtulissent, reuerenter excepi, atque intra ambitum metropolitanae, cui gratia Dei praesideo, ecclesiae

Canterbury, and it follows that Canterbury could have been the place where the Wilfridian additions were first added to the *HE*. This remains highly speculative, but the hypothesis gains some credence if we remember that the copy of the *HE* into which these annals were first added was textually related to C, which was almost certainly a Canterbury manuscript, and that William of St. Calais, who had Dur made for the Durham library, certainly could have obtained its exemplar somewhere in the South. The final words of the annal for 705, moreover, which as has been noted are perhaps suggestive of a saint's cult, may also suggest the site of an active cult of Wilfrid as a more likely place of origin. Canterbury is one place, though certainly not the only place, where Wilfrid would have been remembered as a saint in the later Anglo-Saxon period.[44]

As noted above, Wilfrid's career took him to many places, and his monastic network extended from Northumbria, through greater Mercia, all the way to Sussex. But since the additions lack much in the way of local information, we must rely on the manuscripts themselves for further clues as to their place of origin. Win is first attested at Winchester in the fourteenth century, and its earlier provenance is unknown. As noted above, Dur was given to Durham by William of St. Calais, but it could have been copied at Durham, elsewhere in Northumbria, in the south of England, or even in Normandy, although there is otherwise no evidence that the Wilfridian additions ever made their way to Normandy. The *Carmen de abbatibus* may also have been in Δ, which might suggest a Northern connection, but it is equally possible that it was first paired with the *HE* in Win. The associated contents in Dur provide no clues, since the core of the book (containing just the *HE*) was the original gift to the Durham community, and its other contents are later additions.[45]

---

collocaui, presertim cogente illo euangelistae testimonio, meo uidelicet apologetico, quia ubicumque fuerit corpus, congregabuntur et aquilae. [I]taque tantae, tamque Deo dignae affinitatis delectatus uicinitate, et editiore eas entheca decusare, et excerptis de libro uitae eius flosculis, nouo opere pretium duxi carmine uenustare." The text is from Alistair Campbell, ed., *Frithegodi monachi Breuiloquium vitæ beati Wilfredi et Wulfstani cantoris narratio metrica de sancto Swithuno* (Zürich: Thesaurus Mundi, 1950), 2–3. The allusion is to Matthew 24:28/Luke 17:37. On Frithegod, see Michael Lapidge, "A Frankish Scholar in Tenth-Century England: Frithegod of Canterbury/Fredegaud of Brioude," in idem, *Anglo-Latin Literature, 900–1066* (London: Hambledon Press, 1993), 157–81, 481.

[44] Despite the events of 948, the rebuilt community of Ripon continued to claim to possess Wilfrid's relics, and, later on, Peterborough claimed to possess some of his bones as well. If we assume that the full text of the Wilfridian annals predates the addition of the corrupt version of the 658 annal to C (see above, n. 16), then a mid-tenth-century Canterbury context for their composition is no longer plausible, as the hand that inserted the annal in C seems earlier than s. x.

[45] To judge by the quire marks and other indicators, the original core of Dur appears to have been just the first nine quires (altogether 76 fols., now numbered imperfectly as fols. 36–120) of what is today the second section of the MS. These nine quires are of a

The manuscripts would thus seem to provide little concrete evidence, though there remains one tantalizing clue, namely the annal for 667 mentioned above. Plummer held that the 667 annal was to be expanded "noster abbas scripsit" ("our abbot wrote"), and he does not appear to have entertained the possibility that the passage might be corrupt.[46] He even indulged in a bit of speculation about the annal being a reference to the writing of the Lindisfarne Gospels. According to this hypothesis, the annal would be a reference to Bishop Eadfrith of Lindisfarne (698–721), who is famously credited by the volume's tenth-century colophon with having had a hand in its production. But even if we assume, as we probably should, that Eadfrith would have served as a scribe only prior to becoming bishop, the date 667 would be rather too early, as Plummer himself admits.[47] On the contrary, the most likely explanation for the cryptic 667 annal is probably that Δ was in some way corrupt or unclear at this point, and that the scribes of both Dur and Win have done their best to make sense of what was in front of them. If that is so, then they arrived a fairly consistent solution, only diverging in one letter (*nr̄ ab̄b̄ scr̄ī* vs. *n̄r̄ hab scr̄ī*). That *nr̄* ought to be expanded "noster" seems clear enough. Further, I would argue that Win's "ab̄b̄" is easier to explain (i.e., as "abbas") than Dur's "hāb", and I have adopted that reading in the text above. The last word of the annal is the most problematic. The reading "scr̄ī" is found in both witnesses. Rather than expanding this as "scripsit" as Plummer did, I would argue that it seems equally possible, if not more likely, that it ought to be expanded "scribit."[48] Indeed, there is no reason why we need assume that what has been

---

noticeably smoother, less opaque type of parchment than the subsequent quires. Interestingly, fol. 77, a singleton inserted into the fifth of the original nine quires, is of thicker, more opaque parchment, very much like that of quires ten and following, even though there is no apparent disruption of the text on fol. 77, and it has been written by the same scribe and seemingly as part of the same writing campaign. We know that this scribe, William, worked in both England and Normandy, and one wonders if he may have carried blank parchment with him during his travels, only to be forced subsequently to resort to locally-made parchment in order to supply an additional leaf in one of these imported quires. Dur is a complex and important manuscript that deserves to be better understood; for our purposes, however, it is sufficient to note here that there is a clear break after the ninth quire in this core section of the MS. These nine quires originally contained just the *HE*, and all the many other texts in this manuscript are later additions.

[46] Though the fact that he does print the unexpanded text ("nr̄ ab̄b̄ scr̄ī") suggests some lingering doubt on his part.

[47] Recent scholarly opinion would place the creation of the Gospels in the period c. 710–725, and would credit Eadfrith with a supervisory rather than a scribal role in its production; see Michelle P. Brown, *The Lindisfarne Gospels: Society, Spirituality, and the Scribe* (Toronto: University of Toronto Press, 2003), 10.

[48] A third option, of course, is that the word has been truncated by chance (perhaps a bit of runover went unnoticed by the scribe of the parent manuscript), in which case *scribit* and *scripsit* (or indeed any word beginning 'scri-') would be equally plausible. For

preserved as an annal for the year 667 in our manuscripts was originally meant to be a record of past events at all. It might just as easily have been a scribal notation that was intended to indicate that the abbot was writing, or was planning to write, annals to be added to Bede's text at this point.

This hypothesis moves from the realm of speculation to that of plausibility when we examine more closely the full contents of Win. At the end of the text of the *HE*, after the usual closing prayer found in manuscripts of Plummer's c-type (*Praeterea . . . inueniam.*), the same scribe continues by repeating two annals from *HE* v.24. The annals are those for 653 and 655, which recount, respectively, the conversion of the Middle Angles under Peada, son of Penda, and the subsequent death of Penda and conversion of the Mercians two years later. The second annal is followed immediately by two year numbers (AD 653 and 654) the inclusion of which may have been brought about by an erroneous reading of the year number of the second annal as AD 652 (for 655). The following line is blank, and then year numbers for AD 656 to AD 675 are written out continuously over five lines.[49] It seems clear that these numbers are meant to represent the twenty years following the two annals copied out from Bede's text just before, but it is difficult to see what purpose they were meant to serve written continuously in this way. We know, however, that Win is not the manuscript into which the Wilfrid additions were first copied. It is therefore possible that these year numbers have been taken by the scribe of Win from our manuscript Δ, and that in that manuscript they were not written out continuously as in Win, but rather on consecutive lines, leaving space for the annals themselves to be added later, as the events of the individual years were worked out from various sources. If this is the case, then these year numbers may represent the remains of an unrealized plan by the anonymous abbot referred to in the 667 annal to write out a supplement to *HE* v.24. The Wilfrid annals that do survive may have been a first foray into the

---

valuable insights into the interpretation of the manuscripts here, I owe thanks to Professor F. A. C. Mantello, and likewise to the participants of the 2008 Marco Manuscript Workshop at the University of Tennessee, Knoxville. I alone am responsible for the conclusions I have drawn.

[49] The text is found on fol. 108v, col. b: "Anno DCLIII [as noted by Ker and Piper (*Medieval Manuscripts in British Libraries,* 4:578), the MS appears to read DCLVI here, but if this is indeed the case, then it is an error] medil engli sub principe peada fidei mysteriis sunt inbuti. Anno DCLV [according to Ker and Piper, DCLII, but this too, would then be an obvious error—I have seen the manuscript in microfilm but not in person, and the number of minims would allow either reading] penda perit et merci sunt facti Christiani. DCLIII. DCLIIII. D(?). . . [the text trails into the gutter here]. There follows a blank line, and then the following numbers written out continuously over five lines: "DCLVI. DCLVII. DCLVIII. DCLVIIII. DCLX. / DCLXI. DCLXII. DCLXIII. DCLXIIII. DCLXV. / DCLXVI. DCLXVII. DCLXVIII. DCLXVIIII. / DCLXX. DCLXXI. DCLXXII. DCLXXIII. DC / LXXIIII. DCLXV [an error for DCLXXV].

writing of annals, which the abbot had intended to continue for the period from 653 to at least 675.

But if we accept this hypothesis, can that help us to locate the place of origin of the Wilfrid additions? If the numbers copied at the end of Win were meant to be the beginning of a series of annals, then it seems that the conversion of the Mercians under Peada and after the death of Penda was meant to serve as the starting point for the series. Looking ahead to the last year in the series (675) we note that it is in that year that Bede records the death of King Wulfhere (658–674), first Christian king of the Mercians. It is perhaps not a coincidence that the first annal in the series of Wilfridian additions is the annal for 658 recounting that Wulfhere was "set up" upon the throne (an accurate description of his accession as described in *HE* III.24). It is well known that Wilfrid was active in Mercia, and that he struck up friendships with both Wulfhere and his successor Aethelred (675–704). The Wilfridian addition for the year 692 might be taken to reflect a fairly good knowledge of the locus of Wilfrid's activities in that period (among the Middle Angles as opposed to the Mercians).[50] The traces of this series of incomplete annals found in Win would seem to point toward a Mercian monastery, perhaps a foundation of Wilfrid, as the place of origin of the Wilfridian additions. It is just possible that the additions represent the humble beginning of what was originally envisioned as a more ambitious project: a Mercian supplement to Bede's annals recounting their Christianization and the career of their first Christian king, Wulfhere.

---

[50] Further evidence of interest in Mercian affairs may be sought in Δ's version of Bede's annal for 704, which recounts King Aethelred's retirement. Both Dur and Win place this annal under 703, and both alter the length of Aethelred's reign from Bede's thirty-one years. Dur gives the length as thirty years, while Win gives thirty-two (or, depending on how one interprets the minims, perhaps thirty-five) years. These changes could, of course, be the result of scribal confusion and need not necessarily be interpreted as an attempt to improve Bede's information.

Appendix:
A Supplement to Mynors' "Textual Introduction,"
Concerning the Transmission of Bede's *Historia*
ecclesiastica gentis Anglorum[51]

(1) Aschaffenburg, Hofbibliothek, 39 (A.D. 1472, Speyer; later seemingly at Freiburg im Breisgau, Johannisberg [OCarth]);

(2) Berlin, Staatsbibliothek Preußischer Kulturbesitz, Lat. fol. 378 (s. x/xi, Germany?);

(3) Bloomington, Indiana, Lilly Library, MS. 47 (*olim* Poole MS. 98–7, and Phillipps MS. 13153; s. ix²/³, "Maingegend oder Hessen"; see Bernhard Bischoff, *Katalog der festländischen Handschriften des neunten Jahrhunderts [mit Ausnahme der wisigotischen]*, 2 vols. [to date] [Wiesbaden: Harrassowitz, 1998–2004], no. 644);

(4) Deventer, Stadsarchief en Athenaeumbibliotheek, 111 E1 KL (Van Slee I. 94; *olim* MS. 1781; s. xv^med, Heer Florenshuis Deventer; this MS contains the *Continuatio Bedae* annals);

(5) Durham, North Carolina, Duke University Library, lat. 140 (Nonantola, s. ix; a single leaf from the former Bodmer MS now Rome, Biblioteca Nazionale Centrale Vitt. Em. 1452);

(6) Düsseldorf, Universitätsbibliothek, Fragm. K01:B216 (Werden?, s. ix¹/³; Bischoff, *Katalog*, no. 647; a fragment of an excerpt, not a once-complete text);

(7) Florence, Biblioteca Nazionale Centrale, Conv. Soppr. A. 1. 450 (s. xi/xii, by A.D. 1489 at Florence, S. Maria Novella [OP]);

(8) Florence, Biblioteca Nazionale Centrale, Conv. Soppr. 2671 C7 (date?, Badia Fiorentina [OSB]);

(9) Leipzig, Universitätsbibliothek, Haenel 3518 (s. xiii, Germany?; with Geoffrey of Monmouth);

(10) Madrid, Real Biblioteca, *olim* 2 C 2 (s. xiv, current shelfmark unknown; listed by Laistner, but silently omitted by Mynors; to judge by the description in *Neues Archiv* 6 [1881]: 344, it may in fact contain just I.27 [the *Libellus responsionum*] and Cuthbert's letter on the death of Bede);

---

[51] Colgrave and Mynors, *Bede's Ecclesiastical History*, xxxix–lxxvi. I owe the reference to the Leipzig manuscript to Professor Michael Reeve, and the references to the Schøyen MSS to Michael Gullick. I have not included here those manuscripts discussed in Colgrave-Mynors that have changed hands since its original publication, four of which were noted by Michael Lapidge in the revised edition (1991), ix, nor have I endeavored to supplement systematically Laistner's list of MSS containing excerpts from the text (M. L. W. Laistner and H. H. King, *A Hand-list of Bede Manuscripts* [Ithaca: Cornell University Press, 1943], 103–12).

(11) Mainz, Stadtsbibliothek, Hs. I 181, pp. 290–342 (palimpsest from Mainz, s. ix$^{2/4}$, under a 14th-c. *Rhetorica*; see Bischoff, *Katalog*, no. 2669);

(12) Mainz, Stadtsbibliothek, Hs. frag. 1 (fragment of *HE* iv.29–30 from Mainz, s. ix$^{[ca. 2/4]}$; see Bischoff, *Katalog*, no. 2674);

(13) Munich, Clm 118 (A.D. 1549, Florence; perhaps a copy of BNCF, Conv. Soppr. A. 1. 450);

(14) Munich, Georgianum (Sammlung Karl Ziegler), Fragm. 2 (a fragment, s. ix$^{1/2}$, containing *HE* iii.14; it was lost in 1944; see Bischoff, *Katalog*, no. 3513);

(15) Münster, Universitäts- und Landesbibliothek, Fragmentensammlung, Kaps. 1,3 (s. viii^2, Northumbria; prov. Werden);

(16) Nuremberg, Stadtbibliothek, Cent. III 57 (A.D. 1462, Nuremburg Augustinians);

(17–18) Oslo and London, The Schøyen Collection, MS. 033 (s. xiv, England; *HE* books i-iii, with other historical and genealogical materials), and MS. 102 (ca. A.D. 900, Germany, a single-leaf fragment of *HE* i.1);

(19) Trier, Priesterseminar, H 215,1 (s. ix^1, Lotharingia, prov. incunable-binding from Prüm; two bifolia containing parts of *HE* iii.14–19);

(20) Vatican Library, Reg. lat. 692 (s. xii^2; listed in *Archiv* 12 [1874]: 303, and by Laistner, but silently omitted by Mynors, perhaps because it is fragmentary, containing just i.1–10 of the *HE*, together with Geoffrey of Monmouth and Einhard).

The Old English Boethius, the Latin Commentaries, and Bede

Joseph Wittig

In *The King's English*, her recent book studying the OE *Boethius*, Nicole Guenther Discenza reviews the state of the question concerning the Alfredian translation's use of Latin commentaries.[1] Georg Schepss and later Kurt Otten had argued that material added in the translation clearly came from widely-circulating Latin glosses. Others have questioned that conclusion. Some twenty-five years ago I examined one brief passage, the Orpheus meter (3m12), and concluded that the Latin glosses probably contributed little to the Old English version:[2] what was shared by OE and glosses was fairly commonplace information; much in the glosses, including some of their main concerns, was ignored in the OE or sometimes at variance with its additions; and one could find independent additions in the OE without parallel in the glosses but traceable to other sources. Most significantly, such correspondences as do occur between the OE and Latin glosses are found, not in one or two manuscripts, but widely scattered across many of them. Other scholars have come to similar conclusions since then; Discenza, based on

---

[1] Nicole Guenther Discenza, *The King's English: Strategies of Translation in the Old English* Boethius (Albany: SUNY Press, 2005); see "Appendix: the Commentary Problem," 131–35, where the relevant bibliography is listed. Alfred's personal involvement in this translation, and indeed any connection with it on the king's part, has recently been reexamined by Malcolm Godden, "Did King Alfred Write Anything?" (*Medium Aevum* 76 [2007]: 1–23). Godden carefully analyzes the evidence *pro* (quite insubstantial, especially in the light of the Carolingian context for attribution of authorship) and *con* (the overwhelming implausibility that King Alfred could have produced this work). I find his arguments persuasive. Although *pietas* changes slowly, and many scholars will continue to associate this work with the plan for translations announced in the "Preface" to the *Pastoral Care* and continue to use the term "Alfredian" for this translation, one should nevertheless be prepared to consider that the Old English *Boethius* may indeed have been produced after 900.

[2] Joseph S. Wittig, "King Alfred's Boethius and its Latin Sources: A Reconsideration," *Anglo-Saxon England* 11 (1983): 157–98. (Please note two errors in my list of manuscripts on 188: P2 is BN lat. 6769; P6 is BN lat. 14380.)

---

her work for *Fontes Anglo-Saxonici*, concluded that, though there are occasional instances of very similar content, "the great majority of . . . additions and changes have no parallel in the commentaries" she has studied.[3]

A fundamental problem in reaching a final answer to this question is the diversity of these Latin glosses. Courcelle's conclusion that there were two dominant early commentaries, the "St. Gall" and the "Remigian,"[4] blurs very considerably when one examines the early manuscripts closely. "St. Gall" exists in at least two main versions, and most manuscripts show much variation.[5] As for the "Remigian" commentary, there is really no evidence for ascribing it to Remi d'Auxerre; and the MSS in its tradition show clear evidence of individual glosses, gradually collected, accruing into longer clusters which are distinguishable into at least four "families," and there is much variety in the MSS glosses.[6] But by the tenth century there existed a body of "commentary" in two distinguishable traditions, each of which shows much common content; but each seems more likely to reflect a gradual accumulation of glosses over time rather than two original "commentaries" which were subsequently subject to dispersal and dissolution.

My conclusions about the Latin glosses are based on an examination of most of the manuscripts and on my transcription and edition of the glosses of several limited sections.[7] One of these provided the basis for my examination of the

---

[3] Discenza, *The King's English*, 134. Cf. *Fontes Anglo-Saxonici: A Register of Written Sources Used by Anglo-Saxon Authors* (CD-ROM Version 1.0, ed. David Miles, Rohini Jayatilaka, and Malcolm Godden, Fontes Anglo-Saxonici Project, 2002). See under Alfred, Boethius, *The Consolation of Philosophy*.

[4] Pierre Courcelle, *La Consolation de Philosophie dans la tradition littéraire: antécédents et postérité de Boèce* (Paris: Études augustiniennes, 1967). He discusses St. Gall on 275–78 and 403–4, "Remigius" on 278–90, 405–6.

[5] Courcelle did not closely compare manuscripts (see *Consolation*, 275, n. 6), and two of the three he used most (Einsiedeln 179 and St. Gall 845) are continuous copies of the glosses, later and "sophisticated" versions, the latter a direct and often careless copy of the former (see Appendix below).

[6] Joseph Wittig, "The 'Remigian' Glosses on Boethius's *Consolation of Philosophy* in Context," in *Source of Wisdom: Studies in Old English and Medieval Latin in Honor of Thomas D. Hill*, ed. Charles Wright, Fred Biggs, and Thomas Hall (Toronto: University of Toronto Press, 2007), 168–200. For previous studies of the glosses see notes 1–4 above and Malcolm Godden, "The Latin Commentary Tradition and the Old English Boethius: The Present State of the Question" (given at the first annual symposium of The Alfredian Boethius Project, Oxford University, July 2003, and retrievable from http://www.english. ox.ac.uk/boethius/Symposium2003.html).

[7] Originally intending to edit the "Remigian commentary," I was attempting to discover the relationship among the many varying manuscripts. The sections on which I have worked most intensively are 3p9.86 through 3m9 and 3p12.59 through 3m12. For these sections I have transcribed and edited all the "Remigian" MSS before 1100, most of the St. Gall, and many other early glossed copies of the text. For full lists of MSS see

Orpheus meter in 1983. Invitations to participate in symposia organized by the Oxford Boethius Project gave me the opportunity to work further on another section, the glosses to the "O qui perpetua" (3m9, Boethius's dense epitome of Plato's *Timaeus*). This essay will examine what light the Latin glosses might shed on the OE version of the meter, with particular attention to MSS of English provenance and to Bede as an important source for the glossators, and in the process attempt to illustrate some features of the Latin glossing tradition.[8]

One of the earliest surviving manuscripts of the *Consolatio* seems also to be the earliest manuscript of the work with an Anglo-Saxon provenance.[9] Vat. lat. 3363 (V1)[10] is a MS written in the Loire valley in the early ninth century, arguably using an Italian exemplar.[11] The text is glossed in three distinct hands (or sets of hands): a few comments in a hand nearly contemporary with the text; a great number of syntax marks and lexical glosses throughout the MS, along with a few longer glosses, in a late ninth-century hand which Parkes identified as "originating from Wales, South-West England or Cornwall";[12] and some glosses on the earlier folios in tenth-century hands associated with Glastonbury.[13] I wish

---

Appendices A, B, and C in Wittig, "The 'Remigian' Glosses on Boethius's *Consolation*," 184–96.

[8] The new edition of the OE *Boethius* produced by the Oxford Project, edited by Malcolm Godden and Susan Irvine, with a chapter on the Metres by M.S. Griffith, is being submitted to Oxford University Press as I write. It will contain its own massive commentary on the text, which I have not seen. The present analysis is based on my edition of the Latin glosses and Walter John Sedgfield's edition: *King Alfred's Old English Version of Boethius* De consolatione philosophiae (Oxford: Clarendon Press, 1899; repr. Darmstadt: Wissenschaftliche Buchgesellschaft, 1968).

[9] For an account of this MS see Malcolm Godden, "Alfred, Asser, and Boethius," in *Latin Learning and English Lore: Studies in Anglo-Saxon Literature for Michael Lapidge*, ed. Katherine O'Brien O'Keeffe and Andy Orchard, 2 vols. (Toronto: University of Toronto Press, 2005), 1: 326–48.

[10] For the sake of efficiency, MSS will usually be referred to hereafter by sigils, which are resolved in the Appendix.

[11] M. B. Parkes, "A Note on MS Vatican Bibl. Apost., lat. 3363," in *Boethius: His Life, Thought and Influence*, ed. Margaret T. Gibson (Oxford: Blackwell, 1981), 425–27. Fabio Troncarelli has written extensively on this MS; for a discussion of his contributions see Godden, "Alfred, Asser and Boethius," 327–29.

[12] Parkes, "A Note," 425. As the title of Godden's article suggests, these late ninth-century glosses may indicate that the MS was in Anglo-Saxon England at that date, although it is possible that this hand wrote its glosses on the Continent (cf. Godden, "Alfred, Asser and Boethius," 343). As Godden points out, the MS contains not a "commentary" but an accumulation of notes compiled over a century or more, and there is no evidence whatsoever to associate the Welsh glosses with Asser (cf. Wittig, "King Alfred's Boethius," 160–61 and n. 20).

[13] Godden, "Alfred, Asser, and Boethius," discusses the three sets of glosses on 330–37.

to discuss one gloss in particular, a comment written in the late ninth-century Welsh hand that appropriates a substantial passage from Bede's *De Temporum Ratione*. I have seen this gloss in only two other MSS, both Anglo-Saxon, written at Abingdon, ca. 1000 (A C4),[14] which for the most part contain a distinctly English revision of "Remigian" type glosses.[15]

Bede is invoked to explain the challenging words of the meter: "media anima triplicis naturae" (13) which "circuit et simili convertit imagine caelum" (17).[16] Bede's subject is how the "gentiles," having gotten the idea of the seven days of the week from the Hebrews, renamed the days after their own gods. The gloss as I have edited it reads as follows:

> <1A> existimabant enim se habere a sole spiritum, a luna corpus, a *mare* fervorem, a mercurio sapientiam et verbum, a iove temperantiam, a venere voluptatem, a saturno tarditatem. credo quia sol in medio planetarum positus totum mundum, spiritus instar, calefacere et quasi vivificare videtur, ecclesiaste testante qui de ipso loquens ait: girans girando vadit spiritus et in circulos suos *vertitur* [cf. Eccles. 1:6]. luna per humoris ministerium cunctis incrementum corporibus suggerit. martis stella utpote soli proxima *calore* simul et natura est fervens. mercurius perpetuo circa solem discurrendo quasi inexhausta sapientiae luce radiari *putatur*. iuppiter frigore, *saturnus* et ardore, martis hinc *inde*. venus luminis venustate quam ex solis vicinitate percipit suo cernentes allicit aspectu. saturnus eo tardior caeteris planetis quo et superior incedit (V1 Ac C4)

> [Bede, *De Temporum Ratione*, Chap. 8, "De Hebdomada." Italicized words are variants from Jones's edition, discussed below.][17]

---

[14] The gloss occurs in V1 (Vatican City, Biblioteca Apostolica Vaticana, MS. lat. 3363. Text s. ix[1], Loire region), A (Antwerp, Museum Plantin-Moretus, MS. M. 16. 8 [olim lat. 190]. s. x[ex]/xi[in], Abingdon), and C4 (Cambridge, University Library, MS. Kk. 3. 21. s. x[ex]/xi[in], Abingdon).

[15] The first to call attention to this Anglo-Saxon version was Diane K. Bolton, "The Study of the *Consolation of Philosophy* in Anglo-Saxon England," *Archive d'histoire doctrinale et littéraire du Moyen Âge* 44 (1977): 33–78; it is discussed and illustrated futher in Wittig, "The 'Remigian' Glosses," 173–74 and passim.

[16] "The middle soul of tripartite nature" which "circles [the profound mind] and causes the heavens to turn in similar pattern." Translations into modern English are my own; all quotations from the *Consolatio* are taken from *Anicii Manlii Severini Boethii Philosophiae Consolatio*, ed. Ludwig Bieler (Turnhout: Brepols, 1957).

[17] For Bede's text see *Bedae Venerabilis Opera, Pars VI: Opera Didascalica*, ed. Charles W. Jones, Corpus Christianorum, Series Latina 123B (Turnhout: Brepols, 1977), 301, ll. 36–50.

inc simili in imagine i. in similitudine aequali. quare cur hoc dicit in imagine simili, nisi forte imago similis sit mundi, quia in orbis similitudinem factus est, quia orbis similis est sibimet undique, ut dicitur. mundus est universitas omnis creaturae, quae constat ex caelo et terra, quattuor elementis in speciem et in similitudine orbis absoluti conglobatus, et haec quattuor elementa habent inter se invicem concordiam, ut ignis et terra, et aer et aqua, et ignis et aer, et aqua et terra, quia utraque *et aer et ignis quia utraque* [sic] frigida sunt A C4.

[In C4 this addition is written as a separate block; "existimabant . . ." begins a second block on a new line. A writes the whole as one continuous gloss.]

<1B> [translation (the text most relevant for Boethius is in italics):] For they thought they had soul from the sun, body from the moon, heat from [Mars], wisdom and speech from Mercury, moderation from Jove, pleasure from Venus, slowness [dullness?] from Saturn. *I believe [they thought this] because, positioned in the middle of the planets, the sun seems to heat and as it were vivify the entire world, like a spirit, as Ecclesiastes bears witness speaking about the sun: "wheeling in gyres the spirit turns its circles."* The moon through the ministry of moisture furnishes increase to all bodies. The star of Mars, since closest to the sun, is glowing both by heat and by nature. Mercury, by perpetually running about the sun, is thought to shine with an inexhaustible light of wisdom. Jupiter [is moderated] by the cold of Mars, and Saturn by his heat, to opposite effect. Venus, by the beauty of light which she obtains from the closeness of the sun, attracts the discerning by her appearance. Saturn is slower than the other planets to the extent that he marches higher.

The six words italicized in the Latin gloss are all variants from the text printed by Jones,[18] and only one of them (the gloss *calore* for Jones's *colore*) is reported by him as a variant occurring in other copies of Bede.[19] Given the shared variants,

---

[18] V1 at this point (fol. 29r, margin lower left and bottom) is very badly faded, but digital enhancement of microfilm combined with the texts of A and C4 allow me to read it with enough confidence to reject Troncarelli's reconstruction of V1's text, which relied on Bede as published (Fabio Troncarelli, *Tradizioni perdute: La "Consolatio philosophiae" nell'alto medioevo* [Padua: Antenore, 1981], 182–83).

[19] (1) The variants are: *mare*, Jones *marte* (obviously correct in context); (2) *vertitur*, Jones *revertitur*; (3) *calore*, Jones *colore*—Jones reports *calore* in 4 MSS (and *calore* is printed in the *PL* text); (4) *putatur*, Jones *putabatur*; (5) *saturnus*, Jones *saturni*; (6) *inde*, Jones *inde temperatur*. In his introduction to the text, Jones notes that "the variations among the many texts which existed a century and a half [after Bede's death] are very slight. Bede's words were venerated and protected by careful scribes and assiduous collation" (241). In this case the number of shared variants in these few lines significantly adds to the evidence for the interdependence of these three MSS.

I suspect that V1 was used directly by the Abingdon glossators. Given the material both A and C4 added at the beginning (as the apparatus reports), along with the shared dittography at the end of this addition (bold italic in the apparatus), I conclude that one of these two MSS was copied from the other. The fact that the glosses are combined in A but written as two separate blocks in C4 leads me to think it more likely that A was copied from C4. Both C4 and A collect glosses not found in other copies of the "Anglo-Saxon" revision. Godden has documented the fact that C4 frequently has glosses found in V1, and other late Anglo-Saxon MSS also borrow from it.[20] With the help of C4 and another coeval Anglo-Saxon MS I can read the immediately preceding gloss in V1 (which is badly faded and partially overwritten by a later cursive note), a gloss on *animas* of line 18 which I have found nowhere else:

<2A> [ANIMAS:] intelligentiae et ratione spiritus superiores hominum (V1 Ge C4)[21]

(which I take to mean:)

<2B> [SOULS:] intelligences and spirits of men superior because of reason

(— as distinct from the *vitasque minores* of the same line: another instance of V1 being used as a source of glosses in England around the year 1000).

The Welsh scribe wrote the extract from Bede in V1; since the passage appears only in two other Anglo-Saxon MSS arguably derived from V1 (C4 from V1, A from C4), the gloss was apparently not in wide circulation. There is no way to know whence it came to V1: direct consultation of Bede seems possible (the *De temporum ratione*, as we will see, seems the most likely source for other glosses on the *Consolatio*), but there is not much other evidence that the Welsh scribe was combing through sources. It may be that V1 preserves an excerpt from an "auctor" which somehow came to his attention or that he found it as a gloss, already stripped of attribution. The passage provides context for an idea attested

---

[20] Godden, "Alfred, Asser, and Boethius," 337–40. Godden reports that of the later Anglo-Saxon MSS, C4 appropriated V1's glosses most frequently, and P9 second most with about half as many borrowings. Godden seems to think it likely that C4 and P9 consulted V1 independently, though he does not insist on this (339–40). His examples come chiefly from Books 1 and 2, where all three phases of glossing (early Carolingian, late ninth-century Welsh, and tenth-century Glastonbury) are active, and he does not mention this instance.

[21] Ge: formerly Geneva, Bibliotheca Bodmeriana, Cod. 175, s. x^{ex}/xi^{in}, England (St. Augustine's, Canterbury?). Troncarelli, in his provisional transcription, had offered "Intelligent . . . [cum] ratione spiritus . . ..eri oper hominum" (*Tradizioni perdute*, 182).

in the earliest MS of the *Consolatio* extant[22] where we find, among its relatively few glosses, the following on the *mediam animam*:

<3A> connectens animam. id est solem qui cuncta fovet suo calore ac splendore qui per consona membra currit id est lunae et stellarum (On)

And glosses in the St. Gall and Remigian tradition show similar ideas:

<3B> solis qui lucet, fovet, incendit, vel caeli, terrae marisque (N E1 *par* L4)

L4: qui lucet, nutrit, incidit {*inl* at TRIPLICIS}; **marisque**: et maris E1[1], ac maris E1[2].

<3C> 1 vis animae omnem molem corporis regit. philosophi animam mundi solem esse dixerunt quia sicut calefacit et vivificat corpus anima, ita solis calore vivificantur omnia, eiusque calor diffusus per creaturas facit eas gignere. 2 et re vera ut philosophi dicunt calore illius omnia et gignunt et gignuntur pariter cum humore, deo ita disponente . . . (B Ma P9 T L4b V5 Ab E1 M P3 P4 V7 B1)[23]

<4.1–2>[24] 1 quidam philosophorum animam mundi solem dixerunt quod, sicut anima corpus humanum, ita calore illius vivificantur omnia nascentia eiusque calor diffusus per creaturas facit eas gignere, et re vera calore illius omnia et gignunt et gignuntur pariter cum humore deo ita disponente. 2 quem solem triplicis naturae esse dixerunt videlicet quia est eius substantia, calor quoque et splendor. sed non satis praesenti loco congruit hanc animam accipi quoniam non potest prosequi ratio. . . . (L V6 P8 P5 P1 V2 P10 Es A P V3 P6 Ge C4)

It is possible that Bede was an original source for this idea; but Latin commentary on the *Timaeus* seems to underlie other glosses on this meter, even though its ideas

---

[22] Orléans, Bibliothèque municipale, 270, s. ix[in], glosses ix[1], Fleury. On's glosses interpret the *anima* of the meter as either the sun or the human soul, as do nearly all other early glosses.

[23] Variants, except those among Anglo-Saxon MSS which might conceivably bear on the OE text, have been omitted here to save space; I have printed some of these same glosses with full variants in Wittig, "The 'Remigian' Glosses," 176–81. As will emerge from following examples, many of the longer glosses are made up of shorter explanations which have accreted into clusters; within the text of these I have used (boldface) numbers to divide them into subsections.

[24] This is the first part of a long gloss cluster the rest of which will be quoted below as 4.3–7 and 4.8–10.

underwent considerable simplification in the ninth and tenth centuries, in which case V1's gloss may invoke Bede as a supplementary, more familiar source.[25]

V1 is a carefully-prepared copy of the *Consolatio* which was subsequently glossed by several generations of readers. Later Anglo-Saxon manuscripts are, for the most part, designed as glossed texts from the outset: the manuscripts have generous margins all around, and have been ruled for both interlinear and marginal glosses.[26] P9 is a copy of the "Remigian" glosses to which glosses of the Anglo-Saxon revision have been added (P9b); other copies of the Anglo-Saxon version of the Remigian glosses, especially A Ge and C4, collect still other glosses, as the above examples from V1 and Godden's study attest. Noteworthy is the fact they are collecting glosses, rather than consulting "auctores" directly, and likely consulting one another: thus C4 from V1, A from C4. Equally noteworthy is the

---

[25] Calcidius, commenting on the *anima mundi*, wrote: "Illud uero, quod a meditullio porrecta anima esse dicitur, quidam dici sic putant, ut non tamquam a medietate totius corporis facta dimensione porrecta sit, sed ex ea parte membrorum uitalium in quibus pontificium uiuendi situm est ideo que uitalia nuncupantur. Non ergo a medietate corporis, quae terra est, sed a regione uitalium, id est sole, animae uigorem infusum esse mundano corpori potius intellegendum pronuntiant, siquidem terra immobilis, sol uero semper in motu; item que uteri medietas immobilis, cor semper in motu, quando etiam recens extinctorum animalium corda superstites etiam tunc motus agant. Ideo que solem cordis obtinere rationem et uitalia mundi totius in hoc igni posita esse dicunt" (*Commentarius in Platonis Timaeum*, ed. J.H. Waszink, Plato Latinus 4 [London and Leiden: The Warburg Institute and Brill, 1975], 151, l. 12 – 152, l. 2). The likelihood that this passage or something derived from it circulated in connection with 3m9.13 as the teachings of the *philosophi* is suggested by glosses circulating in both the St. Gall and in the "Remigian" tradition. St. Gall: ". . . quod anima sit media quia philosophi affirmant quod anima cor maxime complectat, quod per medietatem corporis infixum esse liquet, et illo quoque cogitationes inhaerent. non minus vero sol pro anima accipitur quia medietatem videtur possidere" (L4 Ma E1); Remigian (the first part of a long gloss cluster the rest of which will be quoted below as 8.2, 8.3–7, 8.8–12): <8.1>"1 media dicitur anima non quod a meditullio corporis, i. ab umbilico, sit porrecta sed quia in corde sedes illius proprie est ubi est pontificium vitae. . . ." (B Ma P9 T L4b V5 Ab E1 M P3 P4 V7 V6 V2 B1).

[26] On the basis of the glosses I have studied, I would distinguish two subsets of the Anglo-Saxon version of the glosses: Es C2 O, and P9b A P P6 Ge C4. Of the first group, Es does not look as if it were intended for glosses: the margins are relatively small and unruled. Ruling has either largely vanished from the folios of C2 or it was usually unruled. O was designed for glosses but these were only sporadically completed, and the folios do not appear to have been ruled where there are no glosses. By contrast the MSS of the second subset were all designed to be glossed texts, with generous margins, ruled for both interlinear and marginal glosses (with two lines of gloss to each line of text). For the *Consolatio*'s emergence as a "school" text, see Günter Glauche, *Schullektüre im Mittelalter: Entstehung und Wandlungen des Lektür Kanons bis 1200 nach den Quellen dargestellt*, Münchener Beiträge zur Mediävistik und Renaissance-Forschung 5 (Munich: Arbeo-Gesellschaft, 1970), 13–14, 29–30, 55, 59–61, 76–77, 91–93.

fact that C4 and A, which already had the gist of V1's gloss (see example **4.1–2** above) chose to collect the excerpt from Bede. What explains the fact that, of the Anglo-Saxon MSS with (direct or indirect) access to this gloss, only C4 and A copied it? What explains the fact that Ge took the gloss on *animas* of 3m9.18 but not the gloss from Bede? Were these deliberate acts of selection (by scribe or teacher), or the accidents of V1's circulating through Anglo-Saxon scriptoria? If deliberate acts, do they show intellectual curiosity or a magpie mentality? In any case, here we see gleaning from earlier glossed *Consolations* rather than a survival from an original "master commentary" or the fresh consultation of original sources. There are other examples of extracts from authoritative sources circulating as glosses on, or in close association with, the *Consolatio* which never became part of a standard gloss set. And there is no sign that this early gloss from Bede, very likely available in England in the late ninth century, influenced the OE translation.

Indeed, contrasting the OE rendering of 3m9.13–14 with the Latin glosses is instructive:

<5>   Þu eac
þa ðriefealdan sawla on geðwærum limum styrest, swa þæt ðære
sawle þy læsse ne bið on ðam læstan fingre ðe on eallum þam   p. 81, 15
lichoman. Forþi ic cwæð þæt sio sawul wære þreofeald,
forþamþe uðwitan secgað þæt hio hæbbe þrio gecynd. An ðara
gecynda is þæt heo bið wilnigende, oðer þæt hio bið irsiende,
þridde þæt hio bið gesceadwis. Twa þara gecynda habbað netenu
swa same swa men; oðer þara is wilnung, oðer is irsung.   20
Ac se mon ana hæfð gesceadwisnesse, nalles nan oðru gesceaft;
forði he hæfð oferþungen ealle þa eorðlican gesceafta mid
geðeahte 7 mid andgite. Forþam seo gesceadwisnes sceal wealdan
ægðer ge þære wilnunga ge þæs yrres, forþam hio is synderlic
cræft þære saule.[27]

That the soul is distributed throughout the body to the smallest finger is, I think, a commonplace, though it does have a striking parallel in a short gloss found in two Anglo-Saxon MSS: "quia [anima est] nec minus in digito quam in toto

---

[27] "You also guide the threefold soul in harmonious members, so that there is no less of the soul in the least finger than in all the body. I say that the soul is threefold for this reason, because the learned say that it has three natures. One of those is that it is concupiscible, another that it is irascible, the third that it is rational. Beasts have two of these natures as well as men do; one of those is concupiscible, the other is irascible. But man alone has reason, not any other earthly creature; therefore man has surpassed all earthly creatures with thought and with intelligence. Therefore rationality ought to rule both concupiscence and ire, because it is the distinguishing power of the soul."

corpore" (Ge C4).[28] That the soul has a threefold nature, *wilniende, irsende, gesceadwis* (*concupisciblis, irascibilis, rationalis*), the last of which distinguishes it from the beasts and should rule the other two, is a commonplace.[29] Although the Remigian glosses employ it, they do so with a moral emphasis absent from the OE.

One of them, only tangentially relevant for the OE, nevertheless illustrates what seems to have been the typical trajectory of a gloss's development, and if Bede was a source for the soul as sun it would to a certain extent parallel what occurred in that instance. This Remigian gloss is based on a passage from Gregory:

> <6> Tres quippe vitales spiritus creavit omnipotens Deus: unum qui carne non tegitur; alium qui carne tegitur, sed non cum carne moritur; tertium qui carne tegitur, et cum carne moritur. Spiritus namque est qui carne non tegitur, angelorum; spiritus, qui carne tegitur, sed cum carne non moritur, hominum; spiritus, qui carne tegitur, et cum carne moritur, jumentorum omniumque brutorum animalium. Homo itaque sicut in medio creatus est, ut esset inferior angelo, superior iumento, ita aliquid habet commune cum summo, aliquid commune cum infimo, immortalitatem scilicet spiritus cum angelo, mortalitatem vero carnis cum jumento . . .[30]

---

[28] Compare a gloss in three other Anglo-Saxon MSS: "et hic est ordo. tu deus resolvis i. dividis animam quae est triplicis naturae, quae quasi in medio infusa corpori inest, *movens cuncta illius membra ita ut nullum membrorum inspiratione expers sit*" (Es C2 O). Ambrose says something very similar, in the process of making an argument by an analogy which seems taken for granted: "animae tamen uigor per corpus omne diffunditur, siue manus siue pes siue digitus particeps sensus est" (*Expositio psalmi cxviii*, ed. Michael Petschenig, CSEL 62 [Vienna: Tempsky, 1913], 443, ll. 3–5). The idea appears also in Claudianus Mamertus, *De statu animae* which suggests it was indeed a common one: "nec alia pars animae sentificat oculum et alia uiuificat digitum, sed sicut in oculo tota uiuit et per oculum tota uidet, ita et in digito tota uiuit et per digitum tota sentit" (ed. Augustus Engelbrecht, CSEL 11 [Vienna: Tempsky, 1885; repr. New York: Johnson, 1966], 155, ll. 13–26).

[29] Malcolm Godden has identified a passage in Alcuin's *De animae ratione* which closely parallels the OE, lines 16–25: "Triplex est enim animae, ut philosophi volunt, natura: est in ea quaedam pars concupiscibilis, alia rationalis, tertia irascibilis. Duas enim habent harum partes nobiscum bestiae et animalia communes, id est, concupiscentiam, et iram. Homo solus inter mortales ratione viget, consilio valet, intelligentia antecellit. Sed his duobus, id est, concupiscentiae et irae, ratio, quae mentis propria est, imperare debet" (*PL* 101. 639D-640). See Malcolm Godden, "Anglo-Saxons on the Mind," in *Learning and Literature in Anglo-Saxon England: Studies Presented to Peter Clemoes on the Occasion of his Sixty-fifth Birthday*, ed. Michael Lapidge and Helmut Gneuss (Cambridge: Cambridge University Press, 1985), 271–98, at 274.

[30] *Dialogorum libri quattuor*, ed. Adalbert de Vogüé, Sources Chrétiennes 265 (Paris: Editions du Cerf, 1980), IV.III.1–2, (22–24, ll. 1–13).

One MS has this passage, very slightly recast, as a part of a continuous gloss on 3m9:

<7> . . . sed quod beatus gregorius in dialogorum libro dicit melius hoc loco congruit. nam ut ipse testatur tres utiles spiritus creavit omnipotens deus: unum qui nec carne tegitur nec cum carne moritur, i. angelorum; alium qui carne tegitur sed non cum carne moritur, hominum; tertium qui et carne tegitur et cum carne moritur, brutorum animalium. homo vero, sicut in medio est conditus, ita habet aliquid commune cum infimo, immortalitatem quippe spiritus cum angelo. mortalitatem vero carnis habet cum iumento, et ideo recte anima media dicitur . . . (L)

L's gloss preserves the attribution to author and work ("quod beatus gregorius in dialogorum libro dicit"). It explicitly selects this explanation over others ("sed . . . melius hoc loco congruit"), and it remains a relatively straightforward adaptation of Gregory's text. Where it does not reproduce Gregory verbatim, it simply omits a word or two or reflects a minor variant (for example, Gregory's "Tres quippe vitales" becomes L's "Tres utiles," "carne non" becomes "nec carne," "itaque" becomes "vero"), while in the middle of the passage L slightly abbreviates and rearranges Gregory's text. L retains Gregory's organizing "one, two, three" and only once tinkers by adding a "moritur" or "tegitur."

With L's adaptation of Gregory contrast the version which circulated widely in a group of mainly continental MSS preserving a version of the "Remigian" glosses:

<8.2> . . . 2 aut certe media dicitur quod sit anima rationabilis media inter animam pecudum et spiritum angelorum. omnis autem spiritus aut carne tegitur et cum carne moritur, aut carne quidem tegitur sed cum carne non moritur, aut nec carne tegitur nec moritur. anima pecudum carne tegitur et cum carne moritur, anima hominis carne quidem tegitur sed cum carne non moritur, spiritus angelorum nec carne tegitur nec moritur. . . . (B Ma P9 T L4b V5 Ab E1 M P3 P4 V7 V6 V2 B1)

This version deliberately reshapes Gregory's ideas. *Media*, the lemma from 3m9.13, has been promoted to the beginning and explained first: "rationabilis anima" is situated between animals and angels. Then, working "upwards," the gloss relates the three souls to flesh and death; but unlike Gregory, it restates the ideas in deliberately parallel clauses, in each of which "tegitur" and "moritur" are repeated. Instead of Gregory's simple "one, two, three" it uses balanced and correlated connectors: "omnis *autem* spiritus *aut* carne tegitur *et cum* carne moritur, *aut* carne *quidem* tegitur *sed cum* carne *non* moritur, *aut nec* carne tegitur *nec* moritur." And finally, as Gregory did, it applies this explicitly to beasts, humans, and angels—but again, in carefully parallel clauses in each of which "tegitur" and "moritur" are repeated.

Thus while example 7 seems focused on the *auctor* and his matter, 8.2 seems a deliberately "stylized" recasting, one more attentive to its own form than to its *auctor*—the attribution has vanished. And the MSS show this gloss circulating both as a distinct extract from a "source" (in L) and in gloss clusters of various length offering alternative interpretations ("aut certe . . ." it begins).[31] Thus do these glosses develop.

But while it serves to illustrate a typical gloss's development, the passage from Gregory sheds little or no light on the OE version; the only real point of correspondence between Gregory and the OE is that between *netenu* (passage **5**, line 19) and Gregory's mention of beasts with the kind of soul which dies with the flesh. One does find in the Latin glosses the triple division of the human soul into concupiscible, irascible, and rational. There are several versions of this among the Remigian glosses:

<8.8–12> 8 iste ergo minor mundus habet animam triplicis naturae, est enim irascibilis concupiscibilis rationabilis. irascibilis ut vitiis irascatur et corporis voluptatibus, concupiscibilis est ut deum diligat et virtutes appetat, rationabilis est ut inter creatorem et creaturam, inter bonum et malum discernere possit. 9 quae tria si rationabiliter fuerint custodita coniungunt creaturam creatori. si vero fuerint permutata mentem debilem reddunt. 10 si illa pars fuerit corrupta quae irascibilis dicitur fit homo tristis, rancidus, felle amaritudinis plenus. 11 si autem illa pars vitiata fuerit quae concupiscibilis dicitur fit homo ebriosus, libidinosus et voluptatum servus. 12 si vero illa pars animae corrumpatur quae vocatur rationabilis fit homo superbus, hereticus, omnibus subiectus vitiis (Ma T L4b V5 Ab E1 M P3 P4 V7 V6 B1)

<4.8–10> 8 iste minor mundus i. homo habet animam triplicis naturae quoniam secundum quod augustinus et cassianus in collationibus claudianus quoque atque cassiodorus dicunt est rationabilis, irascibilis, concupiscibilis, quae tria dum rationabiliter disponuntur coniungunt creaturam creatori. 9 si vero permutata fuerint removent eum longe a creatoris contemplatione, quoniam si ratio pervertatur excrescit in superbiam et vanam gloriam, si ira in tristitiam et accediam, si concupiscentia in libidinem et gastrimargiam. 10 debet enim ratione uti discernendo creatorem a creatura, bonum a malo; debet sibi irasci ne consentiat corpori; et debet summum bonum rationabiliter concupiscere (P8 P5 P1 P10 Es A P V3 P6 Ge C4)

<9> ideo dixit anima hominis triplicis naturae quia est rationabilis, irascibilis, concupiscibilis. 2 media anima dicitur quod sit media inter animam pecudum et spiritum angelorum. omnis autem spiritus aut cum carne tegitur [et] cum carne moritur sicut pecudum, aut cum carne tegitur sed cum

---

[31] In all the MSS listed as containing example **8.2**, this gloss follows the one quoted in note 22 as 8.1, "media dicitur anima non quod a meditullio corporis." In MSS B, V6, and V2 the cluster ends at the end of example 8.2; in P9 these two begin a slightly longer cluster. In the other MSS this is part of a string of alternative explanations which occupies some 30 printed lines, 8.1 through 8.8–12.

ea non moritur ut hominis, aut nec carne tegitur nec moritur ut spiritus angelorum (P10 L1)

Thus the Latin glosses clearly show that the commonplace of the threefold soul circulated widely. Both **8.8–12** and **4.8–10** offer slightly different recastings, and example **9** shows both Gregory's "tegitur . . . moritur" triplet and the concupiscible, irascible, rational triad circulating as a separate gloss. **8.8–12** and **4.8–10** surely develop from a common original. Both begin identically, making their transition from a gloss on *homo* as *minor mundus* (which we will examine shortly) to this new one on the soul of a triple nature, but **4.8–10** adds the list of alleged *auctores*. Then these glosses turn to the moral implications of the triad, each treating the same four topics in slightly different styles: these three "natures" being used well collectively, being used well individually, their being perverted collectively, their being perverted individually.[32]

Despite the **4.8–10** gloss's alleging Augustine, Cassian, Claudianus, and Cassiodorus as sources, I have found nothing in those authors corresponding to this gloss, in the language of either version. Possibly the claim is a "professorial" gesture, implicitly confirming how familiar the idea was. That the three passions should be used properly was another commonplace which can be found, for instance, in a gloss on Matthew's gospel which circulated very widely and which goes back at least to Jerome. The verse is Matt. 13: 33, on the leaven which the woman hides in three measures of flour:

> <10> Et nos ergo si acceperimus fermentum euangelicum sanctarum scripturarum de quo supra dictum est, tres humanae animae passiones in unum redigentur ut in ratione possideamus prudentiam, in ira odium contra uitia, in desiderio cupiditatem uirtutum et hoc totum fiet per doctrinam euangelicam quam nobis mater ecclesia praestitit.[33]

---

[32] **4.3–7** begins with a list of their individual intended and proper use (we have them *ut*); it then states the effect of their collective proper use; it goes on to the results of collective improper use — proper and improper in parallel "if" clauses. **4.3–7**'s closing section is a series of "if . . . then" statements about the results of their individual perversion. The order of specifying the individual appetites is always: irascible, concupiscible, rational. After its opening, **8.3–7** begins with the summary of proper use (a "while" rather than an "if" clause, but otherwise nearly identical with the corresponding section of **4.3–7**). Then an "if" clause about their perversion — again sharing much wording with **4.3–7**. The list of individual perversions follows, "if" clauses sharing the single verb *pervertatur*; and this gloss concludes with a series of *debet* clauses stating how each individually ought to be employed. **8.3–7** always gives the powers in the order: rational, irascible, concupiscible.

[33] *Commentariorum in Matthaeum libri iv*, ed. D. Hurst and M. Adriaen, Corpus Christianorum, Series Latina 77 (Turnhout: Brepols, 1969), 109, ll. 905–910. Matt. 13:33 reads: "Aliam parabolam locutus est eis simile est regnum caelorum fermento quod acceptum mulier abscondit in farinae satis tribus donec fermentatum est totum." This

The glosses' specifying the vices which derive from the perversion of each of the passions echoes a passage from one of the alleged authorities, Cassian's *Collations*[34] — and a very similar passage occurs in Alcuin *De animae ratione*,[35] shortly following the parallel with the OE to which Godden called attention (n. 29 above). The OE, we should notice, rather than following this well-beaten track, pursues other interests.

And so the glosses serve to highlight features of the OE because their priorities are so different from those of the OE translator. In the St. Gall and "Remigian" glosses, it is lines 13–17 of the meter which attract the longest and most elaborate explanations. By contrast the OE devotes only 29 of its 112 lines to this part of the meter. Both St. Gall and Remigian traditions reflect earlier attempts to understand the *anima* somehow as the "world soul" by understanding it as the sun; in the St. Gall glosses sun predominates, in the Remigian sun is proposed but human soul is preferred, as the following extracts from the Remigian glosses will show. In the OE only the human soul is proposed. And the OE makes no mention of an idea, crucial in the Remigian glosses, connecting human soul to *anima mundi* through man as microcosm:

<8.3–7> 3 prudentioribus autem videtur hoc loco potius animam rationabilem debere intellegi quae magnam concordiam habet cum mundo, unde et homo graece microcosmos dicitur, i. minor mundus. sicut enim mundus

---

gloss was often repeated. Hrabanus Maurus: ". . . tres humanae animae passiones in unum redigentur, ut in rationabili possideamus prudentiam, in ira odium contra uitia, in desiderio cupiditatem uirtutum" (*Expositio in Matthaeum*, ed. Bengt. Löfstedt, CCCM 174 [Turnhout: Brepols, 2000], 393, ll. 21–24); Otfrid of Wizanburg, *Glossae in Matthaeum*: "Ille passiones redigantur in unum, ut possideamus rationabile in prudentia, iram in odio uitiorum, desiderium in cupiditate uirtutum" (ed. C. Grifoni, CCCM 200 [Turnhout: Brepols, 2003], 189–90, ll. 309–311); Paschasius Radbertus, *Expositio in Mattheo libri xii*: ". . . tres istas humanae animae passiones, in unum fuerint redactae et conspersae fermento iustitiae ita ut in ratione uigeat prudentia in ira odium perfectum surgat contra uitia in desiderio uero uel concupiscentia caritas Dei et proximi commutetur ut sit semper in homine uirida cupiditas uirtutum" (ed. Beda Paulus, CCCM 56A [Turnhout: Brepols, 1984], 716–17, ll. 851–85); Sedulius Scotus, *Kommentar zum Evangelium nach Matthäus*: ". . . tres humanae animae passiones in unum redigentur, ut in ratione possideamus prudentiam, in ira odium contra uitia, in desiderio cupiditatem uirtutum" (ed. Bengt Löfstedt, 2.2 [Freiburg: Herder, 1991], 355, ll. 14–16).

[34] *Conlationes*, Conlatio 24, cap. 15 (ed. Michael Petschenig, CSEL 13 [Vienna: Geroldi, 1886], 691, ll. 15–24).

[35] "Concupiscentia data est homini ad concupiscenda quae sunt utilia, et quae sibi ad salutem proficiant sempiternam. Si vero corrumpitur, nascitur ex ea gastrimargia, fornicatio, et phylargiria. Ira data est ad vitia cohibenda, ne impiis, id est, peccatis, homo serviat dominis . . . ; ex qua corrupta, procedit tristitia, et acedia. Ratio data est, ut diximus, omnem hominis vitam regere, et gubernare, ex qua si corrumpitur, oritur superbia, et cenodoxia": *PL* 101. 640 C-D.

quattuor elementis et quattuor temporibus constat ita et homo quattuor humoribus et quattuor temporibus. videamus ergo mundi et hominis concordiam. quattuor sunt elementa, aer ignis aqua terra. **4** aer calidus et humidus
est, ver calidum et humidum similiter, et humidus sanguis qui est in puero
aeque calidus et humidus, pueritia calida et humida. **5** ignis calidus est et
siccus, aestas calida et sicca, colera rubea quae abundat in adolescente calida
et sicca, adolescentia etiam calida et sicca. **6** terra frigida et sicca, autumnus
frigidus et siccus, melancolia i. colera nigra quae est in iuvenibus frigida et
sicca, iuventus frigida et sicca. **7** aqua frigida et humida est, hiems frigida et
humida, flegma quae abundat in senibus frigida et humida, senectus frigida
et humida. . . . (Ma T L4b V5 Ab E1 M P3 P4 V7 B1 *par* P9)[36]

<4.3–7> **3** dixerunt et de hoc loco diversi diversa, quorum opiniones omit-
tentes quod prudentioribus visum est succincte dicamus. homo graeco vo-
cabulo microcosmus appellatur i. minor mundus, habet siquidem concordiam cum mundo huiusmodi. **4** mundus constat ex quattuor elementis et
quattuor temporibus et homo similiter, habet enim corpus ex terra, sanguinem ex igne, humorem ab aqua, flatum ab aere. **5** potest et aliter dici.
concordiam habet cum aere et vernali tempore, quae habent humorem et
calorem, in pueritia et sanguine; **6** cum aestate et igne, quae habent calorem
et siccitatem, in adolescentia vel iuventute et in colera rubea; cum autumno
et terra et melancholia, quae habent ariditatem et frigus, in senectute; **7**
concordat cum aqua et hieme et flegmate, quae habent frigus et humorem,
in decrepita aetate — proprium est enim senibus frigidos esse. (V6 P5 P1 V2
P10 A P V3 P6 Ge C4 *par* Es)[37]

Glosses **8.3–7** and **4.3–7** are very similar, **4.3–7** a slight recasting of **8.3–7**. Both
begin with similar gestures: both will follow "the more prudent" opinion (staying
away from the dangerous idea of a world soul). **8.3–7** is explicit about identifying
anima as human, whereas **4.3–7** begins with what one might take as a professorial
flourish (we will leave aside multiple diverging opinions and succinctly say what
seems best). Both then state that *homo* is a *microcosmus i. minor mundus* with great
concord with the macro *mundus*. They identically state the observation that the
world has four elements and four seasons. (**8.3–7** is more verbose than **4.3–7**'s
"et homo similiter.") **4.3–7** adds the idea that the elements correspond to human
body, blood, wetness, and breath, then it returns with "potest et aliter dici." **8.3–7**

---

[36] P9 has most of this gloss (*partim*): sections 3–4 conclude one block, 5–6 appear
in another, where at 6 P9 diverges into what amounts to a conflation with other glosses:
"terra frigida triplicis naturae est videlicet propter substantiam calorem splendorem, habet enim tria officia in se inluminati [sic] aduret fovet {cf. "vis animae"}. ALITER anima
triplicis naturae irascibilis concupiscibilis rationabilis."

[37] Es has section 3, with variants, and ends (*homo . . . appellatur*): Homo quia grecis
microcosmos i. est minor mundus appellatur, habet (and Es resumes, after eyeskip, with
"habet" (see gloss 4.8–10 "[iste enim minor mundus] habet . . .").

gestures "videamus" and names the elements without reference to body parts. Then, using different verbal structures, each spells out the relations between two qualities, an element, a season of year, a humor, and an age of man.

The closest analogue I have found for these glosses' presentation of micro-cosm / macrocosm is a passage from Bede's *De temporum ratione*, chapter 35, "De quattuor temporibus, elementis, humoribus," where we find, in one passage, that *homo* is a *microcosmus i. minor mundus*, with a body tempered by these same quali-ties the elements have, and by a succession of related dominant humors, in suc-cessive stages of life:

<11A> Tempora sunt anni quattuor, quibus sol per diuersa caeli spatia discurrendo subiectum temperat orbem diuina utique procurante sapien-tia, ut non semper eisdem commoratus in locis feruoris auiditate munda-num depopuletur ornatum, sed paulatim per diuersa commigrans terrenis fructibus nascendis maturandisque temperamenta custodiat. A quo tem-peramento uidetur temporibus inditum nomen; uel certe quia quadam suae similitudine qualitatis ad inuicem contemperata uoluuntur, tempora recte uocantur. **Hiems** enim, utpote longius sole remoto, *frigidus est et humidus*; *uer*, illo super terras redeunte, *humidum et calidum*; *aestas*, illo superferuente, *calida et sicca*; *autumnus*, illo ad inferiora decidente, *sic-cus et frigidus*. Sicque fit ut, amplexantibus singulis medio moderamine quae circa se sunt, orbis instar ad inuicem cuncta concludantur; quibus aeque qualitatibus disparius quidem per se sed alterutra ad inuicem socie-tate connexis, ipsa quoque mundi elementa constat esse distincta. *Terra* namque *sicca et frigida, aqua frigida et humida, aer humidus et calidus, ignis est calidus et siccus*; ideoque haec autumno, illa hiemi, iste ueri, ille com-paratur aestati. Sed et *homo ipse, qui a sapientibus microcosmos, id est mi-nor mundus, appellatur*, hisdem per omnia qualitatibus habet temperatum corpus, imitantibus nimirum singulis eius quibus constat humoribus, mo-dum temporum quibus maxime pollet. *Sanguis* siquidem, qui uere cres-cit, humidus et calidus; *cholera rubea*, quae aestate, calida et sicca; *cholera nigra*, quae autumno, sicca et frigida; *phlegmata*, quae hieme, frigida sunt et humida. Et quidem *sanguis in infantibus* maxime uiget, *in adolescenti-bus cholera rubea, melancholia in transgressoribus*, id est fel cum faece nigri sanguinis admixtum, *phlegmata dominantur in senibus*. Item sanguis eos in quibus maxime pollet facit hilares, laetos, misericordes, multum ridentes et loquentes; cholera uero rubea faciunt macilentos, multum tamen come-dentes, ueloces, audaces, iracundos, agiles; nigra bilis stabilis, graues, compositos moribus, dolososque facit; phlegmata tardos, somnolentos, obliuiosos generant. Horum autem principia temporum diuerse ponunt diuersi . . . [38]

---

[38] Bede, *De Temporum Ratione*, "XXXV De quattuor temporibus, elementis, humo-ribus" (ed. Jones, 391–93), emphasis added.

<11B> [translation:] The seasons of the year are four, in which the sun, by running through different regions of the heaven, tempers the subject orb, by the guidance of divine wisdom, so that not always tarrying in the same places the decked-out earth be depopulated by fierceness of heat but little by little migrating through different regions it might keep proper measures for earthly fruits to be born and matured. From which moderation the name for the seasons seems to have been assigned; or certainly they are rightly called *tempora* because they are evolved successive to one another by a certain similitude of their quality. For winter, in as much as the sun is very far removed, is cold and wet; spring, the sun returning upon the lands, is wet and hot, summer, it being especially hot, is hot and dry, autumn, it declining to the southern regions, is dry and cold. And thus it happens that, the individual [seasons] embracing through a mediating control, which [controlling qualities] encircle them, all things are mutually contained as if in an orb; in the same way, by these qualities very unlike in themselves yet joined by association each one to another [i.e. wet and cold, cold and dry, dry and hot, hot and wet, wet and cold] the very elements of the world are known to be differentiated. For earth is dry and cold, water cold and wet, air wet and hot, fire hot and dry; and so the first is like autumn, the second like winter, the third like spring, the last like summer. But also man himself, who by the wise is called microcosm, that is, little world, has a body tempered entirely by these same qualities, [qualities] wonderfully imitating the individual ones [of seasons and elements], by which humors of his he exists, in the manner of seasons / ages, in which he especially has power. Blood indeed which arises in spring is wet and hot; red choler, which [rises] in summer, hot and dry; black choler, which [rises] in autumn, dry and cold; phlegm, which [belongs] in winter, are cold and wet. And indeed blood flourishes most in infants, red choler in adolescents, melancholy, that is bile mixed with sediment of black blood, in those transitioning, phlegm rules in the old. Likewise blood makes those in which it is most potent cheerful, happy, merciful, much given to laughter and talk; red cholers make people lean, eating much nevertheless, quick, bold, irascible, agile; black bile makes people steady, grave, regular in habit, and cunning; phlegms produce the slow, the sleepy, the forgetful. Different authorities, however, set different beginnings for these seasons.

The chief difference between glosses 8.3–7 and 4.3–7, beyond verbal rearrangement and the addition in 4.3–7,[39] is their assignment of human ages in the last

---

[39] As noted briefly above, 4.3–7 adds the idea that the elements correspond to human body, blood, wetness, and breath, not in Bede but a commonplace: "homo . . . habet enim corpus ex terra, sanguinem (sanguinem: *A-S MSS* A P V3 P6 Ge C4 calorem), ex igne, humorem ab aqua, flatum ab aere." Nearly identical correspondences are listed by Lactantius, *Diuinae Institutiones,* 2. 12. 5 (ed. Samuel Brandt, CSEL 19 [Vienna: Tempsky, 1890], 156, ll. 11–14), Isidore, *Etymologiarum sive Origines Libri XX,* 11.1.6 (ed. W.M. Lindsay [Oxford: Clarendon Press, 1911]) and *Liber Differentiarum XVII,* 48

three sections: **8.3–7**'s adolescence vs. **4.3–7**'s adolescence *or* youth; **8.3–7**'s youth
vs. **4.3–7**'s old age; and finally **8.3–7**'s old age vs. **4.3–7**'s *decrepita aetas*. Bede
uses a relatively unusual term for those in the stage of life between adolescence
and old age: *transgressoribus*, those transitioning from youth to age. It is possible
that the gloss was drafted by one reader of Bede, and subsequently another, re-
consulting Bede, decided on a different interpretation of Bede's term. That possible explanation for the disagreement might be further evidence that Bede was
indeed the source and also suggests independent consultation of him. But Bede's
interest in and emphasis on the special mediating nature of these interlocking
qualities, with which his chapter begins, is left behind by the glosses which, as
seems characteristic of them, focus on a neat, teachable set of categories and correspondences.

Given the widespread circulation of Bede's *De temporum ratione* one might
suppose that Bede's succinct presentation of man as microcosm would probably
have been available to the Anglo-Saxon translator, but the OE shows no trace of it.
Rather, in that translation the longest elaboration on Boethius's 3m9 concerns not
lines 13–17 but lines 10–12: "Tu numeris elementa ligas, ut frigora flammis, / arida
conueniant liquidis, ne purior ignis / euolet aut mersas deducant pondera terras."[40]
Most MSS have short notes, often interlinear, on lines 10–12 identifying the elements and their associated qualities. More elaborate glosses address the idea of the
"immediate" and "mediate" relationships between elements. The most common
gloss in what I take as the earlier form of the Remigian collection is given (without
apparatus) as example **12**. As Example **13** I give the next most elaborate, one found
across families and standard in the A-S one (with apparatus):

> ‹12› [TU NUMERIS ELEMENTA] **1** id est quattuor monadibus nam
> quattuor sunt elementa quorum coniunctiones sex sunt quas [syzygias][41]
> vocant, quarum quattuor sunt immediatae et duae mediatae. **2** immediatae
> sunt istae. aer calidus et humidus est, huius caliditas coniungitur caliditati
> ignis qui est calidus et siccus. **3** ignis calidus est et siccus, huius caliditas
> aeris caliditati coniungitur, siccitas autem terrae copulatur quae est frigida
> et sicca. **4** terra frigida est et sicca, huius siccitas ignis siccitati iungitur, fri-
> giditas vero aquae frigiditati nectitur. **5** aqua frigida est et humida, eius fri-
> giditas terrae frigiditati, humiditas autem aeris humiditati sociatur. **6** me-
> diatae [syzygiae] hae sunt quae contrariae sunt nec possunt coniungi sine

---

(ed. Maria Adelaida Andrés Sanz, Corpus Christianorum, Series Latina 111A [Turn-
hout: Brepols, 2006], 34, ll. 45–9); and those given by Heiric of Auxerre, *Homiliae per
circulum anni*, Pars hiemalis, Hom. 28, correspond exactly with the list in the A-S MSS,
with *calorem* for *sanguinem* (ed. Richard Quadri, CCCM 116 [Turnhout: Brepols, 1992],
229, ll. 49–52).

[40] "You bind the elements by numbers, so that the cold coexists with the hot, the dry
with the wet, lest the purer fire fly away or mass weigh down the overwhelmed lands."

[41] MSS spellings vary: synzygi-, sinzigi-, synzugi-, synzugi-, sinzi-.

aliqua medietate. 7 ignis et aqua contraria sunt quia ignis calidus et siccus est, aqua frigida et humida. nam ut frigiditas aquae ignis conveniat caliditati terrae frigiditas est media; ut autem aquae humiditas siccitati ignis aptetur aeris humiditas media intervenit (Ma P9 T L4b V5 Ab E1 M L An O2 P7 P10)

<13> ideo ligas elementa ut mutua connexione compacta sint, ne ignis subtilioris naturae suam ad sedem evolet, aut pondera terrarum deducant ipsas terras ad nihilum ut subsidant. ignis enim habet obstaculum duo crassiora elementa, aquam et aerem, et terra aeque duo sibi leviora quibus sustentatur, aqua videlicet et aere, hinc inde (P3b P8 P5 P1 V2 C2 O A P V3 P6 Ge C4)

> *ideo*: inde P1 *ignis*: *ad.* qui est P3b. *suam ad sedem evolet*: suam evolet ad sedem P8, ad suam sedem evolet P1 A P V3 P6 Ge C4, ad sedem suam evolet C2 O, a sua sede evolet P3b. *pondera*: pondere P8. *terrarum*: *ad.* ne P3b. *obstaculum*: *om* P3b. *crassiora elementa*: ~ C2 O A P V3 P6 Ge C4. *et terra . . . inde*: TERRAS s. sustentantur duobus levioribus elementis et aqua videlicet et aere P3b. *duo*: *om* P8 V2 C2 O A P V3 P6 Ge C4. *leviora*: leviorem A P V3 P6 Ge (C4 illegible). *sustentatur*: sustendatur A P V3 P6 Ge C4. *hinc*: *ad.* atque C2 O.

The OE translation reads as follows:

> <14> 7 þeah þone anne noman þu todældest on feower
> gesceafta; an þæra is eorðe, oðer wæter, ðridde lyft, feorþe fyr.   80, 1
> Ælcum þara þu gesettest his agene sunderstowe, 7 þeah ælc is
> wið oðre genemned 7 sibsumlice gebunden mid þinum bebode, swa þæt
> heora nan oðres mearce ne ofereode, 7 se cile geþrowode wið ða
> hæto, 7 þæt wæt wið þam drygum. Eorðan gecynd 7 wæteres is   5
> ceald; sie eorðe is dryge 7 ceald, 7 þæt wæter wæt 7 ceald. Sie
> lyft þonne is genemned þæt hio is ægþer ge ceald ge wæt ge
> wearm. Nis hit nan wunder, forþam ðe hio is gesceapen on þam
> midle betwux þære drygan 7 þære cealdan eorþan 7 þam hatan
> fyre. Þæt fyr is yfemest ofer ellum þissum woruldgesceaftum.   10
> Wundorlic is þæt þin geðeaht, þæt ðu hæfst ægþer gedon: ge þa
> gesceafta gemærsode betwux him, ge eac gemengde þa drigan
> eorðan 7 þa cealdan under þam cealdan wætere 7 þam wætan,
> þæt þæt hnesce 7 flowende wæter hæbbe flor on þære fastan
> eorðan; forþampe hit ne mæg on him selfum gestandan. Ac seo   15
> eorðe hit helt 7 be sumum dæle swilgð, 7 for þam sype heo bið
> geleht þæt hio grewð 7 blewð 7 westmas bringð; forþam gif þæt
> wæter hi ne geðwænde, þonne drugode hio 7 wurde todrifen mid
> þam winde swa swa dust oððe axe. Ne mihte nanwuht
> libbendes þære eorþan brucan ne þæs wateres, ne on nauðrum   20
> eardigan for cile, gif þu hi hwæthwegununga wið fir ne

gemengdest. Wundorlice crafte þu hit hæfst gesceapen þæt þæt
fyr ne forbærnð þæt wæter 7 þa eorþan, nu hit gemenged is wið
ægðer; ne eft wæter 7 seo eorðe eallunga ne adwæsceð þæt fyr.
Þæs wateres agnu cyð is on eorþan, 7 eac on lyfte, 7 eft bufan   25
þam rodore. Ac þæs fyres agen stede is ofer eallum woruldgesceaftum
gesewenlicum, 7 þeah hit is gemenged wið ealle
gesceafta; 7 þeah ne mæg nane þara gesceafta eallunga forcuman,
forþamþe hit næfð leafe þæs almihtigan. Sio eorþe þonne
is hefigre 7 þiccre þonne oðra gesceafta, forþam hio is nioðor   30
þonne ænig oðru gesceaft buton þam rodore; forþam se rodor hine
hæfð ælce dæg utane, þeah he hire nawer ne genealæce; on
alcere stowe he is hire emnneah, ge ufan ge neoðon. Ælc þara
gesceafta þe we gefyrn ær ymbe spræcon hafþ his agenne
eard onsundron; 7 þeah is alc wið oðer gemenged, forþamþe   35
nan ðara gesceafta ne mæg bion buton oðerre, ðeah hio unsweotol   81, 1
sie on þære oðerre. Swa swa nu eorðe is 7 water sint swiðe
earfoðe to geseonne oðð to ongitonne dysgum monnum on fyre, 7
swaþeah hi sint ðærwið gemengde. Swa is eac þær fyr on
ðam stanum 7 on ðam wætere, swiðe earfoðhawe, ac hit is þeah   5
þara. Þu gebunde þæt fyr mid swiðe unanbindendlicum racentum,
þæt hit ne mæg cuman to his agenum earde, þæt is to þa mæstan
fyre ðe ofer us is, þylæs hit forlæte þa eorðan; 7 ealle oðre
gesceafta aswindað for ungemetlicum cile, gif hit eallunga
from gewite. Ðu gestaðoladest eorðan swiðe wundorlice 7   10
fastlice, þæt heo ne helt on nane healfe ne on nanum eorðlicum
þinge ne stent; ne nanwuht eorðlices hi ne healt þæt hio ne sige,
7 nis hire þeah þonne eðre to feallanne ofdune þonne up.[42]

---

[42] "And nevertheless you divided that one name into four creatures; one of them is
earth, another water, a third air, the fourth fire. For each of them you established its own
separate place, and nevertheless each is defined with respect to another and bound with it
in a peaceable manner by your command, so that none of them transgresses the boundary
of another, and the cold suffers in the face of the hot, and the wet in the face of the dry.
The nature of earth and of water is cold: the earth is dry and cold, the water wet and cold.
The air then is defined so that it is both cold and wet and warm. This is no wonder, because it is created in the middle between the dry and cold earth and the hot fire. The fire
is highest over all these worldly creatures. Wonderful is that thought of yours, that you
have done both: you have both distinguished the creatures amongst themselves, and also
mixed the dry and cold earth under the cold and wet water, so that the yielding and fluid
water might have a base on the firm earth; because it cannot stand on its own. But the
earth supports it and to some extent drinks it, and because of that sip it is moistened so
that it grows and flourishes and brings forth fruits; because if the water did not moisten it
then it would dry up and become driven by the wind just like dust or ashes. Nor could any
living thing make use of the earth or the water, nor dwell on either because of the cold, if
you did not commingle it to some extent with fire. With wonderful skill you have created
so that the fire does not burn up the water and the earth, now that it is mixed with both;

Early in this passage (80, lines 5–10) we find what seems an oddity: earth is dry and cold, water is wet and cold, but air is *cold* and wet and warm,[43] between the dry and cold earth and the hot [and dry] fire. In the Latin MSS a few glosses wrongly assign a quality, though never this way. [44] But when one notices the focus of the translator, one senses how the "aberration" may have arisen: that focus is the wonderful commingling of the elements whereby they are distinct and distributed, yet at the same time harmoniously commingled. Unlike the Latin glosses which tend to give primacy to sets of neatly corresponding labels (illustrated by examples 8.3–7 and 4.3–7 on man as microcosm and example 12 on the "syzygiae"), the OE is concentrating on a larger concept, and indeed seems to have more in common with the spirit of the *De Temporum Ratione* than the glosses that may have been extracted from it. One notes the praise of divine wisdom in Bede's opening lines, the reference to the earth being temperate and flourishing shortly after that; Bede emphasizes how divine wisdom has made the earth to exist and to vary in moderation, and that central to this moderation are the shared qualities, common to seasons and to elements, which exercise a mediating control; though in themselves very unlike, they are able to join by association one with another: "And thus it happens that, the individual [seasons] embracing through a mediating control, which [controlling qualities] encircle them, all things are mutually contained as if in an orb; in the same way, *by these qualities very unlike in themselves yet joined by association each one to another, the very elements*

---

nor on the other hand do the water and the earth entirely extinguish the fire. Water's own natural place is on the earth, and also in the air, and also above the firmament. But the fire's own place is above all visible worldly creatures, and nevertheless it is mingled with them all; and nevertheless it cannot destroy any of those creatures, because it does not have permission from the Almighty. The earth, then, is heavier and thicker than other creatures, because it is lower than any other creature except the firmament; because the firmament holds itself each day from without, although it nowhere approaches it [touches the earth?]; in every place it is even with it, both above and below. Each of the creatures about which we spoke earlier has its own separate home; and nevertheless each is mingled with another, for none of those creatures can exist without the others, even though it may be indiscernible in the other. Just as now earth and water are difficult to see or to understand for foolish men in fire, and nevertheless they are mingled with it. So also is the fire in the stone and in the water, very hard to be seen, but it is nevertheless part of them. You bound the fire with very indissoluble fetters, so that it cannot not come to its own homeland, that is to the greatest fire which is above us, lest it abandon the earth, and all other creatures perish because of immoderate cold, if [fire] depart entirely. You established the earth very wonderfully and firmly, so that it does not decline on any side nor stand on any earthly thing; and nothing earthly supports it so that it not sink, and yet it is no more inclined to fall down than it is to move upward."

[43] The usual qualities of air are wet and hot, as in example 12, section 2.

[44] The most common mistake is assigning "humida" to earth: for example, "terra humida et frigida . . ." (A P6 Ge C4 P9b).

of the world are known to be differentiated." [45] Bede's initial topic is the seasons, then
he moves on to the elements; the OE translator has the elements before him in
Boethius's lines and focuses on them. But like Bede, and quite unlike the glosses, the translation celebrates a harmonious association of differentiated elements
rather than sets of corresponding categories.

There are a few other places where Latin glosses show correspondences to
the OE translation. 3m9 lines 15–17 become:

<15> Swa ðu gesceope þa saule þæt hio sceolde   81, 25
ealne weg hwearfian on hire selfre, swa swa eall þes rodor
hwerfð, oððe swa swa hweol onhwerfð, smeagende ymb hire
sceoppend, oððe ymbe hi selfe, oððe ymbe þas eorðlican gesceafta.
Þonne hio þonne ymbe hire scippend smeað, þonne bið hio
ofer hire selfre; ac þonne hio ymbe hi selfe smeað þonne bið   30
hio on hire selfre; 7 under hire selfre hio bið þonne ðonne hio
lufað þas eorðlican þing, 7 þara wundrað. [46]

One gloss found in three Anglo-Saxon MSS expresses similar ideas:

<16> quae cum secta duos r[otat]. i. quicquid cogitat *anima* sive bonum sive
malum de se cogitat et *in se ipsam sic redit ut rota.* sunt duae illius rotae vel
orbes, i. in semetipsam et in profundam mentem i. in deum. philosophi dicunt quod deus sit quaedam mens regens mundum, et *quando anima redit in
se, amans caduca et vana, sub se est* et tunc peior, tunc ancilla peccatorum efficitur, non domina, quia peccatis servit. *quando vero ad deum cogitando redit
supra se est* et tunc beata efficitur (Ac Ge C4)

---

[45] Emphasis added. "Sicque fit ut, amplexantibus singulis medio moderamine quae
circa se sunt, orbis instar ad inuicem cuncta concludantur; quibus aeque qualitatibus dis-
parius quidem per se sed alterutra ad inuicem societate connexis, ipsa quoque mundi elementa constat esse distincta" (see passages 11A and 11B, above). The beginning of Bede's
chapter also has an echo in the opening of the OE meter: "Eala, Dryhten, hu micel 7 hu
wunderlic þu eart, þu ðe ealle þine gesceafta gesewenlice 7 eac ungesewenlice wunderlice
gesceope 7 gesceadwislice heora weltst" (79, ll. 10–12; "Behold, Lord, how great and how
wonderful you are, you who wonderfully created all your creatures, visible and invisible, and
govern them reasonably. . .")

[46] "You so created the soul that it ought always to turn on itself, just as all the firmament turns, or just as a wheel turns, meditating about its creator, or about itself, or
about earthly creatures. When it thinks about its creator, then it is above itself; but when
it thinks about itself then it is in itself; and it is under itself when it loves these earthly
things, and wonders at them." Lines 15–17 of the meter read "quae [anima] cum secta
duos motum glomerauit in orbes, / in semet reditura meat mentemque profundam / circuit et simili conuertit imagine caelum" ("which [soul], when divided, gathers motion
into two circles, moves, and about to return to itself, circles the profound mind and causes
the heavens to turn in similar fashion").

quicquid . . . malum: quicquid cogitat anima suum bonum suum malum
Ac, anima quicquid cogitat sive bonum sive malum Ge, {gramm. signs over
first 3 words in pattern a a b}, anima sū bonum sū malum C4. *quando (bis)*:
qn—o Ac C4, qm—Ge.

The italicized phrases in the gloss are strikingly like the OE, but otherwise,
gloss and OE diverge significantly. One notes the symmetrical triads in the OE
(thinking about creator, self, earthly creatures; when doing the first is above self,
when the second in self, beneath self when doing the third). Such symmetry, including the deliberate word order variation in the last clause, is indeed frequent
in glosses, and it may be based on a written Latin source;[47] but it is also a pattern
of patristic and medieval style, which the translator might have assimilated independently of a specific written Latin source for this passage.

Lines 18–21 of the meter speak of "animas" and "vitas minores," the higher
of which the creator provides with light chariots and strews in heaven.[48] The OE
translator rendered the lines:

<17>   Hwæt þu,   81, 32
Drihten, forgeafe þam sawlum eard on hiofonum, 7 him þær
gifst weorðlice gifa, ælcere be hire geearnunge; 7 gedest þæt
hi scinað swiðe beorhte, 7 þeah swiðe mistlice birhtu, sume
beorhtor sume unbyrhtor, swa swa steorran, ælc be his geearnunga.[49]   82, 1

The Latin glosses reflect four main lines of interpretation: the "animas" and "vitas minores" are, respectively, angels and humans, or the wise and the foolish,
or the rational and vital souls, or even stars and moon. The Anglo-Saxon revision of a Remigian gloss reflects several of these, including some neo-Pla-
tonic speculation.[50] Other Anglo-Saxon glosses more nearly reflect the OE
version's focus on human souls, "wise and foolish," better and worse:

---

[47] I have not yet found one.

[48] "Tu causis animas paribus uitasque minores / prouehis et leuibus sublimes curribus aptans / in caelum terramque seris, quas lege benigna / ad te conuersas reduci fa-
cis igne euerti" ("You bring forth by like causes souls and lesser lives and, furnishing
the higher with light chariots, you sow them in heaven and earth; those, by benign law
turned towards you, you cause to be led back by a guiding fire").

[49] "Behold, you, Lord, gave to these souls a homeland in heaven, and there will give
to them valuable gifts, to each according to its merits; and you will cause them to shine
very brightly, and yet with quite varying brightness, some more bright, some less, just like
the stars, each according to its merits." I am indebted to Dr. Leslie MacCoull for pointing
out the bases of this interpretation in Matt. 13:43 and 1 Cor. 15:41.

[50] **1** vitas minores homines dicit: sive animas eorum quae diffunduntur per corpora
hominum et ad comparationem angelicae animae parvissimae aestimantur; sive animae
intellege spiritus, vitas autem minores homines. **2** possumus etiam de stellis et hoc accipere. visum est platoni quod antequam deus se mentem faceret animarum, superimposuit

<18A> [CAUSIS]:-meritum (O2); meritis (P9b Ge C4)

<18B> :-illi qui dicendi sunt animas, i. boni, et illi qui dicendi minores vi-
tas, i. illi qui tendunt ad corpus tantum, provehis paribus causis, i. merit[is],
et aptans illos qui dicendi sunt animas sublimes levibus curribus, i. altis co-
gitationibus, quibus petunt alta, et seris illos sublimes in caelum et minores
vitas in terras (O2)

But all one can finally say here is that some glosses reflect the same interpretative
focus as the OE translation.

As was the case with the Orpheus meter, when one compares the OE
translation with the Latin glosses, one finds some points, sometimes admittedly striking points, of similarity. But one also finds a different focus in the
translation than in the glosses. Even when similarities exist between interpretations in the Anglo-Saxon glosses and in the OE translation, one wonders if,
rather than being regarded as "sources" for the OE, they should not rather be
regarded as reflections of current interpretation which both translation and
glosses reflect. Put another way, rather than being taken as the complete record of available understanding of the *Consolatio*, extant glossed manuscripts
might better be regarded as imperfect snapshots of interpretative activity which
is also reflected in the OE translation. Boethius' *Consolatio* was becoming an
important text, increasingly studied in monastic schools, to which activities
both translation and glosses can attest.[51]

---

deus singulis stellis singulas animas, ut isdem vehiculis universae rei naturam spectarent,
illud docens quod sine divinitatis adminiculo ipsa per se anima nil posse considerare di-
vinum (C2 O A [P] P6 Ge C4)
    {P has key, but gloss cropped at bottom of leaf.} 1 *vitas*: vitasque A P6 Ge C4. *sive
animas eorum*: *om* A [P] P6 Ge C4. *angelicae*: mundanae A [P] P6 Ge C4. 2 *accipere*: ex-
cipere A P6 Ge C4. *est*: *ad.* enim A [P] P6 Ge C4. *singulas animas*: singulas animam C2
O (by corr.). *docens*: docentes A Ge. *nil*: nihil A P6 Ge C4.

[51] Malcolm Godden's "King Alfred and the Boethius Industry" appeared after this
essay was written (in *Making Sense: Constructing Meaning in Early English*, ed. Antonette
DiPaolo Healy and Kevin Kiernan [Toronto: Pontifical Institute of Mediaeval Studies,
2007], 116–38). Godden traces the re-emergence of the *Consolatio* in the ninth century
and lucidly situates the OE translation within the context of that text's becoming a "standard" in the monastic schools. He points out that, since nearly all the extant MSS of the
Consolatio contain at least some glosses, the MS(S) used by the Anglo-Saxon translator
probably contained glosses. In this essay he offers (124–25) one example of a striking
parallel between an addition in the OE and a Latin gloss in two MSS of Anglo-Saxon
provenance (P9 and C4 in the Appendix here); the idea is a commonplace but the wording of it in Latin and OE is indeed close. He offers (125–28) two instances where both
OE and Latin glosses add the name "Theoderic" where it is not in Boethius (one gloss is
in a MS of the twelfth century, apparently of Irish provenance, the other in a MS of the
tenth century of uncertain provenance); these instances seem to me indicative of ideas in

Appendix:
List of MSS and Sigils Referred to in this Essay

MSS are listed in alphabetical order by sigil.
Abbreviations in this list:
Gloss type:
    R (version of "Remi")
    G (version of anon. Sancti Galli)
    O (other early glosses)
other abbrev:
    CPh = Consolatio Philosophiae
    inl (interlinear)
    mg (marginal)
    f (fragmentary or incomplete copy of version)
<u>W</u>, <u>X</u>, <u>Y</u> and <u>Z</u> refer to versions of "R" reflected by MSS groupings.

A   Antwerp, Museum Plantin-Moretus, M. 16. 8 (olim lat. 190). s. x^{ex}/xi^{in}, Abingdon. Gloss: R. (CPh with inl and mg glosses on fols. 1–116. At least 2 glossing hands, approx. contemporary with text: [a] wrote first, keys and mg glosses = MS P—see below; b wrote second and perhaps in several stages and seems to have written the inl glosses; c looks exactly like a, but wrote after a, adding <u>W</u> glosses in inner mg and on an added half sheet, fol. 55.) III.9.85-m.9 on fols. 53v–56r.

An   Alençon, Bibliothèque municipale 12. s. x, France (at St-Évroul from c. 1100). Gloss: R. (CPh with inl and mg glosses on fols. 1–57v. A hand contemporary with text writes the R glosses, but none after III.m.9,12; another hand, transcribed separately and not reported here, looks s. xii and writes most of the inl glosses on III.m.9.) III.p.9,85-m.9 on fols. 25v–26v.

B   Bern, Bürgerbibliothek, Cod. 179. s. ix^2, Brittany? (at Fleury by s. xi). Gloss: R,f. (CPh with inl and mg glosses on fols. 1r-63v. Glossing heavy until I.p.4,fol. 5, then nothing until fol. 8; heavy on II.p.1 to III.p.2, and again

---

the air surrounding the interpretation of the text. Godden also remarks that the cases in which OE and Latin glosses diverge are "in some ways the most interesting" (129). It seems to me—and I think Godden would agree—that the OE translator was very much engaged in "the Boethius industry," and that no single glossed MS is likely to account for everything in the OE version. Until many striking parallels are found between OE and glosses, parallels which go beyond shared commonplaces and which occur in one extant MS or scattered among a group of closely related MSS (e.g. those of Anglo-Saxon provenance), I do not think one can argue that we have identified "the glosses" which were in the translator's copy of the *Consolatio*. But one must certainly agree with Godden that the relationship between the OE translation and Latin glosses will be best resolved by a comparison of the entire OE translation with a complete record of those glosses.

on III.p.3-III.p.10. Thereafter both inl and mg rare and some in later hands. The few on III.m.9 are R type.) III.p.9,85-m.9 on fols. 31r-v.

B1 Bern, Bürgerbibliothek, Cod. 181. s. xi. Gloss: R III.m.9; O. (CPh on fols. 1–83v, R continua on III.m.9 inserted after the meter in text hand; some inl and mg glosses through fol. 19, thereafter very few.) III.m.9 on fols. 43r–45r.

C2 Cambridge, Trinity College O. 3. 7. s. x^2, St. Augustine's, Canterbury. Gloss: R. (CPh with inl and mg glosses on fols. 1r-51v.) III.p.9,85-m.9 on fols. 24v–25r.

C4 Cambridge, University Library Kk. 3. 21. s. x^{ex}/xi^{in}, Abingdon. Gloss: R. (CPh with inl and mg glosses on fols. 1r–103r.) III.p.9,85-m.9 on fols. 49r–50r.

E1 Einsiedeln, Stiftsbibliothek 179. s. x, St. Gall. Gloss: G, R III.m.9. (continuous commentaries on pp. 96a-185b. There is a second copy of the G continua on III.m.9, "ITEM ANNOTATIONES TERTII LIBRI," at the end of the complete G version; the R continua is inserted in the full G version immediately after the first glosses on III.m.9.) III.p.9,85-m.9 on pp. 143b–145b (E1^1,first copy of G), pp. 145b–149a (E1,R), pp. 185b-187b (E1^2, second copy of G).

Es El Escorial, Real Biblioteca, e.II.1. s. xi^1, England (at Horton). Gloss: R. (CPh with inl and mg glosses on fols. 8v-117r.) III.p.9,85-m.9 on fols. 63r–64r.

Ge *olim* Geneva, Bibliotheca Bodmeriana, Cod. 175. s. x^{ex}/xi^{in}, England (St. Augustine's, Canterbury?). Gloss: R. (CPh with inl and mg glosses on 1v–111v.) III.p.9,85-m.9 on fols. 54r–55r. Sold through Sotheby's 7 July 2005 to an anonymous buyer.

L London, BL, Add. 15601. s. x^{ex}/xi^{in}, S. Germany? (at Avignon). Gloss R,f; O. (R continua on I.m.1-III.m.9, fols. 1–16v, followed by CPh fols. 17–59r with frequent inl and, except on III.m.9, rare mg note = R and transcribed separately.) 3.9.86–ix on fols. 15v–16v.

L1 London, BL, Add. 19726. s. x^{ex}/xi^{in}, Germany (at Tegernsee s. xi^{med}). Gloss: R. (CPh with inl and mg glosses on fols. 2–57.) III.p.9,85-m.9 on 28v–29r.

L4 London, BL, Harley 3095. s. x^1, Rhineland (Cologne?). Gloss: G,R. (CPh with inl and mg glosses on fols. 1v–112v. Both R and G glosses written inl and mg throughout, but only G inl and mg at the text of III.m.9, after which the continua of Bovo of Corvey is inserted and, ironically, on the lemmata of this the R glosses are written. The continua of the anon. of Einsiedeln 302 follows on fols. 59r–61v. Closely related to Ma though not its direct exemplar. Glossing hand [a] writes G inl and mg with the text, in several passes; R is written, for III.m.9, "inl" and mg, keyed to the lemmata in the Bovo continua by a hand not always clearly distinguishable from [a], but which I identify as "L4b.") III.p.9,85-m.9 on fols. 46r–47r (G), 47r–59r (R).

M Munich, Bayerische Staatsbibliothek, clm 14836. s. xi, Germany. Gloss: R III.m.9. (Continua in a miscellany of "mathematical" works.) III.m.9 on fols. 10v–15v.

Ma Kraków, Biblioteka Jagiellońska, Lat. Quarto 939 (<u>olim</u> Berlin, Staatsbibliothek der Stiftung Preussischer Kulturbesitz, lat.4o, 939, <u>olim</u> Maihingen, Bibliotheca Wallersteiniana, I, 2, Lat. 4o 3). s. x^{ex}, Tegernsee. Gloss: G, R. (CPh with inl and mg glosses on fols. 4r–57v; continua on CPh on fols. 60r–112r. Fromund copied the text and the G glosses at Cologne; his students wrote the R continua at Tegernsee. Derived from a MS much like L4 though not directly.) III.p.9,85-m.9 on fols. 28r–29r (G), 85v–87v (R).

N Naples, Biblioteca Nazionale, IV G. 68. Text s. ix, France (Tours?), glosses s. x, St. Gall. Gloss: G. (CPh with inl and mg glosses on fols. 4v–92r.) III.p.9,85-m.9 on fols. 46v–47v.

O Oxford, Bodleian Library, Auct. F. 1. 15. x^2, St. Augustine's, Canterbury. Gloss: R,f. (CPh with inl and some mg glosses on fols. 5r–77r. Several glossing hands: one contemporary with text if not identical glossed I.m.1-I.p.3,26, on 5r-8r, fully and III.m.9, on 39v–40r; another wrote glosses for V.p.2-V.m.4, on 66v–72v; a third supplied inl glosses and keys—only—for mg glosses for I.m.5,44-II.p.1,35, on 13r–17r.) III.p.9,85-m.9 on fols. 39v–40r.

O2 Oxford, Corpus Christi College 74. s. xi^1. Gloss: R. (CPh with inl and mg glosses on fols. 1r–61r.) III.p.9,85-m.9 on fols. 30r–31r.

On Orléans, Bibliothèque municipale, 270. s. ix^{in}, glosses ix^1, Fleury. Gloss: O. (CPh with inl and some mg glosses on pp. 3–229. Glosses in three or four hands, two nearly contemporary with text; I have transcribed the glosses on III.m.9 with G.) III.p.9,85-m.9 on pp. 108–110.

P Paris, BN, lat. 6401A. s. x^{ex}, Christ Church, Canterbury. Gloss: R. (CPh with inl and mg glosses on fols. 1r–94v.) III.p.9,85-m.9 on fols. 45r–46r.

P1 Paris, BN, lat. 6402. s. xi^{ex}-xii^1. W. or S-W. France (Poitiers-Toulouse?). Gloss: R. (CPh with inl and mg glosses on fols. 1r-71r.) III.p.9,85-m.9 on fols. 35v–36r.

P2 Paris, BN, lat. 6769. s. xiii. Gloss: abbreviated R? (CPh with mostly inl glosses on fols. 1v–54r; on III.m.9 only short inl, reduced or incipient R; transcribed separately.) III.p.9,85-m.9 on fols. 26v–27r.

P3 Paris, BN, lat. 8039. s. x^2? Gloss: R III.m.9. (CPh with inl and mg glosses on fols. 51r–77v, with R continua on III.m.9 inserted after the meter.) III.m.9 on fols. 63rb–63va (text), 63vb–64va (continua).

P4 Paris, BN, lat. 8308. s. xii. Gloss: R III.m.9. (CPh with inl and mg glosses on 16r-71v with R continua inserted after the meter by the text hand. Like P3 the continua begins with line 13. There are no glosses on the text, at 40v.) III.m.9 on fols. 41v–43r.

P5 Paris, BN, lat. 12961. s. xi^2, E. France (Lorraine, Metz? At Corbie). Gloss: R. (CPh with inl and mg glosses on fols. 2r–90v.) III.p.9,85-m.9 on fols. 44v–45v.

P6 Paris, BN, lat. 14380. s. xi^1, Christ Church, Canterbury. Gloss: R. (CPh with inl and mg glosses on fols. 2r–64v.) III.p.9,85-m.9 on fols. 31v–32r.

P7   Paris, BN, lat. 15090. s. x, St. Evre, Toul. Gloss: R. (CPh with inl and mg glosses on fols. 2v–88v.) III.p.9,85-m.9 on fols. 42v–44r.

P8   Paris, BN, lat. 16093. s. xi^{med}, Loire (Fleury?). Gloss: R. (CPh with inl and mg glosses on fols. 1r–68r. Also continua on III.m.9, fol. 69v, which Courcelle identified as s. xiii Anon. of Erfurt Q 5.) III.p.9,85-m.9 on fols. 35v–36r.

P9   Paris, BN, lat. 17814. s. x^{ex}/xi^{in}, Canterbury. Gloss: R. (CPh with inl and mg glosses on fols. 9r–122v; incomplete at end, expl. V.p.5,114 "quoque"—end supplied s. xviii. Probably several glossing hands contemporary with text and writing in several passes; [a] is much like text and writes version W; b, very similar, adds Z glosses, corresponding to MS P. Trevet's commentary has been added in a later cursive, and some of the original glosses have been erased to make room for it.) III.p.9,85-m.9 on fols. 63r–64r.

P10 Paris, BN, nouv. acq. lat. 1478. s. xi^1, France (at Cluny). Gloss: R. (CPh with inl and mg glosses on fols. 1r–55v.) III.p.9,85-m.9 on fols. 29v–30r.

T   Trier, Stadtbibliothek, 1093. s. xi^m (*recte* x/xi?), Echternach. Gloss: R. (CPh with inl and mg glosses on fols. 118r–168r. On the evidence shared variants, T is closely related to L4b.) III.p.9,85-m.9 on fols. 139v–141r.

V1   Vatican City, Biblioteca Apostolica Vaticana, lat. 3363. Text s. ix^1, Loire region, glosses later—see Parkes in *Boethius*, ed. Gibson, 425–27 and Wittig, "King Alfred's Boethius," 161 n. 20. Gloss: O. (CPh with inl and mg glosses on fols. 1r–60r. Glosses often illegible. Transcribed separately.) III.p.9,85-m.9 on fol. 29r–v.

V2   Vatican City, Biblioteca Apostolica Vaticana, lat. 3865. s. ix^{ex}, France. Gloss: R. (CPh with inl and mg glosses on fols. 1r–57v.) III.p.9,85-m.9 on fols. 28v–29r.

V3   Vatican City, Biblioteca Apostolica Vaticana, lat. 4254. s. xiii^2, France. Gloss: R. (CPh with inl and mg glosses on fols. 4v–80r. This manuscript stands out as a late, and continental?, copy of the English Z version.) III.p.9,85-m.9 on fols. 40v–41r.

V5   Vatican City, Biblioteca Apostolica Vaticana, Pal. lat 1581. s. x/xi, Germany. Gloss: R. (CPh with inl and mg glosses on fols. 2r–69v.) III.p.9,85-m.9 on fols. 34v–35v.

V6   Vatican City, Biblioteca Apostolica Vaticana, Reg. lat. 1433. s. xii. Gloss: R. (CPh with inl and mg glosses on fols. 1r–60r.) III.p.9,85-m.9 on fols. 29v–30r.

V7   Vatican City, Biblioteca Apostolica Vaticana, Reg. lat. 1727. s. xii. Gloss: R III.m.9. (CPh with many inl and a few mg glosses on fols. 1r–23v, R continua inserted after meter in text hand. Mg esp. on I.m.1 and III.m.9; those on III.m.9, closest to Adalbold of Utrecht, transcribed separately.) III.p.9,85-m.9 on fols. 10v–11v.

The Panorama of the Crusades, 1096 to 1218, as Seen in Yates Thompson MS. 12 in the British Library[1]

Jaroslav Folda

The lifelong research of Richard Pfaff into English medieval manuscripts suggested that it would be appropriate to study a wonderful if controversial manuscript in the British Library for his Festschrift. I present my thoughts here in his honor with the hope that he will enjoy this exploration into Crusader studies and what I take to be English manuscript illumination.

The manuscript in question, Yates Thompson MS. 12 in the British Library, first came to light in modern times when it belonged to A. Firmin-Didot in France. Paulin Paris used it along with MS. 142, now in the Walters Art Museum, as the basis of his edition of the Old French text of William of Tyre's *History of Outremer* published in 1879.[2] Henry Yates Thompson acquired this Firmin-Didot manuscript in 1896 and kept it in his select collection of one hundred manuscripts as number 42 until he sold it in 1919. A few years later, finding that he could not do without it, he acquired it again in 1923 — at a significant increase in price — and kept it until 1949, after which time, following his demise, it entered the British Library collection as a gift from his wife.[3]

---

[1] Excellent color illustrations for this manuscript may be consulted in the British Library Digital Catalogue of Illuminated Manuscripts. I urge the reader to go to: http://prodigi.bl.uk/illcat/welcome.htm. Click on "particular manuscript", and select Yates Thompson MS. 12. A few illustrations are on the first screen, but most are on the screen marked "detailed record." When clicking on the reproductions, the first click on the image gives the miniature at actual size; the second click magnifies the miniature to full computer screen size.

[2] Paulin Paris, *Guillaume de Tyr et ses continuateurs*, 2 vols. (Paris: Firmin-Didot, 1879), MS. 'A'.

[3] The basic bibliography for YT MS. 12 after 1879 in chronological order is as follows:
Catalogue Illustré des . . . manuscrits . . . de la Bibliothèque de M. Ambroise Firmin-Didot (Paris: Firmin-Didot, 1881), 87–88.

The Study of Medieval Manuscripts of England: Festschrift in Honor of Richard W. Pfaff, eds. George Hardin Brown and Linda Ehrsam Voigts, MRTS 384 (Tempe: ACMRS, 2010).   [ISBN 978-0-86698-432-4]

The manuscript contains the full Old French text of the *History of Outremer* with a continuation to 1232 also written in Old French. The book is modestly decorated with twenty-five small historiated initials, which typically measure

Charles Riant, "Inventaire Sommaire des Manuscrits de l'*Eracles*," *Archives de l'Orient Latin* 1 (1881): 250, no. 38.

Charles Riant, "Inventaire Sommaire des Manuscrits relatifs à l'histoire et à la géographie de l'Orient Latin," *Archives de l'Orient Latin* 2 (1884): 201, no. 62.

Montague R. James, *A Descriptive Catalogue of Fifty Mss. . . . of Henry Yates Thompson* (Cambridge: Cambridge University Press, 1898), 235–38, no. 42.

One Hundred Manuscripts in the Library of Henry Yates Thompson, vol. 3 (London: Chiswick Press, 1912), iv and plates 49–51, MS. 42.

Seymour de Ricci, "Les Mss. de la Collection Henry Yates Thompson," *Bulletin de la Société Française de Reproductions des Manuscrits à Peintures* 10 (1926): 55, no. 42.

Times Literary Supplement, 20 May 1949, no. 10.

British Museum, Department of Manuscripts, *Miscellaneous Lists* [typescript]: List I, fol. 6; List II, fol. 12.

British Museum Quarterly 16. 1 (1951): 4–6.

Brian Woledge and H.P. Clive, *Répertoire des plus anciens textes en prose française depuis 842 jusqu'aux premières années du XIIIe siècle*, Publications romanes et françaises 79 (Geneva: Droz, 1964), 61.

Jaroslav Folda, "Manuscripts of the *History of Outremer* by William of Tyre: A Handlist," *Scriptorium* 27 (1973): 94, no. 38.

Ruth Morgan, *The Chronicle of Ernoul and the Continuations of William of Tyre* (London: Oxford University Press, 1973), passim.

Jaroslav Folda, *Crusader Manuscript Illumination at Saint-Jean d'Acre, 1275–1291* (Princeton: Princeton University Press, 1976), 32, n. 33, plates 169, 170.

Andrew G. Watson, *Catalogue of Dated and Datable Manuscripts c. 700–1600 in the Department of Manuscripts: The British Library*, 2 vols. (London: British Library, 1979), 1:168 [James' dating rejected].

Alison Stones, review of F. Avril and M-T. Gousset, with C. Rabel, *Manuscrits enluminés d'origine italienne, 2: XIIIe siècle* (Paris: Bibliothèque Nationale, 1984), *Speculum* 61 (1986): 886–90, at 889.

Lilian M. C. Randall, et al., *Medieval and Renaissance Manuscripts in the Walters Art Gallery*, vol. 1, *France, 875–1420* (Baltimore: Johns Hopkins University Press, 1989), 126, 133.

Jaroslav Folda, "Images of Queen Melisande in Manuscripts of William of Tyre's *History of Outremer*: 1250–1300," *Gesta* 32 (1993): 97–112, at 102–3 and fig. 12.

M. Milwright, "The Cup of the Saqi: Origin of an Emblem of the Mamluk Khassakiyya," *Aram* 9–10 (1997–1998): 250, fig. 6.

Peter Edbury, "The French Translation of William of Tyre's *Historia*: The Manuscript Tradition," *Crusades* 6 (2007): 69–105.

British Library Digital Catalogue of Illuminated Manuscripts, accessible as 'Yates Thompson MS. 12'.

[http://.prodigi.bl.uk/illcat/welcome.htm]

c. 4.5 × c. 5.0 cm in the main zone, but often have significant extensions outside the shape of the letter. They are found at the start of each book division of
the text narrative, twenty-one for the original *History* text,[4] and four for the text
of the continuation from 1184 to 1232. The manuscript is written in a compact
gothic hand on 211 folios with small margins. It is not a luxury manuscript, but
it is very handsomely done, and the narrative imagery in the historiated initials is
so remarkable that one can say this codex bids fair to present the grandest panorama of Crusader history in the Holy Land of any extant illustrated thirteenth-
century *History of Outremer* manuscript. What are the characteristics of the cycle
of miniatures that substantiate this claim? Where was this book done, and why
is its attribution so controversial?

The first thing to be said about this codex with regard to the texts of the
Old French translation of the *History* and the Old French continuation is that
both are early examples that are standard and unexceptional in almost every aspect — text editions, text content, text format, orthography, variants — and the
gothic hand, clear and compact, is pleasingly written. That is not to say that the
texts in YT MS. 12 are not important. If, as we shall argue below, this codex was
done in England — one of only two thirteenth-century William of Tyre codices
to have been written in England[5] — it will prove to be a unique early and independent English exemplar in terms of both text and image.

The translation of William of Tyre's original Latin text, which breaks off
in early 1184, must have been composed sometime between the end of the third
Crusade and c. 1232. It was presumably the work of a Western European cleric
who had traveled in the Near East.[6] The continuation to 1232 was then made in
the Latin East based on the so-called *Chronique d'Ernoul* sometime shortly after
1232 and before 1261, probably in the 1230s or 1240s.[7] YT MS. 12 therefore
dates after 1232, probably in the 1240s, or c. 1250 at the latest, given the style
of the script and the style of the miniatures, among other factors. Peter Edbury
argues that the text of the Old French translation of William of Tyre's Latin is
among the earliest extant, as is the text of the continuation to 1232.[8] He has also

---

[4] One historiated initial is missing, that for Book 1, which was apparently gone before the book entered any modern collections.

[5] The other manuscript is in Cambridge, Sidney Sussex College, MS. 93, correctly attributed by Peter Edbury, "The French Translation." MS. 93 is not, however, illustrated.

[6] John H. Pryor, "The *Eracles* and William of Tyre: An Interim Report," in *The
Horns of Hattin*, ed. B.Z. Kedar (Jerusalem: Vad Izhak Ben-Zvi/Israel Exploration Society, 1992; London: Variorum, 1992), 270–93, esp. 288–89.

[7] Morgan, *The Chronicle of Ernoul and the Continuations of William of Tyre*, is the basic study of the complex texts pertaining to the continuations.

[8] My warm thanks to Peter Edbury (Cardiff University) who very kindly provided
me with an advance copy of "The French Translation." My comments on the text of the
Histoire d'Outremer are largely based on his research, which substantially continues the

pointed out that YT MS. 12 has one unique textual feature, namely that certain passages from the *Chronique d'Ernoul* are embedded in the translation of William of Tyre's text, in three places. The problem for our discussion here is that neither the texts, including this special feature, nor the scribal hand in YT MS. 12 are distinctively helpful in attempting to attribute this manuscript to a place of origin or to a particular patron.

We should recall that the *History of Outremer* was one of the most popular secular texts in mid- to late thirteenth-century Europe and the Near East, and we do not lack for comparanda for YT MS. 12. Twenty-six fully illustrated manuscripts survive from the period c. 1240–1300 which contain the Old French translation of William of Tyre's text, of which twenty-four also contain one or another version of the several continuations. Of these twenty-six codices, the most important manuscript to compare with YT MS. 12 is clearly Paris, BNF MS. fr. 9081.[9] This latter codex, done in Paris in the 1240s, also has a very early version of the translation of William of Tyre's text, but no continuation, and it has a very lavish miniature cycle, also in the format of historiated initials, with one exception where a rectangular panel appears instead. Besides significant differences in the choices made for the scenes that illustrate each text division found in MS. fr. 9081 as compared to YT MS. 12, it is also notable that in the Paris codex the historiated initials regularly have two episodes represented in a double-decker format, unlike what we find in YT MS. 12. Finally, the style of the miniatures in MS. fr. 9081 is clearly related to the *Bibles Moralisées* made in Paris in the 1220s to the 1240s. And at least one art historian has proposed that MS. fr. 9081 may have been done for King Louis IX himself. In all of these features, the place of origin, the format of the historiated initials, the style, and the patronage, YT MS. 12 is also distinctive and important, but different.[10]

We can state nonetheless that the most remarkable feature of the Yates Thompson manuscript is its cycle of historiated initials, which is complete except for the opening illustration. Sadly, the miniature for Book 1 was lost before the

---

work begun in the seminar in Jerusalem on which John Pryor reported in "The *Eracles* and William of Tyre."

[9] See Robert Branner, *Manuscript Painting in Paris during the Reign of Saint Louis* (Berkeley: University of California Press, 1977), 59, 207, fig. 90 (Initial "A" for book 15).

[10] For the attribution of MS. fr. 9081 to Louis IX, see Alison Stones, "Secular Manuscript Illumination in France," in *Medieval Manuscripts and Textual Criticism*, ed. C. Kleinhenz (Chapel Hill: University of North Carolina Press, 1976), 83–102, here 91.

Please note that all references to the comparanda are documented in the author's doctoral dissertation, and the selection of differing scenes/episodes/events and the variety of interpretation can be consulted as follows: Jaroslav Folda, "The Illustrations in Manuscripts of the *History of Outremer* by William of Tyre" (Ph.D. diss., The Johns Hopkins University, 1968), vol. 1, for the discussion of the art historical issues, and vol. 2, for the full analytical catalogue of all the manuscripts referred to.

manuscript was ever catalogued, so we have no knowledge of the imagery it contained. The extant illustrations in YT MS. 12 are however, quite exceptional and in some cases unique, and these historiated initials will therefore be our focus in order to explore several issues. First, what are the distinctive features of these miniatures: as individual narrative images, as a cycle illustrating these popular texts, and as a program of images referring to the Crusaders in the Holy Land during the period of the First to the Fifth Crusade? Second, in view of the fact that only one artist is involved in the production of these miniatures, what are the distinctive features of the style of these historiated initials? And third, given our findings in regard to the first two issues, where might this artist have been trained and what can be said about where the manuscript might have been produced and when?

The Narrative Imagery of YT MS. 12

The illustrations of YT MS. 12 are presented as historiated initials which appear at the beginning of each of the twenty-two books of William of Tyre's text, and at the start of four parts of the Continuation. They function therefore both as markers for the text divisions and as indicators of some of the significant content to be found in the following text. The fact that the historiated initial format is used is notable. This was the current choice when the illustration of secular manuscripts began in Europe and the Near East in the mid-thirteenth century. This format changed quickly to panel miniatures in the second half of the century, but historiated initials were the choice among artists and patrons for the earliest of the extant William of Tyre manuscripts. Only seven of the extant illustrated manuscripts are decorated this way, and five of these are early, dating between c. 1245 and c. 1260: one is from Paris,[11] one is from southern France,[12] one is from Acre,[13] one is from Antioch,[14] and the fifth one is YT MS. 12, which I am provisionally dating to c. 1250. The other two manuscripts in this group with

---

[11] Paris, BNF, MS. fr. 9081, from the 1240s (see above, n. 9).

[12] Paris, Ministère des Affaires Etrangères, Mem. et Documents, MS. 230bis, from the 1260s. See Folda, "The Illustrations in Manuscripts of the *History of Outremer* by William of Tyre," 1: 161–67 and 2: 35–44.

[13] Paris, BNF, MS. fr. 2628, from the 1260s. See Jaroslav Folda, *Crusader Art in the Holy Land, from the Third Crusade to the Fall of Acre, 1187–1291* (Cambridge: Cambridge University Press, 2005), 346–50, 404–6.

[14] Rome, Biblioteca Apostolica Vaticana, MS. Palatina Latina 1963, from the 1260s. See Jaroslav Folda, "A Crusader Manuscript from Antioch," *Atti della Pontificia Accademia Romana di Archeologia*, ser. 3, *Rendiconti*, 42 (1969–1970): 283–98.

historiated initials are much later, dating c. 1300, and they represent a later development of the format.[15]

The task facing each artist in the early stages of the illustration of William of Tyre's text in the absence of any pre-existing program of miniatures was, of course, the choice of episode or experience to depict at the beginning of each book as selected from the text of that book. Not surprisingly, many artists chose an episode from one of the first several lines of the text of each book, and the artist of YT MS. 12 certainly did this as well, sometimes. But more often he selects something more deeply embedded in the text of an individual book, an episode that is more representative of what the book in question is about, and possibly an episode that contains more historical significance or major historical figures for the reader or has more of an impact in some other way. What is notable about his illustrations in every case however, is their distinctiveness — created with sensitivity and even drama. Some examples will demonstrate these points.

At the start of Book 2 (fol. 9r), the YT MS. 12 Master depicts a generic scene that becomes more or less standard at this point in manuscripts of William of Tyre's text. It is an image of pilgrims setting out for the Holy Land (Fig. 11.1). It is a common theme, although the majority of the thirteenth-century manuscripts have an image of Godefroy de Bouillon and his men, which is the most immediate and literal reflection of the first lines of text.[16] Some later manuscripts also include Bishop Adhemar of Le Puy with this group. The fact is, however, that Adhemar, the papal legate, traveled with Count Raymond of Toulouse, not Godefroy, so those examples constitute an ahistorical conflation of chapters 1 and 16/17 where Adhemar first appears.

The YT MS. 12 Master focuses on something different in any case, and he does it in a distinctive way. At the right side of the image some mounted pilgrims set out for the Holy Land; they are warmly dressed for travel, wearing coifs, or hoods, or a cap. These travelers are laymen, not soldiers; we do not even see a cross affixed to their clothes. But the message of the image is clear. At the left there are three women who must stay behind. They stand in the gate of the city to see their men off. Compositional and psychological ties bind the two groups together. A woman — the wife? — of the prominent last rider steps just outside the city gate; her form overlaps the hindquarters of his horse. She stands somewhat stooped and holds her tightly clasped hands out to her man in sorrow, worry, and prayer. As she raises her eyes and he looks back in parting, he puts his arm around her shoulder in a tender gesture of affection.

---

[15] These are the two William of Tyre manuscripts in Baltimore, in the Walters Art Museum: MS. 137, c. 1295, and MS. 142, c. 1300. See Randall, *Medieval and Renaissance Manuscripts in the Walters Art Gallery*, 1: 123–27, cat. 50, figs. 102–104 (MS. 137); 133–38, cat. 53, figs. 109–111 (MS. 142).

[16] Paris, ed., *Guillaume de Tyr*, 1: 55.

F_IG. 11.1. Book 2, Pilgrims leaving for the Holy Land.

Strictly speaking this miniature is not drawn from any specific text passage, but instead is an interpretation of a widespread human experience during the Crusades. With this representation, our master has successfully expressed in this simple image the human pathos of the separation of a young couple, poignantly captured. This image of parting becomes a time-honored theme in later medieval art found in both painting and sculpture, but no image at Book 2 in any other illustrated thirteenth-century William of Tyre manuscript focuses on this exact theme nor achieves the content of this artistic result.

Another example of a commonly chosen episode for which our master produces a particularly sensitive narrative portrayal is found at Book 14 (fol. 82v). It is the coronation of King Fulk and Queen Melisende in 1131 (Fig. 11.2). Coronations belong to the stock-in-trade of artists working with these manuscripts, along with certain other scenes, such as marriages, funerals, battle scenes, and sieges of cities. The challenge to all of these artists was how to make an image that was distinctive and carried ideas of specificity and the individual circumstances of the event; one that was not simply a formulaic depiction with no recognizable historical identity and no historical message.

FIG. 11.2. Book 14, Coronation of King Fulk and Queen Melisende.

The YT MS. 12 Master treats this coronation with remarkable specificity. He also gives it monumentality and importance through the quality of his early gothic style and the way he flexibly shapes the initial being decorated to accommodate the scene. In the challenge to balance the image of the episode with the ornamental shape and decoration of the initial, the YT MS. 12 artist consistently chooses to emphasize the image of the event. In this case, by expanding the 'R' horizontally he is enabled to locate the principals, King Fulk and Queen Melisende enthroned, with Patriarch William standing inside the letter. The acolyte who holds the apron for the clergyman, a much less important figure, is placed outside the confines of the letter to the left.

The coronation of Fulk is a common choice for the start of Book 14, drawn from the text that appears at the end of chapter 2.[17] But YT MS. 12 is unique in depicting both Fulk and Melisende in the coronation ceremony at this point.

---

[17] Paris, ed., *Guillaume de Tyr*, 2: 5. The text of the Old French is in fact simpler and more concise than that of the Latin original.

Furthermore, the specific imagery of the coronation is remarkable. The patriarch, having poured the chrism into a small liturgical vessel, anoints Fulk's forehead with the two blessing fingers of his right hand. No indication is given in the text to account for such details or for the acolyte with the apron. As sources of inspiration one might suggest that this artist has closely observed such a liturgical ceremony, and also possibly seen artistic representations of such a ceremony, on the one hand, and that he used familiar biblical iconography as the basis for his image on the other.

In regard to the latter, one thinks of Psalter illustrations, and especially English Psalter illustrations, where it is common to have a crowned and seated David anointed by Saul.[18] In regard to the former it is equally possible that the emphasis on the anointing was also reinforced by his English circumstances. Recall that in 1215 Innocent III had attempted to ban the use of chrism in all royal coronation ceremonies, both French and English.[19] The French ignored this directive, based on the fact that their practice was so well established and went back to the eighth century. England did not have such a long-standing tradition to fall back on, so they maintained their weaker tradition by various means, including emphasis on the iconography of anointing in artistic representations.[20] Our artist may reflect this development as part of his English artistic outlook.

A third example of a commonly-chosen episode is the humiliation of the patriarch of Antioch on the citadel of Antioch by Raynauld de Chatillon, for Book 18 (fol. 120r). This text appears in chapter 1 and is a very popular choice for the image at the start of Book 18. Again the YT MS. 12 Master finds a way to portray this abusive scene with special vividness and explicit specificity (Fig. 11.3). Portraying the patriarch as a kind of stylite figure wearing his miter, the artist

---

[18] Meyer Schapiro, "An Illuminated English Psalter of the Early Thirteenth Century," *Journal of the Warburg and Courtauld Institutes* 23 (1960): 179–89, here 181 ff. By contrast, in French Psalters David is usually standing and uncrowned.

[19] H.G. Richardson, "The Coronation in Medieval England," *Traditio* 16 (1960): 111–202, here 117.

[20] On the anointing issue, see Marc Bloch, *Les Rois Thaumaturges* (Paris: Armand Colin, 1961), 216–24, 224–45; Percy E. Schramm, *A History of the English Coronation* (Oxford: Oxford University Press, 1937), 115–40; and Walter Ullmann, *The Growth of Papal Government in the Middle Ages* (London: Methuen, 1955), 143 ff.

The best-known coronation scenes in English painting in the thirteenth century are later than the miniature in YT MS. 12, e.g., in the Great Painted Chamber at Westminster (c. 1267–1268), now destroyed; in the manuscript of *La Estoire de St. Aedward le Roi* (before 1264); and in the Manchester copy of the *Flores Historiarum* by Matthew Paris (late 13th century). For an illustration of the *Flores Historiarum*, see Nigel Morgan, *Early Gothic Manuscripts 1250–1285*, vol. 2 (London: Harvey Miller, 1988), 50–52, illus. 6–8.

I am only suggesting that the YT MS. 12 artist as, very likely, an Englishman would be aware of this specific English iconography.

FIG. 11.3. Book 18, Abuse of the Patriarch of Antioch by Count Raynauld de Chatillon.

depicts him symbolically, to be sure, but tied securely with strong ropes, a detail
not found in the text.[21] A cloud of large black insects gathers around his head
awaiting Raynauld's order to have the miter removed and the patriarch's pate
smeared with honey in the heat of the day, as the text specifies. This exact scene
is chosen by the artist of Paris MS. fr. 9081 as well, and the notes for the artist
in that codex make clear what the iconographic details should be. The differences
between the Paris miniature and that in YT MS. 12 are rooted in the more dry,
didactic approach taken in the former, and the more dramatic, symbolic confron-
tation of the venerable clergyman and the malicious count in the latter. Again
the YT MS. 12 Master has selected a specific moment in the event and represented it with intense immediacy over against the traditional symbolism of this
stylite figure drawn from Early Christian tradition and Byzantine icon painting.
We are also impressed by how the artist "fills" the initial full of the figures depicting this episode, not letting the initial dominate the diminutive scenes the

---

[21] Paris, ed., *Guillaume de Tyr*, 2: 191. The patriarch is described as aged and an in-
valid, so the ropes are a special addition for dramatic effect, to show that Raynauld forced
the clergyman to stay all day on the summit of this tower of the citadel.

way it does in Paris MS. Fr. 9081. Again, this is part of this artist's design sensibility and a product of his artistic vision.

These three examples are all cases of miniatures that contain images depicted widely among the various thirteenth-century cycles of William of Tyre manuscripts, most of which were done later in the century as compared to YT MS. 12. But there are more numerous cases where the YT MS. 12 Master creates images that are unique, and are not found in any other William of Tyre manuscript.

One prime example is found at the start of Book 6 (fol. 29r). This book is the second of three books dealing with the momentous events of the First Crusade at Antioch (Fig. 11.4). In this miniature the YT MS. 12 Master selected an event that is found among very few thirteenth-century miniature cycles in William of Tyre codices, namely, the Crusaders battling the Turkish army that had besieged them (28 June 1098) soon after they succeeded in taking the city (3 June 1098). This event is drawn from the text of chapter 17 toward the end of this book. The YT MS. 12 Master's achievement is to choose an important event and give it distinctive historical and visual significance by his unique imagery.

The YT MS. 12 historiated initial "I" at Book 6 (fol. 29r) is brilliantly expanded with a dragon's neck forming the ground line for a battle scene worthy of the Morgan Old Testament picture book, Morgan MS. 638, albeit on a much smaller scale.[22] Packed into this relatively small scene we have the suggestion of the city gate of Antioch through which the Crusader army is emerging to engage in battle with the Turks commanded by Korbugha. The main feature of this encounter is the appearance of the papal legate, Bishop Adhemar of Le Puy, riding out with the army and carrying the holy relic of the Sacred Lance. By these choices, our artist has combined the presence of one of the most important figures at Antioch, Adhemar, with the first recorded instance of the Crusaders carrying a holy relic into battle, in this case the Holy Lance. The Lance had been discovered only a few days before this battle and was the inspiration for the Crusaders to march out boldly and face their foe with confidence and determination. Despite the importance of the Holy Lance for the history of the First Crusade at Antioch, it is found in no other Book 6 miniature among the illustrated thirteenth-century William of Tyre manuscripts.

A second unique image is found at the start of Book 9 (fol. 46r) where we find the elevation of Godefroy de Bouillon to be the first ruler of what was to become the Latin Kingdom of Jerusalem, an event recounted in chapter 2 (Fig. 11.5). One of the special merits of the YT MS. 12 Master's depiction is that it remains true to the text of William of Tyre, which points out at chapter 9 that

---

[22] On Morgan MS. 638, see William Noel and Daniel Weiss, eds., *The Book of Kings: Art, War, and the Morgan Library's Medieval Picture Bible* (Baltimore: Walters Art Museum, 2002); see especially Cathleen Fleck and Richard Leson, "Catalogue of the Exhibition," 142–206.

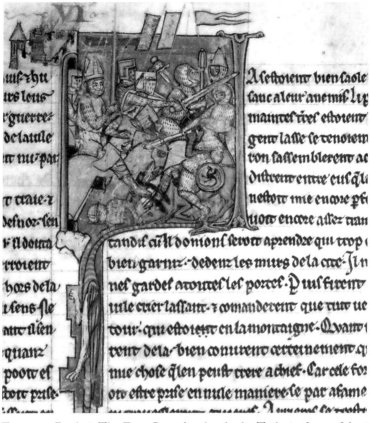

FIG. 11.4. Book 6, The First Crusaders battle the Turks in front of Antioch, led by
Bishop Adhemar of Le Puy carrying the Holy Lance.

Godefroy refused to wear the crown of a king with gold and jewels in the city
where Jesus had worn the crown of thorns.[23]

In a deceptively simple image the artist, in effect, frames the initial "S" with
an architectural setting, and then populates the initial with thirteen nobles, four
of whom hold Godefroy aloft in a prayful, standing position. Godefroy wears
no crown; only his ermine-lined cloak distinguishes him as a noble, a garment
worn by one other noble in this image. Godefroy is made to look like all the other
nobles who voted him into office, a rendering in keeping with the spirit of Godefroy's acceptance.

---

[23] Paris, *Guillaume de Tyr*, 1: 309.

FIG. 11.5. Book 9, Godefroy is elected *advocatus Sancti Sepulchri.*

Given the fact that the text speaks mostly of Godefroy's election, one wonders what the YT MS. 12 Master's inspiration for the image of elevation might have been. Other artists mostly depict Godefroy praying at the Holy Sepulchre, or a conference of the nobles about who the new leader should be, or even introduce a coronation, paying no attention to the fact that Godefroy refused the crown. Our artist has focused on that last fact and he has attempted to represent his election quite explicitly by representing a literal elevation. One possible artistic source for this might be Byzantine biblical miniature painting. Hugo Buchthal and Kurt Weitzmann have discussed how the ancient Roman custom in the late Empire of naming a new ruler by acclamation and raising the new emperor on a military shield was practiced by the soldiers and the imagery was subsequently incorporated into Byzantine biblical miniatures.[24]

Another unique image indicating our artist's interest in holy relics is found at the start of Book 12 (fol. 67v). Book 12 presented a challenge to most artists

---

[24] Hugo Buchthal, *The Miniatures of the Paris Psalter* (London: Warburg Institute, 1938; repr. New York: Kraus, 1968), 24–25, fig. 6; Kurt Weitzmann, *Illustrations in Roll and Codex* (Princeton: Princeton University Press, 1970), 169, 170, 178–79, fig. 187.

because either they could repetitiously depict a coronation of the new king, Baldwin II, whose reign this book discussed, or they could select a variety of local battles to represent, none of which was particularly memorable. Very few showed much imagination in choosing events of historical and visual significance. The Paris BNF MS. 9081 double-decker miniature for this book, for example, depicts a scene of great historical significance, the grant of a house to Hues de Paiens and Godefroy de St. Omer near the Temple for their new order, an image, in effect, of the founding of the Templar Order. But the artistic rendering is completely pedestrian, simplified, and insignificant. By contrast, the YT MS. 12 Master selects an event that is important both historically and liturgically, and gives it a memorable representation.

In chapter 12 of Book 12, William of Tyre discussed how King Baldwin II marched north to Antioch to engage the army of the Turkish satrap Il-Ghazi and help defend the Principality, responding to the urgent plea of Prince Roger. A memorable battle took place at Danith, just east of Antioch, on 14 August 1120, in which the Crusaders were victorious with the aid of the relic of the Holy Cross. Afterwards, the king was forced to stay at Antioch so he could protect the northern Crusader territory, but he sent the relic of the Cross back to Jerusalem. As the text says,

> Li Rois envoia la vraie croiz en Jherusalem par l'arcevesque de Cesaire, cui il bailla bone compaignie, si qu'ele fu receue en la ville a bele procession et a grant joie, le jor de la feste Sainte Croiz, en septembre. [25]

Despite the exigencies of the moment, the king was mindful that the True Cross relic had to be returned to Jerusalem for the feast of the Exaltation of the Holy Cross on 14 September. It was a liturgical festival of great importance in the Holy City, commemorating the return of the relic from Persia by Emperor Heraclius in 629.

The YT MS. 12 Master created an impressive historiated initial to focus attention on this important event recounted in Book 12 (Fig. 11.6). Taking the unusual initial "X", for "Xerses . . .", the artist has placed it at the center of a much larger miniature which expands both to the left and to the right. The "X" of the text appears as a counterpoint to the enormous relic of the True Cross held by Archbishop Ebremar of Caesarea. It is as if the relic was in fact reincarnated as the entire Holy Cross of Christ, in the same manner that Ridley Scott presented the relic of the Holy Cross in his 2005 film *Kingdom of Heaven* as the actual cross covered with precious metal. The genial archbishop marches forth toward Jerusalem accompanied by a 'bone compaignie' to be welcomed by the patriarch of Jerusalem and many citizens of the Holy City. It is a unique and remarkable historical moment which is given visual resonance by the way the artist integrates the

---

[25] Paris, ed., *Guillaume de Tyr*, 1: 452.

FIG. 11.6. Book 12, Bishop Ebremar of Caesarea returns to Jerusalem carrying the relic of the True Cross.

initial into the image, and by the way the familiar iconography of Christ's entry into Jerusalem, known from both Eastern and Western artistic sources, is evoked by the kneeling youth in front of the archbishop and the citizens who follow the patriarch.[26] And while we cannot say that the artist has given an incontrovertibly unique English interpretation to the forms of this image, there is no doubt that, for example, the low, wide, and three-dimensional design of the episcopal miters and the rectangular outlines of the marginal extension of the initial are typically found in mid-century English miniatures.[27]

Among the many memorable images in this codex, two others are also of special interest. At Book 21 (fol. 152v) we find a unique image of King Baldwin IV as a boy, with his mentor, Archbishop William of Tyre (Fig. 11.7). And at Book 24 (fol. 188v), one of the four images added to the basic cycle to illustrate

---

[26] Gertrud Schiller, *Iconography of Christian Art*, transl. J. Seligman, vol. 2 (Greenwich, CT: New York Graphic Society, 1972), 18–23, figs. 31–49.

[27] The miters are similar to those found in the work of Matthew Paris, and the rectangular 'stepped' borders of the initial's extension is found in a number of examples. See, e.g., Morgan, *Early Gothic Manuscripts, 1250–1285*, 2: figs. 120, 47, 41.

FIG. 11.7. Book 21, William of Tyre discovers symptoms that suggest the young Baldwin has leprosy.

the Continuation to 1232 in this manuscript, we find the most famous English Crusader of all, Richard Coeur de Lion (Fig. 11.8).

The historiated initial at Book 21 is memorable because of the extraordinary and tender subject. Inside a lovely 'M' on a pink and blue field, which is set in a rectangular panel anchored by a dragon down the central interval, the artist has visualized the report given by Baldwin IV's tutor, Archbishop William of Tyre. When Baldwin was nine years old, William observed him playing with his friends. When the boys pinched each others' arms, even drawing blood, Baldwin endured it as if he felt nothing, while the others cried out in pain. William then inspects his arm closely. The text reports the sad news:

> . . . il estoit au commencement de la maladie qu'il ot puis, and qui mout
> se descovri quant il comença a venire en aage d'ome; de que les genz du
> roiaume avoient grant duel, quant il le regardoient.

FIG. 11.8. Book 24, King Philippe II welcomes King Richard I and Queen Berengaria to Acre.

Baldwin had a type of the dreaded disease of leprosy. Four years later, in 1174, he became king at the death of his father.[28] In March of 1185 he died overcome

---

[28] The most recent account of Baldwin IV is by Bernard Hamilton, *The Leper King and His Heirs: Baldwin IV and the Crusader Kingdom of Jerusalem* (Cambridge: Cambridge University Press, 2000). Piers Mitchell, the foremost historian of medicine in the Crusades (*Medicine in the Crusades: Warfare, Wounds and the Medieval Surgeon* [Cambridge: Cambridge University Press, 2004]) has discussed "the course of King Baldwin's disease" in detail, in an appendix to Hamilton, *The Leper King*, 249–53. According to Mitchell's interpretation, at the time of the discovery of numbness in his arm as a boy, Baldwin was probably experiencing the primary polyneuritic (PP) subtype of the disease, which is associated with nerve damage. This is what is represented in the miniature in YT12. Later, after he was crowned king in 1174, the nerve damage led to serious muscle weakness and blindness. Baldwin managed to survive until 1185, when he died at the age of twenty-three.

by his disease, just after William of Tyre had died, breaking off the text of his *History* in 1184.[29]

The overwhelming choices for a scene to begin Book 21 were either the death of King Amaury, or, secondarily, the coronation of Baldwin IV. The YT MS. 12 Master is the only thirteenth-century artist who illustrated these William of Tyre manuscripts to depict the learned archbishop with his young charge. A number of other artists represented the leprous king being crowned or in some other event, but no one else attempted to depict the heart-wrenching discovery of symptoms that the boy, Baldwin, soon to become King Baldwin IV, had the horrible disease of leprosy. The choice of such a poignant scene must have been made with the consent or by the directive of the patron, whoever he or she was. The ability of the artist to carry it out sensitively yet with such objective detachment is an impressive demonstration of his ability to master the new gothic naturalism.

The final scene chosen for consideration here is the historiated initial for Book 24 (fol. 188v). This is the only miniature for the Continuation we discuss here, and it must be said at the outset that there was very little consistency in the choice of scenes for this text. Nonetheless, the YT MS. 12 Master once again chooses a unique image (Fig. 11.8). It illustrates the episode at Acre during the Third Crusade where King Philippe II Augustus welcomes King Richard and his new Spanish bride of only one month, Queen Berengaria, to the city in June 1191. There are numerous manuscripts with illustrations showing Philippe and Richard meeting earlier, in Messina or Palermo, but no other artist depicts this meeting in Acre with Berengaria. It clearly is a choice that directly reflects the text of the Continuation, which describes the cordial welcome Philippe gave the English royal couple in Acre. It also focused attention on an important reconciliation, because Richard had at one time been betrothed to Philippe's sister, Alice.[30] It is notable because it is an unique image which put special emphasis on the newly-married English royal couple, and can reasonably be considered as another aspect of the Englishness of this miniature cycle.

The final issue to discuss with regard to the imagery of the miniatures and the overall program of the cycle is the selection of scenes in terms of what was depicted relative to the texts, and what was depicted with regard to historical personages, events, and places. As for the first issue, it is striking that although the text of the continuation takes the story of the Crusades up to 1232, the last event selected for illustration in this book was the successful attack on Damietta during the Fifth Crusade, in 1218–1219. This means that the patron apparently wished to end the pictorial cycle on a positive note, with the last major Crusader

---

[29] Peter Edbury has reopened the argument that William died on 29 September 1184. See Peter W. Edbury and John G. Rowe, *William of Tyre: Historian of the Latin East* (Cambridge: Cambridge University Press, 1988), 22 and n. 33.

[30] Jonathan Riley-Smith, *The Crusades: A History*, 2nd ed. (New Haven: Yale University Press, 2005), 142.

military victory prior to when the text of the Continuation ended in 1232. The complicated story of the Crusade of Frederick II in 1228–1229 was conspicuously not chosen to be depicted, despite the diplomatic success that Frederick achieved in regaining access to the Christian Holy Places by negotiation.

With regard to the program of images chosen, we can observe that in these new secular manuscripts the artists quickly develop a basic repertoire of images which focus on certain common scenes, as we have mentioned above: coronations, marriages, funerals, battle scenes, and sieges of cities. But in the case of the YT MS. 12 Master, we find that in his hands the choices result in a remarkable program that includes important experiences or major events—not incidental or merely convenient choices—that took place at significant places in the Latin Kingdom of Jerusalem and the other Crusader States, where major historical figures appear. The collective result is a program that forms the most impressive panorama of the Crusades found in any codex of the *History of Outremer* illustrated in the thirteenth century. In no other manuscript of William of Tyre's *History* do we see so many illustrious and historically significant figures as Duke Godefroy de Bouillon, Bishop Adhemar of Le Puy, King Baldwin I, Duke Bohemond of Antioch, Bishop Eberhard of Caesarea, King Fulk and Queen Melisende, Emperor John II of Byzantium, Emperor Conrad III of Germany, Count Raynauld de Chatillon, Patriarch Aimery of Antioch, Sultan Nureddin, King Amaury, Sultan Saladin, King Baldwin IV, King Philippe II of France, King Richard I of England and Queen Berengaria. They are included as appropriate in events taking place in Nicaea, Antioch, Edessa, Jerusalem, Bethlehem, Tyre, Tripoli, Acre, and Damietta. More importantly, in no other illustrated William of Tyre text do we find such an impressive array of these figures and others depicted in scenes of such naturalistic immediacy, human poignancy, and historical significance. For a brief outline of the personages, places, and dates of the events that appear for each of the book divisions of the text, see the Appendix below.

Having seen a selection of these remarkable miniatures containing unique imagery, it is important to note that the evidence appears to indicate that this artist was, I think, working somewhere in England. In regard to this argument, three important points can be made. First, the artist was apparently not exposed to other cycles in manuscripts of William of Tyre's text; we see no strong influence on his miniatures from other examples of the illustrated *History of Outremer* text. Second, he executes his artistic work with great success: his miniatures are handsomely painted, and they are original and creatively formulated with striking content. And third, equally notable, other artists did not know his work after its completion; we see no reflection of his iconography, his pictorial cycle, or his painterly style in other illustrated *History of Outremer* manuscripts. With these points in mind, the question that remains to be considered here is what additional evidence there may be for this artist as being English and working in England. Beyond the Englishness of some of the imagery and of some of the choices of miniatures, what do his art, his conception of historiated initials, and his painting style tell us about where he was trained and where he may have executed his work?

The remarkable miniatures of YT MS. 12 have excited much interest over the years and various opinions have been expressed about its origin. Attributions to London,[31] northern France,[32] and Rome[33] have been proposed, all with interesting discussion. None of these suggestions can be sustained, however, with particularly convincing evidence. To return to basic considerations, I think the YT MS. 12 Master can be discussed effectively on two levels. The first pertains to his basic style, his artistic quality, and his artistic creativity with regard to the treatment of historiated initials, some of which we have already touched on. The second refers to his technique and fundamental characteristics of his figural style as well as characteristics of his imagery.

The basic style of this artist is one of gothic naturalism, that is, he is among those early gothic painters who began to observe nature closely and started to record telling aspects of what he saw. Gothic naturalism began perhaps in France with artists like Villard de Honnecourt, who worked in northern France in the 1230s, and is often associated with the 'hairpin loop' style of drapery design. The style develops in major, apparently royal, commissions like the Morgan Old Testament picture book, carried out by several artists and attributed to royal patronage in Paris in the 1240s. This codex is now in the Morgan Library, in New York, MS. 638. The YT MS. 12 Master demonstrates the same interest in naturalistic observation, representation of monumentally conceived figures, and detailed narrative imagery found in a manuscript like Morgan MS. 638. But the YT MS. 12 Master has created his miniatures on a much smaller scale, and his work is not French in its style of linear design and soft, painterly draperies, or in technique, or in colorism. I am proposing that he is an English artist with his own stylistic characteristics of linear design, of colorism, and of technique, one who is also working around 1250, possibly in the 1240s, but for whom we have no other known exemplar of his painting.

If we look closely at the figural style of the YT MS. 12 Master, we find an artist who knows the gothic repertoire in ornamental initials. In colorism he uses basic gothic combinations of pink and blue in decidedly un-French hues combined with other primary colors like orange, red, yellow, green, and occasionally lavender. We note the new naturalistic figure style, and the basic two-dimensional surface designs with some suggestion of interest in three-dimensional representation reflected in the modeling or highlighting of some colored draperies, where the surface of the miniature has not been rubbed or abraded. His figures

---

[31] Folda, "Illustrations in Manuscripts of the *History of Outremer* by William of Tyre," vol. 1, and idem, "Manuscripts of the *History of Outremer* by William of Tyre," 90–95 (at 94, no. 38).

[32] Randall, *Medieval and Renaissance Manuscripts in the Walters Art Gallery*, 1:126, 133.

[33] Stones, review of Avril and Gousset, *Manuscrits enluminés*, 889.

have drapery that is defined in terms of line, but is also modeled in darker hues of the basic color. His technique is clearly one based on a linear drawing style. There is linear articulation of the faces, most of which are seen in a three-quarters view; the draperies are strongly outlined in black, and the folds are created with black linear elements defining a ridge of the fold associated with the darker hue of the base color of the fabric to create the troughs of the folds. These folds have a variety of shapes, mostly irregular and sometimes appearing almost as separate patches on the garment, but occasionally we find these painterly folds to be approximating a hairpin loop configuration (cf. fol. 82v, Book 14; Fig. 11.2). Thus the fundamentally two-dimensional and quite ornamental coloristic treatment of these scenes is relieved by some strong indication of three-dimensional modeling, by suggestions of highlighting, usually in white over the surface of some figures, and by the overlapping of figures to suggest depth.

The colorism of this artist is especially notable. Despite the basic gothic pink and blue combinations that exist in his figural ensembles, this artist has slightly different preferences when dealing with the initials themselves. Most of his initials are orange, often with red infilling and white highlights. These initials are placed on a medium light-blue ground. Very few are the standard pink on medium blue, or the reverse, as we find in French manuscripts. Furthermore, he seems to think of the historiated initials as panel miniatures, in the sense that almost all of his initials are set on light medium-blue grounds that extend beyond the limits of the letter, and sometimes are quite extensive, as at fols. 51 (Book 10), 67v (Book 12), and 90 (Book 15).[34] Furthermore, some of his initials are given formal frames which encircle the initial and its ground in separate colors, as at fol. 46 (Book 9) and fol. 152 (Book 21). Only one initial, the 'F' on fol. 67r (Book 12), has the blue ground contained inside the letter. It is also clear how creatively and flexibly the artist thinks of his initial letters, manipulating them to facilitate the compositions of figural designs to be placed inside and on either side of them. Sometimes, for example in the 'Rs', the initials are widened significantly and opened up in the center. Nonetheless the artist still retains a strong sense of the ornamental, evidence of which is seen in the decorations he places on the stem components of these initials, and on the frequent appearance of long slender dragons that bite the initials and extend up or down the central interval, or in the margins to help mark the text break more emphatically.

There is no doubt that the fundamental focus of the compositions is on the figural designs; architecture, ground lines, and other indications of nature, even horses, are usually quite secondary and subordinate. The impressive aspect of the figures is their monumentality in scenes where only a few major figures appear, their dynamism in scenes of battle, their substantiality in terms of

---

[34] For all of these coloristic points, I recommend again that the reader consult the British Library online digital illustrations for YT MS. 12 available at the following address: http://prodigi.bl.uk/illcat/welcome.htm.

proportions—basically a 5.5 or 6 to 1 ratio in the large important figures, overall length to head height—and the clarity of their narrative imagery. Finally, we should emphasize that the naturalism of these figures is in a beginning stage of gothic development, and of course while we do not as yet see expressions of emotion on the faces of the figures, the bodies and gestures are expressive, the compositions are full and tight, and there is often dynamic interaction among the figures.

The artist also shows certain interests and preferences in the visual material he deals with and how he paints his miniatures. He is interested in heraldry, employing a number of interesting charges on shields, standards, and caparisons. He uses the architecture effectively as a prop for staging the scenes and for its coloristic variety. He often shows thrones supported on low colonnades. Although the miniatures are basically well preserved in this book, it is a shame nonetheless that many paintings display rubbing or flaking which often rob the figural drapery of its fully-modeled effect.

Despite the high quality of this artist's work, it is difficult to find parallels for this style and this artist in contemporary manuscripts. Certainly no other codex painted by the YT MS. 12 Master is known or has yet been identified. The question I would like to pose, therefore, as a possible approach to finding a new attribution for localizing this codex is this: Given the fact that we have here an early example of a major secular text which has a cycle of high-quality miniatures, what centers in England can we think of where production of both religious and secular illustrated books might be found in the mid-thirteenth century? In asking this question one thinks of the parallels in France, in Paris and the north of France where such centers are found, and where some of the same artists can be found working in both religious and non-religious books. In England the choice of centers is perhaps smaller, but a number of possible candidates present themselves. Besides the problematic case of London, one can think of Oxford and East Anglia, and—I think—a very interesting possibility is Salisbury. We of course know about Salisbury when it comes to a number of religious books very handsomely decorated, but we do not know anything as yet about whether Salisbury produced early secular illustrated books or not. When it comes to concrete examples of illustrated religious books from Salisbury that have interesting parallels with the YT 12 codex, there are three excellent manuscripts to be considered. I refer to the Wilton Psalter (London, Royal College of Physicians, MS. 409),[35] the Missal of Henry of Chichester (Manchester, John Rylands Library, MS. lat. 24),[36] and the Amesbury Psalter (Oxford, All Souls College, MS. 6),[37] all dated c. 1250.

[35] Morgan, *Early Gothic Manuscripts, 1250–1285*, 2: 55–57, cat. 99.
[36] Morgan, *Early Gothic Manuscripts, 1250–1285*, 2: 57–59, cat. 100.
[37] Morgan, *Early Gothic Manuscripts, 1250–1285*, 2: 59–61, cat. 101.

All of these manuscripts are luxury books with substantial amounts of gold, in contrast to YT MS. 12, which has no gold. This is of course a typical distinction between religious and secular illustrations at this time. Because these Salisbury manuscripts are religious in nature, either prayer books or service books, they are therefore more traditional in their format, unlike the new secular history books, and they lack aspects of the individuality we find in the YT MS. 12 Master's approach and style. These books also have large-format miniatures as well as smaller compositions, a program of painting perhaps done by more than one artist. But until we find other secular books from Salisbury with a program of historiated initials to compare with YT MS. 12, we can look at the historiated initials of the Wilton Psalter, the Henry of Chichester Missal, and the Amesbury Psalter, and, *mutatis mutandis*, imagine what their counterparts might have looked like as a program of secular paintings. So it is the smaller compositions in, for example, the initials of the Amesbury Psalter, that seem interesting as comparanda. See the initial 'E' on fol. 96r and the initial 'D' on fol. 126v from the Psalter illustrations in this manuscript (Figs. 11.9 and 11.10). Certainly we can point out that these Salisbury historiated initials show a monumentality shared by those in YT MS. 12. Some aspects of the figure style are similar in terms of drapery design and the way the figures appear in the initials, and the technique has certain similarities even if the results are often rather different. What we are proposing is not necessarily that the YT MS. 12 Master worked in Salisbury when he did this manuscript, but that he might have been an artist trained or influenced by the Sarum Master, or one of a number of his assistants.

Nigel Morgan observes the following about the Sarum Master: "The full development of the Early Gothic style occurs in a group of manuscripts perhaps produced at Salisbury (the Sarum Master group). . . ."[38] "His style is characterized by monumental forms with heavily troughed folds strongly delineated in black lines. The figures are elongated in proportion and have a combination of delicacy with graceful nobility. The facial types are in the tradition of works around 1200 such as the Westminster Psalter and there may be conscious revival of work of this period. . . . The work of the Sarum Master is full of iconographic invention both in narrative imagery and devotional types."[39] He also refers to certain aspects of the colorism which is relevant to YT MS. 12. Speaking about the Amesbury Psalter, Morgan says: "A change from the early manuscripts of the Sarum Master's workshop . . . is in the colour palette; there is a tendency to eliminate red, and let orange, a dull pink and blue predominate."[40] This orange is certainly one of the features of the YT MS. 12 painted initials.

---

[38] Morgan, *Early Gothic Manuscripts, 1190–1250*, vol. 1 (London: Harvey Miller, 1982), 28.

[39] Morgan, *Early Gothic Manuscripts, 1250–1285*, 2: figs [II], 21.

[40] Morgan, *Early Gothic Manuscripts, 1250–1285*, 2: 60.

FIG. 11.9. Psalm 80, Jacob wrestling with the angel, Jacob's Dream.
By courtesy of the Warden and Fellows of All Souls College, Oxford.

These points having been made, it remains to be seen whether future research can uncover some more specific indicators for localizing and dating YT MS. 12. We would like to know about the patron of this remarkable codex. Furthermore, the fact that this manuscript is an early example of secular book illustration at a point when the shift from traditional monastic scriptoria to lay workshops was in progress in thirteenth-century England makes it difficult to associate it with existing centers. If the artist is somehow linked to Salisbury, as we are suggesting, the fact is he very well might have been trained there but working elsewhere, e.g., in Oxford or in London, in his own style where the market for secular books was beginning to develop. Our discussion therefore presents a tentative proposal in regard to the place and date where this artist might have been trained, but, lacking any indication of who the patron was, without being able to specify where this book might necessarily have been done. However, despite these qualifications, I think the evidence we have provides important indications that the artist of YT MS. 12 is English and that the book was written and illustrated in England. I think, as discussed above, that its Englishness is reflected in the miniature cycle in terms of style, execution, technique, colorism, and especially in the creativity and imagination shown in its imagery. This book is a remarkable production containing the history of the Latin Kingdom of Jerusalem illustrated for an unknown English patron somewhere in England at mid-century.

What we have seen in discussing the images which illustrate this codex includes the following: Let me review some of the main points of the achievement of the YT MS. 12 Master. He is an artist who carries out his project to illustrate

Fig. 11.10. Psalm 109, The Trinity.
By courtesy of the Warden and Fellows of All Souls College, Oxford.

this text without reference to any other known cycle of miniatures of the *History of Outremer* text. Indeed, his is a remarkably independent artistic production by a very able English painter otherwise unknown. He impressively captures the content and substance of William of Tyre's newly-translated text and its continuation. He visually portrays the various episodes with a noble simplicity and an engaging directness, yet with a great sense of humanity in the spirit of the new 'gothic naturalism' of the mid-thirteenth century in England. His expressive and naturalistic style distinguishes him as an attractive artist of great originality and creative imagination who, despite the fact that we cannot as yet find his hand in any other extant work, deserves to be recognized for a signal achievement in his miniatures in this manuscript. In illustrating this codex he has provided us with a major early example of the new secular book illustration in England, just as Paris BNF MS. fr. 9081 provides us with a major early example of the new secular book illustration in Paris. Indeed, the remarkable achievement of the YT MS. 12 artist is that he presents us with the most impressive panorama of the Crusaders in the Holy Land between 1096 and 1218 found in any extant thirteenth-century codex. Here we find the grandest array of *dramatis personae* from the Crusades and the Holy Land in any thirteenth-century William of Tyre codex, combined with events depicted in the most important places for the Crusaders, such as Jerusalem, Nicaea, Antioch, Tyre, and Damietta, for the First, Second, Third, and Fifth Crusades. It is a work of important historical narrative seen through the eyes of a sensitive, able, well-informed, and observant English painter. Would that we had a colophon that would let us know his name and that of his no doubt interesting and important patron, and more about where and when he worked! The history of English manuscript painting in the thirteenth century has heretofore rested mainly on the foundations of analysis of religious books, with some conspicuous exceptions. Until we know more about the history of English secular book illustration in this period, a fuller story about the YT MS. 12 Master is not likely to be told. But even if we do not know exactly who this artist is, he—or she— seems to be English, and we certainly can admire the high quality of the painting in this codex.

Appendix

Major Events, Major Places, and Major Historical Personages in YT MS. 12 at the start of the major text divisions:
    The basic 22 books of the *History of Outremer* text:

Bk. 1: · lost

Bk. 2: Pilgrims set out for the Holy Land (c. 1096 f.)

Bk. 3: The First Crusade armies at Nicaea (1097)

Bk. 4: Baldwin of Boulogne is welcomed to Edessa (1098)

Bk. 5: The First Crusade army besieges and enters Antioch (1098, June)

Bk. 6: The First Crusade army confronts the Turkish army at Antioch, with Bishop Adhemar of Le Puy carrying the relic of the Holy Lance (1098, June)

Bk. 7: The funeral of Bishop Adhemar of Le Puy at Antioch (1098, August)

Bk. 8: The First Crusade besieges Jerusalem (1099, July)

Bk. 9: Duke Godefroy de Bouillon is elected to rule the Latin Kingdom of Jerusalem (1099, July)

Bk. 10: The funeral of Godefroy de Bouillon, and the coronation of King Baldwin I in Bethlehem (1100)

Bk. 11: Patriarch Daimbert and Count Bohemond of Antioch sail to the West (1104, fall)

Bk. 12: Ebremar, archbishop of Caesarea, carries the relic of the True Cross back to Jerusalem where he is met by the patriarch of Jerusalem (1120)

Bk. 13: The Crusaders assault the city of Tyre; the head of Balak, slain by Count Joscelin, is brought to Tyre to encourage the Christians and demoralize the Muslims (1124)

Bk. 14: The coronation of King Fulk and Queen Melisende (1131, September)

Bk. 15: The Count of Edessa attempts to propose diplomatic measures to the Byzantine Emperor, John II (1138)

Bk. 16: The Crusaders kill an Arab satrap, son of Morel, returning from Bostrum (1146)

Bk. 17: Emperor Conrad of Germany cleaves a Turkish soldier in two with one blow of his sword (1147)

Bk. 18: Raynauld of Chatillon abuses the patriarch of Antioch on a tower of the citadel (1153)

Bk. 19: Nureddin escapes attacking Crusaders after his defeat near Tripoli (1163)

Bk. 20: King Amaury marries the Byzantine Princess Maria, with the patriarch of Jerusalem officiating (1167, August)

Bk. 21: Baldwin IV at play as a boy; William of Tyre inspects his wounds

Bk. 22: Saladin's army invades Crusader territory around Tripoli (1183)

Continuation:
Bk. 23, chap. 6:   The fountain of Siloam outside of Jerusalem
Bk. 24:   King Philippe II Auguste welcomes King Richard and his
                   queen, Berengaria, to Acre during the Third Crusade (1191)
Bk. 25:   Saladin's son, sultan of Egypt, falls from his horse and breaks
                   his neck
Bk. 26:   The Fifth Crusade besieges Damietta by land (1218–1219)

WILLIAM REED, BISHOP OF CHICHESTER
(D. 1385)—BIBLIOPHILE?

RODNEY THOMSON

A medieval bishop who conscientiously performed the duties of his office without cutting a figure as a writer, as a great servant of the Crown, or as a participant in the political or theological issues of his day may now be faceless to us, and we easily assume that he was always so. Such a one would be William Reed, bishop of Chichester 1368–1385, were it not for one highly unusual activity in which he engaged, and for which there happens to exist a substantial body of evidence. Activity and evidence are not only of the greatest interest in themselves, but they make us wish that we knew more about the personality which lay behind them.[1] For what Reed did was, in the first instance, to assemble by far the largest collection of books owned by a private person in fourteenth-century England—perhaps in all Europe—and then, systematically and deliberately, to give it all away. In general terms this has been well known for a long time; however, closer inspection of the documents and surviving books shows that Reed's collecting and donating was on an even grander scale than has been realized, and also reveals something of what motivated him.

Little is known of his origins. His family, certainly well off and highly ramified, was based in Devon with perhaps some representatives in Kent.[2] We learn of members of his kin, in general and some by name, who went to Oxford

---

[1] For his biography, see Alfred B. Emden, *Biographical Register of the University of Oxford to A.D. 1500*, 3 vols. (Oxford: Oxford University Press, 1957), 1556–60 (henceforward *BRUO*); John D. North, *The Oxford Dictionary of National Biography*, ed. H. C. G. Matthew and Brian Harrison, 60 vols. (Oxford: Oxford University Press, 2004), 46. 254–5; F. Maurice Powicke, *The Medieval Books of Merton College* (Oxford: Oxford University Press, 1931), 28–32, 162–82; Rodney M. Thomson, *A Descriptive Catalogue of the Medieval Manuscripts of Merton College, Oxford* (Cambridge: D.S. Brewer, 2009), xxiv–xxx. Emden, Powicke and North spelled his surname "Rede." "Red" or "Reed", however, were the preferred spellings of the man himself, as evidenced by the autograph *ex libris* inscriptions in his books, while his clerk Walter Robert used the form "Reed" for the *ex dono* inscriptions (see below, pp. 286–7).

[2] His will (see below, n. 10) mentions, as "consanguinei et affines mei in Deuonia uel alibi," "Iohannem filium seniorem Roberti fratris mei," M. Richard Pestour and

---

University, where they attached themselves to Exeter and Merton Colleges.[3] It may be that something happened to his parents and that he was orphaned, for in his will he says that he was brought up, and his education supported, by Nicholas of Sandwich, a wealthy cleric who had inherited extensive estates in Kent, and who spent much of his life as a gentleman-scholar at Oxford.[4] We do not know whether Sandwich was related to Reed, or what other reason he might have had for his philanthropy, which was ongoing and was clearly part of a close personal friendship. For much of Reed's adult life, Sandwich seems to have supplied him with books and the means with which to purchase them. It may be that, between the two of them, they developed a plan with respect to the books' ultimate destination. Supported by Sandwich, Reed went up to Oxford, and we find him there in 1337, as a fellow of Merton by 1344, still in 1357; by 1362 he was a doctor of theology and, to briefly summarize the rest of his career, he was archdeacon of Rochester 1359–1368 and provost of the collegiate church of Wingham in Kent 1363–1368, ending his career and life as bishop of Chichester. Again, we do not know whether his career unfolded in Kent and Sussex, rather than Devon, because of family connections or because of Nicholas of Sandwich.

His time at Oxford obviously made a deep impression on him, and in certain respects shaped the remainder of his career. Already during his fellowship, Reed was interested in the College books. This is revealed in the account roll from his term as subwarden (1353–1354). Significantly, it is the only roll from Merton's extensive medieval archive that includes a separate section specifying expenditure on the books and library.[5] He was, of course, at Merton during the period when the College enjoyed European-wide celebrity on account of that extraordinary group of fellows who made important contributions to the fields of what we should now call physics or mechanics (the laws of motion), mathematics, and astronomy.[6] Although not an original thinker himself, Reed obviously swam happily in this pool, compiling a set of astrological tables, of which the respectable number of twenty copies survives, and later presenting to the College his

---

"dominus" John Bampton, three children of another brother and a sister, and another "cognatus" named "dominus Henricus."

[3] For kin at Exeter and Merton Colleges in general, see below, p. 284–6. M. Richard Pestour was fellow of both places.

[4] *BRUO*, 1639–40. He was alive in 1347; the date of his death is wholly unknown.

[5] Merton College Records 970d; H. W. Garrod, "The Library Regulations of a Medieval College," *The Library*, n.s. 8 (1927): 312–35, at 322.

[6] Geoffrey H. Martin and J. Roger L. Highfield, *A History of Merton College* (Oxford: Oxford University Press, 1997), 46–73; J. A. Weisheipl, "*Repertorium Mertonense,*" *Mediaeval Studies* 31 (1969): 174–224; David C. Lindberg, *The Beginnings of Western Science* (Chicago: University of Chicago Press, 1992), 294–307.

astronomical instruments, one or two of which may still survive.[7] Two contemporary fellows and members of the "Merton school," Simon Bredon and William Heytesbury, served as canons of Chichester during Reed's episcopate.[8]

Of his episcopal activity we know only that he made two compilations of provincial statutes, only one of which survives.[9] More of his character may be inferred from silences in the meager data about his career: unusually, he was not a pluralist, nor was he a "civil servant." In his will he asked for his funeral to be celebrated "sine pompa," and that document shows that his wealth, though considerable, was concentrated almost entirely in a narrow range of movables: in vestments and altar plate on the one hand, and in his books on the other.[10] The dispositions of his will show that he was not much concerned to enrich his cathedral church, nor the members of his family beyond what was reasonable. Foremost in his mind was a vision, which he had begun to realize long before his death, and which he now sought to further after it.

This vision concerned the dispersal of his extraordinary collection of books among the colleges of the English university which he had attended, in order to

---

[7] Copies of his astrological tables are listed in Richard W. Sharpe, *A Handlist of the Latin Writers of Great Britain and Ireland before 1540* (Turnhout: Brepols, 1997), 802–3, and the work evaluated by John D. North (see n. 1 above). A copy, now lost, was apparently still at the College in 1615: Francis Godwin, *De Praesulibus Angliae*, ed. William Richardson (Cambridge: Cambridge University Press, 1743), 508: "Astronomicas tabulas in praedicto Collegio reliquit, etiamnum hodie (ut ferunt) visendus, una cum Imagine ipsius ad vivum depicta." Bodl. Lib.MS. Digby 176, one of the books presented by Reed to Merton College (see below, p. 287, n. 22), includes a number of items demonstrating his relations with other members of the "Merton School": (1) John Ashendon, *Prognosticatio de eclipsi uniuersali lunae* (1345), "quas m. W. Reed calculauit et m. Io. Ashedene pronosticauit," (2) "Almanak solis pro quatuor annis" (1341–1344) "per W. Reed anno Christi 1337 calculata et scripta," and (3) a letter from Reginald Lambourne (fellow of Merton in 1353, still in 1357; *BRUO*, 1086–87) to Reed about the conjunction of Saturn, Jupiter and Mars in 1367, with prognostications of consequential unhappy events to occur between 1368 and 1374. William D. Macray, *Catalogus Codicum MSS Kenelmi Digby*, Catalogi Codicum Manuscriptorum Bibliothecae Bodleianae pars nona (Oxford: Clarendon Press, 1883), rev. Richard W. Hunt and Andrew G. Watson (Oxford: Bodleian Library, 1999), 189–90, and "Notes on Macray's Descriptions . . .," 81–82; Sharpe, *Handlist*, 206, 457. The astronomical instruments are mentioned at the end of the 1374 indenture gifting books to Merton (see n. 14 below).

[8] For Bredon, see *BRUO*, 257–58 and Sharpe, *Handlist*, 610–12. He willed his "smaller astrolabe" to Reed: Powicke, *Merton College*, 84. For Heytesbury, see *BRUO*, 927–8 and Sharpe, *Handlist*, 775–7.

[9] A collection of statutes made by him survives in the *Liber Cicestrensis*, Bodleian Library, MS. Ashmole 1146.

[10] Printed in Powicke, *Merton College*, 87–91. The document will be re-edited with commentary, along with the other documents cited below, in my forthcoming edition of Oxford medieval booklists for the *Corpus of British Medieval Library Catalogues* (London: The British Library, 1990–).

enhance the education of the clergy which they offered. Let us begin with the documentary evidence for this. Reed's will was made in 1382: to his successors as bishops of Chichester he bequeathed sixteen books (probably service books); to his relative Richard Pestour, fellow of Exeter and Merton Colleges, one hundred books for the use of scholars of his kin at Oxford, after Pestour's death to be kept and lent out by the heads (rector and warden respectively) of Merton and Exeter. To Merton College itself he left one hundred books; to New College another hundred, of which fifty, in theology and canon law, had earlier been promised to Chichester Cathedral; twenty to Exeter College; ten each to Balliol, Oriel, and Queen's; thirteen to Arundel College in Kent (recently founded by the Earl of Arundel), and more than eighteen single books, mostly unspecified, to persons and churches unconnected with Oxford (a more precise number cannot be speci- fied since in one case an untotalled list is referred to).[11] The grand total of books to be distributed is (a few more than) 398, of which 350 were to go to Oxford. One notes the bishop's change of mind about the books which were to have gone to Chichester, now diverted to New College. This suggests an earlier state of the will, and a change of decision that parallels the intentions of later bishops such as Flemyng of Lincoln (d. 1431) or Gray of Ely (d. 1478), whose books went, not to their cathedrals, but to Lincoln and Balliol College respectively.[12] By this time educated bishops realized that their cathedrals were never going to become im- portant as seats of learning; their books were better bestowed elsewhere.

Reed had conceived and had begun to realize his vision well before he was organizing his legacy. From October of 1374 we have two indentures, evidently made on the same occasion in London. One records the gift and delivery of twen- ty-five books to Exeter College;[13] the other records the delivery of one hundred (actually ninety-nine) volumes to Merton.[14] In both cases the books are itemized,

---

[11] Powicke, *Merton College*, 88: "Item lego ecclesie de Otteham j calicem et certos libros eidem ecclesie."

[12] For Gray, see *BRUO*, 809–14, and Roger A. B. Mynors, *Catalogue of the Man- uscripts of Balliol College Oxford* (Oxford: Oxford University Press, 1963), xxiv-xlv; for Richard Flemyng, see *BRUO*, 697–99. The same was true of his nephew, Robert (*BRUO*, 699–700), dean of Lincoln (d. 1431), and similarly Bishop John Russell (d. 1494), who gave his books to New College (*BRUO*, 1609–11).

[13] Oxford, Exeter College Archives, E. V. 2 1374, previously printed in Susan Ca- vanaugh, "A Study of Books Privately Owned in England 1300–1450" (Ph.D. diss., Uni- versity of Pennsylvania, 1980), 708–10, and Andrew G. Watson, *A Descriptive Catalogue of the Medieval Manuscripts of Exeter College Oxford* (Oxford: Oxford University Press, 2000), 138–39, with annotations, and a photograph, plate 4 (facing p. 101).

[14] The original, formerly in the possession of Merton College, has not been seen since 1955. It was not known to Powicke, who consequently underestimated the total size of Reed's library by that number (Powicke, *Merton College*, 31). The indenture was reproduced, with identifications, in Cavanaugh, "Books," 691–700. Her source appears to have been a pre-publication version of H. W. Garrod (ed. J. Roger L. Highfield), "An

with short titles and, even better, secundo folios, thus enabling the identification of a number of surviving volumes. There was presumably once a similar document relating to Queen's College, since among its accounts for 1374–1375 are payments for the journey of two fellows to London to receive books and money from Reed, and for the carriage of five books back to Oxford.[15] As I shall explain in greater detail shortly, it is important to understand that what these documents record is the practical implementation and hence conclusion of a process that must have been envisaged and initiated some time before; the interval between Reed conceiving the idea of the gifts and the final handover might easily have been as long as a year or more.

Thirdly, another indenture, unfortunately badly damaged by damp, records the delivery in 1400, by the bishop's kinsmen John Bampton and Richard Pestour, to the rector and fellows of Exeter College, of forty-five books for the use of his kin there.[16] Obviously, this represents part of the execution of that provision of the bishop's will by which one hundred books were to be given to Pestour for the use of the bishop's kin studying at Exeter and Merton. The will states that after his death their administration was to be jointly in the hands of the heads of Merton and Exeter. But how would this have worked in practice? The surviving indenture shows that—whether by Reed's decision or his executors'—the joint gift was simply split in two, half to be housed in, and administered by, each College. Prefacing the list of titles is a substantial set of rules for the management of the books assigned to Exeter, unfortunately badly damaged. However, it is

---

Indenture between William Reed, bishop of Chichester and John Bloxham and Henry Stapilton, fellows of Merton College, Oxford, London 22 October 1374," *Bodleian Library Record* 10 (1982): 9–19, at 14–19 (without identifications).

[15] Queen's College Archives, Long Roll 2 P 23:

Expence forincecc'. Item de vijs ijd pro expensis Middelworth et Johanni Spenser versus London' et ibidem quando receperunt ab episcopo Cicestren' libros et donar' dat' domui.

Item de vjd pro cariag' quinque librorum a London' ad Oxon'

Item de ijd ob' pro prandio equi portante eosdem

Conductio equorum. In primis r' de iiijs pro duobus equis vsque London' pro Middelworth et Johanne Spencer qui fuerunt cum episcopo Cicestren' pro libris et aliquibus donariis in negoc' domus.

[16] Exeter College Archives, E. V. 2 1400, unprinted. Between the late seventeenth century and the present the document was badly affected by damp, and most of it is illegible to the naked eye. I have to thank the College Librarian, Julia Chadwick, for allowing me to transcribe it using ultra-violet light in the darkness of the Library's closed stacks, in March of 2007. By this means I was able to make out about ninety per cent of the text. In 1665 the document, obviously in a better state, was seen and brief but helpful notes made from it by the Oxford antiquary Anthony Wood (Bodl. Lib., Wood d. 2, p. 74). The statement by Watson, *Exeter*, xv n. 1, that this document represents a donation to Merton is erroneous.

clear that the use of the books was to be in strict order of priority: Richard Pestour during his lifetime, then Reed's kin at the College, then the other fellows. The books were not to stray beyond the College's confines, and penalties were prescribed for their loss or damage. The Exeter document apparently originally included a reference to its expected Merton counterpart, which contained a corresponding set of regulations.[17] The final piece of documentary evidence is a catalogue of the library of New College, made c. 1385.[18] This catalogue, which is probably incomplete, includes sporadic references to donors, and Reed's name is attached to seventy-three volumes. These were presumably some of the volumes bequeathed in his will.[19]

In combination, the indentures, accounts, and library catalogue yield a total of 248 volumes, of which at least 137 definitely do not figure in the will because they had already been gifted and delivered. The combined evidence of the will and the other documents, then, gives us a minimum total of 536 volumes which Reed owned at some period of his life. The implied caveat is important, for we need not suppose that Reed had all of these books in his possession at one and the same time.

From the documents I move to the surviving books, identifiable not only from their secundo folios, but because they bear Reed's *ex libris* and *ex dono* inscriptions. At Merton College there are thirty-two survivors from the 1374 inventory.[20] But in addition there are another eleven surviving volumes which do

---

[17] Fragments of the reference to Merton College in the Exeter indenture are still visible. They are fortunately made intelligible by Anthony Wood's note on the document: "wherin tis said yt [William Reed] had giuen books to Merton Coll. wch were to be kept & used as expressed in this said indenture as at Exeter Coll." (Bodl. Lib., Wood d. 2, p. 74).

[18] Oxford, New College Archives 9654 (*Liber albus*), fols. 3v–17v, with gaps and later additions. The list was previously printed, without annotations, by Alfred F. Leach, "Wykeham's Books at New College," in *Collectanea III*, ed. M. Burrows, Oxford Historical Society 32 (Oxford: Clarendon Press, 1896), 223–41. Most of Reed's donations were printed by Powicke, *Merton College*, 91–92. These and more are in Cavanaugh, "Books," 703–8, based upon copies of Leach's transcription re-collated and annotated by N. R. Ker and R. W. Hunt.

[19] Bequests of books were not always implemented in full, and it may be that not all of the intended 100 volumes reached the College. Note that the Exeter College indenture of 1400 lists 45 volumes, presumably of the intended 50, and the Merton College indenture of 1374 lists 99 titles of the intended 100. Merton College Records 3771, the bursar's account roll for 1452, unfortunately badly damaged, has an entry "Et [. . . equit]ando libros Cycetre ad Collegium viii d." Could it be that books from Reed's bequest were still arriving at the College at this late date?

[20] Merton Coll., MSS. 8, 19, 27, 66, 103, 105, 149, 158, 166, 168–172 (169 and 170 were each originally two separate books), 194, 216, 227, 237–239, 241, 249, 279, 281–282, 291, 294–295, 305, Bodl. Libr., e Mus. 19.

not appear there, one inscribed "ex legato."[21] I think that these must all be survivors from the hundred bequeathed to the College in Reed's will. There are five
survivors from among the books assigned to Pestour, two from the 1374 gift to
Exeter College, two from the bequest to Balliol, thirteen from the New College
catalogue, and one from the bequest to Arundel College.[22] Four of the New College books (New Coll., MSS. 120, 134, 264, 306) have an unusual form of *ex
dono* inscription which includes the words "to be chained in the common library
and for the common use of the scholars of the same and especially of those to
be taken in future from the diocese of Chichester by the kindness of the bishop
of Winchester." Richard Hunt was surely right to think that these are survivors
from the fifty volumes which Reed had initially intended for his cathedral.[23] An
inexplicable puzzle is Merton Coll. 259, with Reed's *ex dono*, the words "(Liber)
aule de Exon" expunged but not replaced. It does not figure in either of the Exeter College indentures, let alone the Merton one. BL, MS. Cotton Julius B. iii,
fols. 31–42, was owned by Reed, but it is a mere fragment, and whether or to
whom it was gifted is unknown. The total of surviving books is sixty-eight, all
but two of which figure, probably or certainly, in the documents.

Before leaving the extant manuscripts, something must be said of the volume numbers that appear in some of them. These numbers were written by

---

[21] MSS. 35, 77, 137–138, 190, 234, 252, 297, 311. MS. 281 part 2, a separate volume
before the early seventeenth century, is the one inscribed "ex legato." If my interpretation
is correct, then it is striking that there are 32 survivors of the 100 donated in 1374 but
only eleven of the 100 bequeathed after his death. This too makes one wonder (see above,
n. 19) whether all of the intended bequest was located and delivered.

[22] Pestour/Exeter College list (nine secundo folios are partly or wholly illegible):
Exeter Coll. 19 and Merton Coll. 257 are certain survivors. Merton Coll. MSS. 78 and
242 may be from its lost Merton counterpart, and Bodl. Lib., MS. Digby 176, certainly
is. Exeter College 1374 list: Merton Coll. 224, Douai, Bibl. de la ville 860. Balliol College gift: Balliol Coll., MSS. 94, 285. New College gift: New Coll., MSS. 55, 70, 92,
96–97, 106, 120–121, 124, 134, 171, 264, 306. Arundel College gift: BL, Royal 10 A.
xi. Another book from the Pestour/Exeter College list must have survived into the seventeenth century, for Anthony Wood in 1665 recorded (Bodl. Lib., Wood D. 2, p. 106):
"In the front of a MS in the lib. [of Exeter College] in folio thus: Liber mei [*sic pro* magistri?] Will: Rede prepositi ecclesiae collegiatae de Wyngham & Liber scolar de genere
ven. patris domini Willelmi Reed episcopo Cicestr. Oxoniae successive student' ex dono
ven. patris predicti per custodem et rectorem de Merton et Stapleton in Oxonia uel per
earum librarie eiusdem scolaribus iuxta facultates et merita ipsorum cuiusque ad tempus
sub cautione iurato cum prouide liberandus." This inscription does not appear in any surviving book.

[23] Richard W. Hunt, "The Medieval Library," in *New College, Oxford, 1379–1979*,
ed. John Buxton and Penry Williams (Oxford: The Warden and Fellows of New College,
1979), 317–45, at 320.

Reed's clerk M. Walter Robert, and usually follow the *ex dono* inscriptions.[24] Ten of the eleven Merton books not in the 1374 indenture have them, so do the four New College books with the inscription relating to Chichester diocese, and so does the book given to Arundel College.[25] The numbers range from ii to xxxiii. As there are no repetitions, they clearly derive from a single series, and as they generally follow the *ex dono* inscriptions, they must relate not to Reed's ownership but to his bequest. The solution to the problem, it seems to me, lies with the four numbered New College manuscripts. I suggest that Reed had all the books he had originally destined for his cathedral, then diverted to New College, given these numbers. His executors, however, found these books difficult to locate and group together, so they were distributed randomly.[26] This, of course, is no more than a guess.

Five hundred and thirty-six volumes was not an extraordinary figure for the number of books owned in fourteenth-century England by a large corporate institution (it was far exceeded, for instance, at Christ Church Canterbury and Durham Cathedral Priory),[27] but it was remarkable for a private individual. However, we must remember that Reed dispersed at least 129 of them during his lifetime and presumably acquired some that figured in his will later than this, so that at any given time his library may not have been as large as it seems when computed across the whole of his adult life. Both when and how he acquired his books can sometimes be ascertained from the inscriptions which, fortunately, are almost invariably written in those of his books that survive with their flyleaves intact. These are generally of two sorts. Firstly, Reed himself usually wrote an *ex libris* in his own hand, often with an account of where and how he obtained

---

[24] Invariably in the case of the Merton books; in the case of the New College books the numbers follow Reed's *ex libris* and precede his *ex dono*.

[25] Merton Coll., MSS. 35 "xxvii uolumen," 77 "ii uolumen," 137 "xxxi uolumen," 138 "xxxiii uolumen," 190 "vi uolumen," 234 "ix uolumen," 252 "xi uolumen", 297 "xxviii uolumen", 311 "xix uolumen." New Coll., MSS. 120 "xxvi volumen," 134 "xx volumen," 264 "xxiii," 306 "xvi volumen." BL, MS. Royal 10 A. xi "xii volumen."

[26] This interpretation of the Merton and New College volume numbers was first made by the late R. W. Hunt, and is contained in a letter of 26 Jan. 1979 to J. R. L. Highfield. I have to thank Dr. Highfield for making this letter known to me, and James Willoughby for checking the information about the New College manuscripts against the originals.

[27] For Canterbury, see the early fourteenth-century library catalogue compiled under Prior Henry of Eastry, in Montague R. James, *The Ancient Libraries of Canterbury and Dover* (Cambridge: Cambridge University Press, 1902), 13–172; for Durham, Alan J. Piper, "The Libraries of the Monks of Durham," in *Medieval Scribes, Manuscripts & Libraries: Essays Presented to N. R. Ker*, ed. Malcolm B. Parkes and Andrew G. Watson (London: Scolar Press, 1978), 213–49, at 218.

the book.[28] Some of these accounts are quite circumstantial, as the following examples testify:

> (Merton Coll. 234, fol. iv^v) Liber M. Willelmi Reed episcopi Cicestrie cuius partem primam habuit ex dono reuerendi domini sui M. Nicholai de Sandwyco, secundam uero emit ab executoribus uenerabilis patris domini Iohannis de Schepeya episcopi Roffensis, sed tertiam emit ab executoribus uenerabilis patris domini Simonis de Islip archiepiscopi Cantuariensis.

> (Bodl. Libr., Digby 176, fol. 1v) Liber M. Willelmi Reed episcopi Cicestrie cuius partem habuit ex dono reuerendi domini sui M. Nicholai de Sandwyco, partem emit de executoribus reuerendi patris domini Thome de Bradewardina archiepiscopi Cantuarie, partem emit de executoribus M. Ricardi Camsale, partem ipse M. Willelmus scripsit et partem scribi fecit.

Later, when he had determined on the destination for a book he wanted to give away, his clerk M. Walter Robert wrote a formal *ex dono*, sometimes including the same sort of information, together with a request for prayers for Reed and all the faithful. So often was Walter Robert called upon to do this that he complained about it in Merton College, MS. 168.[29] On the basis of these inscriptions I list below the sources from which Reed obtained his books, in order of numbers.

> from Thomas Trillek, bishop of Rochester 1365–1372,[30] thirty books: Merton Coll. 27, 77, 78, 149, 158, 166, 168–172, 190, 237–239, 242, 248 (with money from Sandwich), 249, 252, 295 (part), 311; Bodl. Libr., Digby 19; BL, Roy. 10 A. xi; Douai, Bibl. de la ville, 860; New Coll. 55, 70, 92 part 2, 96, 97, 120.

> from Nicholas Sandwich, fourteen books: Merton Coll. 216 (while provost of Wingham), 227, 234 pt. 1, 259 (while archdeacon of Rochester), 281, 282, 291, 305; Bodl. Libr., Digby 176 (part), Digby 216; Exeter Coll. 32;

---

[28] Balliol Coll. 94, 285; Exeter Coll. 32; Merton Coll. 8, 19, 27, 35, 66, 77–78, 137–138, 140, 149, 158, 166, 168–172, 190, 216, 227, 234, 237–239, 242, 248–249, 252, 259, 281–282, 291, 294–295, 297, 305, 311; New Coll. 55, 70, 92, 96–97, 120, 134, 264, 306; Bodl. Libr., Digby 19, 176, 216, e Mus. 19; BL Roy. 10 A. xi; Douai, Bibl. de la ville, 860.

[29] For Walter Robert, see *BRUO*, 1579. Merton Coll. 168, fol. iii^v: "Orare eciam dignemini pro Waltero Roberti scriba et notarius dicti uenerabilis patris, qui suprascriptos titulos et titulos aliorum 99 librorum per dictum patrem eidem domui datorum ad emendacionem librarie eiusdem inscripsit et circa eosdem libros et alios quamplures per diuersa collegia uniuersitatis Oxon' per ipsum uenerabilem patrem distributos diligenter insudauit."

[30] *BRUO*, 1906–8.

Balliol Coll. 94; New Coll. 92 part 4 ("quam Oxoniam reportari fecit"), 264.

using money given by Nicholas of Sandwich, nine books: Merton College 8 (while archdeacon), 35 (from a stationer), 137 (from an Oxford chest), 138, 294, 295 (part); Bodl. Libr., e Mus. 19; Balliol Coll. 285; New Coll. 134 ("scribi fecit" at Merton while fellow).

by exchange with William Lyneham (former fellow of Merton, d. by July 1361),[31] two books: Merton Coll. 19 (while provost), 140.

from the executors of John of Sheppey, bishop of Rochester (1352–1360),[32] two books: Merton Coll. 234 pt. 2; New Coll. 92 parts 1 and 3.

from the executors of Archbishop Simon Islip (d. 1366),[33] two books: Merton Coll. 234 pt. 3, 297; New Coll. 306.

from the executors of Archbishop Thomas Bradwardine (former fellow of Merton, d. 1349):[34] Bodl. Libr., Digby 176 (part).

from the executors of Richard Camsale (fellow of Merton, d. in or after 1326):[35] Bodl. Libr., Digby 176 (part).

from the executors of M. John Burcote (fellow of Merton, d. 1349),[36] paid for by Nicholas Sandwich: Merton Coll. 66.

wrote or caused to be written part of Bodl. Libr., Digby 176.

For the most part these inscriptions are the only evidence for the ownership of these books by those from whom Reed obtained them; in the case of Bishop Trillek this is quantitatively important. About Reed himself the surviving books and their inscriptions reveal a number of things. Firstly, he did not commission books to be made for him but obtained them (presumably more cheaply) at second hand, generally from persons with whom he was in touch in the various localities in which he lived, studied, and worked. Only fourteen of the surviving manuscripts do not have the inscriptions that supply the evidence for this,

---

[31] *BRUO*, 1193.
[32] *BRUO*, 1683–84.
[33] *BRUO*, 1006–8.
[34] *BRUO*, 244–46.
[35] *BRUO*, 344–45.
[36] *BRUO*, 306.

several because they have lost their flyleaves.[37] Secondly, and most unusually for someone in his position, he was evidently not much concerned with the appearance, or even the legibility, of his books. On the one hand, only one or two have decoration of any note, and on the other some of the collections of sermons are and must always have been desperately difficult to read.[38] This impression may be skewed. One would expect some at least of the service books mentioned in the bishop's will to have been highly decorated, but as it happens none survive to confirm this. A copy of John Balbus's *Catholicon* which he left to Boxley Priory is certainly described as "preciosissimum,"[39] but the bishop also describes the fifty books of law and theology he willed to New College as "preciosi," in this case presumably referring to their contents rather than their appearance. Thirdly, although Reed clearly bought his books for their contents, his personal use of them was not sufficiently intense to be expressed in annotation, even of those texts, of astronomy and mathematics, in which he must have had a quasi-professional interest.[40] This raises once again the question of the purpose for which he acquired them, specifically of whether he bought at least some of them, not for his own instruction or for the purpose of building up a great personal library, but *in order to* give them to Oxford colleges, in the service of what I have called his educational "vision." One piece of evidence for this is the short interval of time between the acquisition of some of the books and his parting with them again. We can see this most clearly in the case of some of those given to Exeter and Merton Colleges in 1374: Merton Coll. 19 was acquired by Reed between 1359 and 1361, and Exeter College 32 between 1363 and 1368. More tellingly, Merton Coll. 27, 149, 158, 166, 168–172, part of 295, and 237, 238, 239, and 249 were all acquired from Bishop Trillek, therefore later than the start of his episcopate in 1365 and probably nearer to his death in 1372. In other words, some of Reed's books were in his hands for only about five to ten years before he disposed of them, and this makes it very likely that he acquired them *in order to* dispose of them in the way that he did.

This impression is supported by the contents of the books individually, and of the collection as a whole. First of all, there is a high correspondence between the contents of Reed's books and the requirements of the University curriculum

---

[37] Merton Coll. 33 (flyleaves possibly replaced in the 15th cent.), 105 (flyleaves lost), 194, 197, 224 (flyleaves lost), 241, 257, 279 (the front flyleaf with Reed's inscriptions mutilated), 281 part 1; New Coll. 106, 121, 124, 171; BL, Cotton Julius B. iii, fols. 31–42.

[38] The copy of Philippe de Thaon's Bestiary in Merton Coll. 249 has rather homely unframed illustrations in pen and ink, and Bodl. Libr., e Mus. 19, colourful but unsophisticated illustrations of medical procedures. On the other hand, the collections of sermons in MSS. 234 and 238–239, though important, were written in uncalligraphic anglicana hands that sometimes degenerate into scribble.

[39] Powicke, *Merton College*, 88, 138.

[40] He occasionally made tables of contents: e.g., Merton Coll. 35.

in the Faculties of Arts and Theology. One can see this correspondence in micro-cosm in the classifications employed in the 1374 indentures, with arts texts fol-lowed by texts of theology, with further subdivisions. The Exeter gift comprised books *de philosophia* (5 titles), *de medicina* (5 titles), *de mathematica* (5 titles), and *de theologia* (10 titles). The Merton list, five times longer, includes *de grammaticis et poeticis* (10 titles), *de phisicis naturalibus* (15 titles, most of them commentaries on Aristotle's *Libri naturales*), *de medicinalibus* (5 titles), *de mathematica* (9 titles, including astronomy), *de legendis istoricis et chronicis* (10 titles, beginning with hagiographical writings), *de epistolis et dictaminibus* (5 titles), *de concordanciis, dis-tinctionibus et tabulis* (5 titles), *de sermonibus et collationibus* (10 titles), *de questioni-bus et lecturis scripture* (10 titles, mostly commentaries on Peter Lombard's *Sen-tences*), *de originalibus et tractatibus* (10 titles, various but broadly theological), and *de postillis* (10 volumes of biblical commentary, headed "Nicolai de Gorham super totam Bibliam"). There are no law books in the Merton gift, doubtless because the study of law was prohibited by the founder's statutes. There are two volumes of canon law in the gift to Exeter, whose founder's statutes allowed one member of the College at a time to proceed to the study of law or (preferably) theology.[41] The founder of New College, on the other hand, wished to encourage the study of both theology and canon law, so Reed's gift included at least nine books of canon law and probably many more.[42]

These variations suggest that he had the particular needs of each College in mind, and that the final choice and delivery of the books must have been pre-ceded by a process of discussion between the bishop and the Colleges about the desired emphases and the gaps in their collections. In this respect, too, the num-bers of books in each gift are probably relevant. Merton College got the largest number, two hundred volumes, not only because it was Reed's old College but because it was large (some forty fellows) and because its fellows were required to pursue the advanced study of theology. Exeter should have been next-closest to his heart, but attracted only forty-five volumes because it was much smaller (a dozen fellows) and because its fellows were to proceed no further than the arts degree. New College, on the other hand, was given one hundred because, as a potentially large College (its statutes provided for seventy fellows) founded as recently as 1379, it needed to build up its library resources quickly from scratch. Reed was probably more generous to it in books than was its founder, William of Wykeham, who after all had purchased the site and was financing its build-ing programme.

But though Reed chose his books with the University curriculum and the needs of individual Colleges in mind, he also had views of his own about what

---

[41] In his statutes of 1316, Bishop Stapledon permitted a single chaplain to study one of the higher disciplines of law or theology, preferably the latter.

[42] For whatever reason, the New College library catalogue rarely specifies donors for the law books, and Reed's own name appears only in informal marginal notes.

constituted desirable reading material for students who were clerics. The group of dictaminal texts in his 1374 gift to Merton reminds us of the "business" schools that had developed alongside the University proper in fourteenth-century Oxford.[43] The purpose of these texts was practical: to assist students to develop those writing skills which would aid them in the composition of letters of instruction, advice, and diplomacy which they might have to write later in their careers. And then there was the much larger group of texts concerned with pastoral rather than academic theology. Among them are the usual practical manuals of confession and spiritual advice,[44] but even more noticeable are the thick volumes of sermons. Take, for instance, Merton Coll. MSS. 237–239, acquired by Reed as a "set" from Bishop Trillek. All of the volumes were written in Paris in the 1270s, and contain collections of sermons preached in the University, mainly by mendicants: 145, 294, and 158 sermons respectively. MS. 248 contains a similar collection made by or for Bishop Sheppey while he was studying at Oxford, comprising another 155 items.[45] Many of the items in these collections are known only from these copies, and this makes the point that among Reed's books generally are some rare or unique titles, suggesting that he was on the lookout, not only for standard texts (of which multiples might be needed), but also for others that were scarce but useful: for instance Merton College MSS. 27 ("Moralitates excerpta de libris Origenis") and 103 (William Ware on the Sentences); and New College MS. 134 (Thomas of Buckingham).

Reed's gifts and bequests to the Colleges of Oxford University, in combination, were princely. In addition to the two hundred volumes assigned to his own old College—not to mention the fifty for the use of his kin—he gave and bequeathed at least £200 "ad reparacionem librarie ibidem." In this way he facilitated the construction of Merton's so-called "Old Library," the oldest surviving library room in western Europe, and his principal monument today.[46]

---

[43] H. G. Richardson, "Business Training in Medieval Oxford," *American Historical Review* 46 (1940–1941): 259–80; T. A. Ralph Evans, "The Number, Origins and Careers of Scholars," in *The History of the University of Oxford*, vol. 2, ed. Jeremy I. Catto and T. A. Ralph Evans (Oxford: Oxford University Press, 1992), 485–538, at 526–28.

[44] E.g., Exeter Coll. 19 (William de Pagula, *Summa summarum*), Merton Coll. 1374 list, no. 89, *Speculum iuniorum*.

[45] The items in MS. 238 are listed in Johannes B. Schneyer, *Repertorium der lateinischen Sermones des Mittelalters für die Zeit von 1150 bis 1350*, 11 vols., Beiträge zur Geschichte der Philosophie und Theologie des Mittelalters 43 (Münster: Aschendorff, 1969–1979), 6: 25–30; the others are listed, for the first time, in Thomson, *Merton*.

[46] On which see John Willis Clark, *The Care of Books*, 2nd ed. (Cambridge: Cambridge University Press, 1902), 172–79; Burnett H. Streeter, *The Chained Library* (Oxford: Oxford University Press, 1931), 130–49; Martin and Highfield, *History of Merton College*, 88–92; Thomson, *Merton*, xxix–xxx.

WHO WAS GILBERT THE ENGLISHMAN?

MICHAEL McVAUGH

The most famous English medical writer of the thirteenth century was undoubt-edly Gilbertus Anglicus, Gilbert the Englishman. His *Compendium medicine* was arguably the first great Latin survey of medical knowledge to have been com-posed after the arrival of Greek and Arabic texts in western Europe, and it en-joyed immediate popularity. At least thirty-eight manuscripts of the Latin work survive today, and it was translated in whole or in part into Middle English, German, Catalan, and Hebrew in the later Middle Ages.[1] It figured among the works that Chaucer famously used to epitomize the Physician's learning:

> Wel knew he the olde Esculapius,
> And Deyscorides, and eek Rufus,

---

[1] The work begins variously "A/De/In morbis universalibus propositi nostri." The following list of manuscripts containing the work (much of which I owe to the generosity of Monica Green) is surely incomplete:

Antwerp, Musée Plantin-Moretus 49; Basel, Univ. bibl. D II 13; Bernkastel-Kues, Bibl. d. St. Nikolaus-Hosp. 305, fols. 1–191v; Bruges 469, fols. 1–244v; Cambrai, Biblio-thèque municipale 906, fols. 1–241; Cambrai 909 (808), fols. 1–292; Cambridge, Pem-broke College 169, fols. 1–233v; Cambridge, Peterhouse 52, fols. 1–92v; Cambridge, University Library Ff.II.37, fols. 1–196; Erfurt, Amplonian F 77a, fols. 38–101; Flor-ence, Bibl. Med. Laur. Ashburnham 148, fols. 5–212v; Florence, Riccardiana 731, fols. 1–231v; Gloucester, Gloucester Cathedral Library 6, fols. 1–84v (Books I and VII); Lon-don, BL Royal 12.G.iv, fols. 5–127r; London, BL Sloane 272, fols. 2–262v; London, Royal College of Physicians 395, fols. 1–186v; Madrid, BN 1199, fols. 1–175; Madrid, Univ. 120, fols. 19–167v; Munich, Bayerische Staatsbibliothek, CLM 28187, fols. 1v-201r; New Haven, Yale University, Medical School Library, Cushing-Whitney 19, fols. 1–178rb; Oxford, All Souls College 79, fols. 1–164v; Oxford, Bodley 720, fols. 1–156v; Oxford, Merton College 226, fols. 1–207v; Oxford, New College 165, fols. 1–242; Ox-ford, St. John's College 108, fols. 1–351v; Paris, Arsenal 1028, fols. 1–137; Paris, BN lat. 6955, fols. 1–241; Paris, BN lat. 10239, fols. 1–136v; Paris, BN lat. 16194, fols. 1–194; Paris, BN n. a. l. 160, fols. 1–355v; Rouen 984, fols. 1–225; Vatican City, BAV Regin. lat. 1132; Vendôme 173, fols. 1–159; Vendôme 235, fols. 14–146; Vienna, ÖNB 1634, fols. 35v-55; Vienna, ÖNB 2279, fols. 1–239v; Worcester Cathedral F. 145, fols. 1–99v.

The Study of Medieval Manuscripts of England: Festschrift in Honor of Richard W. Pfaff, eds. George Hardin Brown and Linda Ehrsam Voigts, MRTS 384 (Tempe: ACMRS, 2010).　　　　[ISBN 978-0-86698-432-4]

Olde Ypocras, Haly, and Galyen,
Serapion, Razis, and Avycen,
Averroes, Damascien, and Constantyn,
Bernard, and Gatesden, and Gilbertyn.[2]

Chaucer here linked Gilbert's name with that of another English physician, John of Gaddesden, but Gilbert's *Compendium* was certainly a more influential work than Gaddesden's *Rosa medicine*, not merely narrowly in England but in Europe generally.

Scholars have been able to say very little about the life and career of so important a figure; even the decade in which he wrote is uncertain. But there has emerged a broad, if vague, biographical consensus. H. E. Handerson (1918) worked from the many citations of other works in the *Compendium* to conclude that Gilbert was born c. 1180, studied at Salerno, practiced in England, and then went to the Continent, where he composed his great work about 1240 and died ten years later.[3] Charles Talbot and E. A. Hammond (1965) followed Ernest Wickersheimer (1936) in calling attention to the text in Bruges MS. 469, dated 1271, where the author of the compendium is named "Gilbertus de Aquila," and in concluding that he was probably the "Gilbertus del Egle" who is documented as attending Archbishop Hubert Walter (d. 1204).[4] Subsequently (1967), on the basis of Gilbert's citation of Arabic authorities and of his scholastic methods of argument, Talbot looked to "the first quarter of the thirteenth century as his most active period" and declared that "he may have studied at Paris, [but] it is much more likely that he was a product of Salerno and Montpellier."[5] More recently Faye Getz has gone over the evidence several times and has worked it into a narrative for the *Oxford Dictionary of National Biography* (2004) that essentially conforms to these earlier accounts: that Gilbert went on to serve King John after Hubert Walter's death and was then summoned from England to Rome in 1214, and remained there; that he is likely to have studied on the Continent, perhaps at Paris or Salerno but more likely Montpellier; that the *Compendium* "cannot have been completed before about 1230–40"; and that his death "cannot have been

---

[2] *The Poetical Works of Chaucer*, ed. F. N. Robinson (Boston: Houghton Mifflin, 1933), 24.

[3] Henry E. Handerson, *Gilbertus Anglicus: Medicine of the Thirteenth Century* (Cleveland, OH: Cleveland Medical Association, 1918), 24; Emile Littré, "Gilbert l'Anglais, médecin," in *Histoire Littéraire de la France*, vol. 21 (Paris: Osmourt/Didot, 1847), 393–400.

[4] Ernest Wickersheimer, *Dictionnaire biographique des médecins en France au Moyen Age* (Paris: Droz, 1936), 191–92. (An *un*documented tradition of his attendance on Walter goes back to John Pits.) C. H. Talbot and E. A. Hammond, *The Medical Practitioners in Medieval England: A Biographical Register* (London: Wellcome Historical Medical Library, 1965), 58–60, did not themselves pronounce on the date but simply repeated that "Handerson would date the *Compendium* about 1240."

[5] C. H. Talbot, *Medicine in Medieval England* (London: Oldbourne, 1967), 72, 73.

much after 1250."[6] In a certain sense, these later studies merely tinker with the general picture worked out by Handerson on the basis of the sources cited by Gilbert, and all concede that their conclusions are merely "probable." But Handerson wrote ninety years ago, and in the intervening period historians have learned a great deal about the patterns of transmission and assimilation of the Greco-Arabic works that Gilbert cites so freely. Let us therefore look systematically at Gilbert's sources in the light of these patterns, to see whether they have anything new to offer to the picture of his career.[7]

An arts education? Aristotle

We should begin by acknowledging, perhaps with a little surprise, how important a source Aristotle was to the author of the *Compendium medicine*. Gilbert does not just mention Aristotle's name in passing, he cites many of his specific works, and they cover an impressive range: the *Topics* (126vb, 175rb); *De sophisticis elenchis* (144va); *Predicamenta* (144ra); *Ethics* (158ra); *Physics* (157va); *De generatione et corruptione* (244ra); *Meteorologica* (5ra); *De anima* (127va, 256ra); and *De animalibus* (248ra, 284rb).[8] The first three of these are the core of the *trivium* of the medieval schools, the basis for further advanced study; the rest are constituent of the higher, quadrivial studies. As a working hypothesis, merely on the basis of his broad familiarity with Aristotle we may reasonably imagine Gilbert to have pursued an arts course at a medieval university with some diligence, and perhaps indeed to have taken an arts degree.

Is there any sign in the sources he cites that he had also formally studied medicine in the schools? As is now recognized, a core body of seven medical texts (known as the *articella* or *ars medicine*) grew up in the twelfth and early

---

[6] Faye Getz, "Gilbert the Englishman," in *Oxford Dictionary of National Biography*, 60 vols. (Oxford: Oxford University Press, 2004), 22: 163–64. In Getz's *Medicine in the English Middle Ages* (Princeton: Princeton University Press, 1998), she reviews the evidence and dates the *Compendium* to about 1230 (39–42); earlier, in *Healing and Society in Medieval England: A Middle English Translation of the Pharmaceutical Writings of Gilbertus Anglicus* (Madison, WI: University of Wisconsin Press, 1991), she had opted for "about 1240" (liii).

[7] Unless otherwise noted, my references to Gilbert's *Compendium* will be to the folios of the sixteenth-century edition: *Compendium medicine Gilberti Anglici tam morborum universalium quam particularium* (Lyons, 1510). I have systematically checked the passages cited against the text in Bruges MS. 469, fols. 1–244vb (the earliest datable manuscript, copied in 1271), and found the two versions to agree closely.

[8] Gilbert's familiarity with contemporary philosophical literature is explored in detail, from a different perspective, by Marian Kurdziałek, "Gilbertus Anglicus und die psychologischen Erörterungen in seinem Compendium Medicinae," *Sudhoffs Archiv* 47 (1963): 106–26.

thirteenth centuries and became established as the essential curriculum for the important European medical faculties, meaning by the thirteenth century Paris and Montpellier (Salerno's educational importance was primarily a feature of the twelfth century): commentaries on these texts were the formal basis of medieval medical instruction.[9] Significantly, all these texts are well known and often cited by Gilbert: Johannitius's *Isagoge* (202vb, 284va); Galen's *Tegni* (217vb, 219ra); the *Urines* of Theophilus (30va, 238vb); the *Pulses* of Philaretus (285ra); and Hippocrates' *Aphorisms* (257vb, 275va), *Prognostics* (70vb), and *Regimen acutorum* (218ra, 290va). Moreover, his references to the *Aphorisms* are often to the text as accompanied by Galen's commentary (15rb, 62ra, 75va, 257vb), the form of the *Aphorisms* that became integral to teaching at thirteenth-century Paris. Gilbert's preparation in a medical faculty thus seems quite as plausible as his formation in an arts faculty, and indeed there is no inconsistency between the two: it was normal in thirteenth-century Paris, for example, for a student to move on to a medical degree after training in arts.[10]

Where might Gilbert have studied these subjects, and when? For the study of Aristotle there would seem to be two leading candidates, Oxford and Paris, and each reacted differently to the quadrivial works of Aristotle, the natural-scientific books that had been unknown to twelfth-century scholars. At Paris, as is well known, there was an early reaction against Aristotelian naturalism which led to an episcopal prohibition on the teaching of these works, and they only began to be taught de facto about 1240 or so, as Roger Bacon tells us. At the much smaller Oxford, where episcopal authority was weaker, the new Aristotle began to be studied a little earlier; the chief figure in its introduction there has traditionally been taken to be Robert Grosseteste, who certainly lectured on the *Posterior Analytics* while still an arts master, perhaps ca. 1210; but we have no sign of his knowledge of Aristotle's physical works until his teaching of theology in the 1220s, and there seems to be no good evidence that *arts* students at Oxford were already being broadly exposed to Aristotle by that time.[11]

---

[9] Cornelius O'Boyle, *The Art of Medicine: Medical Teaching at the University of Paris, 1250–1400* (Leiden: Brill, 1998), chap. 3.

[10] See Danielle Jacquart, *La médecine médiévale dans le cadre Parisien XIVe–XVe siècle* (Paris: Fayard, 1998), 131–32; Pearl Kibre, "Arts and Medicine in the Universities of the Later Middle Ages," in *Les universités à la fin du Moyen Age*, ed. J. Paquet and J. Ijsewijn (Louvain: Institut d'Etudes Médiévales U.C.L., 1978), 213–27; reprinted in eadem, *Studies in Medieval Science: Alchemy, Astrology, Mathematics and Medicine* (London: Hambledon Press, 1984), no. XII.

[11] A useful survey of the process by which the thirteenth-century universities began to assimilate Aristotelian writings is given in Michael Haren, *Medieval Thought: The Western Intellectual Tradition from Antiquity to the Thirteenth Century*, 2nd ed. (Basingstoke: Macmillan, 1992), 143–59.

A decade later, however, the situation at Oxford was different. Charles Burnett has pointed out that in the late 1230s and early 1240s Adam of Buckfield was lecturing there on the whole of the Aristotelian "corpus vetustius," the collection of Arabic-Latin translations including among others the *Physics, De caelo, De generatione, Meteorologica,* and *De anima.* Indeed, Burnett has proposed that Adam may have been the first to do so, "providing a new set of commentaries for a new generation of scholars at Oxford" while referring in the process to Averroes' commentaries on Aristotle more often than to any other authority.[12] These are largely the Aristotelian works that Gilbert knows and cites (although he also knows the *De animalibus,* on which Adam did not lecture), so that he might possibly have studied at Oxford ca. 1240, perhaps even with Adam—especially since Gilbert demonstrates a knowledge of Averroes' commentary on the *Metaphysics.*[13]

Yet some consideration should also be given to Montpellier as a possible source of Gilbert's knowledge of Aristotle, though it is far more famous for its medical faculty than for its arts teaching. Papal statutes for the former were issued in 1220 and revised in 1239 and 1240, but the first statutes for an arts faculty appear in 1242. Luke Demaitre has considered the evidence and argued for an intermingling of the liberal arts with medical teaching there in the first part of the thirteenth century: among other reasons, he has called attention to a provision of the 1240 statutes that no student of medicine should be presented for his degree who had not studied medicine at Montpellier or some other famous place for at least three and a half years, unless he had been a master of arts at Paris (or another famous place), in which case he could be presented after only two and a half years—that is, an arts education elsewhere corresponded to a portion of medical education as it was understood at mid-thirteenth-century Montpellier.[14] Might a medical student there have been exposed systematically to the new Aristotle as part of his training?

---

[12] Charles Burnett, "The Introduction of Aristotle's Natural Philosophy into Great Britain: A Preliminary Survey of the Manuscript Evidence," in *Aristotle in Britain during the Middle Ages,* ed. John Marenbon (Turnhout: Brepols, 1996), 40–42; idem, *The Introduction of Arabic Learning into England* (London: British Library, 1997), 73–75; D. A. Callus, "Introduction of Aristotelian Learning to Oxford," *Proceedings of the British Academy* 29 (1943): 255–56.

[13] *Compendium,* fol. 259ra. See below, p. 304.

[14] "Item, nullus magister presentet aliquem, nisi ille audierit medicinam in Montepessulano vel in alio loco famoso ad minus per tres annos et dimidium, nisi idem fuerit magister in artibus Parisius vel in alio loco famoso; et talis possit post duos annos et dimidium presentari": *Cartulaire de l'Université de Montpellier,* vol. 1 (Montpellier: Ricard Frères, 1890), 187 (doc. 5). On the early relation between arts and medicine at Montpellier, see Luke Demaitre, "Bernard de Gordon (ca. 1258-ca. 1318): A Representative of the Montpellier Academic Tradition" (Ph.D. diss., City University of New York, 1973), 57–63.

The evidence seems to suggest that he would have been. The effective start-ing point for medical education within the *articella* was Johannitius's *Isagoge*, a broad schematic introduction to medical theory. We possess commentaries on this work by two Montpellier masters, Henry of Winchester and Cardinalis, both of whom are mentioned by name in the revised statutes of 1240, where Henry is further identified as "chancellarius."[15] Henry's relatively senior posi-tion in 1240, together with the restricted range of authorities cited in his com-mentary, incline me to believe him the older man and to date his commentary on the *Isagoge* as decidedly earlier than Cardinalis's; we might perhaps take them as representing the school's teaching ca. 1230 and in the 1240s, respectively. Henry refers to Aristotle's *De caelo, De generatione, De anima,* and *Topics* directly, and cites his opinion seven more times in what may be no more than secondhand ref-erences. A decade or two later, commenting on the same work, Cardinalis uses, in addition to the books cited by Henry, the *Metaphysics, Posterior Analytics, De animalibus, De somno et vigilia, De sophisticis elenchis, Meteorologica,* and even the pseudo-Aristotelian *Liber de causis.*[16] This seems to indicate that a Montpellier student at the beginning of his medical education had already been given a ba-sic appreciation of Aristotle's physical thought and a familiarity with his writ-ings, and makes Montpellier 1230–1245 a possible setting for Gilbert's train-ing—"Henry *of Winchester*" shows that Gilbert would not have been the first Englishman to make his way there. In any case, leaving open for the moment the question of where it was obtained, at Oxford or Paris or Montpellier, if we as-sume that his close knowledge of the curricular texts of arts and medicines is a reflection of academic training, we can infer that he must have received his edu-cation—arts schooling typically began at the age of fifteen or so—at some point in the years 1225–1245, probably later in that period than earlier.

Even this preliminary conclusion makes it virtually impossible to accept the identification of the Gilbert of the *Compendium* with the Gilbertus de l'Egle who served Hubert Walter and King John during the years (at a minimum) 1205–1214.[17] Because, as we have seen, the quadrivial works of Aristotle that our Gil-bert knows so well were not taught in the schools of England and France before the second quarter of the thirteenth century at the earliest, his presumed forma-tion in arts and then medicine (occupying altogether perhaps five to ten years of his life) would have to be placed *after* his period of English professional activ-

---

[15] *Cartulaire,* 1:186 (doc. 5).

[16] My references to Henry are based on my reading of the text of his commentary in Oxford, New College MS. 171, fols. 1–18v; to Cardinalis, to his commentary in Bernkas-tel-Kues, Bibl. d. St. Nikolaus-Hosp. MS. 222, fols. 1–48.

[17] Ortrun Riha, "Gilbertus Anglicus und sein 'Compendium medicinae': Arbeits-technik und Wissensorganisation," *Sudhoffs Archiv* 78 (1994): 59–79, here 62, interprets Talbot and Hammond as making this point, but as I read their account (*Medical Practi-tioners,* 59) they are still conflating the two Gilberts.

ity. Accepting that identification would require us to posit an individual accomplished enough to be made physician to the Archbishop of Canterbury before 1205, when he could surely have been no younger than twenty-five or so, who subsequently, in what would have been his late thirties at the earliest, turned his back on his earlier success and decided to launch upon a basic arts program that was aimed at fifteen-year-olds and taught by masters far younger than he. It is barely conceivable, perhaps, but incredible. If our Gilbert began his studies 1225–1245, one would expect him to have been born 1210–1230—the son, not implausibly, of Hubert Walter's "Gilbertus," who followed his father's career but did so by pursuing the new medical education of the day.

A medical bachelor? Averroes

Historians have acknowledged the likelihood that Gilbert had academic medical training, but for some reason they have never been much interested in the possibility that he went on to make his career as a medical master in the schools; they may have been distracted by the tradition of his association with elite medical practice.[18] Their failure to pursue this possibility is the more surprising because a formal academic commentary exists under his name in at least nineteen copies, a commentary upon the poem *De urinis* composed by Giles of Corbeil.[19] Giles had taught at Salerno and Montpellier in the later twelfth century but found both schools wanting, and had moved on to teach at Paris before his death, which occurred sometime after 1200.[20] His *De urinis* was sometimes attached to the *articella* as an occasional part of formal medical education, but it was not at the

---

[18] Getz (*Medicine*, 42) contends that "Gilbert himself never seems to have taught at any university"; Talbot and Hammond suggest (*Medical Practitioners*, 59) that "it is quite possible that Gilbert both studied and taught at Salerno." Talbot (*Medicine*, 73) speculates on Gilbert's studies but not the possibility of his teaching career.

[19] I have located the following manuscripts (the list does not pretend to be exhaustive): Admont, Stiftsbibliothek 496, fols. 1–24; Auxerre, Bibliothèque muncipale 241, fols. 67–90; Bruxelles, Bibliothèque Royale 6123; Bruxelles, Bibliothèque Royale 15627; Erfurt, Amplonian F.276, fols. 42–66; Krakow, Bibl. Jag. 805, fols. 251–274v; Leipzig 1174, fols. 1–18; London, Lambeth Pal. 409, fols. 88 (89)–100v; London, Wellcome 547, fols. 104–145v; Moulins, Bibliothèque municipale 30, fols. 1–44; Munich, Bayerische Staatsbibliothek, CLM 267, fols. 2ra–46ra; Munich, Bayerische Staatsbibliothek, CLM 276, fols. 2–45; Munich, Bayerische Staatsbibliothek, CLM 3875, fol. 52; Munich, Bayerische Staatsbibliothek, CLM 11322, fol. 38; Oxford, New College 170, fols. 257–279; Paris, Bibliothèque de l'Arsenal 1080, fols. 255–277; Paris, BN lat. 6988, fols. 107vb–144rb; Paris, BN lat. 15457, fols. 191ra–216vb; Paris, BN lat. 16188, fols. 307ra–355va; Reims 1002, fols. 90–124; Vienna, ÖNB 5312, fols. 6–41v; Wiesbaden, Hessische Landesbibliothek 56, fols. 122–149. See also Riha, "Gilbertus Anglicus," 64–65.

[20] Wickersheimer, *Dictionnaire biographique*, 196–97.

heart of the curriculum; because Giles's book was optional rather than required for students, Gilbert's decision to draw up a commentary on it should perhaps be understood as an expression of his own particular interests.[21]

The text, beginning "Sicut dicit Constantinus in Pantegni," is typically attributed in manuscript to a "Gilbertus" whom historians have assumed to be Gilbertus Anglicus, and there is internal evidence to confirm this assumption, as we will see. It has never been edited, but Ruth Harvey is preparing a study of the work and has generously shared with me her preliminary transcription of the text in London, Wellcome MS. 547. Gilbert begins the commentary with a short introduction of his own on the physiological nature and production of urine, and then turns to the analysis of Giles's poem, devoting most of his attention to the twenty different colors of urine described there: to what causes the colors, and what they signify. Gilbert frequently cites other authors in the course of the commentary, just as he does in the *Compendium medicine*, and this naturally invites a comparison between the patterns of citation in each. The results of such a comparison, the similarities and differences between the two works, prove to have a significant bearing on our understanding of Gilbert's possible career.

It is noteworthy, for example, that while we find Gilbert referring frequently to Aristotle in the commentary, just as he does in the *Compendium*, he almost never cites a specific work by the Peripatetic. Once he explicitly mentions "Aristotelis in libro de animalibus"[22]—thus establishing that the commentary, like the *Compendium*, must have been written after 1220 (and for the same reason)—but the other twelve mentions of Aristotle are of his name alone. One might therefore wonder whether Gilbert had gained a fuller knowledge of the Aristotelian corpus after commenting on *De urinis*, and this may indeed be the case, though the evidence is a little equivocal. It is possible to trace several of the commentary's generic references to their source: some are to the logical writings that were an unquestioned part of thirteenth-century study, while one is evidently to one of Aristotle's minor works of natural philosophy (*De somno et vigilia*).[23] Others are to *De animalibus*. One unattributed quotation from Aristotle in the commentary will be used again in exactly the same way in the *Compendium*, and

---

[21] O'Boyle (*Art of Medicine*, 112–13) suggests that at Paris Giles's text was frequently attached to the *articella*, and that Gilbert's commentary was often associated with that text in Paris manuscripts. Jacquart (*Médecine médiévale*, 162–63) makes the point that the Paris statutes of 1270–1274 specified that the *De urinis* was not "de forma"—that is, that it was not a required part of the Paris curriculum.

[22] London, Wellcome MS. 547, fol. 142v. I am deeply grateful to Ruth Harvey for allowing me to quote from her unpublished transcription here and below.

[23] Thus at fol. 122rb, the passage referred to is evidently *Posterior Analytics* 68b22; the passage at 107vb is (as Georgia Machemer has pointed out to me) from *De somno et vigilia* 457b6.

there Gilbert identifies its source as the *Meteorologica*[24] — confirmation, if it were desired, that the two works are indeed by the same author. But as far as I can tell, none of Gilbert's references to Aristotle is to his most important writings on the subject, like the *Physics* or *De anima*, works that were certainly known to the author of the *Compendium*.

The *Meteorologica* will be a favorite authority for the *Compendium*, and the Giles-commentary helps us to understand why: Gilbert refers in that commentary no fewer than three times to an earlier commentary by him on the *Meteorologica*. The natural assumption might be that Gilbert had previously lectured on that book in an arts faculty and that it was still fresh in his mind, but in fact that may not be the case; in the fourteenth century, Paris medical bachelors were prohibited from lecturing upon any Aristotelian books *except* the *De animalibus* and the *Meteorologica*, and if this was already the case in the thirteenth century, Gilbert's lectures on *both* the *Meteorologica* and Giles's *De urinis* could have been delivered as a bachelor in medicine at Paris in the 1230s.[25]

A comparison of the strictly medical sources referred to in the two works is also suggestive. In his commentary on Giles, Gilbert draws on almost all of the works comprising the *articella* — not at all surprisingly, if the work he was commenting on was being studied as an adjunct to that body of material. He also knows and quotes freely from Avicenna, who is indeed his favorite source. But with his references to Galen the case is rather different. Whereas the *Compendium* makes regular use of a wide range of named Galenic works, in the commentary there are scarcely more references to Galen than there are to Aristotle, and they do not suggest a broad acquaintance with the former author: some seem to be made at second hand, taken from passages in Avicenna or Constantine the African, others are to a Galenic work long familiar in the *articella*, the *Aphorisms*-commentary, and only two are to other named works: *De crisi* and *De iuvamentis membrorum*. And there are no references here to the other Arabic authors who will be so important to the *Compendium*, Rhazes above all.

There is one other important authority who appears in both the *Compendium* and the Giles-commentary: Averroes. Historians ever since Emile Littré[26] have remarked on Gilbert's references in the *Compendium* to Averroes, specifically to his commentaries on the *Physics* (259ra) and the *Metaphysics* (228va). We now believe that Averroes' commentaries on Aristotle, in translations probably made by Michael Scot after 1220, began to enter Western intellectual life in the next decade. Two Parisian authors (William of Auvergne and Philip the Chancellor) have been found making brief references to a few of the commentaries in the 1230s, and then Albertus Magnus ca. 1240 manifests a much wider

---

[24] Wellcome 547, fol. 113va; *Compendium*, fol. 37va.
[25] No Aristotelian commentaries by a "Gilbertus" are identified by Charles H. Lohr, "Medieval Latin Aristotle Commentaries: Authors G-I," *Traditio* 24 (1968): 149–245.
[26] Littré, "Gilbert l'Anglais," 399.

acquaintance with them.[27] Marian Kurdziałek was the first to examine Gilbert's references carefully, and she discovered that the one that cited Averroes' *Physics*-commentary in the printed edition of 1510 was in fact a quotation from the so-called *Questiones Nicolai peripatetici* which in manuscripts of the *Compendium* was ascribed merely to "Averroes in sua ph'ia" (philosophia?).[28] The passage cited from the *Metaphysics*-commentary, however, she determined to be authentically Averroistic, and on that basis she concluded that the *Compendium* could have been written no earlier than 1230–1240, when Averroes was just becoming known in the West.[29]

What Kurdziałek could not have known, not having looked at Gilbert's commentary on Giles of Corbeil, was that that commentary also refers—four times!—to Averroes:

> Vnde dicit Auerois quod est quoddam celum quod miscet vel quod format, et proprie a quinto datur forma substantialis quam sequitur propria complexio et propria forma;

> propter hoc dicit Aueroys: continuam a forma oportet a materia sumus discontinuati;

---

[27] Fernand van Steenberghen, *La philosophie au XIIIe siècle* (Louvain: Publications Universitaires, 1966), 111–15.

[28] Kurdziałek, "Gilbertus Anglicus," 113–17. Gilbert also refers directly to the *Questiones Nicolai* elsewhere in the *Compendium* (e.g., at fol. 106va).

[29] Kurdziałek, "Gilbertus Anglicus," 114 n. 3. Marie-Thérèse d'Alverny, "La tradition manuscrite des 'Quaestiones Nicolai peripatetici'," in *Medieval Learning and Literature: Essays Presented to Richard William Hunt*, ed. J. J. G. Alexander and M. T. Gibson (Oxford: Oxford University Press, 1976), 200–19, here 204 and n. 1, believed that the author of the *Questiones* already knew Michael Scot's translations of Averroes, and accepted this date as conforming chronologically to the diffusion of the Averroistic texts. Recent studies are suggesting that the first Parisian citations of Averroes may need to be pushed back into the late 1220s (Haren, *Medieval Thought*, 226), but this does not affect the conclusion that his influence began to be felt only in the 1230s. Riha ("Gilbertus Anglicus," 67) contends that the use of Averroes' commentaries is characteristically Parisian, and believes it to be significant (78) that the Sorbonne library possessed a copy of the *Compendium* by 1338.

Both the Giles-commentary and the *Compendium*, then, quote Averroes, but only the latter cites the *Questiones Nicolai*, which means that it is no longer safe to assume on its evidence that the *Questiones* were circulating by the 1230s, as their modern editor did: Stanisław Wielgus, "Quaestiones Nicolai Peripatetici," *Mediaevalia Philosophica Polonorum* 17 (1973): 57–155, esp. 62–63. In fact, certain features of the *Questiones*—their interest in sublimation and distillation (86, 95), their citations of Rhazes (122, 132)—suggest to me that they may have been composed nearer to mid-century.

et hic dico cum Auaroys quia ex luciditate et splendore superiorum corporum per mediocritatem elementorum, scil. ignis et aeris, imprimitur seu
efficitur aut derelinquitur; quid calor qui est uite principium; unde aliquis
uocat ipsum uitalem;

que est materia omnium colorum quoniam fiunt in aqua et aere a natura
corporum supracelestium dantium elementis suam diaphanitatem, que est
res sicut dicit Aueroys que nominari non potest.[30]

I have not identified all these references (though the first and third seem to echo
Averroes' commentary on *Metaphysics* 12, which is also the source of the reference to Averroes in the *Compendium*),[31] but the fourth is unmistakably based on
his *De anima*-commentary.[32] Applying Kurdziałek's reasoning to the evidence of
Gilbert's Giles-commentary, therefore, we can reinforce what we have already
inferred: that the commentary was probably composed by the 1230s, at an early
stage in Gilbert's teaching career, and very possibly in Paris, where the sources
he cites were available and where the books he was lecturing on were apparently
part of the curriculum, but before he had acquired any real familiarity with the
new Galenic literature.

A mature medical author

Gilbert's commentary on Giles, then, evokes a young medical master — conceivably even still a bachelor — bringing his recent arts and medical training to bear
on his teaching of uroscopy, using Aristotle and Avicenna tentatively (and hence
perhaps in the 1230s) to interpret the pathology underlying the phenomena manifest in patients' urines. The *Compendium medicine* gives us indications of a somewhat different figure, of someone who is a mature member of a learned medical
community and who is actively engaged in a broad range of its discussions. The

---

[30] The passages are found, respectively, in Wellcome MS. 547, fols. 104rb, 109rb,
118va, and 144va.

[31] The first of these passages suggests fol. 304a (or perhaps fol. 320ra) in *Aristotelis Metaphysicorum Libri XIIII cum Averrois Cordubensis in eosdem commentariis* (Venice,
1562; repr. Frankfurt am Main: Minerva, 1962); the third appears to echo fol. 305ra-b.

[32] "Idest, et quia diaffonitas non est in sola aqua neque in solo aere, sed etiam in corpore celesti, fuit necesse ut diaffonitas non sit in aliquo eorum secundum quod illud est illud quod est, v.g. secundum quod aqua est aqua aut celum celum, sed secundum naturam
communem existentem in omnibus, licet non habeat nomen": *Averrois Commentarium
Magnum in Aristotelis De anima libros*, ed. F. Stuart Crawford (Cambridge, MA: Mediaeval Academy of America, 1953), book 2 text 68 (235). Wielgus, "Quaestiones," 59–60
n. 10, compares passages from the *Questiones* and the *Metaphysics*-commentary, and the
latter are much more strongly evocative of the first citation above.

most obvious of these indications is the recurrent use in the *Compendium* of the techniques of scholastic debate. Gilbert routinely pauses in the middle of his exposition of medical issues to raise scholastic *questiones* ("Utrum . . .") and to resolve them magisterially (46v). In so doing he often indicates that the question being posed is one that is debated among the *magistri* (284va), whose various answers he sets out (306ra). That his *magistri* are contemporary figures in the schools, not just authors he has found in his books, is made clear when at one point he discusses the difficult symptomatology of salt phlegm: "what the prolongation of a paroxysm signifies is ambiguous; masters disagree about it, and appeal to authority doesn't resolve it."[33]

For Charles Talbot, Gilbert's scholasticism was tedious and regrettable, and to demonstrate its weakness he held up to ridicule one passage in particular on the nature of sight where, he implied, Gilbert did no more than give an exegesis of Aristotelian language.[34] In fact, looked at carefully, the passage in question is a commentary on a quotation from Avicenna, which Gilbert is interpreting in the light of a passage from Aristotle's *De anima* (perhaps 431b23).[35] Whether or not we wish to mock the scholastic method, we must recognize that the passage shows Gilbert to have been capable of applying it effectively, and of having been able not only to understand his Avicennan source but to bring an appropriate passage from Aristotle to bear upon it. The evidence thus suggests that he is likely to have been, not a freshly minted master, but the possessor of some experience in the schools.[36]

---

[33] "Ambiguum igitur esse videtur signum sumptum a prolongatione temporis paroxismi, et est hec contrarietas inter magistros, nec auctoritas soluit": *Compendium*, fol. 40r.

[34] Talbot, *Medicine*, 74–75.

[35] "Viso de instrumento visus videamus de ipso visu quia sicut in instrumento ita et in visu accidit nocumentum medicatione indigens, quem Avicenna sic diffinit: Visus est vis ordinata in nervo concavo ad comprehendendum formam eius quod informatur in humore cristallino ex similitudinibus corporum coloratorum venientibus per corpora radiosa in effectu ad superficies corporum tersorum. . . . Per hoc quod dicit humore cristallino notat secundum quod visus organum immutatur scilicet secundum formam eius quod formatur et non id quod formatur, per hoc notans non ipsas rerum proprietates recipi in organo visus sed similitudines proprietatum, unde Arist.: Non sunt in anima species rerum sed species specierum, unde subiungitur ex similitudinibus corporum coloratorum proprium subiectum visus. Cum enim dicit formatur notat propria obiecta et communia, unde non color proprie sed coloratum, cum visus sit sensus corporeus comprehenditur. Cum dicit venientibus notat distantiam exigi inter rem visibilem et videntem. Et cum dicit corpora notat diversa esse media et per plurale notat extrinseca inter rem visibilem et videntem sicut aera et aquam": *Compendium*, fol. 126rb, va. Essentially the same passage is in Bruges MS. 469, fol. 80rb-va.

[36] The same point, it seems to me, is implicit in Riha's discussion of Gilbert's methodology ("Gilbertus Anglicus," esp. 76–77).

This tends to be confirmed by Gilbert's awareness and intelligent discussion in the *Compendium* of technical issues in mid-century medical thought. One of these is the problem of medicinal degrees, *de gradibus.* Early thirteenth-century medical masters knew from the Greco-Arabic tradition that different drugs were of different strengths—they existed in four degrees each of hotness and coldness, plus a state of neutrality or temperancy—but these writers found it very difficult to master the philosophical analyses of medicinal degree that their much more sophisticated authorities had worked out; they were just beginning to grapple with the very concept of qualitative intensity. If the temperate state results from a balance of hotness and coldness in the drug, what is the relation between the two qualities in a drug that is hot in the second degree, for example? These early masters preferred to explore more practical questions—e.g., how may one empirically distinguish between drugs hot in the second and in the third degree?—and barely touched on the theoretical issues involved.[37]

The most abstruse of their authorities, the Arab philosopher al-Kindi (d. 873), had written an entire treatise to show that the different degrees arose from a geometrical increase in the ratio of hotness to coldness ($1° = 2{:}1$, $2° = 4{:}1$, $3° = 8{:}1$, etc.) and he went on to use this proportionality to explain what medicinal degree was produced when given weights of two drugs of different intensity were combined. His work was translated into Latin by Gerard of Cremona before 1187, and scholastic authors were referring to it in the first half of the thirteenth century, but their language does not suggest that they had the book before them, much less understood it: they merely give a stock "Alkindian" definition of *gradus* that they appear to have taken from some intermediate source (it does not occur in al-Kindi's own treatise) before moving on to other matters. The first appearance of this definition so far known is in Henry of Winchester's Montpellier commentary on the *Isagoge*, in a section he devised to explore the nature of medicinal degree: "Iacobus alkindri describit gradum hoc modo: gradus est sexdecupla proportio vel alia submultiplicium partium eius que continua proportionalitate distinguitur." Henry struggled briefly and unclearly to explain what this phrase meant before turning to other subjects—what divisions there were within a degree, what intensity was, and how degrees could be determined in practice.[38] Thirty or so years later, Peter of Spain can be found quoting the same stock passage in his commentary on Isaac's *Diete universales*, although again with no sign that he has read al-Kindi's treatise or that he understands the mathematical application of the rule.[39] Apparently a brief reference to al-Kindi's work was

---

[37] Arnau de Vilanova, *Aphorismi de gradibus*, ed. M. R. McVaugh, *Arnaldi de Vilanova Opera Medica Omnia* (hereafter *AVOMO*) 2 (Granada-Barcelona: Universitat de Barcelona, 1975), chaps. 1–2.

[38] Michael McVaugh, "An Early Discussion of Medicinal Degrees at Montpellier by Henry of Winchester," *Bulletin of the History of Medicine* 49 (1975): 57–71.

[39] Arnau de Vilanova, *Aphorismi de gradibus*, 60.

a not uncommon feature of discussions in thirteenth-century medical faculties, though it was not something of importance to the practicing physician.[40]

Therefore it is highly suggestive to find Gilbert making place in the *Compendium* for an extended account of medicinal degrees (162va-163vb), an account very much like those of Henry of Winchester and Peter of Spain, perhaps even a little fuller than theirs. He discusses the nature of intensity with great care, distinguishing three different ways in which something can be said to be hotter than something else; explores the nature and extent of intensive range or latitude (already used in this sense as a technical term by Henry); and repeats the definitions of "degree" offered by a number of earlier authorities, including the stock "Alkindian" formulation, "gradus est sexdecupla proportio vel aliqua simplicium partis eius que continua proportionalitate distinguuntur," once again without making an understanding use of the statement.[41] Gilbert evidently had a contemporary master's appreciation of the dimensions of the topic, and of the sources it was traditional to use in analyzing it. It might be added that while medical writers in the years 1230–1270 seem to have been content to make mere passing reference to al-Kindi, Roger Bacon, writing (it would seem) in the 1260s, complained that they did not appreciate the utility of his theory:

> [The degree of a compound medicine] can only be determined by the method taught by Alkindi *de gradibus*, one extremely difficult and almost entirely unknown among Latin physicians these days, as everyone is aware.[42]

---

[40] In mid-century Montpellier, Cardinalis made no reference to the work in his commentary on the *Isagoge*, but he did do so in his commentary on the *De pulsibus* of Philaretus: "Legitur enim in libro de gradibus Iacobi Archindi quod minus calidum additum magis calide infrigidat ipsum, unde si aqua tepida addatur aque multum calide reprimit caliditatem ipsius" (Bernkastel-Kues MS. 222, fol. 89vb). Indeed, he did so again in his commentary on Galen's *Tegni*: "Dicit Jacob Alquin. in libro graduum: equale calidum additum equali calido nec intendit nec remittit caliditatem, ut patet in aqua ferventissima" (ibid., fol. 72va). Needless to say, there is nothing specifically Alkindian about these statements, and they do not testify to an understanding of his theories, but they do suggest that al-Kindi's name was a kind of mantra for Montpellier at mid-century.

[41] Discussions like these make it difficult for me to agree with Getz (*Medicine*, 41) that "Gilbert's book, save for the first chapter on fevers, is not that of a university professor like Taddeo Alderotti. Gilbert sought out the best texts of his time, but did not try to criticize them or analyze them in any depth."

[42] Roger Bacon, *De erroribus medicorum*, in *Fratris Rogeri Bacon De retardatione accidentium senectutis*, ed. A. G. Little and E. Withington (Oxford: Clarendon Press, 1928), 166. Another translation is given in M. C. Wellborn, "The Errors of the Doctors According to Friar Roger Bacon of the Minor Order," *Isis* 18 (1932): 26–62, here 43.

It would remain for Arnau de Vilanova at 1290s Montpellier to study al-Kindi's actual work and to explain his theory (and its application to compound medicines) in detail.

The date of the *Compendium*

I believe we must conclude from this evidence of medical sophistication that Gilbert was writing in the *Compendium*, not merely as someone who had once been exposed to scholastic medical instruction, nor even as a junior instructor, but as an active teacher with considerable experience in a medical faculty. If so, if he was an academic medical master of some maturity when he wrote the *Compendium medicine*, when and where was he teaching? Let us turn back to his citations of medical and philosophical authorities, to see if they can carry us any further. The thirteenth century was a time of rapid change in medical texts and ideas, yet relatively few of its Latin writings can be dated with any precision; this is a further reason why even a tentative dating of Gilbert's activity is so important, since it would go some way towards providing a kind of benchmark on all aspects of thirteenth-century medical thought. The latest of the datable texts he cited in the *Compendium* was apparently the *De animalibus* of Aristotle, translated by Michael Scot shortly before 1220;[43] and if the date given in Bruges MS. 469 is sound, the work was composed before 1271. When in that fifty-year period was it finished? Historians have really been guessing when they have proposed 1230, 1240, or 1250. Can we do better?

One suggestive indicator is the use Gilbert made of Avicenna's medical encyclopedia, the *Canon*. Like al-Kindi's work, this was translated by Gerard of Cremona before 1187, but it was too sophisticated and complex for the early medical faculties to use easily (they found understanding the pure Galen even more difficult). At Montpellier, Henry of Winchester made no use of Avicenna at all in his commentary on the *Isagoge*; for him, it was Constantine the African, with his translations of Isaac, who was the indispensable guide to interpreting the *articella*. Further north, at Paris, it was again Constantine and the *articella* that were the standard medical references listed by Alexander Nequam shortly after 1200; he made no mention at all of the *Canon*.[44] Virtually the only Parisian medical

---

[43] Lynn Thorndike, *Michael Scot* (London: Nelson, 1965), 24. Manuscripts of the translation indicate that it was executed at Toledo, where Scot is known to have been (translating) in 1217; he had left by 1220, when he is found in Bologna.

[44] The document in which these texts were listed was published—as "Sacerdos ad altare"— by Charles H. Haskins, *Studies in the History of Medieval Science* (Cambridge, MA: Harvard University Press, 1924), 374–75. Haskins judged it to have been written before 1194; subsequently, R. W. Hunt, *The Schools and the Cloister: The Life and Writings of Alexander Nequam (1157–1217)*, ed. and rev. Margaret Gibson (Oxford: Oxford

master we know from the first part of the thirteenth century, Gerard of Berry or Bourges ("Bituricensis"), boasted of his use of Avicenna in his commentary on Constantine's *Viaticum*,[45] but unfortunately we cannot date his work with any precision; Danielle Jacquart suggests "il n'est pas postérieur à la première moitié du XIIIe siècle" and, because of its lack of scholastic argument, thinks we ought not "trop avancer la date de composition au delà des années 1230."[46] Indeed, it seems to be in the 1230s that medical teachers began to perceive the attractions of the *Canon*, and we can follow its gradual integration into Latin thought in a series of stages: from extracts from the work incorporated nearly verbatim into another text without acknowledgement (Gerard's regular practice),[47] to isolated references to his name (e.g., by Henrik Harpestræng, d. 1244),[48] to embodied citations with Avicenna's name attached (as in the *Summa medicinalis* of Walter Agilon),[49] and finally to incorporation into academic thought and debate (Cardinalis). By the end of the century writers like Arnau de Vilanova at Montpellier will take Avicenna for granted and will be moving on to the pure Galen.

Against this sequence, Gilbert the Englishman certainly does not appear to have been an early figure, selective or hesitant in his employment of the *Canon*: he makes consistent intelligent use of Avicenna, debating with him and thinking about his ideas; we have already found him using Aristotle to explicate Avicenna's account of the nature of sight. In one particularly revealing example, we can see Gilbert integrating Avicennan detail into his account of *febris ethica* (hectic fever) (65va-66vb). Handerson indeed commented that "in the discussion of this last variety [of fever] we are introduced to the *ros* and *cambium* of

---

University Press, 1984), accepted Nequam's authorship but dated the work to the first decade of the thirteenth century. Nequam was at Paris ca. 1180 and taught in the Oxford schools during the 1190s.

[45] *Breviarium Constantini dictum Viaticum cum expositione Gerardi Bututi* (Venice, 1505), fol. 89va.

[46] Danielle Jacquart, "La réception du *Canon* d'Avicenne: Comparaison entre Montpellier et Paris aux XIIIe et XIVe siècles," in *Histoire de l'Ecole Médicale de Montpellier*, Actes du 110e Congrès national des sociétés, Section d'histoire des sciences et des techniques, 2 vols. (Paris: C.T.H.S., 1985), 2:69–77, here 73.

[47] Arnau de Vilanova, *De amore heroico*, ed. M. R. McVaugh, *AVOMO* 3 (Barcelona: Universitat de Barcelona, 1985), 22. For examples of Gerard's practice, see Mary Frances Wack, *Lovesickness in the Middle Ages: The* Viaticum *and its Commentaries* (Philadelphia: University of Pennsylvania Press, 1990), 200–1, at nn. 13, 14, 15, 16. Based on its citation by an author whose own date is uncertain, Wack proposes (52–54) a date of 1180–1200 for Gerard's commentary, but this seems to me to be impossible to reconcile with the textual and institutional evidence.

[48] Henrik Harpestræng, *Liber herbarum*, ed. Poul Hauberg (Copenhagen: Vilhelm Priors, 1936), 104/5–106/7.

[49] *Gualteri Agilonis Summa medicinalis*, ed. Paul Diepgen (Leipzig: Barth, 1911), 84, 85, 86, etc.

Avicenna, apparently varieties of hypothetical humors,"[50] but he was not aware that those terms show Gilbert to have been responding to one of the most influential innovations in thirteenth-century medical theory. The language comes from *Canon* I.i.4.i, where Avicenna identifies a hierarchy of *humiditates* (not to be equated with the four humors), present in all the bodily members, that explain life and growth: one (*ros*) is able to be converted into nutriment, another has been converted into nutriment but is not yet transformed into the substance of the member, and the third is a moisture present in the members from birth that is responsible for their continuity, which he refers to as a *humiditas radicalis*. Adapting a Galenic image, he explains that the various kinds of hectic fever arise when the moisture are consumed one after the other by an unnatural heat, as a flame devours the oil in a lamp, and that the third moisture, the *humiditas radicalis*, is comparable to the lamp's wick: just as when all the oil has been used up and the flame consumes the wick itself, the lamp will go out, so the consumption of the *humiditas radicalis* will result in the death of the individual.[51] This language and image appear at Montpellier in Cardinalis's commentary on the *Isagoge* (they had not been used in Henry of Winchester's earlier discussion of hectic fever) and show how important the *Canon* had become to the school by mid-century; after 1250 they would be staples of natural-philosophical as well as medical explanation. Gilbert's references to *ros* and his use of the lamp-metaphor make it plain that he, like Cardinalis, had engaged with the discussion in the *Canon*. Gilbert's account, indeed, evokes a lively scholastic setting in which "quidam" and "alii" are reported as proposing alternative metaphors to the Avicennan lamp that Gilbert prefers.

Still another way of trying to get at Gilbert's date is by placing his knowledge of the specialized Galenic writings (that is, those not included in the *articella*) against that of other thirteenth-century writers. Europe's familiarity with these texts grew relatively slowly. Henry of Winchester mentions *De crisi* in his Montpellier *Isagoge*-commentary, while Walter Agilon knows not only that work but *De interioribus* as well.[52] At mid-century, Cardinalis's various commentaries on the *articella* contain references to *De crisi*, *De interioribus*, *De complexionibus*, and *De simplici medicina*.[53] Not only does Gilbert cite all these Galenic writings,[54] he also refers to *De criticis diebus* (257va), *De iuvamentis membrorum* (284vb), and, most interestingly, *De morbo et accidenti* (1vb, 338vb), a work that seems to have

[50] Handerson, *Gilbertus Anglicus*, 29.
[51] Michael McVaugh, "The 'Humidum Radicale' in Thirteenth-Century Medicine," *Traditio* 30 (1974): 265–68.
[52] *Gualteri Aguilonis Summa medicinalis*, 158 and 84.
[53] Bernkastel-Kues, Bibl. d. St. Nikolaus-Hosp. MS. 222, fols. 47rb; 58va and 81ra; 19ra, 73ra, and 94rb; and 68ra.
[54] *De crisi* at 15va, 22rb; *De interioribus* at 103rb, 270rb; *De criticis diebus* at 257va; and *De simplici medicina* at 174vb.

become important to the medical faculties only towards the end of the thirteenth century.[55] This pattern of Galenic citation suggests, again, a relatively late date for the *Compendium*.

This conclusion can be reinforced by positioning Gilbert against a somewhat different tradition, that of a series of thirteenth-century Latin surgical writings, which are (uniquely) datable: it moves from the commentary on Ruggero Frugardi's *Surgery* (c. 1170) by Rolando da Parma, about 1230; to the first version of Teodorico Borgognoni's *Surgery* in the 1240s; to the *Surgery* of Bruno in 1252; and to revisions by Teodorico to his work in the 1250s and again the 1260s.[56] In fact, the line between surgery and learned medicine was not yet sharply drawn, and these surgical writers were discovering and assimilating the same Greco-Arabic authors being read by physicians, in order to move their craft closer to the emerging academic world. Teodorico in the 1240s constructed his surgery largely out of Galen's *De ingenio sanitatis* (he cited only the surgical books) and Book IV of Avicenna's *Canon*, with a few references to Albucasis and Rhazes; by the 1250s he had mastered the works of Rhazes and was quoting them fully (they were already to be seen mentioned briefly by Bruno), and by the 1260s he was taking over not just Rhazes' manual operations but also his chemical preparations.

This pattern—first an appreciation of Avicenna, subsequently an interest in Rhazes—is repeated in Latin medical as well as surgical writers, though their activity cannot be dated so precisely. Gerard of Berry mentions Rhazes only half a dozen times in a hundred folios, while citing Avicenna six times as often. Moreover, he almost always refers to Rhazes in connection with another author; he does not yet really distinguish Rhazes' teaching from that of Avicenna or Isaac.[57] Likewise Agilon's *Summa medicinalis* spices its general dependence on Avicenna with a mere seven scattered references to Rhazes. Cardinalis, just before mid-century, is another indicator: though he refers repeatedly to Avicenna, he never mentions Rhazes. It would seem that Rhazes was a somewhat recherché authority even in 1250. Indeed, writing in the 1260s, Roger Bacon seems to believe that Rhazes is still not sufficiently appreciated as a corrective to Avicenna's excessive philosophizing.[58] Hence Gilbert's practice of enthusiastically introducing long excerpts from "verba Rasis" into his text (310ra, 319vb) would be exceptional before 1250, though it perhaps suggests that Gilbert had not yet entirely digested Rhazes' thought.

Historians have tended to comment with apparent surprise on Gilbert's interest in surgical matters, but it is scarcely remarkable, given the overlap between

---

[55] Arnau de Vilanova, *De intentione medicorum*, ed. M. R. McVaugh, *AVOMO* 5.1 (Barcelona: Universitat de Barcelona, 2000), 178–79.

[56] Michael McVaugh, *The Rational Surgery of the Middle Ages* (Florence: SISMEL, 2006), chap. 1.

[57] Jacquart, "Réception du *Canon*," 73.

[58] Bacon, *De erroribus medicorum*, 162; Wellborn, "Errors of the Physicians," 38–39.

the fields still existing at mid-century—one of Teodorico Borgognoni's contemporaries, Guglielmo da Saliceto, composed separate introductions to both medicine and surgery as late as the 1270s.[59] Gilbert's discussions of surgical material have their own important contribution to make to our argument. Unfortunately he makes no mention of Teodorico's surgical treatise—determining which version Gilbert knew would have gone a long way toward narrowing down the date of the *Compendium*; on the other hand, Gilbert's work did become known to Teodorico, who quoted from it in the third recension of his *Surgery* (IV.7), datable to after 1262,[60] and this slightly reduces our *terminus ante quem* at the same time that it underlines the European impact of the *Compendium*. The surgical authority that Gilbert quotes from most often, though without naming it, is Ruggero's work of the late twelfth century, and in a version that does not contain Rolando's later additions (as Handerson suggested and I can confirm),[61] and hence has nothing to contribute towards the establishment of a *terminus post quem*. However, he does quote an arsenic-based recipe from the "Four Masters" (225rb), a surgical commentary upon the Rolando-Ruggero combination. The Four Masters' work cannot yet be dated (it is referred to once by Walter Agilon),[62] but they knew and used Avicenna, which Rolando did not, and they quoted half a dozen

---

[59] Riha, "Gilbertus Anglicus," 74, makes this point; and see McVaugh, *Rational Surgery*, chap. 1.

[60] McVaugh, *Rational Surgery*, 16–21. Teodorico's reference is to Gilbert's version of *oleum benedictum*, on which see below. See also *The Surgery of Theodoric*, ed. Eldredge Campbell and James Colton, 2 vols. (New York: Appleton-Century-Crofts, 1955–1960), 2:211.

[61] Handerson (*Gilbertus Anglicus*, 58; and see also 23–24) concluded this because Gilbert showed no awareness of Rolando's several explicit criticisms of Ruggero. In further support of this conclusion, I have found that a number of other passages in the *Compendium* appear to be quoting Ruggero's phraseology rather than the expanded version in the *Rolandina*. Thus, for example, in describing the operation for bladder stone, Rolando added to Ruggero's account the injunction not to cut the perineal raphe: see Salvatore De Renzi, *Collectio Salernitana*, 5 vols. (Naples: Filiatre-Sebezio, 1852–1859), 2:484–85, for Ruggero's original text and Rolando's annotated additions, and 688–89 for Rolando's subsequent incorporation of those additions into his own composition, the *Rolandina*. In the *Compendium* (309rb), Gilbert follows Ruggero's language nearly verbatim, but does not repeat the phrases later incorporated by Rolando. Handerson conceded that on at least one occasion Gilbert had dealt with a subject covered by Rolando but not by Ruggero (the condition known as *testudo*), but Rolando's reference is much briefer and very different from Gilbert's, and Handerson's conclusion that Gilbert was here probably drawing on another surgical source is surely correct.

[62] Agilon's citation of the Four Masters refers to their recipe for a troche against diarrhea (*Gualteri Agilonis Summa medicinalis*, 156) that is quite different from this arsenical troche taken from them by Gilbert. The date of 1230 given to the Four Masters' commentary by Riha ("Gilbertus Anglicus," 67), arises from a misunderstanding of the text; 1230 is the date of the text on which they are commenting.

times from Rhazes. It is hard to imagine their commentary as having been composed much earlier than 1240, and this again suggests the relative lateness of Gilbert's *Compendium*.

Gilbert's adoption of this and other arsenical medicines exemplifies his keen interest in the chemical materials and methods that were beginning to have a strong impact on surgery in the 1250s: thus he explains the use of an alembic for the distillation of water for sea crossings (362vb),[63] and employs sublimation with an alembic to produce *oleum benedictum*, a petroleum product that was exciting much interest in the 1260s.[64] It is not implausible, then, that the *Compendium* should be dated to the decade of the 1250s, twenty years after he began to teach, conceivably even as late as 1260. Earlier historians who identified him with the physician who attended Hubert Walter before 1205 were forced as a result to date his birth to no later than 1180, which made 1240–1250 the latest they dared to put the *Compendium*; but if we conclude that the two men are not the same person, and that our Gilbert must have been born 1210–1230, and had begun his teaching career in the 1230s at the earliest, there is nothing at all improbable about dating the work to the academic world of the 1250s.

Did Gilbert practice in the Kingdom of Jerusalem?

This, then, is an argument for the "when" of the *Compendium medicine*; but what about "where"? A remarkable story included in the printed edition (137ra) has sometimes been taken as offering a fixed point in Gilbert's life and travels around which the rest of his life might be reconstructed: it describes a salve (*collyrium*) that the author used to treat the eye disease of a man identified as Bertram, son of Hugh of Jubail in the Kingdom of Jerusalem. Piers Mitchell has looked particularly carefully at this story, trying to reconcile its detail with the standard account of Gilbert's life, and he has proposed two theories with which it seems to be consistent: that it relates either to the time of the Third Crusade (1189–1192), or, alternatively, to that of the 1220s, when a Bertram of Jubail, son of Hugh, is known to have been alive.[65] Neither of these theories, of course, is congruent with our revised understanding of Gilbert as born 1210–1230 and a student 1225–1245. But a third theory is now possible in the light of our reinterpretation of the evidence. Since Mitchell reports that Bertram of Jubail died in 1259, it is perfectly conceivable that a Gilbert who had finished his studies by the mid-1240s subsequently went out to the Holy Land, practiced there for a time

---

[63] Talbot, *Medicine*, 78, recognized that the passage was from Rhazes, but was not aware of any implications of that fact.

[64] *Compendium*, fol. 318vb; McVaugh, *Rational Surgery*, 191–94.

[65] Piers D. Mitchell, *Medicine in the Crusades* (Cambridge: Cambridge University Press, 2004), 21–23.

(treating Bertram before the latter's death), and returned to publish his *Compendium* in the 1250s.

Obviously it is dangerous to build too much on this one case. In the printed edition, the story is headed "Additio," as Handerson (and J. F. Payne before him) pointed out, which would seem to make it suspect as a source for Gilbert's career.[66] Ernest Wickersheimer went further: recognizing that it would be interesting to see whether the episode was reported in manuscript versions of the *Compendium*, he looked at the text in Paris, Bibl. nat. lat. MS. 6955, and concluded that it was missing there.[67] Nevertheless, the story *is* present in the earliest known copy of the *Compendium*, Bruges MS. 469 (at fol. 87ra), and there it appears *without* the ostensibly damning label "Additio." And what are we to make of the printed *Compendium*'s section on *Humiditas oculorum* (138rb), which is also preceded by an "Additio?" Is it too to be interpreted as someone else's later contribution? The situation is evidently not quite as straightforward as it appeared to Handerson and to Wickersheimer.

My close inspection of seventeen manuscripts of the *Compendium* has led me, instead, to understand the printed text as the product of a last-minute authorial revision.[68] In this view, the late thirteenth-century copy at Yale is close in form to what the final version of Gilbert's text must have looked like. The Yale copy has a number of what appear to be glosses in its bottom margins, most but not all of them written in what seems to be the original copyist's hand, glosses ranging in length from two or three to fifty lines. On examination, one of these proves to contain the text of the printed *Compendium*'s discussion of *humiditas oculorum*; another is a passage beginning with the prescription for Bertram of Jubail's collyrium but continuing on for another column or so. The longest of these marginal "additions" (none of them actually bears that heading in the Yale

---

[66] Handerson, *Gilbertus Anglicus*, 22; J. F. Payne, "English Medicine in the Anglo-Norman Period. The FitzPatrick Lectures for 1904," *Lancet* 1904 (2): 1327–30; the same lectures were also reported in essentially identical language in the *British Journal of Medicine* 1904 (2): 1281–84. Payne went on to declare that the story instead "refers to an entirely different person, one Zacharias, who wrote a treatise on disease of the eye." He did not give his reason for believing this, and I have been unable to find confirmation of it in *Magistri Zacharie Tractatus de passionibus oculorum*, ed. P. Pansier, Collectio Ophthalmologica Veterum Auctorum, fasc. 5 (Paris: Ballière, 1907).

[67] Wickersheimer, *Dictionnaire biographique*, 192.

[68] I have paid particular attention to the manuscripts at Bruges; Oxford, All Souls College; Oxford, Bodleian Library; and Yale. I will refer to them in what follows by these abbreviated labels, but their full shelfmarks can be found in n. 1 above. My conclusions have been reinforced by my examination of another thirteen manuscripts of the *Compendium*: Cambridge (CUL, Pembroke College, and Peterhouse); Oxford (Merton, New College, and St. John's); London (College of Physicians and British Library, Royal and Sloane); and Paris (BN lat. 6955, 10239, 16194, and n. a. l. 160).

manuscript) is one belonging to Gilbert's chapter in Book VI on bladder stone and gravel, where it can be found incorporated smoothly into the printed text.

It will be convenient here to identify ten of the most substantial "additions" by their first and last words (with their location in the Yale copy):

1. Omnis dolor . . . quam ante (48vb)
2. Dicitur epilentia . . . aggregationem virtutis (57ra)
3. Tholomeus dicit . . . Ysaac secundum verum (57rb)
4. Materia in cerebro . . . yrundinum (58va, vb, 59ra)
5. Signa communia . . . omnibus capitibus (57ra, 56vb)
6. Collyrium quod feci . . . in contusione oculi (71r)
7. Humiditas oculorum . . . pulvis ad oculos (72r)
8. Cataracte sunt . . . doloris cogatur (73r)
9. Emoroyde sunt . . . cum sagiminibus (120v-121)
10. Galienus in principio . . .ex sanguine coagulato (137v)

The first, dealing with pain, and the next four, which amplify the discussion of epilepsy, occur in Book II of the *Compendium*; nos. 6–8, on eye ailments, come in Book III; and the last two, on hemorrhoids and bladder stone, come in Books V and VI, respectively. If we look systematically for these passages in the printed edition of 1510, we find that nos. 1–5 are missing but 6–10 are present, with the word "additio" prefixed only to nos. 6–7.[69]

Looking at early manuscripts of the *Compendium* helps us to better understand the process by which the marginalia were ultimately incorporated into the text represented by the printed edition. The collyrium-passage (no. 6), for example, which Wickersheimer thought was missing in BN lat. 6955, is indeed not included there as part of the text proper, but it *is* found written separately at the bottom of fols. 91r and 91v, very much as it appears in the Yale copy. The same passage has been integrated into the text of the All Souls manuscript with the word "additio" set in the margin opposite the beginning of the passage; in the Bodleian copy the word "Addi" precedes it in the text itself (the origin of this word is suggested by the fact that other additions in Bodley have "Addi" in the margin opposite their beginning and "cio" opposite their end); in the College of Physicians, Merton, St. Johns, New College, and Peterhouse copies, any indication that the passages were later insertions has disappeared. The independence of the *additiones* from the original text is further evident from the fact that they have not always been inserted in the same place: the Bodleian and All Souls manuscripts have both moved no. 7 from the margin into the text, each with the marginal note "additio," but they have inserted it at different places. The scribe of the Cambridge University copy placed the passage on stone (no. 10) earlier in the

---

[69] I have not supplied the texts of these *additiones* in order not to lengthen this study unduly, but those of nos. 6–10 can thus be found in the 1510 edition of the *Compendium* (at fols. 137ra, 138r-v, 140r-v, 232v-233, and 270v-271, respectively).

text than do any of the other manuscripts, but when he arrived at the spot where most of the others have it he wrote in the margin (fol. 140rb) "hic deberet inscribi additio scripta ex altera parte folii ante [hoc] capitulum."

The Bruges manuscript shows us very clearly how inconsistently the *additiones* were dealt with by scribes from the very beginning. Here the first *additio*, on pain, is left as a marginal gloss at the bottom of the leaf; the next four, expanding Gilbert's account of epilepsy, are present neither in the margin nor in the text; the sixth, Bertram's collyrium, is incorporated into the text with no sign that it is an addition; the seventh, on *humiditas oculorum*, is placed in the same spot as in the Bodley copy with the word "Addi" prefixed to it; the eighth, on cataract, is also introduced with "Addi," while the ninth, on hemorrhoids, is linked to the previous phrase by the word "additio" in such a way as to make it appear that it is part of Gilbert's own sentence. The tenth, on stone, has again been omitted; it has been lost from the margin but has not been copied into the text.

I interpret all this evidence as showing that the original text of the *Compendium* was accompanied by marginal passages that subsequent scribes either recopied in the margin, or inserted into the text where they thought it appropriate to do so, or, as in the Bruges manuscript, omitted to copy. Passages 1–5 and 6–10 seem to have had different histories, for in manuscripts and printed text alike the former group is copied much less consistently and the word "additio" is found attached only to members of the latter group. In BN lat. MS. 16194, nos. 1–5 are each found copied at the bottom of a leaf, while nos. 6–10 are integrated seamlessly into the text. Perhaps passages 1–5, which scribes came upon first and which tend to be shorter, were not recognized as intended to be part of the text. I must stress, however, that virtually every one of the manuscripts in the sample I have examined—roughly one-half of those known to survive—contains at least half of these ten additions, either as marginalia or incorporated into the text.[70] It would appear that an unadorned version of the *Compendium*, the pure un-annotated framework, was never put into circulation.

How should we understand these originally marginal additions? It is possible, of course, that they were supplied by another author who came upon Gilbert's uncirculated text after his death, but it seems to me far more likely that they were Gilbert's own last-minute amplifications of a text that he had already prepared for publication. The body of the text may well have been composed by him as late as the 1250s, as we have seen, and yet the *additiones* had already been incorporated into the text by 1271, when we know the Bruges manuscript was

---

[70] The exception to this is Paris, BN n. a. l. MS. 160, a copy of the early fourteenth century, which has none of the additions in either text or margins—indeed, its margins are essentially devoid of any annotation whatsoever. It is possible, certainly, that this one copy descends directly from an unannotated Gilbertian original, but it sems to me equally conceivable that its scribe decided to copy the text shorn of its apparently accumulated marginalia.

copied. This would mean, therefore, that the story of Bertram's collyrium really is Gilbert's own work, and that he did at least briefly practice his art in the Latin East, perhaps after drafting the original version of the *Compendium*.[71] It is worth remembering that three of the ten *additiones* concern different eye ailments, and we may wonder whether Gilbert had acquired in Syria some of the ophthalmological knowledge for which Arabic medicine was famous and appended it to his treatise once he returned to Europe. Cataract, for example, is not a condition described in Gilbert's principal surgical source, Ruggero Frugardi's *Chirurgia*, and a belated decision to add something about this complaint could easily have arisen out of his recent experiences in the East.[72] In that case, his observation in the collyrium-*additio* that "Saracens and Syrians confirm that, according to the testimony of their books, serapinum and euforbium are of greater benefit in blows to the eye" could then be a recent personal observation, not a generalization drawn from some other source.[73]

---

[71] Payne passed on another, rather more problematic story about Gilbert's stay in the Holy Land, reporting Gilbert's tale of a conversation in Tripoli with a canon suffering from rheumatism (Payne, "English Medicine," *Lancet*, 1328; *British Medical Journal*, 1282). The story would fit well enough with his preparation of Bertram's Syrian collyrium, but no historian has ever been able to find a source for it in the *Compendium* (cf. Riha, "Gilbertus Anglicus," 62). Payne himself owned a manuscript of Gilbert's work and bequeathed it to the Royal College of Physicians, whose Harveian Librarian he was: it is now the College's MS. 395. He might not implausibly have worked from this copy in mining the *Compendium* for information, and I have examined it carefully in the hope that Payne might have left some pointer there to the rheumatic canon. In fact, there is a penciled cross in the margin of the manuscript with a line drawn to the story of the collyrium (Book III, fol. 10rb; each book in this manuscript has been foliated separately), and the word "charm" is penciled in the margin a little further on, both marks apparently made by Payne, but he seems to have left no other mark in the manuscript. The canon of Tripoli will have to remain an unproven mystery until some documentary evidence of his existence is located.

[72] In Michael McVaugh, "Cataracts and Hernias: Aspects of Surgical Practice in the Fourteenth Century," *Medical History* 45 (2001): 319–40, I remarked upon the novelty of Gilbert's discussion of cataract, as well as its mild incoherence, "as if produced in the earliest stages of Western attention to the condition" (327 n. 18), without of course appreciating that the cataract-material had been added to the original text. Handerson (*Gilbertus Anglicus*, 35) pointed out that Gilbert had gone beyond his usual sources here, as well as in his description of actual surgical intervention in eye conditions rather than the simple application of collyria and ointments; this too might be the consequence of his experiences in the East.

[73] "Sarraceni et surriani confirmaverunt serapinum et euforbium magis conferre in ictibus oculorum secundum auctoritatem suorum librorum": *Compendium*, fol. 137va.

At what school did Gilbert teach?

In trying to decide where Gilbert worked we are left, therefore, with speculation based on inference and probability. It is remarkable, and probably no coincidence, that the *Compendium* was already being quoted in the 1260s by two
men associated with the papal court, Teodorico Borgognoni and Peter of Spain,
who seem to have had several scientific interests in common, not just medicine
but also the new chemical technology beginning to spread through Latin Europe: both found Gilbert's chemical knowledge (acquired mostly from Rhazes
and *Meteorologica* IV) of great interest.[74] This is very early in the history of the
Compendium's diffusion, of course, and we might wonder whether Gilbert himself was associated with the court—it was a lively and attractive center of intellectual activity in the mid-thirteenth century—and produced his *Compendium*
there; but Agostino Paravicini Bagliani has turned up no evidence of a medical
"Gilbertus" there in the 1250s or 1260s,[75] and it is more likely that a copy of the
Compendium happened fortuitously to have arrived at the court at just the moment when there was an interested audience for it.

A much more probable setting for Gilbert is in one of the European medical faculties, Paris or Montpellier—but which one? Almost no evidence survives
about the Paris school in the first half of the thirteenth century—its members
seem to have taken virtually no interest in literary activity there until the time
of Jean de Saint-Amand, in the century's final decades[76]—with the exception of
Gerard of Berry's long commentary on Constantine the African's *Viaticum*, already referred to: Gerard tells his readers that he drew up the work "a sociis roga-
tus Parisiis."[77] Many of the patterns of citation in Gerard's commentary certainly
bear comparison with those in the commentaries of Cardinalis at Montpellier.
He refers to most of the constituent works of the *articella*, for example; he makes
use of Avicenna (though it is often unacknowledged), and he occasionally mentions Rhazes' name, though not in connection with chemical procedures—indeed, as we have seen, Gerard boasts in his prologue about his knowledge of these
two authors. In these respects Gerard might be understood as writing somewhat
earlier than Cardinalis, perhaps ca. 1230.

---

[74] McVaugh, *Rational Surgery*, 193 (n. 31 on that page, referring to a distilled product taken by Peter from Gilbert, is mistaken, and should read "Rocha Pereira, 281"). Mi-
chela Pereira, "Prima Materia: Echi Aristotelici e Avicenniani nel *Testamentum* pseudo-
lulliano," in *Aristoteles Chemicus: Il IV libro dei "Meteorologica" nella tradizione antica e
medievale*, ed. Cristina Viano (Sankt Augustin: Academia, 2002), 145–64, gives an over-
view of the excitement produced in Europe by *Meteorologica* IV, ca. 1250.

[75] Agostino Paravicini Bagliani, *Medicina e scienze della natura alla corte dei papi nel
duecento* (Spoleto: Centro Italiano di Studi sull'Alto Medioevo, 1991), esp. 23–31.

[76] Jacquart, *Médecine médiévale*, 21–22.

[77] *Breviarium Constantini dictum Viaticum cum expositione Gerardi Bututi*, fol. 89va.

What distinguishes Gerard of Berry most obviously from the Montpellier masters (and also from Gilbert), however, is the almost complete absence in his work of any references to Aristotle, and (less sharply) the relative paucity of references to Galenic works beyond those in the *articella*.[78] As we have seen, at Montpellier before 1250 both Henry of Winchester and Cardinalis were already making consistent reference to a wide range of Aristotelian texts in their commentaries, just as Gilbert does in his *Compendium*. It is tempting to speculate that the Parisian reserve towards Aristotle's natural works delayed their citation even by the medical masters; but whatever the reason for this silence, what little evidence we have seems to indicate that Gilbert the Englishman's use of Aristotle in his *Compendium* resembled the practice at Montpellier more than it did that at Paris.

And in one instance there appears to be not just a parallelism but an apparent linear connection between Gilbert and the Montpellier masters in their use of Aristotle. Steven Williams has emphasized the importance of medical writers in spreading a knowledge of the [pseudo-] Aristotelian *Epistola ad Alexandrum*, and cited Henry of Winchester, in his *Isagoge*-commentary, as the first one who can be identified as referring to it, though Williams himself was unable to locate Henry's exact quotation.[79] The next author found by Williams to have used the work was Gilbert in the *Compendium* (247ra):

> unde prohibetur in epistola ad Alexandrum ne ulterius differatur refectio, quam saliva incipiat in ore immutari. Dat enim intelligi humores trahi in stomachum per ieiunium qui salivam immutant.

I have now been able to identify the passage in the *Isagoge*-commentary where Henry of Winchester refers to the *Epistola*, and it proves to be this very one: that is, Gilbert was paraphrasing the same passage from the *Epistola* in exactly the same words as Henry before him![80] This is surely no coincidence, and the easiest way to explain it is by assuming that this quotation was current at Montpellier in

---

[78] He refers to Galen's *De crisi* on fols. 174rb, 174vb, and 176vb; and to the *De interioribus* on fols. 97va, 101vb, and 157va.

[79] Steven J. Williams, *The* Secret of Secrets*: The Scholarly Career of a Pseudo-Aristotelian Text in the Latin Middle Ages* (Ann Arbor, MI: University of Michigan Press, 2003), 185.

[80] Williams drew on Talbot, *Medicine*, 61–62, to assert Henry's use of the *Epistola* in his commentary on the *Isagoge*, but Talbot did not give a specific reference to the passage. I have now found it in the text of the commentary given in Oxford, New College MS. 171, fol. 6v: "Ar. in epistola ad Alexandr. precipit quod non ulterius defferatur refectio quam saliva incipiat immutari. Dat enim intelligi homines trahi in stomachum per ieiunum qui salivam immutant."

the second quarter of the thirteenth century, as a kind of digestive *topos*, and that Gilbert, like Henry, picked it up here—if not directly from Henry himself.[81]

There is another point suggesting Gilbert's affinities to mid-century Montpellier thought. Avicenna several times in his *Canon* described how he conceived of the methodology appropriate to physicians, contending that they should not seek the absolute truth of natural philosophy, because as physicians they needed only to know what was necessary to allow them to heal the body, even if this practical knowledge might appear to be inconsistent with philosophical truth. This medical "instrumentalism" was recognized and explained by Cardinalis to his mid-century Montpellier students, and it became the basis in the 1290s for an extended treatise *De intentione medicorum* by Arnau de Vilanova.[82] Gilbert has come to understand Avicenna in exactly this way. In his discussion of [the causes of] dropsy, he adds:

> But this statement is far removed from what physicians believe, and therefore Aristotle's opinion leads physicians into error, since he is speaking of philosophical truth [*secundum veritatem*] but physicians of what the senses reveal, and for them this way is better. Disregarding *veritas* does no harm to the physician, for the route to healing is revealed through the senses.[83]

This passage is contained in the original version of the *Compendium*, but the distinction was apparently still of great importance to Gilbert when he made his last-minute additions: in relating epilepsy to celestial motions (no. 3) he explains that on this subject "Ptolemy speaks *secundum apparitionem et sensus*, while Isaac does so *secundum verum*," and he concludes no. 10 by saying that "quod autem moderni investigant magis pertinet dyalectico quam rationi, cum nihil iuvaminis nobis in medicando largiatur." Gilbert's medical "instrumentalism" is certainly not inconsistent with a possible membership in the Montpellier faculty.

---

[81] Both Williams and Kurdziałek ("Gilbertus Anglicus," 112) recognize that Vincent of Beauvais in his *Speculum historiale* of ca. 1245 associated the *Epistola* with dietetic advice, but Vincent did not refer to a specific passage from the work.

[82] See Arnau de Vilanova, *De intentione medicorum*, esp. 145–54.

[83] "Sed ista dictio valde remota est a sententiis medicorum, eo quod sententia Aristotelis facit medicos errare, eo quod ipse loquitur secundum veritatem, medici secundum manifestationem in sensu, in *quibus autem via est maior*. Veritatis autem occultatio non nocet medico, cum via secundum manifestationem pateat curationis": *Compendium*, fol. 248rb; Bruges MS. 469, fol. 163va-b. In the printed edition of the *Compendium* (fol. 248rb) the italicized words are replaced by "communibus autem maior via"; in the Yale manuscript (fol. 128vb), by "communibus que maior via." The philosopher/physician contrast crops up once in Gilbert's earlier Giles-commentary, but with at most only a hint of the instrumentalist interpretation: "Urine naturali prius datur substantia quam color, de qua urina loquitur philosophus; medicus enim loquitur de innaturali, cui prius datur calor quam substantia" (Wellcome MS. 547, fol. 104va).

The likelihood that Gilbert was teaching at Montpellier is further strengthened by one of his recipes. At one point in the *Compendium*, immediately following his longer recipe for *oleum benedictum*, the author gives a prescription for a laxative medicine, "benedicta Guillermi de Congeniis":[84]

> Rx: turpeth, 1 ounce; sugar, 18 drachms; cinnamon, lavender, leaf of pennyroyal, savory, polypody, saxifrage, hermodactyl, each 4 drachms; clove, ginger, black pepper, long pepper, cardamom, *amomum*, celery seed, rock salt, each 2 drachms; cooked scammony, 2 drachms; honey as needed.[85]

William de Congeniis is best known to us from two sets of student notes on his teaching of surgery at Montpellier—once more we are reminded that surgery and medicine were not always sharply distinguished in the thirteenth century.[86] Karl Sudhoff, who published those notes, subsequently found a reference to a master "*R. de Congimis*" as *medicus* to Simon de Montfort (d. 1216), assumed that the two men were the same, and consequently inferred that William had to be placed at the beginning of the century. Against this supposition should be set the facts of his student's knowledge of Rhazes' *Liber almansoris* and of his own reported use of an "unguentum Rasis,"[87] both of which imply a much later date for his activity. But what is more important than his date is the fact that William was active at Montpellier, where he was evidently highly esteemed as a teacher, though he himself left no written work and his teachings did not circulate widely. It would seem entirely possible that Gilbert's knowledge of a *benedicta de Congeniis* was gained from his exposure to local Montpellier tradition, particularly since I cannot find the recipe in the student accounts of William's surgical teaching.[88]

---

[84] The first name is given in the All Souls ("guillermi de congeniis," fol. 150vb) and Bodleian ("guillermi de geniis," fol. 143vb) manuscripts, as well as in BN lat. 10239 ("guillermi de congeniis," fol. 129rb) and BN lat. 16194 ("gilleemi de congenis," fol. 177va), though not in the other thirteen manuscripts mentioned or in the printed edition. It also reads "guill'mi de congeniis" in Gloucester Cath. 6 (fol. 66v).

[85] "Rx turbith oz. i; zuccare dr. xviii; cinamomomi, spice, folii pulegii, satureie, polipodii, saxifrage, hermodactili, ana dr. iiii; gariofili, zinziberis, menalop., macrop., cardamomi, amomi, seminis apii, sal. gem. ro. ana dr. ii; scamonee cocte dr. ii; mellis quantum sufficit": *Compendium medicine*, fol. 329va. The Bruges and Yale manuscripts give essentially the same recipe at fols. 221v and 163vb respectively, with only a few minor variations.

[86] *Domini et magistri Willehelmi de Congenis ... scriptum cirurgiae*, in Karl Sudhoff, *Beiträge zur Geschichte der Chirurgie im Mittelalter*, 2 vols. (Leipzig: Barth, 1918), 2:297–384.

[87] *Willehelmi ... scriptum*, 383.

[88] It ought to be noted that P. Pansier, "Catalogue des manuscrits médicaux des bibliothèques de France," *Archiv für Geschichte der Medizin* 2 (1908): 1–46, here 21, reported the presence of a "benedicta magistri Guillelmi de Conieniis" in Carpentras MS. 323,

Conclusion

My answer to the question that I posed in my title—who was Gilbert the Eng-lishman?—is obviously highly conjectural, but it is at least consistent with a broad range of evidence that the traditional answer does not fit. I propose that he was born in England after 1210, perhaps to a physician-father of the same name, that he had finished training in the arts at Paris after 1230, and that he subse-quently received a medical education either there or at Montpellier; that if he afterwards went out briefly to the Kingdom of Jerusalem, he soon returned and established himself as a regent master of medicine, probably at Montpellier; and that his great work, the *Compendium medicine*, is likely to have been published in the 1250s, conceivably even the late 1250s. This outline is supported by his par-ticular choice of authorities at different stages in his career, and by his knowledge of specific academic debates.[89] There is no thirteenth-century "Gilbertus" in the Montpellier *chartularium*, but that is no obstacle to my answer: no medical mas-ters at all are named in that *chartularium* between 1240 and 1260, the period in which Gilbert is most likely to have been active there.

And assuming that this answer is correct puts a later episode in Montpel-lier's history in a new light. In the 1290s, as we have seen, its medical faculty included Arnau de Vilanova, who had previously been a student there (about 1260),[90] and by century's end was moving beyond its old Avicennism to a medi-cine more centered on Galenic texts. Arnau's work *De consideracionibus operis medicine*, attempting to explain his new understanding of the method and scope of medicine, begins by criticizing those who

> do not study the writings that pass on the aforesaid art—that is, those of Galen and Hippocrates, to whom we find medicine to have been accu-rately and perfectly revealed by divine favor; instead, [they study it] in huge books and enormous summas, like Gilbert's tales, or Ponce's and Walter's fables.[91]

---

fol. 27r. This raises a number of questions: Might this be the same *benedicta*? Does the Carpentras manuscript testify to William's particular fame in southern France? Is the codex a southern manuscript?

[89] Littré, "Gilbert l'Anglais," 395, identified Gilbert's slips into the vernacular as neo-Latin expressions and interpreted them as therefore suggesting a life on the Conti-nent rather than in England.

[90] Arnau testified in 1306 that he had seen a certain practice observed at Montpel-lier "entre les maistres, bachelliers et escoliers, il y avoit plus de quarante cinq ans": *Cartu-laire de l'Université de Montpellier*, vol. 2 (Montpellier: Lauriol, 1912), 61–62.

[91] "Non in scripturis student in quibus ars traditur supradicta Galieni et Ypocratis videlicet quibus medicinam divina concessione veraciter et perfecte novimus revelatam, ymmo pocius in cartapellis et summis que potissime magni voluminis sunt, sicut in histo-riis Gilleberti et fabulis Poncii et Galteri": Arnau de Vilanova, *De consideracionibus operis*

What was it that brought these three authors together in Arnau's mind? A case has been made in another connection for Ponce de St.-Gilles's association with Montpellier, and the same thing has been proposed for Walter Agilon;[92] Gilbert the Englishman would complete the trinity. Was Arnau perhaps deliberately citing his predecessors at Montpellier, masters whose works were still remembered in the school—and whom he himself might even have known, as a student?

medicine, ed. Luke Demaitre and Pedro Gil-Sotres, *AVOMO* 4 (Barcelona: Universitat de Barcelona, 1988), 133.

[92] The fourteenth-century Montpellier master Jean de Tournemire referred to Agilon as a former member of the school: P. Pansier, "Les maîtres de la faculté de médecine de Montpellier au Moyen Age," *Janus* 9 (1904): 443–51, 499–511 (here 505–6), 537–45, 593–602; 10 (1905): 1–11, 59–68, 113–21. Pansier also supposed (508) that St.-Gilles must have been a member of the Montpellier faculty rather than that of Paris, since the town of St.-Gilles is located in the south of France, in the modern department of Gard.

The Monks of Westminster
and the *Peculium*[*]

Barbara F. Harvey

St. Benedict of Nursia (c.480–c.550) requires every new entrant into the monastery to surrender whatever property he owns, and he condemns any subsequent claim to property as the evil that is above all others to be eradicated. No monk may give or receive anything without the abbot's permission: not even a codex, tablets, or stylus—a book, wax tablets, or the appropriate implement for writing on these—may be acquired except from the abbot or with his permission.[1]

St. Benedict forbids his monks to have *aliquid proprium*. Later, however, as distinctions were made, the need was felt for a more elaborate vocabulary and it will be helpful to introduce these refinements at the beginning of this essay. From the late twelfth century onwards in the west, as it became common for monks to possess money, the latter was referred to as the *peculium*—the word used in the Digest of Roman law, authorised by the emperor Justinian in 533, of property that a son or slave may hold and use but does not own.[2] This usage was given wide currency by the Third Lateran Council of 1179. In a canon which passed into the Decretals of Gregory IX, the Council defines the circumstances in which a monk may lawfully possess the *peculium*—only with the abbot's permission and for a specific purpose—and the word is evidently used here in the sense of money.[3] Omitting the need for a special purpose, late medieval sources

---

[*]I am greatly indebted to the Dean and Chapter of Westminster for permission to use their muniments, to Richard Mortimer, Christine Reynolds, and Tony Trowles for many kindnesses as I have done so, and to Caroline M. Barron, Miriam T. Griffin, and F. Donald Logan for their expert advice and help in other ways.

[1] *Rule of St Benedict*, chaps. 33, 58.

[2] *Digest* 15.1; Adolf Berger, *Encyclopedic Dictionary of Roman Law* (Philadelphia: American Philosophical Society, 1953), 624.

[3] *Decrees of the Ecumenical Councils, 1 (Nicaea I to Lateran V)* ed. Norman P. Tanner, S. J. (London and Washington, DC: Sheed and Ward and Georgetown University Press, 1990), 217, chap. 10; *Decretals of Gregory IX* (1234), III. 35, chap. 2. Cf. Council of London, 1074/5, chap. 2 in *Councils and Synods with Other Documents Relating to the*

tend to use the word in the sense of money that a monk possesses with his superior's permission; and this permissible state is contrasted with *proprietas*, the sin of a monk who possesses property in secret.[4] The money consisted mainly, though not exclusively, of allowances made by the monastery from its own funds, or from funds given by benefactors but earmarked for this purpose.

In this essay, the word *peculium* is used in the late medieval sense, and the allowances, which were in common use from the twelfth century onwards, will be referred to as wages.

The Growth of the *Peculium*

The Rule of St. Benedict did not become the unchallenged point of reference for monastic life in western Europe until the eleventh century. It did so then after a period when the distinction between, on the one hand, a solemn rule regulating normative behaviour for the monastery in question and, on the other, the mutable customs that every monastery also needed to guide it through the rocks and shoals of daily life was less clear than it later became.[5] In the early eighth century, the eclectic rule of the monastery at Jarrow, in Northumbria, which drew on the customs of no fewer than seventeen monasteries on the Continent known to its founder, Benedict Biscop, enabled Bede, who spent his adult life as a monk there, not only to possess a small store of pepper, napkins, and incense, and a box to keep it in, but also to distribute these possessions to his friends on his deathbed, as though they were his own to give.[6]

In this early period it was not anomalous and may not have been unusual for monks and nuns to hold and to administer family property, and especially alodial

---

English Church, 1 (A. D. 871–1204), ed. D. Whitelock, M. Brett, and C. N. L. Brooke, 2 pts. (Oxford: Clarendon Press, 1981), *2 (1066–1204)*: 613 [2].

[4] *Documents Illustrating the Activities of the General and Provincial Chapters of the English Black Monks, 1215–1540*, ed. W. A. Pantin, 3 vols., Camden Society, 3rd ser., 45, 47, 54 (London: Royal Historical Society, 1931–1937) (hereafter *Chapters of English Black Monks*), 2: 43; *Visitations of Religious Houses in the Diocese of Lincoln*, ed. A. Hamilton Thompson, 3 vols., Canterbury and York Society 17, 24, 33 (London: Canterbury and York Society, 1915–1927), 1: 55, 243; 2: 140.

[5] Giles Constable, "Monasteries, Rural Churches and the *Cura Animarum* in the Early Middle Ages," *Settimane di Studi del Centro Italiano di Studi sull'alto Mediœvo* 28 (1980): 344–95, here 351–52.

[6] *Historia Abbatum*, in *Venerabilis Baedae Opera Historica*, ed. C. Plummer, 2 vols. (Oxford: Clarendon Press, 1896), 1: 374–75; *Bede's Ecclesiastical History of the English People*, ed. and trans. Bertram Colgrave and R. A. B. Mynors, Oxford Medieval Texts (Oxford: Clarendon Press, 1969), 584–85.

property, on which no lord had a claim, after their profession.[7] As we learn from Domesday Book, there were such monks in England in the late Old English period. The land in their possession may have provided their keep in the monastery, and in the case of the monk of Abingdon Abbey who held land at Sparsholt, we are told that this was so.[8] A century later, the practice was remembered as one of the abuses of the pre-Conquest church.[9] But in an age of increasingly monetized economies, family money given to members of the family after their profession as monks or nuns may have proved harder to eliminate than gifts of family land. Such gifts may not at first have been clearly distinguished from entry gifts made to the monastery itself in the form of money; and these were only with great difficulty brought under control by higher authority in the course of the late twelfth century and the early thirteenth.[10] Was it also in this period that a gap, later to become conspicuous, opened between the appropriate limits of family support for monks on the one hand and nuns on the other? This seems possible, for already in the thirteenth century it was quite common for nuns to receive, as individuals, testamentary bequests of money, but much less common for monks to do so.[11] The degree of importance to be accorded to family money, and to money given by friends, in life or death, represents a serious gap in our present knowledge of the development of the *peculium* for monks. Yet the early acceptability of gifts of money from external sources for the few may explain how it was that wages for all later came to seem appropriate.

In the classic account of the growth of a wage-system in English monasteries, David Knowles pointed to the period 1150–1250 as that in which it became

---

[7] S. M. Wood, *The Proprietary Church in the Medieval West* (Oxford: Oxford University Press, 2006), 126–27, and for tithe owned by a monk, 503. For St. Dunstan of Canterbury's interim possession of family lands as a monk, see Eadmer of Canterbury, *Lives and Miracles of Saints Oda, Dunstan, and Oswald*, ed. and trans. Andrew J. Turner and Bernard J. Muir, Oxford Medieval Texts (Oxford: Clarendon Press, 2006), 74.

[8] Domesday Book, 1: 59a; see also 90a, 155a, 174d, 196a, 202b, cited in David Knowles, *The Monastic Order in England* (Cambridge: Cambridge University Press, 1963), 81, n. 4. For the absence of the term *alodium* 'or the like' from genuine Anglo-Saxon charters, see George Garnett, *Conquered England: Kingship, Succession, and Tenure 1066–1166* (Oxford: Oxford University Press, 2007), 28 and n. 212.

[9] *Historia Ecclesie Abbendonensis: The History of the Church of Abingdon*, ed. and trans. John Hudson, 2 vols., Oxford Medieval Texts (Oxford: Clarendon Press, 2002–2007), 1: 212.

[10] J. Lynch, "Efforts to Combat Monastic Simony in the Early Thirteenth Century," *Revue Bénédictine* 85 (1975): 132–47.

[11] Michael M. Sheehan, *The Will in Medieval England: From the Conversion of the Anglo-Saxons to the End of the Thirteenth Century* (Toronto: Pontifical Institute of Mediaeval Studies, 1963), 261–62. Cf. Eileen Power, *Medieval English Nunneries c.1275 to 1535* (Cambridge: Cambridge University Press, 1922), 324–37; Claire Cross, "Yorkshire Nunneries in the Early Tudor Period," in *The Religious Orders in Pre-Reformation England*, ed. James G. Clark (Woodbridge: Boydell Press, 2002), 145–54.

customary for monks to receive small sums of money, not only to distribute in alms, but also to pay for small indulgences, including spices. He also identified three other forms of wages that were eventually important: money given in lieu of clothing; gifts from obedientiaries (office-holders with departmental responsibilities) from their surplus funds, in addition to small customary gifts marking a monk's First Mass and other notable occasions in his life; and payment for work done by monks outside the normal course of duty.[12] In the wider church, the canon of the Third Lateran Council referred to above directs our attention to the first half of this period, the late twelfth century, as that when existing restraints on wages, whatever the pretext for such payments, became inadequate; and in England other signs point in this direction. It was, for example, almost certainly in this period that the practice of giving money in lieu of a routine issue of items of clothing gathered momentum in Benedictine houses. Only in this way can we explain how it was that at its first meeting, in 1219, the General Chapter of the English Black Monks forbade chamberlains to adopt this practice.[13] As this episode implies, obedientiaries, who now handled considerable sums of money but were not yet subjected to a rigorous system of account, were susceptible to pressure to share their responsibilities and some of their income with monks within the community.

Eventually, a formal distinction was drawn between sums of money sufficient to cover small necessities, such as spices, and larger sums sufficient for food, drink, clothes, and other major necessities. The former might be received as favours or "graces", the latter not at all: for these, monks must depend on the appropriate obedientiaries who would administer them in kind. In effect, pocket money was no longer to be regarded as a form of private property contravening the Rule. These distinctions were enshrined in the legislation of the Provincial Chapter of the English Black Monks in 1338.[14] But in practice they had long been anticipated. At the Abbey of Bury St. Edmunds, in the time of the redoubtable Abbot Samson (1182–1211), we already glimpse a tolerance for small sums of money in the possession of individual monks, and perhaps a recent period when the monks had actually possessed more. Realizing that his monks possessed chests and other receptacles in which it was possible to conceal private property, Samson called in all the keys, but permitted each monk to possess up to 2s.—the equivalent of several days' wages for a skilled craftsman of this

[12] David Knowles, *The Religious Orders in England*, 3 vols. (Cambridge: Cambridge University Press, 1948–1959), 1: 287–89; 2: 240–44. Cf. idem, *Monastic Order in England*, 484.

[13] *Chapters of English Black Monks*, 1: 11; cf. *Councils and Synods with Other Documents Relating to the English Church, 2 (A. D. 1205–1313)*, ed. F. M. Powicke and C. R. Cheney, 2 pts. (Oxford: Clarendon Press, 1964), *1 (1205–1265)*: 121–22 [48].

[14] *Chapters of English Black Monks*, 2: 11.

period — to give to needy relatives or put to other pious uses, provided only that he had received the money himself in the way of charity.[15]

The legislation of the General and Provincial Chapters of the English Black Monks was normative for monasteries, though not necessarily to be observed to the letter. But not even Benedict XII's unequivocal condemnation of clothes money in his decrees for Black Monks, published in 1336, interrupted the use of this form of wages for long.[16] In the later Middle Ages, canon law on this matter was contradicted by practices commonly sanctioned by abbots and priors, for which some bishops on visitation seem to betray, though never to express, a measure of sympathy even as they reiterated the law. At Ely, in 1403, Archbishop Thomas Arundel restored the issue of new habits and tunics each year, abolished the so-called pension previously given in lieu of the habit, but allowed the monks to keep another pension, given in lieu of the tunic every year, which payment, however, he now renamed as a grace.[17] Finally, in 1421, Henry V's reforming commissioners effectively approved the wage-system in its entirety.[18]

The *Peculium* at Westminster Abbey

The setting

The Benedictine foundation at Westminster owed its great wealth initially to Edward the Confessor (1042–1066), who chose the abbey church already in existence there as his place of burial and provided lavish endowments for the community of monks, numbering about eighty, which was to pray there in perpetuity for his soul.[19] Although Edward's cult as a saint developed slowly, his burial in the abbey church ensured that his successors would be crowned there. His

---

[15] *The Chronicle of Jocelin of Brakelond*, ed. and trans. H. E. Butler (London: Thomas Nelson, 1949), 38–39; and for Samson's relations with his monks, see Antonia Gransden, *A History of The Abbey of Bury St Edmunds, 1182–1256: Samson of Tottington to Edmund of Walpole* (Woodbridge: Boydell Press, 2007), 32–43. Cf. Seiriol J. A. Evans, ed., *Ely Chapter Ordinances and Visitation Records, 1241–1515,* Camden Miscellany 17, Camden Society, 3rd. ser., 69 (London: Royal Historical Society, 1940) (hereafter *Ely Chapter Ordinances*), 9 [7–8].

[16] D. Wilkins, *Concilia Magnae Britanniae et Hiberniae ab anno MCCLXVIII ad annum MCCCXLIX*, 4 vols. (London, 1737), 2: 604–5, no. 18.

[17] *Ely Chapter Ordinances*, 55 [9].

[18] *Chapters of English Black Monks*, 2: 131–32; Knowles, *Religious Orders*, 2: 241.

[19] Barbara F. Harvey, *Westminster Abbey and its Estates in the Middle Ages* (Oxford: Clarendon Press, 1977) (hereafter Harvey, *Estates*), 22–28; for the earlier minster on the site, and for St. Dunstan's probable foundation at Westminster, see now John Blair, "The Minsters of the Thames," in *The Cloister and the World: Essays in Medieval History in Honour of Barbara Harvey*, ed. idem and Brian Golding (Oxford: Clarendon Press,

canonization in 1161 was followed in the next century by a spectacular recovery
of royal favour under Henry III, who built a new shrine for the Confessor and a
gothic church to house it, and by the resumption of royal burials, beginning effectively with that of Henry himself, in 1272.[20] Anniversaries commemorating
the deaths were an inevitable concomitant of these, and in the case of the three
with the largest endowments—those of, respectively, Eleanor of Castile, Richard II and Anne of Bohemia, and Henry V—the monks succeeded, though not
without an initial struggle with Abbot Wenlok (1283–1307), in establishing a
claim to share among themselves the surplus income remaining each year after
the customary distribution to the poor.[21] A privilege of Alexander IV, granted in
1255, permitted the abbot of Westminster to dispense his monks from observance of the statutes of the Chapters of the Black Monks except where the Rule
forbade dispensation.[22] As a monastery directly dependent on the see of Rome,
the Abbey had long been exempt from episcopal visitation.

This unique combination of circumstances explains how it was that Westminster Abbey was always one of the wealthiest monasteries in England, and
both the community of monks and, as will appear, the wages they enjoyed unusually large. In 1535, with a net income of *c.* £2,800 per annum, the Abbey was
second only to Glastonbury Abbey in wealth.[23] As happened generally among
Benedictines, the number of monks at Westminster declined after the mid-
twelfth century. Yet in the thirteenth century the community here probably still

1996), 5–28, here 25, and *Chronicle of John of Worcester,* 2, ed. R. R. Darlington and P. M.
McGurk, Oxford Medieval Texts (Oxford: Clarendon Press, 1995), 406–8.

[20] Paul Binski, *Westminster Abbey and the Plantagenets: Kingship and the Representation of Power, 1200–1400* (New Haven: Yale University Press, 1995), 1–51; D. A. Carpenter, "King Henry III and Saint Edward the Confessor: The Origins of the Cult," *English Historical Review* 122 (2007): 865–91.

For the burial in the abbey church of Katharine, daughter of Henry III and Eleanor
of Provence, in 1257/8, see Margaret Howell, "The Children of Henry III and Eleanor of
Provence," *Thirteenth Century England* 4 (1992): 57–72, here 64.

[21] John Flete, *The History of Westminster Abbey,* ed. J. Armitage Robinson (Cambridge: Cambridge University Press, 1909), 117–19; Harvey, *Estates,* 28–36; eadem, *Living and Dying in England 1100–1540: The Monastic Experience* (Oxford: Clarendon Press,
1993), 25–27.

[22] *Calendar of Papal Registers: Papal Letters,* 1 (*1198–1304*), 316; cf. Barrie Dobson,
"The Monks of Canterbury in the Later Middle Ages, 1220–1540," in *A History of Can-
terbury Cathedral,* ed. Patrick Collinson, Nigel Ramsay, and Margaret Sparks (Oxford:
Oxford University Press, 1995), 69–153, here 102.

[23] Cf. the higher figure for 'clear value' (£3,470 per annum) in the *Valor Ecclesiasti-
cus.* The figure in the text allows for expenses imposed on the Abbey by the several royal
foundations but not allowed as reprises in the *Valor:* Harvey, *Estates,* 62–63; and for gross
income in 1535, and the rank order of monasteries by that criterion, Knowles, *Religious
Orders,* 3: 473.

numbered fifty to sixty, and in the later Middle Ages, when forty-eight was regarded as the optimum figure, it was still relatively large. Remarkably, it managed to attain this figure again after the Black Death of 1348–1349, in which half the community died, although recovery was slow.[24]

By contrast, the town of Westminster was of middling size: in 1300, when it was at its medieval peak, and again, after many vicissitudes, in the early sixteenth century, the population probably numbered about 3,000.[25] But it was unusual among English towns as the site of a royal palace and unique as the seat of government. As landlords, consumers, and employers, the monks had daily contacts with the townsmen and townswomen. In religious matters, however, the Abbey was less important to the town by 1500 than in 1200, such was the success of the parish church of St. Margaret's, adjacent to the Abbey, in supplying the religious needs of the urban population by the later date and in fostering a strong sense of community among its members.[26] Inside the monastery, the life of the community changed profoundly in the course of this long period. The decline of the common life that now occurred, though seen most clearly in the lives of the obedientiaries and other monks living in private chambers, affected the entire number. Even the so-called cloister-monks, who still ate the common meals, slept in the common dormitory, and, more frequently than other monks, participated in the Divine Office in choir, now enjoyed a degree of singularity in their lives that an eleventh- or twelfth-century monk would have found astonishing.[27]

Family money and receipts from other external sources

In the time of Abbot Laurence (1158–1173), a monk of Westminster named Peter Wyndesore possessed a house in Fishmarket, in the city of London, and gave it to the monastery on condition that it be granted to Richard of Ilchester, archdeacon of Poitiers, and his heirs.[28] But the first monk known to us who possessed

---

[24] *Documents Illustrating the Rule of Walter de Wenlok, Abbot of Westminster, 1283–1307*, ed. Barbara F. Harvey, Camden Society, 4th ser., 2 (London: Royal Historical Society, 1964) (hereafter *Documents*, ed. Harvey), 198, 203; Flete, *History of Westminster Abbey*, 128; Harvey, *Living and Dying*, 73.

[25] Gervase Rosser, *Medieval Westminster 1200–1540* (Oxford: Clarendon Press, 1989), 167–69, 177–79.

[26] Rosser, *Medieval Westminster*, 251–74, and J. F. Merritt, *The Social World of Early Modern Westminster: Abbey, Court and Community, 1525–1640* (Manchester: Manchester University Press, 2005), 18–25.

[27] For wider changes, see James G. Clark, "The Religious Orders in Pre-Reformation England," in *Religious Orders in Pre-Reformation England*, ed. idem, 3–33; cf. Knowles, *Religious Orders*, 2: 240–44.

[28] Westminster Abbey Muniments (hereafter cited as WAM), Muniment Book 11 (known and hereafter cited as Westminster Domesday), fol. 368, *Westminster Abbey Charters, 1066–c. 1214*, ed. Emma Mason (London Record Soc. 25, 1988), no. 277. Richard

money acquired outside the monastery and administered it—and, indeed, the last known to us for some time—occurs in the early thirteenth century. Between 1222 and 1226, Abbot Richard de Berking instituted an anniversary for William le Gras, Richard le Gras, William's son, and Richard's relatives. He did so at the instance of Richard, who was himself a monk of Westminster. On the day of the anniversary, there was to be a refection of wine and a "good pittance" in the refectory, and to pay for this Richard had acquired a messuage and lands in Stevenage (Herts.), where the Abbey already held property.[29] Richard's retention of his family name in religion, in a period when locative names indicating place of origin became common at Westminster, suggests that his family was well known or of high status, or both. His father may have been William le Gros, alias Gras, a knight in the service of the Marshal earls of Pembroke in the early thirteenth century. Richard himself probably received a university education. Later, although, as far as we know, after his departure from Westminster to become Prior of Hurley, he became an influential royal servant and counsellor.[30] Abbot Berking's provision that after Richard's death the anniversary should be moved to that date from 28 February, the interim date, suggests that Richard and not his father was the person to be principally commemorated. If so, the money with which he purchased the property at Stevenage may have been family money in a special sense: it was money of his own which he had brought with him when he entered the monastery. Whatever the truth on this point, the episode shows that it was still possible in the early thirteenth century for a well-connected monk not only to possess, for however short a time, money acquired outside the Abbey's nascent wage-system but also to administer it in person. Thirty years and more later, under Abbot Richard de Ware (1258–1283), a monk of Westminster might still enjoy the spiritual benefit of an individual anniversary, financed by family or friends, or by both, but no longer, it appears, did he administer the money or participate as a principal in the purchase of the endowments: the abbot and convent corporately now fulfilled these roles.[31]

As far as we know, the capacity of monks of Westminster to receive, as individuals, post-obit gifts of money and administer them still lay in the future. To

---

of Ilchester gave the abbot and convent of Westminster ten marks (£6 13s. 4d.) and the transaction between these two parties was probably a sale.

[29] WAM 5399*. For Richard le Gras (alias Crassus), who had left Westminster for Hurley Priory by a date early in 1226, see *The Heads of Religious Houses in England and Wales, 2 (1216–1377)*, ed. David M. Smith and Vera C. M. London (Cambridge: Cambridge University Press, 2001) (hereafter *Heads of Religious Houses, 2*), 41, 113.

[30] Carpenter, "King Henry III and Saint Edward the Confessor," 875–76.

[31] See transactions relating to the anniversaries founded, respectively, for John le Fundur and Gregory Tayleboys (Westminster Domesday, fols. 252r, 460v, 461r): E. H. Pearce, *The Monks of Westminster* (Cambridge: Cambridge University Press, 1916) (hereafter Pearce, *Monks*), 52–53.

be recognized, it required acceptance within the monastery that such bequests would not incur the taint of *proprietas*; and acceptance on the part of the testator's family that a monk might share in the portion of movable goods now by custom reserved for the wife and children of the testator. Such bequests tend to occur in our sources in the second half of the fourteenth century and subsequently.[32] If, in accordance with a common testamentary procedure, the money was to be raised by the sale of immovable goods, the responsibility for the sale might be entrusted to the monk himself, as supervisor of the will. In 1432, John Cambridge was named as a legatee in the will of his father, Roger Kyche of Cambridge, and as supervisor. His bequest of £5 was to take effect on the death of Alice Kyche, Roger's widow, when he was to sell the tenement in which Roger's will gave her a life-interest, distribute identical bequests to two other sons, and distribute the remaining proceeds for the good of Richard's soul.[33] But bequests of money were not received only from relatives. In 1392/3, Matilda Penne, a London widow living in Wood Street, in the parish of St. Peter Westcheap, who continued her husband's business as a skinner, bequeathed 6s. 8d. each to John Wrotting and John Stowe.[34] The Abbey held substantial property in Wood Street, and it is likely that Matilda became acquainted with the two monks when they came to collect the Abbey's rents or inspect the property.

Family opposition to a bequest to a monk of Westminster came to the surface as late as the end of the fifteenth century, when the brother and two sisters, the surviving siblings, of Thomas Gardiner, who entered the monastery in 1492/3, attempted to reclaim the sum of £25 which he had received as his portion under the will of his father, William Gardiner, a Londoner.[35] But it seems likely

---

[32] For bequests of money to monks of Westminster in, respectively, the wills of Richard Ruthyn, a London mercer, in 1361, and Henry Sudbury, a London skinner, in 1375, see London Metropolitan Archives, Husting Roll, 89 (126), and 110 (4); and for summaries, *Calendar of Wills Proved and Enrolled in the Court of Husting, London, A. D. 1258-A.D. 1688*, ed. R. R. Sharpe, 2 vols. (London: J. C. Francis, 1889–1890), 2: 34–35, and 225.

[33] WAM 25364; Pearce, *Monks*, 136–37. The will is dated 26 Sept. 1432.

[34] Elspeth Veale, "Matilda Penne, skinner (d. 1392/3)," in *Medieval London Widows 1300–1500*, ed. Caroline M. Barron and Anne F. Sutton (London: Hambledon, 1994), 51. Stowe also received a basin and ewer. Wrotting/Wratting had been collector of the Abbey rents in Wood Street, 1355–1362 (Pearce, *Monks*, 99).

[35] The National Archives, Public Record Office, C1/252/12, a petition in Chancery dated on the dorse 18 Feb. 1502. William Gardyner/Gardiner had two sons and three daughters with Ellen, his wife, but one of the daughters died before litigation began. The surviving siblings apparently claimed that Thomas had entered religion before their father's bequest of £100, to be shared equally among his children as each became of age, took effect. The petitioners, Peter Watson, a London draper, and William Sybson, the second husband of Ellen, who was herself an executor of William Gardiner's will, disputed this claim. Watson was surety for Sybson. For Thomas Gardiner, see Nigel Ramsay,

that in the later Middle Ages the monks normally received the bequests that are recorded and that testators made such arrangements in the knowledge that they were acceptable to all parties. In fact, even in the later Middle Ages, family money did sometimes find its way into the *peculium* in this monastery.

The wage-system

The forms of wages noted by Knowles in the wider monastic Order can easily be recognised at Westminster, but nothing is known here about the origins of the earliest among them. Spice money has left no trace in abbey sources until the 1280s. Then, as part of the endowment of his anniversary, Abbot Wenlok granted his monks £4 per annum from rents received by the Abbey from its fair at Westminster, to provide every professed monk with one shilling for spices on the morrow of the feast of St. Barbara (13 December), any surplus to be kept by the monks for wine and a pittance.[36] We can be confident that what was new at this relatively late date was not spice money but the proposal to endow it in such a way that there would be a surplus each year, and it is of interest that despite Wenlok's undertaking, this proposal had not taken effect at the time of his death.

Similarly, clothes money was older than the first reference to it in our sources and its future development still uncertain in the late thirteenth century. The first reference occurs in the Abbey's *Customary*, completed in 1266, and it relates to a complicated scheme, best understood as a product of piecemeal change over a considerable period of time, designed principally to enable the chamberlain to live within his income. At this date most items of clothing were still issued as a matter of routine or, like breeches and shirts, whenever needed, but a number were now provided on a rota, and when a monk's turn came on the rota he could opt for money in lieu. Each year, twenty-eight monks were entitled to new coverlets for their beds or to 6s. in lieu, forty-four to new tunics (2s.), and fifty to new fur-lined hoods (probably 1s.). In lieu of the pelisse, a garment lined with sheepskin, which was no longer, it appears, issued routinely to anyone, each monk received 2s. 6d. per annum.[37] By the early fourteenth century, winter and summer

---

"Gardiner, Thomas," in *Oxford Dictionary of National Biography*, 60 vols. (Oxford: Oxford University Press, 2004), 21: 445.

[36] *Documents*, ed. Harvey, 20. For spices, see Christopher Dyer, *Standards of Living in the Later Middle Ages: Social Change in England 1200–1520* (Cambridge: Cambridge University Press, 1998), 62–63.

[37] *Customary of the Benedictine Monasteries of Saint Augustine, Canterbury, and Saint Peter, Westminster*, ed. Edward Maunde Thompson, 2 vols., Henry Bradshaw Society 23, 28 (London: Harrison & Sons, 1902–1904) (hereafter *Customary*), 2: 149. I have interpreted this difficult passage in the light of the similar but clearer one relating to clothes and clothes money at St. Augustine's, Canterbury (*Customary*, 1: 196). The omission from the Westminster Customary of money in lieu of fur-lined hoods is probably accidental;

boots had been put on the rota; and although every monk was still entitled to a new outer habit every year, he could now opt for money (7s. or 8s.) in lieu.[38] All such payments ceased at Westminster on the publication of Benedict XII's decree in 1336, condemning clothes money; but the introduction of a new allowance of 10s. per annum to every monk in the 1350s may well represent delayed compensation for this earlier loss. This sum was added to an existing payment by the treasurers of 10s. per annum, and both together are said initially to be *pro camera* but are later described as a stipend.[39]

Clothes money, however, was soon eclipsed in importance as a component of a monk's wages at Westminster by the surplus issues of the major royal foundations. At first, per capita shares in these fluctuated markedly according to three variables: the annual returns from the estates comprised in the endowments, the number of monks in the community when the distributions were made, and perceptions, which became notably less generous in the course of this period, of the appropriate claims of the poor on the issues of the fund before the surplus was distributed. By 1400, however, a senior monk—that is, a monk who was a priest, and no longer under instruction—could expect to receive £3 per annum or thereabouts from the funds then in existence, and by 1500, £4 per annum, with more soon to come from the foundation of Henry VII.[40]

To these sums we must add many smaller ones, and among them payments for various kinds of work and, by the fifteenth century, for virtually every kind of work not implicit in the essential routine of a Benedictine monk. A major obedientiary could now expect to receive an *ex gratia* payment of £2 per annum for his "good labour," and other senior monks engaging in occasional forms of work outside their ordinary duties could probably earn as much if they were so minded. Thus a monk on the rota to celebrate the daily masses of a chantry in the Abbey earned 1s. per week, and 1s. 8d. in the case of Margaret Beaufort's; and the private founders of anniversaries typically provided 1s. or 2s. for distribution to each

---

for 1s. as the later rate, see WAM 18719–20, and for the pelisse, Barbara F. Harvey, *Monastic Dress in the Middle Ages: Precept and Practice* (Canterbury: William Urry Memorial Trust, 1988), 20.

[38] WAM 18718–20.

[39] WAM 19853–57, and later treasurers' accounts; a rota for the issue of certain items of clothing continued in use. Cf. *The Chronicle of Glastonbury Abbey*, ed. James P. Carley, trans. D. Townsend (Woodbridge: Boydell Press, 1985), 254—an early fourteenth-century reference, where *camera* clearly denotes clothes money paid by the chamberlain.

[40] For 1400, see WAM 23726–43 (Eleanor of Castile), and WAM 23973–4, 23985 (Richard II and Anne of Bohemia); for 1500, WAM 23901–15 (Eleanor of Castile), WAM 24063–73 (Richard II and Anne of Bohemia), and WAM 24178–86 (Henry V). For wages from Henry VII's foundation, see below, n. 44.

monk on the day of the anniversary.[41] A number of anniversary payments, together with some rents, were placed in a fund from which annual shares, known as dividends, were distributed to each monk.[42] In 1460, Thomas Millyng, a student at Oxford, received 6s. 8d. for preaching the Palm Sunday and Good Friday sermons in the abbey church, and twice this amount when he preached in 1464, since he was now a graduate in theology.[43]

By 1500, with these and other sources to draw on, a senior monk of Westminster enjoyed wages amounting to at least £8 per annum; and even a junior monk, not yet a priest, could expect to receive not less than half this amount. And within two or three years, a senior monk's £8 would rise to at least £10 per annum, and those of a junior monk proportionately, as Henry VII's founda tion began to pay wages.[44] In addition to their wages, those who lived in private chambers might receive a pension of 16s. to 20s. per annum, to cover the cost of light and fuel, and a monk of special distinction, as, for example, a graduate, might receive as much as £4 per annum.[45] We may compare these sums with the pensions granted to seven ex-monks of Westminster following the dissolution of the monastery in January 1540—that is, at a time when the mid-Tudor inflation was well under way. These ranged from £3 6s. 8d. to £10 per annum; but only one was as high as £10.[46] In the town of Westminster in the early sixteenth century, a master craftsman, with a household to keep, would probably have considered himself fortunate to earn a steady £7 per annum.[47] Nor must we forget that, notwithstanding his wages, every monk was entitled to the monastery's

---

[41] For *ex gratia* payments to obedientiaries, see e.g., WAM 18888–18890, 18896 (cellarer); WAM 19514, 19459, 19468 (infirmarer); WAM 19747, 19754, 19764 (sacrist). For the weekly rotas and stipends of monks serving the chantries of, respectively, Margaret Beaufort and John Estney, 1505–1509, see WAM 33293, fols. 7–21r; and for the range of payments for chantry and anniversary masses *c.* 1500, WAM 23126–28.

[42] The fund existed by 1366, WAM Muniment Book 1, known and hereafter cited as *Liber niger quaternus*, fol. 99v.

[43] WAM 19710, 19712; A. B. Emden, *Biographical Register of the University of Oxford to A. D. 1500*, 3 vols. (Oxford: Clarendon Press, 1957–1959), 2: 1282–83.

[44] Senior monk: major royal anniversaries, £4; other anniversaries, 15s. 8d.; dividend, 6s. 8d.; stipend, £1; payment for work, £2. A junior monk received *c.* £2 from royal anniversaries, little payment for work, but otherwise comparable payments. From Henry VII's foundation, and beginning in 1502 , a senior monk who attended on all the prescribed occasions received £1 16s. 2d. per annum, and a junior monk *pro rata* (WAM 24236–50).

[45] Pearce, *Monks*, 140, 147–48, 150, 151, and passim.

[46] *Letters and Papers of Henry VIII*, 15: 69 (2), cited in C. S. Knighton, "King's College," in *Westminster Abbey Reformed, 1540–1640*, ed. idem and Richard Mortimer (Aldershot: Ashgate, 2003), 16–37, here 17, n. 5.

[47] On making ends meet in the world at this time, see Dyer, *Standards of Living*, 222–28.

common meals, if he cared to eat them, and to the items of clothing provided by the chamberlain. By 1500, the wage-system placed at least £370 per annum of the Abbey's total net income under the private control of its monks and outside the constraints normally encountered by all forms of monastic expenditure. The sum represents 14–15 percent of the Abbey's total net income at this time.[48]

Spending the peculium

A monastic wage-system implies the existence of an internal market in the monastery in question, where obedientiaries supplied the singular needs of individual monks, and the monks themselves engaged in transactions with each other to the same end. We know that at Westminster in the late Middle Ages, books were sometimes bought and sold in this informal way—as in 1507, when Thomas Sall, a senior monk, sold a book to John Langham, a novice, for one shilling.[49] But here, as in other monasteries, transactions of this kind have left all too few traces in the surviving sources for our purpose: the sources focus more often on the corporate life of the monks than on individuals and their private spending. The more informal the document, however, the greater the possibility that it will record this kind of transaction and others in which monks spent their wages; and some informal and intimate sources recording details of this kind survive. Among these are the accounts of the disposal of the goods of, respectively, Richard Exeter (d.1396/7) and John Canterbury (d.1400), each of whom was a senior monk living in private quarters at the time of his death.[50] With due caution, we can identify many of the uses to which monks of Westminster of varying status in the monastery devoted their personal incomes in the period 1250 to 1540.

In the wider monastic world, the claims on monastic charity of poor relatives outside the cloister were one of the seeds from which the wage-system grew. At Westminster, towards the end of the thirteenth century, the experience of Abbot Wenlok alerts us to the lengths to which family claims could be taken, although he was by no means dependent on the fourfold wages which he received as abbot, for he enjoyed a much larger income from his separate portion of lands. He supported his mother, the widow of an apothecary, a sister, a niece, and at least three nephews, two of the latter being for a time at Oxford, and probably several more

---

[48] An estimate allowing for 32 senior monks and 16 juniors in addition to the abbot, who received fourfold wages, and the prior, who received double, and a total net income in 1500—that is, before the monks began to receive the surplus of Henry VII's foundation—of £2,560. The comparable figure in 1535, when the Abbey had a net income of £2,830 per annum, was £460 to £470 per annum, and this represented 16–17% of the whole.

[49] WAM 18793, fol. 41v.

[50] WAM 6603, 18883A; Pearce, *Monks*, 101–2, 107–8.

relatives.[51] To have nephews in need of support was a hazard of ecclesiastical promotion in the Middle Ages. But life-cycle poverty was also an ever-present feature of medieval life, and as widow and orphan Wenlok's mother and sister may indeed have experienced straitened circumstances. William Boston, the last abbot of Westminster before the Dissolution, has left fewer sources for the study of his abbacy than Wenlok of his and may also have had fewer dependent relatives. In 1538, however, he paid 6d. for each of two pairs of shoes and 10d. for a primer, for one Elizabeth Benson. Abbot Boston's family name was Benson, and Elizabeth was no doubt a relative.[52] In general, family piety of this kind is rarely in evidence in our sources, and the same is true of other kinds of discriminating charity that we might expect to be in favor with monks who had money to spare in the later Middle Ages. At the time of his death, Richard Exeter, who had formerly been prior but had resigned this office fourteen or fifteen years previously, was paying fees for two boys at the Abbey's almonry school, at a total cost of 6s. per annum. A modest outlay, we may think, on the part of one who enjoyed a pension of £3 6s. 8d. per annum in addition to the double wages to which a former prior, no less than a serving one, was entitled, and who left £4 13s. 4d. in gold among his goods.[53] But a monk's private charity, whether directed towards relatives or more widely, is more likely than any other possible use of the *peculium* to escape notice in our sources, and its actual extent in this context is an open question.

The desire for spiritual benefits, to ease or shorten the passage of a monk's soul through Purgatory, has left more traces in our sources than has charity. It was the universal Benedictine practice to offer both community and private masses for a deceased monk for a period, often for thirty days, after his death, and each year, on the anniversary he was commemorated with others who had died on the same day in the calendar. At Westminster, moreover, from 1391, and probably from an earlier date, a daily mass for deceased monks was celebrated by a rota of monks at St. Andrew's altar in the abbey church.[54]

But more was sometimes desired, and in a long fourteenth century and much shorter fifteenth, indulgences seem to have taken the place previously occupied by private anniversaries in the spiritual strategies of a number of monks. These were at first collective indulgences, granted by some of the archbishops and bishops who existed on the periphery of curial life at Rome or Avignon to all who should visit

[51] *Documents*, ed. Harvey, 52, 88 (127), 210, 213, 246 and n. 8.

[52] WAM 33332, fols. 2v, 4v. The cost, 10d., suggests that the primer was printed. Cf. Eamon Duffy, *Marking the Hours: English People and their Prayers 1240–1570* (New Haven: Yale University Press, 2006), 4.

[53] WAM 6603. The sum of 13d. was distributed in alms at Exeter's funeral. See also R. Bowers, "The Almonry Schools of the English Monasteries c.1265–1540," in *Monasteries and Society in Medieval Britain*, ed. Benjamin Thompson (Stamford: Paul Watkins, 1999), 177–222, here 215–16.

[54] WAM 18525–30.

the abbey church on prescribed days in the calendar, but with benefits extending explicitly to those praying for a particular monk, who was in fact the prime mover in obtaining the indulgence. Family and friends might also be included. Alexander de Pershore, sent to Rome in 1298 to pursue entirely different business on behalf of the Abbey, seized the opportunity to obtain such an indulgence from fifteen archbishops and bishops. It benefited in particular those who should pray for him and for the soul of Thomas de Lenton (evidently a former friend), or walk round Lenton's tomb in the monks' cemetery at Westminster.[55] While at Avignon in 1334, no doubt on business for the Abbey, Philip de Brightwell obtained a similar collective indulgence, benefiting in particular those who should pray for himself, his deceased parents, his relatives, and those present at masses and other services at St. Agatha's church at West Brightwell (Berkshire), and the church's benefactors.[56] In such cases, only a small part of the total cost of the indulgence, if as much, came from the *peculium* of the monk obtaining the indulgence: the main cost was in the journey to Rome and Avignon, residence there, and necessary expenditure at the curia, and for all of these the abbot and convent, who had sent the monk as their proctor for other reasons, paid.

Later, and inevitably, plenary papal indulgences were more sought after than episcopal indulgences, and in the exceptional years 1349 and 1351, a total of ten monks of Westminster obtained such indulgences, either individually or as members of a group, although, it is unlikely that more than two of the ten — Simon Langham, abbot-elect, and Benedict de Chertsey, Langham's successor as prior — actually travelled to Avignon or Rome.[57] Later still, monks of

---

[55] Westminster Domesday, fol. 403. The indulgence is dated 18 July 1298, and in common with the other collective indulgences mentioned in the text, it survives in a cartulary copy. Pershore also obtained for the abbot and convent a collective episcopal indulgence, dated 4 Feb. 1299, of the normal kind, benefiting those who visited or helped the Abbey (Westminster Domesday, fol. 403v; and for the expenses of obtaining it, WAM 9243). For collective episcopal indulgences, see P. N. R. Zutshi, "Collective Indulgences from Rome and Avignon in English Collections," in *Medieval Ecclesiastical Studies in Honour of Dorothy M. Owen*, ed. M. J. Franklin and Christopher Harper-Bill (Woodbridge: Boydell Press, 1995), 281–93, and R. N. Swanson, *Indulgences in Late Medieval England* (Cambridge: Cambridge University Press, 2007), 38–41.

[56] Westminster Domesday, fol. 407v. The indulgence is dated 28 Feb. 1334. For similar indulgences obtained, by or for, respectively, Hugh de Papworth, with the same date, and Adam de London, dated 25 Oct. 1342, see fols. 407v, 408r; and for Brightwell, Papworth, and London, Pearce, *Monks*, 79, 81–82, 89.

[57] *Calendar of Papal Registers: Papal Letters*, 3 *(1342–1362)*: 159, 310–11, 327, 410; *Calendar of Papal Registers: Petitions*, 1 *(1342–1419)*: 171. In this paragraph, I have not attempted to distinguish between the various forms of benefit in plenary indulgences that occur in the sources. For the indispensable account of the system, see Swanson, *Indulgences in Late Medieval England*, 30–34, 114–22; and for a brief account of late medieval developments, Diana Webb, "Pardons and Pilgrims," in *Promissory Notes on the Treasury*

Westminster, though not in great numbers, were among those taking advantage of the availability of such indulgences, as a matter of routine, to those who did not leave England. Between 1397 and 1436, eleven, to our knowledge, obtained plenary indulgences under these conditions, and after a long interval, two more did so, in 1468.[58] In all these cases, we can assume that each monk met the cost of the actual indulgence together with any additional expenses incurred in a transaction involving a pardoner or other kind of agent, or paid his share if the transaction involved a group.

As, in the mid-fifteenth century, plenary indulgences from Rome became less attractive to the monks of Westminster, or simply harder to obtain, so did the monks begin to seek spiritual benefits through membership of fraternities or guilds in the town of Westminster and the City of London. At least eleven were members of the Assumption guild of St Margaret's church in Westminster in the fifteenth century or the early sixteenth, and, since the records of this guild are far from complete, the actual number may have been larger.[59] Between 1448 and 1521, however, nearly forty monks of Westminster joined the Fraternity of St. Nicholas, the guild of the parish clerks of London, or had already been admitted by the earlier date, when the records of this guild begin. For an entry fee probably amounting to a few shillings, and a quarterly subscription of perhaps no more than a few pence, each one acquired a share in the prayers offered daily for members of that fraternity at the altar of St. Nicholas in the chapel of the London Guildhall.[60] Nevertheless, for some monks older forms of spiritual benefit retained their attraction. The settlement of the debts of Humfrey Litlyngton, a cloister-monk, after his death in 1502, shows that he had purchased the jubilee indulgence of 1500, for two shillings;[61] and when, in 1529, Thomas Ledgold and Christopher Godehappes made the pilgrimage to the shrine of St. Thomas the

of Merits: Indulgences in Late Medieval Europe, ed. R. N. Swanson (Leiden: Brill, 2006), 244–63. For costs, see W. E. Lunt, *Financial Relations of the Papacy with England, 1327–1534* (Cambridge, MA: Medieval Academy of America, 1962), 457–59.

[58] *Calendar of Papal Registers: Papal Letters*, 5 *(1396–1404)*: 41, 122, 126, 148, 231; 6 *(1404–1415)*: 335; 7 *(1417–1431)*: 329, 330, 332, 333; 8 *(1427–1447)*: 615; 12 *(1458–1471)*: 614.

[59] Accounts of the Westminster guilds of the Virgin's Assumption, 1474–1477, 1487–1490, 1505–1508, 1515–1521 (unnumbered WAM), fols. 15v, 16r. For the names, see Rosser, *Medieval Westminster*, 261 n., but add W. Milton and J. Flete. For the special form of friendship cultivated in this as in other guilds, see G. Rosser, "Party List: Making Friends in English Medieval Guilds," in *London and the Kingdom: Essays in Honour of Caroline M. Barron*, ed. Matthew Davies and Andrew Prescott, Harlaxton Medieval Studies 16 (London: Shaun Tyas, 2008), 118–34, here 127.

[60] *The Bede Roll of the Fraternity of St Nicholas*, ed. N. W. and V. A. James, 2 vols. (London: London Record Society, 2004), 1: xxviii. The monks in question are identified by the editors in the annotated roll.

[61] WAM 33288, fol. 20v.

martyr at Canterbury, we can assume that each monk met his expenses from his own resources.[62]

Material goods purchased with the *peculium* tended to be more expensive, item for item, than the later forms of spiritual benefit. Monks living privately had more need of these than those who still followed the common life, and since private hospitality was a concomitant of living privately, they had more opportunity than others to display their possessions. By the end of the fourteenth century, there were probably fourteen or fifteen so-called chambers for their use. These ranged in size from a spacious apartment, which might be shared by more than one occupant, to a single room. Although each chamber was provided with basic furniture and furnishings, more could be added or better substituted. On the death of the monk in question, however, all such additions were either assigned by the abbot or prior as he saw fit, to deserving departments in the monastery or to its dependent cells or manor houses at a distance, or sold under his direction to other monks with their own chambers to furnish. John Canterbury was cellarer and granger until a few days before his death on 15 August 1400, and evidently he died in the cellarer's chamber. We need not doubt, however, that all the fittings and furnishings now inventoried and distributed under the prior's direction had been acquired by Canterbury from his own resources.[63] These included a featherbed (now assigned to the infirmarer), its two canvases (one to the prior, and one to John Colandwode), and three mattresses (severally, to the prior, the hosteller, and the infirmary), a coverlet, tester, canopy, and three curtains of red worsted (to a chamber in the refectory), another coverlet and tester (to John Sandon, now demitting office as refectorer), and two old and worn curtains (to John Colandwode), four basins and ewers, which were probably of silver (one sent to the manor house at Steventon,[64] one to the prior, and one to John Sandon), six mazers, one with a silver gilt cover, weighing eleven and a half ounces (to the prior), six pieces of silver, weighing sixty-eight ounces (one, with a cover, to the abbot), a silver powder box weighing eight ounces (to the abbot), twenty-four silver spoons weighing twenty-nine ounces (twelve to the abbot), two silver saltcellars, of which one was covered, weighing eleven ounces (to the misericord, the alternative refectory used for meals where flesh-meat was consumed), four tablecloths of Paris work (one to the hostelry, one to the refectory, and two to the misericord), and many other items.

---

[62] For this and other pilgrimages made in the years around 1500, see Harvey, *Living and Dying*, 80–81, and n. 37.

[63] For the following details, see WAM 18883A. John Colandwode, who is mentioned, may have been one of the cellarer's senior servants.

[64] The manor house at Steventon (Berks.) was used by monks of Westminster studying at Oxford for recreation, and on visits to preach in the parish church (WAM Lease Bk. 1: fol. 137r; Bk. 2: fol. 149v).

As a former prior, Richard Exeter may have occupied quarters that were even more spacious than Canterbury's, and hall, buttery, kitchen, chamber, and study are all mentioned in the inventory of his goods made after his death.[65] In accordance with custom in the case of privately owned books, his diverse collection, including a "book of Marco Polo," apparently bound with Higden's *Polychronicon*, and Richard Rolle's *Incendium Amoris*, would now have been assigned to the monastic library.[66] Other goods were dispersed, and in many cases sold, again under the prior's direction. Exeter had less silver than Canterbury—thirteen spoons, for example, compared to Canterbury's twenty-four—and apparently nothing of this kind that the abbot wished to have. His gold signet was sold to Ralph Tonworth, who had just taken up his first major obedience, that of the sacrist, for £2;[67] his *pannus de Maria et David'*, a hanging, perhaps depicting the genealogy of Jesus, was given to John London, the abbey recluse.

How far monks who did not live privately emulated those who did by themselves spending money on fittings and furnishings, if not on household goods, is uncertain. From the early fourteenth century onwards, every monk sleeping in the dormitory, as these did, occupied his own cubicle, or cell, separated from its neighbours by muslin or buckram curtains. In the wider Benedictine world, cells in dormitories were scarcely older than the expressed belief that they were used for the concealment of illicit possessions.[68] They were indeed the only private place that most monks of Westminster enjoyed. We can be confident that clothes were kept there, and very likely books, including some that had been purchased with the *peculium*, and the monk's savings: by the sixteenth century even the abbot kept money in a chest in the dormitory.[69] But what other material goods such monks possessed, we do not know, nor is it possible to assign any of the books with an *ex libris* inscription surviving from Westminster to a monk who was to our knowledge always a cloister-monk, though many such books may have existed.[70]

---

[65] WAM 6603.

[66] *English Benedictine Libraries: The Shorter Catalogues*, ed. R. Sharpe, J. P. Carley, R. M. Thomson, and A. G. Watson, Corpus of British Medieval Library Catalogues 4 (London: The British Library in association with The British Academy, 1996), 611, 627–29.

[67] For Tonworth, who spent a total of £6 on this occasion, see Pearce, *Monks*, 116.

[68] *Chapters of English Black Monks*, 2: 47–48; also 88, 224; and Harvey, *Living and Dying*, 77, 130.

[69] WAM 24281, attachment. For books in monastic dormitories in this period, see James G. Clark, *A Monastic Renaissance at St Albans: Thomas Walsingham and his Circle c.1350–1440* (Oxford: Clarendon Press, 2004), 130–32, and for reading on one's bed at the siesta, *Customary*, 2: 146. On the paucity of evidence relating both to the monastic library and to books in private possession at Westminster, see *English Benedictine Libraries: The Shorter Catalogues*, ed. Sharpe et al., 609–10.

[70] Cf. Clark, *Monastic Renaissance at St Albans*, 88.

In the matter of clothing it is clear that the wage-system put diversity and quality within the reach of all monks, whatever their status. In monastic life, fashion did not stand still, although it moved very slowly.[71] In Westminster Abbey, rising standards of living outside the cloister were reflected in the desire for the use of better materials in garments long established as parts of a monk's wardrobe, and sometimes in the addition of new kinds of garment to the latter. At his death, Richard Exeter possessed two frocks and three cowls, the first of these garments being the formal and the second the informal outer garment. It made sense and had long been customary to have two of each. But two of the cowls and one frock are described as livery: they represented the chamberlain's normal issue, and at this date he probably used serge for the purpose. The third cowl was made of worsted, a superior cloth, and this was no doubt also true of the second frock, which is described as Exeter's best frock.[72] It seems clear that Exeter had provided himself with the superior cowl and frock at his own expense.

A century later, even junior monks had best wear at their own expense. In 1502, for example, a serge cowl was purchased for Thomas Stowell at a cost of 4s. 6d., but in the following year, a worsted cowl at a cost of 16s. 8d. Stowell had been a monk since 1498/9, but he was still engaged in formal studies and, in status, a novice.[73] It seems very likely, too, that all monks paid for the separate nightclothes, consisting of coats, caps, and kerchiefs, that were now a feature of their wardrobe, and may long have been so, but never appears as an item of expenditure in the chamberlain's accounts. For many years, they had, almost certainly, met out of their own resources the cost of several necessary items of clothing—tunics, fur-lined hoods, and summer hose—that the chamberlain himself no longer issued or for which he substituted clothes money.[74] With privatization went some small departures from the regular dress of a Benedictine monk, including, in Richard Exeter's case, a tunic with a striped lining—a source of pleasure presumably hidden from every eye except Exeter's own.[75]

Many gifts to the abbey church and its shrine or to the monastic buildings and their furnishings are recorded. Monks seem to have given individually to the shrine, and some, like Christopher Godehappes, who entered the monastery in 1506/7, gave relics: in this case, a relic of St. Christopher.[76] But behind many

---

[71] Harvey, *Monastic Dress*, 7–14; and for uniformity of dress among Augustinian canons as an end and not a beginning, Alison D. Fizzard, "Shoes, Boots, Leggings and Cloaks: The Augustinian Canons and Dress in Later Medieval England," *Journal of British Studies* 46 (2007): 245–62.

[72] "frocum bonum" (WAM 6603). Modern Benedictine practice reverses the medieval use of the terms cowl and frock.

[73] WAM 33288, fol. 22.

[74] Harvey, *Monastic Dress*, 16, and for nightclothes, 27–28.

[75] Harvey, *Monastic Dress*, 21; cf. *Customary*, 2: 147.

[76] WAM 9485; Westlake, *Westminster Abbey*, 2: 501.

gifts of this kind lay a corporate decision to support a good cause by a levy on every member of the community; the obligation might continue for several years or be for a short term and in this case give rise to an ad hoc subscription list. In 1492, the repair of two so-called seyny books was achieved by such a list: these were the books provided for monks recovering from a blood-letting, who were allowed to sit during the Divine Office in a place outside the choir of the church. On this occasion, the agreed subscription was evidently three shillings and four pence for a senior monk and two shillings for a junior, but special arrangements were permitted. In lieu of a standard subscription, Thomas Flete paid for "stuff"—perhaps the three white and four red skins purchased at a total cost of two shillings and eight pence—and William Lokynton for "peecyng." We should probably understand by the latter term the copying from other exemplars of quires or folios that were needed to replace worn originals in the seyny books now under repair.[77] Flete also provided board and Lokynton a bed for the so-called "writer" whose services were needed.[78] From 1468 to 1522, all monks contributed at a per capita rate of 13s. 4d. per annum to the new work in the nave;[79] and in 1509 another subscription list, though one to which others beside monks contributed, produced the sum of £7 0s. 4d. for the dismantling of the temporary wall screening the new work from the choir of the church, the latter having continued in use while the new work was in progress.[80]

It was also possible to harness the contributions made by monks individually to a large design, and this, it seems clear, happened at Westminster in the later fourteenth century. The process of renovating and, in one or two cases, building chapels in the ambulatory and transepts of the abbey church probably began in the mid-1360s, or a little earlier, and in ignorance of the fact that the rebuilding of the nave of the church, made possible by the gifts and bequests of the exceedingly wealthy Cardinal Langham, formerly abbot of Westminster, would begin in the mid-1370s.[81] Although the sacrist is not explicitly identified with this project in our sources, a central role for him can be assumed, since he was the

---

[77] Cf. Graham Pollard, "The *pecia* System in the Medieval Universities," in *Medieval Scribes, Manuscripts and Libraries: Essays Presented to N. R. Ker,* ed. M. B. Parkes and Andrew G. Watson (London: Scolar Press, 1978), 145–61, here 152–56.

[78] WAM 9326, printed in J. Armitage Robinson and M. R. James, *The Manuscripts of Westminster Abbey* (Cambridge: Cambridge University Press, 1909), 9–11; and see *Customary,* 2: 43, 239, 241.

[79] R. B. Rackham, "The Nave of Westminster," *Proceedings of the British Academy* 4 (1909–1910): 33–96, here 64–65, 91.

[80] WAM 33293, fol. 38v. On this occasion, not all the contributors were monks.

[81] Flete, *History of Westminster Abbey,* 132; Rackham, "Nave of Westminster Abbey," 38–39. The departure of William Bromley, a donor, for Hurley Priory, which probably occurred in 1365, provides an approximate term for the beginning of the work on the chapels (*Heads of Religious Houses,* 2 [*1216–1377*]: 114).

obedientiary principally responsible for the church's altars other than that in the Lady Chapel. We should perhaps see the fine new inventory of the vestry, a sub-department of the sacristy, which was completed by four senior monks in 1388, as itself a feature of the current renovation of altars and chapels.[82]

These improvements and a smaller number relating to the furnishing and decoration of parts of the cloister, the chapter house, and St. Katherine's chapel in the infirmary are recorded in a list of donors preserved in the abbey register known as the *Liber niger quaternus*. The list is composite and draws on at least two earlier sources of a similar kind. In this, its final form, no donor who entered the monastery after 1387/8 is mentioned; and since it is noted that the painting of the Apocalypse in the chapter house, given by John Northampton, was not yet finished, a date of compilation before Northampton's death in 1404 or not long after that event seems likely.[83] If so, the opening years of the fifteenth century may provide the term for the completion of the entire enterprise beginning in the 1360s. Monks participating in any of the works comprised in it could hope to find a means of expressing, not only their devotional sympathies, but also their aesthetic perceptions. This is implied in the choice of words in the list, where it is said of each monk donor, in respect of the work or works for which he paid, *fecit* or *fieri fecit*, meaning, in all probability, that he commissioned it; if so, we should probably understand that his views counted in the orders given to the masons and artists involved.[84]

Fifteen monks[85] are named in the list, and we know from other sources that their monastic careers varied widely, from that of Richard Merston, who was an obedientiary within a few years of entering the monastery in 1346/7 and prior from 1362–1376, to that of John Northampton, who, as far as we know, spent the years from his profession *c.*1372 to his death in 1404 as a cloister-monk.[86] We are told the amounts given by eight donors and a portion of what was given by three

---

[82] J. Wickham Legg, "On an Inventory of the Vestry in Westminster Abbey, Taken in 1388," *Archaeologia* 52 (1890): 195–286, here 274. For the sacrists of the relevant period, see Pearce, *Monks*, 197.

[83] *Liber niger quaternus*, fol. 92v. The title given here, *Sequuntur hic de renovatoribus et benefactoribus capellarum in circuitu infra ecclesiam monasterii Westm'*, omitting as it does the works outside the abbey church, may derive from one of the components. For the names in the list and the particular works associated with each, see Westlake, *Westminster Abbey*, 1: 125–26. Two secular donors are included and a rogue entry relates to John Sutton, a monk of Westminster in the late thirteenth century. For the murals of the Apocalypse and the Judgement in the chapter house, both of which were given by John Northampton and survive, see Binski, *Westminster Abbey and the Plantagenets*, 187–91.

[84] Cf. Paul Binski, "Abbot Berkyng's Tapestries and Matthew Paris's Life of St. Edward the Confessor," *Archaeologia* 109 (1991): 85–100, here 85. The words are not used of the secular donors.

[85] Excluding John Sutton, for whom see n. 83.

[86] Pearce, *Monks*, 95–96, 112.

others. The prior of Westminster had only a small income ex officio, and it seems clear that the capacity of Prior Merston to give one hundred marks (£66 13s. 4d.) to build the altar of St. Blaise, in the south transept, and a further twenty marks (£13 6s. 8d.) to provide a crucifix by the seat of the novice-master in the cloister derived principally from his *peculium*.[87] But among the eight, three others gave sums exceeding a year's minimum wages for a senior monk at this date, as did two of the three for whom we do not have a final figure.[88]

Gifts to the monastic offices, or departments, were more haphazardly recorded than those for the larger design considered above; and on some occasions, to our knowledge, goods assigned by the abbot or prior to such an office, after the death of the monk to whom they had previously belonged, were recorded in the next inventory, to the possible confusion of later historians, as an actual gift of that monk.[89] But there may have been an expectation that an obedientiary in charge of an office would make a substantial gift during that period or later, and some gifts of this kind are recorded. Robert Tonworth, as we learn from the inventory of the vestry that he helped to make, gave a set of vestments for the feast of St Nicholas to that office, and it seems likely that he did so during his earlier term of office as vestry keeper.[90] And John Feryng, who, in 1425/6, met the cost of new paving in the infirmary cloister from his own resources, was infirmarer at the time.[91]

Pious purposes ?

When Abbot Samson of Bury St. Edmunds tried to insist that his monks put the money in their chests or boxes to pious uses, he used a phrase of wide application, inside and outside the cloister. Pious uses were good uses, though probably within the limits of Latin Christendom, and possibilities were manifold.[92] Most of

---

[87] After Prior Merston's death on 24 June 1377, his receiver accounted for gross receipts of *c.* £95 since 14 Sept. 1376; but Merston's wages for this period, and the repayment to his estate of two loans, each of £20, contributed more than half this sum: WAM 9498.

[88] Known individual totals in ascending order: William *de reliquiis* (probably William Pulburgh, who entered the monastery in 1383–1384), 10s.; J. Murymouth, £1 6s. 8d.; R. Cirencester, £4 13s. 4d.; J. Feryng, £6 13s. 4d.; R. de Hertford, £13 6s. 8d.; J. Mordon, £15; John Redyng, £20; R. Merston, £80. W. Bromley gave more than £2; R. Kirton (alias Cretton), more than £10; and J. Northampton, more than £14 6s. 8d.

[89] See e.g., the inventory of the hostelry dated 22 Dec. 1400, where a pair of "good" sheets belonging to the recently deceased John Canterbury, and assigned by the prior to the hostelry, are described as a gift from Canterbury (WAM 9480, 18883A).

[90] Wickham Legg, "Inventory of the Vestry," 27, 29–30; and for Tonworth as *vestiarius*, Pearce, *Monks*, 116.

[91] WAM 19414.

[92] W. Lyndwood, *Provinciale* (Oxford, 1679), 180 (gloss on *piæ causæ*); Sheehan, *Will in Medieval England*, 261–62; Swanson, *Indulgences in Late Medieval England*, 46–76; and

the uses of the *peculium* known to us at Westminster would probably have passed the test without difficulty. Not even the purchase of a silver powder bowl and a silver-gilt lid for a mazer cup by an obedientiary for his chamber would certainly have been excluded, for whatever the article in question, the monastery would eventually take possession and benefit accordingly. At Westminster, moreover, as the case of William Sudbury suggests, the canonical requirement that a monk's possessions be approved by his abbot may never have become a dead letter. In 1399, Sudbury, who as a graduate in theology was entitled to occupy a private chamber, considered it fitting to obtain a papal privilege permitting him to keep all his books, jewels, and other goods for life, provided they were saved for the monastery thereafter. He was, perhaps, a little uneasy about the abbot's view of his extensive possessions.[93]

Saving

Yet the monks' savings are as remarkable as their spending. In 1350, John de Ashwell, who had contracted plague in the course of the previous year but recovered, gave the sum of £10 to the high altar as a thank-offering, although his wages at this date were probably less than half this sum.[94] When John Mordon, the infirmarer, died in office in 1379, money amounting to £16 was found in his chamber and assigned to Walter de Warfield, his successor, who took over an office burdened with quite serious debts. In Warfield's first account, however, the sum was distinguished from the normal income of the infirmary: almost certainly, it represents Mordon's personal savings.[95] At his death in 1399, John Canterbury left, in addition to the goods noted above, gold amounting to £11 7s. 8d.; and those administering his estate had now to call in debts owing to him which amounted to £18 16s. 10d. Most of these probably represented loans which he had made, and several debtors now forfeited the pledges they had given.[96] A practice of saving is indeed implied in the capacity of monks to give relatively large sums to the good causes they chose to support.

---

for the wide reference of "pious works" within Latin Christendom, Robert W. Shaffern, "The Medieval Theology of Indulgences," in *Promissory Notes on the Treasury of Merits*, ed. Swanson, 11–36, here 16–17.

[93] *Cal. Papal Registers: Papal Letters*, 5 (*1396–1404*): 197. Cf. Knowles, *Religious Orders*, 2:173.

[94] Oxford Bodleian Library MS. Top. Surrey, d. 4 (R).

[95] WAM 19355–56.

[96] WAM 18883A. At his death, twelve persons owed Canterbury debts to a total amount of £18 16s. 10d. Of these, the two obedientiaries, who together owed £7 10s. 9d., had probably borrowed to meet a need for cash in their official capacity; most of the rest were small debtors.

A wider interest?

The *peculium* at Westminster Abbey remained to some extent insecure until the mid-fourteenth century when, for a time, the monks had neither clothes money nor any monetary compensation for its loss. The calm passage that it enjoyed subsequently is a potent symbol of the decline of the common life, now at an advanced stage here, as in the wider Benedictine world. If we could compile a rank order of *per capita* wages in English Benedictine monasteries in the later Middle Ages—a task for which we do not have the necessary information—the exceptional share obtained by the monks of Westminster in the surplus funds of a number of royal anniversaries would probably ensure a place for them near the top, and quite possibly at the very top. But we have to ask whether arrangements in such a privileged monastery can shed light on the wider scene, or are of merely anecdotal interest.

The striking feature of arrangements at Westminster is the tendency of a monk's wages—always the main component from year to year of the *peculium* in the period for which we have evidence—to move in a circle. In the course of a monk's lifetime, his gifts to the monastery might well return a substantial portion of what it had earlier given to him under this form; and after his death, the monastery took whatever remained of his possessions in cash or kind and disposed of them as the abbot or prior directed. Such a tendency was, no doubt, more conspicuous where wages were large, as at Westminster, than in other monasteries. Where they were small, the monks, though equally loyal towards their monastery, could do less during their lifetime for the fabric of their church than the monks of Westminster, and obedientiaries probably left fewer expensive furnishings in their chambers when they died than their counterparts at Westminster. But the tendency of the monastic wages to move in a circle may have been a common feature of Benedictine life. The wages themselves never ceased to be irregular in the strict sense of the word: they were contrary to the Rule of St. Benedict. By contrast, the return to the monastery after a monk's death, for disposal by the abbot or his deputy, of everything that he had purchased for his own use, and of all his savings, expressed the enduring influence of St. Benedict's peremptory prohibition of private property. Did the knowledge that so much comprised in the *peculium* would in the end return to the monastery, and do so for this reason, help to calm whatever unease still persisted in the cloister about this most irregular feature of monastic life? It seems possible.

CURIOSITIES FROM A SERMON BOOK

SIEGFRIED WENZEL

Medieval sermon books often carry matters of some interest to students other than those focusing on the history of preaching. Thus the study of Middle English literature has received a good deal of input from contemporary sermons that, for instance, throw light on possible sources behind some of *The Canterbury Tales*, or establish the popularity of a putative historical allusion in *Piers Plowman*, or rectify proposed allegorical readings of a medieval song.[1] Other fields of research or intellectual history, too, occasionally benefit from some material preserved in a sermon book, whether it appears actually within a sermon or next to it. Such is the case with MS. Gg.6.26 in the Cambridge University Library. It is a small volume made up irregularly of paper and parchment, with some parchment strips.[2] Its 167 folios measure roughly 160 by 110 mm. with some variation. The texts are written in one column, by various hands of the later fifteenth century. The name John Dotmotte appears several times throughout the volume, and on fol. 4 (medieval 1) Dotmotte of Lewes in Sussex confirms the gift of twenty pounds to John Dayme.[3]

---

[1] The pioneer work in suggesting such a connection was done by G. R. Owst, especially in *Literature and Pulpit in Medieval England: A Neglected Chapter in the History of English Letters and of the English People* (Cambridge: Cambridge University Press, 1933; 2nd rev. ed. Oxford: Blackwell, 1961). Among many other things, Owst suggested that a longer passage in Langland's *Piers Plowman* with the fable of the rats' parliament may have been influenced by a sermon of Bishop Brinton (*Literature and Pulpit*, 583, and earlier in idem, "The 'Angel' and the 'Goliardeys' of Langland's Prologue," *Modern Language Review* 20 [1925]: 270-79). For an example regarding a Middle English lyric see Siegfried Wenzel, "The Moor Maiden: A Contemporary View," *Speculum* 49 (1974): 69-74.

[2] The volume was rebound in 1981, and a modern collation appears on the modern end flyleaf: "1 in 4 (4 cancelled), 2 in 2 (2 canc.), 3 in 16 (14 canc.), 4 in 10 (1 canc.), 5 in 8, 6 in 14 + 1 (fol. 37, a vellum strip), 7 in 14, 8 in 14 (5 canc.), 9 in 14, 10 in 14 (7 canc.), 11 in 14 (5, a half leaf, 7 canc.), 12 in 14, 13? in 16 (4 leaves? gone between fols. 133 + 134, 1 leaf ? gone between fols. 141 + 142), 14 in 12 (2-3 gone), 15 in 14."

[3] On fol. 167 a barely legible note was entered concerning a *tenementum*, with names of several persons (Simon Dunk, Alicia Poode) and places (parish of Sam'e?, Haws?, Dennes Lane, Stonecrosse). Miss Ringrose, Deputy Keeper of Manuscripts at the

The volume is basically a preacher's book, with many sermons derived apparently from Continental sources, including a partial copy of *de tempore* sermons, from Ascension to the tenth Sunday after Trinity, by the German Dominican Johannes Herolt (1380-1468).[4] The sermons are followed by two collections of *Gesta Romanorum*, the second preceded by a tabula.[5] Outside Herolt's sermons (which preserve a German proverb), the volume contains some Middle English material, ranging from individual words to divisions and verses and an entire sermon, which has recently been edited by Andrew Galloway.[6]

With the sermons, exempla, and occasional notes, the book contains several documents and liturgical prayers that were added into existing blank spaces. These include the following:

1. a testimonial that a couple have made their annual confession and paid their tithes;
2. a testimonial for a group of pilgrims;
3. a papal letter allowing the recipient to receive a benefice;
4. the three main prayers, i.e., Collect, Secret, and Post-Communion, from a votive Mass for a pregnant woman.

Several of these documents bear dates in the 1490s, but the personal names that should appear have been reduced to anonymous N's. The four items in question are written in a variety of Secretary (*cursiva currens*) scripts. Items 2-4 appear in seemingly the same hand, while item 1 is written in a different Secretary hand, apparently the same as that of the sermon that precedes it though in lighter ink and employing greater spacing.

In the following transcriptions I reproduce the medieval spellings but silently expand abbreviations and use modern capitalization, punctuation, and paragraph divisions. Material reproduced between slashes (\ /) appears between lines in the manuscript.[7]

University Library, Cambridge, has kindly informed me that nothing is known about these names or the provenance of the volume, except that it came from the Library of John Moore, bishop of Ely (died 1714).

[4] I have discussed the book and its contents in Siegfried Wenzel, *Latin Sermon Collections from Later Medieval England: Orthodox Preaching in the Age of Wyclif* (Cambridge: Cambridge University Press, 2005), 210-12, and inventoried the sermons on 495-99.

[5] The two series (fols. 119-166v, incomplete) may originally have constituted a separate manuscript. They begin on a new quire, with an enlarged initial (fol. 119), and are written in larger Anglicana hands (i.e., the beginning of the first and all of the second series). There is some overlap of story material.

[6] Andrew Galloway, "A Fifteenth-Century Confession Sermon on 'Unkyndeness' (CUL MS Gg.6.26) and Its Literary Parallels and Parodies," *Traditio* 49 (1994): 259-69.

[7] I am grateful to the Syndics of Cambridge University Library for permission to edit these texts.

1. Parochial testimonial of having made the annual confession and paid tithes.

The unnamed parish priest of a church of St. Nicholas sends *literas commendaticeas* to another equally unnamed parish priest testifying that Robert with his wife Joan have made their Lenten confessions and rendered an account of and paid their tithes. No specific date.

[fol. 16] Reuerendo ac peritissimo viro rectori ecclesie parochialis de N. seu eius in hac parte deputato, perpetuus rector ecclesie parochialis [de N., *probably, canceled*] sancti Nicholai de N., salutem in auctore gracie. Ad vestram noticiam deduco presentibus vel per presentes quod Robertus N. nuper de grege meo semel isto tempore quadragesimali apud me erat confessus vna cum vxore sua Johanna ante eorum recessum, necnon et de decimis suis plenarie compotum fecit et soluit. Ad cuius rogatum literas commendaticeas istas in testimonium sue bone conuersacionis mea propria scripsi manu. Valete. Datum apud N. predict' die, mensis et anno Domini.

To the reverend and most skilled rector of the parish church of N. or to his deputy therein, the perpetual rector of the parish church of St. Nicholas sends greetings in the author of grace. I bring to your attention in the present communication or by means of it that Robert N., recently of my flock, made confession before me once in this Lenten season, together with his wife Joan, before their departure, and that he fully rendered account of and gave his tithes. At whose request I have written this letter of recommendation in testimony of his good conduct with my own hand. Farewell. Given at N. on the aforementioned day, month, and year of the Lord.

The text has been entered in the space after the incomplete sermon G-3, apparently in the same hand.

2. Episcopal testimonial and request to aid pilgrims

An unnamed master, commissary of an equally unnamed bishop of England, writes to all the faithful *litere testimoniales* asking them to aid apparently four unnamed persons who are not excommunicated or interdicted and are undertaking a pilgrimage to Rome. Dated 1494.

[fol. 28v] Vniuersis fidelibus ad quos presentes litere testimoniales peruenerint, salutem in Domino sempiternam.

Noueritis quod infrascripti comparuerunt vt boni Christiani et veri peregrini coram nobis Magistro N., commissario reuerendi patris et domini domini [*sic*] N. N. episcopi infra regnum Anglie. Quare intensiue propter Deum pe-

timus vt ex caritate vestra gratuita velitis hiis subuenire viris, scilicet domino
Jo.[8] [N.c.] N. N. N. Atque vere horum singulorum perhibemus testimonium ac ipsos non esse excommunicatos nec interdictos sed omnium morum
honestate circumductos quamuis Christi pauperes, ad limina \sanctorum/
apostolorum ac alia pia loca sanctorum ex voto et deuocione visitatur' pro
salute animarum suarum atque cunctorum eorum benefactorum qui manus
inopie ipsorum porrexerint adnutrices, vt vos qui ipsis subuenitis vna nobiscum or[aci]onum et peregrinacionum suarum efficiamini participes.

Et in huiusmodi operis meritorii testimonium huic script' officialitatis nostri officii sigillum apposuimus. Dat' London' tali die mensis anno Domini
M'o CCCC'mo nonagesimo quarto.

To all the faithful to whom this testimonial letter should come, eternal
wellbeing in the Lord. You should know that those mentioned below have
appeared as good Christians and true pilgrims before us, Master N., commissary of our reverend father and lord N. N., bishop in the realm of England. We therefore beg intently for the sake of God that you would out of
your free charity help these men, that is, lord Jo. N. and N., N., N. And we
truly give witness for each of them that they are not excommunicated nor
under interdict, but fully guided in true morality as Christ's poor. They are
proposing, by their vow and their devotion, to visit the threshold of the holy
apostles and other shrines of saints, for the salvation of their own souls and
of all their benefactors who might offer their hands to supply their needs, so
that you who will come to their help together with ourselves may share in
their prayers and pilgrimages. And in witness to this meritorious work we
have affixed the seal of our office to this official document. Given in London, on such and such a day and month in the year of Our Lord 1494.

Before this text, sermon G-11 ends on fol. 28 halfway down; the remainder of
28 is blank. Item 2 then appears on fol. 28v, in a seemingly different Secretary
(*cursiva currens*) hand. The last two words ("nonagesimo quarto") are written in a
more formal script (*cursiva libraria*). After a blank space of about ten lines follows
sermon G-12, written in the same script as the document but a touch smaller.

3. Papal letter

Evidently a rescript of Pope Alexander VI (26 August 1492–18 August 1503),
addressed to an unnamed recipient, a Benedictine (or Cistercian?) monk of S. in
the diocese of Lincoln, granting him absolution from any ecclesial censures and

---

[8] The reading "Je." is possible, or even "P.".

license to acquire and freely dispose of any benefice and to wear priestly garments instead of his monastic habit. Dated 13 April 1493.[9]

[fol. 118v] Alexander episcopus seruus seruorum Dei, dilecto filio N. salutem et apostolicam benediccionem.

Religionis zelus, vite ac morum honestas, aliaque laudabilia probitatis et virtutum merita, super quibus apud nos fidedigno commi[n]daris testimonio, nos inducunt vt a specialibus fauoribus et graciis prosequamur.

Hinc est quod nos volentes te premissorum meritorum tuorum intuitu fauore prosequi, graciose te a quibuscumque apostasiis, excommunicacionibus, suspensionibus, et interdictis ac aliis ecclesiasticis sentenciis et censuris, et penis a iure vel ab homine quauis occasione vel causa latis—si quibus quomodolibet innodatus existis—ad effectum presencium dumtaxat [ex, *crossed out*] consequendum harum serie absoluere et absolutum fore censentes, tuis in hac parte supplicacionibus inclinati, tecum in [*possibly erased*] quodcumque beneficium ecclesiasticum, cum cura vel sine cura, per clericos seculares teneri solitum, et si parochialis ecclesia vel eius perpetua vicaria aut cantaria, libera capella, hospitale, vel annuale seruicium eisdem clericis in titulum perpetui beneficii ecclesiastici assignari solitum aut de iure patronatus laicorum fuerit ac cuiuscumque taxe seu annui valoris illius fructus redditus et prouentus existant, si tibi alias canonice conferatur aut presenteris vel alias assumaris illud seu instituaris in eo, recipere, et quoad uixeris retinere, illudque simpliciter aut ex causa permutacionis quando tibi placuerit dimittere, et loco dimissi aliud simile vel dissimile beneficium ecclesiasticum, cum cura vel sine cura, eisdem clericis assignari solitum, similiter recipere et ut prefertur retinere.

Tibique ut supra habitum tue religionis honestam togam siue aliam vestem presbiteralem, honesti tamen et decentis coloris, absque alicuius apostasie nota et aliquarum ecclesiasticarum censurarum incursu deferre libere et licite valeas, et habitum per monachos tui ordinis gestari solitum aliter gestandum non tenearis, nec ad id inuitus compelli nequeas seu eciam quomodolibet cohartari, quibusuis apostolicis ac bone memorie Octoni [*script becomes looser:*] et Octoboni olim in regno Anglie apostolice sedis legatorum ac in prouincialibus synodalibus conciliis editis generalibus vel specialibus constitucionibus et ordinacionibus, statutis quoque et consuetudinibus monasterii de S. ordinis sancti Benedicti Lincolniensis diocesis, cuius monachus et ut asseris ordinem ipsum expressum professus existis iuramento, confirmacione apostolica vel quauis firmitate alia roborat', ceterisque contrariis nequaquam obstantibus, auctoritate apostolica tenore presencium de specialis dono gracie dispensamus.

---

[9] Professor Kenneth Pennington has kindly provided some information about this document.

Nulli ergo *[the scribe having reached the end of the folio and quire, the following is written sideways in the left margin:]* Nulli ergo omnino hominum liceat hanc paginam nostre absolucionis et dispensacionis infringere vel ei ausu temerario contraire. Si quis autem hoc attemptare presumpserit, indignacionem omnipotentis Dei ac beatorum Petri et Pauli apostolorum eius se nouerit incursurum.

Datum Rome apud sanctum Petrum anno incarnacionis dominice M'o CCCCmo LXXXXmo *[corrected from LXXXIX]* iii'o, Idus Aprilis, pontificatus nostri anno primo.

Alexander, bishop, servant of the servants of God, to his beloved son N., greetings and apostolic blessing.

Your zeal for the religious life, the integrity of your life and good moral conduct, and other praiseworthy merits of your probity and virtues, for which you are recommended to us by trustworthy witness, lead us to bestow on you special favors and graces.

For this reason we wish in the light of your forementioned merits to bestow on you favor and absolve you and consider you absolved from any apostasies, excommunications, suspensions, interdicts, and other ecclesial sentences and censures, as well as from any penalties inflicted by the law or by any man on whatever occasion or for whatever cause—should you be bound by any of them in any way—and free to receive the following. We are favorably disposed to your petitions in this regard and grant you to receive any ecclesiastic benefice, with or without cure of souls, that is customarily held by secular clergy, even if a parochial church or its perpetual vicarage or chantry, free chapel, hospital, or annual service has been customarily assigned to those clerics as a perpetual ecclesiastic benefice or else belonged to lay patronage, and of whatever assessment or annual value its fruits, income, or yield may be, if it is canonically conferred on you or you are presented to it or otherwise assume it or are instituted in it—to receive it and retain it as long as you live. Also, you may give it up simply or for the sake of commutation whenever you so please, and in place of what you have given up you may similarly receive and if you prefer retain another ecclesiastic benefice that is similar or dissimilar, with or without cure of souls, that has been customarily assigned to the same clerics.

We further grant by our apostolic authority, through the present letter, as a special grace: that you may wear freely and licitly a decent cloak or other priestly vestment over your monastic habit, as long as it is of a becoming and decent color, without any sign of apostasy or that would incur any ecclesiastic censure. And you are not bound to wear the habit customarily worn by the monks of your order, nor can you be compelled to wear it against your will or likewise be constrained by whatever apostolic constitutions, or by the general or special constitutions and regulations that were issued in provincial synodal councils by the former legates of the Holy See to England, Ottoni and Ottoboni of good memory; nor by the statutes and customs of the Benedictine monastery of S. in the diocese of Lincoln, whose monk you have been and, as you declare, whose order you have professed by oath, apostolic confirmation, or any other affirmation.

Let therefore no man whatsoever violate this letter of our absolution and dispensation or brazenly go against it. But if anyone should insolently try to do so, let him know that he will incur the indignation of almighty God and of his apostles Peter and Paul.

Given at Rome at St. Peter's, in the year of the incarnation of Our Lord 1493, on the Ides of April, in the first year of our pontificate.

The document follows upon the sermons by John Herolt (ending on fol. 118) and, on fol. 118v, a prayer or charm as "remedium contra omnia genera febrium." The latter is written in a different form of *cursiva currens*: more rounded and upright with Anglicana features, whereas item 3 appears in the same Secretary (*cursiva currens*) as items 2 and 4. The calendared papal letters from the beginning years of Alexander VI's reign contain several *Religionis zelus* documents but none with details matching this one.[10]

4. Prayers of a Mass for a pregnant woman.

Collect, Secret, and Post-Communion, presumably from a votive Mass for an unnamed pregnant woman. Undated.

[fol. 30v] Deus qui Beatam Virginem et matrem Mariam in conceptu et partu consecrasti et Jonam prophetam de ventre ceti potenti virtute liberasti, famulam tuam N. grauidam protege et visita in salutari tuo vt proles in ea contenta feliciter in lucem prodeat et perueniat ad graciam lauacri salutaris. Per Dominum.

Secr'. Suscipe quesumus Domine Deus hostias humilitatis nostre et famulam tuam N. scuto proteccionis tue defende, et quam ex tua gracia grauidam esse voluisti hanc adueniente partus sui tempore gloriose libera et ab omnibus perturbacionibus cum prole in ista contenta clementer conserues. Per Dominum.

[10] *Calendar of Entries in the Papal Registers Relating to Great Britain and Ireland: Papal Letters*, vol. 16, ed. Anne P. Fuller (Dublin: Irish Manuscripts Commission, 1986), for example nos. 23, 31, 114, 118, 121, *et passim*.

Adesto supplicacionibus nostris, omnipotens Deus, et famule tue N. largi-
flue proteccionis tue munus concede, vt adueniente tempore parturiendi
gracie tue presidium suscipiat et proles quam ediderit percepto lauacro salutari graciosis incrementis feliciter proficiat. Per Dominum.

God, who consecrated Mary, blessed virgin and mother, in her conception
and birth [i.e., when she conceived and gave birth], and who through your
mighty power set the prophet Jonah free from the belly of the whale, protect and visit your pregnant servant N. in your salvation that the child contained in her may happily see the light and come to the grace of the font of
salvation. Through Our Lord.

Secret. Receive, we pray, Lord God, our humble gifts and defend your servant N. with the shield of your protection. And as you have wanted her by
your grace to become pregnant, as the time of her delivery approaches, de-
liver her happily and preserve her and the offspring within her mercifully
from all mishap. Through Our Lord.

Hear our prayers, almighty God, and generously grant your servant N. the
gift of your protection, that as her time of delivery approaches, she may
receive your aid and the child she will bring forth may, after receiving the
water of salvation, happily grow in grace. Through Our Lord.

Preceding these prayers is sermon G-14, which ends halfway down on fol. 30v.
After two blank lines appear the three prayers, written in a slightly different Secretary *(cursiva currens)* hand from the preceding sermon, but the same as that of
items 2 and 3. That these are Mass prayers is confirmed by the rubric "Secr'." at
the head of the second item. The same texts appear in *Missale ad usum insignis et
praeclarae ecclesiae Sarum*, ed. Francis Henry Dickinson, 3 vols. (Burntisland: E
Prelo de Pitsligo, 1861-1883; repr. in one volume, Farnborough, Hants.: Gregg,
1969), cols. 822*-823*. In some early prints they are attributed to Pope Celestine
(col. 821*, note b).
  That the identity of the woman prayed for here is hidden behind an anonymous "N." is of course typical practice in liturgical texts. But the reduction of the
personal identities in the other three documents to "N."—the recipient of the
papal dispensation, the pilgrims, the couple who evidently moved into another
parish, and the writers—unfortunately deprives these texts of genuine documentary value and would mean that whoever copied them was interested in them
only as models or formulas. Prof. Galloway has suggested that the book bears
"all the marks of a friar's work-a-day sermon book."[11] The small size of the codex and its irregular composition, its miscellaneous contents, and the fact that
its texts were written by several different scribes make that a possibility. But one

[11] Galloway, "Fifteenth-Century Confession Sermon," 260.

wonders what use a friar could have had for the formulas just mentioned, which might equally or even more plausibly indicate a parish priest or member of a monastic order (see the papal letter). The latter possibility—a monastic affiliation of the codex—is strengthened by the fact that at least two sermons in this volume also occur in a collection made at Worcester priory (G-1 and 3) and that G-2 is a sermon for the visitation of a (Benedictine) monastery.[12]

---

[12] G-3 is the same as W-123 but ends incomplete after the beginning of its third part; see Wenzel, *Latin Sermon Collections*, 155-56, 211.

Moral Philosophy in England after Grosseteste: An "Underground" History

Charles F. Briggs

During the thirteenth century the arts curriculum at the English universities achieved the form that it would retain, albeit with minor modifications, throughout the remainder of the Middle Ages. Upon successful completion of the arts course, a student would have become familiar with the subjects of the *trivium*, the *quadrivium*, and the three philosophies, natural, moral, and metaphysical. The time and energy devoted to these several *divisiones scientiarum* was hardly evenly distributed, however, with the undergraduate years being overwhelmingly dominated by logic and the baccalaureate by natural philosophy and some of the related subjects of the *quadrivium*.[1] By the middle years of the fourteenth century Oxford had become especially famous for the achievements of its masters of arts in the fields of logic and the closely related area of speculative grammar and, especially at Merton College, in scientific inquiry.[2] As the century wore on a kind of *usus Oxoniensis* developed, as Oxford and Cambridge scholars increasingly studied and developed "the work of their predecessors" and became "less receptive to concepts and material produced on the continent."[3] What, then, became of the poor relations of the arts curriculum, rhetoric, moral philosophy, and metaphysics? According to the evidence of its statutes, Oxford, in 1431, made an effort to redress this imbalance in studies when it issued a revised arts curriculum stipulating three terms each for rhetorical and moral philosophical studies and two for metaphysics.[4] Yet, according to J.M. Fletcher, the 1431 statute, which

---

[1] James A. Weisheipl, "Curriculum of the Faculty of Arts at Oxford in the Early Fourteenth Century," *Mediaeval Studies* 26 (1964): 143–85.

[2] J. M. Fletcher, "The Faculty of Arts," in *The History of the University of Oxford*, vol. 1, *The Early Oxford Schools*, ed. Jeremy I. Catto (Oxford: Clarendon Press, 1984), 364–99, here 393–95.

[3] Fletcher, "Faculty of Arts," 395–96.

[4] The prescribed rhetorical texts were either Aristotle's *Rhetoric*, or the fourth book of Boethius's *Topics*, or the pseudo-Ciceronian *Rhetorica ad Herennium*, or Ovid's *Metamorphoses*, or Vergil's poetry. Those for moral philosophy were Aristotle's *Nicomachean*

was probably compiled in response to the humanist predilections of the university's powerful patron, Humfrey Duke of Gloucester, seems to have gained little traction, so that arts teaching continued to be "supplied from texts written by Oxford logicians and, to a lesser extent, by Oxford scientists of the fourteenth and early fifteenth century." Much the same can be said of the curriculum at Cambridge.[5]

It would be wrong, however, to write off these less prominent arts subjects just because they took a back seat to logic and natural philosophy in the taught curriculum. For studied and used they certainly were. Rhetoric, we now know, flourished in dictaminal studies in late medieval Oxford, while metaphysics received serious attention from theologians.[6] Texts of moral philosophy retained an important place in the arts curriculum and continued to be read and used by arts graduates, whether in their theological studies or out in the world.[7] Still, if scholars have long recognized the substantial contributions of the Englishmen Robert Grosseteste and Walter Burley to moral philosophical studies in the later Middle Ages, no attempt has been made, so far as I know, to examine closely the manuscript evidence for the reception of Aristotle's moral philosophy in England during the two and a half centuries after Grosseteste's death. This essay attempts

---

Ethics, Economics, or *Politics*; and, for metaphysics, Aristotle's *Metaphysics*: J. M. Fletcher, "Developments in the Faculty of Arts, 1370–1520," in *The History of the University of Oxford*, vol. 2, *Late Medieval Oxford*, ed. Jeremy I. Catto and Ralph Evans (Oxford: Clarendon Press, 1992), 315–45, here 323–24.

[5] Fletcher, "Developments," 341, 345. See also the conclusion of J. A. Weisheipl, "Science in the Thirteenth Century," in *History of the University of Oxford*, 1: 435–69, here 438: "Even after the 'three philosophies' were recognized as essential courses in the arts faculty, neither moral philosophy nor metaphysics ever played an important role at Oxford; the mainstay of Oxford education in the middle ages was always logic and the natural sciences, mainly based on the *libri naturales* of Aristotle." For Cambridge, see Damien R. Leader, *A History of the University of Cambridge*, vol. 1, *The University to 1546* (Cambridge: Cambridge University Press, 1988), 157.

[6] On rhetoric, see R.J. Schoeck, "On Rhetoric in Fourteenth-Century Oxford," *Mediaeval Studies* 30 (1968): 214–55, here 214–25; P. Osmund Lewry, "Rhetoric at Paris and Oxford in the Mid-Thirteenth Century," *Rhetorica* 1 (1983): 45–63; Martin Camargo, *Medieval Rhetorics of Prose Composition: Five English "Artes Dictandi" and Their Tradition*, MRTS 115 (Binghamton: Medieval and Renaissance Texts and Studies, 1995); John O. Ward, "Rhetoric in the Faculty of Arts at the Universities of Paris and Oxford in the Middle Ages: A Summary of the Evidence," *Bulletin DuCange* 54 (1996): 159–231. For theology, see Jeremy I. Catto, "Theology and Theologians 1220–1320," in *History of the University of Oxford*, 1: 471–517, here 497; idem, "Theology after Wycliffism," in *History of the University of Oxford*, 2:263–80, here 266–76.

[7] Leader, *History*, 1: 163–67; Charles F. Briggs, *Giles of Rome's "De regimine principum": Reading and Writing Politics at Court and University, c. 1275–c. 1525* (Cambridge: Cambridge University Press, 1999), 91–107.

to survey that evidence in order to begin the reconstruction of what might be termed the "underground" history of Aristotelian moral philosophy in later medieval England.[8]

The Latin translations of moral philosophical works by or purporting to be by Aristotle, these being the *Nicomachean Ethics* (and the earlier incomplete translation, dating from the late twelfth and early thirteenth century, of bks. I-III, which circulated as the *Ethica nova* and *Ethica vetus*), *Politics*, and pseudo-Aristotelian *Economics*, provided the set texts of the curriculum for moral philosophy in Europe's medieval universities. Several other texts of the *Corpus Aristotelicum* came also to be attached unofficially to this area of study, namely the *Rhetoric*, the *Magna moralia*, *De bona fortuna* (a confection consisting of *Eudemian Ethics*, VII.14, and *Magna moralia*, II.8), and the Aristotelizing works of Arabic origin, the *Summa Alexandrinorum* (an abridged *Nicomachean Ethics*) and *Secretum secretorum*.

Before the close of the thirteenth century, the importance of moral philosophy, or at least of the *Ethics*, in the arts curriculum of the University of Oxford seemed firmly established. Robert Grosseteste had, after all, translated the *Nicomachean Ethics*, as well as a number of Greek commentaries on the work, during the latter half of the 1240s. In addition to this, he penned several brief notes, or *notulae*, on the text and its commentaries, and compiled a chapter summary, the *Summa Ethicorum*.[9] Oxford scholars of the generation after Grosseteste maintained a high level of activity in the teaching of moral philosophy. The Dominican Robert Kilwardby (d. 1279) is the likely author of a commentary on the *Ethica nova* and *Ethica vetus*. Although this work is likely associated with his teaching at Paris in the early 1240s, he continued to demonstrate his familiarity with the *Ethics*, now in the version of Grosseteste, in his teaching as Dominican lector in theology at Oxford.[10] By 1283 the Merton MA John Dinsdale

---

[8] I have borrowed and adapted the term and concept of "underground history" from the "underground tradition" of Aristotle's social philosophy developed by Cary J. Nederman, "Aristotelian Ethics Before the *Nicomachean Ethics*: Alternate Sources of Aristotle's Concept of Virtue in the Twelfth Century," in idem, *Medieval Aristotelianism and its Limits* (Brookfield, VT: Ashgate, 1997), 55–75, here 74.

[9] René-Antoine Gauthier, trans., *L'Éthique à Nicomaque* (Louvain: Publications universitaires, 1970), 1.1, "Introduction," 120–24; S. Harrison Thomson, "The 'Notule' of Grosseteste on the Nicomachean Ethics," *Proceedings of the British Academy* 19 (1933): 195–218; Daniel A. Callus, "Robert Grosseteste as Scholar," in *Robert Grosseteste, Scholar and Bishop: Essays in Commemoration of the Seventh Centenary of His Death*, ed. idem (Oxford: Clarendon Press, 1955, repr. 1969), 1–69, here 62–65; Richard W. Southern, *Robert Grosseteste: The Growth of an English Mind in Medieval Europe* (Oxford: Clarendon Press, 1986), 287–90.

[10] P. Osmund Lewry, "Robert Kilwardby's Commentary of the *Ethica nova* and *Ethica vetus*," in *L'Homme et son univers au moyen âge*, vol. 2, ed. Christian Wenin (Louvain-la-Neuve: Éditions de l'Institut supérieur de philosophie, 1986), 799–807.

(*alias* Tytynsale / Didenshale / Didneshale) compiled the *Questiones IV librorum Ethicorum*, a work which doubtless stems from his own teaching of moral philosophy.[11] Other possible thirteenth-century Oxford commentators on the *Ethics* are the Augustinian friar John Wilton (d. ca. 1310) and the Franciscan Robert de Cruce (d. after 1285), though their works do not survive.[12] Sometime after 1269 but before the end of the thirteenth century, the Oxford author of a speech given at the inception of a master of arts felt confident enough of the superiority of Oxford as a center of moral philosophical studies that he could boast, "He first crossed to that place [by which the author probably means Paris] where employment in logic flourishes with sophistry; where grammarians, teaching well-ordered speech, laid the first foundations of wisdom. As was fitting, however, he did not delay unduly over these matters. . . . Secondly, he turned to the *studium* at Oxford, where he was more fully instructed in natural philosophy, ethics and metaphysics."[13]

Still, despite this promising start, it must be said that, when compared with the output of continental authors, the sum total of surviving texts associated with the study of moral philosophy firmly attributable to English authors of the fourteenth and fifteenth centuries is hardly impressive. The most successful of these are Walter Burley's commentaries on the *Ethics* and the *Politics*, extant respectively in some eighteen copies and in thirty-six integral copies and five fragments.[14] Burley, who had completed his studies in arts as a student and fellow of Merton College and gone on to study theology at Paris, was a prolific commentator on Aristotle's works. He composed his moral philosophical commentaries late in life, around 1334, by which time he had become a seasoned royal servant and joined the household of the bibliophile bishop of Durham, Richard

---

[11] The earliest manuscript of this work, Durham Cathedral Libr. C.IV.20A, was copied at Durham Priory in 1283. Other surviving MSS are Cambridge, Gonville & Caius 611/341 (s. xiii^ex) and Oxford, Oriel 33 (s. xiv^1): Richard Sharpe, *A Handlist of the Latin Writers of Great Britain and Ireland before 1540* (Turnhout: Brepols, 1997), 236; P. Osmund Lewry, "Grammar, Logic, and Rhetoric 1220–1320," in *History of the University of Oxford*, 1: 401–33, here 421 n. 4.

[12] For Wilton, see Charles H. Lohr, "Medieval Latin Aristotle Commentaries," *Traditio* 27 (1981): 251–351, at 303. For de Cruce, Sharpe, *Handlist*, 533. Sharpe, *Handlist*, 296, accepts the ascription to John Pecham, OFM (d. 1292) of a commentary on the *Ethica nova* and *Ethica vetus*, but neither Gauthier, *L'Éthique*, 116–17, nor Gernot Wieland, in *The Cambridge History of Later Medieval Philosophy*, ed. Norman Kretzmann, A. Kenny, and J. Pinborg (Cambridge: Cambridge University Press, 1982), 658, credits this attribution.

[13] Lewry, "Grammar, Logic and Rhetoric," 411.

[14] The manuscripts are listed in Sharpe, *Handlist*, 718–20, though Christoph Flüeler, *Rezeption und Interpretation der Aristotelischen "Politica" im späten Mittelalter*, vol. 2 (Amsterdam and Philadelphia: B.R. Grüner, 1992), 13–15, gives a more complete list of *Politics* commentary manuscripts.

Bury. Both works, Burley tells us, were composed at the instigation of Bury and another member of Bury's coterie, Richard Bentworth, a longtime royal servant and bishop of London.[15]

Also from Bury's circle comes the *Quaestiones morales super X libros Ethicorum* of Richard Kilvington (d. 1361). Kilvington, like Burley, had studied and taught arts at Oxford, probably at Oriel College, and completed his studies in theology there by 1339, by which time he enjoyed Bury's patronage and had become a clerk of Edward III. His questions on the *Ethics* comes from his Oxford years, so it is indeed curious that none of the ten manuscripts is found today in an English library.[16] The last surviving English moral philosophical text, the questions on the *Ethics*, or *Questiones moralis philosophie* of John Dedecus, though certainly associated with teaching at either Oxford or Cambridge, may have been composed by a visiting Portuguese Franciscan. Five copies are extent, all in English libraries, and another four are attested in medieval English collections.[17]

At first this may seem a rather anemic showing. Still, it should be stressed that all these works proliferated and had some influence, especially those of Burley. Moreover, there are ascriptions to Englishmen of lost works. A commentary *In libros Ethicorum* by the Carmelite Oxford scholar John Baconthorpe (d. ca. 1348) was attested by Leland in the library of the London Carmelites.[18] Copies of a *Conclusiones Ethicorum libros X* of the Cistercian William Slade (d. ca. 1415), who likely was an Oxford D'Th, were attested by Bale at Magdalen College, Oxford, and, under the name of *Flores moralium*, by Leland at Buckfast Abbey, where Slade had been abbot, and at Fountains Abbey.[19] The "Tabula Deveroys super Ethica" bequeathed by Thomas Markaunt to his college, Peterhouse, Cambridge in 1439, was almost certainly compiled by John Deverose, who had been a fellow there ca. 1383–1400.[20]

---

[15] For Burley's life and works, see Connor T. Martin, "Walter Burley," in *Oxford Studies Presented to Daniel Callus*, Oxford Historical Society, n.s. 16 (Oxford: Clarendon Press, 1964), 194–230; and M.C. Sommers, "Burley, Walter (b.1274/5, d. in or after 1344)," in *Oxford Dictionary of National Biography*, 60 vols. (Oxford: Oxford University Press, 2004), 8: 870–74.

[16] Sharpe, *Handlist*, 485–86. On Kilvington, see Katherine Walsh, "Kilvington, Richard (c. 1305–1361)," *Oxford Dictionary of National Biography*, 31: 579–80.

[17] Sharpe, *Handlist*, 234; J.P.H. Clark, "John Dedecus: Was He a Cambridge Franciscan?" *Archivum Franciscanum Historicum* 80 (1987): 3–38.

[18] Sharpe, *Handlist*, 208.

[19] Sharpe, *Handlist*, 810.

[20] Christopher R. Cheney, "A Register of MSS Borrowed from a College Library, 1440–1517: Corpus Christi College, MS 232," *Transactions of the Cambridge Bibliographical Society* 9 (1987): 103–29, at 107. The college received one, and probably two more copies of Deverose's *tabula* from another of its fellows, John Tittleshall, who died in 1458. A fourth copy made its way to Oxford: Peter D. Clarke, *The University and College Libraries*

Perhaps most interesting, though, are the lost works of John Kervyle OESA, who had been the Augustinian friars' regent master of theology at Oxford in 1388. Sometime before ca. 1435, one of the friars of the York convent, John Bukwode, donated a book to the library there containing, among other things, "Kervyle super libros politicorum Aristotelis cum duabus tabulis Egidii de regimine principum" and an "abbreviatio prefati magistri Kervyle super libros politicorum sancti Thome."[21] As will become apparent in this essay, the combination of Aristotle's works of moral philosophy with Giles of Rome's mirror of princes, the *De regimine principum*, was a practice not limited to Giles's Augustinian confreres, but was a more generalized feature of moral philosophical study in later medieval England. Other ascriptions, to Nicholas Trevet, Richard de Lavingham, Roger Swyneshead, John Dumbleton, and Thomas Netter, are either spurious or tenuous enough to be discounted for the purposes of this essay.

This concludes what is known as far as concerns authorship of works by Englishmen who were associated with the teaching and learning of Aristotelian moral philosophical texts in the thirteenth through the fifteenth centuries. Of course, a look at surviving manuscripts and medieval library catalogues and book lists tells a far richer and more varied story. I have to date found 125 manuscripts containing integral texts or fragments of Aristotelian moral philosophical works originating in England, having been executed by English scribes either in England or on the continent (primarily at Paris), or with clear signs of English medieval ownership or use, by both individuals and institutions (see Table 1).[22] Beginning with the texts of the *Corpus Aristotelicum*, the best represented work in this group is the *Ethics* in Grosseteste's translation, extant in twenty-nine copies. To these can be added the nine complete copies of the *Ethica nova* and *Ethica vetus* and two each of the *Ethica nova* (both fragments) and *Ethica vetus* standing alone. Given that the *Ethica nova/vetus* translation predates the complete Grosseteste version, it comes as no surprise that most and perhaps all copies were made before 1300. Most copies of the complete translation also are early products, fifteen having been made in the thirteenth century and another seven in the years on either side of 1300. Only two copies of this version of the *Ethics* date from after the middle of the fourteenth century.

---

of Cambridge, Corpus of British Medieval Library Catalogues (hereafter CBMLC) 10 (London: British Library, 2002), 185.

[21] K.W. Humphreys, *The Friars' Libraries*, CBMLC 1 (London: British Library, 1990), xxviii–xxix, 82. See also Briggs, *Giles of Rome's "De regimine principum"*, 101–3.

[22] This list does not include those manuscripts containing either Giles of Rome's *De regimine principum* or the *Secretum secretorum* unaccompanied by other texts of Aristotelian moral philosophy. For the manuscripts of the former, see Briggs, *Giles of Rome's "De regimine principum"*, 152–71. On the *Secretum secretorum*, see Steven J. Williams, *"The Secret of Secrets": The Scholarly Career of a Pseudo-Aristotelian Text in the Latin Middle Ages* (Ann Arbor: University of Michigan Press, 2003).

Signs of ownership and use in many of these copies make it apparent, however, that they continued to be read throughout the later Middle Ages. By the middle of the fifteenth century, demand for humanist texts prompted the making of five copies of Leonardo Bruni's *Ethics* translation. Far less well represented are the other texts of Aristotelian moral philosophy. Only six copies of the *Politics*, six of the *Magna moralia*, and four each of the *Rhetoric, Economics,* and *De bona fortuna* survive. This disparity supports the evidence of the Oxford statutes, which give pride of place to the *Ethics* in the prescribed curriculum.[23] Yet these copies show signs of sustained use in the form of annotations and inscriptions; this is especially true of the *Politics,* a work which became increasingly popular in the fifteenth century with Bruni's translation, of which eight copies with ties to later medieval England are extant.

Evidence for the study of moral philosophy is hardly confined to the *originalia,* however. Copies of commentaries and *quaestiones* abound. Table 1 records seventeen copies of Thomas Aquinas's *Ethics* commentary, as well as three of his and Peter of Auvergne's commentary on the *Politics.* Thirteen manuscripts have the collection of the commentaries of Eustratius and other Greeks on the *Ethics,* translated by Grosseteste. Walter Burley's commentaries on the *Ethics* and *Politics* are extant in eight and thirteen copies respectively, Giles of Rome's on *De bona fortuna* and the *Rhetoric* in three and one copies, Albert the Great's *Ethics* commentary in two copies, and Kilwardby's *Ethica nova/vetus* and Bruni's *Isagogicon moralis disciplinae* each in a single copy. To these can be added the *quaestiones* on the *Ethics* of Dinsdale (four copies) and of Dedecus (five copies), and single copies each of Richard Kilvington's and Jean Buridan's questions on the *Ethics.* Two anonymous commentaries on the *Rhetoric* and a set of *quaestiones* on the *Ethics* also survive. To these can be added a dizzying plethora of texts compiled as aids to the study and teaching of moral philosophy. With the exception of Aquinas's *tabula* on the *Ethics* (three copies) and Grosseteste's *Summa in Ethicam* (three copies) and his *Notulae* which are found in several copies of the *Ethics,* these works are silent about their authorship. Yet these anonymous works, variously entitled *tabulae, abbreviationes, conclusiones, notabilia, propositiones,* or *extractiones,* as humble and derivative as they no doubt are, remain as some of our most eloquent witnesses of *studia moralis philosophiae* in medieval England.

Three early examples are found in MSS. St. John's 120, Bodleian Digby 55, and Merton 292. In the first of these manuscripts, an English scribe of the second half of the thirteenth century has penned a brief *Tractatulus de virtutibus cardinalibus* (fols. 182–183v) drawn from a number of authorities, including Cicero, *De inventione,* pseudo-Cicero, *Ad Herennium,* Augustine, and Aristotle's *Ethics,* followed by a curious hybrid *abbreviatio* (fols. 184–195) of the *Ethica nova/vetus* and *Ethics* bks. VI–X.3 (thus leaving out bks. IV and V, and the last nine chapters

---

[23] Fletcher, "Faculty of Arts," 384–85.

of bk. X). Extensive glosses, from a source I have not yet identified,[24] accompany the second book, while the third book incorporates some of the glosses that frequently are found in copies of the *Ethica vetus*. Likewise, where the *Ethica vetus* breaks off before the end of bk. III (in chap. 15, Bekker no. 1119a34), this version (fol. 191rv) adds a paraphrase of the missing material, drawn from Grosseteste's completed version.[25]

The next two manuscripts are of interest not only for their Aristotelian apparatus but also for the graduation speeches each contains which make reference to moral philosophy.[26] In Digby 55 (fols. 178–180v), extracts from the *Rhetoric* and *Ethics* are accompanied by a "sketch of a commentary" on the *Rhetoric*, which Osmund Lewry suggested "may . . . represent an earlier stage in the assimilation of the material," from that represented in Giles of Rome's commentary, completed probably by 1273. It may also simply represent an independent English reading of the text prior to the circulation there of Giles's Parisian commentary.[27] The manuscript's two graduation speeches (fols. 203–204v) show a familiarity with the *Rhetoric*, *Ethics*, and *De bona fortuna*, and with the *Ethics* commentaries of Eustratius et al. Merton 292 includes a table of contents of the *Ethics* (fol. 365rv) as well as two graduation speeches (fols. 372v–373) which also show a familiarity with Aristotle's moral philosophy, citing the *Rhetoric* and *Ethics*.[28]

When viewed together, these three manuscripts reveal an aspect of the study of moral philosophy in the English universities that is not apparent from the statutes, this being the tendency to blend Aristotelian and non-Aristotelian *materia moralis*. Thus the *Ethics* abbreviation in St. John's 120 follows immediately upon the *Tractatulus de virtutibus cardinalibus*; also in the manuscript, though in a fourteenth-century hand, are extracts from John of Salisbury's *Policraticus*. The speeches in the two Oxford manuscripts mix references to Aristotle with those to other moral *auctores*, including Boethius, *De consolatione philosophiae*, Cicero, *De officiis*, the moral letters of Seneca, Vegetius, and the *Ad Herennium*. Furthermore, the Digby manuscript includes Martin of Braga's *Formula honestae vitae*,

[24] The language of the glosses has affinities with the language of Kilwardby's *Ethics* commentary in Peterhouse 206: Lewry, "Robert Kilwardby's Commentary," 800–1.

[25] The *Ethica nova/vetus* and Grosseteste's version have been edited by René-Antoine Gauthier: *Ethica Nicomachea*, Aristoteles Latinus 26.2–3 (Leiden: Brill, 1972).

[26] P. Osmund Lewry, "Four Graduation Speeches from Oxford Manuscripts (c. 1270–1310)," *Mediaeval Studies* 44 (1982): 138–80.

[27] Lewry, "Four Graduation Speeches," 151–52. Lewry assumes a *terminus ad quem* of 1282 for the completion of Giles's commentary, while my dating is derived from the assessment of Costantino Marmo, "L'Utilizzazione della traduzione latina della 'Rhetorica' nel commento di Egidio Romano (1272–1273)," in *La rhétorique d'Aristote: traditions et commentaires de l'Antiquité au XVIIe siècle*, ed. Gilbert Dahan and Irène Rosier (Paris: Librairie Philosophique J. Vrin, 1998), 111–34, at 111–13.

[28] Lewry, "Four Graduation Speeches," 168–80.

which is a treatment of the four cardinal virtues thought in the Middle Ages to have been a work of Seneca, as well as extracts from Seneca's moral letters.

This habit is also revealed in later manuscripts. The *Extraccio compendiosa dictorum in Politica Aristotilis* in Bodleian, Bodley 292 (fols. 180–219) proceeds chapter by chapter through the *Politics*, beginning each chapter summary with a lemma followed by several *conclusiones* and *notabilia*. Each chapter of bk. I is also accompanied by a set of *auctoritates*, drawn from Cicero, Seneca, Aristotle's *Magna moralia*, Zenocrates, Proclus, Vegetius, and the Eustratius et al. commentaries. The most frequently cited of the authorities is Cicero, especially the *De officiis*. Extracts from Seneca's moral letters accompany those from the *Ethics*, *Politics*, *Rhetoric*, and *Poetics* in BL Royal 5.C.iii (fols. 44v-50), a manuscript which also includes an *abbreviatio* and alphabetical *tabula* of Giles of Rome's *De regimine principum*. A manuscript now in Hereford Cathedral Library (MS. O.VI.2), but coming from mid-fifteenth-century Cambridge (it bears an inscription naming John Otteley, elected a fellow of Clare Hall in 1466), combines John of Wales's *Communiloquium* and *Breviloquium* with Engelbert of Admont's *Speculum virtutis pro Alberto et Ottone Austriae ducibus*. These three texts together provide a considerable amount of material on the cardinal virtues, drawn from a wide array of patristic, classical, and medieval sources. But what is interesting for our purposes here is the fact that the scribe responsible for completing the *Speculum virtutis* appended an excerpt from Aristotle's *Politics* (fol. 92). Another Hereford manuscript, P.III.6, pairs an anonymous commentary on the *Rhetoric* (which draws heavily on Giles of Rome's commentary) with the *De consolatione philosophiae* and Nicholas Trevet's commentary thereon.

These abbreviations, indexes, and collections of extracts reveal another aspect of studies in the later medieval schools: the desire for mediated access to authoritative texts. This mediation aided comprehension, simplified access, and increased speed and efficiency of reference.[29] Included in Balliol 108, in an English hand of the middle years of the fourteenth century, is an anonymous collection of *conclusiones* and *notabilia* on each chapter of the *Ethics* (fols. 106–26v). The *conclusiones* and *notabilia* are each numbered serially, and early marginal notes suggest there had been an intention to rearrange the material, perhaps alphabetically under headwords. A short paragraph immediately following the *explicit* discusses the subject of human happiness and virtue, while pencilled notes of the late fourteenth century on fols. 127–128v deal with questions on moral philosophy.

---

[29] Malcolm B. Parkes, "The Influence of the Concepts of *Ordinatio* and *Compilatio* on the Development of the Book," in *Medieval Learning and Literature: Essays Presented to Richard William Hunt*, ed. J.J.G. Alexander and Margaret T. Gibson (Oxford: Clarendon Press, 1976), 115–41; Mary A. Rouse and Richard H. Rouse, "*Statim invenire*: Schools, Preachers, and New Attitudes to the Page," in eidem, *Authentic Witnesses: Approaches to Medieval Texts and Manuscripts* (Notre Dame: University of Notre Dame Press, 1991), 191–219.

Mynors thought it likely that this book was already at Balliol by around 1370, when William Feryby, whose name appears on fol. 128v, was a fellow there.[30] It certainly was there by the 1380s.

Another book now at Balliol (MS. 146a), copied in the early fifteenth century, contains a compendium of the *Politics* (fols. 238–281). Its anonymous author explained why he went to the trouble:

> By the grace of God I intend to extract, according to my judgment, the more fruitful sum of Aristotle's *Politics*, respecting the order in which that material appears in the original, and to redact it in easier Latin, while not varying the style very much from that of its expositors, so that anyone who would wish to detract from my words in this work by gnawing away at them, should know that he instead condemns the very words of the expositors. Three things command me to undertake this work. The first is the dearth of books of one's own, so that if I am not able to have at hand the whole text of the *Politics* or its expositors, I shall at least have the best bits available in a booklet. The second is that those who are unable to consider the text itself owing to the difficulty of its style or its extensiveness, might be enabled to get to the heart of the matter in its abridged form. The third is that, if not many, at least some may, through *mores*, be led back to the study of and zeal for philosophy.[31]

Viewed in its entirety, this manuscript has the look of what one might call a "book of politics," since it also includes the *De re militari* of Vegetius, the *Secretum secretorum*, John of Paris's *De potestate regia et papali*, and Giles of Rome's *De regimine principum* (accompanied by an alphabetical *tabula*). A second, contemporary, copy of this compendium survives in BL Royal 10.C.ix (fols. 145–173), one of whose readers took enough interest to annotate it fairly extensively through the first several leaves. This book also contains a copy of Giles of Rome's mirror of princes, as well as an alphabetical *tabula* thereon (although a different version from that in

---

[30] Roger A.B. Mynors, *Catalogue of the Manuscripts of Balliol College Oxford* (Oxford: Clarendon Press, 1963), 89.

[31] "Per dei gratiam intendo summam Aristotilis de libris politicorum magis fructiferam secundum iudicium meum iuxta librorum ordinem extrahere, et in facilius latinum redigere non multum variando stilum a verbis expositorum, ut qui verbis meis in hoc opere voluerit corrodendo detrahere nouerit se nedum ipsa sed expositorum verba contempnere. Et ad istud monent me tria. Primum est carencia librorum de propriis ut, quia [nec] textum integrum politicorum nec expositores super eodem habere mihi valeo, habeam saltem spicas eius maturiores in fasciculum conspicatas. Secundum est ut qui dictum textum pro difficultate stili nequiunt vel propter eius diffusionem ipsum respicere non optauerint medullam summe valeant in breuibus hic habere. Tertium est ut si non multi ad minus aliqui ad studium et zelum philosophie pro [*sic*] mores reddantur." The text here is that found in BL Royal 10.C.ix (fol. 145).

Balliol 146a), and various apparatuses on the *Retractationes* of Augustine, the *Oculus moralis* of Peter of Limoges, and the *De disciplina scolarium*.

Included among the many texts in Gray's Inn 2 is an alphabetical *tabula* of the *Ethics*, *Politics*, and *Rhetoric*, as well as a brief summary of the *Politics* and, as far as I am aware, the only copy of English origin of the *Summa Alexandrinorum*. One of this book's scribes (and, perhaps, compilers), Ralph Wyche, a Franciscan friar, apparently gave this book to his order's convent at Chester towards the end of the fourteenth century. Moral philosophy commentaries and *quaestiones* might also become fodder for the compiler. Thus the first 158 folios of Gonville & Caius 462/735 are devoted to alphabetical *tabulae* on the texts of and standard commentaries on the *Ethics*, *Politics*, and *Rhetoric*, complete with a helpful numbered list of headings at the end. These *tabulae* refer both to the text of Aristotle and to the *expositiones* of their commentators, St. Thomas and Giles of Rome (he does not mention Peter of Auvergne's contribution to the *Politics* commentary). Thus the first entry, s.v. "Adulator," has: "Adulator est amicus superexcessus, hoc est minor eo cui adulatur, si sit eius amicus, vel fingit se talem illi. Et amatores honorum amant tales 1 · 8 · c · 8 · ph." This refers to Thomas's commentary on Aristotle's discussion in *Ethics* VIII.8 of flatterers and why they are so appealing:

> Ex hoc enim, quod multi magis volunt amari quam ament, procedit, quod multi sint amatores adulationis; qui scilicet delectantur in hoc, quod aliquis eis adulatur. Adulator enim, vel in rei veritate est amicus superexcessus, quia minorum est adulari, vel adulando aliquis fingit se talem, et quod magis amet quam ametur.[32]

This entry, and indeed the entire enterprise, efficiently summarizes the *intentio* of both author and expositor, and thus acts as a useful substitute for the passages in the complete works.

Peterhouse 208 is a miscellany of many and various philosophical and theological texts copied in the second half of the fifteenth century. The most lengthy of its contents is a copy of Leonardo Bruni's translation of the *Ethics*, preceded by a list of contents and accompanied by Aquinas's commentary (fols. 34–170v). Also included, however, are alphabetical *tabulae* on the *Politics* and *De regimine principum*, a brief *Tractatus* on *De consolatione philosophiae*, and a series of *notabilia* extracted from several texts, including a set of *quaestiones* "cuiusdam venerabilis doctoris super libros ethicorum," the *Ethics* itself, and Giles of Rome's *De bona fortuna* and *Rhetoric* commentaries, the *Rhetoric*, the *Politics*, and Peter of Auvergne's commentary on the *Politics*.

Certainly, these and other derivative products of late medieval English scholarship, like the *Ethics* contents summary in Oxford, Corpus Christi 230

---

[32] Thomas Aquinas, *In Decem Libros Ethicorum Aristotelis ad Nicomachum Expositio*, ed. R.M. Spiazzi, 3rd ed. (Rome: Marietti, 1964), 435.

and the abridged *Economics* in BL Royal 12.C.xx, are hardly as impressive as the great commentaries and *quaestiones disputatae* of Parisian luminaries like Aquinas or Jean Buridan. They do nonetheless show that moral philosophy was hardly a moribund topic of study at England's universities. They also suggest that the entire canon of Aristotelian moral philosophy, and not just the *Ethics*, received the attention of English scholars. This impression is confirmed by the evidence of surviving booklists and library catalogues from medieval England (see Table 2). A survey of published booklists and catalogues reveals 177 lost or unidentified manuscripts containing Aristotelian moral philosophical texts.[33] Just as is the case with the surviving manuscripts, here we find that the 64 certain or likely copies of the *Ethics* (53 of the Grosseteste version, four of Bruni's, one *Ethica nova/vetus* and one *Ethica nova*, and five probable *Ethics* manuscripts) far outnumber those of the *Politics* (11), *Economics* (6), *Rhetoric* (9), *De bona fortuna* (5), and *Magna moralia* (2–3). Commentaries on the *Ethics* also dominate, with twenty-four certain and likely copies of the commentary of Aquinas, ten of Burley, and seven of Eustratius et al. as compared to five and six copies respectively of the *Politics* commentaries of Thomas Aquinas/Peter of Auvergne and of Burley, four and three respectively of Giles's *Rhetoric* and *De bona fortuna* commentaries, and two commentaries on the *Economics*, one certainly and perhaps both being the commentary of Bartholomew of Bruges (completed at Paris, 1309).

Yet if medieval English libraries kept more copies of the *Ethics* and works devoted thereto, they rarely lacked books containing other moral philosophical texts. And as we have seen with the extant manuscripts, the lost and unidentified books exhibit a great variety of texts attesting to the vitality of moral philosophical studies at the universities. In the library of the Austin Friars at York, in addition to John Kervyle's commentary on the *Politics* and *abbreviatio* of Thomas Aquinas's commentary, mentioned above, are a "Tabula super philosophiam moralem Aristotelis" and a "Tabula super 5 libros Boecii de consolatione philosophie et super 8 libros poleticorum."[34] Other intriguing titles are the "Summa politicorum" which John Langton LicCnL gave to Pembroke College, Cambridge in 1447, the "Nove questiones super libros ethicorum," at King's Hall, Cambridge, by 1450, a set of *quaestiones* on the *Politics*, listed among the books of Queen's College, Cambridge in 1472, and a no doubt mistakenly ascribed "Exposicio lyncolniensis super libros politicorum," at Syon Abbey by

---

[33] This includes 145 definite and twelve probable manuscripts containing works of Aristotelian moral philosophy as well as a further twenty manuscripts containing Giles of Rome's *De regimine principum*. Thanks to Paul G. Remley of the University of Washington for supplying me with information regarding the medieval catalogues of Canterbury Cathedral Priory, St. Augustine's, Canterbury, and Canterbury College, Oxford, from M.R. James, *The Ancient Libraries of Canterbury and Dover* (Cambridge: Cambridge University Press, 1903).

[34] Humphreys, *The Friars' Libraries*, 63–64.

1524. The monastic library of St. Augustine's, Canterbury, possessed a copy of the *Ethics*, which included an "abbreviacio compendiosa" on that text, as well as a "compendium notabile principalium proposicionum libri Ethicorum" and some "questiones extracte summarie de singulis capitulis libri Ethicorum per modum conclusionum et notabilium."[35] Also notable is the "Liber moralis philosophie" bequeathed by Thomas Markaunt MA, BTh to his colleagues at Corpus Christi College, Cambridge in 1439.[36] This massive collection of texts covering all aspects of Aristotelian moral philosophy and including such interesting titles as "Questiones mote super .8. libros politicorum," was, at £10, the most expensive of Markaunt's seventy-five books.[37] That the fellows of the college found the book useful is likely, since it seems to have been loaned out every year, usually as the first pick, from the time of Markaunt's bequest until the early 1500s.[38] This interest in moral philosophy shown by the fellows of Corpus was hardly unique. At Merton College, which has the most complete surviving evidence of *electiones sociorum*, the fellows consistently showed a preference for borrowing books of moral philosophy.[39] The same can be said for the fellows of Lincoln College and All Souls, and for the monks of Canterbury and Worcester (and, very likely, St. Augustine's Canterbury).[40]

The medieval catalogues also suggest that English academic readers turned to Giles of Rome's *De regimine principum* as a work of moral philosophy. A register of books donated to Cambridge University Library during the second quarter of the fifteenth century lists a copy of it among the "Libri moralis philosophie"; this same volume still shared a shelf with other works of moral philosophy in the register of 1473.[41] The 1418 Peterhouse catalogue also classifies its library's copy of *De regimine principum* as a book of moral philosophy;[42] evidence of the same practice appears at Dover Priory, and in the libraries of All Souls College

---

[35] James, *The Ancient Libraries*, 310.

[36] Clarke, *Libraries of Cambridge*, 184–85.

[37] Markaunt also bequeathed a book containing the *Ethics* and *Magna moralia*, as well as a Giles of Rome's *De regimine principum* and the *Tabula Ethicorum* of John Deverose.

[38] Cheney, "A Register of MSS," 108.

[39] F.M. Powicke, *The Medieval Books of Merton College* (Oxford: Clarendon Press, 1931); N.R. Ker, "The Books of Philosophy Distributed at Merton College in 1372 and 1375," in idem, *Books, Collectors and Libraries: Studies in the Medieval Heritage*, ed. A.G. Watson (London and Ronceverte, WV: Hambledon Press, 1985), 331–78.

[40] For the Canterbury monks studying at Oxford, see James, *The Ancient Libraries*; Roberto Weiss, "The Earliest Catalogues of the Library of Lincoln College," *Bodleian Library Quarterly* 8 (1937): 343–59; N.R. Ker, *Records of All Souls College Library 1437–1600* (Oxford: Oxford Bibliographical Society, 1971); Rodney M. Thomson, *A Descriptive Catalogue of the Medieval Manuscripts in the Worcester Cathedral Library* (Cambridge: D.S. Brewer, 2001), xix, xxv–xxvix.

[41] Clarke, *Libraries of Cambridge*, 21, 39.

[42] Clarke, *Libraries of Cambridge*, 496.

and Lincoln College, Oxford.[43] So too when a *tabula* on *De regimine principum* is found in a volume containing multiple items, its immediate neighbors belong to the category of moral philosophy. Thus we find the two *tabulae* on *De regimine principum* in the volume of Kervyle's writings at York, and the combination of a *tabula* on *De regimine principum* with one on the *Policraticus* and a copy of the *Speculum regis Edward III* in a book at Syon Abbey.

The same habit of combining Giles's mirror of princes with other moral philosophical texts is apparent in surviving books. It is paired with Walter Burley's commentary on the *Politics* in CUL Ii.II.8, Pembroke 158, and Balliol 282, and with Aquinas's *Ethics* commentary in Gonville & Caius 508/387, Bodleian Auct. F.3.3 (along with Vegetius, *De re militari*), and Bodleian Hatton 15; it shares a manuscript with a summary of the *Politics* (as well as Vegetius, John of Paris, and the *Secretum secretorum*) in Balliol 146a. A look at Table 1 also reveals that *tabulae* on *De regimine principum* appear in Peterhouse 208, and BL Royal 5.C.iii and Royal 10.C.ix.

That English scholars frequently turned to *De regimine principum* as an authority on moral philosophy goes a long way toward explaining the text's popularity with this audience.[44] It may also modify the import of the overwhelming preponderance of surviving and lost/unidentified copies of the *Ethics* and related texts versus those of the *Politics*, *Economics*, and *Rhetoric*. In *De regimine principum* Giles achieved the most successful and extensive medieval appropriation of Aristotle's moral philosophical corpus.[45] The work's organization into three

---

[43] William P. Stoneman, *Dover Priory*, CBMLC 5 (London: British Library, 1999), 30; Ker, *Records of All Souls*, 38; Weiss, "The Earliest Catalogues," 353. For the same practice in continental libraries, see Hiver de Beauvoir, ed., *La librairie de Jean duc de Berry au Chateau de Mehun-sur-Yevre, 1416* (Paris: Auguste Aubry, 1860), 35–42; Gilles Meersseman, "La bibliothèque des Frères Prêcheurs de la Minerve à la fin du XVe siècle," in *Mélanges Auguste Pelzer* (Louvain: Bibliothèque de l'Université, 1947), 605–34, here 630; *Corpus Catalogorum Belgii: The Medieval Booklists of the Southern Low Countries*, ed. Albert Derolez and Benjamin Victor, vol. 2, *Provinces of Liège, Luxembourg and Namur* (Brussels: Paleis der Academiën, 1994), 148–61.

[44] The sixty extant manuscripts from medieval England are described and discussed in Briggs, *Giles of Rome's "De regimine principum"*. Here it should be noted that in this earlier publication I mistakenly cited Durham Cathedral Library B.III.31 as B.IV.31, and was unaware of a *tabula* of *De regimine principum* in B.IV.43. The twenty lost/unidentified *De regimine principum* manuscripts listed in Table 2 include the "Tractatus de regimine principum" given by John Lenne to Clare Hall, Cambridge. Other lost/unidentified copies, not included in Table 2, can be found in Briggs, *Giles of Rome's "De regimine principum"*, 54, 61–62, 66–67, 70, 94–95, 97, 99, 106.

[45] Roberto Lambertini, "A proposito della 'costruzione' dell'*Oeconomica* in Egidio Romano," *Medioevo* 14 (1988): 315–70; idem, "'Philosophus videtur tangere tres rationes': Egidio Romano lettore ed interprete della *Politica* nel terzo libro del *De regimine principum*," *Documenta e studi sulla tradizione filosofica medievale* 1 (1990): 277–325; idem, "Il

books manifests the tripartite division of moral philosophy into ethics, economics, and politics that is a commonplace of medieval *divisiones scientiarum*.[46] It is, moreover, the most thoroughgoing source of citations from Aristotle's *Politics*, *Ethics*, and *Rhetoric*, with some 235, 185, and 90 named citations respectively.[47] And, despite Giles having written it before the translation into Latin of the *Economics*, he nonetheless manages in book two to construct a fully (though nonetheless modified) Aristotelian economics on the basis of material drawn from the *Politics* and Aquinas's commentaries thereon.[48] I do not think it at all far-fetched to suggest that medieval English scholars were aware of this text's utility as a source of Aristotle's *corpus moralis philosophiae*, and that they employed it as such. One sixteenth-century cataloguer even went so far as to list the *De regimine principum* in CUL Ii.2.8 as "Egidio super Politicam."[49]

This essay has argued that Aristotelian moral philosophy was not nearly so neglected a subject of study at England's later medieval universities as might appear to be the case from the evidence of both the statutes and works of known English authorship. English scholars of the fourteenth and fifteenth centuries regularly applied themselves to the study of moral philosophy and even made contributions, albeit frequently anonymous and derivative, in aid of this study. True, Oxford and Cambridge did not produce the Aristotelian fireworks of Paris-based polemicists like John of Paris and Marsilius of Padua or vernacular translations like those of Nicole Oresme, but English knowledge and understanding of the moral lore of the Philosopher occasionally rises to the surface in sermons, penitential texts, political speeches, and books of advice for princes.[50]

---

filosofo, il principe e la virtù: Note sulla ricezione e l'uso dell' *Etica Nicomachea* nel *De regimine principum* di Egidio Romano," *Documenti e studi sulla tradizione filosofica medievale* 2 (1991): 239–79; Ubaldo Staico, "Rhetorica e politica in Egidio Romano," *Documenti e studi sulla tradizione filosofica medievale* 3 (1992): 1–75; Janet Coleman, "Some Relations between the Study of Aristotle's *Rhetoric*, *Ethics* and *Politics* in Thirteenth- and Early Fourteenth-Century University Arts Courses and the Justification of Contemporary Civic Activities (Italy and France)," in *Political Thought and the Realities of Power in the Middle Ages*, ed. Joseph Canning and Otto G. Oexle (Göttingen: Vandenhoeck and Ruprecht, 1998), 127–57; Briggs, *Giles of Rome's "De regimine principum"*; idem, "Aristotle's *Rhetoric* in the Later Medieval Universities: A Reassessment," *Rhetorica* 25 (2007): 243–68, at 247–50; Matthew S. Kempshall, *The Common Good in Late Medieval Political Thought* (Oxford: Clarendon Press, 1999), 130–56.

[46] James A. Weisheipl, "The Classification of the Sciences in Medieval Thought," *Mediaeval Studies* 27 (1965): 54–90, here 65–66.

[47] Briggs, "Aristotle's *Rhetoric*," 247.

[48] Lambertini, "A proposito," 335–50.

[49] Clarke, *Libraries of Cambridge*, 92.

[50] Siegfried Wenzel, *Latin Sermon Collections from Later Medieval England: Orthodox Preaching in the Age of Wyclif* (Cambridge: Cambridge University Press, 2005), 424, 473, 560, 564, 612, 620, 622, 654; idem, ed. and trans., *Summa virtutum de remediis anime*

Their active engagement with these texts, moreover, contributed to what Alastair Minnis has recently termed a "practical philosophy" of "international lay culture" in England.[51] In so far as moral philosophy was concerned, then, the *usus Oxoniensis* was no more than a variant of broader European intellectual currents.

(Athens: University of Georgia Press, 1984), 52–54, 148, 158, 270; idem, ed. and trans., *Fasciculus morum: A Fourteenth-Century Preacher's Handbook* (University Park: Pennsylvania State University Press, 1989), 128, 259, 499, 619, 703; Beryl Smalley, *English Friars and Antiquity in the Early Fourteenth Century* (Oxford: Blackwell, 1960), 311, 322, 330, 334, 336, 353; Jean-Philippe Genet, ed., *Four English Political Tracts of the Later Middle Ages*, Camden Fourth Series 18 (London: Royal Historical Society, 1977), 170, 180; John Watts, "*The Policie in Cristen Remes*: Bishop Russell's Parliamentary Sermons of 1483–84," in *Authority and Consent in Tudor England: Essays Presented to C. S. L. Davies* (Aldershot: Ashgate, 2002), 33–59, esp. 35 and 53 n. 4. John Wyclif relies on the *Ethics* in his discussion of the virtues in the *Trialogus*, bk. III (I thank Stephen Lahey for alerting me to this and sending me a typescript of his forthcoming translation of the *Trialogus*).

[51] Alastair J. Minnis, "'I speke of folk in seculer estaat': Vernacularity and Secularity in the Age of Chaucer," *Studies in the Age of Chaucer* 27 (2005): 25–58.

Table 1
Moral Philosophy MSS of Medieval English
Origin/Provenance, or with Evidence of English
Scribal Activity

In Table 1 and Table 2, only moral philosophical texts are mentioned. Most of the biographical information for Table 1 is derived from A.B. Emden, *A Biographical Register of the University of Oxford to 1500*, 3 vols. (Oxford: Clarendon Press, 1957), and idem, *A Biographical Register of the University of Cambridge to 1500* (Cambridge: Cambridge University Press, 1963). Most information relating to institutional ownership of extant manuscripts is derived from N.R. Ker, *Medieval Libraries of Great Britain: A List of Surviving Books*, 2nd ed. (London: Royal Historical Society, 1964). In both tables, the following abbreviations are used:

C	Commentary
Dbf	*De bona fortuna*
DRP	*De regimine principum*
E	*Nicomachean Ethics*
En	*Ethica nova*
Env	*Ethica nova* and *Ethica vetus*
Ev	*Ethica vetus*
P	*Politics*
Po	*Poetics*
Q	*Quaestiones*
R	*Rhetoric*
Ss	*Secretum secretorum*
Y	*Economics*

Avranches, Bibl. municipale
222 (xiii^ex; Engl. scribe) **E, Notulae**

Bruges, Grootseminarie
106/145 (xiii^ex/xiv^in; Engl. or Flemish scribe) **Thos EC**

Cambridge, University Libr. (CUL)
Ee.II.29 (xv^med) **Geremia da Montagnone** *Compendium moralium notabilium*
Hh.I.6 (xv) **Bruni E**
Ii.II.8 (xv^in; Mr Richard Bury, scribe) **Burley PC, Giles DRP**; Cambridge Univ. Libr. (by 1557)

Cambridge, Corpus Christi College
398 (xv²) **Bruni P**

Cambridge, Gonville & Caius College

289/273 (xiii^{ex} + xiv^{1}) **E, Thos EC**

341/537 (xiii; Engl. scribes) **Env**

369/591 (AD 1465–67; John Howson MA, scribe) **Dedecus EQ**

458/396 (xiii^{ex}) **Env**; Richard Pulham BCL — Gonville Hall (by ca. 1400) — Bayham Abbey (during 1400s)

462/735 (xv^{in}) **Thos EC tabula, Thos/Peter PC tabula, Giles RC tabula**

490/486 (xiv^{ex}) **Burley PC, Burley EC**

494/263 (xiii^{med}) **Env**; Peter Blome — Gonville Hall (1400s)

505/383 (xiv^{2}) **Burley PC**; William Asplyn MA, BTh Oxford — Syon Abbey (by 1485)

508/387 (xiv^{in}; English or French scribes) **Thos EC, Giles DRP**

510/388 (xiii; German or NE French scribe) **Albert EC**; John Loppham — William Wyot — Gonville Hall (1450)

611/341 (xiii^{ex}) **Dinsdale EQ**; ?Michael Causton MA, SchCL — Gonville Hall (by late 1300s)

Cambridge, King's College

11 (AD 1480; Robert Hacumblen MA, DTh, scribe) **E**; King's College (by 1528)

Cambridge, Pembroke College

130 (xiv^{in}; N French or Engl. scribes) **M, E, P, R, Mm, Ss**; Thomas Wryght DTh — Pembroke (by 1490)

157 (xiv^{2}) **Burley EC, Burley PC**; John Clenche MA, DTh — Pembroke (by ca. 1430)

158 (xv^{1}) **Burley PC, Giles DRP**; Thomas Lavenham LicCnL — Pembroke (by ca. 1435)

Cambridge, Peterhouse

57 (xiii^{ex}/xiv^{in}) **M, E, P, R**; Walter de Blacollisley MA — Peterhouse (by ca. 1330s)

82 (xiii^{ex}) **Giles DbfC, Thos EC, Thos/Peter PC, Giles RC**; Mr John Malebraunch — Walter Boseville OFM — Peterhouse (by ca. 1315)

90 (xiii^{ex}/xiv^{in}; N French scribes) **Dbf**; Thomas Arundel, abp. of Canterbury — Peterhouse (by 1414)

93 (xiv^{2}) **Burley EC, Burley PC**; Peterhouse

116 (xiii^{ex}) **Grosseteste E Summa, E, Eustratius EC, Notulae**; John Malebraunch — Peterhouse (by ca. 1315)

143 (xiii^{ex}/xiv^{in}; English and/or N French scribes) **Giles DbfC**; Peterhouse (by 1418)

184 (xv) **Thos E tabula**; Peterhouse (by 1418)

206 (xiii^{ex}/xiv^{in}) **Kilwardby EnvC**; Peterhouse (by 1418)

208 (xv^med) **Bruni E, Thos EC, P tabula, Giles DRP tabula, EQ notabilia, E notabilia, Giles DbfC notabilia, R notabilia, Giles RC notabilia, P notabilia, Peter PC notabilia**

Cambridge, St. John's College
120 (xiii²) *Tractatulus de virtutibus cardinalibus*, Env abbrev, E bks VI-X abbrev, *Policraticus* extracts

Cracow, Bibl. Jagiełłońskiego
501 (xiii^ex/xiv^in; Engl. scribes) **E** w. Albert EC and Eustratius EC annotations, **Thos EC, Mm** (last two items s. xiv¹)

Dublin, Trinity College Libr.
C.2.8 (xiii^med) **E** (fragments of parts of bks. VII-X)

Durham Cathedral Libr.
B.I.23 (xiv) **Thos EC**; Durham Priory
C.IV.20A (AD 1283) **Dinsdale EQ**; Durham Priory

Eton College
122 (xiii²) **Eustratius EC, Notulae**; William Horman—Eton (by 1535)

Florence, Bibl. Laurenziana
Plut. LXXIX, 13 (xiii^ex; Engl. scribe at ?Paris) **E, Eustratius EC, Notulae**
Florence, Bibl. Nazionale
Conv. Soppr. B.6.1681 (xiv¹; Engl. scribe) **Kilvington EQ**
Conv. Soppr. G.5.1290 (xiii^ex; Engl. scribes) **E, Mm** (both texts with annotations in Engl. hands)
Conv. Soppr. I.5.21 (xiii^ex; Engl. scribe and annotator); **Eustratius EC, Notulae**; Coluccio Salutati—Cosimo de' Medici—Dominican Convent of San Marco, Florence

Hereford Cathedral Libr.
O.VI.2 (xv^med) **Engelbert of Admont** *Speculum virtutis*, **P excerpts**; John Otteley MA Cambridge (1468)
P.III.6 (xv^in) **RC, R chapter summary**; Owen Lloyd DCL—Hereford Cathedral (1478)

London, British Libr. (BL)
Burney 304 (xiv^ex/xv^in) **Burley PC**
Royal 5.C.iii (xv^med) **Giles DRP tabula, Giles DRP abbrev, Propositiones from many texts incl. E, P, R, Po and Seneca ad Lucilium**; John Pye, London bookseller—Thomas Eborall DTh Oxford (d. ca. 1470s)

Royal 9.E.i (xv^{med}; William Reynoldson MA DTh Cambridge, scribe) **Bruni E,
Thos EC, Thos E tabula**
Royal 10.C.ix (xv^{in}) **Giles DRP tabula, Giles DRP contents summary, Giles
DRP, P summary**
Royal 10.C.xi (xiv^{ex}) **Burley PC**
Royal 12.C.xx (xv^2) **Y abbrev, Bruni** *Isagogicon in libros morales Aristotelis*, **Ss**
Royal 12.D.ii (xiii^{ex}/xiv^{in}) **En** (fragment)
Royal 12.D.xiv (xiii^{ex}) **Env;** John Sheppey, bp. of Rochester—Rochester Cathe-
dral Priory (by 1360)
Royal 12.F.xix (xiii^{ex}) **En** (fragment); Reading Abbey

London, Gray's Inn Libr.
2 (xiv^{ex}) **Tabula of E P and R, P synopsis, Sa;** Ralph Wyche OFM—Chester
Franciscan Convent (late 1300s)

Naples, Bibl. Nazionale
VIII.G.4 (xiii^{med}; Engl. scribe and annotator) **E, Eustratius EC;** Dominican
Convent of Santa Lucia, Fabriano

Oxford, Bodleian Libr.
Auct. F.3.3 (xiv^2) **Thos EC, Giles DRP, Vegetius** *De re militari*; Reading Abbey
Auct. F.5.27 (xv) **Bruni P**
Auct. F.5.29 (xiii^{med}) **Ev;** Henry Jolypace, chamberlain of St. Paul's, London—
New College (by early 1400s)
Auct. F.6.2 (xv) **Bruni P**
Barlow 42 (xv) **Bruni P**
Bodley 292 (xiv^2) *Extraccio compendiosa in Politica Aristotelis*; St. Albans (by 1400s)
Digby 55 (xiii^2) **Martin of Braga** *Formula honestae vitae*, **Seneca, R extracts,
RC, E extracts;** Oxford (1300s)
Digby 150 (xiii^2; N France) **Giles DbfC;** Oriel College (by 1474)
Hatton 15 (xiv^2) **Giles DRP, Thos EC;** Oxford (by mid 1400s)
Rawlinson D.1218 (xiv^{ex}/xv^{in}) **Y**
Selden supra 24 (xii^{ex}; N France) **Ev;** St. Albans (by early 1200s)

Oxford, All Souls College
84 (xiii^2) **Grosseteste E Summa, E, Eustratius EC, Notulae, Thos EC glosses;**
John Stokes, warden of All Souls—All Souls (ca. 1465)
88 (xv^1) **Dedecus EQ;** Walter Hopton—All Souls (by 1459)

Oxford, Balliol College
93 (xv^{in}) **Dedecus EQ;** William Gray, bp. of Ely—Balliol (by 1478)
95 (xiv^2) **Burley EC, Burley PC;** John Malvern DTh—Balliol (by 1422)
108 (xiv^{1-med}) **E conclusiones;** Balliol (by ca. 1370)

112 (xiv^in) **P, Mm, Y**; Elias de Ashby DTh—Balliol (by 1319)
115 (AD 1442–44; Cologne) **Buridan EQ**; William Gray—Balliol (by 1478)
116 (xiii^ex) **E, Eustratius EC**; Balliol (by ca. 1380)
117 (xv) **Dedecus EQ**; George Nevill, abp. of York—Balliol (by 1465)
146a (xv^in) **Vegetius** *De re militari*, **Ss, John of Paris** *De potestate regia et papali*, **Giles DRP** w. tabula, **P summary**
241 (xiii^ex/xiv^in; Paris) **Thos EC** (Engl. scribe); Balliol (by late 1300s)
242 (AD 1444–54; Italy) **Bruni E, Bruni P**, (formerly also contained **Bruni Y**); William Gray—Balliol (by 1478)
250 (xiii^ex; France) **R**; Balliol (by late 1300s)
277 (xiii^ex; Engl. or French scribe) **E**; Balliol (by late 1300s)
278 (xiii^ex/xiv^in; Paris, at least one Engl. scribe) **Thos EC, Thos PC**; Balliol (by late 1300s)
282 (xiv^med) **Giles DRP, Burley PC**

Oxford, Christ Church
Evelyn Collection h.65 (xiv^in) **Thos EC** (fragment)

Oxford, Corpus Christi College
230 (xv^ex) **E notabilia**
398 (xv) **Bruni P**

Oxford, Lincoln College
21 (xv) **Bruni E**; Robert Fleming—Lincoln (1465)

Oxford, Magdalen College
49 (AD 1472; John Gold MA, scribe) **Bruni E, Bruni P**; John Gold—Magdalen
178 (xiii^ex/xiv^in) **Thos EC**; Oxford (by 1470s)
189 (xv^2) **Bruni E, Y, Bruni P**; Nicholas Good DTh—Nicholas Attewater—Magdalen (by late 1400s)
205(xv^2) **Burley EC, Burley PC**
265 (xiv) **Thos EC** (fragment)

Oxford, Merton College
2 (D.3.10) (xiv) **Thos EC** (fragment); Merton (before 1521)
14 (A.3.2) (xiii^2) **Grosseteste E Summa, Notulae**; William Burnell, dean of Wells—Merton (by 1304)
21 (B.2.9) (xv^2) **Thos ET, E chapter summary**; Merton (before 1385)
273 (O.3.5) (xiv^1) **Thos PC**; Merton (ca. 1360)
276 (H.2.8) (xiv^1) **Mm**; Merton (before 1385)
281 (O.3.1) (xiv^in) **Giles DbfC**; William Rede, bp. of Chichester—Merton (1374)
292 (O.1.8) (xiv^in) **E conclusiones**; Merton (before 1385)

Oxford, New College
242 (xiv^2; John Balne, scribe) **Burley EC, Burley PC**; Thomas Chaundler DTh, warden of New College—New (by 1490)

Oxford, Oriel College
25 (xiii^{ex}/xiv^{in}) **E, Dbf, R**; John Cobbledik MA—Oriel (by 1337)
33 (xiii^{ex}/xiv^{in}) **Dinsdale EQ**; William Walcot MA (d. 1323)—Oriel
57 (xiv^2 + xiv^{ex}) **Burley EC, Burley PC**; Oriel (by 1400s)

Paris, Bibl. Mazarine
3458 (xiii^2; N France with some glosses in Engl. hand) **Dbf**
3470 (xiii^2; N France with many glosses in Engl. hands) **Env**; French possessors in 1300s and 1400s
3473 (xiii^{ex}/xiv^{in}; mostly Engl. scribes) portion of **Eustratius EC**; Saint-Jacques, Paris

Paris, Bibl. nationale de France
lat. 6459 (xiv^2; England) **E, Burley EC**
lat. 6576 (xiii^{ex}/xiv^{in}; Engl. scribe) **Env**
lat. 8802 (xii–xvi^{in}; England) **Ev** (s. xiii), **Dbf** (s. xvi^{in}); names of Bryghtman, Thomas Allen, John Caspar, and Kenelm Digby
lat. 12950 (xiii^{ex}/xiv^{in}; Engl. scribe) **Env**; Saint-Germain des Prés, Paris
lat. 14698 (xiii^{ex}/xiv^{in}; Engl. scribe) **EQ**; Saint-Victor, Paris (by 1400s)
lat. 17811 (xiv^1; several scribes, including fr. William of Lincoln and fr. Alan Wythybrcht) **E tabula**
lat. 17832 (xiii^{ex}/xiv^{in}; Engl. or French scribe) **E, Eustratius EC, Grosseteste E Summa, Mm**; College de Navarre (by 1400s)

Princeton, University Libr.
Garrett 102 (xiv^{in}; Italian scribes) **E, P**; fr. Thomas Ratford OFM, DTh—Lincoln Franciscan convent (1340s)

Rome, Bibl. Apostolica Vaticana
Ottob. lat. 2214 (xiii^{ex}; Engl. scribe) **E**
Pal. lat. 1017 (xiv^{in}; Engl. scribes) **E**; Paris (by ca. 1400)
Pal. lat. 1024 (AD 1329; Engl. scribe) **Thos EC summary** ("Summarium Vaticanum")
Urb. lat. 1325 (xiv^1; Engl. scribe) **E, Notulae**; France (by ca. 1350)
Vat. lat. 2171 (xiii^{ex}; Engl. scribe) **E, Eustratius EC, Notulae**

Rouen, Bibl. municipale
923 (xiii^{ex}/xiv^{in}; many glosses in Engl. hand) **E, P**; Fécamp (by ca. 1400)

Saint-Omer, Bibl. municipale

598 (xiii^{ex}/xivⁱⁿ; Paris with some Engl. scribes) **Mm, Averroes PoC, Y, P, Env, E**

619 (xiii^{ex}; Paris with glosses in Engl. hand) **E, Thos EC**; Saint-Bertin

625 (xiii^{med}; England) **Env**; Saint-Bertin

Venice, Bibl. Marciana

Lat. VI, 122 (xiii²; Engl. or N French scribe with annotations in Engl. hand) **E, Eustratius EC, Notulae**; Ioachimus Turrianus of Venice OP—Dominican convent of SS. John and Paul (1487–1500)

Worcester Cathedral Libr.

F. 63 (xiii^{ex}) **E, Notulae** (copied in by fr. Richard Bromwych in early 1300s); Worcester Cathedral Priory (by early 1300s)

F. 86 (xvⁱⁿ) **Dedecus EQ**; Worcester Cathedral Priory (probably made in Oxford for the priory's monks)

F. 138 (xiii^{ex}) **Thos EC**; Worcester Cathedral Priory (by late 1200s)

F. 169 (xivⁱⁿ) **M, E**; Worcester Cathedral Priory (by early 1300s)

Table 2
Lost and Unidentified Manuscripts

The information for this table is derived from the appropriate volumes of CBM-LC. The only exceptions are Beriah Botfield, *Catalogi veteres librorum ecclesiae cathedralis Dunelmensis*, Publications of the Surtees Society 7 (London: J.B. Nichols and Son, 1838); N.R. Ker, "Books at St. Paul's Cathedral before 1313," in *Books, Collectors and Libraries*, 209–42; William J. Courtenay, "The Fourteenth-Century Booklist of the Oriel College Library," *Viator* 19 (1988): 283–90; and from the books and articles, cited in preceding notes, of James (for Canterbury Cathedral Priory, St. Augustine's, Canterbury, and Canterbury College), Ker (for All Souls College and Merton College), Mynors (for Balliol College), Weiss (for Lincoln College), and Powicke (for Merton College), and Thomson (for Worcester Cathedral Priory).

Bullington Priory, Lincolnshire
Giles DRP (ca. 1530)

Cambridge University Library
Giles RC, Thos EC, Thos PC (ca. 1440; Hugh Parys)
Giles DRP w. tabula (ca. 1440; Thomas Paxton)
Dbf (ca. 1440; James Matissale)
P tabula (1473)
E (1473)
"Textus moralis philosophie" (?E; 1434; Robert Fitzhugh)

Clare Hall, Cambridge
Thos EC (before 1496; John Hurt, fellow 1432)
"Tractatus de regimine principum" (?Giles DRP; 1375; John Lenne)

Corpus Christi College, Cambridge
"Liber moralis philosophie," containing: Burley EC, Eustratius EC, Burley E conclusiones, E, Thos EC, Y, Bartholomew of Bruges YC, Bernard of Clairvaux *De laude novae militiae*, PQ, P, Peter PC, R, Giles RC, Dbf, Giles DbfC, *De vita Aristotelis*, *De pomo*, Ss, Roger Bacon *Tractatus ad declarandum quaedam obscure dicta in libro Secreti Secretorum* (1439; Thomas Markaunt)
John Deverose E tabula (1439; Thomas Markaunt)
John Deverose E tabula (1458; John Tittleshall)
John Deverose E tabula (1458; John Tittleshall)
E, Mm (1439; Thomas Markaunt)
Giles DRP (1439; Thomas Markaunt)

Godshouse, Cambridge
Giles DRP (1476; John Hurt)

King's College, Cambridge
Bruni E (ca. 1457)
Bruni P (ca. 1457)
Burley PC (ca. 1457)
Thos EC (ca. 1457)
Dedecus EQ (1475; William Wyche)
E (1475; William Wyche)

King's Hall, Cambridge
E (borrowed ca. 1390 by Henry de Knyveton, fellow)
Thos EC (ca. 1390)
"Nove questiones super libros ethicorum" (1449–50)

Pembroke College, Cambridge
E, P (1406–28; John Sperhawk)
Giles DRP (1406–28; John Clenche)
"Summa Politicorum" (1447; John Langton)
"Grosseteste cum commento super libros Ethicorum" (probably E w. Eustratius
    EC; 1487; Thomas Wryght)

Peterhouse, Cambridge
Dedecus EQ (1456; William More)
E (1418)
E, Thos EC (1418)
E (1418)
"bagg continens questiones philosophie moralis et naturalis incomplete" (1418)
"bagg cum tabulis logice Ethicorum et aliorum librorum philosophie" (1418)

Queen's College, Cambridge
Thos EC, Thos ET (1472)
PQ (1472)
Thos/Peter PC (1472)
Burley EC (1472)
Giles DRP (1491–92)

St. Catherine's Hall, Cambridge
E (late 1400s; Robert Wodelarke)
Averroes EC (late 1400s; Robert Wodelarke)
R, Y, Ss (late 1400s; Robert Wodelarke)
P (late 1400s; Robert Wodelarke)

Canterbury Cathedral Priory
E (1291/2; William de Resham, monk)
E (1299; John de London, monk)
Thos EC (1331; William de Ledebery, monk)
E (1331; William de Ledebery)
E (1328; Walter de Norwyco, monk)
"Liber de regimine principis" (probably Giles DRP; 1331; Henry Eastry, prior)
E, P, R (1508)
P (1508)
E (1508)

St. Augustine's Abbey, Canterbury
Thos E tabula (by 1405; William Welde, abbot)
"Ysagoge in moralem philosophiam" (?Bruni, *Ysagogicon in libros morales Aristotelis*; late 1400s)
"Textus Ethicorum et in eodem libro duplex exposicio super eosdem" (late 1400s; John de Bucwell, monk)
"Textus ethicorum de noua translacione et in eodem quedam abbreviacio compendiosa super libros predictos. Item quoddam compendium notabile principalium proposicionum libri Ethicorum. Item questiones extracte summarie de singulis capitulis libri Ethicorum per modum conclusionum et notabilium" (by 1309; Thomas Findon, abbot)
E (by 1334; Ralph de Bourne, abbot)
P, R (by 1309; Thomas Findon)
Averroes EC "et in eodem libro concordancie Ethicorum," Y (by 1299; John de London, monk)
Albert EC (by 1309; Thomas Findon)
Eustratius EC (by 1309; Thomas Findon)
Eustratius EC, Thos EC (by 1343; Thomas Poucyn, abbot)
Henry of Friemar EC (by 1334; Ralph de Bourne)
Burley EC, Burley PC (by late 1400s; John of Canterbury, ?monk)
"Questiones super iiij libros Ethicorum" (probably Dinsdale EQ; ?early 1300s; Thomas Sprott, monk)
"Questiones super viij libros Ethicorum" (by 1299; John de London)
"Abbreviacio exposicionis super libros Ethicorum" (by late 1400s; Thomas de Salteford, ?monk)
"Conclusiones et notabilia Ethicorum" (by late 1400s; T. de Wyvelesberghe, ?monk)

Dover Priory
E (1389; Michael de Aldin, monk)
E (1389; Salomon, monk)
Giles DRP (1389)

Durham Cathedral Priory
EQ (1392)
E (1392)
Giles DRP (1395)

Ely Cathedral Priory
"Lecture super libros morales Aristotelis, videlicet super libros Ethicorum,
Polethicorum, et libelum de bona fortuna in [uno] volumine" (probably Thos
EC, Thos/Peter PC, and Giles DbfC; returned to Ely 1329 after lifetime
loan to Roger of Huntingfield, fellow of Peterhouse by 1310)

Evesham Abbey, Worcestershire
Burley PC (1392; Nicholas of Hereford, prior)
Giles DRP (1392; Nicholas of Hereford)

Glastonbury Abbey
E conclusiones (1375; Walter de Monington, abbot)

Leicester Abbey
E (mid 1300s; John Sadyngton, cellarer)
E (by late 1400s)
Thos EC (by late 1400s)
Giles DRP (by late 1400s)

London, St. Paul's Cathedral
"moralia Aristotelis" (probably Mm; ca. 1300)

Meaux Abbey, Yorkshire
Thos EC (by 1396)

Norwich Carmelite Convent
R (by ca. 1530)

All Souls College, Oxford
Burley EC, Burley PC (1437; King Henry VI)
"Philosophia moralis et naturalis" (first item either E or a group of moral phil.
texts; by 1443)
E (by 1443)
"Tabula philosophie moralis" (by 1443)
Burley EC (1466–7; John Norfolk, first vice-warden)
". . . ethicorum" (probably E; by ca. 1495)
E (1485; John Saunder)
"Textus moralis philosophie" (late 1400s; Richard Topclyffe)

Balliol College, Oxford
"Leonardus Aretinus super libros Ethicorum" (either Bruni E or Bruni *Isagogicon in libros morales Aristotelis*; 1474; Alexander Bell, fellow)
E (1474; Alexander Bell)

Canterbury College, Oxford
Thos EC (1524)
E, P, R (1524)
Giles DRP (1524)
E (1524)
"Textus de singulis causis libri Ethicorum" (1524)
"Textus ethicorum nouiter translatus" (1524)
"Ysagoge in moralem philosophiam" (?Bruni, *Isagogicon in libros morales Aristo-telis*; 1524)
E (1524)

Lincoln College, Oxford
Bruni *Isagogicon in libros morales Aristotelis* (1465; Robert Fleming, fellow)
Giles DRP (by 1474; John Marchall, fellow)
E w. Thos EC (by 1474; John Tylney, prebendary of Lincoln)
Burley EC (by 1474; Thomas Gascoigne)
Dedecus EQ (by 1476)
Giles DRP (by 1476)
Burley EC (by 1476)

Merton College, Oxford
E (by 1320s; John Martyn, fellow)
E (by 1320s)
Thos PC (by 1320s)
E (by 1320s; Brice de Sharsted, fellow)
Dbf (by 1320s; Stephen Gravesend, bp. of London)
Thos EC (by 1320s; Stephen Gravesend)
"Questiones morales" (probably *quaestiones* on the *Ethics*; by 1320s; Stephen Gravesend)
E (ca. 1360)
E (by 1372)
Thos EC (by 1372)
Thos EC (by 1372)
E (by 1372)
E (by 1372)
Eustratius EC (1366; William Arderne to Merton, in return for a loan)
E (by 1375)
"Textus moralis" (?E; by 1410)

Thos EC (by 1410)
EQ (by 1410)
E (redeemed by Merton 1432)
"Textus moralis philosophie" (?E; by 1451)
EQ (by 1451)
"Expositio moralis philosophie" (by 1451)
EQ (by 1483)
Y w. YC (by 1483)

Oriel College, Oxford
"Textus poleticorum vel de problematibus" (either P or Aristotle *Problems*; by
    1337; John Cobbledik)
"Expositio Methaphisice et Ethicarum" (probably Aquinas's commentaries on
    the *Metaphysics* and *Ethics*; by 1337; John Cobbledik)
"Sententie super libros Rethoricorum Aristotelis" (probably Giles RC; by 1337;
    John Cobbledik)

Peterborough Abbey
Env (by late 1300s)
En (by late 1300s)

Ramsey Abbey
E (by mid 1300s; Hugh de Aylingtone, monk)
Thos EC (early 1300s; Walter de Lilleford, monk)
E (early 1300s; Walter de Lilleford)

Syon Abbey, Middlesex
Dbf (by 1485; William Asplyn)
Dbf, E, P, R, "Proposiciones 10 librorum Ethicorum," and "Tabula peroptima 10
    librorum Ethicorum" (late 1400s; J. Pynchebek)
Dedecus EQ (either 1487 from Richard Grene or 1508 from John Grene)
Bruni E (perhaps the book printed in Cologne 1470; either Richard Grene or
    John Grene)
E, P, R, Mm (ca. 1420; John Bracebrigge)
Giles DRP w. tabula (ca. 1420; John Bracebrigge)
Burley EC (ca. 1420; John Bracebrigge)
E (by 1488; Thomas Westhawe)
Book of all natural philosophy, metaphysics, moral philosophy, and parts of old
    and new logic (by 1524)
Bruni E (by 1513; Stephen Saundre)
Book containing, among other things, Giles DRP tabula, a "tabula Policratici,"
    and William of Pagula *Speculum regis Edwardi III* (by 1524)

"Exposicio lyncolniensis super libros politicorum," Giles RC (the identity of the first text is unclear; by 1524)
Burley EC (by 1524)

Titchfield Abbey, Hampshire
E (by 1400)
E (by 1400)

Winchester Franciscan Convent
Eustratius EC (by ca. 1530)

Worcester Cathedral Priory
Bruni E, Bruni P (mid 1400s; Nicholas Hambury, monk, and John Suckley, monk)

St. Mary's Abbey, York
Thos EC (by mid 1400s)

York Austin Friars Convent
Giles DbfC (by 1372)
"Tabula super philosophiam morale Aristotelis" (by 1372)
"Tabula super 5 libros Boecii de consolacione philosophie et super 8 libros poleticorum" (by 1372)
E (by 1372)
E, R, Y (by 1372)
Giles DRP (by 1372)
Thos EC (by 1372)
Giles DRP (by 1372)
"Libri ethicorum quinque" (apparently an incomplete copy of E; by 1372)
E (by 1372)
Thos EC (by 1372)
Y, Eustratius EC (by 1372)
Thos EC (by 1372)
E bks. II–VII (by 1372)
"Kervyle super libros politicorum Aristotelis cum duabus tabulis Egidii de regimine principum" and "abbreviatio prefati magistri Kervyle super libros politicorum sancti Thome" (presumably John Kervyle OESA compiled some sort of commentary on the *Politics* as well as an *abbreviatio* of Aquinas's *Politics* commentary; 1435; John Bukwode OESA)

Richard W. Pfaff,
Publications, 1970–2009

Books

New Liturgical Feasts in Later Medieval England (Oxford: Clarendon Press, 1970).

Montague Rhodes James (London: Scolar Press, 1980).

Medieval Latin Liturgy: A Select Bibliography (Toronto: University of Toronto Press, 1982).

The Eadwine Psalter: Text, Image, and Monastic Culture in Twelfth-Century Canterbury, ed. and contrib. M. T. Gibson, T. A. Heslop, and R. W. Pfaff (London: Modern Humanities Research Association, and University Park, PA: Penn State University Press, 1992): chap. iii, "The Calendar" (62–87); chap. iv, "Tituli, Collects, Canticles" (88–107).

The Liturgical Books of Anglo-Saxon England, ed. and contrib. R.W. Pfaff. OEN Subsidia 23 (Kalamazoo: Medieval Institute Publications, 1995): "Mass-books" (7–34) and, with J.L. Nelson, "Pontificals and Benedictionals" (87–98).

Liturgical Calendars, Saints, and Services in Medieval England (Aldershot: Variorum, 1998). Thirteen articles (one in two parts): eight published, asterisked below, and five unpublished, abbreviated below as *LSCCME*.

The Liturgy in Medieval England: A History (Cambridge: Cambridge University Press, 2009).

Articles

"The Library of the Fathers," *Studies in Philology* 70 (1973): 329–44.

*"The English Devotion of St. Gregory's Trental," *Speculum* 49 (1974): 74–90.

"Anglo-American Patristic Translations 1866–1900," *Journal of Ecclesiastical History* 28 (1977): 39–55.

"M. R. James on the Cataloguing of Manuscripts: A Draft Essay of 1906," *Scriptorium* 31 (1977): 103–18.

*"William of Malmesbury's *Abbreviatio Amalarii*," *Recherches de Théologie ancienne et médiévale* 47 (1980): 78–113 (commentary) and 48 (1981): 128–71 (text).

*"Some Anglo-Saxon Sources for the 'Theological Windows' at Canterbury Cathedral," *Mediaevalia* 10 (1984/1988): 49–62.

"Psalter Collects as an Aid to the Classification of Psalters," in *Studia Patristica* 18.2, ed. E. A. Livingstone (Leuven: Peeters, 1989–1991), 397–402.

*"*De Cella in Saeculum*: the Liturgical Aspects [St. Hugh of Lincoln as a Liturgical Person]," in *De Cella in Saeculum: Religion and Secular Life and Devotion in Late Medieval England*, ed. M.G. Sargent (Woodbridge: D. S. Brewer, 1989), 17–27.

"The Hagiographical Peculiarity of Martha's Companion(s)" [paper to Oxford Medieval Group, 1990; *LCSSME*, no.IV, 22]

"Why Do Medieval Psalters Have Calendars?" [paper to London Medieval Manuscripts Seminar, 1990; *LCSSME*, no. VI, 15]

*"Lanfranc's Supposed Purge of the Anglo-Saxon Calendar," in *Warriors and Churchmen in the High Middle Ages: Essays Presented to Karl Leyser*, ed. T. Reuter (London: Hambledon, 1992), 95–108.

*"Eadui Basan: *Scriptorum Princeps?*" in *England in the Eleventh Century: Proceedings of the 1990 Harlaxton Symposium*, ed. Carola Hicks (Stamford: Paul Watkins, 1992), 267–83.

*"Prescription and Reality in the Rubrics of Sarum Rite Service Books," in *Intellectual Life in the Middle Ages: Essays Presented to Margaret Gibson*, ed. Lesley Smith and Benedicta Ward (London: Hambledon, 1992), 197–205.

*"Bede Among the Fathers? The Evidence from Liturgical Commemoration," *Studia Patristica* 28, ed. E. A. Livingstone (Leuven: Peeters 1993), 225–29.

"Martyrological Notices for Thomas Becket" [paper to Kalamazoo Congress, 1993; *LCSSME*, no. VIII, 10]

"Liturgical Studies Today: One Subject or Two?" *Journal of Ecclesiastical History* 45 (1994): 325–32.

"N.R. Ker and the Study of English Medieval Manuscripts," in *Basic Readings in Anglo-Saxon Manuscripts*, ed. Mary P. Richards (New York: Garland, 1994), 55–77.

"Bishop Baldock's Book, St Paul's Cathedral, and the Use of Sarum" [paper to Medieval Academy of America, 1995; *LCSSME*, no. XI, 20]

"The Patristic Diet of Cranmer's Generation," *Studia Patristica* 30, ed. E. A. Livingstone (Leuven: Peeters, 1997), 319–24.

"The Study of Medieval Liturgy "[purpose-written introduction, 1998; *LCSSME*, no. I]

"The 'Sample Week' in the Medieval Divine Office," in *Continuity and Change in Christian Worship*, ed. R.N. Swanson. Studies in Church History 25 (Woodbridge: Boydell, 1999), 78–88.

"The Anglo-Saxon Bishop and his Book," Toller Memorial Lecture, University of Manchester; in *Bulletin of the John Rylands University Library of Manchester* 81 (1999): 3–24; also published separately.

"The Lavington Manual and its Students," *Bodleian Library Record* 17 (2000): 10–23.

"M.R. James and the Liturgical Manuscripts of Cambridge," in *The Legacy of M.R. James*, ed. L. Dennison (Donington: Shaun Tyas, 2001), 174–93.

(with Michael Gullick) "The Dublin Pontifical (TCD 98[B.3.6]): St Anselm's?" *Scriptorium* 55 (2001): 284–94 and pl. 58–60.

"The Kenilworth Missal (Chichester Cathedral, MS Med. 2)," in *Music and Medieval Manuscripts. Paleography and Performance. Essays dedicated to Andrew Hughes*, ed. J. Haines and R. Rosenfeld (Aldershot and Burlington, VT: Ashgate, 2004), 400–18.

"Telling Liturgical Times in the Middle Ages," in *Procession, Performance, Liturgy, and Ritual*, ed. N. van Deusen (Ottawa: Institute of Medieval Music, 2007), 43–64.

"The Glastonbury Collectar," in *Tributes to Nigel M. Morgan. Contexts of Medieval Art: Images, Objects and Ideas*, ed. M. Michael and J. Luxford (London: Harvey Miller, 2009), 31–38.

"St. Richard of Chichester and the Kenilworth Missal," in *Richard of Chichester, 750th Anniversary Essays*, ed. P. Foster Otter Memorial Papers 25 (Chichester: University of Chichester, 2009), 14–21.

Forthcoming Article

"Liturgical Books," in *Cambridge History of the Book in Britain*, vol. I: *to A.D. 1100*, ed. R. Gameson (Cambridge: Cambridge University Press, 2010).

Contributions to Reference Works

Westminster Dictionary of Church History, ed. J.C. Brauer (Philadelphia: Westminster Press, 1971): "Common Prayer, Book of" (222–23), "Cranmer" (244–45), "Whitgift" (865–66) and forty-five other entries, mostly on 16th-century English ecclesiastical figures.

McGraw-Hill Encyclopedia of World Biography, 12 vols (New York: McGraw-Hill, 1973): "Douglas, Sir James" (3:420–21), "James I [of Scotland]" (5:524–25), "James III" (5:525–26), "Robert I" (9:217–18), "Robert II" (9:218–19), "Robert III" (9:219–20).

Dictionary of the Middle Ages, ed. J.R. Strayer, (New York: Scribner, 1987): "Marian Feasts," 8:134.

Medieval England: An Encyclopedia, ed. P.E. Szarmach, M.T. Tavormina, and J.T. Rosenthal (New York: Garland, 1998): "Feasts, New Liturgical," 295; "Liturgy," 446–48.

Dictionary of Literary Biography, vol. 201, ed. W. Baker and K. Womack (Detroit: Gale, 1999): "M.R. James," 148–61.

Blackwell Encyclopaedia of Anglo-Saxon England, ed. M. Lapidge et al. (Oxford: Blackwell, 1999): "Liturgical Books," 290–91; "Liturgy," pp. 292–93.

Dictionary of the Middle Ages, Supplement, I, ed. W.C. Jordan (New York: Scribner, 2004): "Liturgical Year, Western," 330–32.

Oxford Dictionary of National Biography, ed. H.C.G. Matthew and B. Harrison (Oxford: Oxford University Press, 2004): "Abbo of Fleury" (1.10–11), "Grimbald of St. Bertin's" (24:19–20), "James, M.R." (29:723–26), "Ursula [St.]" (55:958–59), "Werferth" (58:166–67), "Wilson, H.A." (59:559).

Oxford Dictionary of the Middle Ages, ed. R. Bjork et al. (Oxford: Oxford University Press, 2010): "Liturgy."

Book Reviews

AHR = *American Historical Review*; *CH* = *Church History*; *HRNB* = *History. Review of New Books*; *JEH* = *Journal of Ecclesiastical History*; *TMR* = *The Medieval Review* [electronic journal; word-lengths supplied in place of page references]. Book-notes of under 200 words are not included.

1971
T.W. Jones, ed. *The Becket Controversy* (New York, 1970): *CH* 40:215

P Hunter Blair, *The World of Bede* (London, 1970): *CH* 40:477–78.

1972
G. Wegner, *Kirchenjahr und Messfeier in der Würzburger Domliturgie des späten Mittelalters* (Wurzburg, 1970): *Speculum* 47:151–52.

P. Clemoes and K. Hughes, ed., *England before the Conquest: Studies in Primary Sources presented to Dorothy Whitelock* (Cambridge, 1971): *CH* 41:404–05.

1973
H. Mayr-Harting, *The Coming of Christianity to England* (New York, 1972): *CH* 42:172–73.

T. Bailey, *The Processions of Sarum and the Western Church* (Toronto, 1971): *Speculum* 48:337–39.

1974
P. Clemoes, et al., ed. *Anglo-Saxon England* I (Cambridge, 1972); II (1973): *CH* 43:97–98 and 389–90.

R.B. Dobson, *Durham Priory, 1400–1450* (Cambridge, 1973): *AHR* 79:773–74.

C.R. Cheney, *Medieval Texts and Studies* (Oxford, 1973): *CH* 43:390.

1975

J.T. Rosenthal, *The Training of an Elite Group. English Bishops in the Fifteenth Century* (Philadelphia, 1970): *AHR* 80:94–95.

P. Clemoes, et al., ed. *Anglo-Saxon England* III (Cambridge, 1974): *CH* 44:398–99.

1976

M. Brett, *The English Church under Henry I* (Oxford, 1974): *CH* 45:379.

D. Parsons, ed., *Tenth-Century Studies. Essays in Commemoration of the Millennium of the Council of Winchester* . . . (London, 1975): *CH* 45:525–26.

1977

J.J.G. Alexander and M. T. Gibson, eds., *Medieval Learning and Literature: Essays Presented to Richard William Hunt* (Oxford, 1976): *AHR* 82:73–74.

M. Warner, *Alone of All Her Sex. The Myth and Cult of the Virgin Mary* (New York, 1976): *CH* 46:234–36.

1978

R.C. Finucane, *Miracles and Pilgrims: Popular Beliefs in Medieval England* (Totowa, 1978): *AHR* 83:.1238–39.

B. Harvey, *Westminster Abbey and its Estates in the Middle Ages* (Oxford, 1977): *CH* 47:443.

C. Haigh, *Reformation and Resistance in Tudor Lancashire* (Cambridge, 1975): *Societas — a Review of Social History* 8:162–63.

1979

R.E. Reynolds, *The Ordinals of Christ from Their Origins to the Twelfth Century* (Berlin and New York, 1978): *Speculum* 54:622–24.

R.M. Haines, *The Church and Politics in Fourteenth-Century England: the Career of Adam Orleton, c. 1275–1345* (Cambridge, 1978): *Speculum* 54:381–82.

M.P. Lillich, *The Stained Glass of Saint-Père de Chartres* (Middletown, Conn., 1978): *CH* 48:338–39.

C. Jones, G. Wainwright, and E. Yarnold, ed. *The Study of Liturgy* (New York, 1978): *CH* 48:359–60.

1980

D. Hill, ed. *Ethelred the Unready: Papers from the Millenary Conference* (BAR British Series 59, 1978): *Speculum* 55:581–82.

J.J. O'Donnell, *Cassiodorus* (Berkeley and Los Angeles, 1979): *CH* 49:320–21.

F. Barlow, *The English Church, 1066–1154* (London, 1979): *CH* 49:452–53.

C. Donaldson, *Martin of Tours: Parish Priest, Mystic, and Exorcist* (Boston, 1980): *HRNB* 8:212.

1981

J.C. Dickinson, *The Later Middle Ages; from the Norman Conquest to the Eve of the Reformation* (London and New York, 1979): *Speculum* 56:376–78.

M.G. Cheney, *Roger, Bishop of Worcester, 1164–1179* (Oxford, 1980): *AHR* 87:164–65.

J.M. Gilbert, *Hunting and Hunting Reserves in Medieval Scotland* (Atlantic Highlands, NJ, 1980): *HRNB* 9:190–91.

B. Hamilton, *The Medieval Inquisition* (New York, 1981): *HRNB* 10:40.

1982

M. Brett, C.N.L. Brooke, D. Whitelock, ed. *Council and Synods . . . relating to the English Church, 871–1204*, 2 vols. (Oxford, 1982): *HRNB* 11:8.

G. Duby, *The Three Orders: Feudal Society Imagined.* transl. A. Goldhammer (Chicago, 1980), *Anglican Theological Review* 64:104–05.

R. Grégoire, *Homiliares liturgiques médiévaux: Analyse de manuscrits* (Spoleto, 1980): *Speculum* 57:899–900.

M. Perham, *The Communion of Saints: An Examination of the Place of the Christian Dead in the Belief, Worship, and Calendars of the Church.* Alcuin Club Collection 62 (London, 1980): *CH* 51:472–73.

P. Salway, *Roman Britain* (Oxford, 1981): *HRNB* 10:106–07.

M. Todd, *Roman Britain, 55 B.C.-A.D. 400* (Atlantic Highlands, NJ, 1981): *HRNB* 10:103.

1983

W.F. Coleman, ed. *Philippe de Mézières' Campaign for the Feast of Mary's Presentation: Edited from Bibl. nat. MSS Latin 17330 and 14454* (Toronto, 1981): *Speculum* 58 (1983), 521–22.

W. Davies, *Wales in the Early Middle Ages* (Atlantic Highlands, NJ, 1982): *HRNB* 11:153.

G. Duby, *The Age of the Cathedrals; Art and Society, 980–1420*, transl. E. Levieux and B. Thompson (Chicago, 1981): *CH* 52:205–06.

J. John, *Chartres. The Masons who Built a Legend* (Boston, 1982): *HRNB* 11:220.

C. Thomas, *Christianity in Roman Britain to A.D. 500* (Berkeley, 1981): *CH* 52:493–94.

1984

D.L. Edwards, *Christian England: Its Story to the Reformation* (Grand Rapids, 1983): *CH* 53:531–32.

A. Gransden, *Historical Writing in England*, II: *c. 1307 to the Early Sixteenth Century* (Ithaca, 1982): *CH* 53:242–43.

R.M. Thomson, *Manuscripts from St Albans Abbey, 1066–1235*, 2 vols. (Woodbridge, 1982): *Speculum* 59:445–47.

1985

R. Bartlett, *Gerald of Wales, 1146–1223* (Oxford 1982); with B.F. Roberts, *Gerald of Wales*, (Cardiff, 1982): *Speculum* 60:117–19.

M. Chibnall, *The World of Orderic Vitalis* (Oxford, 1985): *HRNB* 13:161.

C. de Hamel, *Glossed Books of the Bible and the Origins of the Paris Booktrade* (Woodbridge, 1984): *TLS: Times Literary Supplement* 16 Aug., 911.

R.W. Hunt, ed. M. Gibson, *The Schools and the Cloister: the Life and Writings of Alexander Nequam* (Oxford, 1984): *CH* 54:394.

J.E. Sayers, *Papal Government and England during the Pontificate of Honorius III (1216–1277)* (Cambridge, 1984): *CH* 54:516–17.

C. Stancliffe, *St. Martin and his Hagiographer: History and Miracle in Sulpicius Severus* (Oxford, 1983): *CH* 54:92–93.

N.P. Tanner, *The Church in Late Medieval Norwich, 1370–1532* (Toronto, 1984): *AHR* 90:665–66.

F. Wormald, *Collected Writings*, I: *Studies in Medieval Art from the Sixth to the Twelfth Centuries*, ed. J.J.G. Alexander et al. (London, 1984): *Speculum* 60:1069.

1986

M. Curran, *The Antiphonary of Bangor and the Early Irish Monastic Liturgy* (Dublin, 1984) *CH* 55:89–90.

J.N.L. Myres, *The English Settlements*. Oxford History of England (Oxford, 1986): *HRNB* 14:143.

J. Steane, *The Archaeology of Medieval England and Wales* (Athens, GA., 1985): *HRNB* 14:106.

A.K. Warren, *Anchorites and their Patrons in Medieval England* (Berkeley and Los Angeles, 1985): *AHR* 91:1181.

1987

F. Barlow, *Thomas Becket* (Berkeley, 1986): *CH* 56:245–46.

C.W. Brockwell, Jr., *Bishop Reginald Pecock and the Lancastrian Church: Securing the Foundations of Cultural Authority* (Lewiston, NY, 1985): *AHR* 92:645–46.

B. Colgrave, ed. and tr., *The Earliest Life of Gregory the Great*; *Two Lives of St. Cuthbert*; *The Life of Bishop Wilfrid by Eddius Stephanus*; *Felix's Life of St. Guthlac*, 4 vols., repr. (Cambridge, 1985): *CH* 56:239–40.

D. Dumville and M. Lapidge, ed. *The Anglo-Saxon Chronicle, a Collaborative Edition*, 17: *The Annals of St. Neots with Vita Prima Sancti Neoti* (Cambridge, 1985): *CH* 56:111–12.

H. Vollrath, *Die Synoden Englands bis 1066* (Paderborn, 1985): *CH* 56:388–89.

1988

S. Cruden, *Scottish Medieval Churches* (Edinburgh, 1986): *CH* 57:535–36.

R. Taft, *The Liturgy of the Hours in East and West: the Origins of the Divine Office and its Meaning for Today* (Collegeville, Minn., 1986): *Speculum* 63:478.

R. Thomson, *William of Malmesbury* (Wolfeboro, N.H., 1987): *Albion* 20:79–80.

1989

J.M. Beers, ed. *A Commentary on the Cisterican Hymnal/ Explanatio super hymnos . . .*, Henry Bradshaw Soc. 102 (London, 1987): *Speculum* 64:657–58.

W Goffart, *The Narrators of Barbarian History (A.D. 550–800): Jordanes, Gregory of Tours, Bede, and Paul the Deacon* (Princeton, 1988): *CH* 58:372–73.

A. Kenny, ed. *Wyclif in his Times* (New York, 1986): *AHR* 94:429.

M.R. Moyes, ed. *Richard Rolle's* "Expositio super Novem Lectiones Mortuorum," 2 vols. (Salzburg, 1988): *CH* 53:508–09.

C. Tyerman, *England and the Crusades 1095–1588* (Chicago, 1988): *HRNB* 17:114.

1990

J.H. Burns, ed. *The Cambridge History of Medieval Political Thought, c. 350–1450* (Cambridge, 1988): *CH* 59:82–84.

C. Morris, *The Papal Monarchy: The Western Church from 1050 to 1250*, Oxford History of the Christian Church (Oxford, 1988): *CH* 59:543–45.

C.A. Newman, *The Anglo-Norman Nobility in the Reign of Henry I: the Second Generation* (Philadelphia, 1988): *HRNB* 18:160.

S.J. Ridyard, *The Royal Saints of Anglo-Saxon England: a Study of West Saxon and East Anglian Cults* (Cambridge, 1988): *AHR* 95:1513.

R.N. Swanson, *Church and Society in Late Medieval England* (Oxford, 1989): *Journal of Interdisciplinary History* 21:313–14.

C. Waddell, ed. *The Paraclete Statutes* "Institutiones nostrae": *Troyes, Bibl. municipale, MS 802, fo. 89r-90v* (Gethsemani, Ky., 1987): *Speculum* 65:1073–74.

J.M. Wallace-Hadrill, *Bede's "Ecclesiastical History of the English People": Historical Commentary* (Oxford, 1988): *CH* 59:228–29.

1991

E.B. Foley, ed. *The First Ordinary of the Royal Abbey of St-Denis in France* (Fribourg, 1990): *Worship* 65 (1991): 478–79.

J. Gerchow, *Die Gedenküberlieferung der Angelsachsen. Mit einem Katalog der Libri Vitae Necrologien* (Berlin, 1988): *CH* 90:528.

G.McM. Gibson, *The Theater of Devotion: East Anglian Drama and Society in the Late Middle Ages* (Chicago, 1989): *AHR* 96:1184–85.

J.T. McNeill and H.M. Gamer, eds. *Medieval Handbooks of Penance* (New York, 1990, repr. of 1938 original): *HRNB* 20:41.

C. Wilson, *The Gothic Cathedral* (New York, 1990): *HRNB* 19:93.

1992

L. Abrams and J.P. Carley, eds. *The Archaeology and History of Glastonbury Abbey: Essays in Honour of . . . C.A. Raleigh Radford* (Rochester, NY, 1991): *Albion* 24:455–56.

M. Camille, *The Gothic Image: Ideology and Image-Making in Medieval Art* (Cambridge, 1990): *CH* 61:83–85.

P. Sims-Williams, *Religion and Literature in Western England, 600–800* (Cambridge, 1990): *AHR* 97:178–79.

D. Welander, *The History, Art and Architecture of Gloucester Cathedral* (Wolfeboro, NH, 1991): *Albion* 24:307–08.

1993

N. Cantor, *Inventing the Middle Ages: the Lives, Works, and Ideas of the Great Medievalists of the Twentieth Century* (New York, 1991): *Speculum* 68:122–25.

D.N. Dumville, *Wessex and England from Alfred to Edgar* (Woodbridge, 1992): *HRNB* 21:158.

M. Lapidge and M. Winterbottom, eds. *Wulfstan of Winchester, Life of St Æthelwold* (Oxford, 1991): *CH* 62:247–48.

A.G. Martimort, *Les "ordines," les ordinaires, et les cérémoniaux*, Typologie des Sources du Moyen Age Occidental, 56 (Turnhout, 1991): *Speculum* 68:537–38.

V. Ortenberg, *The English Church and the Continent in the Tenth and Eleventh Centuries: Cultural, Spiritual, and Artistic Exchanges* (Oxford, 1992): *Albion* 25:282–84.

A. Paredi, *Storia del rito ambrosiano* (Milan, 1990): *Speculum* 68:552–53.

W. Rodwell, *The Archaeology of Religious Places. Churches and Cemeteries in Britain* (Philadelphia, 1990): *CH* 62:258.

C.P. Schreiber, *The Dilemma of Arnulf of Lisieux: New Ideas versus Old Ideals* (Bloomington, IN., 1990): *CH* 62:389–91.

1994

D. Abulafia, M. Franklin, M. Rubin, eds. *Church and City 1000–1500: Essays in Honour of Christopher Brooke* (Cambridge 1992): *Jnl. Interdisciplinary Hist.* 24:690–91.

D.N. Dumville, *Liturgy and the Ecclesiastical History of Late Anglo-Saxon England. Four Studies* (Woodbridge, 1992): *Speculum* 69:1158–59.

C.W. Dutschke, *Guide to the Medieval and Renaissance Manuscripts in the Huntingdon Library*, 2 vols (San Marino, CA, 1989); Paul Saenger, *A Catalogue of the Pre-1500 Western Manuscripts at the Newberry Library* (Chicago, 1989): *The Library/ Transactions Bibliographical Society* 6th ser. 16:234–36.

M. Harvey, *England, Rome and the Papacy 1417–1464. The Study of a Relationship* (Manchester, 1993): *Journal of Theological Studies* n.s. 45:391–93.

E.A. Lowe, ed. *The Bobbio Missal . . .* with notes and studies by A. Wilmart, E.A. Lowe, and H.A. Wilson (Woodbridge, 1991; repr. of HBS 58, 61, 1920–24): *Mediaevistik* 7:342–43.

R.H. Rouse and Mary A. Rouse, eds. *Registrum Anglie de libris doctorum et auctorum veterum*, Corpus of British Medieval Library Catalogues (London, 1991): *The Library* 6th ser. 16:335–37.

R.V. Turner, *King John* (London, 1994): *HRNB* 23:70–71.

1995

P. Cramer, *Baptism and Change in the early Middle Ages, c. 200- c. 1150* (Cambridge, 1993): *JEH* 46:130–32.

E.U. Crosby, *Bishop and Chapter in Twelfth-Century England. A Study of the 'Mensa Episcopalis'* (Cambridge, 1994): *TMR* 95.05.04 [2726].

R. Gameson, ed. *The Early Medieval Bible. Its Production, Decoration and Use* (Cambridge, 1994): *The Library*, 6th ser. 17:172–74.

K. Ottosen, *The Responsories and Versicles of the Latin Office of the Dead* (Aarhus, 1993): *Speculum* 70:185–86.

E. Palazzo, *Le moyen âge. Des origines au XIIIe siècle*. Histoire des livres liturgiques (Paris, 1993): *JEH* 46:356.

1996

H. Belting, *Likeness and Presence; A History of the Image before the Era of Art* (Chicago, 1994): *CH* 65:99–101.

A. Corrêa, ed. *The Durham Collectar* (Henry Bradshaw Society 107, 1992): *Cahiers de civilisation médiévale* 39 (1996): 166–67 (transl. Janet T. Sorrentino).

A. Davril, ed. *The Winchcombe Sacramentary* (Henry Bradshaw Society 109, 1995): *JEH* 47 (1996): 717.

R.A.B. Mynors and R.M. Thomson, *Catalogue of the Manuscripts of Hereford Cathedral Library* (Woodbridge, 1993): *The Library* 6th ser. 18:55–56.

A.E. Nichols, *Seeable Signs: the Iconography of the Seven Sacraments 1350–1444* (Woodbridge, 1994): *CH* 65:87–88.

H. Leith Spencer, *English Preaching in the Late Middle Ages* (New York and Oxford, 1993): *AHR* 101:170.

D. Walker, *The Normans in Britain* (Oxford, 1995): *HRNB* 24:70.

1997

B. Bischoff and M. Lapidge, ed. *Biblical Commentaries from the Canterbury School of Theodore and Hadrian* (Cambridge, 1994): *CH* 66:893.

B. Bischoff, *Manuscripts and Libraries in the Ages of Charlemagne*, ed. and tr. M.M. Gorman (Cambridge, 1994): *Papers of Bibliographical Soc. of America* 91:247–49.

K.L. Jolly, *Popular Religion in Late Saxon England: Elf Charms in Context* (Chapel Hill, 1996): *AHR* 102:797–98.

M. Lapidge, ed. *Archbishop Theodore: Commemorative Studies on his Life and Influence* (Cambridge, 1995): *Speculum* 72:852–54.

R.C. Love, ed. and tr. *Three Eleventh-Century Anglo-Latin Saints' Lives*: Vita S. Birini, Vita et Miracula S. Kenelmi *and* Vita S. Rumwoldi (Oxford, 1996): *TMR* 97.09.10 [1448].

M. Metzger, *Les Sacramentaires*, Typologie des Sources du Moyen Age Occidental, 70 (Turnhout, 1994): *Speculum* 71:200–01.

W. Noel, *The Harley Psalter* (Cambridge, 1995): *Early Medieval Europe* 6:109–10.

R. Sharpe, J.P. Carley, R.M. Thomson, and A.G. Watson, ed. *English Benedictine Libraries. The Shorter Catalogues*, Corpus of British Medieval Library Catalogues 4 (1996): *The Library* 6th ser. 19:258–60.

A.P. Smyth, *King Alfred the Great* (New York and Oxford, 1996): *HRNB* 25:72.

1998

G. Constable, *The Reformation of the Twelfth Century* (Cambridge, 1997): *Jnl. of Interdisciplinary History* 29:94–95.

R. Etaix, *Homéliaires patristiques latins. Recueil d'études de manuscrits médiévaux* (Paris, 1994): *JEH* 49:538–39.

I.B. Milfull, *The Hymns of the Anglo-Saxon Church. A Study and Edition of the 'Durham Hymnal'* (Cambridge, 1996): *Early Medieval Europe* 7:246–47.

1999

M. Budny, *Insular, Anglo-Saxon and Early Anglo-Norman Manuscript Art at Corpus Christi College: An Illustrated Catalogue*, 2 vols. (Kalamazoo, 1997): *TMR* 99.02.05 [1700].

L. Larson-Miller, ed. *Medieval Liturgy. A Book of Essays* (New York, 1997): *Cistercian Studies Quarterly* 34:118.

M. Thompson, *Medieval Bishops' Houses in England and Wales* (Aldershot, 1998): *CH* 68:978–79.

T. Webber and A.G. Watson, ed. *The Libraries of the Augustinian Canons*, Corpus of British Medieval Library Catalogues 6 (1998): *TMR* 99.01.01 [1320].

A. Williams, *Kingship and Government in Pre-Conquest England, c. 500–1066* (New York, 1999): *HRNB* 27:18.

2000

C.A. Jones, *Ælfric's Letter to the Monks of Eynsham* (Cambridge, 1998): *Catholic Historical Review* 86:309–10.

R. Gameson, *The Manuscripts of Early Norman England (c. 1066–1130)* (Oxford, 1999): *Envoi* 9.i:34–37.

M. Gretsch, *The Intellectual Foundations of the English Benedictine Reform* (Cambridge, 1999): *English Historical Review* 115:924.

P. McGurk, ed. and tr. *The Chronicle of John of Worcester*, III: *The Annals from 1067 to 1140* (Oxford, 1999): *TMR* 00.01.05 [980].

N.K. Rasmussen, *Les Pontificaux du haut moyen âge. Genèse du livre de l'évêque* (Louvain, 1998): *JEH* 51:385–86.

2001

L. Casson, *Libraries in the Ancient World* (New Haven, 1991): *HRNB* 29:181–82.

M. Clayton, *The Apocryphal Gospels of Mary in Anglo-Saxon England* (Cambridge, 1998): *JEH* 52:535.

M. Harvey, *The English in Rome, 1362–1420: Portrait of an Expatriate Community* (Cambridge, 1999): *Albion* 33:81–83.

2002

J.A.A. Goodall, *God's House at Ewelme. Life, Devotion and Architecture in a Fifteenth-century Almshouse* (Aldershot, 2001): *CH* 71:653.

N. Saul, *The Cobham Family and their Monuments, 1300–1500* (Oxford, 2001): *HRNB* 31:22.

2003

M.B. Bedingfield, *The Dramatic Liturgy of Anglo-Saxon England* (Woodbridge, 2002): *TMR* 03.05.07 [2070].

H.E.J. Cowdrey, *Lanfranc: Scholar, Monk, and Arhcbishop* (Oxford, 2003): *HRNB* 32:17.

R.M. Thomson, *A Descriptive Catalogue of the Medieval Manuscripts in Worcester Cathedral Library* (Cambridge, 2001): *TMR* 03.01.14 [1913].

Tongeren, Louis van, *Exaltation of the Cross. Toward the Origins of the Feast of the Cross and the Meaning of the Cross in Early Medieval Liturgy* (Leuven, 2000): *JEH* 54:121.

2004

N. Hiscock, ed. *The White Mantle of Churches. Architecture, Liturgy and Art around the Millennium* (Turnhout, 2003): *CH* 73:686.

R. Kieckhefer, *Theology in Stone: Church Architecture from Byzantium to Berkeley* (New York and Oxford, 2003): *HRNB* 33:39–40.

D. Knowles, C.N.L. Brooke, V.C.M. London, eds. *The Heads of Religious Houses, England and Wales*, I: *940–1216* (2nd ed. [1st edn. 1972]), and D.M. Smith and V.C.M. London, II *1216–1377* (both Cambridge, 2001): *Speculum* 80:925–27.

A. Linder, *Raising Arms: Liturgy in the Struggle to Liberate Jerusalem in the Late Middle Ages* (Turnhout, 2003): *English Historical Review* 119:1398–99.

A. Thacker and R. Sharpe, eds. *Local Saints and Local Churches in the Early Medieval West* (Oxford, 2002): *TMR* 04.01.13 [2167].

2005

D. Keene, A. Burns, and A. Saint, ed. *St Paul's: The Cathedral Church of London, 604–2004* (New Haven, 2004): *CH* 74:866–67.

M. Lapidge (et al.), *The Cult of St Swithun. Winchester Studies* 4.ii (Oxford, 2003): *TMR* 05.01.05 [1276].

R.M. Thomson, *William of Malmesbury*, revised edn (Woodbridge, 2003): *Antiquaries Journal* 85:421.

Y. Hen and R. Meens, ed. *The Bobbio Missal: Liturgy and Religious Culture in Merovingian Gaul* (Cambridge, 2004): *The Library*, 7th ser. 6:455–56.

2006

P. Binski, *Becket's Crown. Art and Imagination in Gothic England 1170–1300* (New Haven, 2004): *TMR* 06.10.06 [1610].

2007

G.W. Bernard, *The King's Reformation. Henry VIII and the Remaking of the English Church* (New Haven, 2005): *Sixteenth Century Journal* 38:1229–30.

P. MacCulloch, ed. *Lancelot Andrewes. Selected Sermons and Lectures* (Oxford, 2005): *Sixteenth Century Journal* 38:868–69.

M. Staunton, *Thomas Becket and his Biographers* (Woodbridge, 2006): *CH* 76:831.

2008

K. Anheuser and C. Werner, ed. *Medieval Reliquary Shrines and Precious Metalwork* (London, 2006): *Mediaevistik* 21:527–28.

2009

M.F. Giandrea, *Episcopal Culture in Late Anglo-Saxon England* (Woodbridge, 2007): *Catholic Historical Review* 95:134–35.

M. M. Reeve, *Thirteenth-Century Wall Painting of Salisbury Cathedral* (Woodbridge, 2008): *TMR* 09.01.03 [1887].

F. Tinti, ed. *Pastoral Care in Late Anglo-Saxon England* (Woodbridge, 2007): *Mediaevistik* 22: 408–09.

D. M. Smith, ed. *The Heads of Religious Houses. England and Wales, III: 1377–1540* (Cambridge, 2008): *Speculum* 85: 1111–12.

About the Contributors

CHARLES F. BRIGGS, Lecturer in History, University of Vermont and Affiliate of the Leslie Humanities Center, Dartmouth College, is author of *The Body Broken: Medieval Europe, 1300–1520* (2010) and *Giles of Rome's "De regimine principum": Reading and Writing Politics at Court and University, c. 1275–c. 1525* (1999), and editor, with D.C. Fowler and P.G. Remley, of *The Governance of Kings and Princes: John Trevisa's Middle English Translation of the "De Regimine Principum" of Aegidius Romanus* (1997). His most recent articles and chapters are "History, Story and Community: Representing the Past in Latin Christendom, 1050–1400," in *The Oxford History of Historical Writing*, vol. 2 (2010); "*Philosophi in Adiutorio Fidei*: Pastoral Uses of Pagan Moral Teaching in the Later Middle Ages" *LATCH* 1 (2008); "Aristotle's *Rhetoric* in the Later Medieval Universities: A Reassessment," *Rhetorica* 25 (2007); "Translation as Pedagogy: Academic Discourse and Changing Attitudes toward Latin in the Thirteenth and Fourteenth Centuries," in *Frontiers in the Middle Ages* (2006); "Moral Philosophy and Dominican Education: Bartolomeo da San Concordio's *Compendium moralis philosophiae*," in *Medieval Education* (2005).

JAROSLAV FOLDA is N. Ferebee Taylor Professor of the History of Art Emeritus at the University of North Carolina. Since 1995 he has written a series of articles on medieval figural art and ornament including work on manuscript illustration, icon painting, architectural sculpture, çintamani, and chrysography. His three most recent books include: *Crusader Art: The Art of the Crusaders in the Holy Land, 1099–1291* (Lund Humphries, 2008); *Crusader Art in the Holy Land, from the Third Crusade to the fall of Acre: 1187–1291* (Cambridge University Press, 2005); and *The Art of the Crusaders in the Holy Land, 1098–1187* (Cambridge University Press, 1995).

BARBARA HARVEY was for nearly forty years Fellow and Tutor in Medieval History at Somerville College, Oxford, and is now an Emeritus Fellow of the College. At earlier stages of her career, she taught History in the University of Edinburgh and at Queen Mary College in the University of London. She has wide interests in the economic and social history of medieval England, and in particular in the interaction between monasteries, which then had secular concerns on a scale undreamt of today, and society outside the cloister. Much of her work has explored these themes in the rich archives of Westminster Abbey. Her most important publications in these fields are *Westminster Abbey and Its Estates in the Middle Ages* (Clarendon Press, Oxford, 1977) and *Living and Dying in Medieval England, 1100–1540: The Monastic Experience* (Clarendon Press, Oxford, 1993). The latter book was joint winner of the 1993 Wolfson Foundation Prize for History. She was elected a Fellow of the British Academy in 1982.

ANDREW HUGHES, University Professor Emeritus, Faculty of Music and the Centre for Medieval Studies, University of Toronto, writes on the liturgy and plainsong. His works include a monograph on newly composed medieval liturgical offices, *Breviary*, vol. 1 (*Lambeth Palace Library Sion College MS. L1*); *Late Medieval Liturgical Offices: Resources for Electronic Research* (1994); *Medieval Manuscripts for Mass and Office: A Guide to Their Organization and Terminology* (1982); *Medieval Music: The Sixth Liberal Art* (1974).

CHRISTOPHER A. JONES, Professor of English, the Ohio State University, is author of *A Lost Work by Amalarius of Metz* (2001) and *Aelfric's Letter to the Monks of Eynsham* (1998), as well as numerous essays on various early medieval topics, appearing in journals such as *Traditio, The Journal of Medieval Latin, Mediaeval Studies, Speculum*, and *Anglo-Saxon England*.

WILLIAM PETER MAHRT, Associate Professor of Early Music, Stanford University, specializes in the theory and performance of medieval and Renaissance music. He has written articles on Gregorian chant, troubadours, medieval performance, Machaut, Dufay, Lasso, Dante, Brahms, English cathedrals, and conducts workshops in Gregorian chant and Renaissance polyphony. He is president of the Church Music Association of America and editor of its journal *Sacred Muse*.

MICHAEL MCVAUGH, William Smith Wells Professor of History Emeritus, University of North Carolina, writes on thirteenth- and fourteenth-century medicine; his works include *The Rational Surgery of the Middle Ages* (2006) and *Medicine before the Plague: Practitioners and their Patients in the Crown of Aragon, 1285–1345* (1993). He has edited the *Inventarium sive Chirurgia Magna* of *Guy de Chauliac* (1997), and he has been a general editor of the *Arnaldi de Villanova Opera Medica Omnia* since their founding in 1975.

NIGEL MORGAN, Professor Emeritus of Medieval Art History, University of Oslo, Honorary Professor of History of Art, University of Cambridge, is a prolific author on medieval art, including *Illuminated Manuscripts in Cambridge, I*, editor with Stella Panayotova (2009); *The Medieval Imagination: Illuminated Manuscripts from Cambridge, Australia and New Zealand*, editor with Bronwyn Stocks (2008); *Cambridge History of the Book in Britain*, vol. 2, editor with Rodney M. Thomson (2008); *The Douce Apocalypse: Picturing the End of the World in the Middle Ages* (2007); *The Trinity Apocalypse*, with David McKitterick, Ian Short and Teresa Webber (2005); editor of *Prophecy, Apocalypse and the Day of*

Doom: Proceedings of the 2000 Harlaxton Symposium (2004); *The Lambeth Apocalypse : Manuscript 209 in Lambeth Palace Library: A Critical Study* (1990); *Early Gothic Manuscripts, 1(1190-1250) (1982); 2(1250-1285)* (1988); and *The Medieval Painted Glass of Lincoln Cathedral (1983).*

SHERRY REAMES, Professor of English Emerita, University of Wisconsin-Madison, is author of "Reconstructing and Interpreting a Thirteenth-Century Office for the Translation of Thomas Becket," *Speculum* 80 (2005); "Origins and Affiliations of the Pre-Sarum Office for Anne in the Stowe Breviary," in *Music and Medieval Manuscripts: Paleography and Performance* (2004); *Middle English Legends of Women Saints* (annotated collection of texts, edited with the assistance of Martha G. Blalock and Wendy R. Larson, 2003); "The Second Nun's Prologue and Tale," in *Sources and Analogues of the Canterbury Tales* (2002); *The Legenda Aurea: A Reexamination of Its Paradoxical History* (1985); and a number of other articles on Chaucer, hagiography, and liturgical manuscripts.

JANET SORRENTINO, Associate Professor of Early European History, Washington College, has, with the title "Liturgy and Ritual for Medieval Nuns," provided excerpts from the *De ecclesiasticis officiis* of the Order of Sempringham, for *Women's Lives in Medieval Europe: A Sourcebook*, ed. Emilie Amt, 2nd ed. (2010), and has written "The Gilbertines," for the *Women and Gender in Medieval Europe: An Encyclopedia* (2006); "In Houses of Nuns, In Houses of Canons: A Liturgical Dimension to Double Monasteries," *The Journal of Medieval History* 28 (2002): 361–372; and *"Pena brevior et levior*: A New Expression of Concern for the Dead in Medieval Missals," in *Death, Health and Sickness in the Middle Ages* (2000).

ELIZABETH C. TEVIOTDALE, Assistant Director, The Medieval Institute, Western Michigan University, has written on the *Stammheim Missal* at the J. Paul Getty Museum (2001), and has published as well articles on manuscripts, art, and liturgy.

ALAN THACKER was, until his retirement in 2009, Reader in History at the University of London and Executive Editor of the Victoria County History. Now a Senior Research Fellow at the University of London, Institute of Historical Research, he is the author of numerous articles on the early medieval church. His most recent publications include "Bede, the Britons and the Book of Samuel," in *Early Medieval Studies in Memory of Patrick Wormald*, ed. Stephen Baxter, Catherine Karkov, Janet Nelson, and David Pelteret (2009); "Gallic or Greek? Archbishops in England from Theodore to Ecgberht," in *Frankland: Essays in Honour of Dame Jinty Nelson*, ed. Paul Fouracre and David Ganz (2008); "Rome of the Martyrs: Saints' Cults and Relics, Fourth to Seventh Century," in *Roma Felix*, edited by Éamonn Ó Carrigáin and Carol Neuman de Vegvar; and *Bede and Augustine of Hippo*, the Jarrow lecture (2005)

RODNEY M. THOMSON is Professor Emeritus of Medieval History and Honorary Research Associate in the School of History and Classics, University of Tasmania. He has written extensively on books, libraries, and learning in medieval England. His published works include *A Descriptive Catalogue of the Medieval Manuscripts of Merton College*, Oxford (2009); (with Nigel J. Morgan) *The Cambridge History of the Book in Britain 2: The Manuscript Book c.1100–1400* (2008); (with Michael Winterbottom), *William of Malmesbury, Gesta Pontificum Anglorum*, 2 vols. (2007), *Books and Learning in Twelfth-Century England: The Ending of 'Alter Orbis'. The Lyell Lectures for 2000–2001* (2006), *William of Malmesbury* (2nd ed. 2003), *The Bury Bible* (2001), and *Manuscripts from St Albans Abbey 1066–1235*, 2 vols. (1985).

SIEGFRIED WENZEL is Professor Emeritus of English at the University of Pennsylvania. He has held fellowships from the National Endowment for the Humanities, the American Council of Learned Societies, and the Guggenheim Foundation. A Fellow of the Medieval Academy of America, he was awarded the prestigious Charles Homer Haskins Medal for his contributions to medieval literature and religion. His many publications include *Preaching in the Age of Chaucer* (2008); *Latin Sermon Collections from Later Medieval England* (2005); *Macaronic Sermons: Bilingualism and Preaching in Late Medieval England* (1994); and *Preachers, Poets and the Early English Lyric* (1986).

JOSHUA A. WESTGARD, Haslam Postdoctoral Fellow of the Marco Institute for Medieval and Renaissance Studies at the University of Tennessee, Knoxville, is the author of several articles on medieval historical writing and the manuscripts and transmission of Bede's works, most recently "Bede and the Continent in the Carolingian Age and Beyond," in the *Cambridge Companion to Bede* (forthcoming). He is currently completing an edition and study of the set of annals known as the *Continuatio Bedae*, and is preparing a monograph on the transmission and reception of the *Historia ecclesiastica gentis Anglorum*.

JOSEPH WITTIG is Professor of English at the University of North Carolina at Chapel Hill. His publications include "The 'Remigian' Glosses on Boethius' *Consolatio Philosophiae* in Context," in *Source of Wisdom: Studies in Old English and Medieval Latin in Honor of Thomas D. Hill*, ed. Charles Wright, Fred Biggs and Thomas Hall (2007); *Piers Plowman: Concordance. A Lemmatized Analysis of the English Vocabulary of the A, B and C versions* (2001); *William Langland Revisited* (1997); "Piers Plowman B, Passus IX–XII: Elements in the Design of the Inward Journey," *Traditio* 28 (1972), 211–80; "Figural Narrative in Cynewulf's Juliana," *Anglo-Saxon England* 4 (2008), 37–55; "The Aeneas-Dido Allusion in Chrétien's *Erec et Enide*," *Comparative Literature* 22 (1970), 237–53; "'Homiletic Fragment II' and the Epistle to the Ephesians," *Traditio* 25 (1969), 358–63.

Index of Feasts

Index of Manuscripts

Auct. F.5.29: 378
Auct. F.6.2: 378
Barlow 41: 181
Barlow 42: 378
Bodley 163: 211
Bodley 292: 367, 378
Bodley 302: 211
Bodley 719: 66
Bodley 720: 295n1, 315n68, 316, 317, 322n84
Can. lit. 215: 177, 182
Digby 19: 289, 289n28
Digby 55: 365, 366n67, 378
Digby 150: 378
Digby 176: 283n7, 287n22, 289, 289n28, 290
Digby 216: 289, 289n28
Don. b.5: 147, 154n55
Douce 136: 18
e Mus. 2: 111n25, 168n13
e Mus. 19: 286n20, 289n28, 290, 291n38
e Mus. 222: 66
Hatton 15: 372, 378
Hatton 43: 210n2
Hatton 113: 78n49
Hatton 114: 78n49
Junius 121: 78n49
Lat. lit. b.7: 182
Lat. lit. c.36: 182
Lat. lit. e.39: 179
Lat. lit. f.29: 180, 180n44
Lat. liturg. f.5: 79n55, 84n99
Laud misc. 3a: 147n33
Laud misc. 299: 178, 181n47, 183
Lyell 40: 67
Rawlinson C.73: 171n23, 174n30, 177, 181, 183, 184
Rawlinson C.489: 181
Rawlinson D.1218: 378
Rawlinson liturg. d.3: 145n7
Selden supra 24: 378
Top. Surrey d. 4 (R): 347n94
Wood d.2: 285n16, 286n17
Christ Church College, Evelyn Collect. h.65: 379

Corpus Christi College
74: 243, 248, 251
230: 369n70, 379
232: 363n20
279: 211
398: 379
Exeter College
19: 287n22
32: 289n90, 289n28, 291, 293n44
Lincoln College 21: 379
Magdalen College
49: 379
178: 379
189: 379
205: 379
265: 379
Merton College
2: 379
8: 286n20, 289n28, 290
14: 379
19: 286n20, 289n28, 290, 291
21: 379
27: 286n20, 289, 289n28, 291, 293
33: 291n37
35: 287n21, 288n25, 289n28, 290, 291n40
66: 286n20, 289n28, 290
77: 287n21, 288n25, 289, 289n28
78: 287n22, 289, 289n28
103: 286n20, 293
105: 286n20, 291n37
137: 287n21, 288n25, 289n28, 290
138: 287n21, 288n25, 289n28, 290
149: 286n20, 289, 289n28, 291
158: 286n20, 289, 289n28, 291
166: 286n20, 289, 289n28, 291
168: 286n20, 289, 289n28, 291
169: 286n20, 289, 289nn28n29, 291
170: 286n20, 289, 289n28, 291
171: 286n20, 289, 289n28, 291
172: 286n20, 289, 289n28, 291
190: 287n21, 288n25, 289, 289n28
194: 286n20, 291n37
197: 291n37
216: 286n20, 289, 289n28
224: 287n22, 291n37
226: 295n1, 315n68, 316

lat. 12950: 380
lat. 12961: 231, 236, 239, 243, 251
lat. 14380: 225n2, 231, 232n26,
    236, 239, 243, 245n44, 248n
    50, 251
lat. 14698: 380
lat. 15090: 243, 252
lat. 15457: 301n19
lat. 16093: 230n20, 231, 232,
    232nn25n26, 235, 236, 239,
    243, 245n44, 248, 248n51, 252
lat. 16188: 301n19
lat. 16194: 295n1, 315n68, 317,
    322n84
lat. 17294: 184
lat. 17811: 380
lat. 17832: 380
nouv. acq. lat. 160: 295n1, 315n68,
    317n70
nouv. acq. lat. 1478: 231, 236, 239,
    243, 252
Ministère des Affaires Étrangères,
    Mem. et Documents
    230bis: 257n12
Parma, Bibl. Palatina 98: 145n7
Princeton, University Library, Garrett
    102: 380

R

Rheims, Bibl. mun.
    9: 75n38
    1002: 301n19
Rome
    Bibl. Nazionale Centrale V.E. II,
        1452: 222
    Bibl. Vallicelliana, C. 64: 65
Rouen, Bibl. mun.
    923: 380
    984: 295n1
    Y.6 (Jumièges Missal): 8

S

Saint-Omer, Bibl. mun.
    598: 381
    619: 381
    625: 381

Salisbury, Cathedral Library
    135: 52, 64, 65
    152: 180, 180nn43n44, 182, 183
    154: 42n44, 47, 50n51, 54n55, 62
    224: 146, 156, 166n9, 168, 173, 174,
        180n84 passim, 181, 182
San Marino, Calif., Huntington Library,
    HM 19918: 147, 154
Southwark, Roman Catholic See 1: 179,
    184
Stonyhurst College
    40: 179
    44: 179, 181, 181n47, 182, 184
    52: 165, 179, 180

T

Trento, Mus. Prov. d'arte del Castello del
    Buon. 1590 (Trento Sacramen-
    tary): 8
Trier
    Priesterseminar H 215,1: 223
    Stadtbibl. 1093: 231, 232n25, 235,
        236, 239, 243, 252

U

Ushaw, St Cuthbert's College 18: 147, 152

V

Vatican Library
    lat. 3363: 227, 228n14, 229, 233, 252
    lat. 3865: 231, 232n25, 235, 236n31,
        239, 243, 252
    lat. 4254: 231, 236, 239, 243, 252
    Ottobon. lat. 145 (Monte Cassino
        Manual): 7
    Ottobon. lat. 2214: 380
    Pal. lat. 98: 67
    Pal. lat. 482: 67
    Pal. lat. 554: 192n29
    Pal. lat. 1017: 380
    Pal. lat. 1024: 380
    Pal. lat. 1581: 231, 232n25, 235, 236,
        239, 243, 252
    Pal. lat. 1963: 257n14
    Reg. lat. 73: 67
    Reg. lat. 692: 223

General Index

A

Abbots
  duties of, 206n7
  numbers of, 197n98
Aberdeen Breviary, 176n83 passim
Abingdon Abbey, 228, 230, 327
Acca, 187n88
Acre, 257, 269, 270, 271, 280
Acton Burnell Missal, 147, 153
Adalbold of Utrecht, 252
Adam of Buckfield, 299
Adderbury church, 155
Addi, count, 199n70
Adhemar of Le Puy, bishop, 258, 263,
    271, 279
Adomnan, 187
Advent season, 133n34
Ælfric, 47, 189
Æthelheah, 196
Æthelheard, archbishop, 196n97
Æthelstan, bishop, 78
Æthelthryth, 216n38
Æthelwulf, *Carmen de abbatibus*, 211n8,
    217, 218
Aelred of Rievaulx, 14n36
Aethelred, King, 221, 221n50
Ages, human, 241n42
Aidan, bishop, 187, 200
Aimery, patriarch, 271
Albert the Great, 303n4
    Aristotelian commentaries, 365, 376,
        377, 384
Albinus, 12
Albucasis, 312
Alcuin, 190, 195
    De animae ratione, 234n29, 238
Aldfrith, King, 213, 215n16

Aldhelm, 188
Aldin, Michael de, monk, 384
Aldwulf, bishop, 197
Alexander III, 14, 15, 16n17
Alexander IV, 330
Alexander VI, 352n55
Alexander, bishop, 11, 12
Alexander Nequam, 309
Alfred, King, 225
Alfred of Lincoln, 11n17
Alhfrith, King, 194n95
Alkindi, 307n9
All Souls College, Oxford, 371, 385
Allen, Thomas, 380
Alverny, Marie-Thérèse d', 304n29
Amalarius
    Canonis missae interpretatio, 45n14
    Geminus codex, 44n46, 51, 52, 55
    Liber de ordine antiphonarii, 46
    Liber officialis, 41n67 passim
    lost work *De triduo,* 41n67
    Versus marini, 44
Amaury, King, 270, 271, 279
Ambrose, St, 234n28
Amesbury, 149n46
Amesbury Psalter, 274n75
Angoulême Sacramentary. *See* Paris, Bibl.
    nat., lat. 816
Anima, 231n39, 246n48. *See also* Soul,
    human
    as human, 239
    as world soul, 238
Annales Cambriae, 189
Anne of Bohemia, 330, 335n40
Anniversaries, 332, 332n31, 335n36, 338
    royal, 348
Anointment, 261

Bruni, Leonardo
  on *Ethics,* 365, 369, 370, 375n79 passim,
    383n88 passim
  Isagogicon in libros morales Aristotelis, 378
  Isagogicon moralis disciplinae, 365
Bruno, St, 35, 36n37
Bruno Longobucco, *Surgery,* 312
Bryghtman, 380
Buchthal, Hugo, 265
Buckfast Abbey, 363
Buckland church, 155
Bucwell, John de, monk, 384
Bukwode, John, 364, 388
Bullington Priory, 382
Burcote, John, 290
Buridan, Jean: Aristotelian commentaries,
    365, 370, 379
Burley, Walter, 360
  Aristotelian commentaries, 362n63,
    365, 370, 372, 375n88 passim
Burnell, William, 379
Burnett, Charles, 299
Bury, Richard, bishop, 362n63
Bury St Edmunds, 328, 346
Bute: Foulis Easter breviary, 176n84 passim
Byzantine miniatures, 265

C
Cælin, 194n44, 195
Calcidius, 232n25
Calendar, Sarum Use, 143n62
Caligula Troper, 70n71
Cambridge, Eric, 201n91
Cambridge, John, 333
Cambridge (city): Fitzwilliam Museum,
  The Cambridge Illuminations, 69
Cambridge University. *See also* individual
    colleges
  curriculum, 359, 360
  University Library, 370n33, 371, 382
    The Cambridge Illuminations, 69
Camsale, Richard, 289, 290
Canon tables, 70, 71n72, 75, 82
Canterbury, John, 337, 341n42, 346n89, 347
Canterbury (city), 196, 214n17, 217n18
  cathedral priory, 370n33, 371, 384
  library, 288

Convocations, 161n68
  province, 143, 159
  shrine of St Thomas the martyr, 340n41
Canterbury, St Augustine's, 334n37,
    370n33, 371, 384
Canterbury College, Oxford, 370n33, 386
Canticles, 73
Cardinal virtues, 366n67
Cardinalis, 300, 308n40, 310, 311, 312,
    319, 320, 321
Carmelites, 363
Carolingians, 72, 189, 192
Carthusian Missal. *See* Grenoble, Bibl.
    mun., 386 (olim 71)
Carthusian Order: lay brothers, 35n37, 40
Caspar, John, 380
Cassian, 237
  Collations, 238
Cassiodorus, 237
Cataract, 318
Causton, Michael, 376
Cavanaugh, Susan, 284n14
Cedd, bishop, 194n44, 200
Celestine, pope, 356
Ceolfrid, abbot, 202
Ceolfrith, abbot, 194nn44n47, 202
Cernel Abbey, 47
Chad, 194n44
Chadwick, H. Mary, 193
Chaplains, 199
Chartres cathedral, 130n3
Chaucer, Geoffrey, *Canterbury Tales,*
    295n96, 349
Chaundler, Thomas, 380
Chazelle, Celia, 46n19
Chelsea: Council of (816): 190, 194
Chemical technology, 319
Chertsey, Benedict de, abbot, 339
Chertsey Abbey, 179
Chester, 369
Chichele Breviary, 171n24
Chichester, 168n15, 282, 284
  provincial statutes, 283
Chichester Missal, 274n75
Christ
  baptism, 80
  genealogy, 82n83

F

Famuli, 19, 22
Farne, 200
Feasts. *See also* separate Index of Feasts
  double, 133
  new, 160n61, 164
  regional, 163n84 passim
Feologeld, 196
Feryng, John, 346, 346n88
Fever, 355
  hectic, 310n11
Findon, Thomas, abbot, 384
Firmin-Didot, A., 253
Fischer, Bonifatius, 73n21
Fitzhugh, Robert, 382
Fladbury minster, 198
Fleming, Robert, 379, 386
Flemyng, Richard, bishop, 284
Fletcher, J. M., 359n60
Flete, Thomas, 344
Florence: cathedral, 130n3
Flüeler, Christoph, 362n14
Fontevrault, Order of, 3
Fordham, 14
Fountains Abbey, 363
Four Masters, 313n14
Franciscan Order, 362, 369
Frankia, 192, 198, 199, 201, 206, 207
Frederick II, 271
Frere, Walter Howard, 131n7, 132, 138
Frithegod, 217
Frithuric, 206
Frodesley church, 153
Fromund, 251
Fulda Sacramentary. *See* Göttingen, Universitätsbibl., Cod. theol. 231
Fulk, King, 259n61, 271

G

Galen, 303, 309, 310, 320, 323
  De complexionibus, 311
  De crisi, 303, 311, 320n78
  De criticis diebus, 311
  De ingenio sanitatis, 312
  De interioribus, 311, 320n78
  De iuvamentis membrorum, 303, 311

  De morbo et accidenti, 311n12
  De simplici medicina, 311
  Tegni, 298, 308n40
Galloway, Andrew, 350, 356
Gameson, Richard, 78n49, 80n58, 81n63, 83, 212n10
Gardiner, Thomas, 333
Gardiner, William, 333
Gascoigne, Thomas, 386
Gatch, Milton McC., 43n9
Gateshead, 198
Gaul, 187, 189, 194, 203
Gauthier, René Antoine, 362n12
Gellone Sacramentary. *See* Paris, Bibl. nat., lat. 12048
Geoffrey, chaplain, 12
Geoffrey of Monmouth, 223
Gerard, lay brother, 14, 15
Gerard of Berry (or Bourges), 310, 312, 319n20
Gerard of Cremona, 307, 309
Geremia da Montagnone, *Compendium moralium notabilium*, 375
Gerent, King, 188
Gesta Romanorum, 350
Getz, Faye, 296n97, 301n18, 308n41
Gilbert de Gant, 11n17
Gilbert of Sempringham, 3, 10n20, 26, 27n29, 32
  canonization dossier, 4, 17n18
  Vita, 12n20 passim, 25
Gilbert the Englishman, 295n324
  Compendium medicine, 295n323 passim
    additiones, 315n18
    dating of, 309n14
Gilbertine Order
  conversi (lay brothers), rebellion of, 3n40
  foundation narrative, 10n14
  Institutes, 18, 29n32
  Mass books, 4, 5n10
  Ordinal, 29n106
  Rule, 39
Gilbertus del Egle, 296, 300n301
Giles of Corbeil, *De urinis*, 301n5
Giles of Rome